Y0-CCX-023

Teacher Compensation and Motivation

EDITED BY
LARRY E. FRASE, Ed.D.
Professor, Organizational Psychology
San Diego State University

TECHNOMIC
PUBLISHING CO., INC.
LANCASTER · BASEL

Teacher Compensation and Motivation
a TECHNOMIC® publication

Published in the Western Hemisphere by
Technomic Publishing Company, Inc.
851 New Holland Avenue
Box 3535
Lancaster, Pennsylvania 17604 U.S.A.

Distributed in the Rest of the World by
Technomic Publishing AG

Printed in the United States of America
10 9 8 7 6 5 4 3 2 1

Main entry under title:
  Teacher Compensation and Motivation

A Technomic Publishing Company book
Bibliography: p.

Library of Congress Card No. 91-58005
ISBN No. 87762-813-0

Teacher Compensation and Motivation

Contents

7. School District Planning for Teacher Incentive Pay   185

RICHARD M. BRANDT– *University of Virginia*
BRUCE GANSNEDER – *University of Virginia*

8. The Effects of Financial and Nonfinancial Rewards: 217
Program Description and Research Results

LARRY E. FRASE – *San Diego State University*

PART IV: TEACHER EVALUATION

9. Designing Evaluation Systems for Performance Pay   241

ROBERT W. HETZEL – *Superintendent, Catalina Foothills School District, Tucson, Arizona*

**10. Performance Appraisal in Education: 261
A Strategic Consideration**

SHARON C. CONLEY– *University of Arizona*
SAMUEL B. BACHARACH – *Cornell University*

PART V: ADMINISTERING THE ALTERNATIVE COMPENSATION SYSTEM:
          THE PRACTITIONERS' PERSPECTIVE

**11. Administering an Alternative Compensation System: 277
Reflections on the Tennessee Plan**

CHARLES BURKETT– *University of Tennessee*
ROBERT McELRATH – *East Tennessee State University*

19. Kyrene Career Development Ladder: A Case Study   483

CAROLYN J. DOWNEY—*Superintendent, Kyrene Public Schools, Tempe, Arizona*
CAROL PARISH—*Assistant Superintendent, Kyrene Public Schools, Tempe, Arizona*

20. Paying for Performance in Lake Forest, Illinois   541

ALLEN J. KLINGENBERG—*Superintendent, Lake Forest Public Schools, Illinois*

**21. The Career Ladder Plan of the Cave Creek Unified   573
School District: A Case Study**

DAVID ALEXANDER—*Superintendent, Cave Creek Unified School District, Arizona*
RICHARD P. MANATT—*Director, School Improvement Model, Iowa State Univ.*

Introduction

LARRY E. FRASE — *San Diego State University*

THE history of merit pay and other innovations in teacher compensation in this country evokes the image of Sisyphus rolling massive boulders up a steep mountain — in this case, the mountain of teacher compensation reform. Whether the boulders were called merit pay, career ladders, differentiated staffing, incentive pay, or restructuring, they have nearly always rolled back down the mountain.

This book provides reasons for the ebb and flow of alternative compensation programs, the turbulent love–hate relationship with the desire to reward performance, and the success and failure of alternative compensation programs. Practitioners who have designed and operated successful alternative compensation programs and academics who have assisted them offer their wisdom and insights on the subject.

This book of readings provides the most comprehensive compilation of information to date on alternative compensation and motivation systems. This book is prepared for all professionals interested in learning more about compensating and motivating teachers. Practicing administrators and school board members interested in designing alternative programs will find the examples and suggestions for program development and implementation in this book highly useful.

University professors interested in providing graduate students with both academic and practical perspectives on alternative compensation systems will find this book a valuable tool. A full array of topics related to alternative compensation systems is addressed by experts, both practitioners and theoreticians.

Educators and lay people alike have debated for centuries the plethora of promises and problems surrounding teacher compensation and motivation. The more recent love affair with alternative compensation was launched in 1983 with *A Nation at Risk* in the "first wave" of educational reform. The first wave popularized alternative compensation and motivation programs with innumerable claims of mystical powers for "merit pay." The charge was led by President Reagan and backed by highly regarded associations such as Phi Delta Kappa, American Association of School Administrators, and National School Boards Association. Their publications and convention agendas were filled with discussions of merit pay and career ladders as the "new cures" for the traditional ills of teacher compensation programs and problems reportedly related to poor student achievement. Even long-time opponents of merit pay, such as the presidents of the two major teacher associations, expressed willingness to "check it out." Albert Shanker, president of the American Federation of Teachers and an ardent opponent of any compensation system other than the single salary schedule, voiced a willingness to consider the new cure in Rochester called restructuring with its new salary cap (Rivera, 1989). Mary Futrell, president of the NEA, expressed her approval of merit pay in Fairfax County Schools (Spillane, 1991).

The desire to recognize quality teaching has been present for centuries. As early as 1867, Aaron Sheeley, superintendent of Adams County, Pennsylvania, lamented the injustices of compensation systems that required the same pay for all teachers, without recognition of performance. His lament was reiterated in 1957 in the *Scholastic Journal*:

> As a pure matter of justice, there is nothing more unfair than paying unequals equally. (p. T 1)

In 1958, Clarence Hines, superintendent of schools in Eugene, Oregon, wove this bias into the fabric of the American work ethic:

> Compensation or reward according to the quality of service rendered is basic to the American system. . . . The public is opposed to paying average or mediocre teachers as much as it is willing to pay superior teachers. . . . (p. 9)

Politicians entered the fray in earnest in the early 1980s in President Reagan's pet report, *A Nation at Risk* (1983). Other politicians followed suit. Possibly the most adamant was Tennessee's Governor Lamar Alexander (1983) and now Secretary of Education who stated:

> Our schools would be better if we paid our best teachers more than our worst. (p. 4)

This apparent basic drive is not an American invention. One year before the statement by Superintendent Aaron Sheeley, the parliament of Australia debated their practice of paying teachers an additional eight shillings for each child who passed the basic examination in literacy and numeracy and an extra four shillings for each who passed in grammer and geography (Dear, 1975, p. 89).

The nineteenth and twentieth centuries have been characterized by three periods of high activity with alternative compensation systems: 1918–1928, 1948–1959, and 1979–present. The desire to compensate teachers on the basis of performance has led to over 125 years of trial, error, retrial, and frequent failure.

Merit pay activity peaked during the 1920s when 99 percent of the cities in the U.S.A. with populations over 25,000 operated merit rating programs (*NEA Proceedings, 1925*). In the same year a survey conducted by the Research Bureau of the University of Minnesota discovered rating plans in operation in forty-six of the then forty-eight states (Brighton and Hannan, 1962). This peak period (1918–1928) and the second period of activity were followed by periods of reentrenchment in the comfortable single salary schedule.

The single salary schedule and its relationship to teaching performance has become the object of numerous research studies. Pay on a single salary schedule is determined by years of teaching experience and graduate training. Opponents believe that teacher pay as determined by these criteria bears no relationship to teaching performance, while supporters believe that it not only reflects performance but also protects teachers from arbitrary and capricious decisions about pay.

The research conducted on this issue strongly supports the former point of view. As early as 1952, McCall's study found no positive or negative correlation between either of the two criteria and teaching performance (McCall, 1952). These results have been replicated many times through more tightly controlled and better conceptualized studies (Murnane, 1975; Bridge, Judd, and Moock, 1979).

At first glance, past efforts in teacher compensation and motivation appear unrelated to today's reform efforts to restructure teaching. But the goal remains the same — *to enhance student learning*.

Unlike the ones in the past, today's reform efforts are stimulated by both educators and noneducators. Literature reflects little involvement of the private sector in past teacher compensation plans, but today's efforts to restructure schools and implement performance pay plans are spurred by many members of private enterprise, government, and educators. According to Galagar, some businesses feel the future of the United States of America lies in the balance:

> That business cannot flourish in the future in the international economy with large populations of citizens unequipped to fill the available jobs has become conventional wisdom, and business leaders are beginning to bring pressures for change in a chronic condition that has so far defied the solution of both the public and private sectors.

> Business is not in a mood to be timid or fuzzy about changing the education system. At least a million workers a year are coming into the job market not knowing how to read or write, and corporations collectively are spending millions teaching them basic skills. One out of three companies offers basic skills training, and the number of such programs has doubled in the past ten years.

One indicator of the private sector's commitment to education is seen in the fact that American industry spent $210 billion last year for on-the-job remedial skills programs (Merl, 1990).

Industry leaders have strengthened their appeal with grants of money and time to schools. Over 140,000 partnerships between schools and industry have been formed. Panasonic is supporting restructuring in San Diego and Xerox is supporting restructuring in Rochester.

Sadly, industries are now questioning the wisdom of their investments. Virgil Roberts, chair of the Los Angeles partnership and entertainment industry executive, stated that there is a growing sense of frustration that the reform efforts haven't worked and that more radical steps are needed. It is difficult to sustain corporate interest in demonstration projects and other reform programs unless they get wider dissemination—and results (De Witt, 1991; Merl, 1990).

Although restructuring has expanded the focus from alternative compensation only, as in the peak days of merit pay, alternative remuneration remains a major factor. The National Governors Association (Siegel and Smoley, 1988) has suggested that education borrow two powerful concepts from industry: collaborative management and rewarding performance. The latter is simply a reaffirmation of the century-old intent to pay teachers, at least in part, on the basis of the quality of their work. This intent has not died; it has taken new clothing and shares the spotlight with other reform efforts.

What is the prognosis for alternative compensation systems? Some of the more highly touted are waning; one has received an apparent fatal decision from its board of education; one has received a negative teacher vote; some are dead; and many continue to live healthy lives. Answers to this question are provided in this book.

Sisyphus is on the move. He has a new boulder, one with expanded meaning and implications. His boulder is now called reform or restructuring, and it is heavier than before. But Sisyphus is on the move up the mountain. America's energy to improve its educational system is boundless, and there are many people who share Sisyphus' boulder. This book is written by those people, about those people, and about their programs. It shares the broad picture and the gritty and delicate details of alternative compensation and reform, Sisyphus' current load.

REFERENCES

1983. *A Nation at Risk: The Imperative for Educational Reform.* Washington, D.C.: U.S. Department of Education, National Commission on Excellence in Education, David P. Gardner, Chairperson.

Alexander, L. 1983. "Issue: Should Single Salary Schedules for Teachers Be Replaced by Provision for Differentiated Teaching Scales and Salaries?" *ASCD Update,* 25:4–5.

Bridge, R. G., C. M. Judd, and P. R. Moock. 1979. *The Determinants of Educational Outcomes.* Cambridge, MA: Ballinger Publishing Company.

Brighton, S. F. and C. J. Hannan. 1962. *Merit Pay Programs for Teachers.* San Francisco: Fearon Publishers.

Dear, K. 1975. "Payment by Results and the Status of Teachers in Victoria 1862–1872," *Melbourne Studies in Education,* S. Murray-Smith, ed., Melbourne University Press.

Dearns, D. and D. Doyle. 1988. *Winning the Brain Race: A Bold Plan to Make Our Schools Competitive.* San Francisco, CA: ICS Press.

1957. "Debate Merit Pay," *Scholastic Teacher,* 70(6):1T–3T.

De Witt, K. 1991. "Brought to You by Exxon-School Reform," *New York Times* Editorial (July 21).

Galager, P. 1988. "Joining Forces: Business and Education Take on Competition," *Training and Development Journal* (July).

Hines, C. 1958. "To Merit Pay or Not to Merit Pay," *The American School Board Journal,* 117:9–43.

McCall, W. A. 1952. "Measurement of Teacher Merit," *Bulletin No. 284,* North Carolina Department of Public Instruction.

Merl, J. 1990. "Corporations Find NO Easy Education Cure," *Los Angeles Times,* A-3, March 28.

Murnane, R. J. 1975. *The Impact of School Resources on the Learning of Inner City Children.* Cambridge, MA: Ballinger Publishing Company.

National Education Association. 1925. *Proceedings.* Washington, D.C.: NEA, 202–215.

Rivera, M. "The Rochester Plan," Keynote presentation at the *Restructuring Conference, San Diego State University, San Diego, California, July 20, 1989.*

Spillane, R. 1991. "Pay for Performance in Fairfax County, Virginia," In *Teacher Compensation and Motivation,* L. Frase, ed., Lancaster, PA: Technomic Publishing Co., Inc.

Overview

THIS book is comprised of twenty-one chapters organized into seven sections. A brief overview of each chapter is provided in this section.

PART I—HISTORY, POLICY, AND MOTIVATIONAL ISSUES

Professor Fenwick English begins the book with a thorough and insightful review of the history of alternative compensation systems from the nineteenth century through the twentieth century with analysis of merit pay, staff differentiation, and career ladders. Many questions are posited in his answer to the very basic question, "Why do people work?" This is followed with an assessment of the characteristics and effectiveness of the many compensation programs implemented to address concerns with pay and teacher motivation. He addresses related assumptions regarding concepts of equity and control and offers an insightful perspective of how workers (teachers) interact with alternative pay schemes from an organizational context.

Professor Tom Timar addresses policy issues surrounding alternative compensation programs at the local, state, and national levels. He provides an extensive examination of the value, efficacy, and philosophical assumptions of alternative compensation systems from political, policy, and operational perspectives. A practical yet academic analysis of these perspectives is provided in light of teacher incentive pay programs conducted in Texas, Utah, and California. Each of the following are assessed in relation to the assumptions and the advantages and disadvantages of the integrated, programmatic, procedural, and *pro forma* modes of implementation:

- features of incentive programs

- issues relevant to the implementation stage
- likelihood of improving organizational competence

Professors Rod Ogawa and Mary Rhodes provide a critique of the "first wave" of educational reform through three lenses: 1) three conceptualizations of human motivation (expectancy theory, a job-characteristic model, and goal theory); 2) contextual factors based on the relationship of work structures and alienation; and 3) early attempts to motivate teachers via manipulation of the work conditions. Their review of motivational theory and their critique of the "First Wave" of reform provides practitioners and academics with the basic building blocks for designing and implementing alternative compensation and motivation programs.

PART II—FINANCING AND DEVELOPING COMPENSATION SYSTEMS

Professors William Castetter and Richard Heisler provide a "how to" chapter on developing alternative salary structures. Detailed steps involving PLANNING (Strategic Design), IMPLEMENTATION (Operational Design), and EVALUATION are provided. Based on years of experience in helping school districts to develop alternative salary structures, they provide both the quantitative and qualitative dimensions of a compensation model. Examples with clear, concise explanations are provided.

The editor and Professor William Poston explore the efficacy of diversity and effectiveness in teacher incentive programs without external funding. Drawing from their research findings and highly successful experience in designing and managing alternative compensation and reward systems for teachers, the authors present six conditions that are key to successful teacher incentive and alternative compensation systems:

- absence of legislative-level political involvement
- nonreliance on external funding
- teacher organization cooperation sought when appropriate
- presence of clear, attainable objectives
- freedom of school system to determine the form of rewards
- presence of local, "grass roots" initiative to undertake the program

Based on these conditions, the authors offer recommendations to leg-

islators and practitioners to assist in the successful implementation of
teacher incentive programs.

Legislatures should

- shift control to the local level
- limit external requirements
- offer support and assistance
- invest in risk

School administrators and boards should seize the opportunity to
utilize the freedom and support to design bold new strategies for compensating and rewarding teachers.

PART III—THE RESEARCH BASE ON ALTERNATIVE COMPENSATION SYSTEMS

In light of the fact that alternative compensation systems traditionally
have not been the recipients of sound research efforts, three excellent
studies on alternative compensation systems are presented in this section. These studies address the effect of performance pay on teacher
motivation, the planning that is crucial to successful implementation of
alternative compensation programs, and the effects of non-salary and
salary rewards.

Professors Schwab and Iwanicki share the results of a year-long evaluation of a collectively bargained performance based salary program
(PBSP) for teachers. While addressing a broad range of issues relating
to merit pay, the authors also provide a clear focus on the perceptions
of administrators and teachers regarding the success of programs in
providing a motivational work climate for teachers. The study assesses
attitudes toward teaching, perceived accuracy of performance ratings
(evaluation), attitudes toward PBSP, impact of PBSP, teacher burnout,
and job satisfaction as affected by PBSP.

Professors Brandt and Gansneder examine a critical component in
any program, *planning*. To date, very little information has been presented on this most important function. The authors fill this chasm
with an examination of planning for incentive pay programs and the variety of plans that have emerged in Virginia. Specifically, answers to
the following questions are provided:

- Why are such plans started? Who originates them?
- What factors influence their development?
- How much support or resistance can be expected from various

> stakeholders such as administrators, teachers, and especially board members?
>
> - What kind of planning has taken place?
> - What were the effects?
> - Who was involved?
> - What provisions were made for funding?

Their answers will assist planners by providing information crucial to successful program implementation.

The editor provides the only known study which compares the effects of salary and non-salary teacher rewards. Based on a teacher reward program structured around Herzberg's Motivation–Hygiene Theory, the study focuses on the effects of two rewards (cash versus travel for professional development) on teacher recognition and opportunities for job enrichment. A thorough review of theory is provided along with implications for practice. A description of the program this research is based on is also presented in this chapter.

PART IV—TEACHER EVALUATION

Dr. Robert Hetzel addresses teacher evaluation, the oft-cited culprit in the demise of alternative compensation systems. He provides a lucid and straightforward explanation of steps and key ingredients found in successful teacher evaluation programs that have withstood the rigors associated with performance based compensation.

The following topics are addressed:

- clarity of purpose
- inter-rater reliability
- validity of instrumentation
- competency of evaluators
- political cost

Examples of the tools of teacher evaluation are provided, e.g., critical incidence logs, data analysis guides, planning conference guides, and observation guides.

Professors Conley and Bacharach analyze the requisites to successful performance appraisal. They contend that efforts must be made to design compensation and performance appraisal systems to capitalize on teachers' intrinsic motivations to teach. The authors utilize their backgrounds in private industry and education to answer three questions:

(1) What should be evaluated in teaching—teachers' skills or student achievement scores?

(2) How should performance appraisal be linked to organizational rewards?

(3) How can performance appraisal reflect the work of teaching?

PART V—ADMINISTERING THE ALTERNATIVE COMPENSATION SYSTEM: THE PRACTITIONERS' PERSPECTIVE

Professors Burkett and McElrath discuss the role of the school principal in the implementation of alternative pay plans. They remind us that the school principal is the key element in educational reform, and they outline the many political forces that affect principals' administration of alternative compensation systems. Research findings on these topics from the Tennessee Career Ladder Plan are utilized to highlight major points. A detailed list of recommendations for principals is provided.

Professor Poston utilizes his experience as principal and superintendent in creating and administering alternative compensation systems to provide clear guidelines for avoiding dangerous pitfalls. Each of the following topics is addressed:

- focus on demands
- teacher role expansion
- determining and managing results
- administrative obstacles to overcome
- organizational dissonance
- deficient motivation and reinforcement practices

This chapter provides insight regarding the day-to-day problems and considerations which make or break compensation systems.

Mr. John Littleford offers the private school perspective of alternative compensation systems. In this chapter, he provides an overview of independent school salary administration policies and practices over the past fifteen years and the recent shift to the career ladder concept. The author compares public and independent school salary programs and offers a comparative analysis of the innovations taking place. He further suggests that the two systems are coming together in a career ladder structure that provides predictability of future earning power with some degree of performance recognition.

PART VI—ALTERNATIVE COMPENSATION PROGRAMS IN ACTION

Dr. Lynn Cornett has tracked Career Ladder Programs in the United States for the past eight years. In this chapter, she states and analyzes the trends and issues in incentive programs for teachers and administrators. Current programs are assessed on the basis of the following questions:

- Are attitudes of teachers and administrators toward incentive pay changing?
- Is education improving because of these programs?
- Will states and school districts continue the commitments to incentive pay programs for the long term so that their effectiveness can be evaluated?

Chapter 15, by Professor Ann Hart, offers a comprehensive view of the Utah Career Ladder Programs. Professor Hart draws heavily on the job-characteristics model and work redesign in her analysis of the Utah plans. A hard-hitting prognosis is offered for career ladders in Utah as she offers the following prescriptions:

- discrete assessment of work and pay feature available in Career Ladder Plans
- avoidance of general statements about "The Career Ladder"
- increased focus on outcomes and less on procedural and *pro forma* compliance with regulation
- stable long-term approval and funding
- constant emphasis on the school level impacts of reforms on instruction and the psychosocial environment in schools, which shape these impacts

Professor Hart's chapter complements Chapters 8 by Frase and 11 by Conley and Bacharach in that both approach the topic of compensation systems by analyzing the teachers' interaction with work and the resulting impact on teacher motivation levels.

Dr. Robert Spillane began a pay-for-performance program in 1984 in Fairfax County Schools. In this chapter, he outlines the processes utilized beginning with a pilot test, establishment of a "Blue Ribbon Committee," and involvement of the school board, teachers, and community leaders. The goal was to provide a program that ensures an excellent teacher in every classroom, gives help to the marginal teacher, terminates the ineffective teacher, and provides financial incentives to the very best teachers. The processes utilized to accomplish this goal and the political roadblocks encountered are described.

PART VII—RESTRUCTURING AND COMPENSATION PROGRAMS IN ACTION

Restructuring does not fit, in the traditional sense, the category of alternative compensation programs. Restructuring programs may not offer pay for performance or career ladders, and money may not be used as a motivational carrot, but restructuring does focus on teacher motivation, with the ultimate outcome being better learning for students. Indeed, teacher compensation has found the limelight in some restructuring projects and attempts are afoot to link pay with student outcomes.

Five projects were chosen for inclusion in this book: Rochester, New York; San Diego City Schools, California; Kyrene Public Schools, Arizona; Lake Forest, Illinois; and Cave Creek Unified School District, Arizona. These are five of the largest and most widely recognized projects in the nation and offer tremendous promise for restructuring education.

The Rochester restructuring project is described by Dr. Manuel Rivera, deputy superintendent of the Rochester City School District. Although the highly touted $69,500 teacher salary ceiling has captured much press, there are other more intricate and possibly more valuable aspects of this project. One is the peer assistance and review program, and another is the career in teaching program, which serves to restructure the teaching profession in Rochester. Detailed explanations are provided regarding the use of the teachers' contract as a vehicle for bringing about these changes through active participation with teachers. Three elements are crucial to the success of these reforms: 1) all efforts must be directed towards improving student performance, 2) the efforts must be accompanied by parent and community satisfaction with the quality of service provided, and 3) student achievement will serve as the barometer for measuring success.

Dr. Thomas Payzant offers a blueprint of "restructuring" in San Diego. He begins with work with the board, community groups, and the teachers' union. Board policies and union agreements are presented in their entirety. School site waivers are a major element in the San

Diego plan and are explained in detail through a Waiver Process Flow Chart. An effort not only to involve employees but to give them ownership of the project is a hallmark and is stressed through shared decision making. Assessment of the impact of restructuring on students is highlighted. Traditional norm-referenced tests are eschewed in favor of authentic assessment, e.g., portfolios.

Superintendent Carolyn Downey and Assistant Superintendent Carol Parish offer a thorough description of the Career Ladder Program in the Kyrene Public Schools in Tempe, Arizona. The authors offer the Kyrene strategies used to negate factors that have been the demise of many career ladder and other compensation programs. The following, among others, are discussed: poor teacher evaluation procedures, teacher opposition, poorly prepared evaluators, and quotas. A concise review of the Kyrene teacher evaluation system is provided.

The Kyrene career ladder and companion salary schedules are compared to other career ladders, traditional salary schedules, and basic tenets of motivational theory such as

- Focus on professional growth.
- Provide a plan for all staff, rather than the exceptional few.
- Foster collegial efforts and cooperation.
- Focus rewards on *classroom instruction.*
- Offer teachers a variety of rewards to choose from.

All of the above and practical descriptions of how teachers advance through the steps of the career ladder are discussed in detail.

District 67, the Lake Forest Public Schools in Lake Forest, Illinois, has successfully operated a merit pay program for teachers for over forty years. Superintendent Allen Klingenberg provides key insights into this very successful plan. He compares the corporate and school district government model and highlights the Lake Forest evaluation plan, which, as in the Kyrene model, focuses on *quality of classroom instruction*, not extra duties. The evaluation instrument is research based, a modified MBO system is in place for both teachers and administrators, and student and parent feedback is utilized.

Superintendent Klingenberg outlines the theoretical assumptions and tenants of the Lake Forest merit pay system, the basic commitments required of the governing board and concludes the chapter with a review of the results of evaluations of the project from the eyes of teachers, parents, and students.

Superintendent Alexander and Professor Richard Manatt offer a thorough and critical review of the Cave Creek Career Ladder Program. In his third month as superintendent, David Alexander was confronted with news from the Arizona State Department of Education: the Cave Creek Career Ladder Program was not in compliance with State requirements and funding was to be terminated. With that challenge, he teamed up with Professor Manatt's School Improvement Model (SIM) located at Iowa State University to redesign the program, particularly the teacher evaluation system.

The outcome is a research based teacher evaluation system that incorporates peer evaluations, principals' evaluations, student achievement and feedback, and a professional growth plan. The results are very positive. Cave Creek has been granted continued funding. Teachers have accepted the program with positive enthusiasm, and there is evidence that the plan has resulted in increased student achievement.

PART I

HISTORY, POLICY, AND MOTIVATIONAL ISSUES

CHAPTER 1

History and Critical Issues of Educational Compensation Systems

FENWICK ENGLISH – *University of Cincinnati*

No one would be concerned about compensation systems at all if they were not connected to work. While it is true that people believe they work for money, money is but a very small part of the complexity of issues surrounding work.

Human work extends far back into the misty origins of the human species on earth. It is known that early people were nomadic and roamed in groups to find game as food. The hunting group was probably the first true *work group* (Henderson, 1976, p. 11). Hunting groups were a necessity for prehistoric peoples to survive. It is in the social bonds of the hunting group that some of the most powerful aspects of human work were revealed. Here, as today, work was inherently *social* involving *recognition, cooperation, and rewards.*

The hunting group involved teamwork and that in turn rested upon developing and adhering to instructions depending upon the nature of the animal and the means used to kill it. It was an occasion to use judgment, cunning, and creativity, which blended in with actions taken by others. At the end of the kill, a person earned recognition and appreciation of individual effort.

When early Homo sapiens learned the tasks of agriculture in growing crops and domesticating animals for slaughter instead of hunting them, the true rise of civilization began. Agriculture initiated the development of special skills, the formation of social classes, and extended learning of special groups of leaders who became the ruling priest class (Henderson, 1976, p. 13).

While the nature of work has changed, the fact that it consumes between 30 and 80 percent of the waking time of most people is still as true today as it was millions of years ago.

The genesis of modern day compensation systems was the development of factories as harbingers of the industrial revolution. Throughout several hundreds of years, compensation became attached to the money-centered economy. The money economy meant that the *value* and *meaning* of work was translated into and often defined by *money*. And as the industrial revolution redefined wealth, large masses of people moved away from the brink of daily starvation to extended lines of food supply. Today, most people look upon their work as being *more than* physically required simply to survive. Work today is inherently *psychological*. The fundamental purpose of work then lies in its capability to be mentally fulfilling. This is especially true for people who are involved in a profession (see Etzioni, 1969).

Early teachers were hired directly by members of boards of education. They were paid in money, with free room and board ("boarding around" as it was called) (Tyack, 1974, p. 19), and with gratitude. The low pay was also indicative of the low status of teachers.

As free public schooling became accepted as a norm of the nation, the demand for a large supply of *cheap* teachers also escalated. In this respect, a sexist society determined that teaching was a respectable occupation for a woman (hence the definition of teaching as "woman's work") as long as the teacher was not married (see Kaufman, 1984). When teachers married, they were forced to retire from the classroom. When principals, who were usually male, were added to schools, the large presence of unmarried females signaled to some historians that schoolhouses were "pedagogical harems" (Spring, 1986, p. 136).

Because women were denied work almost everywhere else in society, salaries could be kept low. The teaching profession is filled with long diatribes regarding the chronic low pay of classroom pedagogues. J. P. Wickersham, state superintendent of Pennsylvania, wrote in his report for the year 1866:

> Let facts tell the story. Of the whole number of persons examined as teachers in the year 1865, 12,171 received provisional certificates, and 388 professional certificates, and 1,351 were rejected. The large number of provisional certificates given indicates either a general want of scholarship, or of experience, or both. It indicates no doubt a want of both, for the average grade of such certificates in the State was 2 1/8 in a scale of 5, and this average was probably rather too high than too low, and there were as previously stated, 4,682 teachers who had never taught at all, or had taught less than one year, 5,641 who had never read a book relating to their profession, and 10,336 who had never attended any kind of Normal school. . . . The average age of all the teachers examined was twenty-three and a third years. (Wickersham, 1866, p. xiii)

The state superintendent then went on to indicate the remedy for these conditions:

The inducement of longer terms and better salaries must be held out to teachers. . . . Well qualified teachers are constantly leaving the profession and the inexperienced ones are constantly taking their places, and in this state of things no rapid rise in the general standard of qualifications is possible. (p. xiii)

The solution over time was to develop salary schedules and for the respective states to adopt a starting minimum salary below which no individual school system could pay teachers. However, early salary schedules were basically *position-based,* i.e., attached to the level where the teacher worked (Greider, Pierce, and Rosenstengel, 1961, p. 240). The *position-based* salary schedule served to add some uniformity to the matter of pay for teachers, but they were overtly sexist since elementary teachers were paid less than secondary teachers and most elementary teachers were female.

Cubberley attacked such schedules as violative of "sound administrative principles" because they forced teachers to consider the salary attached to a position and not where he/she might do the best job (Cubberley, 1929, p. 380).

Later, after nearly fifty years of labor by the National Education Association, teacher salary schedules became unified by eliminating position as the focus for pay. Instead the "single salary schedule plan" was based on recognizing training and experience as the most important factors to recognize rather than position and experience (Cubberley, 1929, p. 303).

The single salary schedule remains the dominant pay model in the U.S.A. today. At least one sociologist has indicated that this pay model fits perfectly into an *equalitarian* work structure dominated by females (Lortie, 1969, p. 21). The school work structure, which is dominated by a salary mechanism now insensitive to grade, specialization, or competence (and performance), *negates* administrative control over the work cadre as well. Such a pay schedule serves to provide teachers with greater autonomy than if their cadre were capable of being manipulated by such devices (Lortie, 1969, p. 8). The ringing condemnation of any alternative to the single salary schedule by teacher unions or associations is at least in part a fear that the solidarity of the teaching cadre will be seriously undermined as a result. Union power rests upon cadre solidarity. This problem with power over teachers (either by administrators and boards or their own unions) also explains union attacks of any "piece rate" pay plan as opposed to straight time compensation (see Millis and Montgomery, 1945, p. 356).

The American teacher salary schedule has thus evolved over several hundred years to its present structure. Understanding how it got to be the way it is means knowing the socioeconomic and political problems and decisions that led to its formulation, growth, and finally hegemony over all competing forms that might exist today.

SALARY ALTERNATIVES

While the single salary schedule solved some problems, it failed to deal with others. The shortcomings of any salary schedule that was insensitive to performance has also been chronic in U.S. schools. For example, Adams County, Pennsylvania, Superintendent Aaron Sheeley commented in his annual report to the state in 1867:

> I cannot but condemn the practice, prevailing to some extent, of paying all teachers the same wages; the merest tyro in the art as much as the well qualified, experienced teacher. It seems to me that by this course directors actually offer a premium to mediocrity, if not to positive ignorance and incompetency. Inducements should always be held out to teachers to duly qualify themselves for their work; and it seems to me that this can best be done by means of salaries increasing progressively in proportion to the amount and value of the services performed. This would excite the emulation of teachers, and thus could be established a system of promotion advantageous to the schools. (Wickersham, 1868, pp. 8–9)

Not only did Sheeley use arguments that were to become very familiar in the 1980s and the Reagan Administration, but he foresaw the implementation of career ladders by over 100 years (Burden, 1987).

Even the stolid Elwood Cubberley, while conceding advantages to the single salary schedule plan, proffered that it should be augmented "with additional rewards for professional growth and demonstrated efficiency after the common maximum has been reached, [and] offers one of the best means for providing the proper stimulus for further professional development" (Cubberley, 1929, p. 393).

The major challenge to the standard or single salary schedule has been *merit pay*. Merit pay is the idea that a teacher should be paid in whole or in part on the *quality of his or her performance* (ERS, 1979, p. 1). The first recorded attempt at instituting merit pay in a U.S. school system was in 1908 in Newton, Massachusetts (Robinson, 1984, p. 3). Interest emerged again with the election of the Reagan Administration, which made merit pay one of its "bully pulpit" issues (English, 1983–84, p. 72).

Merit pay has been one of the most tracked educational issues in the U.S., due largely to the frequency of its propositions and the hostility engendered to it by organized teacher groups. In a national survey of merit pay and incentive pay plans conducted by the Educational Research Service (ERS) in 1977–78, it was revealed that 183 school systems had tried one and discontinued it after a time. The average number of years that the plans were functional was six (ERS, 1979, p. 39). It must be noted that numerous school districts, such as Catalina Foothills School District in Tucson, Arizona, and the LaDue School District in LaDue, Missouri, continue to operate performance pay plans.

ERS discerned that the reasons for the failure of merit pay plans in its survey were administrative problems (40.2 percent), personnel problems (38.4 percent), collective bargaining (18.0 percent), financial problems (16.7 percent), and a variety of other problems such as adverse publicity when the names of teachers receiving the merit awards were published in the local paper (5.9 percent) (ERS, 1979, p. 41).

Another salary alternative to the single salary schedule was that of differentiated staffing (English and Sharpes, 1972). Differentiated staffing's rationale for different pay for teachers was that they performed different tasks for which they were paid different amounts. Even utilizing the time-worn concept of "additional pay for additional duties" long accepted by unions, the concept was attacked by both the NEA (National Education Association) and the AFT (American Federation of Teachers) as merit pay in disguise (English, 1972).

In the 1980s the concept of career ladders was reintroduced from its old differentiated staffing roots and blended in with the idea of merit pay. The most notable example was the Tennessee Plan where a four-tiered teacher hierarchy model, quite similar to the Temple City Differentiated Staffing Model of the 1970s (Christensen, 1987), was implemented on a state-wide basis.

The Tennessee Plan created a four-tiered teacher "ladder" of offices and jobs, which varied in complexity and time required, and entry was restricted to an assessment of the quality of teaching performance among other things. This was a different twist than the Temple City approach, where initial entry was determined not on merit, but on overall qualifications for a post as determined by a colleague panel. Tennessee used direct evaluations of teachers by trained observers, tests of professional knowledge, and the compilations of dossiers by applicants called "portfolios."

The concept of career ladders drew the familiar battle cries of the organized teacher unions as generally undesirable (Futrell, 1987); however, AFT President Albert Shanker had modified his stance conceding, "It may be time to reexamine some of the ideas that we rejected in the past when conditions were quite different from what they are now. . . . A careful examination of differentiated staffing programs attempted in the past would be useful at this time to provide guidance for decision makers" (Shanker, 1987, p. 238).

One theme runs through the failures of both merit pay and differentiated staffing plans—that is, their first rationale must be to improve instruction and not simply to pay teachers differently (Frase, 1982). Even if most of the plans have failed, they did accomplish paying teachers differently. The real question is, "So what?" The jury is still out on the effects of performance pay (Frase, 1989; Staw, Calder, Hess, and Sandelands, 1980; Deci, 1976). However, districts successfully implementing such programs suggest that rectifying the inequities of the single salary schedule is sufficient justification. Because of this now-established dilemma, anyone contemplating changing an educational compensation system must deal with at least two dimensions of impact. There are those outcomes of the change that impact the individual alone and those that are interactive upon the individual in his or her work group. Some compensation alternatives are destructive both of individual performance and of group performance productivity.

So asking the question, "Can we pay teachers differently?" should be considered answered. The answer is affirmative. The better question is, "Why pay teachers differently?" Other questions might be, "What happens when we pay teachers differently?" or even more significantly, "How can we improve teacher productivity and performance?" If the latter question is asked with an open mind, there are powerful responses that may involve absolutely no change in the compensation system per se. There may be changes in working relationships, working conditions, recognition, and nonmonetary rewards as suggested by Frase (1982, 1989) that might be contemplated, but all *within* the existing compensation system. The issue is too complex to be solved completely with compensation alone. That perhaps is the real failure of all the previous merit pay and differentiated staffing plans of the past—they were unidimensional solutions to multidimensional problems.

ISSUES WITH PERFORMANCE AND PAY

Those interested in changing the current compensation system in schools customarily enter the process by asking, "Shouldn't high performers in our classrooms be rewarded?" The question is framed in such a way as to make anything but a positive answer appear trivial or even contrary to the kind of competitive outlook that built America. Yet the question precludes a more open-ended inquiry that would help in considering workable answers in the end.

Let us take an example of where simplistic approaches have led to something less than anticipated by the change agents of compensation systems. Suppose that in school district "X" the superintendent becomes convinced that outstanding teachers should be recognized and compensated differently. He convinces the board that it is almost a "sin" not to do so. The plan calls for awarding outstanding teachers a bonus of $1500, exemplary teachers $1000, and meritorious teachers $500. Scanning his budget he feels that he can afford approximately ten awards at each level for a total of $30,000. He then has to decide whether these are one-time awards or will be permanently attached to whatever base salary the winners may possess. While he believes that the awards should be one time only, he knows that that idea would be far too revolutionary to be accepted by the teachers as a cadre. So he makes the awards permanent appendages to the base. This means that the additional $30,000 in awards will forever be part of his salary line in the budget. Over ten years the amount becomes $300,000 plus cost of living adjustments, which use the old base in calculating percentage increases. Thus, the district will pay for one year of exemplary teaching until each of the teachers retires in the district.

At the time of the awards, several teachers who are not recognized at all file a grievance with the union alleging "administrative favoritism" in the evaluation process. That results in a hearing in which the district's evaluation process is exposed for being incomplete and subjective in nature. Furthermore, none of the principals are adequately trained, and so the union shows through expert testimony that there were probably a lot of reliability questions asked that could not be properly answered.

Some teachers who receive less than the $1500 award were secretly miffed about it because they believed they deserved the higher award. They vow to work behind the scenes to rid the system of the plan. Some new teachers who didn't expect to be rewarded like the plan but don't know whether to share the fact they were compensated with their older colleagues for fear they will be ostracized by them.

With a mere $30,000 investment the superintendent and the board have succeeded in *lowering* individual productivity of some teachers, even those who won awards, and *lowering* the overall productivity of the entire teaching cadre. They did so all in the name of simply trying to recognize superior performance. What they missed was the multidimensional nature of compensation problems. Teachers do not work in a vacuum. They work individually in a collective, i.e., a group. But that group is divided by separate workplaces, "hidden" from one another. Unlike the primitive hunter groups of our ancestors, they don't get to see "superior performance" in action. All they see is their own performance. Since they are already working as hard as they know how, already exercising every technique they learned, it is difficult to believe anyone else has any other secrets of which they are unaware. Therefore, differences in performance must be attributed more to "favoritism" than anything else.

Any alternative compensation plan that does not recognize the psychosocial nature of work may do more harm than good. It may account for the short life of most merit pay plans that have been tried in the past and are likely to continue to be attempted in the future. Good intentions and traditional American values will not be enough to carry the day. In short, common sense frequently takes a bashing on this issue.

UNLOCKING THE QUESTIONS ABOUT PAY AND PERFORMANCE

A more promising approach is not to begin with the compensation system at all. Compensation systems ought to follow as a solution to a larger issue. That issue is to begin by asking, "Why do people work? What makes people work hard?" and "How do we define, implement, and sustain outstanding work?" For a more detailed discussion of these questions, see Chapter 3.

At the outset any reasonably experienced teacher or administrator has to concede that he or she knows of places where morale is high, educators are working diligently, children are learning, and the compensation system is indifferent to all of those qualities. An open-minded inquiry would not only ask, "How can the system be changed to recognize and reward those qualities?" but equally, "Why do people do what they do now *without* those characteristics of recognition and reward being present in the compensation system?"

If it is possible to create a working situation that appears to maximize human productivity *without* changing the compensation system, can that productivity be *sustained* without any changes as well? To answer that probe means digging around a bit and discerning who it is we may want to motivate, recognize, and reward in our schools.

The bulk of the teaching cadre is female. In 1986, 86.2 percent of the elementary teachers, 61.4 percent of the junior high school teachers, and 47 percent of the high school teachers were women (U.S. Bureau of Census, 1987, p. 129). It has been well-documented that women bring into teaching a different set of values than men (see Zeigler, 1967). Teaching has been called an "in and out" profession for women, i.e., they "drop in" for a while, then they "drop out" to have children. Some return after that initial experience and some do not.

Since teaching has never been a profession or occupation that paid as well as other alternatives, women and men would never enter teaching because of or solely for high pay. This is especially true for women since teaching has historically been a "first choice" profession for females. Lortie (1969) has indicated that teaching, most specifically elementary teaching, "is clearly congruent with feminine socialization, work styles, and familial roles" (p. 21). Lortie quotes Caplow (1954) who states that, "The absence of interpersonal rivalry for monetary rewards fits the socialization experiences . . . attributed to American women" (p. 243). This state of affairs may well offer an explanation as to why it is possible to create a highly productive work environment for teachers without changing the existing compensation system. It seems logical that if the bulk of the teaching force came into teaching for some other reason than salary, it would be possible to motivate individuals and the cadre without substantial changes in the compensation system. It may also explain the historical resistance to such changes by teacher unions/associations who argue that are counterproductive to teacher morale (see Futrell, 1987).

Any proposed plan to alter educational compensation systems must account for how it proposes to deal with the *social context* in which the bulk of teachers are engaged. When educators examine compensation alternatives used elsewhere, as for example, in industrial/business settings, these tend to be working environments in which the largest number of people are male, particularly with business executives. To superimpose a compensation plan from a male-dominated business setting onto a feminine-dominated occupation like teaching is to assume that the context for the work is also similar. That it is clearly not the case ought to be at least in part underscored by the high failure rate of compensation plans used in business, which have been unsuccessfully transplanted into educational settings over eight decades. However, when it comes to merit pay for school administrators, business practices may well have greater applicability in this role level than with classroom teaching. School administration has been male-dominated for many decades, so the likelihood of attitudinal differences existing in the administrative cadre, which are more conducive to monetary differences and potential rivalries, are and have been more acceptable in administration than in teaching (see ERS, *Merit Pay for School Administrators*, 1979).

To complicate matters a bit further and to emphasize the cultural aspects of compensation, a brief glimpse at the world's leaders in productivity may be interesting. Japan has dazzled the world with its record levels of productivity, quality products, and domination of selected industrial and high tech markets. Japanese students have led the Western world in standardized test scores for at least a decade, particularly in math and science. If one were to examine the compensation of Japanese teachers who at least at the secondary level are 80–85 percent male, one finds a system rooted in seniority as the only method of driving pay increases (Rohlen, 1983): "Japanese companies use promotion as a motivating factor. But in high schools only peer pressure, personal pride and informal leadership have influence" (p. 176). Rohlen is also quick to add that because there is no recognition of such differences, particularly in the assumption of extra administrative duties in Japanese teachers' paychecks, "this provokes considerable cynicism, resentment, and disapproval."

Apparently, in spite of such negative attitudes being present in Japanese high schools, student learning is quite high by any standard measure anyway. So there appears to be no "perfect" compensation system that everybody finds acceptable. Perhaps one reason is found in human organizations themselves; i.e., people want different things from their organizations at different times in their lives. Even if a human organization was able to attain a perfect match with the needs and perceptions of its work force, as the needs of that work force shift, the pay structure would soon find itself at odds with that change if it were not adaptable as well. This apparent descriptor of the human condition is perhaps best described in the work of Abraham Maslow (1954) who posited that there appeared to be a kind of hierarchy of human need. At the bottom of that hierarchy were so-called "survival needs." These included needs for safety, food, and other creature comforts. However, as these needs were met, human beings' perceptions and needs escalated to the next level beyond those satiated. In turn, when these needs became satisfied, there was even a higher level. The last level of Maslow's hierarchy dealt with "self-actualization." This pinnacle of need was concerned with reaching one's full potential, the desire to be self-developed and truly creative.

Maslow's concept is truly instructive when considering compensation alternatives. Perhaps the greatest challenge to the design of a compensation system is the flexibility required to adapt to the changing needs of the group whom the system is supposed to motivate and thereby optimize their work performance. The optimization of work performance, particularly at the upper ends of Maslow's hierarchy, will require some significant changes in working conditions as well as compensation in terms of straight salary. For example, for a classroom teacher to fully engage in self-actualization, his or her teaching responsibilities may have to be expanded beyond the four walls of their traditional work space. It may also necessitate the capability of straying away from mandated curricula in order to be truly creative within the act of teaching.

REDEFINING COMPENSATION AND ITS BOUNDARIES

Wages refers to hourly pay and *salary* refers to payment on a longer basis such as weekly or monthly (Greenlaw and Kohl, 1986, p. 282). *Compensation* refers to the entire package a person may receive in the form of money, benefits, and other nonfinancial rewards (Belcher and Atchison, 1987, p. 4). Developing a compensation system means attempting to deal with virtually all of the issues that would bear upon securing people for work in school systems; evaluating their performance in order to make decisions regarding retention, transfer, demotion, or promotion; and developing responses that ensure maximization of their continued loyalty and high productivity over time.

This definition of *compensation system* shifts the focus to a more encompassing question than simply pay. It de-emphasizes pay as the only or even the most important issue within the entire compensation question and focuses on every area that concerns human beings and what makes them want to work and to work well consistently.

Suppose one were going to design a compensation system to fit Maslow's hierarchy of needs. First, such a compensation system would have to have enough internal flexibility to be able to be responsive to changing needs. For example, Maslow's initial level of need is physiological needs, followed by safety needs as the second level. Examining the mix of broad variables within a compensation system, it is at this level that money is probably most important, followed by benefits, most specifically medical benefits. For the beginning teacher nonfinancial rewards might seem fairly far removed from those needs that require some immediate attention.

However, as teachers mature and their pay improves, they may be less responsive to lower level safety needs and more responsive to nonfinancial motivators, such as recognition of outstanding performance, that satisfy esteem needs. A little money will go a lot further at this point of a teacher's career than it would if the teacher were located at a more survival-type benchmark.

A compensation system that had as its first objective the optimization of professional performance would have to recognize the fact that the internal state of the teacher's own motivation to work is the single most important part of sustaining outstanding performance (Steffy, 1989). Therefore the compensation system would have to have the capability to shift and readjust its three major components of money, benefits, and nonfinancial rewards accordingly. A compensation plan that will be successful must understand the psychosocial state of the work force not only to be accepted, but to truly work in improving the overall work productivity of the entire cadre at any point in time.

THE STRATEGIC CONCEPT OF EQUITY

Perhaps from the point of view of a strategic concept, the idea of *equity* is one of the most important factors in constructing a compensation plan. A synonym that most workers would use to describe the concept of equity is *fairness*. From a personnel perspective, "fairness is achieved when the return on equity is equivalent to the investment made" (Wallace and Fay, 1988, p. 14). Adams (1963) has theorized that people in an organization constantly monitor a kind of exchange relationship with that organization. At the heart of the monitoring relationship is the notion of *distributive justice.* This idea means that "the proportionate relation between outcomes and inputs is equal for all persons in the relationship. Thus, distributive justice defines fairness and equity" (Wallace and Fay, 1988, p. 15).

An example of a perceived lack of fairness is cited by Wallace and Fay (1988) regarding star halfback Tony Dorsett, formerly of the Dallas Cowboys. Dorestt was being paid about $450,000 a year, with a benefits package that brought the base pay up to nearly $700,000 per year. This hefty salary and fringe benefit package wasn't enough to stop him from complaining when the Cowboys gave new halfback Herschel Walker, an untried NFL player, a million dollars per year. Dorsett felt he was being unfairly treated and said so (p. 4).

At stake for Dorsett was the concept of distributive justice. He felt that with a proven record of accomplishment for the Cowboys and Walker's unproven performance, he was not being treated fairly. His attitude and performance were affected. So the amount involved does not necessarily guarantee high performance or even good morale, a fact underscored by Herzberg, Mausner, and Snyderman's classic study reported in *The Motivation to Work* (1967).

There are at least three facets of the concept of equity. They are *external equity, internal equity,* and *individual equity. External equity* refers to setting pay for work that corresponds to corollaries in the external marketplace. In this situation one might compare teacher salaries from one district to another nearby or to occupations that involved cores of similar skills possessed by teachers.

The concept of *internal equity* involves setting pay for the value of the work performed *within the organization. Individual equity* revolves around paying employees for merit or performance (Wallace and Fay, 1988, p. 25). Each avenue of equity can be answered separately. However, if this occurs, a school system can work at cross purposes with its own needs. For example, suppose that to secure the professional services of a physics teacher, a school system finds its base salary schedule clearly uncompetitive. Physics teachers often have backgrounds and skills in great demand in private sector jobs. The difference between private and public sectors can be quite marked. So a decision is made based on the idea of *external equity* that since the salary schedule cannot be raised overall to the level required to be competitive for physics teachers, the district will add salary based on market forces in order to become competitive. While universities have a long history of engaging in this practice, it is still not widely used at the elementary and secondary levels.

Suppose that the district is able to hire physics teachers as a result. However, teachers in other disciplines like English, physical education, and foreign language now feel like Tony Dorsett. It isn't that their salaries have been decreased per se; rather, they feel less valuable to the school system than before. They feel they are being treated unfairly. If they withdraw their services, or if their services decrease in quality or quantity, the school system has *both* gained something and lost something.

The same scenario can also occur if a system focuses only on the issue of *individual equity*. Suppose a newly installed performance appraisal system is responsible for some teachers receiving merit increases, while others fail to attain the increases. Because of botched implementation, the attempt to derive individual equity results in a loss to perceived overall *internal equity* within the system at large. A very negative reaction can also affect *external equity*.

A truly effective compensation system must account for all three forms of equity, and it is quite likely to be tilted more on some equity indices than others. For this reason there is going to be tension consistently present inside and outside of school systems on equity issues most of the time. There is probably no compensation plan that can satisfy equally well on all three dimensions all the time. The question is one of balance and priorities. Balance is also one of proportionality rather than strict equality as well.

THE STRATEGIC ISSUE OF CONTROL

Control is a critical and necessary ingredient of changing the traditional compensation system. It is one thing to develop an alternative compensation model; it is quite another to have the control necessary to implement it. To bring about compensation system changes, it is necessary to *manage expectations* and *manage results* (Wallace and Fay, 1988, pp. 78–81).

The management of expectations is firmly grounded in *expectancy theory;* i.e., people in organizations will do well as they come to believe that those actions will be recognized and rewarded by those with the power. At the heart of this relationship lies the *expectation* that action "X" will lead to outcome "Y."

The second issue is searching for rewards that have *motivational value* to induce people to engage in efforts that are desired by the organization and then *linking* the rewards to the work efforts in a compensation system. To carry this off, management has to come into the relationship with the power to control *both* results and the incentives tied to them. Finally, management must make sure that pay actually influences performance (reinforcement theory) or the impact of the system will be negligible.

It is just this kind of managerial power that is in dispute in schools today. The "teacher empowerment" advocates would argue that such raw managerial power has proven unresponsive to the challenge of producing meaningful educational change in schools. They would point out that it is time to alter the power relationships accordingly (see Darling-Hammond, 1986, p. 76). Yet to shift the power relationships to a more egalitarian base may portend losing the very kind of authority necessary to alter the compensation system to make it more responsive to linking pay to performance. If one argues for a group based pay approach, one also has to confront the historical evidence; i.e., there are few examples in the literature where a group that comes into power makes themselves any more accountable or vulnerable than they are forced to be. When medical doctors control hospitals or lawyers run law firms, they are not more accountable than before.

It is also quite clear to teacher unions/associations that the real issue over pay and performance is indeed *control*. Establishing that linkage puts into the hands of the administration and the board greater potential coercive authority than before because there is a more direct and visible linkage between work and salary. The current salary schedule does indeed blunt and thus limit the power of the administration and the board to "tighten" the reins if they so desire. In short, different approaches to compensation will ensure greater compliance to whatever those in authority desire to accomplish. Unions tend to see this development as a threat, while management sees it as an opportunity. The two positions are not implacably opposed, but reconciliation is made infinitely more difficult if both sides are not honest about the real issue at stake, and there is only one—the power to control the rewards in the teaching profession.

ALTERNATIVES TO MONEY MOTIVATIONS

Compensation systems have traditionally relied on money to motivate, whether through the single salary schedule or merit pay. The effectiveness of money as a motivator has been the subject of much debate (see Chapter 9). Contrary to claims by merit pay proponents, there is little or no evidence to prove that money motivates teachers to work harder or better. Indeed, use of extrinsic rewards may stifle intrinsic motivation (Deci, 1975; Daniel and Esser, 1980; Staw, Calder, Hess, and Sandelands, 1980). Based on the absence of data indicating that money is an effective motivator, the only justification for differentiating pay on the basis of performance may be that it is the "right thing to do"—i.e., more should be paid to those who produce more or perform better, as a general principle.

The failure of most merit pay programs and the continuing desire to reward performance has led others to search for rewards with motivational value. A few reward systems of the 1980s have moved beyond monetary rewards (merit pay) in their search for rewards with motivational value. One such program utilized rewards derived from Herzberg's Motivation–Hygiene Theory for outstanding classroom instruction (Frase, Hetzel, and Grant, 1982). Research on this program indicates that rewards such as professional travel have greater motivational value than money (Frase, 1989). The program and related research are described in Chapter 9.

Other alternative programs offered teachers the opportunity to choose the method by which they would be evaluated (Hatry and Griener, 1985), while another offered teachers grants for staff development and curriculum projects (Mann, 1984). Both programs focused on the motivational potential of recognition, one of Herzberg's motivators. Reports on the projects are promising, but no formal research has been reported.

Some Career Ladder Programs have also looked beyond money for effective motivators. The report on the Utah Career Ladder Program in Chapter 15 illustrates the use of the Job-Characteristics Model (JCM) to shape a Career Ladder Program and to restructure the role of the teacher. The JCM is based on the assumption that work can be a powerful motivator and that good performance is satisfying. The strategy of the model is to create work characteristics that allow workers to perform well. Reports on the program are encouraging, although no formal research to assess the effects of the program has been completed.

Certainly, both the Motivation–Hygiene Theory and the JCM offer promising alternatives to the use of money as motivators.

THE SCHOOL SYSTEM AS AN INTERACTIVE VARIABLE: ORGANIZATIONAL CULTURE

How the school system goes about engaging in the process of implementation will determine to a great extent the reactions of people affected by any new pay-for-performance plan. In short, how the organization establishes its alternative says a lot to people about its real motives. People determine motives from actions and not so much from words; actions reveal intent, while words often conceal intent.

One of the first issues regarding process concerns the concept of *organizational culture* (Dean and Kennedy, 1982). Sethia and Glinow (1985) have indicated that there are four basic types of organizational cultures to consider for the purpose of designing a compatible reward system. The four cultures are cross-referenced on two axes—concern for people and concern for performance (p. 409). The *caring culture* is one that has a high concern for people and a low concern for performance. An *apathetic culture* is one that has low concerns for both people and performance. The culture that possesses high concerns for performance but low concerns for people has been labeled *exacting*. A culture that is considered both high in terms of concerns about people and performance has been named *integrative*.

Sethia and Glinow (1985) then examine the kinds of dimensions in a reward system that appear to be congruent with a given organizational culture. For example, in the *apathetic culture,* the worst of the four, status differentials are high, but rewards for career advancement and job content are quite poor. The criteria for rewards in such cultures is determined more by manipulation, politicking, and patronage than by other factors. These behaviors are entirely logical given the fact that within an *apathetic culture* there is little evidence of either concerns about people or concerns about performance.

The *caring culture* exhibits concerns about people for career rewards, but places only compliance minimums on performance. It shows deference to position and to membership in the culture, but little else.

The *exacting culture* places greater emphasis on performance than people. In this culture, performance results are viewed largely in the short term. There is a great deal of stress on measures of efficiency and nonconforming members are viewed as "replaceable." In this culture, management establishes internal competition among individuals, so success is always individual and almost never group based.

The *integrative culture* represents the epitome of an organizational climate that has high concerns for people and performance. Career rewards in this culture are very high; status differentials are quite low. Group and company/firm success is very high and performance results are long-term. In this culture, innovation and independence are valued and equity concerns are prevalent. Nonconforming members are not first viewed as renegades or deviants, but as people with potential as yet untapped by the organization.

It is clear from these descriptions that in order to install any new compensation system successfully, the school system itself cannot be considered a sort of "neutral" or noninteractive variable. School systems and the values they embrace are *major interactive variables* in installing alternative compensation systems. They not only shape which compensation systems will be successful, they also powerfully mold the reactions of people in the organization.

Let us take for example a school system that has for years been dominated by high concerns for people and low concerns for performance. A *caring culture* will also have driven from its embrace administrators and teachers who also demonstrated concerns about performance because of the inevitable conflicts in values, so the system will be staffed by "good hearts." The system may have rationalized its failures on tests and other measures.

Finally, in frustration a board election brings onto the board persons experienced in management who are vitally concerned with test scores. They, in turn, force out the old superintendent and bring in one from a school system that has been dominated by the *exacting culture.* The new superintendent, ignorant of the differences in cultures and anxious to please his board, ushers forth a series of bold proposals to change the compensation relationships dramatically to focus on outcomes. He meets massive indifference and then open hostility. He is accused of "not caring" about people. He is accused of trying to impose an industrial machine model on a "human" enterprise like education.

If the resistance is driven to extremes, it will take to the streets and seek to change the political relationships, beginning with the board itself. This will then again alter the mix in the governance process and may result in the removal of the superintendent. One can find these scenarios dotting the national educational landscape rather frequently, with a discerning investigation.

Few other types of alterations in the compensation system will usher forth such a vitriolic response from the people inside a school system.

If such changes were inconsequential, it would not matter. The power of linking pay to performance is underscored by the animosity it often engenders in the opponents to the idea. The opponents may argue that pay is not a major variable anyway, but their emotions often belie this claim at the outset.

To link some earlier themes in this piece to the one under consideration, the scenario just explicated is quite true to life. If schools are peopled largely by women who come to teaching not for money but for other reasons and if the dominant attitude and values of those in the teaching ranks is one of "nurturance" first and perhaps "performance" second, then it is no small wonder that many school cultures will be quite resistant to movement away from that culture to either the *exacting culture* or the *integrative culture.*

The effective school research movement represents one such challenge to the dominant school culture, which is either *caring* or *apathetic.* The effective school research movement (Edmonds, 1979) placed a major emphasis on performance *with caring* as a preeminent set of goals. The resistance to effective schools may take on the same cloak as do efforts to change the compensation system to embrace performance.

CRITICAL PROCESS VARIABLES

The ERS survey data (1979) on merit pay for teachers indicates that where such plans succeeded, they were marked by teacher input into formulation, which occurred in a climate of trust, honesty and mutual confidence and which was given top priority by school administrators (p. 7).

An emerging view of teacher involvement in the actual construction of a pay-for-performance compensation system is that embraced in the idea of *stakeholders.* A stakeholder is someone who has a vested interest in the outcome of any new innovation and in the outcomes of the organization. Strategic management thought indicates that groups affected by change, internal and external, ought to be involved as a matter of principle (Tichy, 1983).

Another area of involvement hinges upon whether those affected by the linkage of pay to performance ought to have a hand in its actual administration, i.e., decisions made about pay within the parameters of the compensation system as designed.

There are few empirical studies that rigorously and unambiguously shed light on these questions. One study by Locke and Latham (1984) indicated that actual participation in the application of performance plan had the least significant impact on real performance on the job. The most significant impact dealt with individual incentives, primarily money. Group incentives was second, followed by participation in goal setting (p. 117).

Once again, the type of organizational culture may dictate the extent to which people in an organization are involved in the design of a pay-for-performance system. In an *apathetic culture,* there may be no interest in participation. In an *integrative culture,* employee participation would be crucial to its eventual acceptance and success.

ADMINISTRATIVE PROBLEMS

The national ERS data (1979) indicated in those school systems that had tried and dropped merit pay plans, the single largest reason offered was "administrative problems—40.2%" (p. 41). The NEA published a report by Davis (1961) that delved into specific reasons why thirty school districts in cities of 30,000 or more population had discontinued their merit pay programs. The list is instructive and would support the ERS data gathered sixteen years later.

Tops on the list of administrative problems were those pertaining to evaluation. Among the major concerns were the lack of adequate data to support a decision regarding pay, the potential inaccuracy of the actual rating applied, bias and unreliability of the raters (principals), and general instrument rigor.

The next problem areas pertained to the friction and ill will generated and to the fact that the bulk of the teachers received merit or that merit was "passed around" instead of being selective and discriminative. Other areas of dissatisfaction involved the lack of adequate supervision to ensure accuracy, the extensive record keeping involved, and cumbersome administrative procedures. Interestingly enough, the lack of direct teacher involvement in the development/implementation of the plans was the lowest of the reasons given for the plans being shelved, underscoring the study by Locke and Latham (1984) previously cited.

These data are significant in that they indicate that a plan may have larger theoretical or even methodological flaws, but the ultimate test as far as real operational success is how they are finally implemented and how they touch teachers in that process. It strongly suggests that *internal* and *individual equity issues* are ultimately where final success or failure rests. It is within the actual administrative machinery that equity issues are fully revealed to those to be affected by it.

SUMMARY

It is not likely that the debate and dialogue over the proper compensation system in schools will be resolved one way or the other very soon. Two broader value issues are involved, which are immediately understood by educators and the public. The first value upholds superior performance in any guise and posits it should be honored and rewarded. The second value, equally powerful and quintessentially American, is fairness or equity.

These two values, often conflicting in practice, were described eloquently by John Gardner in his classic book *Excellence* (1961). Gardner did not resolve the tensions between the two values. Instead he sought a reconciliation when he wrote, "But neither extreme speaks for the American people, and neither expresses the true issues that pose themselves today. It would be fatal to allow ourselves to be tempted into an anachronistic debate. *We must seek excellence in a context of concern for all*" (p. 77).

A compensation system must honor outstanding work performance, but not at the expense of equity for all because a school system is at once not only individual teachers working alone; it is also a collectivity. That fact may be paradoxical, but it won't be erased by any compensation plan that doesn't recognize concurrently both excellence and equity in its design and more importantly in its implementation. Values are, after all, experienced first and consciously formed second. We know what we live. What we live is what we perceive. What we perceive is what we believe. Compensation is one of the ways we define ourselves. It is in the end *organic* to human life in the psycho-social–economic context of our times. For this reason no change in a compensation system can be considered *tinkering*. Change here is always *fundamental*.

REFERENCES

Belcher, D. W. and T. J. Atchison. 1987. *Compensation Administration*. Englewood Cliffs, New Jersey: Prentice-Hall, Inc.

Burden, P. R. 1987. *Establishing Career Ladders in Teaching*. Springfield, Illinois: Charles C. Thomas Publisher.

Caplow, T. 1954. *The Sociology of Work*. Minneapolis: University of Minnesota.

Christensen, J. C. 1987. "Roles of Teachers and Administrators," in *Establishing Career Ladders in Teaching*. P. R. Burden, ed., Springfield, Illinois: Charles C. Thomas Publisher, pp. 88–110.

Cubberley, E. P. 1929. *Public School Administration*. Boston: Houghton Mifflin Company.

Daniel, T. L. and J. K. Esser. 1980. "Intrinsic Motivation as Influenced by Rewards, Task Interest, and Task Structure," *Journal of Applied Psychology*, 65(5):566–573.

Darling-Hammond, L. 1986. "We Need Schools Able and Willing to Use Carnegie's Teachers for the 21st Century," *The Chronicle of Higher Education* (July 16):76.

Davis, H. 1961. *Why Have Merit Plans for Teachers' Salaries Been Abandoned?* Washington, D.C.: National Education Association.

Deal, T. E. and A. A. Kennedy. 1982. *Corporate Cultures*. Reading, Massachusetts: Addison-Wesley Publishing Company.

Deci, E. L. 1976. "The Hidden Cost of Rewards," *Organizational Dynamics*, 61–72.

Edmonds, R. 1979. *A Discussion of the Literature and Issues Related to Effective Schooling, Volume 6*. St Louis: Cemrel, Inc.

English, F. W. 1972. "AFT/NEA Reaction to Staff Differentiation," *The Educational Forum*, 36(2):193–198.

English, F. W. 1983–1984. "Merit Pay: Reflections on Education's Lemon Tree," *Educational Leadership*, 41(4):72–79.

English, F. W. and D. Sharpes. 1972. *Strategies for Differentiated Staffing*. Berkeley, California: McCutchan Publishing Corporation.

Educational Research Service. 1979. *Merit Pay for School Administrators*. Arlington, Virginia: Educational Research Service, Inc.

Educational Research Service. 1979. *Merit Pay for Teachers*. Arlington, Virginia: Educational Research Service, Inc.

Etzioni, A. 1969. *The Semi-Professions and Their Organization*. New York: The Free Press.

Frase, L. E. 1989. "Effects of Teacher Rewards on Recognition and Job Enrichment," *The Journal of Educational Research*, 83(1):52–57.

Frase, L. E., R. Hetzel, and R. T. Grant. 1982. "Merit Pay: A Research-Based Alternative in Tucson," *Phi Delta Kappan*, 64(4):266–269.

Futrell, M. H. 1987. "Career Ladders: An NEA Perspective," in *Establishing Career Ladders in Teaching*, P. R. Burden, ed., Springfield, Illinois: Charles C. Thomas Publisher, pp. 226–232.

Gardner, J. 1961. *Excellence*. New York: Harper and Row.

Greenlaw, P. S. and J. P. Kohl. 1986. *Personnel Management*. New York: Harper and Row.

Greider, C., T. M. Pierce and W. E. Rosenstengel. 1961. *Public School Administration*. New York: The Ronald Press Company.

Hackman, R. and G. Oldham. 1980. *Job Redesign*. Reading, PA: Addison, Wesley.

Henderson, R. I. 1976. *Compensation Management*. Reston, Virginia: Reston Publishing Company, Inc.

Herzberg, F., B. Mausner and B. B. Snyderman. 1967. *The Motivation to Work*. New York: John Wiley and Sons.

Kaufman, P. W. 1984. *Women Teachers on the Frontier*. New Haven: Yale University Press.

Locke, E. A. and G. P. Latham. 1984. *Goal Setting: A Motivational Technique That Works!* Englewood Cliffs, New Jersey: Prentice-Hall.

Lortie, D. C. 1969. "The Balance of Control and Autonomy in Elementary School Teaching," in *The Semi-Professions and Their Organization*, A. Etizioni, ed., New York: The Free Press, pp. 1–53.

Maslow, A. 1954. *Motivation and Personality*. New York: Harper and Row.

Millis, H. A. and R. E. Montgomery. 1945. *Organized Labor*. New York: McGraw-Hill Book Company, Inc.

Robinson, G. E. 1984. "Incentive Pay for Teachers: An Analysis of Approaches," *Concerns in Education*. Arlington, Virginia: Educational Research Service, Inc.

Rohlen, T. P. 1983. *Japan's High Schools*. Berkeley, California. University of California Press.

Sethia, N. K. and M. A. Von Glinow. 1985. "Arriving at Four Cultures by Managing the Reward System," in *Gaining Control of the Corporate Culture*, R. Kilmann, M. Faxton, and R. Serpa, eds., San Francisco, California: Jossey-Bass.

Spring, J. 1986. *The American School 1642–1985*. New York: Longman.

Steffy, B. E. 1989. *Career Stages of Classroom Teachers*. Lancaster, Pennsylvania: Technomic Publishing Co., Inc.

Staw, B. M., B. J. Calder, R. K. Hess, and L. E. Sandelands. 1980. "Intrinsic Motivation and Norms about Payment," *Journal of Personality*. 48:1–14.

Tichy, N. M. 1983. *Managing Strategic Change*. New York: John Wiley and Sons.

Tyack, D. B. 1974. *The One Best System*. Cambridge, Massachusetts: Harvard University Press.

United States Department of Commerce, Bureau of Census. 1988. *Statistical Abstract of the United States*. Washington, D.C.: U.S. Government Printing Office.

Wickersham, J. P. 1866. *Report of the Superintendent of Common Schools of the Commonwealth of Pennsylvania*. Harrisburg: Singerly and Myers State Printers.

Wickersham, J. P. 1868. *Report of the Superintendent of Common Schools of the Commonwealth of Pennsylvania*. Harrisburg: Singerly and Myers State Printers.

Wallace, M. J. and C. H. Fay. 1988. *Compensation Theory and Practice*. Boston: PWS-KENT Publishing Company.

Zeigler, H. 1967. *The Political Life of American Teachers*. Englewood Cliffs, New Jersey: Prentice Hall, Inc.

CHAPTER 2

Incentive Pay for Teachers and School Reform

THOMAS TIMAR — *University of California at Riverside*

INTRODUCTION

One of the most enduring dimensions of the school reform movement that began in 1983 has been the policy focus on the performance and job orientation of teachers. School reformers representing a variety of interests — business, politicians, and academics — called for improvements in the quality of the teacher work force through a combination of expanded work responsibilities in schools and incentive pay schemes as a step toward overall improvement in primary and secondary education.

A Nation at Risk, the wellspring of a stream of reports calling for reforms in the teaching profession, recommended that teachers' salaries be "performance based" (The National Commission on Educational Excellence, p. 30). The commission also recommended that "salary, promotion, tenure, and retention decisions should be tied to effective evaluation systems that includes peer review so that superior teachers can be rewarded" (The National Commission on Educational Excellence, p. 30). And finally, it urged for development of "career ladders for teachers that distinguish among the beginning instructor, the experienced teacher, and the master teacher." The Carnegie Forum's report, *A Nation Prepared,* reinforced earlier reports of declining quality of the teacher work force. While demand for teachers would increase in the late 1980s and early 1990s, prospects for meeting the demand were discouraging. Not only were fewer college graduates entering the profession, but those who were, were among the students who showed the least academic ability (Carnegie Forum on Education and the Economy, pp. 25–32).

Some states were quick to respond. California, Florida, Tennessee, Texas, and Utah were among the first to develop incentive based pay programs, and, increasingly, state policy began to focus on two objectives: ways of attracting and retaining good teachers and ways to improve the performance of schools. The first objective responded to increasing disaffection with teaching as a profession. Highly qualified college and university graduates were not attracted to careers in teaching, and, among teachers, the best of them tended to leave the profession after five or six years (Stoddard, Losk, and Benson, 1984; Murnane, Singer, and Willett, 1989). Teacher incentive pay schemes are intended to remedy this situation, serving as an incentive to teachers by offering them opportunities and rewards for professional growth and advancement. The second policy objective was to provide school administrators with management tools and marginal resources to improve the productivity and effectiveness of schools.

Those states that developed some incentive pay plan for teachers adopted several strategies to structure the two policy objectives—professional growth and improved productivity and effectiveness. They included the career ladder, master and mentor teacher, and merit pay for teachers and merit schools (incentive money that goes to schools for improved student performance). Whatever they are called, most incentive based pay plans contain very similar provisions. Generally, they embody some variation of pay for performance. The aim of such schemes is to provide incentives to teachers to excel and to make salary not exclusively a function of numbers of course credits and years of teaching amassed. Neither longevity nor numbers of college credits have been positively related to teaching effectiveness (Hanuschek, 1981). Instead, policymakers turned to greater financial and career incentives to keep good teachers in the classroom, more and better teacher evaluations to improve the quality of teaching, and better use of teacher talents outside the classroom as strategies to school reform.

According to the Career Ladder Clearinghouse, at the end of 1986, thirteen states had fully implemented state-wide teacher incentive programs, five more were in the process of developing such programs, thirteen states implemented pilot programs in districts, and eight states allowed local school districts to develop alternative compensation schemes for teachers. Between the fiscal years 1983–87, states spent over $531 million on incentive based pay initiatives. In fiscal year 1987 alone, twelve states funded incentive based pay programs in excess of $232 million (Cornett, 1988). By 1989, Texas was spending over $300 million annually on its Career Ladder Program; California was spending $67 million for its mentor program; and Tennessee was spending over $102 million.

While new programs abound, their impact on school performance is unclear. The important questions for policymakers and educators to ask are: What differences have incentive based pay schemes had on the daily operation of the schools in which they have been implemented? Have those initiatives made schools organizationally more competent than they were five years ago (in the pre-reform era)? Have alternative compensation schemes been uniformly successful? Have some state implementation strategies worked better than others? More importantly, policymakers need to understand the conditions that legitimate alternative compensation policies as school improvement strategies. Hence, a second set of questions asks: Under what conditions are career ladder and merit pay policies incentives to teachers? The political controversies that such policies have engendered demonstrate that teachers have not readily embraced such plans. More importantly, the National Education Association has opposed all merit and differentiated pay schemes for teachers.

FEATURES OF INCENTIVE BASED PROGRAMS

The most common forms of alternative teacher compensation systems fall into two general categories. The extended contract year and job enlargement allow districts to pay teachers for work beyond the regular contract year. Performance bonuses and career ladders, on the other hand, provide for teachers to be paid for expanded job responsibilities and qualitatively better teaching during the regular school year. Merit pay schemes give monetary rewards to teachers for outstanding performance. Performance is typically based upon professional evaluation. No additional duties are required of the teacher to receive the stipend. Utah's state incentive pay program pays performance bonuses to teachers rated as the best in the school or district. This component of alternative compensation has generally been the most controversial and its benefits most difficult to implement. A variation on merit pay is Florida's District Quality Instruction Program. Local districts may qualify for state funding for merit pay for teachers. Districts develop plans for awarding bonuses. Awards may be to all teachers in a particular school or to those teachers whose students show extraordinary gains in academic achievement or to those teachers who teach in areas where there is a critical shortage of teachers.

In contrast to incentive pay, a master or mentor teacher receives extra pay for assuming extra duties and responsibilities. Those responsibilities may include supervision of interns or curriculum development. Teachers are generally selected on the basis of outstanding performance. California's Mentor Teacher Program is available for 5 percent of the state's teachers. Those selected serve for three years, after which they may be selected to serve longer or return to their previous status. Washington state has also established a mentor teacher program that is intended to assist beginning teachers through supervision by an experienced teacher. The mentor teachers—100 in the first year—receive a stipend for the additional supervisory work. A number of districts in Utah have also included mentoring as a component of the Career Ladder Program.

The career ladder is perhaps the most popular strategy for rewarding teaching excellence and encouraging teachers to remain in the profession. There is considerable variation among states in program design and implementation, from Texas' highly prescriptive state mandated program as enacted to Utah's discretionary, locally developed programs (Cornett and Weeks, 1985). Utah provided $15 million in state funding for districts to voluntarily develop career ladders in 1985. In 1987–88, funding exceeded $34 million, which equates to approximately $2200 per teacher and represents about 10 percent of the average teacher salary in the state. All forty of the state's school districts chose to participate. The career ladder advancement provision provided salary boosts and expanded professional responsibilities. Because the program is connected to teacher evaluation, policymakers believe that the program will serve the dual purpose of general school improvement, while it provides teachers opportunities for professional growth and development. To date, two-thirds of Utah's districts have revised their evaluation practices. In some districts, criteria for placement on the ladder are quite subjective, while in others, placement depends more upon quantifiable data. According to state education officials, most districts have begun using evaluation committees—sometimes comprised of peers—as well as administrators who traditionally handled evaluation matters. A teacher's rating now may include student progress. Teachers who have been promoted on the career ladders are used to revise the curriculum and to help train new teachers.

Tennessee's Career Ladder Plan is one of the most comprehensive. The state's ladder consists of five rungs. Beginning with a "probationary teacher" rank—a one-year appointment, followed by promotion to the second rung or dismissal—teachers proceed to the apprentice level and can eventually become Career Level III teachers. A Career Level III teacher can earn bonuses ranging from $1000 to $7000, depending upon the length of the teaching contract. During 1984–85, 90 percent, or approximately 37,000, of Tennessee's teachers elected to participate in the career ladder. Participating teachers received a $1000 salary bonus. Another 1080 teachers qualified for the second rung of the career ladder. Teachers are evaluated at the local level while at the first rung; state evaluations are required for subsequent steps (Doyl and Hartle, 1985).

While teacher participation in Tennessee's Career Ladder Program is purely voluntary, the program itself is characterized by a high degree of standardization and uniformity. Placement criteria, evaluation standards—including who conducts the evaluations and the qualifications of the evaluators—retention on the career ladder, extra duties, and length of service are all prescribed in the law.

California's Mentor Teacher Program offers state-funded stipends for up to 5 percent of the permanent classroom teachers in California. Mentor teachers are nominated by committees comprised of a majority of classroom teachers, with local school boards making the final selection. Mentors receive a $4000 bonus for extra duties, including providing assistance and guidance to both new and experienced teachers and offering staff or curriculum development assistance. Yet, mentors are teachers first, so they must spend at least 60 percent of their time in "direct instruction of students."

IMPLEMENTING TEACHER INCENTIVE PROGRAMS

Though policymakers and educational policy analysts agree on the necessity of reforming the teaching profession, there is little agreement on how to do it. Among policymakers, the prevailing logic of merit pay, career ladders, mentor teachers, or other teacher compensation schemes rests on the assumption that the potential for higher salaries and professional status will both attract and retain good teachers and act as an incentive for teachers to improve their teaching skills. In both instances, policymakers believe that dividends are collected through higher student achievement. Incentive pay also has some intuitive appeal to private sector school reformers because of its apparent simplicity and free market origins. Appealing as it may be to think that an invisible hand can guide school reform, it is misleading. Increasingly, policy researchers point to the difficulty involved in generalizing about the effectiveness of incentive pay and career ladder schemes (Cohen and Murnane, 1985; Rosenholtz, 1987; Timar and Kirp, 1988; Timar, 1990). Translating generalized assumptions into effective programs is even more difficult.

Assessing the implementation effects of various teacher incentive pay schemes can provide some important lessons for policymakers. Among them is the fact that the policy dynamics of school reform have proven to be highly complex—more complex than most policymakers realized. Reform efforts that ignored the complexities most often failed or, in some instances, became parodies of their intended effects. There are no "magic bullets" with which to reform schools. There is no single policy or combination of policies—such as merit pay, career ladders, or mentor teachers—that will automatically transform mediocre teachers into good ones.

The success of reform policies depends on the organizational features of individual schools; schools shape policies as much as policies shape schools. Recognizing the importance of organizational culture, policy researchers have also learned that, while specific policies may not be determinants of school improvement, the strategies that they adopt make a difference to reform outcomes. Finally, the most important lesson to come from reform implementation studies is the need for new policy approaches. School reform policies must focus on schools as organizations, not disparate parts of the system. Hence, alternative teacher compensation plans must be evaluated on their capacity to engender organizational change.

Integrating school reform policies into the organizational consciousness of schools means transforming institutional and individual incentives, behaviors, and attitudes, as well as cultural values. There must also be a logical connection between policy goals and the standards to effect them. Policy goals must be based upon defensible criteria. Policymakers should anticipate the effects of their policies. And organizations must have the capacity to implement those policies. Experience with incentive based pay policies has shown, however, that these conditions are often not realized.

The very size and complexity of the educational sector, its interdependent relationship with other policy sectors, the multiplicity of motives that animate organizational and individual behavior, and competing incentives and priorities all make it difficult to predict policy outcomes precisely. Consequently, efforts to ameliorate one problem may create new ones or exacerbate existing ones. The result is that policies often work at cross purposes to one another. The sheer magnitude of reform efforts in some states creates inevitable tensions among policies.

One of the principal difficulties with incentive based pay plans is that they are theoretically weak, for there is no reliable connection between teacher salaries and student achievement. Devising defensible and generally acceptable criteria for meritorious teaching has so far eluded policymakers. Consequently, efforts to impose state-wide evaluation criteria for what is only vaguely known promise to be problematic at best. What happens instead is that the focus shifts from meritorious teaching efforts to justify merit increases. In those instances, teachers regard such plans as intrusive and unrelated to either professional development or teaching quality.

A recent study shows how merit pay becomes a problem of documentation. One school district's guidelines require "signed statements from (the) departmental chairperson, principal, coordinators, and/or support personnel who are in a position to evaluate (one's) . . . performance as a teacher" (Cohen and Murnane, 1985, p. 18). "Being able to type" gave her a real advantage in her application for merit pay, reported one teacher, while another teacher whose application was turned down on several attempts finally received merit pay after he decided to "play their game . . . documenting things that (he) thought were asinine . . . and finally turned in a notebook with something like 257 pages" (Cohen and Murnane, 1985, p. 18). Teachers seeking merit pay have taken to keeping camaras in their desks, having been instructed that photographs are an acceptable documentation of good teaching. Advice from one teacher to another is entered into the ubiquitous journal as a "shared professional exchange." According to one commentator:

> The word "portfolio" has become part of the educational jargon in many states. These portifolios consist of the mountains of data teachers accumulate to show how deserving they are of merit pay. Typically requiring 40 or more hours of work to assemble, such collections include the snapshots, the journals, the lesson plans designed according to state-approved formats, the names and topics of inservice sessions, and the names of teachers who were given special "consulting" help. Portfolios also contain descriptions of "vivids," another new coinage. A "vivid" occurs when a teacher does something out of the ordinary. One state official who trains merit-pay "evaluators" suggested that a teacher could be "vivid" by wearing an unusual hat to class. (Hipple, 1985)

A common strategy that is available to organizations when objectives cannot be met is to simply change the objectives and substitute objectives that can be attained. Policy means become policy ends. They assume a life of their own, independent of the purpose they were intended to serve. Other manifestations of organizational retreat from unattainable objectives include the displacement of external objectives with more internal procedures and the equalizing or standardizing of outputs, so that the outcomes are measured by organizational effort rather than effect on clients. On the simplest level, this means substituting quantity measures for quality.

Numbers are important in assessing the success of Tennessee's Career Ladder Program. According to former Tennessee Governor Lamar Alexander, that state's Career Ladder Program for teachers is a resounding success *(The Knoxville News-Sentinel)*. But Alexander has only numbers to define success. His conclusion is based upon the fact that state evaluators recommended more than 600 teachers for advancement up the teaching ladder. In all, 40 percent of teachers and administrators who applied for the upper levels of the career ladder completed the requirements "on their first try," and some 400 others "came so close" that most of them would surely complete the requirements. "Even that is not all," according to the article. "Thirty-nine thousand teachers and administrators — 90 percent of those eligible — earned a step on the Career Ladder in the first year: 15,000 of them took standardized tests, 20,000 of them trained in 40 overtime hours of staff development, and the rest submitted to a state approved local evaluation" *(The Knoxville News-Sentinel)*. These numbers have little significance beyond themselves. One has to assume — for there are no data — that those 15,000 teachers who took a standardized test to advance to the first rung of the career ladder are better teachers for having done so.

State-mandated incentive based pay schemes may create tensions between the pursuit of educational excellence and equity. Merit pay, career ladder, and mentor teacher programs are vulnerable to legal challenge on various grounds. The basis for selection may be the focus of challenge: what are the criteria for bonus pay? What are the standards for evaluation for receiving additional pay? In Florida, the state affiliates of both the National Education Association and the American Federation of Teachers sued the state's Associate Master Teacher Program (merit pay) as well as the School District Quality Instruction Incentives Program (merit schools). The merit pay program paid teachers who qualified an additional $3000 per year bonus. The merit schools program gave money to schools in which students excelled on certain tests and other standards developed under the plan. The suit charged that the merit pay program could be implemented in a non-discriminatory fashion because of inequities in the law and the way applications were processed by the state department of education. The teachers' lawyers argued that denying special education teachers, art teachers, teachers of several foreign languages, and counselors opportunity to qualify as "meritorious" was discriminatory.

Suit was almost filed when the Florida Education Department rejected the applications of those teachers who forgot to use zip codes, failed to use social security numbers on their applications, or committed other similarly minor infractions. Nearly 3500 applications were rejected for failure to comply with the language of the rule implementing the program, which required a "complete application." If one of fourteen items on the application form was not completed, the application was rejected. The issue was resolved when, faced with thousands of administrative hearings and possible court appeals, the State Board of Education instructed the Department of Education to give the rejected applicants another chance.

State policymakers in Florida decided to avoid prolonged litigation and conflict over merit pay by abolishing the program at the end of the 1986 school year.

Current efforts to reform the teaching profession are often regarded by unions as efforts to undermine hard-fought employment rights for teachers. The Florida teachers' union challenged the merit schools and merit pay plan on the basis that the merit pay plan abridges the right to collective bargaining. The suit alleged that the merit pay plan abridged that right by making the contract between the teachers' union and the school board subject to scrutiny by the state department of education, thereby giving the state unlawful veto power over local contracts. The union argued that the merit pay plan violated the separation of powers between branches of government. It also insisted that the merit pay plan usurped the constitutional authority of school boards by the department of education, since the department of education is empowered to alter merit pay plans that have been approved by local school boards.

The fact that there is no stable, quantifiable relationship between teacher quality and student achievement and no legally defensible criteria for meritorious teaching makes litigation more likely. That is why the rationally and validity of standards for merit pay are subject to challenge. While Florida required a score in the upper quartile of a subject matter test (or a master's degree if no test is available) and one classroom observation as a qualifying condition for merit pay, there is no demonstrable connection between those requirements and teaching quality.

So far, evidence indicates that questions regarding eligibility for incentive pay are more likely to be based on legally defensible standards than standards of excellence. A substantial body of case law specifying teachers' rights has developed over the past twenty years. Substantive entitlement and due process protections are entrenched and unlikely to be easily dislodged. Professional norms based upon legal rights are attractive because of the protection they offer teachers against administrative caprice.

Merit pay, career ladders, and the like are not ready solutions to complex problems. Changing organizational cultures, teacher job orientations, and social relationships within schools—preconditions for implementing alternative teacher pay policies—is not easily accomplished, particularly not through legislative mandates.[1]

IMPROVING ORGANIZATIONAL COMPETENCE

Educational excellence is fostered by a complex mixture of cultural and institutional factors. It is not likely to be cultivated by disparate policies that aim at various pieces of the educational process. Merit pay for teachers, for example, can be effective but only within the broader context of the school and community. A study of the effects of merit pay for teachers shows that merit increases bear scant relationship to their presumed effects—as an incentive to better teaching. Merit pay can be a positive inducement to teachers but only in relationship to the whole—as a measure of professional competence. The purpose of reform policies should be to create the kinds of institutional arrangements and organizational structures that promote educational excellence. Whether school reforms take hold depends on the degree to which that can be accomplished.

Enacting new rules for schools to follow may just add to the baggage that already overburdens the system. Reforms must create a sense of coherence and direction for schools as institutions. Reform policies may result in producing a crop of new teachers who are better prepared to teach their subjects. But what will prepare them for the indifference, monotony, incoherence, and rampant directionlessness of the insititution itself, the jealousy of colleagues, the blandness of the architecture, and the spiritual sterility of the environment? A school must set a certain tone—which is as real as the classrooms themselves—that will greet the students. That tone, that organizational ethos, determines the character of the school. It sets the expectation for excellence or failure. But it is created by individuals working in schools, not by a panoply of programs.

THE STATE'S ROLE

If real reform can only be achieved by changing the insititutional nature of schools, what then is the role of the state in managing the reform process? The first observation is that state efforts should be targeted at strengthening schools as organizations. In this context the role of the state is to establish professional standards and expectations, to provide support, and to nurture organizational characteristics that foster excellence. The Carnegie Forum has already proposed a massive restructuring of teacher work roles and training. However, just as states regulate the medical, legal, and other professions without presuming to tell lawyers how many cases they need to win or doctors what medication to prescribe to patients, states should regulate the teaching profession without intruding into the process of teaching. The role of the state would be to "articulate principles of institutional design and institutional diagnosis." An appropriate state management strategy would be to create a capacity to determine a harmonious fit between state control agencies and schools: what blend of cognitive, organizational, and political resources schools require for the realization of their purpose.

Since specific policies do not guarantee educational excellence, policymakers must look elsewhere—to the strategies they adopt for promoting reform. Though many states have assumed responsibility for reforming their schools, little is known about the effects of various reform strategies or the problems associated with their implementation. Yet the strategies that states select to manage both the substance and process of educational reform are central to the outcomes of reform efforts. While policy research has focused on the effects of federal education policies on local practices and the effective schools' research has focused on the school as an independent entity, little, if any, research has examined models of state–local relationships and the patterns of influence and support that promote educational excellence on the local level.

The implementation strategies of three state-initiated teacher pay incentive plans illustrate the complex dynamics of state-initiated policy and local responses to it. Teacher incentive pay programs in Texas, Utah, and California illustrate the difficulty of implementing state-initiated reform measures, particularly when those measures receive, at best, only lukewarm reception from those they intend to benefit.

Texas

One of the most significant issues addressed in Texas' school reform measure, House Bill 72, the improvement of the teaching profession, exemplifies the difficulty of reforming from the outside. Ross Perot, the engine of school reform in Texas, hoped to "put a great teacher . . . in every classroom in Texas and keep them there"[2] (Select Committee, 1984). To accomplish that, Perot and the other school reformers believed, required major changes in the quality of education that would be impossible without major changes in the teaching profession. While many teachers applauded the general effort to increase teaching salaries and to improve their professional status, specific policies to that end were greeted with ambivalence by the teaching profession. Some teachers and administrators believed that the overall effect would enhance the quality of teaching. Available evidence indicated, however, that the majority of teachers regarded both the required competency test for all teachers and the career ladder provisions as ineffective at best and an insult at worst. Competent teachers resent policies that treat all teachers as though they were incompetent. They also resent the fact that they were excluded from deliberations on policies that were intended for their benefit.

Teachers in Austin, who had won prior recognition as outstanding teachers, were strongly opposed to the career ladder. Their opposition was based primarily on what was perceived as the divisiveness of the program. The teachers stressed their belief that successful schools depended upon a number of factors: community, common purpose, collegiality, and cooperation. Since only one-third of the teachers in the school district were eligible for placement on the career ladder due to a shortage of funds to place all those teachers who were eligible, relationships among teachers had become competitive and uncooperative. They also argued that at issue was not the additional $1500 per year that teachers would earn, but the recognition they would receive as superior teachers. Because career ladder status had become competitive, teachers were fearful that by helping one another they might actually be hurting their own chances for career ladder placement. Finally, these teachers objected to the standards of selection for merit pay. They feared that placement on the career ladder would be based on superficial standards, not merit: those who documented everything—not necessarily the best teachers—would be the ones to advance. Teachers who considered themselves highly competent felt demeaned by the necessity of calling attention to activities they considered part of their professional responsibilities.

Implementation of the Career Ladder Plan for teachers in Texas was further complicated by the fact that evaluation standards were eventually to be developed by the state. But due to the abbreviated implementation timetable, districts were required to create their own evaluation measures. Implementation was further complicated by the fact that there was not enough state money to place all eligible teachers. Consequently, those districts that could afford to do so paid teachers the full $2000 while other districts paid teachers the minimum $1500. Those districts that had the funds placed all eligible teachers on the career ladder. Elsewhere, only a fraction of eligible teachers could be placed.

Establishing selection criteria for placing teachers on the second rung of the career ladder proved difficult. Once the quantitative selection criteria—college degrees, teaching major and minor, numbers of credits of graduate study or the like—were exhausted, other measures became necessary. In some districts, past evaluations were used. The difficulty there, too, was in quantifying past evaluations to make them legally defensible. Suddenly, past evaluations could be subject to strict scrutiny under due process norms as evaluations became the basis for differential treatment of teachers. In the past, the consequences of evaluation tended to the extremes. Evaluators often give teachers either high ratings, as a means of encouragement, or very low ratings, as a prelude to termination. It is rare to find a range of responses on a teacher's evaluation, particularly if the teacher has tenure. Similarly, the occasional negative comment often goes unchallenged by the teacher because evaluations generally have little consequence in the working life of a teacher. Now, suddenly, small differences in ratings can determine a teacher's career ladder placement. Because of the substantive benefits that attend placement, a higher standard of evaluation becomes necessary.

A potential source of conflict regarding career level placement flows from the mixture of state and local standards used to implement the Career Ladder Program. House Bill 72 establishes criteria for placement on the career ladder but allows local standards, driven ultimately by a district's capacity to fund the program, to further determine placement. Consequently, there is some confusion about placement of teachers who transfer from one district to another. The law states that "(a) A teacher is entitled to transfer a career ladder level assignment between districts, and a district *may* recognize the appraisal of a district previously employing the teacher in determining career level assignment. (b) A teacher may waive entitlement to a particular career ladder level assignment when changing employment from one district to another."[3] Teachers transferring between districts with different standards for placement and levels of compensation may find themselves moving up and down on the career ladder independently of their professional competence and qualifications. As an attorney remarked, "Obviously (state policymakers) did not talk to lawyers who practice employment law before enacting this plan."

According to the statute, a decision of a district concerning career ladder assignment is final and subject to appeal only if the decision of the district was arbitrary and capricious or made in bad faith. According to one legal expert, this provision probably means that a district decision may be appealed to the Commissioner of Education but may not be reversed unless the commissioner finds that it was "arbitrary and capricious or made in bad faith." House Bill 72 is silent as to which decisions may be appealed and who may appeal them. A decision not to recommend a teacher for a higher ladder assignment would surely be a clear case for appeal. But is a performance rating awarded during the appraisal process a "decision of the district" that can be appealed? Can the decision of a district be appealed based upon the validity and reliability of the assessment instrument used for assignment and that is administered and graded by the district? Finally, does anyone other than a teacher have standing to appeal (Bednar, 1984, p. 827)?

The appraisal process for teacher placement on the career ladder is unclear both in its intent and implementation. The "appraisal" is the measure of performance for purposes of assigning and maintaining a teacher's position on the career ladder. The state board of education, upon consulting teachers, is to develop and adopt a state-wide appraisal process and performance criteria. The criteria are to be based on "observable, job-related behavior," which presumably means that they are to measure observable aspects of a teacher's performance on the job (Bednar, p. 824). The statute also specifies five performance categories for teacher appraisal: "unsatisfactory," "below expectations," "satisfactory," "exceeding expectations," and "clearly outstanding." As one commentator points out, "After taking such pains to create an objective appraisal process, it is odd that the legislature spoke in term of 'expectations,' which tend to focus more upon subjective impressions of the teacher's supervisor than objective criteria for measuring performance" (Bednar, p. 825).

Finally, House Bill 72 asserts that assignment to a career ladder is neither a property right nor the equivalent of tenure. A teacher who has earned a certificate at a given level has a right to retain that certificate until it expires, is duly suspended, or is removed. Whether this disclaimer could withstand legal challenge is debatable. While assignment to a position on the career ladder may not confer substantive entitlement to salary, procedural entitlement to placement is conferred by the fact that the state, acting under color of law, establishes different criteria for teacher compensation. These criteria, in turn, affect those individuals' earning capacities and professional status.

As noted earlier, there is considerable ambivalence among teachers regarding the Career Ladder Program—a sign of trouble for a program intended to be an incentive to teachers to work harder and to stay in teaching. The point is not that the Career Ladder Program is inherently bad, but that it is hard to implement if it is not embraced by teachers. School reformers need to realize that alienating workers decreases, rather than increases, productivity.

California

A 1971 effort to institute a system of merit pay in California schools was a failure. Although the legislature created a merit pay plan that allowed school districts to create "Master Teacher Programs," opposition to the plan by the teaching profession succeeded in stifling it. Because of intense opposition by teachers' organizations, not a single Master Teacher Program was ever implemented in any of the state's 1043 school districts.[4]

California lawmakers tried again in 1984 with Senate Bill 813, the state's showcase reform bill. One of the more controversial provisions of SB 813 was the Mentor Teacher Program, which gives stipends to exemplary teachers. The California Teachers' Association opposed the provision because it viewed it as a merit pay plan. Others questioned the measure's substantive provisions, such as the requirement that teachers designated as mentors spend at least 60 percent of their time teaching while carrying out other duties. The intent of the provision is to keep exemplary teachers in the profession. It provides funds to school districts to establish programs that provide 5 percent of the teachers in a district annual stipends of $4000 in return for performing additional duties. In order to qualify for participation in this program, a teacher must have substantial recent classroom instruction experience and have demonstrated exemplary teaching ability.

Senate Bill 813 specifies that while the primary duty of a mentor teacher is to provide assistance and guidance to new teachers, mentors may also help more experienced teachers. Mentor teachers may also provide staff development and develop special curricula. Mentors must spend at least 60 percent of their time in direct instruction of pupils, and they cannot be used to evaluate other teachers.

Initial reactions by local school personnel to the mentor program were mixed. Local school administrators viewed the program as being highly politicized and, so, were reluctant to embrace it. In addition, many local educators mistrusted anything the legislature might propose. Past experience with promised cost-of-living increases that never materialized and fears about the legislature assuming the role of a super school board prompted suspicion. Despite initial concerns, the state department of education reports that in the program's first year, 1983–84, 64 percent of the state's districts (662 out of 1030) elected to participate. In 1984–85, the percent of districts participating rose to 72 percent (Kaye, 1984, p. 13). One study found that district administrators who oversee mentor programs have grown more favorable toward the program since its enactment (Shulman, St. Clair, and Little, 1984).

The initial stages of program implementation required that districts resolve some of the program's problematic issues. The legislation simply specified that the decision to participate rested in the hands of a district's governing board, that the amount of stipend for each mentor teacher was $4000, and that the majority of the selection committee must be teachers (Shulman, St. Clair, and Little, p. 15). Legislators left a variety of issues, significant for their number and potential volatility, to be resolved by districts. These included composition and procedures for the selection committee, duties and responsibilities, method of payment, use of support funds, and a host of other items that related even tangentially to working conditions. Consequently, the most controversial issues tended to be handled at the bargaining table. A California Tax Foundation study found that even the question of participation became an issue for bargaining. The selection of mentors was made problematic by lack of suitable criteria. As the study points out, "No strong precedent exists for singling out teachers on the basis of performance; in addition, the teaching profession has yet to wrestle successfully with the definition of valid selection criteria and procedures that, in the eyes of teachers, will be fair, justifiable, and consistent" (Shulman, St. Clair, and Little, p. 15).

The mentor teacher program has assumed very different forms. Districts that had enjoyed good bargaining relationships with teachers were generally able to implement the program without formal negotiations. In districts where bargaining relationships were difficult or where the program might generate conflict, efforts at implementation were abandoned for the sake of "labor peace."

Other districts saw no real benefit in the program. According to one district:

> There is great difficulty reconciling the extra remuneration for one person and not for others who [also] provide resource services for fellow staff members. Our governing board turned down the program because they felt that we could lose more than we stood to gain. (Shulman, St. Clair, and Little, p. 11)

Given the ambivalence of many teachers and the opposition of their unions to the program, teachers generally concurred when districts decided not to participate in the mentor program. In some of those districts, teachers were reluctant to take on extra duties even at extra pay. Some teachers were already eligible for extra compensation for curriculum development. In the Vallejo City Unified School District, for instance, a staff development program similar to the mentor teacher program was already in place.

Local factors generally color a district's implementation of the mentor program. Selecting mentors, for example, presents the same difficulties as selecting teachers for merit pay and career ladder placement. The absence of objectively defensible criteria for selection promotes suspicions of favoritism, elitism, and political influence. In spite of the fact that the majority of school districts chose to participate in the mentor program, districts did not seem to have a clear idea how mentors were to fit into the schools' structure. In part, the ambiguity flows from the imprecision of statutory definition and purpose. Are mentors to be regarded as instructional leaders or are they being rewarded for meritorious teaching? How districts view the role of mentor certainly shapes mentor behavior. If the goal of the mentor teacher program is to provide an incentive to teachers to stay in teaching, then the mentor program should take on the characteristics of a master teacher program. That is, the program must be structured to provide real professional incentives to individuals. For that to occur, however, schools must be structured so that there is an organizational role for mentors. On the other hand, if the program's purpose is simply to provide a salary bonus for exemplary teachers, no real organizational change is required.

Time and practice may clarify the role of the mentor teacher (Little, 1990). Mentors can provide considerable assistance to a school if given a prescribed function in the instructional process and a place in the school's organizational structure. Unless the program becomes an integral part of the school, however, its long-term benefit as an incentive to teachers is doubtful. Much of the program's eventual success in schools will depend on various factors, all of them critical to maintaining the program's integrity. The program must provide an incentive for superior teachers to apply. If teachers become disenchanted with the program and the pool of qualified applicants shrinks and undistinguished teachers are selected, the program's integrity will suffer. Mentors must also be convinced that their activities make a contribution to the school. To act as a true incentive, the program must be regarded by teachers as an opportunity for challenging work, for professional growth, and prestige. And the program's benefits must be visible. The contribution of the mentor to a school's instructional effort and the mentor's effect on student outcomes should be apparent to teachers and administrators (Shulman, St. Clair, and Little, p. 32). Unless the program demonstrates its effectiveness over time, it is likely to fall into a state of desuetude.

Utah

The financial incentives offered to districts by the Career Ladder System are significant—approximately $2200 per teacher. It is not surprising then that all forty of the state's school districts chose to participate, particularly since districts would not receive any cost-of-living adjustments. Though schools responded uniformly to the program's fiscal incentives, they responded idiosyncratically to its legislative intent. The past twenty years of policy implementation have shown how schools twist state policies to their own needs, and Utah is no exception. From its inception, the program was controversial. The active opposition and hostile indifference of large numbers of teachers threatened the success of the program. It was difficult to predict the overall response. At one extreme, teachers and administrators might regard the program as an intrusive example of increasing state interference in schools. At the other, they might regard the Career Ladder Program as an opportunity to improve the organizational competence of schools through teacher professional development and administrative leadership.

The decentralized design of the Career Ladder System is intended to be responsive to conditions in forty diverse school districts. Over half of the state's school districts are rural, very sparsely populated, and serve large numbers of American Indian and Hispanic students. Other districts serve highly homogenous populations. Aside from the obvious difficulties of designing a single program to suit such divergent school districts, state policymakers eschewed, for political reasons, a single state-mandated program, opting instead for locally designed programs. While the intent of such a strategy is to encourage innovation, it may also open the door for evasion and opportunistic compliance.

However, local responses to state policy initiatives may vary for a number of reasons. Districts may not agree with state program goals; teachers and school officials may disagree over the goals and procedures for implementing the Career Ladder Program; and schools and districts may lack the technical capacity to implement a complex program. Generally, local culture—the aspirations, values, and traditions among teachers, administrators, and the community—is an important determinant in policy implementation. In some instances, districts may subvert state intent by using career ladder funds to satisfy local needs, which may be more pressing than state priorities as defined in the policy. For example, districts may regard career ladder monies as opportunities to improve curriculum and to create new programs. Such improvements may have beneficial effects on school improvement but may not institutionalize opportunities for teacher professional growth and development. Still other districts may regard career ladder monies as opportunities to provide across-the-board salary increases to all teachers.

In order for the Career Ladder Program to succeed as a school reform strategy, local implementation must satisfy two conditions: (1)

it must be connected to school improvement, i.e., improving the organizational competence of schools, and (2) it must be connected to teachers' professional growth and development. The means for achieving these goals is by providing administrators with managerial resources and teachers with a system of rewards and incentives. In order to achieve the first condition, the Career Ladder Program, as implemented, must be tied to programmatic activities that are logically related to school outcomes. The Career Ladder Program will have minimal systematic impact on schools if it is nothing more than a way of funneling money to teachers to increase their salaries. Similarly, activities associated with career ladder components, such as curriculum development, teacher evaluation, teacher in-service, and expanded job responsibilities, must be organizationally integrated so that they become part of teachers' expanded professional responsibilities rather than occasional opportunities for additional work. Similarly, teachers must regard performance evaluations as a source of professional improvement, not as ritual exercises or the price of salary increases.

The career ladder components serve as a system of rewards and incentives to teachers if teachers perceive them as real opportunities for expanding their job responsibilities, improving the quality of their teaching, and developing and improving curriculum and teaching materials. Teachers will resist participation in incentive pay and career ladder schemes if they perceive themselves as "jumping through hoops" for a few extra dollars. Under those conditions, teacher reform strategies demoralize, rather than inspire, teachers. Research on teacher reforms has consistently concluded that teachers reject merit pay on grounds that there are no defensible criteria for determining what is meritorious teaching (Cohen and Murnane, 1985). The evidence from Utah suggests, however, that teachers do not unilaterally reject merit pay. They reject it if they perceive its implementation to be capricious and arbitrary. They accept it when they perceive that it is logically related to a fair process of evaluation that is embedded in an organizational strategy for professional improvement.[5]

Utah's decentralized reform strategy means that decison-making authority is delegated and widely dispersed. As decisions are made at the school and district level about implementation of the Career Ladder Program, there is a greater risk that the policy intent of the Career Ladder Program is eroded. The problems that Utah's policymakers face are those faced by all central policymakers. Policy is comprised of two dimensions: program goals and the rules to effect them. The dilemma for policymakers is that program goals can serve purely parochial needs, while rules can easily become ends in themselves. If, for example, school administrators and teachers convert the career ladder into a latter day spoils system, there is little likelihood that the program will enhance professional growth opportunities for teachers. If schools turn rules into rituals, as they are known habitually to do, they have scant effect on school improvement. Local implementation of state policy achieves state intent when both program goals and rules to effect them serve organizational ends.

IMPLEMENTATION RESPONSES

A study of Utah's Career Ladder Program reveals important insights into the implementation of pay incentive plans and their relationship to school reform. The study by Amsler et al. answers several questions. Under what circumstances do Career Ladder Programs provide real incentives to teachers? Is there a systematic way of understanding variation among districts in implementing incentive programs?

The case studies of twelve districts reveal four implementation responses. They are classified as "Integrated," "Programmatic," and "*Pro forma.*" The categories are based on the relative importance districts attach to rule adherence on the one hand and realization of organizational goals on the other.[6]

The integrated mode of implementation represents an effort to combine allegiance to state policy ends, broadly conceived, and to prescribed means of implementing and balancing those policies – rules (Kagen, 1978). Programmatic implementation emphasizes substantive ends, but without regard to competing values of procedural integrity. Procedural implementation emphasizes procedural regularity and fairness for its own sake, without adequate attention to substantive results. *Pro forma* implementation subverts or ignores state policy purpose in favor of parochial interests. The dimensions of local implementation are displayed in dichotomized form in Table 1.

Which of the four implementation modes characterizes districts' implementation of the Career Ladder Program is colored by the relative importance that school districts attach to adherence to organizational purpose on the one hand, and adherence to rules on the other. School districts may place high or low emphasis on the attainment of organiza-

Table 1. Policy implementation modes.

Emphasis on Realization of Organizational Ends		
	(High)	(Low)
	Integrated	Procedural
Emphasis on Adherence to Rules (High)	Rules are seen as instrumental to organizational purpose, e.g. school improvement, procedural and substantive congruence. Managerial competence and teacher professionalism are means to organizational competence, i.e., school improvement. Teacher evaluation is not only fair, but also leads to improved teacher performance.	Preoccupation with procedural fairness, e.g., a fair system of teacher evaluation; institutional improvement through procedural regularity and fairness, e.g., a "fair" teacher evaluation system that is based on "objective" standards. Focus is on the integrity of the process; "fairness" is equated with "objectivity." Rules and procedures become ends in themselves, to the denigration of organizational and professional interests.
	Programmatic	Pro forma
(Low)	Emphasis is on realization of programmatic ends; process and professional growth concerns are attenuated. There is a preoccupation with "right" results, which are defined in programmatic terms. Focus is on substantive ends without regard to competing values of procedural regularity.	Implementation is ad hoc, particularistic, driven by local needs. Program is regarded as a means of getting funds, but little attention is paid to legislative intent. Focus is on paper compliance; there is a tendency to avoid responsibility for program implementation and outcome. Programs are often used to satisfy private over professional or organizational ends. Rules are manipulated for convenience.

tional goals, or they may place high or low emphasis on adherence to procedure.

The Career Ladder Program promotes school effectiveness if teachers regard the program as a means for professional development and as a source of enrichment of their professional lives by offering them work opportunities that otherwise would not be available to them as teachers, and, most importantly, if teachers believe that career ladder benefits are allocated in a fair way that is consonant with professional competence. Teacher acceptance of the Career Ladder Program is lowest if it is regarded as a series of hoops to jump through to qualify for additional funds. For administrators, acceptance of the Career Ladder Program is highest when they regard it as a means of channeling resources to areas where school improvement is needed. It is lowest if they regard it as a "give-away" program for teachers. Consequently, teachers may be quite satisfied with a "procedural" response to the program as it satisfies their desires to control its implementation. Similary, administrators may be equally satisfied with the "programmatic" response insofar as it satisfies their need to control resources. While the two implementation modes may satisfy teachers and administrators, neither is satisfactory from a broad policy perspective since each satisfies only one of the two conditions implicit in state policy. The tension that is created between teachers and administrators by these two implementation modes may faint or quite pronounced, depending upon a variety of local conditions. The tension is resolved, however, in the integrated mode of implementation.

Integrated

The integrated mode of implementation is the preferred mode because it creates the conditions under which meaningful school improvement is most likely to occur. In this mode, teachers regard the Career Ladder Program as a means of professional growth and development, and school administrators regard improved teacher performance as synonymous with improved organizational effectiveness. In this mode, career ladder components are integrated into the organizational lives of schools and are not regarded as a state mandate that must be satisfied if the district is going to be eligible for state funds. Teacher evaluation is regarded by teachers as a source of improvement and is connected to their effectiveness as teachers. It is not as a ritual exercise. Similarly, administrators regard teacher evaluation as a means of strengthening instruction. Teachers do not regard career ladder components as so many hoops to jump through for extra money, but as opportunities for expanding their professional responsibilities. The integrated implementation response strives for state and local congruence by improving the overall performance of the school through improved evaluation, expanded professional responsibilities, and increased compensation for teachers.

While the integrated mode of implementation is the most desirable, it is also the most difficult to achieve. Of the twelve districts in our case study, only three are classified as integrated in their implementation of the Career Ladder Program.

Programmatic

This model of implementation focuses on the realization of programmatic ends and emphasizes the administrative dimensions of the program at the expense of professional development. This mode of implementation regards the career ladder primarily as an administrative tool. The emphasis is generally on getting the "right results," with little attention to formal procedures for achieving results. How career ladder funds get allocated is determined by administrators, based upon perceived school needs. Administrative discretion is exercised in two areas. Administrators may determine (1) *what activities get funded* and (2) *who is eligible for funding under the various activities.* Local decision makers focus exclusively on producing results that they think best suit the school's purposes. Organizational needs tend to drive decision making at the expense of procedural regularity. Teachers tend to view the allocation of expanded work opportunities, performance bonuses, and the like on the basis of favoritism, rather than merit, based upon an objective and reliable process of selection. As long as teachers perceive bias in the distribution of career ladder benefits, it remains disconnected from professional development since currying favor rather than professional competence establishes the basis for career ladder rewards.

Even in the absence of bias, programmatic implementation has limited organizational effect because it denigrates the corollary values of professional development for the sake of achieving organizational goals. Consequently, lasting, organizational benefits are rare because implementation is idiosyncratic, intended to engender specific *programmatic* rather than *organizational* benefits. The programmatic mode of implementation is oriented toward fragmented problem solving rather than coherent organizational improvement

Procedural

The procedural mode of implementation is generally aligned with teacher, rather than administrative, interests. The preoccupation is with procedural fairness, e.g., development of a "fair" system of teacher evaluation, for example. The implementation focus is on the integrity of the process: fairness and objectivity based upon rules and standardization. School improvement is thought to be synonymous with procedural fairness and objectivity.

Procedural fairness and regularity are important because of the intrinsic value society places upon them and because professional development is impossible in an organizational environment in which benefits are distributed arbitrarily and capriciously. However, rules can become obstacles to the realization of organizational goals. It is possible, for example, to have a fair and regular process for teacher evaluation, which, in turn, is the basis for allocating career ladder benefits, without that process leading to substantive improvements in a school's instructional effectiveness. Rules and procedural regularity can become ends in themselves. While the procedural implementation mode may be a comfortable place for teachers and administrators to land, it may be disconnected from school improvement. Rules frustrate organizational purpose if they become part of the school ritual without any organizational purpose beyond themselves.

Pro forma

This mode of implementation is minimally compliant with state intent. Neither the programmatic nor procedural elements of the Career Ladder Program take root in the district as implementation focuses on technical compliance. *Pro forma* implementation is ad hoc and particularistic. Implementation is manipulated for the sake of convenience to the denigration of professional and organizational ends. This mode of implementation resists program integration. The career ladder exists on paper but has almost no effect on schools organizationally.

One way of differentiating implementation of the Career Ladder Program in districts is by the change they engender in the schools. The integrated mode prompts significant redefinition and realignment of working relationships and roles among teachers and administrators. Hence, it requires substantial organizational change. In contrast, programmatic and procedural implementation can be accommodated by superficial changes that are manifested in increased activity and rule elaboration, but absent changes in organizational behavior. *Pro forma* implementation engenders nominal changes in organizational behavior. Hence, it is the least disruptive. The question that the theoretical implementation models raise is how they affect practice. Do daily routines in districts differ depending on their implementation approaches? Though the boundaries that define district implementation responses are not sharp, there are discernible differences among them. Those differences are observable in the organizational cultures of schools and are reflected in the attitudes of teachers and administrators toward the Career Ladder Program.

Three districts that are classified as *"pro forma"* comprise two groups. Among these districts, one group regards the Career Ladder Program positively as a state supplement to teachers' salaries but resents state intrusion into local affairs by controlling the way teachers are paid. Therefore, the local response to the Career Ladder Program is to effect the most minimal compliance possible to qualify for funds without disrupting established routines. Another group of districts simply did not want the disruption that comes with implementing any new program. Some districts in this group returned career ladder funding to the state rather than wrestle with the complexities of implementation.

One source of local resistance to the Career Ladder Program was annual threats by the legislature to discontinue funding the program. Districts were obviously reluctant to invest heavily in a program that was threatened annually with termination.

School districts that comprise the *pro forma* group do not regard the Career Ladder Program as an opportunity for school improvement. They regard the program as a state-imposed mandate (though it is not) that threatens to disrupt established relationships and entrenched patterns of behavior. They justify their resistance on the basis of organizational stability. They are not willing to buy "the pig in the poke" and especially not if it threatens to foul their own backyards. Collegial and authority relationships are based upon and defined by community morality. School culture is an expression of community norms that supersede professional and organizational norms. In small, rural, culturally homogenous communities, for example, that are rigidly stratified by gender roles and authority relationships, changes in organizational behavior that depend on disturbing those relationships are unlikely.

Reasoning in *pro forma* districts is ad hoc and expedient. It is driven by a need to comply with the letter of state intent to the denigration of program purpose. Decision making and information dissemination are localized and haphazard. In one district, teachers complained about the unfairness and secrecy in the process of awarding bonuses. Administrators reported that they had not given any. In other districts, standards for awarding performance bonuses were nonexistent and, therefore, everyone qualified. In one district, it was reported that teacher wives of state legislators were receiving performance bonuses.

Of the twelve case study districts, two are classified as programmatic. These districts approach the Career Ladder Program as a means for realizing school and district program goals without regard to the policy's intended expansion of the professional roles of teachers. Teachers and administration point to programmatic changes stemming from the Career Ladder Program. These include curriculum development projects, extracurricular programs, and temporary or specialist mentor roles. There is little evidence in these districts, however, of systemic change, either through differentiated teacher work roles or professional career advancement opportunities. Decision making is generally centrally controlled by district administrators or a district committee that is dominated by administrators. The penchant for administrator dominance keeps policy goals focused on programmatic ends with little emphasis on the competing values for teacher professionalism. Because decision making is not widely shared, teachers regard the program as benefitting a select few, members of an "inner circle." If favoritism forms the basis of a system of professional rewards, the benefits to professional development are lost.

Administrators support the programmatic benefits of this implementation mode. Its principal benefit is in marginal resources to carry out school and district goals. From this perspective, overall district and school effects are positive. A view that typifies this approach to implementation was expressed by a principal: "This has changed our school dramatically. . . . I have instructional teams to carry out school goals . . . there is no question that school and district programs are better for it (the Career Ladder Program)." It is noteworthy that the principal made no claims for *school* improvement, but for *programmatic* improvement.

The benefits of this implementation mode are primarily to the school. There are also short-term benefits to teachers through various projects. However, the career ladder components have an ad hoc character to them. They have little impact on organizational structure as this implementation response does not aim to integrate the Career Ladder Program into schools. Asked what they would miss the most if the Career Ladder Program were terminated by the legislature, teachers and administrators pointed to the projects and extra work the program currently supports. Most thought that its elimination would lead to missed opportunities. Few thought of its termination as a professional setback.

While some teachers in programmatic districts were pleased with opportunities to take on additonal projects for pay, others were critical of the administrative arbitrariness that they associated with administrators' goal-oriented pragmatism. Even if decisions about *what* activities were to be carried out under the Career Ladder Program were determined systematically, decisions about *who* would do them were made expediently, as ends take precedence over means. Such an approach may be efficient, but it does not promote long-term organizational improvement. One teacher summed it up by stating that "I see the good things that are happening in the schools and applaud the (career ladder) system . . . *but it isn't keeping the good teachers in the schools. It's just making the schools run better*" (Amsler et al., 1988).

Procedural implementation is the antithesis of programmatic implementation. Where administrators tend to control the Career Ladder Program in districts typed as programmatic, teachers control the career ladder in districts typed as procedural. The goal of teachers and administrators in the four districts that comprise this group was to create fair procedures for allocating career ladder benefits. Program success is measured by objectivity and systematization of procedures, not by school improvement. Organizational energy is process, not task, oriented. Though procedural fairness is important, it can eclipse substantive goals. One principal, for example, found the evaluation process for teachers to be restrictive and, in some instances, unrelated to improving the professional competence of teachers. She did not believe that the district-sanctioned evaluation was useful as a means of assessing teachers' strengths and weaknesses. Teachers were evaluated on a scale of one to five on a long list of items, and a score of three or lower on a single item disqualified a teacher for a performance bonus. Since she believed that it was unfair for a teacher to be disqualified on that basis, she turned in positive evaluation scores. (The exceptions were teachers who she believed should not qualify for merit.) However, in order to have a realistic means of assessing teachers and providing them with information about their professional performance, she used a second set of evaluations that she kept in her desk.

Adherence to procedural regularity has obvious benefits. Administrative discretion to determine both the scope and nature of expanded professional responsibilities for teachers as well as the basis for awarding performance bonuses is limited and systematized by rules. But, it is easy to confuse rules with outcomes, means for the goals they are intended to achieve. One principal stated:

> For teachers it is good to have the opportunity to make more money. . . . Teachers are grateful for the money, but wonder what hoop they have to jump through next to get it. I support it because it pays teachers for extra time. But teachers were good before this . . . the paperwork that they and I have to go through is too time consuming. . . . At least we've worked out a plan that seems fair. (Amsler et al., 1988)

While a results-oriented implementation approach may be threatened by unchecked administrative discretion in the name of "getting things done," a procedure-bound approach is threatened by rules being transformed into ends. The negative side of procedure—proceduralism—is expressed by a teacher:

> So one day I'm good if I structured 20 minutes of my lesson right. Another day I'm good if parents and students have said so, or if I have pasted enough stuff in a so-called "dossier," none of which is an accurate picture of my real strengths or weaknesses. All of it takes too much of an emotional toll with no real professional growth or even accurate feedback for me. (Amsler et al., 1988)

Teachers and administrators in districts typed as procedural believe that the Career Ladder Program in their district is implemented in a fair way. Teachers helped make the rules; they know what they are and can live with them. For all that, however, the effect on the organizational competence of schools may be slight. Rules often become rituals or routines in the process of bureaucratic aging.

The three districts that are classified as professional regarded the state-initiated Career Ladder Program as an opportunity to fundamentally change the conduct of business in their schools. They saw in the Career Ladder Program opportunities to restructure school-level decision making and professional work roles and, simultaneously, to enhance school effectiveness. The animating goal of districts in this category is organizational competence through administrative leadership and teacher professionalism. These districts sought to integrate career ladder components into the organizational life of their schools. The depth of formal change was greatest in these districts. A distinguishing feature of professional districts is that they achieve a high degree of consonance between rules and the ends they are meant to serve. Rules are not ends in themselves as they are in procedural districts or denigrated as they are in programmatic districts, but instrumental in forging an organizational response to state policy that integrates legislative intent with organizational purpose.

Professional districts have decision-making styles that are collegial and inclusive—shared, but not dominated by either teachers or administrators. Teachers and administrators shared responsibility for making decisions about teachers' professional advancement and standards. In these districts, broad involvement in implementing the Career Ladder Program was not regarded by teachers and administrators as poaching on each other's territory. Both groups were confident that shared decision making would result in fair procedures and better programs that would translate into better schools. According to one principal:

> We've had to change some of the ways we operate as a system—strengthening and standardizing evaluation and bite the bullet on determining just what we mean by excellent teaching—and it has required quite a bit of work. But it has been worth it. Teaching practices are improving. The core curriculum is better aligned in schools and from school to school; and schools are delivering better education to students because teachers and principals have time to plan the program together, systematically.

Differences among the four implementation modes is illustrated by variation in districts' approach to the Extended Contract Days component. *Pro forma* districts tended to allocate as much money as they could to that component. All teachers were paid for the maximum number of days for which they were eligible. They did not have to account for or justify the use of their time for those days. Programmatic districts tended to control the use of the extended contract days for work on specific projects. Procedural districts cared less about the content of the activity and more about who approves the use of those days and who decides how those days are going to be used. In the professional districts, the use of extended contract days were determined by teachers and administrators. Some days were allocated to teachers to use for instructional preparation, while others were allocated to school staff development activities. In deciding how extended contract days would be used, teachers and administrators tried to balance competing interests: the desire to achieve organizational goals, professional autonomy, and professional development.

One way to assess the effects of the Career Ladder Program is to ask what has changed as a result of its implementation and, conversely, what difference would it make if the program were terminated. *Pro forma* districts would be least affected since they had made the fewest structural changes. Programmatic districts would go through severe retrenchment. Procedural districts would be left with elaborate bureaucratic structures and nothing to do with them. The effect on professional districts is the hardest to predict. Obviously, the loss of state funds would necessitate curtailing various activities. However, the structural changes that had been initiated in response to state policy might be sufficiently integrated to be immune from changes in funding levels.

CONCLUSION

It is no easy matter for districts to implement incentive pay schemes for teachers as the legislature thought they should. It requires changing existing practices regarding teacher compensation, work responsibilities, and professional advancement. Teacher evaluations, for example, acquire new significance both professionally and legally. In some Utah districts, teachers were never evaluated once they passed probationary status. Now, evaluation becomes a basis for decisions about professional advancement. Evaluation also becomes the basis for determining salary increases, which are no longer dependent exclusively on uniform cost-of-living adjustments, longevity, and earned credits. Increased professional responsibility for teachers requires redefining how teachers spend their time in schools. Schools must change existing decision-making structures by formalizing means for teachers to engage in planning and evaluation. Teachers cannot be held responsible for what they do not control. Therefore, they must have control over the allocation of resources.

I have suggested in this chapter that some school districts — the ones typed as integrated — have been able to effect real changes in their schools through the Career Ladder Program. The best characterization of the decision-making styles in those districts is "purposive." That is, decision making is guided by a sense of institutional purpose. Implementation decisions are driven by the goal of making schools more professionally satisfying for teachers and administrators and improving their effectiveness.

Purposive decision making requires schools to look beyond the immediate programmatic or regulatory dimensions of state policy to their outcomes. Integrated districts look to organizational, rather than programmatic or procedural, outcomes. Integrated districts do not think of merit pay and career ladders as a way of reforming the teaching profession, but as a way of improving schools. Teacher reform measures are just one set of policy instruments to effect better schools.

Even when school districts act in good faith to implement state policies, they may not succeed. The programmatic and procedural districts illustrate the inherent limits of those implementation responses. Consequently, district orientation to state policy becomes a crucial determinant to program success. The good news for state policymakers in that conclusion is that districts can change. There is a certain tension among the four implementation responses, and districts move from one category to another. Some districts changed their initial implementation responses as they became more comfortable with the program and began to appreciate its potential for school improvement. Established patterns of behavior also had to change. The program generated a new vocabulary in the language of teachers and administrators, and both groups had to become comfortable with that language.

How much and under what circumstances districts change depends upon their willingness and capacity to align cultural values with organizational goals. That kind of change takes time and it takes resources. For schools to make investments in major change, they must believe that the transaction costs at least equal the purported benefits.

Educational reform policies are no better than the schools that implement them. Therefore, the object of state policy must be the school. And within schools, the focus must be on the kinds of organizational arrangements that maximize organizational competence. If states are serious about improving educational quality and striving for excellence, they must create the appropriate context in which that can take place. That effort will require fundamental redefinition of various organizational roles. The dichotomized view of local versus state control, for example, is inappropriate and anachronistic if institutional change becomes the focus of reform. The distribution between state and local authority is no longer a zero sum game over specific policy decisions but a cooperative effort aimed at enhancing organizational competence. The effort has to be centered on enhancing institutional effectiveness. The history of educational reform in America is full of innovative strategies that became routine in the process of bureaucratic aging.

REFERENCES

Amsler, Mary, Douglas Mitchell, Linda Nelson, and Thomas Timar. 1988. "Policy Evaluation of Utah's Career Ladder Program," San Francisco: Far West Laboratory for Educational Research and Development.

Bednar, William C., Jr. 1985. "A Survey of the Texas Reform Package: House Bill 72," *St. Mary's Law Journal,* 16.

Carnegie Forum on Education and the Economy. 1986. *A Nation Prepared: Teachers for the 21st Century.* New York: Carnegie.

Cohen, David K. and Richard Murnane. 1985. "The Merits of Merit Pay," *Public Interest* (Summer):80.

Cornett, Lynn. 1990. "Paying for Performance—Important Questions and Answers," *Career Ladder Clearinghouse,* Atlanta, GA: Southern Regional Education Board.

Cornett, Lynn. 1988. "Is 'Paying for Performance' Changing Schools?" *Career Ladder Clearinghouse,* Atlanta, GA: Southern Regional Education Board.

Cornett, Lynn and Karen Weeks. 1985. "Career Ladder Plans: Trends and Emerging Issues—1985," *Career Ladder Clearinghouse,* Atlanta, GA: Southern Regional Education Board.

Doyle, Dennis P. and Chester E. Finn, Jr. 1984. "American Schools and the Future of Local Control," *Public Interest* (Fall):77.

Hanuschek, E. A. 1987. "Throwing Money at Schools," *Journal of Policy Analysis and Management,* 1(1):19–41.

Hipple, Theodore, H. June 19, 1985. " 'Vivids' and Portfolios Do Not a Master Teacher Make," *Education Week.*

Kagen, Robert A. 1978. *Regulatory Justice: Implementing a Wage-Price Freeze.* New York: Russell Sage Foundation.

Little, Judith W. 1990. "The Mentor Phenomenon and the Social Organization of Teaching," *Review of Research in Education,* Vol. 16.

Murnane, R. J., J. D. Singer, and J. B. Willett. 1989. "The Influences of Salaries and 'Opportunity Costs' on Teachers' Career Choices: Evidence from North Carolina," *Harvard Educational Review,* 59(3).

National Commission on Excellence in Education. 1983. *A Nation at Risk: The Imperative for Educational Reform.* Washington, D.C.: U.S. Department of Education.

Nonet, Philippe and Phillip Selznick. 1978. *Law and Society in Transition: Toward Responsive Law.* New York: Harper and Row, p. 111.

Rosenholtz, Susan. 1987. "Educational Reform Strategies, Will They Increase Teacher Commitment?" *American Journal of Education,* 95(4):534–562.

Select Committee on Public Education. April 19, 1984. *Recommendations.* Austin, TX: State Printing Office.

Shulman, Judith, George St. Clair, and Judith Warren Little. 1984. *Expanded Teacher Roles: Mentors and Masters.* San Francisco, CA: Far West Laboratory for Educational Research and Development.

Stoddard, Trish, David J. Losk, and Charles Benson. 1984. *Some Reflections on the Honorable Profession of Teaching.* Berkeley: University of California, Policy Analysis for California Education, Graduate School of Education.

The Knoxville News-Sentinel, June 30, 1985.

Timar, Thomas B. 1989. "A Theoretical Framework for Local Responses to State Policy: Implementing Utah's Career Ladder Program," *Educational Evaluation and Policy Analysis,* 11(4).

Timar, Thomas B. and David L. Kirp. 1988. *Managing Educational Excellence.* Philadelphia: Falmer.

ENDNOTES

1 See, for example, Guy Benveniste, "Implementation and Intervention Strategies: The Case of 94-142" and Paul Berman, "From Compliance to Learning: Implementing Legally Induced Reforms" in *School Days, Rule Days,* David L. Kirp and Donald A. Jensen, eds., New York: Falmer Press; Stanford Series in Education and Public Policy (1987). Larry Cuban, "Transforming the Frog into a Prince: Effective Schools Research, Policy, and Practice at the District Level," *Harvard Education Review,* 54 (1984).

2 Comments by H. Ross Perot to the Select Committee on Public Education.

3 *House Bill 72,* Sec. 13.321. Emphasis added.

4 Several years later, the legislators who authored these measures reminisced about efforts to change schools and "laughed about the transitory nature of these landmark reforms."

5 Merit pay is accepted by teachers if it establishes a standard of professional competence and rewards all teachers who achieve that level. Merit pay is rejected by teachers when it is used to reward a small percent of the teaching force on a competitive basis. The screening effect of the former filters out teachers who do not meet a certain standard. The latter rewards a select few in a school or district regardless of the performance of the other teachers.

6 This classification draws on a typology of regulatory decision making and a typology of laws. See Kagan, 1978: 97 and Nonet and Selznick, 1978: 16–22.

CHAPTER 3

Teacher Motivation, Work Structures, and Organizational Change: Perspectives on Educational Reform and Compensation

MARY RHODES – *University of Utah*
RODNEY T. OGAWA – *University of Utah*

ATTEMPTS to positively affect the academic performance of schools by influencing the motivation of teachers were a prominent part of the first wave of educational reform. As the nation proceeds to the second wave, we have an opportunity to review these efforts. That is the purpose of this chapter. The review will follow a number of themes. First, we review three theories from the mainstream literature on motivation. Second, we discuss two concepts not typically linked to motivation that add to our understanding about the internal states of organizational participants – empowerment and efficacy – that can affect job performance. Third, we move beyond conceptualizations of organizational members' internal psychological states and consider contextual factors that can affect job performance. Fourth, taking a somewhat historical perspective, we describe earlier attempts to alter teachers' work conditions to provide a temporal perspective of current efforts. Finally, we describe two concerted attempts at positively affecting the performance of teachers by altering conditions of work. We close the chapter by offering some observations and recommendations for thinking about the second wave of reform.

MOTIVATION LITERATURE

The concept of motivation is important to any consideration of educational reforms aimed at improving student outcomes because motivation is considered to be an important factor in determining the effectiveness with which work is done. As Miner notes (1980), motivation theory can reveal work conditions that enhance motivation and thereby increase productivity. In a review of the motivation literature, Miskel and Ogawa (1988) discuss potentially useful perspectives on motivation, including expectancy theory, a job-characteristics model, and

61

goal theory. However, they also observe a "lack of diversity characterizing the research in educational administration" (1988, p. 286). To overcome this limitation, we will augment the treatment of teacher motivation with discussions of two related concepts from the management literature: empowerment and efficacy.

Expectancy Theory

Expectancy theory assumes that individuals are motivated by psychological as well as environmental conditions. Decisions are governed by mathematical relations between valence, instrumentality, and expectancy (Vroom, 1964). The perception of positive or negative outcomes determines valence, and the likelihood of attaining the outcome after a particular behavior determines instrumentality. The likelihood of achieving the behavior after a particular level of effort determines expectancy. In verbalizing the mathematical formula, Miskel and Ogawa note that "motivation to behave in a certain way changes as the level of each variable increases or decreases. Because the relationships are multiplicative, if one of the variables is zero, effort is zero" (1988, pp. 281–282). More specifically, if the valence, or perception of rewards, decreases, effort will decrease. Similarly, if the perception of the probability of attaining the outcome or the behavior necessary to achieve the outcome decreases, effort will decrease. Motivation, therefore, can be increased by increasing the reward, the behavior likely to lead to the reward, or the effort likely to lead to the necessary behavior. If any one of these factors is absent, however, effort will be absent.

Perhaps the most pertinent finding of research on expectancy motivation for educators is that it is related to student achievement (Miskel, McDonald, and Bloom, 1983). Implications for educators indicate that rewards, perceptions of possession of behaviors that can lead to rewards, and perceptions that effort can achieve these behaviors can increase effort and thereby increase student achievement. Although the mathematical and technical complexity of expectancy theory limits its usefulness in field settings, the general principles deserve attention and can be enhanced by integration with other motivation theories.

Job-Characteristics Model

The job-characteristics model (Hackman and Oldham, 1976) is based on the concepts of experienced meaningfulness, experienced responsibility, and knowledge of results. Meaningfulness depends on skill variety, task identity, and task significance. While the definitions of skill variety and task significance are inherent in the labels, task identity depends on the relationship the worker has with the entire work process. If the worker, for example, is only involved in a fragmented part of the process, low task identity results. In contrast, a worker involved with an integrated process achieves task identity. Responsibility depends on accountability, and knowledge of results depends on feedback. The combination of these factors produces a motivating potential score.

Research on the job-characteristics model is limited in educational settings (Miskel and Ogawa, 1988), and more general research finds that the motivating potential score reinforces, rather than creates, high performance (Hackman and Oldham, 1980). And yet, because of the current emphasis on attraction and retention of high-performing teachers, reinforcement is a justifiable tenet, and the job-characteristics model contains potentially valuable contributions for educational work structures.

Goal Theory

Goal theory differs from expectancy and job-characteristics theories. It is not as thoroughly developed as the other models (Miskel and Ogawa, 1988), and thus it is ironic that it has found its way into practice in educational settings as frequently as it has.

Goal theory assumes that behavior is based on a purpose, and the goal is the purpose an individual wants to achieve (Lock, Cartledge, and Knerr, 1970; Mento, Cartledge, and Lock, 1980). Research has yielded three generalizations pertinent to a consideration of motivation. Specific goals are more effective motivators than general or absent goals; more difficult goals are more effective motivators than easy goals if they are accepted by the individual; participation in goal setting increases individual satisfaction but not necessarily performance (Miskel and Ogawa, 1988).

Miskel and Ogawa observe that the failure to illuminate determinants of goal acceptance and commitment is a limitation of research but acknowledge the theory's probable value especially when combined with "other theories of work motivation, including expectancy theory and the job-characteristics model" (1988, p. 285).

Empowerment

Empowerment means enabling people to act (Kanter, 1983). Because the concept of motivation emphasizes antecedents to action, empowerment and motivation are related concepts. Although Kanter's research was conducted in corporate settings, that alone does not make her conclusions inapplicable to other organizational settings. In fact, there is precedent for applying lessons learned in one field to another. Kerchner (1988), for instance, considers management techniques such as networking appropriate for loosely coupled schools, and even more strongly, he suggests an entrepreneurial responsiveness to clients as a model for education.

Kanter's primary objective is to empower employees; this means providing employees with the ability to produce (Kanter, 1983). In *The Changemasters,* Kanter explores "environments that stimulate people to act" (1983, p. 18) and identifies factors that are closely related to those highlighted in theories of motivation. She incorporates two concepts discussed in motivation theories: rewards and goals. Rewards are an integral part of expectancy theory, and goals are inherent in goal theory.

Besides providing praise and feedback, Kanter (1983) suggests an augmented view of the role of rewards, one in which rewards are an incentive to act rather than a result of an act. As such, the reward is provided as an encouragement to move in a desirable organizational direction rather than as the result of goal attainment. As in expectancy theory, then, a reward is a motivator. However, while in expectancy theory the reward is a perceived outcome, Kanter suggests that reward is a real and precedent outcome. Although empirical verification of this claim is absent, the concept may be pertinent to answering the question raised by Miskel and Ogawa (1988) about participants' commitment to goals.

Kanter (1983) also provides more direct strategies for increasing commitment to goals. If goals are the product of bargaining, she asserts, they are more likely to gain adherence. She also suggests they are more likely to be embraced if they are close to the individual's territory, a concept that is consistant with the notion of task significance in the job-characteristic model. In addition, Kanter claims that one source of motivation is "the desire to apply a pet idea or carry out a pet project" (1983, p. 30). This is congruent with assertions about goals, bargaining, and territory. If an individual is involved in the goal setting, some commitment is generated. Alternatively, "the motivation to solve problems declines in segmented systems" (1983, p. 29). This is related to task identity in a job-characteristics model and suggests that work conditions that apply principles of integration are worth investigation.

Generally, empowerment means enabling individuals to act by providing access to resources, information, and support. Kanter proposes several strategies to accomplish this. She recommends a "culture of pride" (1983, p. 361), which includes support in the form of visible awards and in allowing innovators to solve other problems in the company. Kerchner (1988) maintains that norms ensuing from such a structure are more effective than bureaucratic rules because they "have the property of situational adaptivity" (1988, p. 389).

As a means of increasing access to information and thereby empowering individuals, Kanter recommends networking. One specific technique — the reduction of hierarchical levels — is particularly appropriate to educational settings because they already are characterized by relatively flat structures. This flatness should facilitate the implementation of another of her recommendations: the improvement of lateral communication produced by lateral mobility.

Kanter's concept of empowerment, combined with empirical evidence concerning expectancy, job characteristics, and goal theory, provides insights to the nature of motivation in educational settings. To summarize, commitment to goals can be enhanced through bargaining, which can result in the adoption of goals that are proximate to participants' domains. The ability to act also is enhanced by having access to critical resources, being embedded in a "culture of pride," and reducing hierarchical levels and increasing lateral communication.

Efficacy

Efficacy is an expectancy construct that derives partially from Rotter's work on locus of control. Rotter's (1966) definition of an individual with an internal locus of control describes an individual with a high sense of efficacy. He states that, "If the person perceives that the event is contingent upon his own behavior or his own relatively permanent characteristics, we have termed this belief *internal control*" (Rotter, 1966, p. 1). Expectancy, then, concerns the extent to which an individual believes that some phenomenon is the result of his/her action.

Thus, teacher efficacy is "the extent to which teachers believe they can affect student learning" (Dembo and Gibson, 1985, p. 173). Although the concept of efficacy has not been linked explicitly to motivation, the two concepts have much in common. For instance, efficacy as defined by Dembo and Gibson (1985) resembles instrumentality in expectancy theory. Instrumentality is the perceived likelihood that an outcome will result from a behavior and is thought to affect effort.

Research identifies two independent constructs involved in teacher efficacy—a sense of teaching efficacy and a sense of personal teaching efficacy (Ashton and Webb, 1986). Teaching efficacy "refers to teachers' expectations that teaching can influence student learning" (Ashton and Webb, 1986, p. 4). Personal teaching efficacy "refers to individuals' assessment of their own teaching competence" (Ashton and Webb, 1986, p. 4).

Investigation of the causal link between efficacy and outcomes indicates that "performance varies as a function of perceived efficacy" (Bandura, 1982, p. 124). Further, Bandura (1982) observes that, "Because people are influenced more by how they read their performance successes than by successes per se, perceived self-efficacy was a better predictor of subsequent behavior than was performance attainment . . . " (p. 125). After reviewing social learning theory, attribution theory, and intrinsic motivation theory, Stipek and Weisz (1981) similarly conclude that, "Success or failure per se might be less important than a child's perceptions of the *causes* of the success or failure. Success enhances self-perceptions of competence only if the child accepts responsibility for that success" (p. 130). The internal attribution, therefore, is an important component of resultant behavior.

Applied to teaching, a sense of efficacy can be expected to affect teaching performance. As Gibson and Dembo (1984) state, "One would predict that teachers who believe student learning can be influenced by effective teaching, and who also have confidence in their own teaching abilities, should persist longer, provide a greater academic focus in the classroom, and exhibit different types of feedback than teachers who have lower expectations concerning their ability to influence student learning" (p. 570).

Findings corroborate such predictions. Besides spending more time with whole-group instruction, "high-efficacy teachers also spent more time monitoring and checking seatwork" (Gibson and Dembo, 1984, p. 576) and more time "in preparation or paperwork than low-efficacy teachers" (Gibson and Dembo, 1984, p. 577). Also, "high-efficacy teachers were more effective in leading students to correct responses through their questioning, whereas low-efficacy teachers would go on to other students or another question (lack of persistence)" (Gibson and Dembo, 1984, p. 577).

Behavioral differences between high-efficacy and low-efficacy teachers result in different student outcomes. This relationship has been investigated empirically. Based on Rotter's internal and external measure,

Rand researchers developed items corresponding to teacher and personal senses of efficacy that related to increased reading achievement (Gibson and Dembo, 1984). Similarly, Ashton and Webb (1986) report that, "Teachers' sense of efficacy is related to student achievement" (p. 138). A somewhat related study on locus of control reports that, "Internal student teachers . . . were more effective in the classroom than those with more external orientations" (Sadowski, Blackwell, and Willard, 1985, p. 353).

While efficacy has been linked to the classroom behaviors of teachers, the conditions that contribute to efficacy are not as clear. Several possibilities have been identified but, as yet, have not been confirmed empirically. Dembo and Gibson (1985) suggest "teacher education and socialization" and "school organization" (p. 177) as possibilities, while Ashton and Webb (1986) focus on school norms, collegial relationships, and school decision-making structures. Rhodes posits that the concept of alienation, operationalized as a perception of external working conditions, provides access to some structural components that covary with efficacy (Rhodes, 1989). This will be discussed later.

To summarize, the concept of motivation shares much with other concepts with which it typically has not been linked. The concept of efficacy suggests that behavior is influenced by expected outcomes. This is consistent with goal theory, which holds that behavior is motivated by expected outcomes. Empowerment emphasizes identification with the task to be completed as a motivator. Research on job characteristics reveals that a motivating potential score reinforces, rather than creates, high performance (Miskel and Ogawa, 1988). This mirrors the findings of efficacy research concerning the relationship between performance and efficacy. As noted previously, empowerment defines some mechanisms that might increase commitment to goals and, therefore, augments goal theory.

What is lacking is an integration of the concepts of efficacy, attribution, and goal setting which addresses the reciprocal effects of these factors (Ashton and Webb, 1986). Theories of motivation may provide frameworks for this integration. For example, expectancy theory has indicated that increased valence, instrumentality, and expectancy can lead to greater effort, which in turn results in improved student achievement (Miskel, McDonald, and Bloom, 1983). Empirical studies have shown that performance varies between high and low efficacy teachers (Gibson and Dembo, 1984) and that high-efficacy teachers differ from low in achieving increased student achievement (Armor et al.,

1976; Gibson and Dembo, 1984; Ashton and Webb, 1986). Current efforts to identify the antecedents of efficacy could be informed by factors identified by motivational theory as affecting expectancy. Similarly, the identification of factors that contribute to efficacy, to the extent that efficacy and expectancy are related, could illuminate further our understanding of teacher motivation.

The discussion of empowerment also provides some possible answers to the question of what contributes to efficacy or expectancy; however, empirical evidence is scanty. Participative decision making, for instance, may resemble Kanter's (1983) parallel goal setting, but there is greater evidence that this strategy results in increased satisfaction rather than in increased productivity. Reform clearly calls for work conditions that can increase motivation in measurably productive ways or increase the attraction and retention of individuals motivated to productive performance.

WORK STRUCTURES: INFLUENCES ON ALIENATION

To this point, the discussion has focused on issues involving the internal states of organizational actors, namely their motivational levels, their capacity to act (or empowerment), and their efficacy. As we noted, each of these internal factors is affected to a degree by conditions in the workplace. Thus, in this section we turn expressly to contextual factors that can affect the performance of organizational participants. The discussion will be guided by the sociological construct of alienation, which offers a perspective on workplace conditions and their relationship to work behaviors, motivated states, and student achievement.

Alienation is defined as a feeling of powerlessness, meaninglessness, normlessness, and isolation (Dworkin, 1987; Aiken and Hage, 1966; Dean, 1961; Seeman, 1959). For the purpose of this discussion, alienation is a perception of the extent to which these conditions exist in the workplace. Low alienation is a perception of the presence of power, meaning, norms, and collegial patterns, while high alienation is the absence of these conditions. Powerlessness, specifically, is a perceived inability to change work conditions. Meaninglessness is a perception that actions are unrelated to work outcomes. Normlessness is an absence of coherent rules, formal or informal, in the workplace, and isolation is a distance between an individual and other workers.

The resulting condition of alienation resembles the fragmented workplace, which Kanter (1983) describes as unresponsive to innovation and creativity. Similarly, some features of the job-characteristic model are antithetical to alienation. Task identity defines a link between the worker and the entire work process, and meaninglessness is a condition defined by separation between actions and outcomes.

Dworkin (1987) has focused attention on alienation by asserting that the findings of his research indicate that alienated teachers do not necessarily underachieve in reference to student outcomes. Reform efforts have envisioned and implemented plans that attempt to increase the power, meaning, norms, and collegial patterns in schools in order to professionalize teaching and increase student gains. Thus, connections between alienation and student achievement are important. At least one reviewer, however, finds the absence of a link between teacher alienation and student outcomes "somewhat difficult to accept" (Firestone, 1988, p. 88). Further, although Apple (1988) does not use the term, he does use a classical definition of alienation as the "process of separating conception from execution" to account for the "*deskilling* of teachers" (p. 276). Because the assertions and controversy are related to motivation and work structures, attention to the issue is addressed. The terms are problematic and paradoxical, but discussions can illuminate which work conditions can be changed in what directions to increase teacher motivation.

The feeling of powerlessness contributes a great deal to the sense of alienation. Power is a broad concept, and as a bureaucratic profession, teaching exhibits some contradictions that have complicated the problem. Teachers are subject to an organization responsible for coordinating the movement of a large number of individuals. Further, certain standards of quality are necessary (Bidwell, 1965), and this requires some relinquishing of individual autonomy. The use of public funds gives power to external constituencies (Bidwell, 1965), and a lay board is another external constraint on professional and collective autonomy for teachers (Lortie, 1969).

The issue of individual autonomy illuminates varying forces in teaching work that confound the definition of power. Moeller and Charters (1966) note, for example, that "a teacher might well feel fully in command of the classroom learning process, but feel essentially powerless to control his fate in the organizational setting" (p. 446). More recent attention to a similar phenomenon has conceptualized the distinction as organizational efficacy and individual efficacy, and while work structures can operate to influence both phenomena in the same direction, some structures can "influence each form of efficacy in different directions" (Fuller, Wood, Rapoport, and Dornbusch, 1982, p. 10). Lortie (1969) has noted that while teachers do retain some instructional autonomy, because this power is not legitimated, it remains fragile. It is probably true that recent trends toward accountability and visibility have threatened that power. In its stead, reformationalists are envisioning "teachers who have the real authority to educate in the best way their collective wisdom dictates" (Soltis, 1988, p. 244).

The issue of power is complex because professionals are working within bureaucratic structures, but power can be considered the ability to influence work conditions. The reform movement is demanding an empowered teaching profession and an empowered teaching individual, but evaluations of the first reform wave are mixed. Futrell (1988) observes that teachers are becoming "fully enfranchised" (p. 375); Boyer (1988) cites a Carnegie Foundation study of 22,000 teachers to support his conclusion that "teachers are not involved in key professional decisions" (p. 314).

A second element of alienation is a sense of meaninglessness. This term is less clearly elaborated in alienation literature and more difficult to use to define teaching work, but based on the above discussions of alienation and power, meaninglessness can refer to work conditions. Because it suggests uncertainty between actions and outcomes, meaninglessness can be defined as work conditions that are unpredictable regarding attainment of intrinsic or extrinsic rewards.

The role of rewards has been examined generally in expectancy theory and in empowerment, but the specific role of rewards in teaching is less clear. In the past, the intrinsic rewards of teaching have been characterized as ambiguous (Lortie, 1975), and extrinsic rewards of teaching such as status or income have been considered relatively lacking. Reformers have addressed both issues. Johnson (1986) states, "There is extensive evidence that teachers regard professional efficacy, not money, as the primary motivator in their work" (p. 55). The emphasis on improved student outcomes (National Commission on Excellence in Education, 1983; Carnegie Task Force on Teaching as a Profession, 1986) could presumably result in improved intrinsic satisfaction for teachers individually or collectively, and in this case the parallel of intrinsic rewards with student achievement can result in rewards being inherently aligned with productivity.

The insistence on improved status and income is clearly related to improved extrinsic satisfaction for teachers (Shanker, 1988; Futrell,

1988). In the case of extrinsics, however, the relationship between satisfaction and productivity is not as blatant. Another pertinent observation about extrinsic rewards is related to a characteristic of power alluded to previously. In some cases, the extrinsic rewards accrued from the status or recognition of mechanisms that increase individual satisfaction may be counterproductive to organizational goals. Time and energy spent in participative decision making, for example, may embellish status and be individually satisfying but detract from the time and energy available for classroom responsibilities. The issue of status is clouded by one more vagary—the demand for status by an occupation does not insure societal compliance. Sources for prestige are not entirely clear, but once granted, they are somewhat self-perpetuating and cyclical in nature. Furthermore, a profession may use its power and status to limit the power and status of other occupations (Ritzer, 1977).

Still, increased salaries may operate in the way that Kanter (1983) suggests is the appropriate role of rewards—as incentives for commitment; also, recruitment and retention of able workers may be improved. A variant role of rewards is advocated by proponents of merit pay. While the idea of merit pay reward programs may not be new, the implementation has not been clearly accomplished, and evaluation of results continues to be elusive.

Norms are operants as complicated as power and rewards, but they are also part of the working conditions of teaching. Some norms of teaching have been the targets of proposed changes, and some have inhibited reform attempts. The equality norm (Lortie, 1969) teachers adhere to professionally and the traditionally flat career paths have probably contributed to the resistance to merit pay attempts. Breaches of this norm involve evaluation of teachers and, therefore, increased visibility and possible erosion of instructional freedom. These are informal norms that have helped teachers preserve some individual autonomy, and some studies even show a preference for formal norms by teachers. Contrary to the hypothesis, teachers in a highly bureaucratized system reported a higher sense of power (Moeller and Charters, 1966). Hoy, Newland, and Blazovsky (1977) found that teachers preferred the predictability of rule codification. It must be noted, however, that while teachers preferred the codification, they were not as interested in enforcement of the codes (Hoy et al., 1977). Of primary pertinence, however, is determination of the effect of norms on teacher productivity, and teacher productivity means enhanced student performance.

A clear and well-established norm of teaching, isolation, is the fourth dimension of alienation. Isolation has always been a characteristic of teaching, and this pattern of teaching work has been at least partially faulted with the occupation's resistance to implementation of other changes (Lortie, 1975). It is perhaps ironic that the combination of a flat level and bureaucratic structure has resulted in workers who do not interact, but it is probably teachers' primary interaction with students that has reduced contact with peers. General corporate literature cites networking and blurred organizational boundaries as conducive to productivity and innovation (Kanter, 1983; Peters and Waterman, 1982), and, as in the case with other elements of alienation, reform has recommended programs to alleviate this condition. Programs that inhibit cooperation are eschewed (Bacharach, Conley, and Shedd, 1986), and research studying work patterns in schools found collegiality a contribution to effectiveness (Little, 1982).

The elements of alienation define work conditions that are descriptive of teaching work. The problem requiring attention is the relationship between the work conditions and productivity. The discussion of motivation emphasized the relationship between behavior and productivity and noted that job satisfaction and productivity were not always parallel. Similarly, while alienation merits examination as a state contrasting with motivation, the relationship between alienation and job dissatisfaction is not as important as the relationship between alienating conditions and productivity.

Dworkin (1987) must be commended for insisting that changes in power, meaning, norms, and collegial patterns of teachers be justified by concomitant increases in student achievement, but empirical links are limited, and those available are not entirely consistent. While Dworkin (1987) reports no correlation between alienation and student outcomes, Rhodes (1989) reports a modest but significant negative correlation between alienation and efficacy. Because efficacy has been empirically linked to student outcomes, this offers some support for the position of some reformists to reduce factors contributing to teacher alienation.

HISTORICAL ANTECEDENTS

Recent efforts to redefine the power, meaning, norms, and collegial patterns of teaching are not without antecedents. Lessons learned from previous attempts to alter the conditions under which teachers work might well inform current efforts. Thus, in this section we review four reform strategies that were implemented before the current wave of reform. One antecedent is differentiated staffing, which was a predominant model in the late 1960s and 1970s and has been remodeled and implemented in the 1980s and, thus, is given extensive treatment here. Others are job enlargement, merit pay, and extended contract. We also review the literature on organizational change, which is relevent to a consideration of altering the organizational characteristics of schools.

Differentiated Staffing

The differentiated staffing movement of the 1960s and 1970s attempted to restructure the work of teaching. A critical examination of the movement reveals its goals, successes, and failures, which can be employed to inform current reform efforts.

In the late 1960s, federal funding for differentiated staffing plans became available through the Education Professions Development Act (Sharpes, 1972) and Title III of the Elementary and Secondary Education Act (Mann, McLaughlin, Baer, Greenwood, McCluskey, Prusoff, Wirt, and Zellman, 1975.) While the EPDA developed the School Personnel Utilization Plan specifically to develop "alternative conceptual staffing projects" (Sharpes, 1972, p. 56), Title III, the "most heavily funded of all change agent programs," supported a variety of locally initiated innovations at a cost of approximately $150 million a year (Mann et al., 1975, p. 1–2).

The rationale was "to reduce through training projects for teachers and administrators, the number of trained personnel leaving teaching by differentiating salary schedules, and by redefining school and teaching responsibilities" (Sharpes, 1972, p. 156). These reasons were based on research, but particular models often lacked empirical referents. Although a general expectation that students would benefit from increased individualized instruction was expressed (*Educational Digest,* 1970), Earl points out a tendency of the literature to emphasize teacher over student benefits (1969, p. 10). Examples include a teacher role in decision making and heightened status possibilities.

The application of such research based observations in differentiated staffing models, however, did not lead to fulfillment of these specific expectations. Significant and lasting changes in organizational structure, teaching behavior, and student gains were not reported. An examination of several models can provide a partial explanation for the limited effectiveness of the differentiated staffing movement, and from there it will be possible to derive the implications for current programs.

Complexity of Differentiated Staffing Models

The complexity of differentiated staffing models was a major dysfunctional element. It was manifested in several different areas. Principally, the number of vertical levels often approached ten or more with paraprofessionals. Sarasota County, for example, added four horizontal function areas to approximately eleven vertical levels. Barber (1971) notes that these kinds of levels go "beyond traditional staff allocations based on common subject matter distinctions and grade level arrangements" (p. 167). Because such traditional distinctions do already exist in teaching work, further delineations may have proven too cumbersome. In a Wagonia model, additional separations between teachers of core and of elective subjects were observed (Mann et al., 1975, IV-146). Although not a formal division, the example may serve to emphasize the abundance of separatist possibilities already in place in teaching.

The complexity of the differentiated staffing structures resulted in complicated authority lines in some models. Informal and formal communication suffered in Venice Junior High (English, 1972). In other models such as Wagonia, participative decision-making mechanisms were time-consuming (Mann et al., 1975), and Venice reported the "creation of divisiveness due to the Academic Senate" (English, 1972).

Detailed job descriptions for teachers and paraprofessionals with twenty and twenty-two duties were reported by Rosemount (1972). These numbers may have proven excessive conceptually and inflexible physically. Even in the absence of such numerous items, "role overload" (Harriot and Gross, 1979, p. 23) was a likely phenomenon.

Other complications were sometimes added to the differentiated staffing program. Open spacing often accompanied plans. Daily time schedules were sometimes manipulated; Temple City reported a 40 percent time block that was "unscheduled for the average secondary student" (Fiorino, 1972, p. 52). Mesa required detailed contractual bids from schools to the board (Fiorino, 1972). When such items combined with the basic plan, the effects may have been unwieldy. Similarly, the detailed guidelines for implementation, management, and evaluation by Fiorino (1972) suggest further possibilities for confusion.

Resulting Teacher Dissatisfaction

For reasons other than complexity, the structure sometimes resulted in individual dissatisfactions. It was noted, for example, that teachers were concerned about aides usurping their roles and about loss of status (English, 1972). Although not strictly a differentiated staffing model, Pew et al. offer some observations of team teaching that may be applicable. In particular, a "lack of complete trust and openness" was cited (1971, p. 4). They also note that students reflected "staff frustrations" (Pew et al., 1971, p. 7). In team teaching, the financial structures are unclear, but differential staffing allocations might be expected to exacerbate such problems. In reference to Temple City, for instance, Stover cautions, "The financial resources are vital if disruptive personnel displacements and associated deterioration of staff morale are not be avoided" (1969, p. 8).

A study by Charters (1973) is particularly relevent to the thematic considerations of work structure and inherent motivation because a sociological framework was used to explore how the structure of differentiated staffing affected teaching behaviors. Although limited to case studies of one experimental and one control group, evidence from other models supports the findings of the Charters study. It is furthermore significant because of the methodological and empirical comparison on claims of differentiated staffing—specifically, dimensions of teaching tasks, working relations, and power redistribution were analyzed. Some of these claims are salient because they are targets of current reform.

Generally, Charters (1973) concluded that the characteristics of the two schools "did not differ" (1973, p. 91). Findings on teaching tasks, for example, indicated the experimental group gained on one and lost on three disciplinary measures (Charters, 1973). Division of instructional labor, interdependence, and communication comprise categories used to measure working relations, and again conclusions illustrated more similarities between schools than differences (Charters, 1973). An analysis of work loads by Conant (1971) similarly found that work roles were not highly changed by aides. Differentiated staffing attempted to redistribute power, but assessment of instructional decision, staff evaluation, and influence and esteem structures of the two schools generally did not support success (Charters, 1973).

Particularly valuable, however, is Charters' identification of "energy diversions" (1973, p. 95). He mentions "heavy meeting attendance, attention to problems of pupil decorum, work in supervising teacher aides . . . amount of discussion devoted to gripes and concerns about work, constraints on teaching of time, space and scheduling" (1973, p. 95). English (1972), in comparing the Venice and Beaverton projects, also reported comments of fatigue and exhaustion. These behavior patterns may be related to the possibility of organizational and personal efficacy operating in opposing directions noted above.

Examination of the models indicates a great amount of complexity that increased teacher work load and energy expenditures. In some cases, job satisfaction was threatened by status hierarchies and presumably by accompanying financial promotions. The introduction of paraprofessionals was similarly unsettling. Charters (1973) notes, incidentally, that using aides productively requires teacher time in a situation where time is unavailable. Otherwise, teacher behavior in regard to tasks, work roles, and relations remained basically unchanged. Advancements in student achievement have not been reported (Hawley, 1988).

Similarities to Recent Reform Programs

Similarities between differentiated staffing programs of the late 1960s and early 1970s and recent reform programs deserve attention. Although the impetus for funding was from the federal level for differentiated staffing and from the state level for career ladders, funds were used, at least in some cases, to support locally developed plans. The rationale of both movements are similar. As noted above, projects hoped to reduce numbers of teachers leaving (Sharpes, 1972), and more recent plans cite the "greater retention of competent teachers" (Reston Teachers Association, 1985, p. 10) as a goal. Means of achieving these objectives sound comparable in the rhetoric—expanded decision-making opportunities, use of paraprofessionals, and increased status and salaries are recommended in documents of both periods (Earl, 1969; Charters, 1973; Shanker, 1988, Futrell, 1988; Boyer, 1988).

Because these proposals are receiving emphatic attention at later dates, however, this suggests that problems were not solved adequately through the mechanisms of the initial movement. Perhaps differences between earlier and more recent reform movements can ameliorate these problems and provide directions for more successful implementation during second wave reform.

One difference between early differentiated staffing schemes and recent reform plans lies in the complexity of the former. Besides implementing several professional and paraprofessional levels, early programs also included experimental time and spatial arrangements, resulting in complicated authority lines as well as communication complications. Recent programs are more likely to limit levels by plans such as mentor teachers. This concept as implemented in the California Mentor Teacher Program is basically a two-level ladder for new and inexperienced teachers to work together (Honig, 1988). Utah mentor teacher programs operate similarly (Malen, Murphy, and Hart, 1987). As a result of fewer levels, tasks of career ladder teachers do not appear to be as fragmented as the job descriptions of differentiated staffing teachers, nor are authority and communication channels as complex. Although "competition among teachers for scarce jobs" (Bacharach et al., 1986, p. 565) is a problem of different teaching levels, the availability and rotation of mentor teacher positions may alleviate this problem and be beneficial to cooperation.

The role of the union in reform plans differs between eras. Teacher unions of the 1960s and 1970s were conceptualized on labor models, and collective bargaining, conflict, and conflict resolution were predominant functions (Cresswell and Murphy, 1980). Specific roles of the union in differentiated staffing literature are passive and scarce. The role of unions in the 1980s is much more active and evident. Kerchner and Mitchell (1986) call for a professional unionism with a changed complexation and different functions such as entrance requirements, examinations, and peer review for teachers. National leaders verbalize work structures they consider supportive of teachers (Shanker, 1988; Futrell, 1988). Local associations participate directly in defining specific plans (Reston Teachers Association, 1985). A more active and cooperative role by the union may help sustain reform efforts.

While rhetorical justifications for reform are similar, contrasts in emphasis are also evident. Early rationales implied that changing teacher work structures would allow for individualized instruction (Fiorino, 1972) and team approaches (Charters, 1973; Williams, 1975). Recent reports prioritize improved student achievement and demand accountability from the teacher (National Commission on Excellence on Teaching, 1983; Carnegie Task Force on Teaching as a Profession, 1986). Hawley (1988) notes that restructuring in general is based on a rationale of increased status, pay, and decentralized decision making for teachers but that effects on students remain ambiguous. The distinction may be subtle, but its importance may contribute to more successful outcomes for current reform than those experienced by early plans.

Merit Pay

Merit pay is a model that has been introduced to some reform plans. Merit pay differs from differentiated staffing models in that differentiated staffing involves increased remuneration for increased responsibilities, while merit pay involves increased remuneration for exemplary performance of duties. The problem of evaluation, however, is shared by both schemes. Although evaluation is the basis of promotion in differentiated staffing and the basis of increased financial rewards in merit pay, evaluation of teachers is problematic "where work is successive, accomplishments are cumulative and cooperation is essential" (Johnson, 1986, p. 62). Rosenholtz reports the importance of intrinsic rewards rather than extrinsic ones in motivating teachers and mentions isolation as a possible result of merit pay plans. Johnson (1986) also cites intrinsic motivators, specifically efficacy, as more powerful than money. In an evaluation of three reform work structures, a merit pay plan was least likely to be attributed with improved working conditions by high-efficacy teachers (Rhodes, 1989).

Job Enlargement

Job enlargement is another model implemented in some reform plans. This plan "ties salary increases to special projects that teachers complete during an extended work day or an extended work year" (Malen et al., 1987, p. iii). This plan has some theoretical merit whether it is implemented individually or in groups. If individual teachers are granted time and financial support to pursue personally defined projects, the motivation may operate as Kanter (1983) suggests—rewards for "pet projects." Alternately, much reform literature advocates the use of teams of teachers for development of programs (Rosenholtz, 1985; Little, 1982).

Extended Contract

One plan not previewed in the outline of job design because of such limited implementation cannot be ignored. The extended contract may be a plan unique to Utah plans, but its diversion from traditional work structures merits attention. As much as 50 percent of state funding for career ladders may be allocated by districts for extended days. These days are allotted for professional duties other than teaching; teachers report to schools, but students do not. As may be expected, teachers are supportive of the program (Malen et al., 1987). At least two factors are responsible for this teacher support. As Charters (1973) noted, teachers work within time restrictions. This mechanism allows time free from student contact to attend to teaching duties. Opportunities for collegial contact and organizational duties are provided without risking time and energy allocated for students. Also, although "status among teachers is not affected" (Malen et al., 1987, p. 30) as it is in differentiated staffing promotions, "status of teachers is enhanced" (Malen et al., 1987, p. 30). Professional and cooperative role definitions, rather than individual and competitive connotations, emerge within the profession.

Many work structures have been altered by reform programs, and specific working conditions such as power, meaning, norms, and isolation have been modified. Techniques to introduce modifications, however, are also an important element in reform.

Change Literature

The combined subjects of inherent motivation and work structures suggest attention to change implementation. If work structures are to be altered to increase motivation, workers must be introduced to modified structures in ways that will facilitate adoption of the structures rather than resistance to them. Examination of problems of educational change and more general change will be followed by promising techniques to overcome the problems.

Again, differentiated staffing provides an opportunity for analyzing attempted changes in educational work structures. Rand and English (1968) assert that the most serious difficulties for differentiated staffing are "subtle limitations in our visions, attitudes and expectations, conditioned by one organizational structure for over 100 years" (p. 268). While recent reformers are changing their visions, the durability of the educational structure is evident. Harriot and Gross (1979) report that "nearly every systematic study of the fate of a specific educational innovation in public schools has concluded that its anticipated outcomes were not achieved, that its educational benefits were minimal, or that it was not fully implemented" (p. 11). More recently, Malen et al. (1987) observe that teachers have attempted with some success to modify innovative theoretical plans to resemble existing mechanisms.

In their examination of Title III programs, Mann et al. (1975) illuminate some pertinent dynamics of educational change. The process itself is "potentially conflictive and political" (p. III-32). Problems arise because change is a threat to existing authority structures. This is probably true whether authority is formal or informal, and it may be that teachers cling more tenaciously to their authority because it has been informal and imperceptible in the classroom and severely limited in the larger organization.

Mann et al. (1975) also state that "projects with precise purposes pointed directly at identifiable groups were more likely to encounter the opposition of those groups" (p. III-26). A related idea emerged in reference to goal specification—"prior identification of the group whose behavior needs to be changed is very likely to increase the resistance of that group to the change efforts" (1975, III-29). This suggests that concepts discussed in goal theory must be implemented with awareness of possible counterproductive results.

Other inhibiting factors included the teachers' organizations, whose purpose has been opposed historically to that of administratively initiated plans. Also, these groups have rarely initiated changes (Harriot and Gross, 1979). More general assessments of the Title III programs elucidated some further findings—"The higher the grade level, the more resistant to training is the teacher" (1975, III-31), and " 'career bound' leaders were more successful than 'place bound' " in effecting change (1975, p. III-41). Efficacy has been found to be a factor linked empirically with successful change (Berman, McLaughlin, Bass, Pauly, and Zellman, 1977).

Beyond such situational properties, the adaptations to the change process exhibit characteristic patterns. With time, projects tend to diminish on factors such as ambition, complexity of treatment, pacing, and commitment to controversial goals. Opposition also had an opportunity to grow. Mann et al. (1975) report findings similar to those of Harriot and Gross (1979), that the "most arresting finding was how little change" (p. III-46).

Miles (1965) lists some adverse properties of schools that deserve attention because some continue to characterize modern educational institutions. Goal ambiguity about output measures (Miles, 1965) is relevant as a target of reform and as a point of teacher resistance. Although goal theory suggests that verbalization of goals can motivate workers toward accomplishing those goals, as noted above, initial resistance resulting, perhaps, from threatened curricular flexibility, must be overcome. Miles (1965) also mentions the variability among teachers and among students, a phenomenon that has probably grown recently as society has become more pluralistic. Role performance invisibility is another characteristic of teaching (Miles, 1965) and one, perhaps, guarded by teachers because of the relative autonomy it provides. Similarly, low interdependence (Miles, 1965) insures some freedom in the classroom. Education's vulnerability (Miles, 1965) results from environmental demands that reduce autonomy.

These factors illustrate points of resistance for educational change. Teacher autonomy is fragile, partly because it is not legally defined (Lortie, 1969). Reluctance to adhere to innovative norms may be due to anxiety over upsetting the delicate equilibrium attained by teachers. Some reform efforts call for measures that pertain directly to the characteristic Miles describes. Attention to measurable outcome involves more teacher accountability and points up the need for objective, rather than subjective, curricular goals. Decreased teacher variability similarly suggests more strictly defined training programs. Increased visibility and cooperative work goals threaten to reduce individual autonomy, and the goal of professional autonomy may be sufficiently ambiguous to remain untenable.

In the past, significant and substantial educational change has been limited. Recent reform movements have differed from earlier ones in some respects—as noted above, reformers today have a shared vision, and the pervasiveness of the movement is perhaps unprecedented. More concretely, teachers' associations have aligned themselves with reform goals, possibly to preserve some ability to protect the teacher autonomy discussed above. In any case, cooperation between administration and teacher associations is more characteristic of recent relationships than is conflict. Further, such a role is being vigorously advocated, and specifications for achieving it are being verbalized (Kerchner and Mitchell, 1986).

Still, some teacher resistance is evident, and reform momentum is abating. At least some evidence, however, attests to success of reform goals. Student achievement has increased (Honig, 1988), and the efficacious teachers are reporting improved working conditions due to reform (Rhodes, 1989). Continued emphasis on reform is justifiable. Attention to problems of teacher resistance and emphasis on change techniques that are congruent with educational structure are likely to revive second wave movements.

Organizational literature provides some guidelines for change implementation applicable to educational organizations. Some general wisdom recommends initiating change internally by working within the existing structure rather than revolutionizing structures. One characteristic of organizational health listed by Miles (1965) is relatively equal power distribution, and this exemplifies the principle stated above. Traditionally, teaching has been characterized by a flat level, and attempts to change that structure have met with resistance. Although Malen et al. (1987) report improved status from redesign programs in Utah plans, two other pertinent effects were noted—some promoted teachers were subjected to negative reactions from peers, and "pressures for uniform allocation of salary through short-term or rotated positions" were observed (Malen et al., 1987, p. 23). Rhodes (1989) finds that efficacious teachers preferred job enlargement plans to vertical job redesign plans. Findings also indicated, incidentally, no difference in efficacy ratings between participants in leadership positions created by job redesign and nonparticipants (Rhodes, 1989). This illustration suggests selection problems for differentiated staffing decisions and may illuminate one reason for teacher resistance.

One more issue relevant to the work structure of teaching must be addressed—while teachers resist vertical promotions, apparently they are not entirely satisfied with the opportunities for horizontal moves. Some authors have characterized teachers as suffering from "lock-in" (Lowther, Stark, and Chapman, 1984; Lowther, Gill, and Coppard, 1981). Similarly, Dworkin (1987) describes many teachers as entrapped. Teachers consider themselves to have less occupational mobility than other workers. In a comparison of practicing teachers with trained teachers otherwise employed, "The variable 'job lock-in' differentiated career teachers from non-teachers. This finding suggests that teachers see themselves as having less horizontal occupational mobility than non-teachers. In effect, teachers feel constrained in finding equivalent alternative positions should they wish to seek them" (Lowther, Stark, and Chapman, 1984, p. 281.) A related study compares teachers with other workers and also finds that teachers report less opportunity for occupational mobility (Lowther, Gill, and Coppard, 1981). Results are similar when the comparison involves other professionals (Lowther, Gill, and Coppard, 1981). Dworkin (1987) uses the term translatable to describe skills that allow teachers to secure other jobs, and he finds that those having such skills often leave teaching.

Evidence suggests, therefore, that teachers are generally dissatisfied with opportunities for horizontal reassignments. It seems they are specifically dissatisfied with vertical assignments.

More than once, reform movements have planned to change the flat structure of teaching, but there is one specific characteristic of the flat structure rather than the structure that is perhaps problematic. Teachers are isolated (Lortie, 1975), and collegial communication suffers. Kanter (1983) considers poor lateral communication to be a factor responsible for resisting change in organizations. Specifically, "information hoarding" and "turf issues" (Kanter, 1983, pp. 80–81) are detriments to innovation. Techniques to combat these behaviors are perhaps more likely to meet with success than large-scale plans to redistribute power into vertical hierarchies.

Similarly, Miles (1965) finds communication adequacy to be an element of organizational health, and he states that the directions of this distortion-free communication must be vertical, horizontal, and across the boundary to the environment. Specific vehicles for change include target setting (Miles, 1965), which, of course, resembles goal setting. Miles does stipulate the agreement of new targets must be between the superior and subordinate workers (1965). Although research indicates this technique leads to employee satisfaction, it may not lead to increased performance (Miskel and Ogawa, 1988). Some evidence suggests that participation in goal setting leads to increased acceptance and increased difficulty, and increased effort may therefore result (Beehr and Love, 1983).

Both Kanter (1983) and Miles (1965) recommend use of teams to innovate successfully. Kanter (1983) is astute in listing problems with team mechanisms. Basically, inequalities among team members pose difficulties, and these difficulties can result from variances in hierarchical status, knowledge, personal resources, or amount of seniority within the group. Techniques to surmount these difficulties improve the productivity of teams.

Implementation techniques are an important element of inherent motivation and work structures. Changes in work structures expected to increase motivation must be accepted rather than resisted, and these techniques can facilitate acceptance.

REFORM

We now turn our attention to current efforts to reform education. Reform is an attempted alteration of work conditions to achieve various goals. Educational reform has defined goals of increased attraction, retention, and performance of teachers, and these goals are related to teacher motivation. If educational structures can increase the attraction and retention of motivated workers or motivate workers to enhanced performance, productivity in the form of improved student outcomes is likely, and reform goals are achieved.

In discussing the current wave of reform, we focus on two specific programs because a description of actual programs can illuminate the theoretical constructs of work design and change implementation with evidence from the world of practice. Moreover, discussions of empirical findings from existing programs can assist them in relation to the thematic concerns raised in this chapter. Thus, we will focus on two contrasting programs in the states of Utah and California.

Utah

Four educational programs are being implemented in Utah (Malen et al., 1987): job design, performance bonus, job expansion, and extended contracts. Job design differentiates teachers by assignment to positions with increased responsibilities, and as such, shares characteristics with differentiated staffing. Performance pay is based on the award of extra money for meritorious teaching and is essentially a merit pay program. Job expansion is also described previously as an opportunity for teachers to participate in enlarged projects and to be compensated for the time involved. Extended contract is the payment of teachers at timely intervals during the school year for days when students do not attend class. The intent of extended contract is for professional development without direct student contact.

Malen et al. (1987) analyzed fourteen studies of Career Ladder Programs and highlighted their central findings. The extended contract differs from the other three aspects of career ladder reform in unequivocal teacher support. This analysis finds performance pay generally unsupported. "Teacher satisfaction with merit pay is related primarily to the ability to convert merit pay plans into uniform salary increases for all or nearly all teachers" (Malen et al., 1987, p. 9). Theoretical recommendations for increased base pay in lieu of merit pay (Rosenholtz, 1985) have apparently, in this case, been achieved if not intended.

Although teachers were categorized as participants and nonparticipants, a general theme that emerged is that job enlargement and job redesign drew mixed reactions. Participants in job enlargement "tend to be more positive than nonparticipants," but overload was a source of complaint (Malen et al., 1987, pp. 17–18). This is reminiscent of the sentiments of teachers involved in differentiated staffing plans. Some nonparticipants reported positive reactions, and some reacted negatively. Similarly, sources of satisfaction and dissatisfaction with job redesign emerged regardless of participation (Malen et al., 1987).

Rhodes (1989), in a study of Career Ladder Programs in two districts, also investigated job redesign, job enlargement, and merit pay plans. In these districts, job redesign linked increased money to new teaching positions, such as mentor teachers, evaluator in one district and teacher leader, teacher specialist, and facilitator in the other. Also, some more traditional positions, such as department chair and cooperating teacher, were included as part of the Career Ladder Plan and designated as job redesign positions. Job enlargement linked increased money to special projects completed during extended hours. Examples of job expansion were teachers working on district projects or on individual projects. Merit pay schemes were described as increased money accompanying an appropriate evaluation of classroom teaching and professional activities.

In some respects, findings were similar to those obtained by Malen, Murphy, and Hart (1987). Rhodes (1989) reports that participation or nonparticipation in a plan failed to predict responses. Participants, for example, were no more likely than nonparticipants to report improved working conditions due to reform. The specific working conditions were power, meaning, norms, and collegial patterns.

However, Rhodes (1989) did find a negative correlation between alienation and efficacy. Participants and nonparticipants in reform leadership positions of all three plans did not differ in efficacy ratings. More importantly, high-efficacy teachers were more likely than low-efficacy teachers to perceive improvements due to reform. Low-alienation teachers were more likely than high-alienation teachers to perceive improvements due to reform. High-efficacy teachers as well as low-alienation teachers were more likely to consider job expansion an improvement as opposed to job redesign or performance bonus.

Because of the empirical links between efficacy and student achievement (Ashton and Webb, 1986; Berman et al., 1977), these findings are provocative. Using the same alienation scale as Dworkin (1987), results indicate connections between low alienation and high efficacy; this, in turn, suggests a connection between low alienating conditions, which have been tied to conditions altered by reform, and student outcomes. Although Dworkin (1987) fails to link alienation and student achievement, Rhodes (1989) indirectly does so.

Further, the results empirically support reform programs based on job enlargement programs because high-efficacy teachers perceived improved conditions attributable to these programs (Rhodes, 1989). Specifically, these teachers reported improved power and collegial relations due to job enlargement programs. Causal connections between low alienation and high efficacy were not ascertained, but, as a Career Ladder Plan preferred by efficacious teachers, job enlargement might be expected to attract and retain teachers capable of improving student outcomes. Also, although causal directions were not determined, the possibility that these programs can contribute to efficacy cannot be empirically rejected.

California

The California reform movement differs from Utah's in some respects. Utah plans allocate financial support to locally derived programs. As described by Honig (1988), the California program is more comprehensive both geographically and ideologically. State-wide coordination is evident, and a "vision" (Honig, 1988, p. 258) is the basis for this movement. Aligned texts, curriculum, and evaluation measures are specific products of reform, but working conditions for teachers have also been altered. As mentioned above, a mentor teacher program has been initiated. In addition, new teachers have been exposed to other means of staff development.

However, the key issue involves the relationship between these work structures, teacher motivation, and student outcomes. Empirical findings resemble those of studies conducted in Utah, although California provides more comprehensive and more direct data on student achievement. Student scores are higher than they have been in years on more than one test, and students are enrolling in more rigorous classes (Honig, 1988). Although not empirically documented, claims of increased professional efficacy also have been made (Honig, 1988).

IMPLICATIONS FOR THE CURRENT WAVE OF REFORM

What does an examination of the reform programs described here through the lenses provided by the motivation, work design, and change literatures reveal? In this section we consider some tentative answers to that question.

Relation of Reform Programs to Motivation Theory

Some themes transcend the discrete categories provided by the review of the literature on motivation. Goals and expected outcomes, ability to produce required behaviors, integration of work tasks, rewards, and effort theoretically are motivating factors. An examination of the implementation of each of these precepts in the Utah and California reform programs will serve to illuminate both theory and practice. The California plan began with a vision (Honig, 1988), clearly an example of verbalization of goals and expected outcomes. The vision was derived from a general sense of public education's responsibilities toward students. Honig (1988) cites responsibilities to students entering a work force, to students as citizens, and to students striving to reach their potential. As mentioned in goal theory and empowerment, participation in goal setting may increase commitment, and Honig (1988) identified and obtained consensus among "key actors" (p. 261). The concepts of goals and consensus were both exemplified by the specification of centralization of curriculum, texts, and tests (Honig, 1988). The California plan also instigated policies to insure that teachers had the ability to produce the required behavior, which was defined as behavior that led to improved student scores; the ability to produce this behavior was enhanced by teacher professionalism plans. Mentor teachers were paired with novices, and staff development was introduced for experienced and inexperienced teachers (Honig, 1988). California also reports some collaboration with higher education institutions on training current faculty (Honig, 1988).

Integration of work task is more difficult to assess. While the entire state program appears more integrated as a result of the comprehensive plan, the scope of responsibility for individuals may have diminished. As texts and curriculum are aligned, the nature of teaching work for individual teachers threatens to become more fragmented. Honig (1988) reports that the state board is collaborating with textbook companies to develop standards. Even though some teachers are involved in augmented responsibilities such as reviewing new curricula and developing instructional strategies (Honig, 1988), the effect in the classroom may be instructional and curricular constraints. This need not necessarily be the case if attention to the fragile balance is maintained and if strategies are recommended rather than mandated. As noted earlier, some professional integration of curriculum is necessary because of the movement of large numbers of individuals through an institution;

still, preservation of task identity for individual workers is justifiable, Apple reports unsavory organizational results of "separating conception from execution" (1988, p. 286) in industrial settings, such as reduced commitment and power. He asserts that similar results are possible in an educational setting (Apple, 1988).

Extrinsic rewards in the California plan seem to consist primarily of higher salaries for beginning teachers, but this was a substantial increase. Entry-level salaries jumped from $15,000 to $22,000 (Kirst, 1988). The mentor teacher program contributes extrinsic rewards of status and intrinsic rewards of increased responsibilities. Improved student scores may also be an intrinsic reward, and increased feedback about these improvements is likely to increase teacher perceptions of ability and efficacy. This can be a powerful motivator. The role of rewards as an incentive to endorse certain behaviors is advocated by Kanter (1983) and may be achieved by increased beginning salaries. Provision of grants and loans are a recommended course for future reforms (Honig, 1988) and are probably justifiable in the above context, but more concrete and behavior-specific examples of this function are currently absent. Further, these incentives are concentrated on recruitment rather than retention efforts. Realizing that this is a profession characterized by ambiguous rewards (Lortie, 1975), some positive steps have been taken in California, but efforts in this arena do not seem as emphatic as those in goal articulation and increasing teacher ability.

Although effort is clearly an inherent element of motivation, means of increasing it are not as clear. Expectancy theory suggests increasing valence and instrumentality, and interpretations of the California plan might consider the expression of student responsibility as increased valence; similarly, the attention to improved teaching skills can be intrepreted as improved instrumentality.

An assessment of the Utah plan using the same motivation concepts offers some contrasting results. In regard to goals and expected outcomes, a primary difference between the plans is revealed. Because Utah allowed each district to design its own program, the vision and comprehensive goal articulation evident in California are absent in Utah. Those goals that were targeted state-wide in Utah also differed in substance from California's goals. Utah intended to change teacher performance and retention through modifications in compensation structures (Malen et al., 1987). While this expected outcome might affect student achievement, it is a more indirect route than the one that California charted.

The Utah goal of improving teacher performance is related to the motivational strategy of producing the required behavior. Mentor teacher programs were probably the most apparent plan effected in this respect, but these programs addressed novice teachers. Some job expansion projects allowed teachers to define projects and share results with colleagues, but results were mixed (Malen et al., 1987). In some cases, recipients of the information were impressed with the professional talents of teachers who developed projects, but in other cases, they were dissatisfied with the delivery of in-service in general and the quality of the projects specifically (Malen et al., 1987). Generally, however, intensive and comprehensive teacher professionalization movements are not clearly perceptible in Utah's reform. Although teacher training programs have been revised, alliances between higher education and public education teachers have not moved beyond traditional individual arrangements.

Task integration has been perhaps more carefully preserved in Utah than in California. While the Utah State Board of Education has issued a CORE Curriculum with standards and objectives for subject areas and grade levels, local districts and teachers retain freedom to choose texts from approved state lists. Furthermore, the discretionary power delegated to districts from the state to develop Career Ladder Plans has protected district power and has probably involved a larger number of teachers in curricular decisions than California's plan. This may enhance task integration for a broader segment of the population, but the same caveat noted for California is applicable in Utah—"When teachers cease to plan and control a large portion of their work, the skills essential to doing these tasks well and self-reflectively atrophy and are forgotten" (Apple, 1988, p. 276). In Utah, however, opportunities to rotate positions were noted (Malen et al., 1987), and this may serve to nurture skills in more teachers. Job redesign in at least some districts tended to be defined by using new titles for traditional roles such as department heads (Rhodes, 1989). In this context, perhaps, less danger of task disintegration exists. It seems likely that Utah plans, by virtue of district authority and the higher proportion of involved teachers, currently exhibit more possibilities for task integration among individual teachers than the California plan.

The Utah plan contains a deviation from traditional educational reward systems. The state allows districts to spend half of their funds allocated for reform on extended days. As a result, Utah's teachers are paid to be at school on designated days throughout the school year when students are not present. Teacher support for the program is strong (Malen et al., 1987). There is no empirical evidence on the effects on teaching. Therefore, we are left to speculate on the impact of career ladders on teaching work. As noted, teaching work is characterized by time constraints (Charters, 1973). The arrangement of "career ladder days" during critical times of the school calendar contributes to a likelihood of productive activity. Furthermore, teachers who are motivated to use regular contract time productively are unlikely to engage in unproductive behaviors on such days. While unproductive teachers may behave unproductively during school days and "career ladder days," motivation literature reports that some rewards reinforce already motivated individuals in positive directions (Hackman and Oldham, 1980). The important point, however, is that highly motivated teachers are rewarded with time to perform necessary educational duties. Diversions from instructional time thereby are diminished.

Teaching is also characterized by isolation (Lortie, 1975). "For most of their working days, teachers are alone with their students" (Boyer, 1988, p. 314.) The extended day may be a convenient means of providing collegial contact. Opportunities to interact informally with peers can inspire creative collaboration for productive teachers. The chance for productive teachers to influence and direct less productive teachers in fruitful directions is made more possible.

Although teachers receive increased money for increased work, the extended day effectively rewards teachers with time and with money beyond contract salaries. It is possible that this plan produces educational outcomes and affects teacher motivation, recruitment, and retention. These effects, however, remain empirically unverified.

Utah has also instituted increased financial rewards by requiring that at least 10 percent of reform funds be used for merit pay plans (Malen and Murphy, 1985). The success of such plans is questionable. As Conley (1988) notes, enthusiasm for merit pay has dwindled. Rhodes (1989) found that they are the plans least preferred by high-efficacy teachers. Inadequate evaluation methods combine with the imprecise nature of teaching to present difficulties with merit schemes. However, although some proponents of differentiated staffing (Rand and English, 1968) identify differences between evaluation for each plan, in reality, the problems are similar. This suggests limited acceptance of job redesign plans that promote teachers, and again Rhodes (1989) found that high-efficacy and low-alienation teachers preferred alternate plans.

Job enlargement resembles extended day in one respect—teachers are given financial rewards for duties other than classroom instruction. However, job enlargement defines responsibilities other than routine teaching. In Utah high-efficacy teachers preferred this plan to job redesign and merit pay (Rhodes, 1989).

Extrinsic rewards for Utah teachers have been primarily financial, although some status distinctions have ensued from job enlargement and job redesign positions. Collectively, some increased professional respect has been reported as a result of extended day programs (Malen et al., 1987). Intrinsic rewards have been considered to be more important motivators than extrinsic ones (Johnson, 1986). As such, a sense of efficacy may have been improved by the extended day. Extended days presumably could contribute to the ability to produce required behaviors.

Because some success has been achieved by some Utah plans in increasing rewards and in constraining fragmentation of tasks, effort of teachers might increase. Instrumentality and valence may be enhanced by extended day and contribute to an embellished professionalism.

Implementation of Work Structure Components in Reform Plans

We discussed work structure in terms of its effect on alienation. Conditions that increase power, meaning, coherent norms, and collegial interaction reduce alienation and covary with increased efficacy (Rhodes, 1989). Also, job redesign, job enlargement, and merit pay are pertinent concepts. Because empirical evidence on these variables is not available for California reform plans, assumptions based on theory and evidence available on Utah plans will be discussed.

Rhodes (1989) found that power, norms, and collegial patterns correlated most strongly with efficacy, and high-efficacy teachers reported that these patterns were most affected by job enlargement plans. Based on this evidence, the components of the California plan that resemble job expansion need to be identified. In Utah, job enlargment included teachers working on district or individual curricular or instructional projects. Some plans also included dispersion of information to colleagues. California apparently included teachers in this fashion on a state-wide rather than a district-wide basis. Fewer teachers and less collegial contact may have resulted. It is interesting to note, however, that although high-efficacy and low-efficacy teachers reported significantly different responses to questions about reform, participants did not differ from nonparticipants (Rhodes, 1989). While this finding does not directly support the centralization of the California plan, it may suggest that participation does not predict endorsement of plans. Still, the increased visibility of participants of local plans may be a variable affecting reports of improvements due to reform.

Merit pay was the least preferred plan among high-efficacy teachers in the Utah study (Rhodes, 1989), and California may have avoided some resistance to reform efforts by eschewing overt merit schemes. Some comparisons between merit pay and job redesign plans also elucidate teacher reluctance to adopt such plans. Bacharach et al. (1986) observe that "job ladders foster competition among teachers for scarce jobs, and like merit pay, inhibit cooperation and sharing of job knowledge" (p. 565). The coexistence of high-efficacy and collegial patterns in teachers (Rhodes, 1989) supports this observation.

One job redesign plan seems exceptional in fostering acceptance among teachers in both Utah and California. It may be that mentor teacher programs have experienced less teacher resistance and more success than other forms of ladders. Some contrasts between mentor teacher positions and other leadership positions may be responsible. One difference alludes to task identity. "Job ladders are bureaucratic devices that break up the tasks people perform" (Bacharach et al., 1986, p. 564). In contrast, the task fragmentation that characterizes some ladders is not apparent in the duties of mentor teaching. Perhaps the most significant difference is the most subtle. Status and pay promotions to duties other than classroom teaching imply these duties are more important than classroom teaching (Bacharach et al., 1986). Conversely, the duties and implications of mentor teaching prioritize classroom teaching. Some districts in Utah rotate mentor teaching assignments. This technique can provide more available positions for the abundance of qualified applicants. Teacher resistance can be expected to be less. Finally, isolation, an alienation variable that correlates negatively with high efficacy (Rhodes, 1989), may be reduced by mentor teacher programs.

Reform plans have incorporated theoretical work structure designs into programs, and empirical evidence is somewhat supportive of the theoretical assumptions. Alienating conditions such as powerlessness, normlessness, and isolation predict low efficacy, and high-efficacy teachers report improved power and collegial patterns for job expansion (Rhodes, 1989). As purported (Rosenholtz, 1985; Bacharach et al., 1986; Johnson, 1986), merit pay and job ladders were not held accountable for improved working conditions by high-efficacy teachers (Rhodes, 1989).

Change Implementation Techniques

Education has traditionally been conservative. Some points of resistance to change have been based on the preservation of autonomy and task integration. Goals and outcome measures, lessened input variability achieved by standardized teacher training programs, and increased demands for accountability have threatened autonomy and task integration. Unions have accepted the role of protecting autonomy and task integration.

Some suggestions for successful implementation of work structure change include improved communication and flat-level structures. Also, change implemented through existing internal structures is more likely to be accepted.

California reform has emphasized articulate and comprehensive goals and outcome measures, lessened input variability in teaching through an alliance with teacher education programs, and established accountability through student performance "linked with local quality indicators" (Honig, 1988, p. 261, Table 1). Although these are threats to autonomy and task integration, they may foster improved communication and, thus, facilitate implementation. The reform has not significantly challenged the flat structure of teaching, so reform thrusts may survive. Reports of improved student performance (Honig, 1988) support the plan, so that only a vague concern with possible detrimental effects of reduced autonomy and task integration on successful implementation remains.

Utah has attempted to improve teacher performance by changing compensation structures (Malen et al., 1987). Movements to lessen input variability through teacher training programs are not evident. Accountability was based on improved teacher evaluation procedures, not student outcome indicators. Theoretical points of resistance to change are less apparent and less direct than California. Accountability centered on student outcome measures linked to school characteristics and is more direct than revamped teacher evaluation systems. Combined with the local retention of curricular and instructional independence, autonomy and task integration appear more stable. Further, the extended day in Utah may reinforce some of these functions indirectly.

At least some of the elements of the Utah plan attack the internal structure of teaching with merit pay and job redesign. This plan threatens autonomy and task integration, but again because of local discretion the threat is somewhat diminished. Still, this is a point of resistance that may influence reduced commitment to the plan. Teachers capable of achieving improved student achievement have reported preferences for alternate plans (Rhodes, 1989). Local variance makes it difficult to assess the existence of improved communications.

The California plan encounters more points of resistance than the Utah plan, but it also implements some change mechanisms such as clear communication and maintenance of internal structure. Utah plans are more passive in terms of confronting points of resistance but are not as clearly adept as California in incorporating change techniques.

There are signs of some resistance by California teachers to the curricular and instructional uniformity. Utah teachers are unlikely to accept attempts to redefine the horizontal structure of teaching. Demands for accountability, whether reported through student outcomes or teacher evaluation systems, may persist. These mechanisms provide feedback for teachers operating in uncertain arenas and may enhance professional efficacy. As such, they are motivators for performance. Lessened input variability is more dependent on higher education levels and less susceptible alterations due to work structure reform. Effective mentor teaching programs, however, may achieve some productive socialization ends.

Predictions can also be based on the history of differentiated staffing and on the history of change in education. Difficulties and lack of supportive evidence point to the conclusion that differentiated staffing did not effect changes in the recruitment and retention of academically talented teachers. Student gains were not documented. Indications of changes in teacher work behavior are also absent. Empirical results from investigations of recent reform combine with knowledge about the process of change to project diminishing interest in vertical plans. It may be that these goals are controversial among teachers, and it is controversial goals that are often eliminated over time. The "energy diversions" (Charters, 1973, p. 95) also suggest declining commitment. In summary, empirical evidence from studies combined with more general knowledge of educational change suggest a declining interest in vertical ladders. A study of these issues, however, provides valuable information applicable to reform practices.

SUMMARY

Several related bodies of literature provide lenses through which recent efforts to influence teachers' motivation and performance can be examined. Theories of human motivation contribute an understanding of factors regarding the internal states of individuals that can affect effort and productivity. In this chapter we reviewed three theories of motivation. Expectancy theory links outcomes, perception of possession of behaviors likely to lead to outcomes, and the likelihood of achieving the behavior after a particular level of effort is made. The job-characteristics model focuses on job meaningfulness, experienced responsibility, and knowledge of results to explain varying levels of motivation. Job meaningfulness, the central concept in this model, is composed of skill variety, task identity, and task significance. The findings of research based on goal theory suggest that specific goals motivate more than general or nonexistent goals and that difficult goals, if accepted, motivate more than easily attainable ones. These theories generally focus on conditions of work rather than extrinsic rewards, such as compensation, as factors that affect motivation and productivity. They seem to suggest that efforts to increase teachers' motivation and performance should emphasize the results of teachers' work and the nature of the work by which these results are attained.

Two concepts that typically have not been included in discussions of the motivation literature are included in this chapter because they add to an understanding of motivation. Those concepts are empowerment and efficacy. The concept of empowerment suggests that an individual's productivity will improve if he/she gains access to resources, information, and support (Kanter, 1983). It also posits a link between goals and rewards and the capacity of individuals to act. Treatments of this concept move beyond describing factors associated with empowerment and specify techniques that can be employed to enhance empowerment. For example, they discuss both the positive and negative results of the use of participative mechanisms in organizational decision making.

The concept of efficacy concerns individuals' perceptions of their capacity to affect outcomes. It is related to motivation in that it too concerns internal states of individuals that affect job performance. Moreover, it is of importance when considering teacher motivation because empirically it has been linked to student achievement scores (Armor et al., 1976; Ashton and Webb, 1986; Gibson and Dembo, 1984) and to behavioral differences between high- and low-efficacy teachers.

Taken together, the concepts of empowerment and efficacy reinforce the emphasis that motivation theories place on individuals' internal states and conditions of work as important factors affecting the willingness of these individuals to engage in productive activity. However, the concept of empowerment provides an interesting twist on the place of rewards in motivating individuals. It suggests that rewards can, under certain conditions, precede the desired action and increase the probability that the action will be taken. The implications of this for thinking through the issue of teacher compensation are intriguing. How could rewards be built into compensation systems such that teachers would be rewarded before completing a desired action or attaining a desired objective?

Research on work redesign provides some evidence of the existence of relationships between factors posited by theories of motivation and the concepts of empowerment and efficacy. One study, for instance, indicates that increased access to power, to coherent norms, and to collegial patterns correlates positively with teachers' feelings of efficacy (Rhodes, 1989). However, studies of previous attempts to alter the work structures of teaching direct attention to the limitations of vertically oriented designs such as differentiated staffing. There is evidence that teachers are reluctant to embrace compensation systems that are based on vertical schemes in which some teachers, in effect, are elevated to superordinate positions. Thus, an important implication of theories of motivation and the empirical findings of previous attempts to tie rewards to altered work structures is that rewards should somehow be linked to nonvertical, or horizontal, structures in school systems. To close, we offer one system of horizontal compensation.

CONCLUSION: A HORIZONTAL COMPENSATION SYSTEM

In this section we describe one example of a horizontal compensation system. We also briefly discuss how this system has the potential to address issues raised in the literature on motivation, empowerment, and efficacy.

The essence of the horizontal system is that teachers are compensated monetarily for opting to transfer between grade levels, schools, or districts. Funds presently allocated to compensation systems that are tied to schools' vertical structures, such as differentiated staffing, are made available to administrators to fund the horizontal system. Administrators use the money as an incentive to attract teachers to openings on faculties. An incentive would be paid as a single sum at the time of the transfer, rather than added to the teacher's salary. Teachers would not be eligible to transfer again for some set period of time.

As principals become aware of their staffing requirements, they write job descriptions that include the amounts of compensation, specific job requirements, and performance targets. Teachers then apply for positions in which they are interested and for which they are suited. They submit applications, resumes, and other documentation of their qualifications for a particular position. As the first set of openings are filled, a second group of teachers are recruited for or shifted to vacated positions. Currently, transfers and attrition are handled within a time frame that could be adapted to accommodate the new procedures. That is, procedures that already are in place would only need to be changed to accommodate increased numbers of transfers.

A probable result of compensating teachers to make horizontal transfers would be increased teacher movement, which in turn could positively affect factors associated with motivation. Let us illustrate by drawing on examples from the literature reviewed in this chapter.

The literature on motivation reveals that goal specificity, perceived ability to produce required behaviors, skill variety, task integration, and rewards contribute to employees' levels of effort to accomplish job-related tasks. The compensation system described previously incorporates each of these factors. The use of job descriptions that detail expectations of available positions could provide specific goals to which teachers would be held accountable. Engaging in new assignments could result in teachers enacting, or confronting, their work situations, which could positively affect their efficacy (Bandura, 1982). As teachers encounter new assignments, they likely will learn new skills, thus adding variety to their repertoires. As teachers become exposed to more and varied colleagues, they may develop broader networks, thus improving their collaborative communication systems—a manifestation of task integration. Also, moving between grade levels could result in teachers expanding their knowledge of curriculum and their awareness of the stages through which students develop. Finally, a horizontal system of compensation avoids the problems that arise from associating rewards with vertical promotions and evaluative functions. Linking incentives to horizontal transfers could eliminate the reluctance of teachers to participate in revised incentive programs, which in the past were associated with vertical promotions or evaluation systems, and avoid the negative effects associated with collegial competition (Johnson, 1986).

A horizontal compensation system, while unconventional, could thus circumvent many of the problems associated with the traditionally vertical structures of school organizations and teacher incentive programs. It would give teachers the power to alter their job situations in a real way if they so chose and would provide monetary rewards without any of the demoralizing subjectivity involved in programs such as merit pay. In short, such a system could foster many of the conditions that contribute to human motivation.

REFERENCES

Aiken, M. and J. Hage. 1966. "Organizational Alienation: A Comparative Analysis," *America Sociological Review,* 31:497–507.

Apple, M. W. 1988. "What Reform Talk Does: Creating New Inequalities in Education," *Educational Administration Quarterly,* 24(3):272–281.

Armor, D., P. Conry-Oseguera, M. Cox, N. King, L. McDonnell, A. Pascal, and G. Zellman. 1976. "Analysis of the School Preferred Reading Program in Selected Los Angeles Minority Schools," Report No. R-2007-LAUSD, Santa Monica, CA: The Rand Corporation, ERIC Document Reproduction Service No. ED 130 243.

Ashton, P. and R. Webb. 1986. *Making a Difference: Teachers' Sense of Efficacy and Student Achievement.* New York: Longman Inc.

Bacharach, S. B., S. C. Conley, and J. B. Shedd. 1986. "Beyond Career Ladders: Structuring Teacher Career Development Systems," *Teachers College Record,* 87(4):563–587.

Bandura, A. 1982. "Self-efficacy Mechanism in Human Agency," *American Psychologist,* 37(2):122–147.

Barber, D. 1971. "Differentiated Staffing: Expectations and Pitfalls," *Differentiated Staffing,* Nassau Regional Office for Educational Planning.

Beehr, T. A. and K. G. Love. 1983. "A Meta-Model of the Effects of Goal Characteristics, Feedback, and Role Characteristics in Human Organizations," *Human Relations,* 36:151–166.

Bidwell, C. E. 1965. "The School as a Formal Organization," in *The Handbook of Organizations,* J. G. March, ed., Chicago: Rand McNally.

Berman, P., M. McLaughlin, G. Bass, E. Pauly, and G. Zellman. 1977. *Federal Programs Supporting Educational Change.* Santa Monica, CA: The Rand Corporation, ERIC Document Service No. ED 140 432.

Boyer, E. L. 1988. "The New Agenda for the Nation's Schools," *Educational Administration Quarterly,* 24(3):310–318.

Bridges, E. M. 1977. "The Nature of Leadership," in *Educational Administration: The Developing Decades,* Nystrand and Hack, eds., Berkeley: McCutchan Corp., pp. 202–230.

Carnegie Task Force on Teaching as a Profession. 1986. *A Nation Prepared: Teachers for the 21st Century.* New York: Carnegie Corporation.

Charters, W. W. 1973. *Measuring the Implementation of Differentiated Staffing.* Center for the Advanced Study of Educational Administration, University of Oregon.

Conant, E. H. 1971. "A Cost-Effectiveness Study of Employing Nonprofessional Teaching Aides in the Public Schools," ERIC Document Reproduction Service No. ED 058 611.

Conley, S. C. 1988. "Reforming Paper Pushers and Avoiding Free Agents: The Teacher as a Constrained Decision Maker," *Educational Administration Quarterly,* 24(4):393–404.

Cresswell, A. M. and M. J. Murphy. 1980. *Teachers, Unions, and Collective Bargaining in Public Education.* Berkeley: McCutchan Publishing Corp.

Darling-Hammond, L. 1984. *Beyond the Commission Reports: The Coming Crisis in Teaching.* Santa Monica, California: Rand.

Dean, D. 1961. "Alienation, Its Meaning and Measurement," *American Sociological Review,* 26(5):753–758.

Dembo, M. and S. Gibson. 1985. "Teachers' Sense of Efficacy: An Important Factor in School Improvement," *The Elementary School Journal,* 86(2):173–184.

Dworkin, A. G. 1987. *Teacher Burnout in Public Schools: Structural Causes and Consequences for Children.* Albany: State University of New York Press.

Earl, S. A. 1969. "Differentiated Staffing," ERIC Document Reproduction Service No. ED 036 885.

1970. *Education Digest.* 36(2):22–24.

English, F. W. 1972. "A Report to Superintendent Regarding the Progress of Venice Junior High School towards Flexible Instructional Organization, or Staff Differentiation," ERIC Document Reproduction Service No. ED 069 614.

Fiorino, A. J. 1972. *Differentiated Staffing: Flexible Instructional Organization.* New York: Harper and Row.

Firestone, W. A. 1988. "Essay Review of *Teacher Burnout in Public Schools: Structural Causes and Consequences for Children,*" *Educational Administration Quarterly,* 24(1):86–88.

Fuller, B., K. Wood, T. Rapoport, and S. Dornbusch. 1982. "The Organizational Context of Individual Efficacy," *Review of Educational Research,* 52(1):7–30.

Futrell, M. H. 1988. "Teachers in Reform: The Opportunity for Schools," *Education Administration Quarterly,* 24(4):374–380.

Gibson, S. and M. Dembo. 1984. "Teacher Efficacy: A Construct Validation," *Review of Educational Research,* 52(1):7–30.

Hackman, J. R. and G. R. Oldham. 1976. "Motivation through the Design of Work: A Test of Theory," *Organizational Behavior and Human Performance,* 16:250–279.

Hackman, J. R. and G. R. Oldham. 1980. *Work Redesign.* Reading, MA: Addison-Wesley.

Harriot, R. E. and N. Gross. 1979. Chapter 1. *The Dynamics of Planned Educational Change.* Berkeley: McCutchan Publishing Corp.

Hawley, W. D. 1988. "Missing Pieces of the Educational Reform Agenda: Or Why the First and Second Waves May Miss the Boat," *Educational Administration Quarterly,* 24(4):416–437.

Honig, B. 1988. "The Key to Reform: Sustaining and Expanding upon Initial Success," *Educational Administration Quarterly,* 24(3):257–271.

Hoy, W. K., W. Newland, and R. Blazovsky. 1977. "Subordinate Loyalty to Superior, Esprit, and Aspects of Bureaucratic Structure," *Educational Administration Quarterly,* 13(1):71–85.

Hoy, W. K. and C. G. Miskel. 1982. *Educational Administration: Theory, Research, and Practice, 2nd ed.* New York: Random House.

Johnson, S. M. 1986. "Incentive for Teachers: What Motivates, What Matters," *Educational Administration Quarterly,* 22(3):54–79.

Kanter, R. M. 1983. *The Change Masters.* New York: Simon and Schuster.

Kerchner, C. T. 1988. "Bureaucratic Entrepreneurship: The Implications of Choice for School Administration," *Educational Administration Quarterly,* 24(4):381–392.

Kerchner, C. T. and D. E. Mitchell. 1986. "Teaching Reform and Union Reform," *The Elementary School Journal,* 86(4):449–470.

Kirst, M. W. 1988. "Recent State Education Reform in the United States: Looking Backward and Forward," *Education Administration Quarterly,* 24(3):319–328.

Little, J. W. 1982. "Norms of Collegiality and Experimentation: Workplace Conditions of School Success," *American Educational Research Journal,* 19(3).

Locke, E. A., N. Cartledge, and C. S. Knerr. 1970. "Studies of the Relationship between Satisfaction, Goal-Setting, and Performance," *Organizational Behavior and Human Performance,* 5:135–139.

Lortie, D. C. 1969. "The Balance of Control and Autonomy in Elementary School Teaching," in *The Semi-Professionals and Their Organization,* A. Etzioni, ed., New York: Free Press.

Lortie, D. C. 1975. *Schoolteacher: A Sociological Study.* Chicago: University of Chicago Press.

Lowther, M. A., S. J. Gill, and L. C. Coppard. 1981. "Worklife Issues of Teachers and Other Professionals," in *Adult Career Transitions: Current Research Perspectives,* R. E. Hill, E. L. Miller, and M. A. Lowther, eds., Ann Arbor: Michigan Business Papers #66, Graduate School of Business Administration, University of Michigan.

Lowther, M. A., J. S. Stark, and D. W. Chapman. 1984. "Perceptions of Work-Related Conditions among Teachers and Persons in Other Occupations," *Journal of Educational Research,* 77(5):277–282.

Malen, B., M. Murphy, and A. W. Hart. 1987. *Career Ladder Reform in Utah: Evidence of Impact, Recommendations for Action.* Unpublished manuscript, The University of Utah: Graduate School of Education, Salt Lake City, Utah.

Mann, McLaughlin, Baer, Greenwood, McCluskey, Prusoff, Wirt, and Zellman. 1975. *Federal Programs Supporting Educational Change, Vol III: The Process of Development.* Rand: Santa Monica.

Miles. 1965. "Planned Change and Organizational Health: Figure and Ground," in *Organizations and Human Behavior: Focus on Schools,* F. D. Carver and T. J. Sergiovanni, eds., New York: McGraw-Hill.

Mento, A. J., N. D. Cartledge, and E. A. Locke. 1980. "Maryland vs. Michigan: Another Look at the Relationship of Expectancy and Goal Difficulty to Task Performance," *Organizational Behavior and Human Performance,* 25:419–440.

Miskel, C. G., D. McDonald, and S. Bloom. 1983. "Structural and Expectancy Linkages within Schools and Organizational Effectiveness," *Educational Administration Quarterly,* 11:38–54.

Miskel, C. G. and R. Ogawa. 1988. "Work Motivation, Job Satisfaction, and Climate," in *Handbook of Research on Educational Administration,* N. Boyan, ed. University of California, Santa Barbara: Longman.

Moeller, G. H. and W. W. Charters. 1966. "Relations of Bureaucratization to Sense of Power among Teachers," *Administrative Science Quarterly,* 10:444–460.

National Commission on Excellence in Education. 1983. *A Nation at Risk: The Imperative for Educational Reform.* Washington, D.C.: U.S. Government Printing Office.

Ollman, B. 1976. *Alienation: Marx's Conception of Man in Capitalist Society,* 2nd ed. New York: Cambridge University Press.

Peters, T. J. and R. H. Waterman. 1982. *In Search of Excellence.* New York: Warnter Books, Inc.

Pew, C. et al. 1971. "Analyzing Teacher Team Effectiveness: A Team Tutorial Approach: A Model," ERIC Document Reproduction Service No. ED 100 916.

Rand, J. and F. English. 1968. "Towards a Differentiated Teaching Staff," *Phi Delta Kappan* (January).

Reston Association of Teacher Educators. 1985. "Developing Career Ladders in Teaching," ERIC Document Reproduction Service No. ED 252 952.

Rhodes, M. 1989. "Work Alienation, Teacher Efficacy, and Career Ladder Reform," Paper presented at the *Annual Meetings of the American Educational Research Association, San Francisco, March 1989.*

Ritzer, G. 1977. *Working, Conflict and Change, 2nd ed.* Englewood Cliffs, NJ: Prentice-Hall.

Rosemount Independent School District 196, Minnesota. 1972. "A Differentiated Staffing Model and Statement of Philosophy for Specially Open Elementary and Junior High Schools," ERIC Document Reproduction Service No. ED 077 578.

Rosenholtz, S. 1985. "Political Myths about Education Reform: Lessons from Research on Teaching," *Phi Delta Kappan* (January):349–355.

Rotter, J. B. 1966. "Generalized Expectancies for Internal Versus External Control of Reinforcements," *Psychology Monographs,* 80:1–28.

Sadowski, C. J., M. W. Blackwell, and J. L. Willard. 1985. "Locus of Control on Student Teacher Performance," *Education,* 105(4):391–393.

Seeman, M. 1959. "On the Meaning of Alienation," *American Sociological Review,* 24:783–791.

Shanker, A. 1988. "Reforming the Reform Movement," *Educational Administration Quarterly,* 24(4):366–373.

Sharpes, D. 1972. "Administering Federal Educational Policy," in *Strategies for Differentiated Staffing,* F. English, ed., Berkeley: McCutchan Publishing Corp.

Soltis, J. F. 1988. "Reform or Reformation?" *Educational Administration Quarterly,* 24(3):241–245.

Stipek, D. and J. Weisz. 1981. "Perceived Personal Control and Academic Achievement," *Review of Educational Research,* 51(1):101–137.

Stover. 1969. "The Temple City Story: New Careers in Teaching: Differentiated Staffing," ERIC Document Reproduction Service No. ED 029 853.

Williams, R. 1975. "Staffing Plan for Upgrading of Rural Schools," ERIC Document Service No. ED 108 770.

PART II

FINANCING AND DEVELOPING COMPENSATION SYSTEMS

CHAPTER 4

Teacher Compensation: A Conceptual Design

WILLIAM B. CASTETTER – *University of Pennsylvania*
RICHARD S. HEISLER – *University of Pennsylvania*

PLANNING PURVIEW OF TEACHER COMPENSATION

No great stretch of imagination is required to realize the importance, as well as the complexity, of a teacher compensation system. Compensation is a vital aspect of organizational life in that it

- constitutes the core of the school budget
- affects satisfaction of the system's needs and goals
- impacts on personnel perceptions of pay equity
- influences the system's ability to attract, retain, motivate, and satisfy personnel aspirations and expectations
- represents what the organization intends to pay for, how it intends to do so, and what it expects in exchange for the pay package

Compensation is complex because it has various dimensions (see Table 1) that must be integrated into a workable combination of mission, strategies, programs, practices, and processes to provide consistent pay decisions and to resolve pay problems within and throughout all levels of the organizational structure.

Compensation: Past, Present, and Future

For the greater part of the twentieth century, models of teacher compensation, by and large, have tended to emphasize

- uniformity of all instructional positions
- equal pay for unequal performance
- a unilateral approach to working conditions
- the inclusion of teaching experience as a determinant of pay increases without regard to performance

105

Table 1. Dimensions of a teacher compensation system.

- **Human Resources Strategy:** Expresses in precise form two fundamental aspects of institutional compensation: (a) the ends for which the system is striving ultimately and (b) the human resources goals that will prevail in order to reach (a).
- **Compensation Strategy:** A plan to translate broad human resources strategy into a program that will: (a) staff the system with competent personnel, (b) provide an environment that will motivate personnel to achieve their potential, (c) establish an equitable pay package, (d) appraise performance in accordance with acceptable standards, and (e) reward outstanding performance.
- **Compensation Policy:** Board-initiated plan designed to provide management with a quasi-discretionary operational framework in order to (a) establish more detailed plans, procedures, processes, regulations, rules, and controls; (b) set strategic guidelines that define system intent, expectations, and operational scope for teacher pay planning and decision making; (c) enhance human resources effectiveness and instructional outcomes; (d) regularize and facilitate the exercise of judgment relating to recurring pay problems; (e) gain internal and external acceptance and support; and (f) respond to internal and external forces of change that impact on the compensation system.
- **Position Structure:** The number, types, levels, and relationships of instructional positions. Determines economic value of positions.
- **Pay Structure:** Establishes the total pay package (base pay, benefits, monetary, and non-salary incentives). The economic value of the position holder is determined by a combination of base pay and incentives.
- **Compensation Administration:** Refers to the implementation, coordination, and maintenance of a compensation system. Includes management of all pay-related activities such as legal compliance, budget preparation, collective bargaining, allocation of responsibilities, cost control, pay equity problems, and return of compensation investment.
- **Compensation Evaluation:** Focuses on extent to which organization goals are being accomplished, how effectively the compensation model operates, and what remodeling is necessary to maintain the quality of educational service anticipated.

- the inclusion of teacher preparation as another determinant of pay increases without regard to performance or type of preparation

and to deemphasize

- the significance of benefits as a form of compensation
- importance of the pay–performance relationship
- the needs of and investments needed for human resources
- the relationship between proper working conditions and teacher motivation

- the importance of continuous organizational planning for its human resources
- acceptance of the importance of the performance appraisal process as basic to effective compensation administration
- the interaction of system mission, human resources, and the compensation design

Forces of Change

Contemporary social, political, economic, and technological developments, especially those that have emerged during the present decade, have brought about considerable efforts to reform long-standing models of teacher compensation. As illustrated in Table 2, these much-maligned models are being recast in order to respond to

- government (federal, state, local) employment regulations
- the negative image of teaching and its rewards
- the competition for competent personnel
- the changing expectations of the teaching corps
- the spread of personnel sophistication relative to work-related conditions
- unionization as a vital force in negotiating compensation and the gamut of factors affecting teaching assignments

It is to the foregoing indicators of change as they impact on teacher compensation that the attention of the reader will be directed in the text following. The focus will be on those elements that are likely to be embodied in present and future compensation models and on how these elements can be unified to improve the effectiveness of teaching and learning in our nation's schools.

REMODELING TEACHER COMPENSATION

The starting line for transforming a teacher compensation system from where it is to where school officials desire it to be is a design—a plan for fashioning its form and structure. A design contains those details or features that are calculated to achieve preconceived teaching and learning objectives through enlightened monetary means.

Table 1 illustrates the dimensions of a contemporary design for teacher compensation. Examination of Table 1 indicates certain important characteristics. These are

Table 2. Focus of change in compensation planning.

Away from . . .	Toward . . .
Compensation based on piecemeal additions and deletions	Compensation based on a comprehensive model, including all personnel on payroll, openly arrived at, fully understood by those affected
Compensation policy shaped by professional negotiators	Compensation based on strategic design, concerned with organization goals and its aspirations for its human resources
Compensation designed for current staff	Compensation encompassing current staff but focused on attracting, developing, and retaining those most capable of contributing to system mission
Benefit package excludes options	Benefit package including options
Position emphasis	Performance emphasis
Market insensitive salaries	Market sensitive salaries
Single salary schedule	Variable compensation structure
Equal salaries for unequal performance	Rewarding quality performance through various options
Cost saving pay plans	Cost effective pay plans
Base pay addends limited to merit	Concept of merit embracing a variety of addends
Reward system limited	Reward system varied to be consistent and to enhance system mission
Merit quota system	Merit available to all who qualify
Equal compensation for all	Disparate compensation to reward specified behavior
Compensation practices which are event-prone (what others pay)	Compensation practices designed to attain educational outcomes
Pay limited to monetary consideration	Non-salary factors included in compensation structure
Performance appraisal focus on process and input	Performance appraisal process focused on output
Union-driven compensation	Compensation tied to achievement of organization, unit, and individual goals; compensation that is value-driven

Source: Castetter, William B. 1988. "Transforming Traditional Teacher Compensation," *National Forum of Educational Administration and Supervision Journal*, 5(3):1–22.

- inclusion of the system mission as one of the key elements in compensation planning
- setting forth management intent regarding purposes, expectations, and quality of work-life aspirations for its human resources
- identification of the several variables involved in teacher compensation, their interrelationships, and their function in bringing about organizational effectiveness
- the presence of policies, programs, processes, practices, procedures, and rules needed to coordinate, maintain, enforce, and enhance the compensation system

The foregoing features help to sharpen the point that contemporary compensation models have greater breadth and depth than earlier models, are mission-oriented, and give greater emphasis to all elements that comprise the pay package, including incentives, pay equity, and pay satisfaction. Moreover, the contemporary model is designed to manage compensation more effectively and efficiently through the use of a compensation process that establishes the economic worth of positions and position-holders, as well as through the creation of plans for coordinating, maintaining, evaluating, and modifying the various elements that give concrete form to the design.

Table 3 presents a teacher compensation model around which the rest of this chapter is woven and which is intended to provide greater specificity to the compensation dimensions outlined in Table 3. Accordingly, the model illustrated in Table 3 consists of three stages (I, II, III). Several salient aims of the model appear below:

- to offer succinct and usable guidelines for planning a compensation design that will serve to detect flaws and absence of linkages and to develop approaches to old compensation quandaries that are ever new
- to provide a panoptic view of all parts that enter into the formation of a compensation design
- to identify the various plans that are embodied in a compensation design, which range from the general to the detailed; from broad intentions and expectations to rules to be enforced; from nonsequential to sequential activities
- to bring into focus planning alternatives to be considered and from which design decisions can be derived and ordered
- to challenge assumptions under which the current model operates

Table 3. Model for designing teacher compensation.

Stage I: Strategic Design (Planning Foundation)
   • System mission
   • Human resources strategy
   • Compensation strategy
   • Compensation policy
 	
Stage II. Operational Design (Implementation)
   • Position structure
   • Pay structure
   • Pay administration
 	
Stage III. Expectations—Outcomes (Evaluation)
   • Model assumptions
   • Purposes of evaluation
   • Criterion variables
   • Performance criteria
   • Compensation system information
   • Compensation system adjustments

• to review compensation aims, variables that influence such aims, and to develop strategies to achieve these aims.

Stage I: Strategic Design

The model offered in Table 3 is a plan that sets forth in advance of action of the system's aspirations and intentions as well as guidelines for facilitating goal achievement.

The three stages of the model shown in Table 3 are given organizational life by means of managerial functions—*planning, implementing,* and *controlling.* Although the elements in each stage are grouped arbitrarily, collectively they represent a unified approach to attain: (a) a high degree of order and certainty in the compensation system, (b) coordination and control of activities involved in reaching defined and agreed-upon goals, and (c) proactive rather than reactive decision making. The constituent elements of Stage I and their significance in compensation planning are treated below.

System Mission

The system mission is the starting point in changing the design of a compensation system. The mission of a school system identifies the purposes for which it has been created and the statutory and related purposes that it is expected to fulfill. Teacher compensation is based on the assumption that its primary function is to support and enhance the system mission. That mission is generally concerned with providing an educational program and supporting services that will benefit the children, youth, and adults served by the school district. Compensation is viewed as an important mechanism for ensuring and enhancing the educational rights of each attendee.

The linkage between mission and money is all-important. For example, the mission

- is the mainspring for generating priorities, strategies, policies, processes, rules, and regulations
- provides a basis for assessing the extent to which progress is being made toward its fulfillment
- establishes the rationale for attracting, retaining, and motivating personnel in order to realize system outcomes
- sets the operational limits within which the educational program and related services are designed, budgeted, and put into operation

Consequently, every dollar for teacher compensation must be viewed in terms of whether it is aimed at attracting, retaining, developing, and motivating personnel who are competent and committed to contributing effectively to mission attainment.

Human Resources Strategy

Compensation may be considered as a transaction between the individual and the school system that involves an employment contract. The contract represents an exchange between the individual and the organization in which each receives something in return for giving something. Human resources strategy expresses the organization's belief system regarding the treatment of personnel in its employ and commitment to their development and self-fulfillment. Illustrations of elements involved in planning such strategy include equitable compensation, position security, equal pay for equal work, competitive salaries, protection against arbitrary treatment, assistance in improvement, and opportunity for advancement. The individual's responsibility in the exchange includes agreement to join, stay, meet role expectations, work independently, achieve self-improvement, cooperate, and adhere to system cultural expectations.

Compensation Strategy

Compensation strategy may be viewed as a set of interrelated decisions focused on directing selected fiscal resources to move the system from its current compensation status to more desirable arrangements. Strategy amounts to a plan that directs attention and resources to the system's critical pay problems such as direct and indirect compensation, incentives, benefits, market conditions, performance-dependent pay, marginal performance, and rewarding outstanding performance. In effect, compensation resources are linked to instructional targets and to the system mission.

Compensation Policy

As noted in Table 3, policy is one of the important dimensions of a compensation system. A policy is considered to be a standing plan (one used over and over again); is more detailed than a mission or strategy statement; is employed to translate broad objectives into more tangible terms and into more specific organizational intents; and is treated as a guideline—recommended practice—rather than a rule to be obeyed. Policy as formalized intent is a major force through which the board of education seizes the initiative and sets the spirit of organizational commitment to effect compensation change and innovation.

Table 4 illustrates the kinds of policy statements that can be designed to translate the broad plans (mission, strategies) that characterize Stage I into intended courses of action.

In the section that follows (Stage II) the reader's attention will be directed toward a set of plans that are more detailed and that are directly subordinate, as well as contributory, to achievement of the broader purposes identified in Stage I. In sum, policies serve to generate greater levels of specificity by which general aims are translated into operational form.

Stage II: Operational Design

Once compensation policy consistent with the district mission has been established, a framework needs to be created wherein monetary, non-salary, and benefit components of individual compensation can be designed and administered. Decisions are needed as to the compensation to be accorded to various instructional positions and position hold-

Table 4. Compensation policy framework.

It is the policy of the Winter Cove School District to maintain a compensation system that will:

- attract and retain personnel capable of performing effectively in positions to which they are assigned
- contribute to attainment of organizational objectives and to the economic, social, and psychological satisfaction of all personnel
- equal or exceed compensation levels prevailing in other school systems throughout the regional market
- compensate personnel equitably in relation to the effectiveness with which they perform the services for which they are employed
- provide balance among compensable factors (base pay, benefits, monetary, and non-salary components)
- comply with government employment standards, statutes, and union–system agreements
- communicate compensation information to enable system members to understand fully the purposes, policies, practices, and processes underlying the pay plan
- reward performance excellence
- gain public and personnel acceptance

ers. The stance taken in the text following is that choices should be systematic and consistent with standards of objectivity and fairness. Three aspects of a decision system governing the compensation process follow: *position structure, pay structure,* and *pay administration.*

Position Structure

During the last quarter of the twentieth century, rapid social evolution and changes in the competitive position of the United States in the world of nations have been accompanied by corresponding changes in demands made on education. Proposed and actual changes in the breadth and depth of the educational program suggest that a diversity of instructional positions will be required to meet existing and emerging expectations. Consequently, it is reasonable to assume that factors such as teacher availability, professional competence, position responsibility, and complexity, as well as market conditions, will need to be taken into consideration in planning the compensation process.

Table 5 illustrates an *instructional position structure.* It is designed to establish *responsibility levels* that form the basis for the *position structure* shown in Table 5. As shown, responsibilities range from

Table 5. Criteria for position placement in the instructional position structure.

Responsibility Level	Placement Criteria
Level 1: Foundation Program[a,b,c]	*Position Candidate*
Instructional positions in this program are intended to carry forward the instructional mission of the school district. The program also provides a base on which to erect incentives toward innovative and model strategies for instructional refinement.	Conforms to controls established by federal, state, and local government Meets entry requirements established by the school district Is eligible for retention in accordance with tenure regulations Carries out responsibilities specified by the designated position guide
Level 2: Developmental Program[b,c]	*Position Candidate*
Instructional positions in this program are intended to supplement those in the foundation program so as to encourage program innovation and development and to provide a climate with incentives for professional advancement.	Leads in devising, testing, and establishing pilot programs or innovative methods Assists in improving and perfecting existing program(s) Helps the system to identify and remedy instructional problems Is instrumental in improving status and instructional effectiveness of colleagues Participates in trial of alternative instructional strategies

(continued)

Table 5 (continued).

Responsibility Level	Placement Criteria
Level 3: Magnet Program[b,c]	*Position Candidate*
Instructional positions in this program are intended to meet needs of the the school district to attract and retain instructional personnel who are in short supply, to establish model instructional standards for selected positions and to motivate the highest achievement of system enrollees and instructional personnel.	Meets criteria established for levels 1 and 2
	Conforms to standards established by search committee
	Represents type, level and/or class of instructional position in short supply (see definitions)
	Chooses to teach among competing, well-compensated positions
	Attracts similarly qualified personnel to the school system

[a]By definition the magnet program will consist of a relatively small number of teaching positions. Incumbents at other levels who qualify for placement are automatically included at the applicable compensation level.

[b]Monetary compensation is determined by ratio to base compensation and addends established for level 3 (see Figure 1).

[c]Designated percentages of instructional time and noninstructional time are set aside for professional, position, and program development. This will require corresponding adjustments in staffing ratios used for projecting the budget.

maintenance of existing program standards (Level 1) through program and professional development (Level 2) to attracting and retaining instructional personnel who are in short supply (Level 3). At each responsibility level criteria are specified for inclusion of positions at that level. *The reader will note that this structure departs from the traditional teacher compensation model, which is based on the untenable assumption that all instructional positions are identical in responsibility and skill requirements.*

Pay Structure

Once the instructional position structure has been established (Table 5), linkages need to be developed among *levels and pay.* In the discussion that follows it is assumed that compensation may consist of (a) monetary payments (base salary and incremental addends); (b) non-salary rewards (such as recognition, position modification, and grants); and (c) benefits (such as those for retirement and health maintenance) (see Tables 6 and 7 for details). Following are their relationships to the position structure discussed previously:

- The compensation structure is found on base pay levels that correspond to the number of levels established for the position structure (see Table 9).
- Base pay at consecutively higher levels of the position structure is linked to that at the lowest level by a compensation index (see Table 9).
- Increased addends to base pay are proportional to the relative amount at the base (see Table 9).
- Budget expenditures for non-salary incentives for each position are porportionate to the pay base of the responsibility of that position (see Table 14).
- Benefits are independent of the position structure.
- The compensation structure expands and is indexed to instructional programs identified in Table 5.

Base Salary Criteria

The three-level responsibility structure illustrated in Table 8 assumes that compensation at the basic (foundation) level consists essentially of elements required by governmental (state) controls and collective

Table 6. Illustration of a compensation structure.

D Performance Perquisites (non-salary incentives)	*Objective.* Enhance individual and group performance. Motivational mechanisms include recognition, position security, latitude for intitiative, appreciation, status symbols, privileges, authority and power, information, proper and pleasant facilities in which to work, absence of close supervision, position–person compatibility.
C Base Compensation Addends (monetary incentives)	*Objective.* Motivate behavior. Variable compensation, payment of which is dependent upon specified behavior. Extends base salary concept. Assumes: positions may differ in status, complexity, and responsibility; position holders vary in performance effectiveness; base salary should be adjusted to account for differences in positions and performance.
B Collateral Benefits (non-salary)	*Objective.* Personnel security, retention, motivation. Indirect forms of non-salary compensation. Generally applies to all personnel. Requires no additional services to be performed beyond those specified in base pay. Considered an organization social obligation.
A Base Compensation (monetary)	*Objective.* Attract, retain competent personnel. Links position values and pay levels. Decisions influenced by pay policy, ability and willingness to pay, legislation, and collective bargaining

negotiations. These requirements are common to all responsibility levels. Optional (discretionary) monetary and non-salary incentives at the higher levels are designed to enhance selected objectives of the school system, namely program and personnel development.

Position–Base Salary Linkage

In the foregoing discussion it has been suggested that base pay be established and maintained as linkage to the responsibility structure (see Table 5) by *indexing.* Table 9 illustrates a plan for developing such

Table 7. Forms of teacher incentive compensation.

I. **For Teacher Performance**
 A. Extraordinary Classroom Performance
  1. *Instructional Delivery* (focus is on major teaching functions: instructional strategies, time management, student behavior, instructional presentation, instructional monitoring, and feedback)
  2. *Instructional Outcomes* (pupil achievement)
 B. Extraordinary Extraclassroom Performance
  1. *Faculty Performance*
   (a) School site service
    e.g., as staff development instructor, school based project leader, extra duty assignment, lead teacher, department head, program coordinator
   (b) System service
    e.g., as teacher monitor, peer observer, staff development instructor, part-time or joint appointment, extra duty assignment, special assistant, teacher assistance project leader
   (c) Extrasystem service
    e.g., as collaborative project leader, community educational project leader, PTA project leader
  2. *Professional Performance*
   (a) School site service
    e.g., as research project leader, experiment project leader, model development planner
   (b) System service
    e.g., as research project leader, experiment leader, special assignment, project consultant
   (c) Extrasystem service
    e.g., for publication: textbooks, articles; teaching professional courses, professional consultation
II. **For Teacher Improvement (Professional Development)**
 A. Intraschool Plan
  Innovative curriculum project; innovative teaching project; extension of position requirements or exceptions; extraordinary professional development through conferences, clinics, seminars, in-service activities, special projects
 B. Extraschool Plan
  Graduate level coursework; advanced degree attainment; recertification; retraining; multiple approaches to professional improvement in addition to those cited above

Table 8. Illustrative criteria for determination of base salaries of instructional personnel at foundation, developmental, and magnet responsibility levels.

Foundation Level Criteria	Development Level Criteria	Magnet Level Criteria
Local minimum established by regulations of government entities	Established by ratio at a level commensurate with position responsibility relative to the foundation and median beginning salary for positions at the magnet level	Norms of beginning salaries for positions of equivalent technical skill and preparation
Regional norms (averages) of beginning salaries paid		Amounts set at a selected level below average earnings of positions of equivalent technical skill and preparation, e.g., 80 percent of average
An amount established by competition to obtain an adequate supply of competent personnel to meet district needs		
An amount determined by regional maximum of beginning salaries paid		Amounts determined competitively by negotiation to satisfy district standards and supply requirements
Regional norms (averages) of beginning salaries paid by school districts of similar size and/or wealth		
An amount determined by regional maximum of beginning salaries paid by school districts of similar size and/or wealth		

See Tables 6 and 7 for incentive addends and benefits that are included in the compensation structures.

Table 9. Derivation of a compensation index for determining base salaries of instructional positions.

(1)	(2)	(3)	(4)	(5)
Responsibility Level	Position Value Differential Units	Cumulative Differential Units	Weighting Constant	Compensation Index 1 + (Col. 3 × Col. 4)
1	0	0	.272727	1.000000
2	1	1	.272727	1.272727
3	2	3	.272727	1.818181

Assumptions: Responsibility levels in instructional compensation structure = 3; minimum base salary = $22,000; maximum base salary = $40,000.

Column 1 derives from responsibility levels in instructional position structure illustrated in Table 5.

Column 2 is based on position value differentials illustrated in Figure 1.

Column 3 represents sum of differentials between level 1 and consecutive levels.

Column 4 derives from difference in base salaries at levels 1 and 3 ($40,000 − $22,000 = $18,000) divided by base salary at level 1 ($18,000/$22,000 = .818182). The resulting quotient is interpreted to mean that the base salary at level 3 is 82 percent higher than at level 1. This figure is divided by the cumulative differential at all levels (3) to relate it to the total number of differential units accumulated in column 3 (.818182/3 = .272727).

Column 5 is obtained by adding to 1 (the reference level) the product of columns 3 and 4.

Note: See note 1 for a reference illustrating a model employing *five* levels of responsibility to compensate *administrative* personnel.

an index. In a three-level structure such as the one indicated, the procedure is obvious:

- The minimum salary for any position in the instructional responsibility structure (Table 5) needs to be determined.
- The base salary at the highest level of the structure needs to be established.
- Base salary at the intermediate level(s) is selected.

These steps are required regardless of the number of responsibility levels recognized.

Essentials for developing a *base pay structure* consist of decisions as to base pay levels at the lowest and highest levels of the compensation structure and as to the number of intervening levels for which base pay must be determined. *Table 8 indicates there are a number of ways in which the minimum salary base can be determined.* If it is to exceed the level required by regulatory agencies, it may be based on normative data, experimentation, or contractual obligations. Base salary at the uppermost level of the structure can be guided by the marketplace for equivalent positions or by experimentation. Just as there are a number of means for determining base pay levels at the extremes of the compensation structure, a number of options exist as to the number of *intermediate levels* to be included in the compensation design. The discussion that follows *illustrates a useful procedure* for determining how many responsibility levels will be incorporated in the organization structure for classroom teachers and linking those to a corresponding pay structure. Details of a procedure for converting responsibility levels to base pay levels are included here since the calculation methodology has been found by the authors to be: (a) applicable to any number of structural levels, (b) adaptable to such sublevels as the organization may define, and (c) perceived as useful in establishing and maintaining equity when applied to multilevel administrative organizations. A method for calculating an index governing the intermediate level or levels of base pay is illustrated in Table 9.

The formula employed in Table 9 serves to concentrate most of the pay differential in the third responsibility level. An intermediate level is created whose salary increase is one-third the range between the first and third responsibility levels. Such a compensation index will provide a strong incentive for teachers to strive to reach the highest responsibility level. Figure 1 has been included to illustrate graphically the relationship between position values and responsibility levels.

Position Value Indicators

Table 10 contains a variety of indicators of position worth. This type of information is useful in determining base pay of selected instructional positions at the third responsibility level, which is illustrated in Table 9. Factors that will influence the choice are

- availability of qualified personnel to fill the position
- financial resources of the school district
- willingness to expend sufficient fiscal effort to sustain required expenditures

Differences in starting salaries for some positions listed in Table 10 suggest two approaches to selecting dollar values for instructional positions at the top of the responsibility structure:

- Set different base values for highly valued positions and those in short supply.

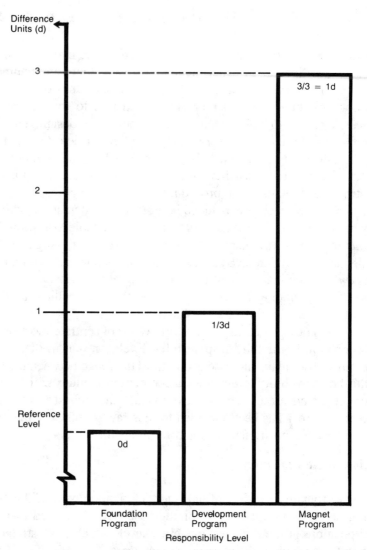

FIGURE 1. Relationship of position values to responsibility levels (from Table 9).

Read as follows:

Position value in foundation program is at *reference level*; position value in developmental program is at one-third of position value range above reference level. Difference in position values in magnet program and developement program is twice as great as difference between position values in developmental and foundation programs.

Example:

Base foundation level salary (reference level) = \$20,000; base developmental level salary = \$22,500; difference units above reference = 1 = \$2500; base magnet level salary = \$27,500; difference units above reference = 3 = \$7500.

Table 10 Monetary compensation benchmarks for selected occupations.

Classroom Teachers	
Elementary, 1987 average	$26,100
Secondary, 1987 average	27,400
Biological Sciences	
Median annual equivalent, 1985 (average)	26,312
Starting offers, all types of employers, 1986 (average)	19,068
Chemistry	
Starting salaries of graduates, 1987 (average)	27,048
Beginning positions, B.L.S. Level I, 1985 (med., private sect.)	22,167
Beginning positions, B.L.S. Level II, 1985 (med. private sect.)	26,400
Federal government positions, 1984 (average)	35,457
All positions, 1985 (median)	30,576
Beginning salary offers to college graduates, 1986	23,376
Physics	
Master's degree with no experience, private industry, 1985	30,000
Bachelor's degree, starting salary in federal government, 1985	15,500
Master's degree, starting salary in federal government, 1985	20,000
Doctor's degree, starting salary in federal government, 1985	30,000
Federal government positions, 1985	41,791
Geology	
Bachelor's degree, starting salary in private industry	21,000
Master's degree, starting salary in private industry	28,000
Bachelor's degree, starting salary in federal government	16,000
Master's degree, starting salary in federal government	28,000
Doctor's degree, starting salary in federal government	29,000
Other Physical and Earth Sciences	
Beginning salary offers to college graduates	25,200
Mathematics	
Starting salaries of graduates, 1987 (average)	25,548
Beginning salary offers to college graduates, 1986	24,444
Federal government positions, 1985	35,613
Computer Science	
Beginning salary, 1987	26,280
Beginning salary offers to college graduates, 1986	26,542
Computer specialist in federal government, 1984 (average)	32,183
Computer program analyst in federal government, 1984 (average)	35,683
Computer programmer, 1985 (median, all positions)	26,104
Computer systems analyst, 1985 (median, all positions)	31,304

Sources:
    U.S. Department of Commerce, Bureau of the Census. "Classroom Teachers," *Statistical Abstract of the United States, 1988 (108th edition).* Washington, DC: U.S. Department of Commerce, pp. 130–131.
    Wright, John W. 1987. "Science and Mathematics," *The American Almanac of Jobs and Salaries (1987–1988 edition).* New York: Avon Books, pp. 7, 138, 303–307, 318, 369.

- Choose the base value that promises to attract maximum support for the totality of positions selected

Differentiation of position values at the uppermost responsibility level would call for creation of indexed sublevels, one or an average of which would then serve as a basis for the determination of the dollar value of the intermediate pay base (level 2).

Magnet Level Base

One of the foregoing methods for calculating the base salary at level 3 (magnet level) is demonstrated in Table 11. Teaching positions that re-

Table 11. Translating reference norms into magnet level instructional compensation base.

Step 1. Select position(s) for which initial compensation is to be determined.
Step 2. Select reference norms appropriate to position guide specifications and system fiscal resources.
Step 3. Determine whether initial compensation is to be applied uniformly, or by position.
Step 4. Set magnet instructional compensation base.

Example:

Step 1. Magnet responsibility level instructional positions in short supply are teachers of life science, chemistry, mathematics in grades 10–12.

Step 2. Reference norms selected are

Life science:	Average starting offers to college graduates, 1987 $19,068—adjusted to June 1988 = $19,823[a]
Chemistry:	Average starting salary of college graduates, 1987 $27,048—adjusted to June, 1988 = $28,119[a]
Mathematics:	Average starting salary of college graduates, 1987 $25,548—adjusted to June, 1988 = $26,560[a]

Step 3. It is decided to apply a uniform compensation base to instructional positions at the magnet level in life science, chemistry, and mathematics.

Step 4. The high of norms obtained for positions under consideration is selected as the magnet level instructional compensation base, $28,119.

[a]Adjustment is made to economic trends by multiplying data for the available year by a factor derived as follows: Consumer Price Index[b] for the most recent month available divided by the Consumer Price Index for the same month of the year represented by the data. The rate of change for the year used in the example is 1.0396. For example, the Life Science Average of $19,068 × 1.0396 = $19,823.

[b]Council of Economic Advisors. 1988. *Economic Indicators, July, 1988.* Washington, DC: United States Government Printing Office, p. 23.

Table 12. Method of transforming position values into dollar values.

Step 1:	Determine base salary range: $22,000 to $28,119 (from Step 4, Table 11)
Step 2:	Determine ratio of the difference to the minimum base: $28,119 minus $22,000 = $6119; $6119/$22,000 = 0.2781.
Step 3:	Determine number of responsibility levels and assign differential units (three levels are assumed for the suggested instructional responsibility structure).
Step 4:	Determine cumulative differential units: 0 + 1 = 1; 1 + 2 = 3.
Step 5:	Determine weighting constant: 0.2781 (from Step 2)/3 (from cumulative total, Step 4) = 0.0927.
Step 6:	Determine compensation index at each responsibility level: 1 + (0 × 0.0927) = 1; 1 + (1 × 0.0927) = 1.0927; 1 + (3 × 0.0927) = 1.2781.
Step 7:	Verify compensation index: Compensation index, level 3 × base salary, level 1 = $28,118 (computed value approximates selected value).
Step 8:	Convert position values into dollar values: Multiply compensation index at each responsibility level by base salary at level 1.

(1)	(2)	(3)	(4)	(5)	(6)
Instructional Responsibility Level	Position Title	Differential Units	Cumulative Differential Units	Compensation Index	Base Salary
1	Foundation Program Teacher	0	0	1.0000	$22,000
2	Developmental Program Teacher	1	1	1.0927	$24,039
3	Magnet Program Teacher	2	3	1.2781	$28,119

quire personnel with special skills sought by the school district are identified—e.g., life science, chemistry, and mathematics (step 1). The positions are referenced to the most recently available market value of equivalent positions in the Consumer Price Index to date (step 2). Since the dollar values thus obtained vary from $19,823 for life science to $26,560 for physics, the high value of $28,119 (chemistry) is chosen as a uniform starting level base for positions at level 3 (steps 3 and 4).

The base salary specified in Table 12 for instructional responsibility level 3 (magnet program) teachers is selected by step 4 of Table 11.

Also needed to complete the task of transforming position values to dollar values are the dollar values for the remaining two levels of the pay structure. It is assumed that the base salary of foundation program teachers at level 1 will correspond to either a mandated or contractual minimum (whichever is higher) – $22,000 in the example. In accordance with the three-tiered structure depicted in Table 12, a compensation index is then derived and verified in steps 1 through 7, which, when applied to the base for the foundation program (level 1), results in a determination of $24,039 as the salary base for positions in the developmental program (level 2).

Position Values to Dollar Values

The following discussion focuses on (a) determination of the total cost of compensation of individual position holders and (b) examination of individual patterns of compensation and their linkage to the entire compensation system. Compensation controls and their relationship to system effectiveness will be addressed in Stage III.

Tables 13 and 14 consider the *compensation of individual positions.* Together they represent a decision system for implementation of compensation policy. Base salaries (BS) in Table 13 are derived as follows: the computer technology teacher associated with the development program (level 2) qualifies for a compensation index of 1.0927. When applied to the foundation program base level of $22,000, this index yields a base salary for the position of $24,039 (see Table 12 for assumptions).

Table 13. Conversion of teacher compensation operational design (Table 5) into base salaries.

Instructional Role	Compensation Level	Compensation Index	Base Salary
Fifth grade teacher	1	1.0000	$22,000
Middle school math teacher	1	1.0000	22,000
Kindergarten teacher	1	1.0000	22,000
Computer technology teacher	2	1.0927	24,039
Senior H.S. chemistry team leader	3	1.2781	28,119
Senior H.S. physics teacher	3	1.2781	28,119
Middle school biology teacher	1	1.0000	22,000

Note: See Table 12 for derivation.

Table 14. Summary computations of individual teacher compensation requirements.

I. Assumptions Underlying Compensation Computations

  A. Base salary range = ($22,000 – $28,119). (For derivation see Table 12.)

  Base salary (*BS*) + across-the-board, if any (*ATB*) + preparation addend (*P*) remain part of salary. Extended service addends (*ESA*) and monetary and non-salary addends are re-earned each year. If performance does not justify addends, salary is frozen at (*BS* + *ATB* + *P*) during the next budget year. Model precludes reduction of *BS* + *ATB* + *P*. When base salaries at responsibility levels are increased across-the-board they should be multiplied by the responsibility index. If not, the ratios used will be diminished.

  B. Number of compensation levels = 3. (For rationale see Table 8.)

  C. Work year = 10 months (union–system contract)

  D. Minimum employment requirement = bachelor's degree + state certification

  E. Monetary addends (required)

   1. Preparation addend = 40% of base salary: M.S. = 20%; doctorate = 40%. Academic course work, specifically approved for instructional objectives, represents incentive addend for teacher improvement (see Table 7).

   2. Extended service addend (*ESA*) = 0–80% (4% per annum)

  F. Monetary incentives (optional). 0–40%. Not to exceed 50% of maximum base salary.

  G. Non-salary incentives = 0–20%. See Table 7 for list of incentives.

  H. Collateral benefits = flexible benefit plan. Each teacher selects desired benefits from approved list not to exceed $6010 (based on 25% of base salary average (Table 13).

II. Formula: Base salary + required monetary addends + monetary incentives + non-salary incentives + collateral benefits = budgetary support required for position.

III. Computation of individual budgetary compensation requirements

(continued)

127

Table 14 (continued).

1	2	3	4	5	6	7	8	9
Position Holder	Compensation Level (From Table 9)	Base Salary (From Table 13)	Preparation Addend (required)	Extended Service (ESA) (required)	Performance Incentives Monetary (optional)	Performance Incentives Non-salary (optional)	Collateral Benefits (required)	Individual Dollar Value Total
Teacher Grade 5	1	$22,000	—	3(.04) = $2640	—	—	$6010	$30,650
Teacher Math Middle School	1	22,000	M.S. = $4400	4(.04) = 3520	(.08) = $1760	(.05 × BS) = $1100	6010	38,790
Teacher Kindergarten	1	22,000	M.S. = 4400	5(.04) = 4400	(.05) = 1100	(.08 × BS) = 1760	6010	39,670
Teacher Computer Technology	2	24,039	M.S. = 4808	2(.04) = 1923	—	(.05 × BS) = 1202	6010	37,982
Teacher S.H.S. Chemistry Chairman								

(continued)

Table 14 (continued).

1	2	3	4	5	6	7	8	9
Position Holder	Compensation Level (From Table 9)	Base Salary (From Table 13)	Preparation Addend (required)	Extended Service (ESA) (required)	Performance Incentives Monetary (optional)	Performance Incentives Non-salary (optional)	Collateral Benefits (required)	Individual Dollar Value Total
Team Leader S.H.S. Physics	3	28,119 M.S. = 5624	2(.04) = 2250	(.10) = 2812	(.05 × BS) = 1406	6010	46,221
Teacher S.H.S. Physics	3	28,119 Doct. = 11,248	—	(.05) = 1406	—	6010	46,783
Teacher Middle School Biology	1	22,000	—	8(.04) = 7040	(.16) = 3520	—	6010	38,570

The dollar values shown in columns 7 and 8 represent indirect payments. For example, collateral benefits and non-salary incentives (research account, tuition, replacement cost for released time, and funds for reading experiment) are teacher costs but are not included in paycheck.

The flexibility of this model provides for adjustment of all compensable components to accommodate changing internal and external organization circumstances.

Note: Column 4 = Col. 3 × (.20) = M.S.; Col. 3 × (.40) = doctorate (see Table 14: Assumptions); Column 5 = Col. 3 × years of experience × .04. (see Table 14: Assumptions); Column 6 = optional percentage × Col. 3 (see Table 14: Assumptions); Column 7 = optional percentage × Col. 3 (see Table 14: Assumptions); Column 9 = Total (Col. 3–8)

Table 14 illustrates the procedure for determining combined dollar values of base salary, monetary and non-salary incentives, and benefits for positions identified in Table 13. The reader will observe that the computer technology teacher qualifies for the following in addition to the base salary of $24,039:

- Twenty percent of the base salary for the Master's degree = $4808.
- Four percent of the base salary times two years of service = $1923.
- Five percent of base salary for non-salary incentive = $1202.
- Collateral benefits = $6010.

Thus, the equivalent cost to the school district of compensable variables may be determined for a given position. This information is of value in estimation of the actual salary as well as the equivalent costs of addends.

Pay Administration

While emphasis has been given previously to the concept that goals are essential components of a compensation system, it is also important to develop formal plans for implementing pay practices. Failure of many compensation plans is due frequently not to poor planning but to poor implementation of plans. Mission, strategies, and policies are worthless unless they are translated into specific plans and administered in a manner to fulfill system expectations. This view takes cognizance of the fact that plans are transformed into real terms through careful allocation and management of resources. It is useful at this point to indicate the kinds of activities frequently associated with implementation of pay plans. Table 15 is designed to reinforce the view that compensation administration is an integral component of a compensation system.

The forces of change that confront modern school systems are numerous and challenging. Analysis of these movements serves to point out that simplistic approaches to compensation planning and implementation do not embrace the conceptual foundation and operational sophistication for coping with internal and external organizational influences affecting teacher compensation.

Table 15. Illustration of activities associated with compensation administration.

- allocation of compensation responsibilities
- benefit management
- collective bargaining
- compensation communication
- compensation budgets
- compensation controls
- compensation grievances
- compensation litigation
- demotion (salary adjustment)
- downgrading (position)
- government regulations (adherence)
- incentives (individual, group)
- inequity situations (internal: individual, inter–intra group)
- pay increases (general, special)
- pay periods
- pay equity (external: professional, regional, national)
- performance appraisal process
- personnel placement (salary scale)
- promotion (salary adjustment)
- return on investment
- transfers
- turnover
- upgrading (position)
- updating (system)

Stage III: Compensation System Outcomes

Model Assumptions

The model of teacher compensation described in Table 3 assumes

- Various forces, both internal and external, continually act upon the compensation system.
- These forces frequently create the need for corrections or adjustments, either major or minor, if the intent of the compensation plan is to be achieved.
- Compensation problems will emerge at individual, group, and organization levels.
- The source of numerous compensation problems may be

structural (plans and planning) or behavioral (individual, intragroup, or intergroup) in nature.

- Some of the forces that impact on compensation systems are beyond institutional control; others are within management parameters. Both kinds of forces create compensation problems and challenges to which management must respond adaptively and creatively for the sake of the organization's well-being.

The discussion that follows is devoted to the importance of and actions involved in (a) analyzing the difference between compensation expectations and outcomes and (b) making adjustments in the system based on the review process outlined in Stage III (Table 3).

Purposes of Evaluation

The evaluation process featured in Stage III is one of the three elements (see Table 3) essential to the design and operation of a compensation system. The cardinal purpose of evaluation is to seek dependable answers to questions such as the following:

- Are the policies, practices, processes, rules, and regulations established in the design being followed?
- To what extent are the goals of the compensation program being attained?
- How effective are the monetary and nonmonetary incentives?
- Is the base pay adequate to attract qualified and competent personnel?
- Is the cost of the benefit plan properly balanced in relation to other compensable elements?
- Is the appraisal process effective?
- Has the operation of the compensation system minimized complaints, litigation, grievances, or anti-organization behavior by the teachers' union?

The elements to be addressed throught the compensation evaluation process depicted in Stage III (Table 3) will be examined in turn in the text following.

Criterion Variables

A compensation system, regardless of its breadth, depth, or level of sophistication, needs some means by which to judge, as well as to ensure, its success (see Fallon, *AMA Management Handbook,* 1983). Two important tools are employed for this purpose — criterion variables and criterion measures. Criterion variables are the performance levels — standards of judgment against which results or expectations of the compensation system are measured. They are considered to be official expectations for which compensation plans are designed to have a positive impact. Table 16 illustrates compensation performance criterion categories and related criterion measures.

Criterion Measures

The criterion measures shown in Table 16 have as their function the evaluation of compensation system performance against its objectives. These measures, it will be observed, are both subjective and objective. Some are based on numerical indices such as rates, ratios, percentages, relationships, estimates, forecasts, and measures of central tendency or dispersion. Others are judgmental and rely heavily on analyses of deviations from established levels of performance; from agreed-upon performance goals; on impressions, observations, personnel behavior patterns, and internal and external complaints about and dissatisfaction with elements of the pay plan.

Various problems are encountered in measuring the impact of compensation on personnel behavior and on pupil learning outcomes. Establishing performance standards for components of the compensation

Table 16. Compensation performance criterion categories and performance criterion measures.

Performance Categories	Performance Measures
Pupil learning outcomes	Pupil achievement measures
Teacher performance	Performance appraisal
School attendance unit performance	Performance appraisal
Compensation equity	Comparative indicators
Recruitment–retention effectiveness	Acceptances–turnover
Terminations	Rate comparison
Tenure/turnover	Rate comparison
Absenteeism	Rate comparison
Compensation costs	Statistical indicators
Personnel satisfaction	Information system
Government regulation compliance	Personnel information system
Union–system relations	Contract settlement provisions

plan (salaries, benefits, incentives) and devising measures to determine their impact are complex and challenging, though not insurmountable tasks. The primary focus of performance measures is to compare progress against objectives or standards and to initiate corrective action when evaluation information indicates decisions relating to upgrading the pay plan are in order.

Compensation System Adjustments

The flow of the preceding steps identified in Stage III (Table 3) leads to a discussion of decision making—what to do about feedback information that indicates certain adjustments are necessary to achieve the desired well-being, stability, effectiveness, and efficiency of the compensation system (see Gibson, Ivancevich, Donnelly, 1982).

When there is dependable evidence that a gap exists between performance and objectives, deviations may derive from various sources: personnel attitudes, skill deficiencies, lack of motivation, organization structure, compensation design features, inadequate resources, supervisory behavior, and so on. Table 17 depicts the kinds of compensation problems to be addressed when there is a disparity between actual and planned results.

In closing this brief discussion on compensation system adjustment, the point should be made that the intent here is not to deal extensively with some of the decisions inherent in Stage III (e.g., identification of alternative solutions, selecting an appropriate course of action, imple-

Table 17. Illustration of compensation problems.

- As compensation expenditures increase, levels of pupil achievement decrease.
- Absentee and turnover rates are well beyond desired levels.
- Incentive compensation is granted to marginal performers.
- Statistical data show that teaching staff numerical adequacy is unsatisfactory.
- Base salary schedule is not conducive to attraction, retention, or motivation of a substantial portion of the teaching staff.
- Benefits amount to 50 percent of salary expenditures.
- Termination of marginal performers is a rare occurrence.
- Individual schools within the system are neither recognized nor rewarded for developing consistent, outstanding learning outcomes.
- System refuses to take action to resolve comparable worth problems—pay gaps between men and women in collateral curriculum activities (i.e., coaching) and personnel with intermittent assignments (see Scarpello, Ledvinka, 1988).

menting the decision, recycling the evaluation process). Rather, the purpose is to stress the importance of continuous review of compensation system outcomes and of developing approaches calculated to motivate teaching personnel in ways that will generate desired teaching and learning.

SUMMARY

The major thrust of this chapter has been to propose a model for designing a teacher compensation system. It began by noting the importance of compensation in organizational life, as well as the shortcomings of models of teacher compensation that have prevailed during the greater part of the twentieth century.

The chapter indicated that there are various internal and external forces at work in contemporary society that necessitate remodeling of existing compensation plans if school systems expect to cope effectively with major influences affecting compensation decisions.

The model offered in this chapter is composed of three stages—*planning, implementation,* and *evaluation.* Stage I lays the foundation for compensation modeling by advancing a set of planning tools (mission, strategies, policies) around which detailed subplans can be fashioned. Stage II includes a discussion of means by which mission, strategies, and policies are operationalized through three approaches—*position structure, pay structure,* and *pay administration.* Stage III of the model focuses on assessment of differences between objectives and outcomes. Results of the assessment are utilized to make needed readjustments in the compensation system. The chapter ended by stressing the importance of continuous review of compensation system outcomes and initiation of adjustments, based upon dependable feedback, which are calculated to improve teaching and learning outcomes.

The Case for Compensation Modeling

The compensation model described in this chapter, as well as alternative models (linear-programming, zero-based, or other add-on approaches (see references), have these objectives in view:

Learning Outcomes: designing the compensation process to attract, retain, and motivate personnel capable of and committed to improvement of learning outcomes.

Planning Base: including the *compensation process* as one of the powerful mechanisms for mission attainment.

Definition: defining each step and substep in the compensation process carefully in order to regularize its operation.

Culturalization: institutionalizing compensation policy and process so that they become important elements of organizational life.

Member Involvement: securing faculty and community support by employing a model to familiarize participants with the nature and operation of the compensation system.

Negotiations: using the compensation model in collective negotiations to define system intent and expectations, as well as to engender proactive attitudes focused on system well-being.

Equity: designing the model to create trust by those affected on the basis of its fairness, objectivity, and policy intent.

Change: building flexibility into the model to make possible the changes necessitated by external and internal developments. For example, a model such as the one described provides an approach for breaking away from the fixed-step salary schedule.

Appraisal: forcing the administration to design the appraisal process to deal with the variety of decisions involved in compensation administration.

Review: requiring continuous review of and feedback about the state of the compensation process so that its updating can take place as needed.

Cost Sensitivity: sensitizing the board of education, administrative officials, faculty, and community to the financial issues involved in designing the compensation budget. How to get the right mix of compensable dollars forces careful scrutiny as to the most effective allocation of school revenues.

REFERENCES

Association for Supervision and Curriculum Development. 1987. *Developing Teacher Incentive Programs*. Alexandria, VA: The Association.

Bernardin, H. John and Richard W. Beatty. 1984. *Performance Appraisal in Organizations*. Boston, MA: Kent.

Biles, G. E. and S. R. Holmberg. 1980. *Strategic Human Resources Planning*. Glen Ridge, NJ: Thomas Horton and Daughters.

Boyer, E. L. "School Reform: Completing the Course," *NASSP Bulletin*, 72(504):61–70.

Bruno, J. E. 1970. "An Alternative to the Fixed Step Salary Schedule," *Educational Administration Quarterly,* 6(1).

Burack, E. H. and N. J. Mathus. 1980. *Human Resource Planning: A Pragmatic Approach to Manpower Staffing and Development.* Lake Forest, IL: Brace-Park Press.

Cascio, Wayne F. 1982. *Costing Human Resources: The Financial Impact of Behavior in Organizations.* Boston, MA: Kent.

Castetter, William B. 1986. *The Personnel Function in Educational Administration,* 4th ed. New York: Macmillan.

Castetter, William B. and Richard S. Heisler. 1974. *Planning the Compensation of School Administrative Personnel.* Philadelphia, PA: University of Pennsylvania [Reference for compensation model for school administrative personnel].

Castetter, William B. 1988. "Transforming Traditional Teacher Compensation," *National Forum of Educational Administration and Supervision Journal,* 5(3):1–22.

Castetter, William B. 1989. "Education Reform and the Compensation Factor," *National Forum of Educational Administration and Supervision Journal,* 6(1):1–18.

Cresap, McCormick, and Paget (n.d.). *Teacher Incentives: A Tool for Effective Management.* Washington, DC: The Authors.

Fallon, William K., ed. 1983. *AMA Handbook, 2nd ed.* New York: American Management Association.

Feldaker, B. 1985. *Labor Guide to Labor Law, 2nd ed.* Reston, VA: Reston.

Flippo, Edwin B. 1987. *Personnel Management.* New York: McGraw-Hill.

Gibson, James L., John M. Ivancevich, James H. Donnelly Jr. 1982. *Organizations, 4th ed.* Plano, TX: Business Publications, Inc.

Gorton, Richard A., Gail T. Schneider, and James C. Fisher. 1988. *Encyclopedia of School Administration and Supervision.* New York: Oryx Press.

Guthrie, J. W. and R. J. Reed. 1986. *Educational Administration and Policy.* Englewood Cliffs, NJ: Prentice-Hall.

Hawley, Willis D. 1985. "Designing and Implementing Performance-Based Career Ladder Plans," *Educational Leadership,* pp. 40–44.

Henderson, Richard I. 1986. *Compensation Management.* Reston, VA: Reston.

Heneman, Herbert G., Donald P. Schwab, John A. Fossum, and Lee D. Dyer. 1983. *Personnel/Human Resource Management.* Homewood, IL: Irwin.

King, William R. and David I. Cleland. *Strategic Planning and Policy.* New York: Van Nostrand.

Lawler, Edward P. III (n.d.). *Merit Pay: An Absolute Policy?* Los Angeles, CA: School of Business Administration, University of Southern California.

Ledvinka, James. 1982. *Federal Regulation of Personnel and Human Resource Management, 2nd ed.* Boston, MA: Kent.

McCaffery, Robert M. 1988. *Employee Benefits.* Boston, MA: Kent.

Mahoney, T. A. 1979. *Compensation and Reward Perspectives.* Homewood, IL: Richard Irwin.

National School Boards Association. 1987. *Rewarding Excellence: Teacher Compensation and Incentive Plans.* Alexandria, VA: The Association.

Scarpello, Vida and James Ledvinka. 1988. *Personnel/Human Resources Management.* Boston, MA; Kent.

Taylor, Raymond G. 1988. "Linear Programming and Alternative Models for Merit Pay

Distributions," *National Forum of Applied Educational Research Journal*, 2(1): 18–24.

Taylor, R. and W. M. Reid. 1987. "Application of Linear Programming and Network Analysis to the Collective Bargaining of Public Administrative Salaries," *Psychology*, 24(1).

Walker, J. W. 1980. *Human Resources Planning*. New York: McGraw-Hill.

Wallace, Marc and Charles Fay. *Compensation: Theory and Practice*. Boston, MA: Kent.

Wallace, M. J., Jr., N. F. Crandall, and C. H. Fay. 1982. *Administering Human Resources*. New York: Random House.

Yoder, Dale and Paul Staudohar. 1982. *Personnel Management and Industrial Relations, 7th ed.* Englewood Cliffs, NJ: Prentice-Hall.

Yoder, Dale and Herbert G. Heneman. 1979. *ASPA Handbook of Personnel and Industrial Relations*. Washington, DC: The Bureau of National Affairs.

CHAPTER 5

Effective Teacher Incentive Programs: Diversity and Effectiveness without State Funding

LARRY E. FRASE—*San Diego State University*
WILLIAM K. POSTON, JR.—*Iowa State University*

FOR a number of years, extra pay for teachers has been viewed as a major mechanism for upgrading education, and educators and politicians alike have implemented plans accordingly. Nevertheless, practitioners and theoreticians remain doubtful of any tangible performance improvement from such plans and rightfully so in light of recent findings (Mathis, 1988; Orlich, 1989; Olson, 1989; Timar and Kirp, 1989; Reinhold, 1987; Cornett, 1991). Central to concerned educators' focus in use of teacher compensation incentives is the matter of what works and what doesn't work in terms of enhancing learning. Guidance for practitioners is in short supply.

Cloaked in a variety of blandishments and often implemented with high-profile political hoopla, many efforts have been made to capitalize on the perceived connection between financial incentives and improved teaching performance. Despite numerous efforts, contradictory findings about the effectiveness of teacher incentive programs (TIPs), such as merit pay and career ladders, persist. For example, Hegebush and Norton (1988) found that some groups of teachers in career ladder districts were no more positive about Career Ladder Programs than were teachers in noncareer ladder districts.

Reyes and Madsen (1989) also found little or no connection between improved teacher job satisfaction and career ladder participation. Interestingly, their view was that organizational incentives are less powerful in promoting morale and satisfaction than is portrayed in what they called "management literature."

Whether such incentives are effective in promoting improved job performance remains a central issue. This article will explore this basic question and define some practitioner viewpoints worthy of note.

In 1988 thirty-four states were either implementing or developing policy relative to teacher incentives, generally in the form of a career ladder (Cornett, 1988). The money being invested was substantial. Iowa, for example, provided over $92 million in new funds for teachers in 1987, with nearly half designated for teacher incentive programs; Tennessee's 1988 funding level was $99 million; and California's 1988 program was funded at $63.5 million (Cornett, 1988). Literally hundreds of millions of dollars are being spent each year on Career Ladder Programs.

TIPs have political, professional, and financial support: the usual magic formula for success in education. Even major teacher organizations have agreed to support teacher incentive proposals. National Education Association head Mary Futrell has supported the Fairfax County, Virginia, pay plan (Spillane, 1990), and Albert Shanker of the American Federation of Teachers has supported the Rochester, New York, plan (see Rivera, 1989). However, little success has been achieved (Olson, 1987), and many teachers have become dissatisfied with their teaching careers despite increased preparation and compensation (Conley, Bacharach, and Bauer, 1989). Enthusiasm for career ladder forms of TIPs appears to be waning, as in North Carolina where the governor and the NEA affiliate battled over the future of the state's Career Ladder Plan and the legislature declined to mandate state-wide implementation of career ladders (Cohen, 1989). The Florida Career Ladder Program died quietly (Mathis, 1988; Cornett, 1988), the Texas state formula has found success in very few of the state's 1000 districts (Timar and Kirp, 1989), and legislation for career ladders in Alabama, Nebraska, and Wisconsin was repealed or struck (Cornett, 1988).

Without a baseline for comparison, the reasons for the dearth of success stories are open to debate. Fortunately, a number of local education agencies across the United States have experienced formidable success with teacher incentive programs (TIPs), indicating that the much-needed baseline may in fact exist.

In an unpublished study by Frase and Inman, five classic TIPs were closely examined, revealing little need for massive external funding or direction for success. These programs have withstood the test of time, having been in existence for between eight and thirty-five years. The five districts had little in common in terms of socioeconomic levels, enrollment trends, ethnicity, or rural-suburban-urban location. Nevertheless, some key similarities were found. Modestly funded with internal resources, the districts' TIPs displayed several significant characteristics in common, including the following:

- Legislative-level political involvement was absent.
- Funding from external sources was nonexistent.
- Teacher organization cooperation during planning was present.
- Clear, attainable objectives were provided.
- Freedom to determine the form of rewards was afforded.
- Local initiative ("grass-roots" development) was extant.

A discussion of each of these characteristics follows.

ABSENT LEGISLATIVE INVOLVEMENT

Absence of politics is the first common ingredient among the five districts. Teachers and others involved in TIPs often report significant political problems. In Tennessee, 93 percent of the teachers polled said the quality of education would be improved if the money proposed for the higher levels of the career ladder were used to reduce class size. Claims were made that teacher tasks were being manufactured to match legislatively defined levels and were creating impractical differences among teachers. Other claimed that Career Ladder Programs resulted in teachers being too far removed from the classroom, while still others asserted that incentives resembled pay for extra work, not greater quality of work (Olson, 1986).

Other claims about state-mandated programs depicted limitations on the numbers of eligible teachers as a disincentive. Teachers were discouraged from supporting TIPs that offered little hope for personal financial gain. Further, in Texas, a key official in the Texas Education Agency lamented unrealistic time lines imposed by politicians for the development of Career Ladder Programs. Texas' Career Ladder Program was established before accompanying evaluation instrumentation was developed. Other states suffered similar time constraints (Olson, 1986).

Moreover, in Tennessee, former Governor Lamar Alexander objected to career ladder monies being bureaucratically expended rather than utilized in classrooms. More than $2 million was used for hiring salaried employees just to manage the Career Ladder Program (Olson, 1987).

Political problems arising from conflicting interests of legislators and others pose overwhelming obstacles to success. So bad has been the career ladder reform movement's political record that the Carnegie publication, *Report Card on School Reform: The Teachers Speak* (1988) reported that 70 percent of the 13,500 teachers surveyed gave a grade of C or lower to the movement. Sixty percent of those responding cited political interference and increased paperwork as major faults.

NO EXTERNAL FUNDING

Despite historical records of under-funding, the five school districts addressed in the Frase–Inman study successfully designed, implemented, and operated their TIPs with only local revenues. State funding was not needed. Although state funding is not inherently pernicious or unnecessary, the point remains that districts accepting external funds have been unduly restricted. Additional funding is needed if most schools are to adopt TIPs, but accompanying political requirements cripple the projects' chances for success (Orlich, 1989). Bureaucratic survival can mean simply meeting the minimum requirements to ensure funding without suffering sanctions. Regrettably, the priority shifts to keeping the funds first. Integrity of the TIPs, the prime reason for seeking funding, comes second. Modifying the TIP to fit the demands for funding becomes another procrustean bed in which educational quality is forced to lie.

TEACHER COOPERATION

Few would disagree that working with members of the organization, in this case teachers, is the most effective way of implementing new programs. Four of the five districts in the Frase–Inman study used the "grass roots" or bottom-up collegial approach and, with cooperative effort, each reported success.

In contrast, one of the five, the Catalina Foothills School District (CFSD) in Tucson, Arizona, implemented a TIP without teacher consultation and, nonetheless, reported success. The CFSD experience demonstrated that when teacher organizations maintain long-held beliefs that only the single salary schedule can be used to determine teacher compensation, other strategies must be employed. The teachers were resolute in insisting upon uniform salary increases based upon years of experience and graduate training, neither of which is firmly connected to measured performance (Frase, 1987).

The perceived unfairness of compensating good and not-so-good teachers equally was not sufficient to warrant development of alternative compensation systems (Megel, no date). Recognizing the intransigence of that position, the CFSD eschewed the collegial approach, believing that negotiation would destroy the TIP's essence. The system of performance rewards was implemented with a top-down strategy, and it worked.

Complaints and resistance were frequent and harsh for two years until the teachers realized the benefits of the program. In the CFSD, the TIP succeeded through sound reasoning and firm commitment from the district leadership, overcoming staff inflexibility and reluctance.

The cooperative approach may be contextual. That is, in some cases it may ensure success, but in other cases it may hinder success. Depending upon the circumstances, the implementation strategies may vary. In the districts studied by Frase and Inman, implementation of the TIPs was achieved with *and* without agreement among parties involved, with comparable successful results.

CLEAR OBJECTIVES

Obviously, externally funded programs must be designed to achieve the external goals and objectives specified by the funding agency. Many school districts in the past have designed career ladder TIPs that parrot objectives fabricated at the state level, thus implementing a "state Career Ladder Model." The resulting sacrifice of local creative integrity is obvious.

However, in the five districts studied, TIPs were designed with authority and pride. The districts owned their program, the program addressed the districts' needs, and political game playing was obviated. Objectives included enhancing teacher recruitment and retention, improving instruction, motivating teachers, remedying inequities of the single salary schedule, rewarding superior teacher performance, increasing teacher recognition, and enriching job opportunities.

All five districts reported success in accomplishing their objectives. Some offered evidence from surveys and interviews, while others offered testimonial endorsement from teachers and administrators.

In the CFSD, the first evaluation revealed several positive and interesting findings (Frase, Hetzel, and Grant, 1982):

- Teachers experienced additional motivation as a result of participation in the TIP.

- Rewards were considered special recognition.
- Recognition was valued.
- Additional rewards were believed accessible given continued teaching excellence.

One negative, but equally interesting, finding was that 55 percent of the participating teachers believed that the CFSD incentive program created dissension among teachers. However, three years later, high levels of satisfaction were noted among teachers, and dissension was not evident. This later evaluation also revealed that the objective, increasing teacher recognition and job enrichment, was secured (Frase, 1989).

Evidence of success in externally, or state, funded programs currently is needed. To date, no program evaluation that links TIPs with teacher performance is available. Now is the time to determine whether externally imposed objectives are being effectively delivered.

FREEDOM IN REWARD SELECTION

Making rewards to fit the district was an essential attribute of the five districts' success. Rewards varied among the districts and included conference attendance, job enrichment, and provision of special materials or equipment in addition to salary schedule advancement and one-time cash rewards. Such diversity of incentive structure has not existed in externally funded TIPs. Typically, incentives were monetary, fit a career pattern, and were prescribed by state legislatures. Recently, one of the Arizona state-funded programs recognized the conflict between motivation research and monetary reward, and the district diversified incentives to include nonmonetary options (Downey, 1991). In spite of the importance, such adaptations with state-funded TIPs are rare (Mitchell and Peters, 1988; Frase, Hetzel, and Inman, 1987).

The five districts reported above, and others (Murnane and Cohen, 1986; Hatry and Griener, 1986), prove that educators can effectively tackle educational problems given local autonomy and noninvolvement of external political bodies. Demonstrated success provides guidelines for practitioners, and it is to these guidelines that this chapter's conclusions are directed.

RECOMMENDATIONS

Based on the findings of the five districts' incentive programs discussed above, some guidelines promise to be of assistance to practitioners interested in TIPs. Pursuit of the guidelines should enhance the possibility of attracting and retaining good teachers, motivating teachers toward instructional improvement, and increasing public respect for teachers.

(1) *Shift Locus of Control.* Practitioners need time to develop, implement, evaluate, and revise their ideas. Legislatures should consider funding local districts with unrestricted "seed money" for the formulation and operation of TIPs at the local level.

(2) *Limit Requirements.* The only required action for funded districts should be annual progress reports, statements of objectives, formal descriptions of the program, and evaluation reports to the state or funding agency.

(3) *Support and Assist.* State legislatures and state or external agencies should provide minimal regulatory functions with maximal support and assistance to local practitioners as they struggle with implementation of their locally developed TIP.

(4) *Invest in Risk.* External funding agencies, or states, should view funding of local districts for TIPs as risk capital or as an investment in the future of American education. Investment without interference will result in valuable outcomes.

(5) *Seize the Opportunity.* Local practitioners should view TIP funding as a golden opportunity to get control of their profession and empirically to elevate instructional practice to new heights of excellence. Achievement will improve the public image of the public schools, as well.

In conclusion, local districts interested in resolving problems of poor instruction, inadequate compensation, and financial limitations must move ahead with teacher incentive programs to reach their objectives. Given much-deserved support and nonintervention from external political or funding bodies, workable solutions to the problems of attaining educational excellence can be reached. Unless local initiative and flexibility are fostered, lofty political goals for teacher incentive programs will be suffocated by cumbersome political baggage and the opportunity to improve public schools with career ladder incentive programs may be lost forever.

REFERENCES

Cohen, Deborah. 1989. "In North Carolina, Pay Raise, But No Career Ladder," *Education Week,* 9(1):16.

Conley, Sharon, Samuel Bacharach, and Scott Bauer. 1989. "The School Work Environment and Teacher Career Dissatisfaction," *Educational Administration Quarterly.* 25(1):58–81.

Cornett, Lynn. 1991. "Trends and Issues: Incentive Programs for Teachers and Administrators," Chapter 15 in *Teacher Compensation and Motivation,* Larry E. Frase, ed., Lancaster, PA: Technomic Publishing Company, Inc.

Cornett, Lynn. 1988. *Is "Paying for Performance" Changing Schools?* Atlanta: Southern Regional Education Board Career Ladder Clearinghouse.

Downey, Carolyn. 1991. "Kyrene Career Development Ladder: A Case Study," Chapter 20 in *Teacher Compensation and Motivation,* Larry E. Frase, ed. Lancaster, PA: Technomic Publishing Company, Inc.

Frase, Larry. 1989. "Effects of Teacher Rewards on Opportunities for Recognition and Job-Enrichment," *Journal of Educational Research,* 83(1):52–57.

Frase, Larry, Robert Hetzel, and Deborah Inman. 1987. "Is There a Sound Rationale Behind the Merit Pay Craze?" *Teacher Education Quarterly,* 14(2):90–101.

Frase, Larry and Deborah Inman. Unpublished. *Teacher Incentive Program Successes without External Funding.* San Diego State University.

Hatry, H. and J. Griener. 1986. *Issues and Case Studies in Teacher Incentive Plans.* Washington, D.C.: Urban Institute Press.

Hegebush, William and Scott Norton. 1988. "Incentive Pay Programs: Does Participation Change Viewpoints?" *The Clearing House,* 62:149–151.

Mathis, Nancy. 1988. "Florida's Incentive Pay Experiment Dies Quietly," *Education Week,* June 22, p. 11.

Megel, Carl (n.d.). *Merit Rating: Educationally Unsound and Why.* Washington, D.C.: American Federation of Teachers, Publication #612.

Mitchell, D. and M. Peters. 1988. "A Stronger Profession through Appropriate Teacher Incentives," *Educational Leadership,* 46(3):74–78.

Murnane, Richard and David Cohen. 1986. "Merit Pay and the Evaluation Problem: Why Most Merit Pay Programs Fail and Few Survive," *The Harvard Education Review,* 56(1):1–17.

Olson, L. 1986. "Performance: New Round for and Old Debate," *Education Week,* 5(26):1.

Olson, Lynn. 1987. "Performance-Based Pay System for Teachers Are Being Re-Examined," *Education Week,* 6(29):1.

Olson, L. 1989. "In North Carolina, Career-Ladder Plan Nears a Crossroads," *Education Week,* 8(19):1–14.

Orlich, D. C. 1989. "Education Reforms: Mistakes, Misconceptions, Miscues," *Phi Delta Kappan,* 70(7):512–517.

Reinhold, R. 1987. "School Reform: 4 Years of Ferment and Mixed Results," *New York Times,* August 10, pp. A1 and A14.

1988. *Report Card on School Reform: The Teachers Speak.* Carnegie Foundation for the Advancement of Teaching. ERIC Documents No. ED 298 099.

Reyes, Pedro and Jean Madsen. "Organizational Incentives, Teacher Commitment, Morale, and Job Satisfaction: Is the Program Achieving Its Goals?" Paper presented at the American Educational Research Association, San Francisco, California, 1989.

Rivera, Manuel. "The Rochester Plan," Keynote presentation at the *Restructuring Conference, San Diego State University, San Diego, California, July 20, 1989.*

Spillane, R. 1991. "Pay-for-Performance in Fairfax County, Virginia," Chapter 17 in *Teacher Compensation and Motivation,* Larry Frase, ed., Lancaster, PA: Technomic Publishing Company, Inc.

Timar, T. and D. Kirp. 1989. "Education Reform in the 1980s: Lessons from the States," *Phi Delta Kappan,* 70(7):504–511.

PART III

THE RESEARCH BASE ON ALTERNATIVE COMPENSATION SYSTEMS

Can Performance Based Salary Programs Motivate Teachers? Insights from a Case Study

RICHARD L. SCHWAB – *Drake University*
EDWARD F. IWANICKI – *University of Connecticut*

MERIT pay. These two words evoke strong emotional reactions from teachers, taxpayers, school administrators, school board members, and even the Secretary of Education. Opponents contend that linking pay to classroom performance causes dissension, low morale, and destruction of collegial relationships, leading to high levels of job stress. Proponents argue that rewarding excellence in the classroom reinforces those who exert extra effort on the job and offers incentives for others to improve their performance. Merit pay, therefore, becomes a motivator for teachers.

Despite the attention given to merit pay programs by national reports, the professional literature, legislators, and the public at large, little systematic research has been conducted that supports or refutes the claims of either side. Most arguments have been based on philosophical beliefs, personal opinion, or experiences of other occupations that have attempted to use such an approach (see for example, Bacharach and Conley, 1987; Hatry and Grenier, 1985; Silk 1984–85). This work shares the results of a year-long evaluation study of a merit pay program for teachers. While the study addressed a broad range of issues relating to merit pay, this chapter focuses on administrators' and teachers' perceptions of success of the program in motivating teachers.

BACKGROUND OF STUDY

In 1984 a New Hampshire school district instituted a Performance Based Salary Program (PBSP) to accomplish the following goals:

This study was partially funded by USDOE funds from the Secretary Discretionary Grant Fund through the New Hampshire School Boards Association. The opinions expressed are solely those of the authors.

Develop a five-year plan for making the professional salary program competitive with like positions of responsibility and educational requirements in the private sector. Develop a Master Teacher Program. Maintain a program of attracting the best and most qualified staff by providing an interesting and motivational climate and providing recognition for excellence through awards, articles, money or other appropriate means. Develop and implement strong and effective standards of excellence for teacher performance including an effective evaluation system which assures the public we are meeting those standards. (Paul, 1985)

The Performance Based Salary Program (PBSP) was negotiated with the local teachers' association, which was not aligned with any state or national association. The contract contained several important components as summarized below:

(1) The contract covered the years 1984–1989. The teachers' work year was extended from 186 days to 192 days over the five years (180 contract days with students).

(2) Teachers were given salary increases of 15 percent for year one, 13 percent for year two, 11 percent for year three, and 10 percent for years four and five. This money was distributed partially as an increment and partially on the basis of performance. The amount distributed by performance level increased as the contract matured.

(3) The contract stipulated that a new teacher evaluation plan had to be designed by a committee of teachers and administrators to determine the performance ratings of teachers. This committee was called the Performance Criteria/Evaluation Process Committee (PC/EPC). It was comprised of seven members recommended by the teachers association and five recommended by the superintendent of schools. This ongoing committee was also charged with revising the evaluation procedures as necessary over the duration of the contract.

STUDY DESIGN

This chapter addresses the question — *What effect has the PBSP had upon the quality of the work environment for teachers?* The study was conducted in two phases. First, all teachers ($N = 165$) and administrators ($N = 24$) in the school district completed a comprehensive survey developed in cooperation with the Performance Center/Evaluation Process Committee. This survey was completed at the end of the second year that the plan was in place. It included the following sections:

(1) Background information—This section requested background information about the respondents.

(2) Performance levels—This part asked teachers to indicate what their performance levels were and if the teachers thought they were accurate.

(3) Attitudes toward Teaching—This section identified reasons why teachers entered and remained in the profession.

(4) Attitudes toward PBSP—This section assessed teachers' and administrators' general attitudes toward the PBSP.

(5) Impact of PBSP—This part assessed teachers' and administrators' attitudes toward specific aspects of the PBSP as implemented at the time of the study.

(6) Attitudes toward Teacher Evaluation—This section contained part of the *Teacher Evaluation Needs Identification Survey* (Iwanicki, 1983), a valid and reliable instrument to measure teachers' attitudes toward the quality of the teacher evaluation process.

(7) Levels of Teacher Burnout—This section contained *The Maslach Burnout Inventory: Educators' Edition,* a valid and reliable instrument to measure perceived levels of job burnout (Maslach, Jackson, and Schwab, 1986).

(8) Job Satisfaction—This section contained the *Teacher Job Satisfaction Questionnaire* (Lester, 1985), a valid and reliable instrument to measure levels of job satisfaction in nine areas.

Responses to the survey were analyzed for the total group and by grade level taught (elementary, middle, high school), years in teaching (1–5, 6–10, 11–15, and 16 or more years), and age (20–29, 30–39, 40–49, and 50 and over). Responses were also examined by performance ratings that teachers received in the end-of-year summative evaluation. Teachers were awarded points based on the summative criteria and then placed into one of seven performance levels. Teachers who did not receive enough points to receive a merit increment received only a percentage raise. A critical aspect of this study was to confirm whether the teachers' self-reported performance levels were valid. The self-reported levels were considered valid because they compared favorably to the distribution of actual ratings received by the teachers.

The seven performance levels combined into categories of levels 1–3 (lower third), level 4 (middle third) and levels 5–7 (upper third) for purposes of analysis in this study.

The second phase of the study consisted of follow-up interviews in November of the third year of the plan with randomly selected teachers ($n = 18$), administrators ($n = 9$), and school board members ($n = 5$). Those interviewed were asked to respond to open-ended questions about the program's effect on aspects of morale, the quality of education in the district, and personal and professional development.

The data collected in this study were analyzed using quantitative and qualitative methodologies. Quantitative analyses of the survey results included the use of chi-square and one-way analysis of variance with Tukey HSD post hoc tests. Interview data were content-analyzed by both authors.

SURVEY RESULTS

Background Information

Table 1 summarizes background information for teachers and administrators. From Table 1 it is evident that the typical teacher is female, aged 37, with a total of eleven years experience in education, and the highest degree held is a bachelors. The typical administrator is male, aged 44, with a total of nineteen years experience in education, and the highest degree held is a masters. It is important to note that statistical comparisons of teacher and adminstrator responses to items included in the survey were not conducted due to the substantial difference between numbers of teachers and administrators who responded. Differences in perceptions between these two groups are discussed as trends in subsequent sections of this paper.

Teachers' Self-Reported Performance Ratings

One of the more important aspects of the PBSP is the performance level rating that teachers receive. Teachers are awarded merit based upon the number of merit points they receive in the spring summative conference. There are seven levels of performance. The amount of merit money received is determined by dividing the money in the merit

Table 1. Background information for the teacher and administrator samples.*

	Teachers (**N = 165)	Administrators (**N = 24)
Sex		
Male	23%	71%
Female	77%	29%
Age		
Mean	37	44
Years of Experience		
Mean	11	19
Grade Level Assigned		
Elementary	42%	22%
Junior High	26%	13%
High School	32%	52%
More than 1 level	—	13%
Highest Degree Held		
Bachelor's	55%	—
Master's	43%	71%
CAGS	1%	8%
Ph.D.	1%	21%

*Figures are rounded to the nearest whole number or percent.

**Please note that for some analyses there was slight variation in sample size due to some incomplete data.

pool by the total number of merit points awarded to teachers in the district. Then each teacher multiplies the rating they received by the dollars set for each point. As one would expect, teachers consider the rating itself to be as important as the money received for that rating. In addition to providing their performance ratings, teachers were asked to indicate (a) the extent to which the rating was consistent with expectations and (b) whether the rating was accurate. From Table 2, it is evident that only about 7 percent of the teachers indicated they received a performance rating that was higher than expected. Depending upon the year, 48–52 percent of the teachers received the performance rating expected, and 41–45 percent of the teachers received performance ratings that were lower than expected. Rating expectations did not differ significantly with respect to grade level, age, or years of teaching experience. Rating expectations did differ significantly with respect to actual performance category. Teachers in the lower performance category (L1–L3) tended to get lower ratings than expected, while teachers in

Table 2. Teachers' performance rating expectations.

	Percent Responding That Their Rating Was		
	Higher Than Expected	About What Was Expected	Lower Than Expected
Spring 1985 rating	6.9	48.1	45.0
Spring 1986 rating	6.4	52.0	41.5
Teachers' Perceptions of the Accuracy of Their Performance Ratings			
	Percent Responding That Their Rating Was		
	Accurate	Not Accurate	
Spring 1985 rating	40.8	59.2	
Spring 1986 rating	39.6	60.4	

the higher performance categories (L4) and L5–L7) tended to receive the rating they expected.

Turning to the second half of Table 2, about 40 percent of the teachers perceived their first and second year performance ratings to be accurate. More teachers in the higher performance categories perceived their ratings as accurate than did those in the lower performance categories. The proportion of teachers who viewed either their first or second year performance ratings as accurate did not differ significantly with respect to grade level, age, or years of teaching experience.

Orientation and Attitudes toward Teaching

Teachers were asked a series of questions focusing on their orientations and attitudes toward teaching. The first of these questions focused on the importance they placed on factors affecting their decision to become a teacher. From the mean responses in Table 3, it is evident that the opportunity to influence children (1.26) and the opportunity to develop professionally (1.49) were very important. Some importance was placed on the opportunity to advance the teaching profession, as well as on a work schedule that can permit travel, family activities, etc. Less importance was placed on salary (2.60) as these teachers made their decision to enter the profession. Comparisons of teacher responses grouped by either grade or performance levels indicated that there were not significant differences in the importance placed on these factors. When grouped by age, it was evident that the work schedule of the teaching profession was a significantly more important factor for teachers in their forties and fifties than for those in their twenties and thirties ($F = 5.51$; $df = 3166$; $p < .01$). While not significant, this trend was also evident when examining the means for teachers grouped by level of experience. Older, more experienced teachers tended to place more importance on the work schedule of teaching when they entered the profession.

When asked what the likelihood was that they would still be in teaching five years from now, responses of teachers were distributed as follows: Strong 40 percent, Good 28.6 percent, Fair 13.7 percent, Doubtful 14.9 percent. For the remaining 2.9 percent of the teachers this item was not applicable due to retirement plans. Thus, about 70 percent of the teachers indicated there was a good to strong chance that they would remain in teaching. When grouped by either grade, experience, or performance levels, there were no differences in the responses of

Table 3. Rank order of factors that influenced teachers to enter the profession.

Rank	Factor Response	Response	Level of Importance
1	Opportunity to influence children	1.26	Very Important
2	Opportunity to develop as a professional	1.49	Very Important
3	Opportunity to advance the teaching profession	1.90	Somewhat Important
4	A work schedule which can permit travel, family activities, etc.	2.03	Somewhat Important
5	Salary	2.60	Of Little Importance

Means are based on a four-point scale, where 1 = Very important, 2 = Somewhat important, 3 = Of little importance, 4 = Not important.

teachers. There was a tendency for those teachers in their twenties who had not invested many years in the profession, as well as those in their fifties who were approaching retirement, to be most skeptical about still being in the teaching profession five years from now.

Table 4 provides an indication of how important teachers believe various factors are in influencing their decision to remain in the teaching profession. All factors were perceived as important. Respect of students, degree of intellectual challenge, and positive relations with peers were perceived as very important in influencing their decision. Factors that were perceived as somewhat important in influencing their decision include positive relations with administrators, adequate instructional materials and resources, support of parents and the community, and salary. It is interesting that teachers perceived salary as being of little importance (mean = 2.60) in influencing their decision to enter teaching, but salary is of some importance (mean = 1.85) in affecting their later decision to remain in teaching. When grouped by either grade, experience, or performance levels, there were no differences with respect to the importance teachers placed on the various factors influencing their decision to remain in teaching. One significant difference emerged when teachers were grouped by age, such that teachers in their fifties found positive relations with peers to be of greater

Table 4. Rank order of factors influencing teachers to remain in the profession.

Rank	Factor Response	Response	Level of Importance
1	Respect of students	1.39	Very Important
2	Degree of intellectual challenge	1.44	Very Important
3	Positive relations with peer teachers	1.48	Very Important
4 tied	Positive relations with administrators	1.56	Somewhat Important
4	Adequate instructional materials and resources	1.56	Somewhat Important
5	Support of parents and the community	1.80	Somewhat Important
6	Salary	1.85	Somewhat Important

Means are based on a four-point scale, where 1 = Very important, 2 = Somewhat important, 3 = Of some importance, 4 = Not important.

Table 5. Teacher and administrator attitudes toward the performance based salary program.

	Percent Responding as Follows:				
	Positive (1)	Mixed (2)	Skeptical (3)	Negative (4)	Overall Mean
Before PBSP was introduced					
Teachers	19.0	32.5	32.5	16.0	2.45
Administrators	25.0	41.7	33.3	—	2.08
When the program was established in 1984					
Teachers	8.3	40.4	32.1	19.2	2.62
Administrators	26.1	52.2	17.4	4.3	2.00
Now in 1986, after the program has been in operation for 2 yrs.					
Teachers	10.3	39.7	17.8	32.2	2.72
Administrators	50.0	50.0	—	—	1.50

Means are based on a four-point scale, where 1 = Positive, 2 = Mixed, 3 = Skeptical, 4 = Negative.

importance than teachers in their forties ($F = 4.75$; $df = 3165$); $p < .01$). A further analysis was conducted to determine whether there was any difference in the importance placed on the factors in Table 4 between teachers who planned to remain in teaching (i.e., good to strong chance) and those who did not (i.e., fair to doubtful likelihood). No significant differences were evident between these two groups.

Attitudes toward the Performance Based Salary Program

Teachers' and administrators' attitudes toward the Performance Based Salary Program (PBSP) are presented in Table 5. These results indicate that while teachers had mixed feelings about PBSP before it was implemented, they grew more skeptical of the process as it was implemented over the past two years. By the end of the second year there was a 50–50 split between those teachers with positive or mixed feelings versus those with skeptical or negative views toward PBSP. For administrators, on the other hand, initial mixed feelings have led to more positive attitudes toward PBSP. All administrators viewed PBSP with positive or at least mixed feelings. Teachers' attitudes over time with respect to PBSP did not differ significantly when they were grouped by either age or level of teaching experience. The only grade level difference was for junior high school teachers who exhibited a significantly more negative attitude toward PBSP than did their colleagues at the high school level ($F = 3.75$; $df = 2163$; $p < .05$). With respect to performance level, teachers in the top performance categories (L5–L7) exhibited significantly more positive attitudes toward PBSP at the end of the second year than did teachers in the middle (L4) or lower (L1–L3) performance categories. The attitudes of teachers toward PBSP over time are summarized by performance level in Table 6.

Impact of the Performance Based Salary Program

In addition to examining general attitudes toward PBSP, teachers and administrators were asked to indicate what they believed had been the impact of PBSP on specific aspects of the school program Teachers' and administrators' responses are summarized in Table 7. Trends in the results provided in Table 7 can be derived through two approaches. The first is to eliminate the "about the same" response and then compare the percent of respondents who have perceived things as improving versus those who have not. For example, 58 percent of the teachers believed things were about the same with respect to the involvement of the principal in their classrooms. Putting this group aside, we see also that 31 percent of the teachers saw an improvement in this area, will 11 percent believe conditions have deteriorated. By taking the difference between

Table 6. Teacher attitudes toward the performance based salary program over time by performance level.

	Overall Means by Performance Level				
	Mean	L1–L3	L4	L5–L7	F-ratio
Before PBSP was introduced	2.46	2.43	2.51	2.45	n/s
When the program was established in 1984	2.62	2.58	2.63	2.65	n/s
In 1986, after the program had been in operation for 2 yrs.	2.74	2.98	2.81	2.45	4.50 $df = 2,165$ $p < .05$

Means are based on a four-point scale, where 1 = Positive, 2 = Mixed, 3 = Skeptical, 4 = Negative.

Table 7. Teacher and administrator perceptions of the impact of the performance based salary program on various aspects of the school program.

	Percent Responding This Aspect			
	Has Improved	Is about the Same	Has Deteriorated	Overall Mean
a) Quality of communications between principals and teachers				
Teachers	31.7	33.5	34.7	3.1
Administrators	79.2	8.3	12.5	2.3
b) Involvement of the principal in your classroom				
Teachers	31.3	57.7	11.0	2.8
Administrators	77.3	18.2	4.5	2.3
c) Quality of staff development activities				
Teachers	28.1	64.1	7.8	2.8
Administrators	58.3	41.7	—	2.4
d) Quality of the teacher evaluation process				
Teachers	49.7	24.2	26.1	2.8
Administrators	95.8	4.2	—	2.0
e) Level of cooperation among teachers				
Teachers	18.0	45.5	36.5	3.4
Administrators	41.7	50.0	8.3	2.7
f) Level of trust between teachers and administration				
Teachers	10.1	27.4	62.5	3.8
Administrators	25.0	45.8	29.2	3.0

(continued)

Table 7 (continued).

g) Quality of instruction in your classroom				
Teachers	43.3	54.9	1.8	2.5
Administrators	68.6	31.3	—	2.3
h) Quality of education in the school district				
Teachers	35.4	57.8	6.8	2.7
Administrators	83.3	16.7	—	2.2
i) Level of financial support for education in the community				
Teachers	33.1	61.3	5.5	2.7
Administrators	58.3	37.5	4.2	2.5
j) Level of community confidence in the quality of teaching				
Teachers	19.3	77.6	3.1	2.9
Administrators	50.0	50.0	—	2.5

Means are based on a five-point scale, where 1 = Improved greatly, 2 = Improved, 3 = Are about the same, 4 = Deteriorated, 5 = Deteriorated greatly. The percents for the "improved" category were determined by combining those who selected responses 1 or 2. Likewise, percents for the "deteriorated" category were determined by combining those who selected responses 4 or 5.

these two percents, we arrive at a net difference of 20 percent in the direction of improvement. A second approach for identifying trends is to examine the group mean. A mean of less than 3.0 provides support for the trend toward improvement, while a mean greater than 3.0 indicates conditions have deteriorated. For example, in going back to the item dealing with the involvement of the principal in the teachers' classrooms, we see that the mean response for teachers is 2.8, which supports the trend toward improvement. In applying both approaches, we see they both support the trend that teachers perceive improvement with respect to the involvement of the principal in their classrooms as a result of PBSP.

In applying these two approaches, it is evident that principals perceived that PBSP has improved all aspects of the school program addressed in Table 7, except for the level of trust between teachers and administration. When applying both approaches for teachers, it appears that PBSP has led to improvements in the following areas:

- involvement of the principal in the classroom
- quality of staff development activities
- quality of the teacher evaluation process
- quality of instruction in the classroom
- quality of education in the school district
- level of financial support for education in the community
- level of community confidence in the quality of teaching

Areas where teachers believed conditions have deteriorated as a result of PBSP are as follows:

- quality of communications between principals and teachers
- level of cooperation among teachers
- level of trust between teachers and administrators

Meaningful significant differences in teachers' perceptions of the impact of PBSP on these aspects of the school program did not emerge when teachers were grouped by either age or level of experience. A strong trend emerged when teacher responses were examined by grade level. More specifically, junior high school teachers believed PBSP had a more negative impact on many aspects of the school program than did either elementary or high school teachers. Junior high school teachers differed significantly from high school teachers with respect to their perception of the impact of PBSP on the following aspects of the school program:

- quality of communications between principals and teachers
- involvement of the principal in the classroom
- level of trust between teachers and administration

Junior high school teachers differed significantly from elementary school teachers with respect to their perceptions of the impact of PBSP on these aspects of the school program:

- level of trust between teachers and administrators
- level of financial support for education in the community

For those aspects where significant differences were evident, the perceptions of the junior high school teachers were more negative than those of either the elementary or high school comparison groups. It is important to note that the junior high school has utilized a team teaching approach to instruction for several years. It is possible that a program that primarily rewards individual effort is less appropriate for schools where team teaching is practiced.

As expected, there were also significant differences with respect to the impact of PBSP when teachers were grouped by performance level. Teachers in the higher performance category (L5–L7) believed that PBSP had a more positive impact on those aspects of the school program listed below than did teachers in the lower performance category (L1–L3).

- quality of communications between principals and teachers
- quality of the teacher evaluation process
- quality of education in the school district
- level of financial support for education in the community

Attitudes toward Teacher Evaluation

Teacher and administrator attitudes toward the teacher evaluation process in the district were assessed using part of the *Teacher Evaluation Needs Identification Survey* (Iwanicki, 1983). More specifically, teachers and administrators responded to a series of items that focused on the following aspects of the teacher evaluation process: 1) performance responsibilities, 2) accountability relationships, 3) evaluation for personal improvement, and 4) feedback. Descriptions of each of these aspects of the teacher evaluation process are included in Table 8. Overall means of the responses for each aspect were calculated for teachers and administrators and are presented in Table 8. From

Table 8. Teachers' and administrators' attitudes toward aspects of the teacher evaluation process.

Aspects of the Teacher Evaluation Process	Mean Response	Is This Aspect Fostered?
1. Accountability Relationships: The extent to which the accountability relationship of each position is defined clearly, such that teachers know who will be evaluating their performance and understand the means by which they will be evaluated.		
Teachers	1.32	yes
Administrators	1.44	yes
2. Feedback: The extent to which the teacher evaluation program makes ample provision for clear, personalized, and constructive feedback.		
Teachers	1.38	yes
Administrators	1.27	yes
3. Performance Responsibilities: The extent to which general responsibilities and specific tasks of a teacher's position are defined comprehensively and are used as a frame of reference for evaluation.		
Teachers	1.86	undecided
Administrators	1.42	yes
4. Evaluation for Personal Improvement: The extent to which the teacher evaluation program takes a constructive approach in considering the personal needs of the teachers as well as the specific nature of the learning environment in which the teacher is involved.		
Teachers	1.96	undecided
Administrators	1.67	undecided

Means are based on a three-point scale, where 1 = agree (yes), 2 = undecided, 3 = disagree (no).

Table 8 it is evident that teachers 1) believed the evaluation process had been clearly defined and communicated to staff, 2) knew who they were accountable to for the purposes of evaluation, and 3) felt the evaluation process provided clear and constructive feedback. Teachers' responses indicated the evaluation process could be improved by 1) specifying more clearly the general responsibilities and specific tasks that serve as the basis for evaluation and 2) placing more emphasis on personal and professional improvement.

With respect to feedback, junior and senior high school teachers differed significantly from elementary school teachers. Elementary school teachers believed less emphasis was placed on the feedback aspect of the teacher evaluation process than did teachers at the higher grade levels. Also, less experienced teachers (one to five years experience) perceived the feedback aspect to be fostered more than did experienced teachers (those with six to ten or sixteen or more years experience). With respect to performance responsibilities, high school teachers perceived this aspect of the teacher evaluation process to be fostered significantly more than did elementary school teachers. Finally, teachers in the upper performance category (L5–L7) believed significantly more emphasis was placed on the personal improvement aspect of the teacher evaluation process than did teachers in the lower performance category (L1–L3).

Teachers' and administrators' attitudes toward including other types of information in the teacher evaluation process are summarized in Table 9. There is good support for peer evaluation and sparse support for using student performance on standardized tests as part of the teacher evaluation process. While only moderate overall support was provided for including student feedback in the evaluation process, this practice received significantly stronger support among high school teachers ($F = 4.11$; $df = 165$; $p < .05$). Attitudes toward including

Table 9. Teachers' and administrators' attitudes toward including additional information in the teacher evaluation process.

	Percent Responding as Follows		
	Support Strongly	Support with Some Reservation	Do Not Support
Evaluation by peer teachers			
Teachers	18.9	50.3	30.9
Administrators	25.0	50.0	25.0
Student Feedback			
Teachers	11.4	47.4	41.1
Administrators	8.3	50.0	41.7
Student performance on standardized achievement tests			
Teachers	6.9	31.0	62.1
Administrators	16.7	33.3	50.0

Table 10. Levels of perceived burnout.*

Factors	Teachers under PBSP Mean (N = 165)	N. H. Teachers Mean (N = 339)	National Teachers Mean (N = 4,125)
Emotional Exhaustion	21.91	22.19	21.25
**Range	average	average	average
Depersonalization	5.36	6.73	11.00
**Range	low	low	average
Personal Accomplishment	40.46	38.06	33.54
**Range	low	low	average

*The scores for the New Hampshire sample were taken from Schwab, Jackson, and Schuler (1986) and the national scores were taken from Maslach, Jackson, and Schwab (1986).
**Range cutoff scores for teachers are reported in Maslach, Jackson, and Schwab (1986).

these types of information in the teacher evaluation process did not differ when teachers were grouped by either age, experience, or performance level.

Perceived Levels of Job Burnout

Levels of teacher burnout were measured by using the *Maslach Burnout Inventory: Educators' Edition* (Maslach, Jackson, and Schwab, 1986). This inventory is designed to measure perceived levels of job burnout for educational professionals. The inventory has three subscales that measure different aspects of job burnout: 1) emotional exhaustion and fatigue, 2) attitutes toward students, and 3) feelings of accomplishment on the job. A person who is experiencing job burnout will have higher feelings of emotional exhaustion and fatigue, more negative feelings toward students, and a low sense of accomplishment from their job. This instrument was utilized to examine if teachers experienced abnormal feelings of burnout while working under PBSP.

Table 10 contains the mean scores on the *Maslach Burnout Inventory: Educators' Edition* for teachers who worked under the PBSP, a random sample of teachers from across the state of New Hampshire, and a national sample of teachers. These results indicate that teachers in the district in this study generally fall into the average category in the area of emotional exhaustion and fatigue when compared to the national teacher sample. On the other two subscales, teachers fall into the low category of burnout when compared to the national sample. This would indicate that teachers who have worked under the PBSP tend to have more positive attitudes toward students and have higher feelings of accomplishment from their job than do teachers in the national sample. As indicated in Table 10, these teachers' scores are similar to those of other New Hampshire teachers (Schwab, Jackson, and Schuler, 1986). Both groups scored in the average range on emotional exhaustion and in the low range for depersonalization and personal accomplishment. No significant differences were found on these subscales when teacher responses were examined by either grade level, age, years of experience, or performance level.

Teacher Job Satisfaction

Teacher job satisfaction was assessed using the *Teacher Job Satisfaction Questionnaire* (Lester, 1985). The *Teacher Job Satisfaction Questionnaire* (TJSQ) assesses teachers' attitudes toward aspects of teaching associated with the job itself as well as those associated with the conditions of the job. Aspects of the TJSQ associated with teaching itself include responsibility, the work itself, recognition, and advancement. Aspects of the TJSQ associated with the conditions of teaching include colleagues, security, supervision, working conditions, and pay. Each of these nine aspects of the TJSQ is described in Table 11.

It is appropriate to apply the motivation theory of Herzberg (1966) when reviewing the results of the TJSQ. According to Herzberg, separate factors in the work environment account for teacher satisfaction and teacher dissatisfaction. Those factors that account for teacher satisfaction are those associated with the job itself, while those which account for teacher dissatisfaction are associated with the conditions of the job. Teacher motivation is enhanced to the extent that the work environment maximizes the satisfiers (i.e., those factors associated with the work) and minimizes dissatisfiers (i.e., those factors associated with the conditions of work).

From the TJSQ means presented in Table 11, it is evident that teachers tended to be satisfied with respect to the factors of responsibility and the work itself, but were satisfied less with respect to recognition and advancement. Also, teachers were not dissatisfied with respect to the factors of colleagues and job security, but were dissatisfied more with supervision and working conditions. Pay was clearly a source of

Table 11. Teachers' levels of satisfaction with respect to various aspects of teaching.

Aspects of Teaching	Mean Response	Are Teachers Satisfied?
*1. Responsibility: Teachers are afforded the opportunity to be accountable for their own work and to take part in policy or decision-making activities.	4.36	Yes
*2. Work Itself: Teachers are free to institute innovative practices, to utilize their skills and abilities in designing their work, to experiment, and to influence or control what goes on in the job.	3.84	Yes
3. Colleagues: The teaching environment is characterized by positive work group relations as well as social interactions among fellow teachers.	3.81	Yes
4. Security: School district policies regarding tenure, seniority, layoffs, pension, retirement, and dismissal provide teachers with a sense of job stability.	3.64	Yes
5. Supervision: The teachers' immediate supervisors are competent and fair, while maintaining positive interpersonal relations during the supervisory process.	3.24	Neutral
*6. Recognition: The reward system which pervades the teaching environment is characterized by the attention, appreciation, prestige, and esteem of supervisors, colleagues, students, and parents.	2.91	Neutral
7. Working Conditions: Teachers pursue their work in comfortable physical surroundings where administrative policies are defined and communicated clearly.	2.85	Neutral
*8. Advancement: School district policies provide teachers the opportunity for improved status, advancement, or promotion in their profession.	2.58	Neutral
9. Pay: Teachers are compensated adequately through a process which recognizes their achievements and contributions.	1.95	No

Means are based on a five-point scale, where 1 = Strongly disagree, 2 = Disagree, 3 = Neutral, 4 = Agree, 5 = Strongly agree. Also, note that aspects of teaching marked with an asterisk (*) are those associated with teachers' work, while the remaining aspects are associated with the conditions of the teachers' work.

dissatisfaction. To facilitate the interpretation of these results, it is appropriate to view a mean in the neutral range as indicative of a moderate level of satisfaction. In summary, these results indicate that teachers exhibited a moderate to respectable level of satisfaction for most aspects of teaching associated with the work itself as well as the conditions of work. The only aspect that emerged as a clear dissatisfier was pay.

Teachers did not differ in their level of satisfaction when grouped by either age or level of experience. Significant differences did emerge when teachers were grouped by grade level. Several significant differences were evident between elementary and high school teachers. High school teachers were more satisfied than elementary teachers with respect to supervision, advancement, and pay. Elementary teachers were more satisfied than high school teachers with respect to the work itself and colleagues. Other significant grade level differences were evident between junior and senior high school teachers. High school teachers were more satisfied than junior high school teachers with respect to working conditions and pay.

Significant differences were evident when teachers were grouped by performance level. Teachers in the higher performance category (L5–L7) were more satisfied than teachers in the lower performance category (L1–L3) with respect to the work itself, security, and recognition.

The Bottom Line

The final question in the survey was—Knowing what you know today about the Performance Based Salary Program, what would your recommendations be to other teachers considering such a program? Teachers responded as follows:

	Percent	N
Recommend enthusiastically	5.1	9
Recommend with caution	46.6	82
Do not recommend the program	48.3	85

From this response it is appropriate to conclude that teacher support for PBSP was marginal at best. Support for PBSP did not differ significantly when teachers were grouped by either grade level, age, years of teaching experience, or even by performance level. In summary, teachers were split fairly evenly on this issue.

INTERVIEWS

The second phase of data gathering consisted of follow-up interviews with randomly selected teachers, administrators, and board members. The final sample of interviewees included eighteen teachers from different schools who have been in the program since it began; nine administrators including principals, assistant principals, department chairpeople from different schools, and representatives from the central office; and five school board members. All three groups were asked to respond to the following questions:

(1) How has PBSP affected education in this district?
(2) How has PBSP affected your role as a teacher/school board member/administrator?
(3) What changes would you make in the PBSP?
(4) Are there any other issues that you want to share with us regarding PBSP?

Content analyses of the interviews identified several common areas where education has been influenced by the PBSP. Because responses tended to be overlapping from question to question, responses to each question are integrated with respect to the categories below.

Quality of Instruction

Board members and administrators were in agreement that the quality of education has improved in the district. Both of these groups attribute this change to holding teachers more accountable for their teaching practices. This has occurred because the principal is in classrooms more often and is taking responsibility for evaluation more seriously. The major changes that have taken place according to administrators were improved planning and instruction, more time on task for students, and more discussion by teachers about what effective instruction is all about. Administrators felt that marginal and weaker teachers have benefited the most from the program.

Teachers' feelings about the effect of PBSP were mixed. Teachers were split between those that felt the program improved instruction in the district and those who felt that it had either no effect or a negative effect. Those who viewed the program positively felt that marginal teachers are forced to pay more attention to what they are doing and are less likely to "write students off." Teachers who felt that the program had no effect or a negative effect felt instruction was hurt because creativity was stifled, more time had to be spent on documenting what they were doing that could have been spent on teaching related activities, and classes were interrupted by evaluation. This group of teachers also felt that the plan had no real effect on instruction because evaluations were only conducted three times a year. They felt many teachers only put on a show for those evaluations and returned to old habits for the rest of the time.

Morale

Overwhelmingly, teachers felt that this program has hurt morale and has distressed teachers a great deal. This was raised as a major concern by all but three of the teachers interviewed. Over half of the teachers interviewed mentioned that they had done well under the plan but questioned whether it was worth it. The following quotes from three different teachers describe these feelings.

> One of the reasons that I originally selected this school and district was because of the family atmosphere that is gone. Instead there is dissatisfaction, tension, mistrust that wasn't there before. I am one of the higher ranked teachers and I feel the joy is gone. I have thought about leaving.

> The effect on the district has been negative; self esteem of teachers has fallen. The only way to survive is to work together and say we will teach in spite of the games they play.

> Right now I am planning to leave, and my scores have been good. There is an attitude of "Who cares if you leave, we can always replace you with someone at the bottom of the scale."

Almost all teachers and some administrators indicated that several of the best teachers in the district have left because of the effect of PBSP on morale. One administrator summarized these feelings with the following statement. "We need to study the turnover issue very carefully; if all we are doing is upgrading mediocrity at the expense of losing our best teachers, then we are going down a self-destruction path." Some administrators disagreed with the contention that many good teachers havc left because of the plan. They believed these teachers have left for personal reasons (i.e., retirement, job transfer of spouse).

Evaluation Plan

All three groups agreed that the strongest point of PBSP was that the teacher evaluation component was improving constantly and that teachers have had a great deal of input into the changes that are made. Most agreed that the plan was as good as or better than any other teacher evaluation plan of which they were aware. The majority of teachers and administrators felt the improvements that occurred during PBSP came about as a result of improved evaluation, not because of the link between performance and financial remuneration. A quote from one administrator summarizes these feelings: "If we [administrators] had done our job evaluating teachers in the first place, we would not have to go through all of this now."

The most frequent concern expressed by teachers was not with the plan but with the competence of the evaluators. About half of those interviewed felt that the evaluators did not have the proper training or expertise to conduct evaluations. Many of these teachers felt that the evaluation plan was ineffective because incompetent evaluators focused only on trivial items that had no effect on student learning. Teachers indicated that administrators did this in order to classify teachers into predetermined categories. Several teachers indicated that evaluations were not fairly administered and that school politics had a major influence on who got rewarded. One are where teachers, administrators, and board members agreed was that more effort is needed to make evaluations more consistent across the district.

Communication

Communication between administrators and teachers has changed since the beginning of the program. All agreed that communication is more formalized now. Some teachers felt this has been detrimental because teachers are less likely to go to administrators when they need help. Other teachers and administrators felt that this formalized role has not hurt because teachers are more likely to work with colleagues to solve problems. School board members felt that communication has improved as a result of the program, since they are now more aware of what is going on in schools.

Staff Development

A significant amount of time has been added to the school calendar for staff development. Board members indicated that they are now more willing to fund staff development. Administrators strongly felt that staff development improved greatly under this program. Teachers did not agree fully. While most indicated that more opportunities are now available, they also expressed concern that more planning needs to go into designing and offering staff development programs that meet their particular needs. Several teachers expressed the concern that some of the extra days that have been added to the calendar for staff development have been virtually a waste of time.

Money

Teachers and administrators indicated overwhelmingly that the money offered under the plan is not sufficient to motivate teachers. This appears to be the result of two phenomena. First, when teachers agreed to the five-year contract, they also agreed to work more days. Many teachers felt that the percent increases the contract provided them each year were inflated because they were working more days than they did under the original contract. The other event that occurred was that surrounding districts gave their teachers similar, if not greater, percentage increases as they negotiated their teachers' contracts. Many teachers indicated that staff in these surrounding communities received similar salary increases without extending the school year and without having to put up with all of the additional stress caused by PBSP. Board members also expressed concern that their plan had become less attractive because other districts provided similar increases without additional responsibility or careful evaluation.

Many teachers also indicated that the extra money received for each increase in level was not worth all one had to do to achieve it. Several teachers indicated that it was much less stressful and more financially rewarding to have a second job and not have to worry about advancing with respect to performance levels.

Effect on Role

Administrators seemed to be affected most in the way their roles changed. They indicated that they were in classrooms more, took evaluation more seriously, and felt relationships with staff were more formalized. One concern expressed by some administrators was that they did not feel they were able to provide the supervisory help that they should because relationships with teachers had become too formalized.

Teachers felt that this plan had not changed their roles, with the exception that some felt they spent more time letting administrators know what they were doing. Board members did not feel that their roles had changed because of the plan.

Community Support

When planning for this program, board members believed that if they were to give teachers the salary increases they deserved, then they would have to provide concrete evidence that the performance of teachers had improved. Board members now felt that the community viewed the district more favorably and was willing to continue to provide appropriate levels of financial support for schools because of PBSP.

DISCUSSION

There is no question that the generalizability of the findings reported in this chapter are limited because of the single district sample and the unique nature of the collective bargaining arrangement that existed in this district. However, the findings do identify many critical issues that need to be resolved before a pay-for-performance program can become a motivator for teachers. The findings also identify issues that need to be addressed through future research.

School board members, administrators, and teachers differ in their perceptions of the success of PBSP. Administrators and school board members believe it contributed to teachers' professional growth as well as to improved student learning. Some teachers do not share these positive perceptions of the program's impact. Teachers who have received average or below average performance ratings are skeptical of the program. Even teachers who have received above average performance ratings have mixed feelings toward the program.

Given the focus of this paper, it is important to examine the positive and negative aspects of PBSP from the teachers' perspective. It is clear that teachers believe that PBSP has had some positive impact. The survey results show that teachers believe that PBSP has led to improvements in the following areas:

- involvement of the principal in the classroom
- quality of staff development activities
- quality of the teacher evaluation process
- quality of instruction in the classroom
- quality of education in the school district
- level of financial support for education in the community
- level of community confidence in the quality of teaching

Further review of the survey results indicates that teachers' stress levels are low and teachers tend to be fairly satisfied with their jobs, except for the area of pay.

Given these beneficial aspects of PBSP, why is there a 50–50 split between those teachers who recommended continuation of the program and those who did not? Insights into this question are provided through a review of what teachers believe to be the negative aspects of PBSP. The survey results indicated that teachers believe conditions have deteriorated as a result of PBSP in the following areas:

- quality of communications between principals and teachers
- level of cooperation among teachers
- level of trust between teachers and administrators

Problems with Performance Appraisal

With respect to teacher evaluation, survey responses indicated that teachers were undecided as to whether their performance responsibilities were defined comprehensively and used as the frame of reference for evaluation. Many teachers were undecided as to whether the evaluation process was responsive to those professional improvement needs that are unique to a specific teacher's classroom situation. Also, the teachers interviewed believed that further training was needed for evaluators to improve the quality and consistency of the teacher evaluation process.

The teachers interviewed made it clear that the performance rating process is a major reason why many staff members disliked PBSP.

Many teachers did not object strongly to being evaluated, to being held accountable, or to being paid on the basis of a differentiated salary scale, but they did object strongly to being rated. These teachers believed they worked very hard to do their best all year only to find themselves rated as average or sometimes below average through an evaluation process that is always somewhat subjective. Teachers felt it was this aspect of PBSP that had the most detrimental effect on teacher morale.

These results reinforce the contention that a performance based salary program cannot be successful without a well-developed, adequately field-tested, and fairly administered teacher evaluation plan. Such plans must be refined over time with teacher involvement. The results of this study identified four critical areas of teacher evaluation. First, teachers noted that clear criteria had not been established for evaluating staff with respect to each performance area. For example, the first performance area is described as follows: "Provides motivation and stimulation for students." Teachers believe clear criteria should be determined to communicate what a teacher must do to receive a top rating on a scale of one to five in this performance area as well as in the other nine areas. This concern is valid. Since the goal of PBSP is excellence in teaching, clear criteria must be determined to guide the teacher evaluation and supervision processes. In developing these criteria, teacher involvement is critical. The works of Streifer and Iwanicki (1987), Streifer (1987), and Bacharach, Conley, and Shedd (1987) offer insights that can help address this issue.

Once clear criteria have been established for evaluating staff with respect to each of the performance areas, procedures need to be planned to guide teacher development with repsect to these criteria. To improve communication as to what constitutes excellence and how teachers can get there, staff could set objectives at the beginning of the year in areas where they wish to improve. Such objectives would indicate clearly the improvements that need to be made to achieve a higher performance rating. Progress toward these objectives would be monitored during the subsequent months. Then achievement of these objectives would be assessed in the spring before performance ratings are assigned. By clearly identifying the expected results early and agreeing to the criteria for achieving these outcomes, it would be possible for teachers to develop a better understanding of what constitutes superior performance and how it can be attained.

A second area of concern among teachers was the belief that quotas may exist, whereby a specific number or proportion of teachers must be classified at each of the seven summative performance levels. While teachers at level one are viewed as at least "reliable and respected members of the staff," staff felt that the typical teacher surpassed this expectation. They believed the performance of the typical teacher was more consistent with level four: "One's overall contribution consistently exceeds goals and expected performance of a fully qualified teacher." Furthermore, teachers believed that many of their colleagues were excellent teachers and deserved to be classified at performance levels 5–7. While staff believed the vast majority of teachers tended to fall at performance levels four to seven, the second year self-reported ratings of teachers wre distributed such that one-third of the staff fell into each of the following performance categories: L1–L3, L4, L5–L7. If the self-reported performance ratings were correct, then the teacher evaluation process places staff at lower levels than they believed were appropriate. This tendency to classify staff into lower performance levels than expected could account for some of the teacher morale problems associated with PBSP. This issue of how staff should be distributed across performance levels as a result of the evaluation process merits close consideration. If PBSP is to motivate staff and foster excellence, then one would expect to see a skewed distribution of performance ratings with the majority of staff falling toward the upper end of the performance continuum.

Another concern raised regarding the teacher evaluation process was the one of administrator bias and the need for further administrator training in the area of teacher evaluation. It is not unusual for some teachers to raise this concern. If you believe you are being evaluated through a process where the criteria are not clear and are receiving a performance rating lower than you expected, one conclusion is that your evaluator is biased, poorly trained, or both. This problem will diminish somewhat as the criteria for evaluation are clarified and the issue of how performance ratings should be distributed is resolved. Even after this is done, teacher evaluation outcomes are always suspect when they are conducted by administrators, directors, and/or department heads. For this reason, consideration should be given to involving peer teachers in the evaluation process. Survey responses indicated that teachers and administrators are receptive to this option. Alternatives could be considered where selected peers are trained as evaluators to fulfill this function in cooperation with building administrators. When qualified, respected, and trained peers begin to have input into the evaluation process, the teachers' suspicions of administrator bias might diminish.

The fourth concern about the evaluation process was that teachers had no recourse regarding their evaluators' summative ratings of their performance. While teachers are free to discuss their performance with their evaluator, the point values assigned by the evaluator to each of the performance areas are not a subject for debate. For example, if a teacher is judged to be professionally competent (3 points) in the area of "utilizes appropriate and varied instructional strategies, teaching methods, and instructional media," the teacher could ask what he or she needs to do to improve this rating. The issue of whether the teacher merits four points in this area is not negotiable. As criteria for evaluation are clarified and as peers become more involved in the teacher evaluation process, the need to discuss why a teacher was assigned a particular point value in a specific performance area should diminish. Although the need for such discussion may diminish, teachers should be afforded the opportunity for dialogue on the issue. Teacher evaluation is perceived as fair and equitable by staff to the extent that opportunities are provided for such frank discussion.

While the evaluation component of PBSP is critical for distributing money on a fair and equitable basis, teachers were concerned that summative evaluation had become the focal point of life in the district. Teachers indicated that their decision to stay in teaching was influenced by the respect they received from students, the intellectual challenge of the teaching profession, and the quality of their interactions with colleagues. Salary is somewhat important, but last on their lists. While improving teachers' salaries is important, attention must be devoted to developing constructive supervisory relationships and processes that result in improved teaching through more effective staff development. Another option is to offer teachers choices of non-salary incentives for outstanding performance. Such incentives could include providing additional time and financial support for conference attendance, monies for purchase of additional instructional material, or compensation for taking specialized training in areas related to teaching.

Level of Compensation

Teachers in this district agreed to a five-year contract, which at that time looked very lucrative (50 percent increase in money for salaries over five years). After the first two years that the contract was in effect, surrounding districts negotiated comparable raises without increasing the length of the school year or having as rigorous an evaluation process. While this problem cannot be linked directly to the concept of paying teachers based on classroom performance, it does raise a major problem for implementing this merit pay program. Districts that implement such programs must be willing to invest the amount of money necessary to make the merit worth striving for. While research has not shown what amount of money is significant enough to be considered to be a motivator, Hatry and Grenier (1985) report that incentives in the $1000 range are viewed as significant. Based on such logic, teachers in this study at the upper end of the performance levels should be paid at least $1000 to $1500 more than they would be if they moved to a neighboring district.

Basic Assumptions Underlying the Compensation System

From the comments of many teachers, it is clear that they view the merit pay program as more of a behavioral than a professional compensation system. The system is behavioral to the extent that fairly uniform performance expectations have been set for classroom teachers across the district, performance with respect to these expectations is monitored through the teacher evaluation process, and salary rewards are determined on the basis of summative evaluation ratings. The message these teachers are hearing is, "Play by the system, if you want to get rewarded." These teachers are not resisting playing by the system but, rather, resisting the system because the system defines teaching too narrowly. Currently, teachers whose strength is classroom performance are being rewarded. While classroom performance is important, some teachers are saying we need a more professional performance based program where other critical factors are considered when assessing teacher performance.

In examining performance based salary programs across the nation, teachers are rewarded for one or some combination of the following factors:

- their *classroom performance*
- the level of *responsibility* or *leadership* they are willing to assume for school program (i.e., serving as curriculum committee chair, team leader, peer coach)

- the amount of *time* they are willing to commit to the school district (i.e., coordinating club or extracurricular after-school activities, serving as liaison with parent or community groups, participating in extended school year staff or professional development workshops).

When the performance based salary program is renegotiated, consideration should be given to including factors of responsibility and time, along with classroom performance, as the criteria for making merit pay decisions. By including these three factors, the performance based salary program will be based on a more professional conception of teaching, which should result in a more equitable distribution of rewards. As one teacher noted,

> Last year I got a 5 [performance level]. I stay after school and work with kids on projects. I come back in the evening for school activities. Over the summer I work on curriculum. The teacher next door is out of here right after school, only comes back at night if we have to, and is gone for the summer. She got a 7 [performance level]. Is that fair? She's a heck of a good teacher in the classroom, but I do a lot of things she doesn't.

SUMMARY

As a result of this study we have identified what teachers expect from a merit pay program. These include clear criteria for achieving merit recognition, teacher involvement from the beginning in the design of the plan, competent evaluators, and significant amount of money to make a difference. These expectations are consistent with the professional literature that has identified the necessary components of an effective process for performance based salary programs (see for example, Hatry and Grenier, 1985). It is apparent that districts contemplating such programs must invest the time, energy, and resources to ensure these basic components are addressed initially and monitored continually.

The findings in this study also challenge some of the concerns expressed by opponents of performance based pay programs. Opponents have argued that such programs will make teachers highly stressed, not trusting of each other, uncooperative, and even less motivated to teach. Consequently, the quality of instruction will deteriorate rather than improve. While teachers in this study expressed concerns with the *pro-*

cess, it does appear that the plan has not been unduly stressful or dissatisfying. In some cases it appears to be at least somewhat motivating, especially for teachers that received higher scores. Finally, teachers, administrators, and school board members agree that some improvement in instruction has occurred as a result of the program.

The question that arises is, "Can all teachers be motivated and satisfied under such a program if the process is refined and improved?" The answer to this question is probably no. Just as some teachers in a school system that does not pay teachers on the basis of performance will experience job dissatisfaction from not being recognized or rewarded for outstanding performance, a segment of the population in a pay-for-performance program will not be satisfied. There are two probable reasons for this dissatisfaction. First, some teachers will not be capable of achieving the higher performance levels. Reasons may vary from limited ability to time constraints on outside-the-classroom involvement with students because of other responsibilities. Second, some teachers will be philosphically opposed to the concept of performance based pay for teachers regardless of the process. The choice these less satisfied teachers face is to remain in the system or to seek a position in a district that does not pay teachers on the basis of performance. Unfortunately, this means that the district may lose some very qualified teachers (and fortunately maybe some marginal ones). In such cases school districts should be careful to hire highly qualified replacements who believe in the concept of performance based pay.

The answer to the many controversies surrounding pay-for-performance programs may lie in maintaining local control of the issue so that teachers and school districts have options. Those districts that strongly believe in the concept and are willing to invest the time, energy, and resources should be able to design plans that fit the needs of their district. Consequently, those that do not believe in either salaried or non-salaried performance based programs can maintain the status quo. Districts that continue to compensate teachers by degree and years of experience offer alternative employment possibilities for teachers who are competent, yet philosophically opposed to incentive programs.

The demand by the public for implementing performance based programs is well-documented. If educators continue to resist attempts to implement such programs, taxpayers may force these programs on districts without considering the many issues that make them work effectively. While pay-for-performance programs are not the simple cure-all that many politicians contend, they are a viable alternative for compensating teachers that is worthy of further consideration and follow-up research.

REFERENCES

Bacharach, S. B., S. C. Conley, and J. B. Shedd. 1987. "A Developmental Framework for Evaluating Teachers as Decision Makers," *Journal of Personnel Evaluation in Education*, 1(2):181–194.

Hatry, H. P. and J. M. Grenier. 1985. *Issues and Case Studies in Teacher Incentive Plans*. The Urban Institute Press.

Herzberg, F. 1966. *Work and the Nature of Man*. New York: World.

Iwanicki, E. F. 1982. "Development and Validation of the Teacher Evaluation Needs Identification Survey," *Educational and Psychological Measurement*, 42:265–274.

Lester, P. "The Validation of the Teacher Job Satisfaction Questionnaire," Paper presented at the *Northeastern Educational Research Association Annual Conference, Kerhonkson, New York*, 1985.

McCarthey, S. J. and K. D. Peterson. 1987. "Peer Review of Materials in Public School Teacher Evaluation," *Journal of Personnel Evaluation in Education*, 1(3):259–269.

Maslach, C., S. E. Jackson, and R. L. Schwab. 1986. *The Maslach Burnout Inventory: Educators' Edition*. Palo Alto, CA: Consulting Psychologist Press.

Murphy, J. 1987. "Teacher Evaluation: A Comprehensive Framework for Supervisors," *Journal of Personnel Evaluation in Education*, 1(2):157–181.

Paul, K. L. "How to Identify and Reward Excellent Teachers," Paper presented at the *Annual Conference of the National School Boards Association, Anaheim, California*, 1985.

Schwab, R. L., S. E. Jackson, and R. A. Schuler. 1986. "Educator Burnout: Sources and Consequences," *Educational Research Quarterly*, 10(3):14–30.

Silk, D. N. 1984–1985. "Are Merit Raises Meritorious?" *The Teacher Educator*, 20:23–26.

Streifer, P. A. and E. F. Iwanicki. 1987. "The Validation of Beginning Teacher Competencies in Connecticut," *Journal of Personnel Evaluation in Education*, 1(1):33–57.

Streifer, P. A. 1987. *Assessment Guide for Select Connecticut Teaching Competencies*. Barrington (Rhode Island) Public Schools.

CHAPTER 7

School District Planning for Teacher Incentive Pay

RICHARD M. BRANDT – *University of Virginia*
BRUCE GANSNEDER – *University of Virginia*

THIS chapter examines the planning of incentive pay programs and the variety of plans that emerged in one state (Virginia). Much information is available today about the nature of various career ladder, merit pay, and other teacher incentive plans. Very little is known, however, about what kind of planning actually goes on, how decisions are reached about whether to have a plan, and, if so, what it should look like.

Teacher incentive pay programs are now in operation or in the planning/pilot testing stage throughout the country. In some states, Tennessee and North Carolina for example, both administration and funding of the programs are primarily a state responsibility. In others such as Utah, where a large number of districts participate, the funding is furnished by the state, but plans are locally designed and operated under general state guidelines. In states where legislative action has provided substantial funding for incentive pay programs, many, if not all, localities participate. In states without substantial state funding for such programs, some school districts have developed plans on their own, but the majority have not. Virginia is one such state. Early state initiatives to stimulate planning and pilot testing of master teacher and pay-for-performance programs lasted only two years. Since then, whatever has developed in Virginia has been the result of local district leadership and action.

A SURVEY OF VIRGINIA SCHOOL DISTRICTS

Why are such plans started? Who originates them? What factors influence their development? How much support or resistance can be expected from various stakeholders – school boards, administrators, and especially teachers?

Answers to such questions were derived from a two-stage survey of

185

all Virginia school districts (Brandt and Gansneder, 1987). First, a one-page letter explaining the study and defining incentive pay practices was sent to every ($n = 139$) superintendent in the state. Superintendents were asked to check on a return postcard one of five statements that best described the status of teacher incentive pay practices in their districts. Incentive pay practices were defined to "include merit pay, pay-for-performance, career ladder, and master teacher programs where the quality of teaching performance provides at least one basis for extra pay."

All districts responded as follows:

- 61 (44%)—We do not have a program, nor have we seriously considered having one.
- 24 (17%)—We considered adopting such a program but rejected the idea.
- 5 (4%)—We once had a program but do not have one now.
- 35 (25%)—We do not yet have a program but are exploring the possibility.
- 11 (8%)—We do have a program.
- 3 (2%)—Not applicable (school services subcontracted, etc.)

Four months later a one-page (back and front) questionnaire was sent to all districts (a longer questionnaire was sent to districts that did have merit pay[1]). Superintendents were asked to indicate the activities and people involved in considering incentive pay; the effect of these activities and involvements on their decision about incentive pay; the percentages of persons in selected groups that they believed wanted incentive pay; the nature of any existing awards for exceptional teaching; existing opportunities for teachers to earn extra money; major restrictions to the development or implementation of a plan; and their opinions as to whether particular results would be achieved from a good incentive pay plan. One hundred two (75%) districts responded to this second questionnaire. Additional information on the size of school districts, per-pupil expenditures, teacher salary averages, and percentages of the budget from local funds (a rough indicator of economic conditions in the district) were taken from state documents. The eleven school districts that had indicated earlier that they had a program were also asked eighteen additional questions about the nature of their particular programs.

The remainder of this chapter will, first, report survey information about the planning process and factors related to the decision to establish an incentive pay program and, second, describe the programs that were launched and compare their major features.

Data about planning were analyzed by grouping districts according to their level of implementation or decision status, as reported on the single-item postcard question, and then comparing responses of the several groups to items on the second questionnaire. School districts were grouped as follows for these comparisons:

- never considered ($n = 41$)
- considered but rejected ($n = 22$)[2]
- considering now ($n = 28$)
- have merit pay ($n = 11$)

PLANNING ACTIVITIES AND EFFECT ON DECISIONS

Each school district was asked to indicate the activities that took place as part of their consideration of a teacher incentive pay plan (see Table 1). Major findings were as follows:

- A considerable majority of the school districts had school board discussions (83 percent), received recommendations from the administrative staff (69 percent), looked at the experiences of other school systems (70 percent), and used literature reviews and professional publications (76 percent).
- Approximately one-half of the districts had a special task force study (49 percent) and reviewed the national reform reports (51 percent).
- A little over one-third held teacher association meetings with the administration (39 percent) and reviewed the state pilot study guidelines (38 percent).
- About a fourth (26 percent) used outside consultants.
- For seven of the nine activities, the four groups differed significantly. In general, those who had *never considered* a plan were least likely to have engaged in any of these activities. They were much less likely than the other three groups to have used task force recommendations, reviewed the literature, or reviewed state pilot study guidelines.
- Those who had *considered but rejected* a plan were more likely to have reviewed the national reform reports and literature on the topic.

Table 1. Percentage of districts that conducted selected studies and consultations, based on the district's status on merit pay.

Status of District with Respect to Merit Pay	Percentage of Districts That Conducted								
	School Board Discussions	Task Force Studies*	Administ. Staff Meetings*	Meetings w/Outside Consultants*	Review of Relevant Literature*	Consult. of Teacher Leadership*	Review of Nat'l Reform Reports*	Study of Other School Systems	Review of State Pilot Study*
Never Considered Merit Pay	73.5	20.6	52.9	11.8	58.8	26.5	32.4	64.7	17.6
Considered Merit Pay, But Rejected It	87.5	70.8	79.2	33.3	91.7	50.0	77.3	75.0	52.2
Currently Considering Merit Pay	85.7	50.0	71.4	21.4	82.1	32.1	50.0	78.6	46.4
Currently Have Merit Pay in Operation	90.9	81.8	90.9	63.6	81.8	72.7	54.5	54.5	45.5
Overall Average	82.5	48.5	69.1	25.8	76.3	38.9	50.5	70.1	37.5

*Differences among these percentages are statistically significant.

- Those who had *considered but rejected* it and those who *have merit pay* were more likely than the other two groups to have received recommendations from a special task force.
- Those *with merit pay* were more likely than the other three groups to have used outside consultants and involved the teacher association leadership.

Superintendents also rated the degree to which each activity affected the final decision, with the following results:

- For only three of the activities did the majority or near majority of the districts who conducted these activities indicate that the activity had a major effect on their decision. These were recommendations of a special task force (59 percent), involvement of the school board (49 percent), and the administrative staff (45 percent). Relatively few districts indicated any of the other activities had a major effect on the final decision, ranging from 6 percent for the national reform reports to 26 percent for other school systems.
- Recommendations from a special task force had a major effect on more of the districts that have *merit pay* (67 percent) or who *considered it but rejected it* (82 percent) but on fewer of the districts who *were still considering* it (47 percent) or who *never considered* it (25 percent).
- The national reform reports had a major effect on more of the districts who *have merit pay* (40 percent) but on almost none for the other three groups.
- The experiences of other school districts had a major effect on more of the districts who are *considering it now* (50 percent) but on few of the other districts (14 percent, 18 percent, and 14 percent).

School districts that made a decision either to have or not to have a plan apparently engaged in more planning activities of almost all kinds than either the districts that reported they had never seriously considered one or those that were still exploring the possibility. However, even a majority of school districts that said they had not given serious consideration to implementing a plan had discussed the notion among school board members, received administrative staff recommendations, reviewed literature on the topic, and looked at what other school systems were doing.

Overall, much planning activity was generated by the notion of teacher incentive pay. More than four out of five school boards discussed it. Literature reviews, examination of other school systems' experiences with it, and administrative staff recommendations took place in approximately three of every four districts. About half the districts consulted the national reform reports and appointed a special task force to consider the matter and make recommendations. Meetings of administrators with teacher association leaders, on the other hand, as well as the use of outside consultants occurred primarily in districts that made a decision to have a plan. The national reform reports were significantly more important influences in districts that decided to adopt a plan than in those that did not. Of those considering a plan but still undecided, half of the districts had special task forces which looked at other school district plans and reviewed both (a) literature and reform reports and (b) other school systems' programs. Not surprisingly, the biggest influences on final decisions to go ahead or not to go ahead were school boards and special task forces.

DESIRE FOR MERIT PAY BY SELECTED GROUPS

Each school district was asked to indicate the percentage of each of the selected groups (e.g., school board) in the district who wanted merit pay (see Table 2). Responses in each case differed by merit pay implementation.

- Those *with merit pay* were more likely to indicate that a higher percentage of each group supported it.
- All (100 percent) of the school districts that *had merit pay* thought that a majority of the school board, central administration, and the community at large wanted it.
- Almost two-thirds of the *merit pay districts* thought that a majority of the principals and teacher association leaders wanted it.
- There was also a greater tendency for districts that were *considering merit pay* to think that a majority of these groups wanted it than there was in those that rejected it or never considered it.
- In no case did a large percentage of the districts think that a majority of the elementary, middle, or secondary teachers wanted merit pay.

Table 2. *Percentage of districts in which merit pay is supported by a majority of the members of selected interest groups, according to the district's status on merit pay.*

Status of District with Respect to Merit Pay	Merit Pay Supported by a Majority of the District's*							
	School Board	Central Administration	Teacher Assc. Leadership	Secondary Teachers	Middle School/ Jr. High Teachers	Elementary Teachers	Principals and Asst. Principals	Community at Large
Never Considered Merit Pay	13.3	3.3	3.7	7.4	4.2	7.4	10.3	10.7
Considered Merit Pay, but Rejected It	31.8	13.0	8.7	0	4.3	4.3	13.0	34.8
Currently Considering Merit Pay	50.0	29.2	16.0	16.0	16.0	16.0	24.0	60.0
Currently Have Merit Pay in Operation	100.0	100.0	62.5	30.0	40.0	40.0	63.6	100.0
Overall Average	39.3	25.0	14.5	10.6	12.2	12.9	21.6	41.9

*In each case differences among these percentages are statistically significant.

The outside pressure for teacher incentive pay is clearly evident in Table 2.

It is likely that the rather extensive planning process noted earlier was necessary not only to work out procedures but to lessen resistance and build support in the education community itself. Teacher sentiment in one district did shift during the first three years from being predominantly negative to a balanced mixture of approval and disapproval (Brandt, 1988). Major change is always slow and arduous in social institutions, and when the stimulus that elicits it is from the outside, as is the case here, even greater resistance than usual can be expected. It is interesting to note back in Table 1 how much attention was paid to other school systems' experiences with incentive pay, especially by those who were waiting to see what happened to the effort.

CURRENT AWARD AND EXTRA PAY OPPORTUNITIES

Two questions focused on the nature of other award structures and extra pay opportunities already in place.

- Less than one-quarter (23 percent) of the districts indicated awards were given for "exceptional teacher performance," half of whom were those that already had merit pay or Career Ladder Programs. Among the others, seven indicated they gave monetary awards to one or just a few teachers. The rest gave certificates or teacher of the year awards, again to very few individuals.
- In the majority of the districts (72 to 92 percent), teachers could earn extra pay for club activity sponsorship (88 percent), graduate degree work (92 percent), summer school teaching (91 percent), and extended contracts for summer (72 percent). This pattern did not vary significantly on the basis of merit pay implementation (see Table 3).
- In about one-third (34 percent) of the districts, teachers could earn extra pay for instructional leadership. Once again, this percentage did not vary significantly by merit pay implementation.
- In districts where these options were available, the percentage of teachers receiving extra pay for graduate degree work (31 percent), instructional leadership (6 percent), and summer contracts (7 percent) did not vary by merit pay implementation.

Table 3. Percentage of districts offering various options for teachers to earn extra money.

Status of District with Respect to Merit Pay	Percentage of Districts Offering Extra Money to Teachers for*				
	Club/Activity Sponsorship	Instructional Leadership	Summer School Teaching	Extended Contracts for Summer	Graduate Degree/ Coursework
Never Considered Merit Pay	85.0	27.5	90.0	65.0	89.7
Considered Merit Pay, but Rejected It	87.5	33.3	95.8	73.9	95.7
Currently Considering Merit Pay	92.9	39.3	89.3	82.1	96.4
Currently Have Merit Pay in Operation	90.9	50.0	90.9	63.6	81.8
Overall Average	88.3	34.3	91.3	71.6	92.1

*Differences among these percentages are not statistically significant.

- The percentages of teachers earning extra money for club activity sponsorship (16 percent) and summer school teaching (6 percent) did differ by merit pay implementation. Districts *with merit pay* had a higher percentage of teachers receiving pay for club activity sponsorship (23 percent vs. 16 percent), while districts that had *considered but rejected it* had a higher percentage of teachers receiving extra pay for summer school teaching (8 percent vs. 6 percent).
- The average amount of money received by teachers for club activity sponsorship ($945), summer school teaching ($1745), extended contract for summer ($2120), and graduate degree work ($1221) was similar across merit pay implementation. Districts *with merit pay*, however, provided significantly higher average amounts of money for instructional leadership. For these districts the average amount of money for instructional leadership was $3704 vs. an average of $1043 for all districts.

It is clear that school districts did provide several ways for teachers to earn extra pay beyond their basic salaries. The vast majority paid extra for sponsoring club activities, teaching summer school or assuming other summer duties, and completing graduate degrees or coursework. About a third paid extra for assuming instructional leadership roles. Other than graduate study, for which almost one-third of all teachers received extra pay, the numbers of teachers awarded it for one of the other roles was rather small: 16 percent for club/activity sponsorship and in the 5–7 percent range for the other options. The amounts of money earned, furthermore, were not substantial. They ranged on average from $945 for club/activity sponsorship to $2120 for extended contracts in the summer. It is noteworthy that the highest extra stipend by far ($3704) in any of the groups was for "instructional leadership" in school districts that had merit pay programs. As will be seen later, initiation of merit pay and Career Ladder Programs often leads to improved evaluation systems and increased involvement of teachers in staff development activities. In such programs teachers are frequently used for both evaluation and leadership purposes.

It is also worth noting that, except for merit pay districts, school districts that had considered but rejected incentive pay reported somewhat higher percentages of teachers earning extra money for club/activity sponsorship and for summer school teaching. These somewhat greater opportunities for earning extra pay by taking on these extra duties might have diminished interest among teachers in incentive pay structures. Those who wanted to work harder and longer in order to earn extra school pay could do so. If these extra responsibilities were assigned to those who were considered the best teachers, through an application, review, and competitive selection process, the beginnings of an incentive pay structure already existed without the label.

MAJOR RESTRICTIONS TO INCENTIVE PROGRAMS

Superintendents were asked to indicate the extent to which a number of frequently cited deterrents were considered major restrictions in the development and/or implementation of a teacher incentive pay plan in their districts (see Table 4).

- None of these factors was seen as a major restriction by a majority of the school districts. However, more than one-third of the school districts felt that the nonavailability of state ·funds (48 percent), the nonavailability of local funds (46 percent), and a potential threat to morale (40 percent) were major restrictions.
- These perceptions differed significantly across level of implementation with regard to availability of state funds and the threat to morale. Only 10 percent of the districts *with merit pay* felt that these two factors were major restrictions compared to much higher percentages for all districts (48 percent and 40 percent respectively).
- Those divisions that had *considered merit pay* but rejected it were most likely (63 percent) to indicate that nonavailability of state funds was a major restriction.

There are indeed many good reasons why careful, thorough planning is needed. A number of major concerns must be resolved before successful development is likely: whether funds are available in the long term as well as the short term, whether administrators are ready to assume new burdens the plan will give them, how teacher morale can be sustained, if not improved, in the face of imposed change and new expectancies, what other priorities may have to be momentarily sidetracked, and how valid the evaluation system is with respect to the new summative demands that are placed on it. Evidence is clearly present in Table 4 that most superintendents in districts that had already

Table 4. Percentage of districts who perceived selected factors to be major obstacles to developing a teacher incentive pay plan.

Status of District with Respect to Merit Pay	Percentage of Districts Who Claimed That Development of Teacher Incentive Pay Plans Was Limited by						
	Availability of Local Funds	Availability of State Funds*	Administrative Burden	Threat to Morale*	Other Priorities	Existence of Adequate Eval. System	Difficulty Developing System
Never Considered Merit Pay	48.6	43.3	27.3	52.9	38.2	24.2	37.1
Considered Merit Pay, but Rejected It	50.0	62.5	16.7	45.8	30.4	12.5	31.6
Currently Considering Merit Pay	50.0	53.6	10.7	28.6	22.2	25.9	20.0
Currently Have Merit Pay in Operation	20.0	10.0	10.0	10.0	0	0	10.0
Overall Average	46.4	47.8	17.9	39.6	28.0	19.4	28.1

*Differences among these percentages are statistically significant.

launched programs did not see these particular concerns as major restrictions. Either they did not exist or these districts were able to overcome them. Although the differences were not statistically significant in all instances, it is interesting that those districts still considering incentive pay indicated less concern over administrative burdens, teacher morale, and developing an adequate evaluation system than those that had never considered or those that had considered but rejected it.

LIKELY OUTCOMES

Districts were asked whether they agreed that selected outcomes were likely if one had a good incentive plan (see Table 5).

- A substantial majority (approximately two-thirds) of the districts agreed that each of these outcomes would occur, except for an improvement of morale (42 percent).
- There were significant differences by merit pay implementation for two potential outcomes—improvement of morale and raising teacher standards.
- While only 42 percent of the total group thought that a good incentive pay plan would result in improved morale, all (100 percent) of those *with merit pay* agreed and even 29 percent of those who *never considered merit pay* agreed.
- While 69 percent of the total group agreed that a good incentive pay plan would result in raising teaching standards, only 53 percent of those who had *considered it but rejected it* agreed as contrasted with all (100 percent) of the districts that *had merit pay*.

It is clear that a large majority of superintendents believed a good incentive pay plan would accomplish a great deal. It would function to attract and retain teachers in a profession noted for much higher than average rates of turnover (Dworkin, 1987). Standards would be raised, along with professionalism among teachers. Teachers would be stimulated to do better, instruction would improve, and students would learn more. The only potential benefit not cited by a majority of the districts was better teacher morale, but even here 100 percent of those with Merit Pay Programs felt improvements would occur.

Since all of the differences cited above were treated as if they were independent comparisons, further analyses were conducted of the dif-

Table 5. Percentage of districts who agreed that the following were likely outcomes of a good teacher incentive plan.

Status of Districts with Respect to Merit Pay	Percentage of Districts Who Agreed That a Good Teacher Incentive Plan Was Likely to									
	Attract Teachers	Retain Teachers	Improve Morale*	Increase Professionalism	Raise Teaching Standards*	Improve Eval. System	Improve Instruction	Stimulate Teachers	Improve Learning*
Never Considered Merit Pay	71.1	65.8	28.9	52.6	64.9	73.0	66.7	58.3	58.3
Considered Merit Pay, but Rejected It	59.1	60.9	34.8	56.5	52.2	87.0	56.5	60.9	47.8
Currently Considering Merit Pay	69.2	61.5	46.2	73.1	76.9	84.6	84.6	80.8	79.2
Currently Have Merit Pay in Operation	90.9	90.9	100.0	90.0	100.0	100.0	90.9	90.0	70.0
Overall Average	70.1	66.3	41.7	62.9	69.1	82.3	71.9	68.4	62.4

*Differences among these percentages are statistically significant.

ferences between the four groups—those that had adopted merit pay, those that had considered but rejected it, those that were still considering it, and those that had not seriously considered it. Through the use of multivariate discriminant analysis, three discriminative functions were identified, which were able to classify correctly 61 percent of the school districts into the four groups (Gansneder and Brandt, 1988).

The classifications were most accurate for districts with merit pay (73 percent) and least accurate for districts that were still considering the adoption of merit pay (39 percent). The three discriminate functions appeared to represent three variables: the desire for merit pay, the ability to support merit pay financially, and the extent of the planning process. Districts with merit pay were most likely to be those (a) in which the people in the district wanted merit pay, (b) which were able to support it financially, and (c) which had gone through a fairly thorough planning process. Districts indicating that they were still considering merit pay were most likely to be those (a) in which the people were perceived as wanting merit pay but (b) in which little of the planning process had occurred and (c) in which financial support for merit pay might not be available. Districts indicating that they had considered but rejected merit pay were most likely to be those in which (a) the people were perceived not to want merit pay, (b) there had been some exploration of the issue, but (c) there might not be financial support for it. Districts that had never considered merit pay were most likely to be those in which (a) people were perceived as not wanting merit pay, (b) there had been little exploration of the issue, and (c) there might not be financial support for it.

In short, merit pay, as may be true of most educational innovations, is most likely to be adopted when it is desired by relevant people, conscientiously considered, and there is money to absorb the expected costs.

NATURE OF TEACHER INCENTIVE PAY PROGRAMS

Two characteristics of the eleven existing programs in 1986–87 complicate efforts to describe them as a group.[3] First is their newness. One plan had been functioning for a decade, one for five years, and two others for four years, but at the time of our second and primary survey, none of the other seven had completed even two years of operation. Three of the programs, in fact, did not receive final go-ahead approval from their school boards until late spring or early summer, 1987.

The recent start-up of most of the plans means that there is only very limited historical information to report. In several instances, one district could not report how many teachers had applied for and received merit pay or promotion the previous year, nor would estimates for the current year be much more than guesses with such a short track record. Thus, participant numbers and cost figures in this study are somewhat unreliable predictors of the future because several plans are still under development. One or possibly two groups of teachers have been promoted to the first rung of a career ladder, for example, but it may be another year or two before people will even be considered for the next step. The first master teacher applicants in Danville, for example, were being reviewed during 1988–1989 for promotion in fall, 1989.

In three Merit Play Plans, furthermore, including one that was in its fourth year, a career ladder feature was either (a) still under consideration for those who had performed well over time or (b) to be added in the fall of 1987. For one plan, the first group of teachers to be selected was composed not of those who were ultimately to be reviewed for merit pay or promotion but of a special cadre of new specialists who were to help do the reviewing. Creation of this new role for some carefully selected teachers was in itself a career advancement with extra pay. This new evaluator position will eventually be eliminated once enough teachers have been promoted on the career ladder to serve in that role. In another division, the first group of teachers who advanced on the career ladder (twenty-eight in 1985–86) included fourteen teachers who act as supervisors for other teachers. They serve three-year terms in this latter capacity after which they may reapply; they do not, however, have to reapply to remain on the career ladder.

The second characteristic that complicates the analysis is the great variation among plans. No two plans are alike. As designated by the superintendents or their assistants in charge of the plans, six are merit pay, four are career ladder, and one is a combination of both types. As indicted in the survey, one of the Merit Pay Programs was adding a career ladder feature the next year, and two other places were considering similar moves. So the distinction often drawn between merit pay and career ladders is not sharp in Virginia.

Merit pay is characterized by some kind of monetary supplement for superior teaching. It is awarded as a bonus to those who have performed particularly well over the past year, with the possibility of other bonuses in subsequent years. With it comes no increased responsibility or extra assignment. Two of the three programs in which mandatory consideration of all teachers occurs are of the merit pay type. Four other Merit Pay Programs are only open to volunteers. Career Ladder Programs, however, are all offered on a voluntary participation basis.

Career ladders typically, but not always, imply extra status and responsibility along with extra money for good or outstanding teaching. For example, in at least two districts, willingness to accept changes in teaching assignments, including transfers to other schools where special expertise is needed, is expected of those promoted.

Of the five Virginia plans with career ladder structure, four had barely started in 1987, and the extra roles, and possibly extra hours or days of work as well, were not yet fully prescribed. In only one of the plans were extended hours or days mandatory. In this plan, teachers in one of the career ladder classifications were supposed to work one-half hour per day and five days a year more than others, observing and assisting teachers and conducting staff development and curriculum/research activities; the other classification in the same district called for no extra duties. Extended hours or days under contract were optional in two plans, not expected at all in one plan, and added later in another.

One's promotion to a rung on a ladder is usually for a longer period than one year — three, four, five years, or perhaps indefinitely. One other feature of all the Career Ladder Plans and at least two Merit Pay Plans is a requirement that teachers have a certain amount of teaching experience, especially in the district itself, before being eligible to participate. In one district it is as much as ten years. In two others, it is six and seven years, respectively, for the first promotion and three more for the final step on the ladder.

DIFFERENCES IN PARTICIPATION AND AWARDS

Vast differences exist in such factors as the size of awards, the basis on which they are given, the percentage of teachers receiving them, and expectations and responsibilities of recipients. The eleven Virginia plans vary greatly on these factors. In one district, 99 percent of the teachers received merit pay last year ranging from $55 to $165. The awards were based on the demonstration of specific teaching skills. In another program with mandatory participation, 97 percent of the teachers received merit pay in 1986–87 in the amount of a 5 percent salary raise, as well as a cost-of-living increase. The percentages of teachers receiving merit pay in various districts ranged downward as follows: 99, 97, 37, 24, and 17.[4] Similar differences exist in the percentages of teachers being promoted on the career ladder, with one school district reporting 75 percent of the teaching staff qualifying for the second step of a three-step ladder and another, only 16 percent.

The amount of the stipend varied inversely, as it often does, with the percentage of teachers participating. The promotion increment for the district with three-fourths of the teachers participating was only $500, one-third of the amount of the increment for one where only a sixth of the teachers was promoted. As with Tennessee's career level I, which more than 90 percent of the tenured teachers have reached, the first rung on some ladders provides relatively small increments for promotion but much greater participation than higher rungs.[5]

Inverse variation of the size of increments with the numbers of teachers participating is apparent also among the merit pay programs. The dollar amounts of teacher pay awards vary from as low as $55 per person in the school district with 99 percent receiving awards to as high as $1300 in one with only 37 percent doing so. The district in which 97 percent of the teachers earned a 5 percent raise is not considered an exception to the inverse variation principle because this amount, along with the 5 percent cost-of-living increase, was really an across-the-board salary increase for all teachers, except those performing very poorly. A similar pattern will probably prevail also in the school district where 75 percent of the teachers made the second rung; promotion to the third step will most likely be more selective and more lucrative once it is implemented.

Three of the programs with career ladder components do not follow the Tennessee pattern of a small increment and wide participation for the first promotion. Promotion increments are substantial, ranging between $2000 and $2500, and the rates of participation are modest and likely to remain so. They were 16 percent in a relatively longstanding program and 7 and 6 percent for the two others after their first year in operation.[6]

Generally speaking, Career Ladder Plans differ from Merit Pay Plans in the size of increments, especially where participation is relatively low. This pattern prevails elsewhere, as well as in Virginia. Supplements for the four Career Ladder Plans (excluding the one with heavy participation at step two) averaged $2167 in 1987, approximately double that of the Merit Pay Programs.

EVALUATION DIFFERENCES

Perhaps the greatest differences among the teacher incentive programs are found not in the money involved or the extent to which people participate, but in the means by which teachers are evaluated. Although similarities are apparent here and there among the various items that make up an evaluation system, each of the eleven systems is quite unique. No topic was more important or provoked more discussion during the design stage than the means by which teachers were to be singled out for extra pay or promotion.

In those school districts where school boards asked that only superior teaching be rewarded, the design of an appropriate evaluation mechanism was especially challenging. Traditional evaluation instruments are notoriously weak. The four- or five-point rating scales that have been used for decades to rate teachers on several dozen general traits ("makes good decisions," "is well organized," etc.) lack both the discriminating power and validity to be very useful for identifying superior teaching. Personnel records based on such scales typically show two-thirds of the teachers receiving top ratings in 90 percent of the categories, and all but 2 or 3 percent receiving nothing below the top two steps on the scale in anything. In many places, furthermore, summative ratings have been made without seeing some individuals teach a full class period even once a year. Once teachers achieve continuing contract status, the classroom door is often shut and their teaching is seldom observed (Goodlad and Klein, 1970).

Where incentive pay programs have been installed, both in Virginia and across the country, teacher evaluation practices have been completely revised. Scales for rating general traits have been replaced by behaviorally specific instruments consisting of carefully selected, research based, precisely defined instructional variables. Teacher manuals describe the variables to be studied, indicators to look for, examples to follow, and forms on which to record observational data systematically. The principal is joined by other school personnel, including teachers, to serve as evaluators. Evaluators are given extensive training in the correct use of the rating or low-inference coding systems.[7] Other sources of data than direct classroom observation may also become an official part of evaluation systems: parent and student surveys and student performance data in particular.

Until the recent reform movement shifted the target from minimum competency to the excellence end of the spectrum, little attention had been devoted to how one identifies outstanding teaching. Most of the previous evaluation scales had been used to assess minimum competency. Even now the lack of valid, well-accepted measures of outstanding, as contrasted with competent, teaching is a major reason why "paying good teachers more" is not easy to do in a systematic and fair way.

In reviewing the eleven Virginia plans, one is impressed with the care and attention that have been given to teacher assessment in school districts, especially for several in which high selectivity is called for. Selectivity refers to the ratio of teachers selected for awards to the total number who are eligible and considered. The lower the proportion of teachers chosen, the higher the selectivity. The evaluation system used in the Florida master teacher program was so highly selective during its first year—one of six applicants succeeded, representing only 3 percent of the teaching force—that it was not politically sustainable. The teacher assessment system that produced these results provoked great criticism, and the legislature ultimately dropped the program.

In at least four Virginia districts, high selectivity is not required and large proportions of teachers are expected to receive awards. Included in this group is the longest standing plan, where one prerequisite to participate is ten years teaching in the system. After that, the majority of teachers choose to participate, and 96 percent succeed in receiving merit pay. Obviously, the underlying rationale for such a plan is (a) to encourage most teachers with seniority and at least average teaching ability to continue to receive a raise and, at the same time, (b) to place a ceiling on the salary of any who are below average. This is a very different plan from one that would attempt to identify and reward outstanding teachers regardless of seniority. Many other Career Ladder Plans, in Virginia and elsewhere, also require a minimum number of years teaching in the district before one is eligible to try for incentive pay. This practice automatically restricts the number of participants to those with a certain amount of seniority and reduces the degree to which teaching performance alone is the primary determiner of merit pay.

Although almost all the Virginia plans require observation of teaching, one or two still depend primarily on high inference ratings by the immediate supervisor of general teaching attributes. This pattern tends to be used mostly in low selectivity systems where the need to distinguish between the best teachers and competent ones is not great, and the prime attention remains on those who are not sufficiently competent.

In five school districts teachers serve directly as evaluators or less directly as recorders of classroom observation data that are ultimately used in the selection process. In two districts, they teach half-time for a two- or three-year period, and in the others they continue to teach full-time with the exception of three or four days of observing during the school year. All evaluators receive special training of several days' duration prior to serving in this capacity.

In those systems where high selectivity is important, the number of times teachers are formally and informally observed each year has increased dramatically. In two of the systems, teachers under consideration for promotion will be observed by at least three observers on not less than four and six different occasions, respectively. A number of conferences with reviewing teams are held as well to consider performance related material.

USE OF STUDENT DATA

In five school districts, student outcome data are an important part of the evaluation system, and in at least one other plan, teachers have the option of presenting such information as part of their evaluation material. In two districts, in fact, student outcome data are really the sole measure of success for merit pay purposes.

In the small rural district that dropped its program because of budget cuts, teachers were to receive a $600 bonus if at least 75 percent of their students maintained or exceeded their normal curve equivalency scores on the relevant SRA tests compared with scores of the previous year. So as to promote collegiality and participation opportunities for nonacademic teachers, all teachers would have received the bonus in a school where 75 percent of the teachers made it.

In the other school district where student achievement is a main determiner of merit pay, end-of-year achievement scores for an entire school are used in relation to targets established early in the year. Virtually all teachers in the school receive $400 bonuses if targets are met. The school board sets targets in the fall based on demographic considerations and past test results. In its fifth year of operation (1988–89), the program was extended from the elementary to middle schools. School objectives were established in other areas besides student achievement, and measures of self-concept, school climate, and other "process" areas were used in addition to or as a substitute for achievement. The school board judges overall progress in the district, however, on the basis of how much change occurs from year to year on standardized achievement tests.

In one district, students and parents are also surveyed to enrich the data base that is used to judge the teaching effectiveness of career ladder candidates. Students are asked about such matters as how fair and impartial a teacher is and how much encouragement this teacher gives them. Also asked is how much they have learned in a particular teacher's class. Parents are asked, among other items, about how much they think their child has learned under a specific teacher, how much communication they have received from this teacher, and how available for conferences he or she has been.

CRITERIA FOR MERIT PAY OR PROMOTION

Underlying the evaluation systems are specific expectations of how teachers should perform both inside and outside the classroom. These performance expectations are the variables on which teacher behavior is to be judged. The primary means of assessing many of them is observation of classroom teaching and recording and/or rating how well they are manifested. Variables selected for assessment are often those that considerable research indicates promote student learning. Some variables have little research backing, however, but are considered by educators as important dimensions of the teaching act.

Not all of what teachers do is seen during classroom teaching. Important dimensions of overall teaching performance include, for instance, the quality of the planning, collegiality with other teachers, and professionalism outside, as well as inside, the classroom. One survey question focused on what criteria were used in determining whether or not an award or promotion was justified. Responders were requested to check all that were so included. The results are presented in Table 6.

The two superintendents who checked "other" indicated that "student achievement" is the sole criterion they use. Among the other nine districts, the quality of lesson plans and the quality of teaching are among the criteria cited in all but one instance. For one district, in lieu of assessing the overall quality of teaching, teachers are observed as they attempt to demonstrate one set of designated teaching practices at a

Table 6. Criteria used in the assessment of teaching performance in eleven school divisions.

	f	%
Attendance of Teachers	5	45.5
Quality of Lesson Plans	8	72.7
Quality of Teaching	8	72.7
Graduate Work Taken/Degree Received	3	27.3
Amount of Extra Curricular Supervision/Activity	3	27.3
Kind/Extent of Professional Development	6	54.5
Professionalism in Attitude/Behavior	6	54.5
Collegiality with Other Teaching Personnel	5	45.5
Leadership Qualities	4	36.4
Other	2	18.2

time, up to three sets a year. Other criteria used by approximately half of the school districts in the assessment of teaching performance are participation in professional development activities, attendance, professionalism, and collegiality with other teachers. Instructional leadership is judged in four evaluation systems, especially when promotion to the highest rungs on a career ladder is being considered. Although nine out of eleven school districts pay a supplement for graduate degrees or course work, they are included as criteria for merit awards or promotion in only three. Similarly, all but one district pay those who sponsor clubs or activities extra money, but these activities count as part of the overall teacher assessment criteria in only three districts.

STANDARDS

Two survey questions requested information about the standards used in determining whether or not an award or promotion is justified. Answers to the first, an open-ended one, typically refer one to the manual, the evaluation plan, or state something about "exceptional performance." In several instances the plans specify a certain proportion of teacher evaluation variables that must be rated as "exceptional," with none judged as below the competency level. For those dependent on student achievement, average gain scores or the percentages of children who should pass specific tests are established ahead of time. In the district in which teacher competency is to be demonstrated in one area of teaching at a time, specific behaviors reflecting that competency are recorded and used for scoring purposes.

The second question asked whether standards included comparisons with (a) other teachers, (b) group averages, or (c) designated performance goals. One superintendent checked group averages and designated performance goals, and seven others checked only the latter. One of the three who did not officially make a selection wrote "SRA test scores." The plan itself, however, specifies certain percentages of students making or exceeding their scores from the previous year. Thus, a second district is really using group averages as well as designated performance. What is most obvious in these answers, however, is the fact that no district indicated teachers were being compared with each other.

The avoidance of direct comparisons of one teacher to another may be one of the most distinguishing features of school personnel practices as contrasted with those in business and industry. Commissions, bonuses, and promotions in the commercial world presumably go to those with the best performance records. Comparing performance records and ranking people from best to worst is quite common in business and industry. In education, ranking people is almost taboo, and singling people out for "teacher of the year" awards is usually done reluctantly, with all sorts of apologies to everyone else (McKenna, Carter, and Berliner, 1987). Such awards were mentioned by less than a fourth of all Virginia districts. Where they had once been given, in several instances, teachers or teacher associations had petitioned to do away with them. Quotas, which would entail direct comparison of teachers, are also severely frowned on as an arbitrary limitation on how many persons can be considered "best."

One of the major dilemmas school systems face in creating a Merit Pay or Career Ladder System stems from this philosophical difference between education and industry. Evaluation practices that would provide the clearest, most discriminating performance data, i.e., information obtained by ranking individuals making forced choices or using sociometric techniques, run completely counter to longstanding educational traditions. The public mandate calls primarily for a relative standard, i.e., reward the best, for an institution in which only absolute standards are acceptable. Not a single Virginia plan has been identified in which relative standards predominate.

Therefore, in order to achieve some discriminatory capability at the positive end of the performance continuum, raters are often instructed to specify teaching behaviors that cause them to assign above average ratings. Special documentation is required for many variables. Precise descriptors of exceptional teaching patterns, as contrasted with good and poor teaching patterns, are also in many instruments. In one system principals are asked, in recommending career candidate applicants, to indicate if they are among the best, second-best, etc., 10 percent of all the teachers they have ever seen with respect to a particular variable. All of these features are designed to minimize the ceiling and halo effects of traditional rating scales and to encourage valid identification of those who perform better than average. To repeat the point above, however, if current evaluation schemes do not seem satisfactory for selecting "the best teachers," as the public desires, it may be partly the fault of a tradition that prevents the use of better assessment methods.

SOURCES OF DATA

One means of dealing with the assessment of teaching problems is to increase the number of data sources on which judgments are based. It was indicated earlier that the number of observations for career ladder candidates increased dramatically over those of previous years. Not only did the number of observations increase, but, in most cases, the sources of data did as well. Table 7 shows the kinds of data used in each of the eleven school districts. Other than two systems that base awards completely on student outcome data, all districts depend on at least two sources, several use three or four sources, and one considers data from six sources. While administrators' observations play a key role in eight of the systems, lesson plans and other records the teacher presents are

Table 7. Sources of data used to assess candidates in eleven school districts.

	1	2	3	4	5	6	7	8	9	10	11
Self-evaluations		X			X	X					
Obs. by Administrators	X	X	X	X	X	X	X	X			
Obs. by Other Teachers	X		X	X	X				X		
Student Performance	X	X		opt.			X			X	X
Student Ratings	X										
Parent Ratings	X										
Teacher Records	X	X	X	X	X	X	X	X	X		

used just as frequently. Student learning and performance data are required in five districts and optional in one other. Observations by other teachers also play a role in the evaluation process in five school districts. Self-evaluation serves as a source of data in three districts, but only one of these districts is highly selective. Although self-evaluation serves a useful function in formative evaluation, its utility in summative evaluation is questionable, especially when it leads to merit pay or promotion. The teacher faces a conflict of interest between providing accurate information and receiving an award.

Only one system includes the clients of education, i.e., parents and students, as a direct data source. Yet, the origin of this movement and the source of ultimate accountability are the consumers of education. It remains to be seen how valuable student and parent ratings are in the assessment of teaching and, particularly, how well they agree with other data.

COST FACTORS

It should be apparent that a great deal of deliberation and effort is needed to install a good teacher incentive plan and the essential evaluation system to make it work. Potential benefits in improved instruction and greater learning may well be worth the effort, but if realistic long-term cost planning for such programs is not done, they will surely fail.

Cost factors ultimately determine what is possible in a particular time period, given all other school district needs and priorities. Virginia school boards recognize at least two major deterrents at the moment to the adoption of incentive pay plans. 1) The state that provides more than half the funding for school budgets, on average, has no special funds for teacher incentive programs. Other priorities currently usurp potential attention in this direction: full funding of the state standards of quality and raising teachers' salaries to the national average. 2) These programs will require substantial outlays over the intermediate, if not long, term if they are to succeed. This movement is imposed on educators, not desired by many of them. If educators are going to respond positively, they must be convinced that the public interest will be backed up by sufficient funding to make it work.

One should be cautious over how to interpret cost figures reported in the survey. Most of the programs are so new that cost projections are particularly difficult. Realistic limits have to be set from year to year on how many people can receive awards or be promoted. As with all school budget items, these limits ultimately reflect the underlying values of those responsible for the budget, which in turn are subject to changing economic and political forces in the community. Priorities must be established yearly. Where teacher incentive pay ranks in relation to other priorities will always vary from community to community and from one year to the next.

Several survey questions focused on cost, which in turn varied with the demographics involved, i.e., the number of people receiving awards and the size of supplements. Five school districts reported the amounts budgeted for incentive pay for the last two years along with the number of teachers receiving it. Two of these have Career Ladder Plans where the amount of average extra pay for those on the ladder was $2500 and $5139 in 1986–87. A third district gave $800 supplements to about one-fourth of all teachers in the district. Average costs per recipient in the two districts with Merit Pay Plans rather than Career Ladder Plans were $362 and $577.

The cost of these supplements in these five districts seems not only more modest but much more alike when calculated against the total numbers of teachers in the districts. Total supplementary pay divided by all the teachers in the districts were $93, $177, $180, $289, and $294. These would have been the average increases in all teachers' pay if these districts had dropped their incentive pay programs and put all the money then going into supplementary pay into across-the-board raises instead. Although several of the supplementary pay increments will rise somewhat above the figures cited above, as programs become fully implemented, the actual percentage of teacher salary totals is likely to remain between 1 and 3 percent. Variations, of course, will depend on the number of teachers participating and the size of the awards.

The source of extra funds for merit pay is an especially sensitive issue. Teachers do not want to feel that any bonus they receive comes from lowering the raises for other teachers. One of the best means of downplaying this potential disincentive is to have a separate source of funding for the awards. Although extra state money was not available, six districts indicated local governing bodies had made special allocations for this purpose. In two districts where merit supplements came only from regular salary allocations, the vast majority (75 percent, 97 percent) of teachers received them, and in one other the average regular salary increase was 12.9 percent, well over the 10 percent state mandate. Of the six districts reporting special outside allocations, one indicated the use of regular salary funds as well, and another indicated that the money was taken in part from other parts of the budget. At least one other district is known to have tapped funds from other parts of the budget than teachers' salaries during 1986–87.

With seven of the districts indicating some use of regular salary allocations for merit supplements and at least two districts already taking funds from other budget priority areas, the threat to long-term funding of incentive programs remains real and could increase with full implementation of new programs, especially during an economic downturn. The lack of extra state funding appears to be an especially severe deterrent in the face of state-mandated salary increases of specific percentages. The eleven districts must either come up with extra funds for incentive pay on their own or take the extra pay out of the regular pay of other teachers, a most undesirable practice according to many teachers.

The final authority for determining how much money is available for teacher salaries, as well as other budget items, is the general public, i.e., how much people are willing to be taxed for the services they receive. Because it is the public that has asked for such programs, the public might be expected to pay extra for them. In order to estimate how real the public commitment might be, the eleven superintendents were asked whether or not "the total amount of money for teachers' salaries [in 1986–87] would have been less without an incentive pay plan." Eight replied "yes" and three "no." One of the latter probably misread the intent of the question, furthermore, because others in his district clearly believed there would have been less overall money without the plan and the special community based allocation that helped launch it. The other two "no" responses came from districts where the vast majority of teachers received merit pay as part of regular salary allocations. It would seem, therefore, that at least in these eleven districts the public is willing to see more money spent for teacher salaries than otherwise if some of it presumably reflects the quality of their teaching.

Cost factors are complex, but vitally inportant. Planning must be thorough and realistic with respect to them.

SUMMARY

Teacher incentive pay in Virginia is a young and diversified movement. Of the eleven programs that were in operation or under development in 1986–87, seven were less than two years old.[8] Plans are still evolving and not fully operational in several cases.

Their diversity reflects the full range of settings to be found in Virginia from Orange County to Fairfax, Danville to Northampton, and Virginia Beach to Hanover County. Differences between plans are great in percentages of teachers receiving incentive pay, in criteria and data sources used to judge outstanding teaching, in the amounts and types of awards, in their voluntary vs. nonvoluntary nature, and in who conducts evaluation.

Teacher evaluation procedures have been improved substantially, especially for the seven plans in which a limited number of teachers are selected for promotion and/or extra pay. Better evaluation takes more effort and resources. Student performance is at least one criterion and data source in approximately half the plans, the sole criterion in two. In five districts teachers, as well as administrators, serve either as recorders of classroom observation data or as full-fledged evaluators.

The great diversity of these eleven plans undoubtedly reflects differences in purpose and intention of those who proposed and endorsed them, but also in political struggles and tradeoffs during the planning process. Career ladders on which almost everybody is promoted require a much less rigorous (and less threatening) evaluation system than those in which only a few are selected. When pay is given primarily for extra duties, longer hours, and extended contracts, rather than for teaching extra well, traditional worker pay patterns still prevail, and teacher association leadership is likely to be supportive.

The data clearly indicate that pressure to install incentive pay programs usually comes from the community or its representative body, the school board, not from professional educators. In all eleven districts that have incentive pay, the majority of school board members and the community at large are considered in favor of the idea, as is true of at least half of those districts where planning is still going on. A relatively low degree of interest in having such plans is expressed for all educators, including central administrators, except in the eleven districts that have an incentive plan. Even in those districts, however, the majority of teachers are thought not to favor the idea.

Throughout Virginia many planning activities have focused on teacher incentive plans even in school districts that indicate they did not seriously consider developing programs. Four of every five school boards discussed the topic. Three of five conducted literature reviews, examined plans in operation elsewhere, and received staff recommendations, and half the districts established special task forces to consider possibilities. More than two dozen districts have not yet made a final decision on whether or not to develop a plan but indicate they have been studying that possibility for at least two years.

School boards should not initiate teacher incentive plans without near-consensus among their members and widespread community support that would endure changes in board membership and school leadership. Installation of teacher incentive pay represents major structural change imposed by outside forces. Public schools are highly institutionalized around bureaucratic, egalitarian traditions and can be expected to resist this change effort strongly. One can expect much fault-finding with new teacher evaluation systems and documentation demands. Longstanding problems in distinguishing outstanding teaching from average and even less than average teaching in consistent defensible ways will be highlighted as reasons why such programs should not be adopted.

School boards need to be firm and unified in their insistence on putting these programs in place if they expect them to succeed. This is especially true for career ladders, which tend to induce more organizational change and new instructional roles than merit pay alone. Merit Pay Programs are more easily dismantled because funding decisions can be made on a year-to-year basis and no long-term change of status commitments are made to teachers.

Resistance to teacher incentive pay focuses primarily on the means of assessment in determining why one person is more deserving than another. Resistance can also be expected over where the extra money is coming from. Even though the amount of money devoted to teacher incentive plans so far represents only a small percentage of total instructional budgets (1–3 percent), the notion that one's bonus might come in part from basic raises for others is not acceptable to most teachers and would act as a disincentive to participation if invoked. In Virginia, several plans have been started only after such major increases as 12 and 15 percent were granted in basic pay for all teachers. Such tradeoffs may be needed to obtain a reasonable amount of teacher acceptance of the plan. Thus, these programs are likely to cost somewhat more, not less, than traditional pay practices, at least in the initial stages.

It would seem advisable to put one "sticky" issue on the table during the early planning stage, i.e., the long-term cost of merit supplements. Perhaps extra funds can be put aside for two to four years, specifically to launch such programs. Eventually, however, such supplements should be considered part of the regular teacher salary budget. The long-term policy that needs early understanding and endorsement is that, while all teachers can be expected to receive some increases based on cost of living, extra duties, and perhaps years of experience, some percentage of teacher salaries will also reflect the quality of their performance. The latter is what the board and community seem to want in those districts that have adopted teacher incentive pay programs.

It is reasonable for school systems to find extra funds for teacher salaries while such programs are being initiated. Indeed, almost all superintendents of districts with plans indicated that less total money would have been available for teacher salaries during 1986–87 without an incentive pay plan. However, to expect school systems to finance merit supplements indefinitely as an added cost to basic salaries suggests that, should budget cuts come, one will suffer from reduction of the other. Such ambiguity regarding the long-term financing of teacher incentive pay programs will itself induce a continuing distrust of the system. It might be better to establish the long-term principle at the beginning, namely, that some fraction of teachers' salaries will eventually reflect performance. With such a principle clearly understood as part of the standard operating procedure, teachers receiving a bonus should not feel that it comes from someone else.

Because highly selective Merit Pay or Career Ladder Systems represent major organizational change, they need to be thought of as long-term, almost irreversible programs that will require continued attention and fine-tuning for years to come. Ten years may well be a minimum period for their development and complete institutionalization. They should be thought of as major vehicles for accomplishing other policy objectives, such as the improvement of instruction, strengthening the quality of teacher applicants, differentiating teaching roles, stimulating staff development, enhancing teacher leadership, and increasing attention to student learning and performance. These, according to most Virginia superintendents, are likely outcomes of a "good" incentive pay plan. For it to be a good plan, it has to be durable over changes in leadership and early skepticism if not outright resistance from at least some of the teachers.

REFERENCES

Brandt, R. M. 1988. "A Study of Career Ladder Planning and Implementation," A report to OERI. Charlottesville, VA: University of Virginia.

Brandt, R. M. and B. Gansneder. 1987. "Teacher Incentive Pay Programs in Virginia," Charlottesville, VA: Curry School of Education, University of Virginia.

Dworkin, A. G. 1987. *Teacher Burnout in the Public Schools.* Albany, NY: State University of New York Press.

Gansneder, B. and R. M. Brandt. "Factors Influencing the Implementation of Merit Pay Plans," Paper presented at the *American Education Research Association Convention, Washington, DC,* 1988.

Goodlad, J. and M. F. Klein. 1970. *Behind the Classroom Door.* Worthington, OH: C. A. Jones.

McKenna, B., C. Carter, and D. Berliner. "The Nature of Selection and Judging for the Teacher of the Year Award," Paper presented at the *American Education Research Association Convention, Washington, DC,* 1987.

ENDNOTES

1 The term *merit pay* is used synonymously with incentive pay unless it is being contrasted with career ladder.

2 The five districts that indicated they "once had a program, but do not have one now" were added to the twenty-four others that had "considered adopting such a program, but rejected the idea." A total of twenty-two responded to the second questionnaire from these two groups.

3 The eleven public school districts with teacher incentive pay programs were in the counties of Bath, Campbell, Fairfax, Hanover, Henrico, Northampton, and Orange and in the cities of Danville, Lynchburg, Newport News, and Virginia Beach. Monitoring of these programs has been continued by phone and correspondence since the survey was completed in February 1987. New information has been added to the original survey responses if programmatic changes have occurred since then. For example, one program was dropped in 1988 because of substantial budget cuts.

4 The lowest of these percentages might have been extra low at the time because plans were not fully implemented. Also, the district reporting 37 percent of the teachers receiving merit pay automatically limits the opportunity to receive it to those who are in the last four steps of a twelve-step pay scale; 99 percent of the 37 percent received it for "outstanding" performance.

5 Tennessee established one of the nation's first career ladders. Many other ladders today function in the same way with the vast majority of teachers achieving the first level.

6 The percentages of the total teacher population of those on the career ladder or in the related teacher evaluator role increased in these latter divisions to approximately 13 percent after the second year for one and 22 percent in the third year for the other.

7 Technically, no low-inference coding systems such as those developed in Alabama or Florida are currently being used in Virginia as the primary tool for assessing teachers, except for those in the Beginning Teacher Assistance Program.

8 Two more districts have started programs since 1987 and one of the eleven has dropped its program.

CHAPTER 8

The Effects of Financial and Nonfinancial Rewards: Program Description and Research Results

LARRY E. FRASE – *San Diego State University*

REWARDING AND MOTIVATING TEACHERS: THE PROGRAM FOR EXCELLENCE

THE desire to reward and compensate high quality teaching has a long but blemished legacy in the U.S.A., as well as other countries. As pointed out in the Introduction to this book and by Professor Fenwick English in Chapter 1, school boards and superintendents have long expressed displeasure with the egalitarian teacher salary schedule and have emphasized the need for differentiated recognition based on quality of work. Although the number of superintendents and boards expressing these views have fluctuated, the ideas have always been present. The board and administration of the Catalina Foothills School District in Tucson, Arizona, is an example of one district's way of rewarding teachers who demonstrate outstanding instructional abilities. The program is called the "Program for Excellence."

Administrators realized that paying for excellence was a worthy goal if the purpose were to benefit individual teachers, the school, and the students. They believed that recompense should be perceived not only as a reward, but also as an incentive, and that the underlying purpose should be to motivate teachers to continue excellent teaching and to make additional improvements. Based on these assumptions, the question became "What motivators can be provided to teachers that will reward and perpetuate the instructional excellence?" Herzberg's (1966) Motivation–Hygiene Theory was used as the organizing center of the board's plan because it provided crucial answers to this very important question.

Contrary to basic assumptions in the literature at the time, Herzberg's theory asserts that two separate and distinct sets of factors account for satisfaction (motivation) and dissatisfaction (hygiene). According to Herzberg's theory, the factors that serve as motivators are tied to work *content*. They include achievement, recognition for

217

achievement, intrinsic interest in work itself, growth, and advancement. These factors serve people's motivational needs.

Hygiene factors account for job dissatisfaction. They are extrinsic to the work content and concern the workers' relationship to the context of the job. Hygiene factors include matters of company policy, administration, supervision, interpersonal relationships, working conditions, salary, status, and security. According to the theory, if the needs are met, dissatisfaction can be avoided. Based on this theoretical foundation, a crucial factor in formulating the program was to provide internal rewards, which in turn serve as motivators.

Assumptions, Funding, Rewards, and Notification Process

Several key assumptions were necessary for implementation of a teacher recognition program, the most significant being that competent administrators are capable of identifying excellence in the classroom. Given the somewhat unsatisfactory history of merit systems and the apparent unpopularity they have with teacher associations, a decision was made to avoid the rigorous and conflict-laden process of governance by committee and the identification of universally acceptable criteria of excellence. Since principals are legally responsible for and usually capable of evaluating instruction, their judgment was used as the means of identifying excellence in the classroom. In practice, principals recommended teachers whose nominations were then reviewed by the superintendent and assistant superintendent.

The funds available for the recognition program were distributed proportionately among the schools. In addition, the size of the award was commensurate with the performance of the teacher, thus resulting in varying types and amounts. Again, administrative judgment was used to place a value on the level of teaching performance. Contributions outside the classroom, service on committees or community projects, and professional attitude and cooperation were minor considerations in a teacher's selection for the program. Excellence in working with students in an instructional setting was the major factor considered.

A variety of awards, such as out-of-state attendance at professional conferences, cash, computers, and instructional materials was granted. In value, awards ranged from $1200 for a conference to $200 for classroom equipment. Award possibilities were discussed in a conference between the teacher and the principal, with great care taken to identify an experience or reward that the teacher would value highly and that would fit a motivator category as described by Herzberg. Whenever feasible, an attempt was made to have the item or money enhance the teacher's ability to assist children in the classroom. According to Herzberg's theory, money is not a motivator. However, due to the obvious importance of money and the commonly held opinion that it is an effective reward, it was included in the list of rewards available to teachers.

The notification process was kept fairly informal and was generally done by the principals. The intent was to reinforce an existing high level of performance, not to demoralize or chastise nonrecipients. This delicate process required tact on the part of the principals in order to avoid conflicts. Dissension over criteria, selection, and the awards were minimized by keeping the program low-key and by selecting teachers whose performance and reputation were beyond reproach.

Program Evaluation

Following the first year of implementation, a questionnaire and interviews were used to evaluate the program, "The Program for Excellence." Each is addressed below.

The Questionnaire

Data regarding teacher opinions and attitudes toward the program were collected via a five-point Likert scale questionnaire. Each program participant (thirty-four in total) was provided a questionnaire. Thirty questionnaires (76 percent) were returned (one was partially completed and three were unusable either because the questions had been altered or no responses were provided). Some questionnaires were returned anonymously, while many teachers chose to sign their names. The questionnaire items are presented below:

(1) I consider the remuneration received through the Program for Excellence as "special recognition" for my teaching excellence.

   Strongly Disagree Disagree Undecided Agree Strongly Agree

(2) The special recognition received through the Program for Excellence served as motivation for me to continue my teaching excellence and to make further improvements.

   Strongly Disagree Disagree Undecided Agree Strongly Agree

(3) I believe the Program for Excellence has caused great dissension among teachers.

Strongly Disagree Disagree Undecided Agree Strongly Agree

(4) I do not value the special recognition received in SY80–81.

Strongly Disagree Disagree Undecided Agree Strongly Agree

(5) I believe I will receive additional recognition if I continue my teaching excellence.

Strongly Disagree Disagree Undecided Agree Strongly Agree

(6) Please provide comments you consider to be appropriate.

Questionnaire Results

Frequency counts are presented in Table 1. A summary of the results follows:

(1) There was considerable agreement that the remuneration received through the Program for Excellence was considered "special recognition" for teaching excellence. Twenty-four of the twenty-seven usable responses were positive (agree or strongly agree).

(2) A large majority of the respondents agreed that the special recognition served as a monitor for them to continue their teaching excellence. There was, however, diversity in the responses: twenty-one subjects agreed that the recognition served as a motivator, two were undecided, and four disagreed.

(3) Fifteen teachers agreed that the Program for Excellence caused dissension among the teachers. Again, the range of responses was wide: one respondent strongly disagreed that dissension had oc-

Table 1.

Item No.	Strongly Agree	Agree	Undecided	Disagree	Strongly Disagree
1.	10	14	2	1	0
2.	6	15	2	1	3
3.	2	13	6	5	1
4.	0	1	4	13	9
5.	7	12	6	0	1

curred, five disagreed, six had no opinion, thirteen agreed, and two strongly agreed. The concern expressed about dissension via the questionnaire is considerably more than that expressed during the interviews or observed throughout the school year. Although dissension is never desired in a school district, the report of dissension was de-emphasized because the majority of teachers valued the recognition received.

(4) A large majority (81 percent) of the respondents valued the special recognition received, four were undecided, and one disagreed.

(5) There was agreement that the recipients believed they would receive additional recognition if they continued their teaching excellence: seventeen agreed, six were undecided, and one strongly disagreed.

The Interview

Twelve teachers, six program participants and six nonparticipants, were randomly selected and interviewed by a professor of educational administration from the University of Arizona. The interviews provided a means for collecting teachers' overall opinions of the program, eliciting suggestions for program improvement, and discovering reasons for the program's attractiveness/unattractiveness. In contrast to the questionnaire, the interviews allowed the investigator to explore the subjects' attitudes and opinions. The interviewer's summary of the interviews are provided below.

> One of the more common perceptions in the interviews was that teachers in the Catalina Foothills School District are of exceptionally high caliber, extremely competent, and do an excellent job; otherwise they would not be there. They were also very positive about the recent salary raise, which was seen as a gesture of appreciation for a job well done.

> Other specific attitudes and suggestions were somewhat mixed. For example, the program was seen as a carrot by some and not really necessary. A number of the individuals thought there ought to be more information disseminated about the program. Others believed that making the program public (highly visible) would defeat its purpose, and those teachers not receiving awards would tend to feel somewhat devalued. The major concensus seemed to be that if the program continues and is well administered, it will generate enough informal publicity to meet the need for visibility. Some believed it would be beneficial if the district would informally publicize the program's purposes and criteria for awards.

In summary, the teachers think very highly of the district, appreciate the fact that a large number of their colleagues are extremely competent, and believe that resources distributed in the form of "awards for excellence" are not particularly high motivators. Most teachers did, however, appreciate the reward received. Comments indicative of this attitude included: "nice to be recognized," "good program," "teachers should be recognized," and "this type of thing keeps you going." While teachers do not see this program as a top priority item, they believe it should be continued. Assuming these comments convey an accurate impression, the district can profitably continue the program and let it generate its own momentum and benefits.

Theoretical Criteria

Edward Lawler (1979) provided the following criteria for use in evaluating reward systems. Data derived from the questionnaire survey, interviews, and observations throughout the school year were used to evaluate the Program for Excellence on the basis of each criterion.

(1) *Importance—Are Rewards Valued?* As stated in the questionnaire results section, there was high agreement that the rewards were valued. The interviews yielded the same finding. The reward most highly valued appeared to be pay for professional conferences; of course, this type of reward is also highly valuable to the school district because the participating teachers gain new skills and later train other teachers during in-service sessions. The reward least valued was money. Teachers seemed to believe that special recognition in the form of money was contrary to professionalism. It is interesting that nonparticipants most frequently voiced this perception.

(2) *Flexibility—Can the Reward Be Individualized?* The rewards or recompense offered varied from pay for national conferences to special classroom equipment and classroom materials to cash. In addition, the following statements from teachers supported the contention that adequate flexibility existed and was appreciated: "The fact that recognition can take many forms was very positive" and "The fact that the rewards are different and can be individualized for each recipient is very positive."

(3) *Visibility—Secrecy vs. Public Knowledge.* The Program for Excellence deliberately had very little visibility during its first year to avoid possible negative responses that are often associated with innovations and gifts from the pedagogical "bandwagon." Teacher

opinions on visibility varied drastically. Some asked for the program to be highly publicized, while others stated it is crucial that the program be kept low-key. Statements included: "Personally I want it public" and "It would be damaging to publicize names of recipients."

(4) *Frequency—How Often Can Rewards Be Given?* In most cases, recompense was provided once throughout the school year. However, for several teachers, rewards were provided on two or three separate occasions. This appeared to be highly advantageous in that the second and third rewards appeared to provide a good mid-year or second semester "pick-me-up."

(5) *Cost—How Much Does the Reward Cost?* In the second year, the program cost was .06 percent of the district budget. This cost is slight in comparison to the benefits. In general, the teachers agreed that the recompense received through the program represented special recognition, that it provided motivation for them to continue their teaching excellence and to make further improvements, that they valued the reward and believed they would gain additional recognition if they continued their teaching excellence.

Summary and Conclusion

Overall, based on the data provided, the program was considered successful. The possibility of dissension within the teaching ranks as a result of this program was a very serious one. Perception of dissension must be considered and its causes reduced where possible. The major source of dissension or negative feelings toward the program came from one school in which a list of teacher's names ranked on the basis of teaching performance was distributed to the faculty. The impact of this practice was negative and therefore was quickly eliminated. Other than this incident, dissension has been minimal, if not absent.

The wide range of opinion regarding visibility of the program warranted further study. Some teachers wanted total secrecy regarding the program, while others suggested providing recipients' names to newspapers to gain high visibility. This aspect of visibility is very closely related to dissension and, therefore, becomes quite crucial. Some teachers believed that greater visibility would cause greater dissension, while other teachers believed it would further enhance the desirability and related prestige of the reward. The latter suggested that a formal letter from the superintendent indicating selection for the Program for Excellence would be gratifying. This practice seemed reasonable and valuable, and when implemented it was well-received. The decision was made to maintain a low profile.

By far the most highly prized form of recognition was conference attendance. Teachers believed their professionalism and value to the school district were greatly enhanced as a result of conference attendance. Use of conference attendance was continued and expanded. Based on statements from teachers, use of financial recognition was considered. Interview data indicated that teachers do not value financial recognition beyond that which they receive from the salary schedule. However, money was retained on the menu of rewards.

The program's success in the view of the school board and the community was dramatically manifested in a 50 percent increase in funding the following year.

THE ROLE OF MERIT PAY: MOTIVATION OR SIMPLY THE RIGHT THING TO DO?

Background

The first major change in the program occurred in 1987 when the menu of rewards was limited to professional travel. When a merit pay program was introduced in the district, cash was eliminated as a reward in the Program for Excellence. Other rewards were eliminated since they were seldom selected.

Theories associated with worker motivation and worker job site interaction continued to develop through the 1970s and 1980s. Battle lines were again drawn between those who believed that money is a powerful motivator and those who believed that money is less powerful a motivator than intrinsic rewards. Both money and intrinsic rewards were offered in the Program for Excellence in an attempt to create a setting for testing the theories.

The remainder of this chapter is devoted to a review of literature on this subject and a description of the research conducted in conjunction with the Program for Excellence.

What Motivates Teachers?

At approximately the same time that Phase I came to an end, demand for higher teacher salaries via merit pay, career ladders, and across-the-board raises came into vogue with the publication of *A Nation at Risk* (1983) and *A Nation Prepared: Teachers for the 21st Century* (1986).

The response to the call for higher salaries was widespread. By 1985, twenty-nine states implemented state-wide Career Ladder or Merit Pay Programs in an attempt to combine pay incentives with new career roles as a means of attracting and retaining teachers and motivating them to improve performance (Cornett, 1985). Teachers, too, supported the general idea of basing pay, at least in part, on performance (Rist, 1983; Feistritzer, 1986).

The common assumption of Career Ladder and Merit Pay Plan proponents was and continues to be that higher pay will more effectively serve to attract, retain, and motivate teachers to improve performance than nonfinancial rewards. Cash incentives were viewed as the "cure-alls" to eduation's personnel ills (Olsen, 1986), although the actual effects of money, as opposed to other rewards, are not known and are still strongly debated in the professional literature. There is considerable evidence that intrinsic rewards are more effective motivators than extrinsic ones such as money (Hackman and Oldham, 1980; Herzberg, 1966; Sergiovanni, 1967; Deci, 1976; Spuck, 1974; Weaver, 1977; Bess, 1977; Wright, 1985; Sherman and Smith, 1984; Daniel and Esser, 1980). In contrast, Schlechty and Vance (1981) and Sykes (1983) argue that extrinsic rewards may be needed to retain better classroom teachers. Further, there is considerable evidence that the use of external rewards reduces internal motivation (Calder and Staw, 1975; Daniel and Esser, 1980; deCharms, 1968; Deci, 1976; Greene and Lepper, 1974; Pinder, 1976; Ross, 1975; Staw, Calder, Hess, and Sandelands, 1980).

The value and importance of intrinsic and extrinsic rewards in the teaching profession have received considerable attention by researchers (Lortie, 1975; Kottcamp, Provenzo, and Cohn, 1986; National Education Association, 1971, 1976, 1981; Fruth et al., 1982). However, the actual effects of rewards have received very little research attention. Many research studies have questioned whether certain job factors and rewards result in a motivational effect or serve to prevent dissatisfaction in the workplace. Frederick Herzberg's (1966) Motivation–Hygiene Theory is a case in point and has been internationally replicated in industry (Myers, 1971; Sergiovanni and Carver, 1980; Herzberg, 1966) and in the teaching field by Sergiovanni (1967), Savage (1967), Wickstrom (1971), and Schmidt (1976) with only minor deviation from the original results. The theory has been criticized by Salancik and Pfeffer

(1977); Campbell, Dunnette, Lawler, and Weick (1970); and House and Wigdor (1967), among others. The primary emphasis of the criticism has been that the theory is bound to the critical-incidence methodology (see Herzberg, 1966), which was utilized for data collection and analysis. The criticisms are not sufficiently serious to disprove the theory or seriously restrict its use; the theory is considered by many to be valid and useful (Miner, 1980; Hoy and Miskel, 1987; Sergiovanni, 1980, 1987; Frase, Hetzel, and Grant, 1982a, 1982b; Hackman and Oldham, 1980; Lawler, 1986).

Research on teachers is supportive of the Motivation–Hygiene Theory in that intrinsic rewards are shown to be more powerful motivators than extrinsic rewards. Oxman and Michelli (1980) found that intrinsic factors affected satisfaction, but extrinsic factors were sources of dissatisfaction. Teachers consistently rated intrinsic or "psychic" rewards, e.g., "knowing that I have reached students and they have learned," as more powerful motivators than extrinsic rewards such as money and fringe benefits (Lortie, 1975; Kottcamp, Provenzo, and Cohn, 1986). Spuck (1974) found that schools that evidence two intrinsic reward variables—a high level of pride of workmanship and a high level of positive social interaction among staff members—tend to experience ease of recruitment and a higher teacher retention rate than other schools.

Two recent studies found intrinsic rewards more powerful motivators than external rewards. Feistritzer (1986) found that teachers ranked the "opportunity to use their minds and abilities" as first in importance, "chance to work with young people" as second, and "appreciation for a job well done" as third. Salary was rated fourth by teachers and first by other employed adults with four-year college educations. Similar results were reported in *The Metropolitan Life Survey of Former Teachers in America* (1985), which found that teachers remain in the classroom for the "satisfaction of teaching."

These results reflect Herzberg's (1966) findings that intrinsic rewards serve as motivators and Sergiovanni's (1967), Wickstrom's (1971), and Savage's (1967) findings that teachers obtain their greatest satisfaction from reaching and affecting students, followed by experiencing recognition for a job well done. Sergiovanni (1967) further stated that caution must be exercised to avoid providing for motivation needs at the expense of hygiene needs. If employees are preoccupied with concerns about unsatisfactory working conditions or the inability to provide adequate food and shelter, positive impact from motivators will not be realized.

Herzberg used the Motivation–Hygiene Theory to develop the concept of job enrichment as a means of motivating employees. The practice has received much attention from industry and educators in the 1960s, 1970s, and 1980s. Lawler (1986) and Hackman and Oldham (1980) claimed that intrinsic rewards were more directly related to performance than external rewards. They claimed that satisfaction, rather than causing good performance, is caused by it. Other researchers (Hackman and Lawler, 1971; Hackman and Oldham, 1976; Turner and Lawrence, 1965) provided further evidence that job characteristics can directly affect emplyees' attitudes and behavior at work. The dominant job design theory during the past two decades has been the Job Characteristics Model, which combines Maslow's Need-Fullfillment Theory of Motivation, Herzberg's Motivation–Hygiene Theory, and Vroom's Expectancy Theory (Vroom, 1964). Primary proponents of the model, Hackman and Oldham (1980), specified three psychological states (feeling of meaningfulness, feeling of responsibility, and knowledge of results) and five job characteristics (skill variety, task identity, task significance, autonomy, and feedback) as requirements for job enrichment and enhancement of internal motivation to perform effectively. Lawler (1986) further asserts that jobs must be enriched both horizontally and vertically before there will be an increase in internal motivation to perform effectively and that individual job enrichment usually has a greater impact on quality of work than on productivity. Reports of job enrichment success are numerous (Kopelman, 1985; Locke, 1980).

In summary, there are sufficient research results and empirically validated theories to question the wisdom of depending on across-the-board or merit raises to enhance significantly the public schools' ability to recruit, retain, and motivate top teachers. This suggests that use of motivation rather than hygiene factors is more likely to yield the results claimed by career ladder and merit pay proponents.

The Research Project

The purpose of the study was to test the Motivation–Hygiene Theory by assessing the likelihood of teachers achieving an increase in job enrichment opportunities and recognition after a reward in the Program for Excellence for meritorious teaching. Two rewards, professional travel for training and cash, were included in the analysis. The former represented the motivator/satisfier category in the Motivation–Hygiene Theory while the latter represented the hygiene/dissatisfier category. Four professional activities were used to assess changes in the number of job enrichment opportunities: 1) conducting workshops for other teachers, 2) chairing special committees, 3) participating on special committees, and 4) redesigning curriculum. Job enrichment opportunities addressed in these questions were derived from the job-characteristics model (Hackman and Oldham, 1980) and met the requirements for job enrichment as stated by Hackman and Oldham (1980) and Lawler (1986).

Four sources of recognition (Herzberg, 1966) in the school environment were used to assess changes in recognition. Items 5, 6, and 7 measured changes in recognition from administrators, teachers, and students, respectively, while item 8 measured changes in advice-seeking from peers.

Two hypotheses guided this investigation:

(1) Opportunities to experience perceived job enrichment will be greater for participants choosing professional travel as a reward than those choosing cash.

(2) Recognition will be greater for those choosing professional travel as a reward than for those choosing cash.

Methodology

Sample

Thirty-eight (ten male and twenty-eight female) high-performing kindergarten through eighth grade teachers in the Catalina Foothills School District in Tucson, Arizona, participated in the study. These teachers were selected by administrators to participate in an established teacher reward program on the basis of their superior classroom teaching performance during the 1985–86 school year (Frase, Hetzel, and Grant, 1982a, 1982b). Participants were asked to choose cash or professional travel as a reward for their high instructional performance. The rewards were valued at approximately $1000 each. Conference subjects selected by teachers included Teacher Expectations and Student Achievement (TESA), mathematics, writing, classroom management, and other educational topics. However, none of the topics directly related to the changes analyzed (see Tables 2 and 3). For example, no teacher attended a conference dealing with conducting a workshop (Criterion 1). Eighteen teachers chose cash and twenty chose travel. The effects of other rewards were not tested due to the small number of teachers selecting them.

In September 1986, the year following the receipt of the reward, participants were asked whether they experienced a decrease, increase, or no change in opportunities to engage in four job enrichment activities: 1) conducting workshops for other teachers, 2) chairing special committees, 3) participating in special committees, and 4) redesigning curriculum. They were also asked whether they experienced an increase, decrease, or no change in recognition from 5) administrators, 6) teachers, and 7) students or 8) advice-seeking from peers. The response rate was 100 percent. The opportunities for job enrichment as defined by Hackman and Oldham (1980) and the sources of recognition as defined by Herzberg (1966) are examples of job enrichment and sources of recognition.

The mean age of participants was 37.1 years with a standard deviation of 8.1. The mean number of years of teaching experience was 10.3 with a standard deviation of 0.9. The mean number of years teaching experience in the school district was 6.2 with a standard deviation of 0.5. The mean undergraduate grade point average was 3.25 on a 4.0 scale with a standard deviation of 0.06. Sixty-nine percent of the participants were married, 28 percent were single, and 4 percent were separated or divorced. The political and practical considerations of administering merit programs in this case did not permit random assignment of rewards to teachers.

The fact that rewards were self-selected by teachers suggests that caution should be taken in making any generalizations from this study. Even so, the means and ranges of demographic characteristics (age, gender, years of experience, grade point average, and marital status) were very similar for those teachers who chose professional travel and those who chose cash. No levels of significance greater than $p = .48$ between the demographic characteristics addressed in this study and the rewards chosen were observed. Therefore, demographic characteristics and rewards chosen were independent of each other.

Analysis

Teacher responses were arranged in 2 × 2 contingency tables, and the relationships between rewards chosen and impact (changes in opportunities to experience job enrichment and perceived recognition) were tested for significance. The chi-square test of significance using the Yates correction factor for continuity was used to assess responses to questions 3, 4, 5, and 8, and the Fisher Exact Probability Test was used to assess responses to questions 1, 2, 6, and 7, since the expected frequency in one or more cells in these tables was less than 5 (Seigel, 1956).

Discussion of Results

Hypothesis 1

Opportunities to experience job enrichment will be greater for participants choosing professional travel as a reward than for those choosing cash.

Criteria 1–4 (see Table 2) were used to assess Hypothesis 1. Each is discussed below.

Criterion 1: Opportunities to Conduct Workshops

The observed differences in proportion of teachers in each group who reported an increase in opportunities to conduct workshops was significant at the $p < .0088$ level. Those who chose cash reported no increase. These opportunities represent the intrinsic motivator labeled "responsibility" in the Motivation–Hygiene Theory and are examples of job enrichment.

Criterion 2: Opportunities to Chair Special Committees

The observed difference in the proportion of teachers in each group who reported an increase in opportunities to chair special committees was significant at the $p < .0725$ level. Those who chose cash reported no increase. These opportunities are intrinsic motivators labeled "responsibility" in the Motivation–Hygiene Theory and are examples of job enrichment. The observed proportion of individuals who selected travel and reported an increase (25 percent) was higher than the proportion for those who selected cash (zero percent).

Criterion 3: Opportunities to Serve on Special Committees

The observed difference in the proportion of teachers in each group who reported an increase in opportunities to serve on special committees was only significant at the $p = .2204$ level. The observed propor-

Table 2.

Question 1. Conducting Workshops			Question 2. Chairing Special Committees		
	Reward			Reward	
Impact	Cash	Travel	Impact	Cash	Travel
No Increase	18	12	No Increase	18	15
Increase	0	8	Increase	0	5

Fisher Exact =
$p < .0088$ $df = 1$

Fisher Exact =
$p < .0725$ $df = 1$

Question 3. Participation on Special Committees			Question 4. Redesigning Curriculum		
	Reward			Reward	
Impact	Cash	Travel	Impact	Cash	Travel
No Increase	15	12	No Increase	12	5
Increase	3	8	Increase	6	15

$x^2 = 1.5015$
$df = 1$ $p < .2204$

$x^2 = 5.074$
$df = 1$ $p < .0243$

tion of individuals who selected travel and who reported an increase (40 percent) was higher than the proportion for those who selected cash (16 percent).

Criterion 4: Redesigning Curriculum in Areas of Expertise

The observed difference in proportion of teachers in each group who reported an increase in opportunities to redesign curriculum in areas of expertise was significant at the $p = .0243$ level. Opportunities to serve on district-wide committees to update curriculum are intrinsic motivators labeled "responsibility" in the Motivation–Hygiene Theory and are examples of job enrichment.

In summary, a significant relationship between type of reward and its impact was found for two of the four opportunities for job enrichment and responsibility. In all cases, the observed proportion of teachers who reported an increase was higher for those who selected travel than for those who chose cash.

Hypothesis 2

Recognition will be greater for participants choosing professional travel as a reward than for those choosing cash. The second hypothesis was tested by questions 5–8 as shown in Table 3.

Criterion 5: Perceived Respect from Administrators

The observed difference in the proportion of teachers in the travel and cash groups who reported an increase in respect from administrators was not significant, $p < .446$.

Criterion 6: Perceived Respect from Teachers

The observed difference in the proportion of teachers in the travel and cash groups who reported an increase in respect from teachers was not significant, $p < .676$.

Criterion 7: Perceived Respect from Students

The observed difference in the proportion of teachers from the two groups who reported an increase in respect from students was not significant, $p < 1.0$.

Criterion 8: Advice-Seeking by Colleagues

The observed difference in the proportion of teachers from the two groups who reported an incrase in advice-seeking from colleagues closely approximated statistical significance, $p < .0522$ level. As with all eight questions, teachers selecting travel reported the higher proportion of increase. The presence of strong internal consistency for all dif-

Table 3.

Question 5. Perceived Respect from Administration		
	Reward	
Impact	Cash	Travel
No Increase	13	11
Increase	5	9

$x^2 = .5808$
$df = 1\ p < .446$

Question 6. Perceived Respect from Teachers		
	Reward	
Impact	Cash	Travel
No Increase	17	17
Increase	1	3

Fisher Exact =
$p < .676\ df = 1$

Question 7. Perceived Respect from Students		
	Reward	
Impact	Cash	Travel
No Increase	18	19
Increase	0	1

Fisher Exact =
$p < 1.0\ df = 1$

Question 8. Advice Seeking		
	Reward	
Impact	Cash	Travel
No Increase	16	11
Increase	2	9

$x^2 = 3.7705$
$df = 1\ p < .0522$

ferences (i.e., all travel effects are in the direction of higher ratings and are greater than the effects of cash) is a strong indication that this difference is due to the effect of the reward. This difference in impact on advice-seeking by colleagues is considered significant.

Advice-seeking from colleagues is an intrinsic motivator known as "recognition" (Herzberg, 1966). Advice-seeking from peers is a very powerful reflection of recognition and achievement. It is interesting to note that teachers electing travel did not report an increase in respect from other teachers but did report a significant increase in teachers seeking their advice, indicating that teachers may not recognize advice-seeking as increased respect. This may be explained by the fact that respect requires a relatively long time to develop. Advice-seeking, on the other hand, is an objective count of times others seek advice and does not require an extended period of time for development.

In summary, the chi-square showed a significant difference between type of reward and its impact on question 8, advice-seeking from peers. In all instances, the observed frequencies of teachers who chose travel were higher than for those who selected cash.

Conclusions and Implications

In comparison to teachers selecting cash, teachers who favored professional travel reported significantly greater increases in the number of opportunities to experience job enrichment in the form of conducting workshops for teachers and redesigning curriculum. These opportunities represent intrinsic motivators that Herzberg labeled "responsibility" and "possibilities for growth." In addition, teachers choosing travel reported a significantly greater increase in advice-seeking from colleagues. This is an internal motivator that Herzberg labeled "recognition." In summary, professional travel as a reward for teaching excellence is associated with significant increases in recognition from peers and opportunities to experience professional responsibilities and opportunities for growth associated with job enrichment. These findings should be viewed with some caution since the impact of self-selection of rewards is uncertain. It is recommended that similar studies in other locations be conducted with a larger sample size. It is also recommended that the future studies analyze the possible effects of self-selection.

Policymakers should consider the differences in effects of these motivators when choosing ways to spend available funds to motivate teachers. Based on this study, intrinsic motivators, such as professional travel, as opposed to extrinsic motivators, such as cash, appear to lead to greater intrinsic motivation, job enrichment, and involvement in professional activities. This study supports earlier contention that intrinsic rewards yield a greater motivational effect than external rewards. In this study, teachers choosing cash reported little or no increase in intrinsic motivation, job enrichment, or involvement in professional activities.

It is important to note that hygiene needs must be satisfied before motivators can have a positive effect (Sergiovanni, 1980; Hackman and Oldham, 1980; Frase, Hetzel, and Inman, 1987). Policymakers are cautioned to ensure that salary levels and other extrinsic factors are adequate to satisfy hygiene needs. This is considered a prerequisite to successful use of motivators.

Higher pay is generally a major request from teacher bargaining groups, and it is likely that their leaders will continue to seek across-the-board raises. However, the findings of this study support the contention that school boards and administrators cannot buy motivation with salary raises. Negotiating a reward system will likely be very difficult; however, the idea of offering a menu of rewards may make it more palatable to teacher bargaining groups. The school district participating in this study implemented the program without conferring with teachers and experienced complaints for eighteen months until the teachers experienced the benefits of the program. Since that time, acceptance has been high. Without an agreement with the teacher group, boards of education and school executives are left with the option of implementing a reward program unilaterally.

Local- and state-level boards of education and executive directors of professional associations need to be aware of the apparent power and influence of intrinsic motivators in comparison to hygiene factors when negotiating with teacher groups, allocating district funds, and formulating lobbying packages for legislatures to improve the prosperity of teachers. Spending all district funds and focusing legislation on hygiene factors may miss the mark when it comes to teacher recruitment, retention, and performance improvement. While improvement in hygiene factors is often needed or desirable, legislation must provide for flexibility at the local level and insure that both motivational and hygiene factors are considered.

REFERENCES

1986. *A Nation Prepared: Teachers for the 21st Century.* New York: Carnegie Forum on Education and the Economy.

1983. *A Nation at Risk: The Imperative for Education Reform.* U.S. Department of Education, National Commission on Excellence in Education: Washington, D.C.

Bess, J. L. 1977. "The Motivation to Teach," *Journal of Higher Education,* 48(3):243–258.

Calder, B. J. and B. M. Staw. 1975. "Self-Perception of Intrinsic and Extrinsic Motivation," *Journal of Personality and Social Psychology,* 31:432–443.

Campbell, J. P., M. D. Dunnette, E. W. Lawler, and K. E. Weick. 1970. *Managerial Behavior, Performance, and Effectiveness.* New York: McGraw Hill.

Cornett, L. M. 1985. "Trends and Emerging Issues in Career Ladder Plans," *Education Leadership,* 43(3):6–10.

Daniel, T. L. and J. K. Esser. 1980. "Intrinsic Motivation as Influenced by Rewards, Task Interest, and Task Structure," *Journal of Applied Psychology,* 65(5):566–573.

deCharms, R. 1968. *Personal Causation: The Internal Affective Determinants of Behavior.* New York: Academic Press.

Deci, E. L. 1976. "The Hidden Cost of Rewards," *Organizational Dynamics,* 61–72.

Feistritzer, C. 1986. *Profile of Teachers in the U.S.* Washington, D.C.: National Center for Education Information.

Frase, L. E., R. W. Hetzel, and R. T. Grant. 1982a. "Merit Pay: A Research Based Element in Tucson," *Phi Delta Kappan,* 64(4):266–269.

Frase, L. E., R. W. Hetzel, and R. T. Grant. 1982b. "Promoting Instructional Excellence through a Teacher Reward System: Herzberg's Theory Applied," *Planning and Changing,* 13(2): 67–76.

Frase, L. E., R. W. Hetzel, and D. Inman. 1987. "Is there a Sound Rationale behind the Merit Pay Craze?" *Teacher Education Quarterly,* 14(2):90–101.

Fruth, M. J., P. V. Bredeson, and K. L. Kaston. 1982. *Commitment to Teaching: Teachers' Responses to Organizational Incentives."* Wisconsin: Wisconsin Center for Education Research, University of Wisconsin, Madison.

Greene, D. and M. R. Lepper. 1974. "Effects of Extrinsic Rewards on Children's Subsequent Intrinsic Interest," *Child Development,* 54:1141–1145.

Hackman, J. R. and G. R. Oldham. 1980. *Work Redesign.* Reading, PA: Addison-Wesley.

Hackman, R. J. and E. E. Lawler. 1971. "Employee Reactions to Job Characteristics," *Journal of Applied Psychology,* 55:259–286.

Hackman, R. J. and G. R. Oldham. 1976. "Motivation through the Design of Work: Test of a Theory," *Organizational Behavior and Human Performance,* 16:250–279.

Herzberg, F. 1966. *Work and the Nature of Man.* Cleveland: World.

House, R. J. and L. A. Wigdor. 1967. "Herzberg's Dual-Factor Theory of Job Satisfaction and Motivation: A Review of the Evidence and a Criticism," *Personnel Psychology,* 20:369–389.

Hoy, W. K. and C. G. Miskel. 1987. *Educational Administration: Theory Research and Practice.* New York: Random House.

Kopelman, K. E. 1985. "Job Redesign and Productivity: A Review of the Evidence," *National Productivity Review,* 14(3):237–255.

Kottkamp, R., E. Provenzo, and M. Cohn. 1986. "Stability and Change in a Profession: Two Decades of Teacher Attitudes (1964–1984)," *Phi Delta Kappan,* 67(8):559–567.

Lawler, E. E. 1986. *High-Involvement Management.* San Francisco: Jossey-Bass.

Lawler, E. E., David A. Nadler, and J. Richard Hackman. 1979. *Managing Organizational Behavior.* Boston: Little, Brown and Company, pp. 69–70.

Locke, E. A. 1980. "The Relative Effectiveness of Four Methods of Motivating

Employee Performance," In *Changes in Working Life,* K. D. Duncan, M. M. Greeneberg, and D. Wallis, eds. Chichester, England: Wiley.

Lortie, D. 1975. *Schoolteacher: A Sociological Study.* Chicago: University of Chicago Press.

Metropolitan Life Insurance Company. 1985. *The Metropolitan Life Survey of Former Teachers in America.* New York: Metropolitan Life Insurance Company.

Minor, J. B. 1980. *Theories of Organizational Behavior.* Hinsdale: Dryden.

Myers, S. 1971. *Every Employee a Manager.* New York: McGraw-Hill.

National Education Association Studies. 1971, 1976, and 1981. Washington D.C.: National Education Association.

Olson, L. 1986. "Performance Pay: New Round for an Old Debate," *Education Week,* 5(26):1–19.

Oxman, W. G. and N. M. Michelli. 1980. *Teacher Stress in an Urban Center: Analysis of a Survey of Morale among Newark Teachers.* NIE Rep. (Contract No. 400-79-0054), Montclair, NJ: Montclair State College.

Pinder, C. C. 1976. "Additivity Versus Nonadditivity of Intrinsic Incentives: Implications for Work Motivation, Performance, and Attitudes," *Journal of Applied Psychology,* 61:693–700.

Rist, M. C. 1983. "Our Nationwide Poll: Most Teachers Endorse the Merit Pay Concept," *The American School Boards Journal,* 170(9):23–27.

Ross, M. 1975. "Salience of Reward and Intrinsic Motivation," *Journal of Personality and Social Psychology,* 32:245–254.

Salancik, G. R. and J. Pfeffer. 1977. "An Examination of Need-Satisfaction Models of Job Attitudes," *Administration Science Quarterly,* 22:427–456.

Savage, R. M. 1967. "A Study of Teacher Satisfaction and Attitudes: Causes and Effects," Unpublished doctoral dissertation, Auburn University, Montgomery, Alabama.

Seigel, S. 1956. *Non-parametric Statistics.* New York: McGraw-Hill.

Schlechty, P. and V. S. Vance. 1981. "Do Academically Able Teachers Leave Education? The North Carolina Case," *Phi Delta Kappan,* 63(2):106–112.

Schmidt, G. L. 1976. "Job Satisfaction among Secondary School Administrators," *Educational Administration Quarterly,* 12:81–88.

Sergiovanni, T. J. 1967. "Factors Which Affect Satisfaction and Dissatisfaction of Teachers," *The Journal of Educational Administration,* 5:66–82.

Sergiovanni, T. J. and F. D. Carver. 1980. *The New School Executive: A Theory of Administration.* New York: Harper and Row.

Sherman, J. D. and H. L. Smith. 1984. "The Influences of Organizational Structure on Intrinsic versus Extrinsic Motivation," *Academy of Management Journal,* 27(4):877–885.

Spuck, D. W. 1974. "Reward Structures in the Public High School," *Education Administration Quarterly,* 10(1):18–34.

Staw, B. M., B. J. Calder, R. K. Hess, and L. E. Sandelands. 1980. "Intrinsic Motivation and Norms about Payment," *Journal of Personality,* 48:1–14.

Sykes, G. 1983. "Public Policy and the Problems of Teacher Quality: The Need for Screens and Magnets?" in *Handbook of Teaching and Policy,* L. S. Schulman and G. Sykes, eds., New York: Longman, p. 98.

Turner, A. N. and P. R. Lawrence. 1965. *Industrial Jobs and the Worker.* Boston: Harvard Graduate School of Business Administration.

Vroom, V. H. 1964. *Work and Motivation.* New York: Wiley.

Weaver, C. N. 1977. "Relationships among Pay, Race, Sex, Occupational Prestige, Supervision, Work Autonomy, and Job Satisfaction in a National Sample," *Personnel Psychology,* 30:437–445.

Wickersham, J. P. 1868. *Report of the Superintendent of Common Schools of the Commonwealth of Pennsylvania.* Pennsylvania: Harrisburg—Singerly and Myers State Printers.

Wickstrom, R. A. 1971. "An Investigation into Job Satisfaction among Teachers. Oregon: Unpublished doctoral dissertation, University of Oregon.

Wright, R. 1985. "Motivating Teacher Involvement in Professional Growth Activities," *The Canadian Administrator,* 24(5):1–6.

PART IV

TEACHER EVALUATION

CHAPTER 9

Designing Evaluation Systems for Performance Pay

ROBERT W. HETZEL – *Superintendent, Catalina Foothills School District, Tucson, Arizona*

TEACHER evaluation has been an ongoing process in public schools since their inception. In some districts it is a somewhat perfunctory procedure occurring each spring and limited to a brief classroom visit, the completion of a rating scale, and a short conference. On the other hand, in many districts teachers and evaluators are involved in a sophisticated clinical supervisory process including frequent classroom observation, peer coaching, and a vast array of professional growth opportunities. Even though educators have a long history of experience to build on and a broad spectrum of models to choose from, the single most frequently mentioned argument against performance based incentive systems for teachers is the absence of an effective teacher evaluation system (Newcombe, 1983). The North Carolina state legislature is currently debating the fate of its highly publicized Career Ladder Plan. Opposition to the plan is being fueled by the state teachers' union, which cites the "inappropriateness" and "rigidity" of the state's evaluation instrument as one of the plan's major flaws (*Education Week,* February 1, 1989). Entering into the realm of performance based incentive systems ensures that a district's evaluation system is no longer perfunctory and will be taken seriously and scrutinized against the highest standards. It is no surprise that Cohen and Murane's (1985) study of districts where incentive pay plans have endured over time revealed that longevity depended on being able to devise ways to "cope with the inherent problems of developing defensible criteria of meritorious teaching and ways of measuring it."

CLARIFYING PURPOSE

Newcombe's study of teacher reward systems found the difficulties in evaluation centered around three major issues: identifying acceptable

241

criteria for superior teaching, ensuring the technical ability of the evaluators, and allaying confusion over the purpose of the evaluation (Newcombe, 1983). The first step in designing a performance based incentive system is to clarify the purpose for evaluation. Five generally acceptable purposes for evaluation have been identified by McGreal (1988):

(1) To provide a process that allows and encourages supervisors and teachers to work together to improve and enhance classroom instructional practices

(2) To provide a process for bringing structured assistance to marginal teachers

(3) To provide a basis for making more rational decisions about the retention, transfer, or dismissal of staff members

(4) To provide a basis for making more informed judgments about differing performance levels for use in compensation programs such as Merit Pay Plans or Career Ladder Programs

(5) To provide information for determining the extent of implementation of knowledge and skills gained during staff development activities and for use in judging the degree of maintenance of the acquired knowledge and skills

Any one of the five is manageable, but typically, evaluation systems are expected to achieve several purposes, if not all five. The problem, McGreal (1988) states, is that, "Each purpose demands a set of practices and requirements that adds complexity and 'weight' to the system." That actual or perceived weight can dramatically lessen the effectiveness of the system, particularly in terms of the commitment of teachers and educators to participate fully and enthusiastically. Duke and Stiggens (1986) concur that performance criteria and standards vary as a function of purpose. They point out that evaluation systems focused on fostering professional growth need to be tailored to the individual capabilities of the teacher and his/her professional development goals, and the concern is with how creditable the evaluation system is to the individual teacher. On the contrary, in evaluation systems designed for the purpose of making personnel decisions regarding termination, compensation, or promotion, the concern is with uniformity across all teachers and whether the system is legally and technically defensible. Performance pay evaluation systems fall into the latter category and emphasize uniformity, minimal standards, and emphasize treating all teachers the same. One system says, "Here is the standard you must meet," and the other says, "We'll take you from where you are and progress onward."

Both purposes for evaluation are essential to any school system. A solution to the dilemma is to develop and implement parallel evaluation systems, one aimed at gathering data for making performance pay and/or personnel decisions and the other aimed at fostering and assessing individual teacher growth. One approach is to evaluate teachers every other year. The first-year focus is on setting uniform standards and identifying areas that need improvement, with the second-year focus being on assessing progress on an individualized growth plan stemming from the first year's evaluation. An evaluation system designed solely for promoting growth may not serve to make compensation decisions. Districts must be aware of the relationship of process to purpose and of the fact that too often educators expect the evaluation system to accomplish multiple purposes.

Clarity of purpose, then, is the first step in developing a successful evaluation system. If the purpose is to determine a teacher's salary, then the standards used to judge the credibility of the system will be high and rigorous. In a recent study of effective evaluation practices, Rand Corporation researchers used three criteria to assess effectiveness: reliability, validity, and utility (Wise, Darling-Hammond, McLaughlin, and Bernstein, 1984). An understanding of these concepts is critical to meeting the rigorous standards performance pay evaluation systems must meet.

ESTABLISHING RELIABILITY

Reliability is the consistency of measurements across observations and evaluators (Wise, Darling-Hammond, McLaughlin, and Bernstein, 1984). Performance incentive plans necessitate the highest degree of reliability possible because teachers must have confidence that their evaluation is not a function of when or who is doing the evaluation. Reliability requires that the indicators for a given criterion be consistent, that an evaluator use these indicators with the criterion consistently over time and across observations, and that different evaluators use those indicators with the criterion consistently when observing the same behavior (The Joint Committee on Standards for Educational Evaluation, 1986). The keys to a reliable evaluation system are

- a high level of specificity in defining criteria
- evaluator training in the specific data gathering techniques to be used
- the gathering of data prior to the observation through a preobservation conference and/or an observation planning guide (The Joint Committee on Standards for Educational Evaluation, 1986)

To tell a teacher you are going to evaluate his/her classroom management skill isn't sufficient. It's only natural to ask that evaluators be more specific, to indicate what they will be looking for as evidence of "good" classroom management. The indicators should operationally define the district's view of competency or good teaching for that criterion. Below is an example of a criterion and its concomitant indicators:

A. Establishes and Reinforces High Standards for Student Discipline

*(1) Manages discipline in accordance with school procedures, school board policies, and legal requirements

*(2) Defines the limits of acceptable behavior, the consequences of misbehavior, and communicates these to students' parents

*(3) Attends to disruptions quickly and firmly

*(4) Demonstrates fairness and consistency in handling student problems, always maintaining the dignity of the students

*(5) Uses a behavior management system based on sound psychological theory and research

*(6) Uses a discipline plan based on the encouragement and recognition of positive, appropriate student behavior

*(7) Uses voice control, cues, hand signals, eye contact, and/or other techniques to establish desired behavior

*(8) Uses procedures and practices to promote self-discipline

The asterisks identify which indicators must be in place for the teacher to be judged competent in the criterion, "Establishes and Reinforces High Standards for Student Discipline." This level of specificity is often criticized as being too mechanistic or restrictive, insensitive to the artistry of teaching. However, when you are determining someone's salary, he/she wants the expectations clearly spelled out. The goal here is high reliability to ensure uniformity, not the promotion of instructional artistry.

Instruments don't evaluate, people do. Performance pay plans falter not because of poorly designed instruments, but because of poorly trained evaluators. Evaluator training is crucial to ensuring reliability and is one of the critical attributes identified in districts with effective evaluation systems (Conley, 1987). Once criteria and indicators have been developed, the specific data gathering technique to be used in assessing them must be determined. McGreal identifies at least eight recognized data collecting techniques:

- paper–pencil testing of teacher knowledge
- self-evaluation
- parent, peer, or student evaluation of the teacher
- student performance
- artifact collection
- observation

Interviewing the teacher is a ninth possibility. Although observation is by tradition and common sense the primary technique used, it is important to recognize that the use of multiple data sources increases reliability (McGreal, 1988). For example, teachers spend as much as 20–30 percent of their time in student assessment and related assessment activities (Stiggens, 1988). Discussing student assessment with the teacher, examining record systems, and using teacher made tests are important data sources when evaluating teacher competency in this area and the data is not attainable through observation. Limiting data gathering to classroom observations alone results in a limited view of a teacher's overall competency (McGreal, 1988). Classroom observations should be the primary data source, but to ignore these alternative sources is to ignore reliability and validity as standards.

Districts must carefully select which data sources to use for which criteria since none are without shortcomings. Paper and pencil tests can be useful to determine basic literacy or content knowledge, and, obviously, people failing to meet minimum literary standards should be denied entrance into the profession. Attempts to use paper and pencil tests to assess a teacher's knowledge of how pupils learn or of instructional theory have not provided any evidence that such scores predict success in applying that knowledge or that they are correlated with student gain scores (Medley, Cohen, and Soar, 1984). Self-evaluation is typically a part of any evaluation process but not as a data source. It is used to engage the teacher in reflection about teaching. Studies have consistently shown that self-ratings show little agreement with ratings completed by students, colleagues, or supervisors on the same set of criteria and so lacks inter-rater reliability (Carroll, 1981).

Use of third party ratings by parents, students, or colleagues is another alternative. The reliability, however, depends upon the specific criteria being evaluated. For example, parents are a legitimate data source on criteria dealing with home–school communication, quality and frequency of homework, and children's attitudes about school (Epstein, 1985). Aleamoni (1981) provides overwhelming evidence that student ratings can be both valid and reliable. Student data, however, should be descriptive rather than evaluative. For example, asking students to rate "My teacher is organized" is not as reliable as asking them to rate "Class starts on time." Student rating instruments can be a rich source of descriptive data. Asking peers to rate a colleague against a set of criteria has been found to be highly unreliable (French-Lazovik, documentary). However, use of peers as trained classroom observers to describe teacher behavior is a rapidly growing practice and can be a useful formative data source in promoting teacher growth. Again, data is neither good nor bad, only useful or not useful, reliable or unreliable depending upon the criteria being evaluated. Third party sources, particularly parents and pupils, can be useful and reliable as one part of comprehensive data collection procedures for specific criteria.

Although the public legislators continually call for measurable outcomes, the use of student performance data in assessing individual teacher effectiveness is highly unreliable (Medley, 1984):

> We may summarize our discussion of the use of pupils achievement test scores for teacher evaluation by saying that both the validity and the reliability of such evaluation procedures are far too low to be useful. The basic difficulty arises from the multiplicity of factors not under the teacher's control that affect pupil achievement, the operation of which prevents the most competent teachers from obtaining the highest scores and the least competent from obtaining the lowest scores. An additional difficulty arises from the fact that available achievement tests do not measure some of the most important outcomes of teaching. The consequence is that the poorer teachers often do as well as or better than the better teachers.

Consequently, of the nine potential data sources discussed above, six have limited reliability in assessing teaching.

The three primary sources of evaluative data are classroom observations, collection of teacher artifacts, and structured interviews. Without question, classroom observations are the foundation of teacher evaluation. Reliable observations require a clear focus on the criteria to be evaluated and a systematic method to record behavioral data. Observational systems fall into three general categories: rating scales, narrative descriptions, and frequency counts (Evertson and Holley, 1981).

Rating scales ask the observer to identify a behavior and, after observing, to rate the degree to which that behavior existed (Medley, 1984). This approach requires a high degree of inference on the part of the evaluator. Medley (1984) points out the flaws in straight rating scales as observer tools:

> What was recorded on the rating scale would depend on (1) what each rater thought the teacher ought to be doing; (2) what behaviors he took into account; (3) the weight he attached to each behavior he observed; and (4) the reference standard with which he compared what he saw in arriving at his rating.

Medley goes on to say that all four factors vary from observer to observer and, thus, so will the rating a teacher gets (Medley, 1984). Affective qualities such as warmth, enthusiam, or energy are typically assessed using such a scale.

Frequency counting systems are a second approach and are often combined with rating scales. In these systems the observer counts the frequency, number, or presence of certain behaviors or events (Evertson and Holley, 1981). These systems are used to document time on task, frequency and type of questions, etc. These are low-inference systems requiring less subjectivity; the behavior is either present or not.

Narrative systems such as scripting are coding systems whereby the observer describes, in writing, classroom events as they happen (Evertson and Holley, 1981). Later, a coding procedure of some type can be used to highlight specific behavior patterns. The emphasis is on patterns rather than on isolated events. Teacher dialogue is usually the focus of the narrative. The strength of the narrative is its holistic perspective, plus the observer has a record of original data to use as a reference in conferring with teachers. This approach can be easily combined with frequency counting systems.

Classroom observations should be the primary data source for evaluating teachers. To increase the reliability of such observations, McGreal emphasizes the importance of the amount and type of information the observer has prior to the observation and the importance of narrowing the focus of the observation to a limited number of behaviors to be rated, counted, or described (McGreal, 1988). Preobservation data can be obtained through the use of a structure interview or planning conference combined with an observation guide prepared by the teacher for the evaluator.

The planning conference allows the evaluator to elicit relevant information about criteria not easily observable and to establish a mental set for what will take place during the lesson. Nonobservable data relevant to these criteria might include questions such as the following: Will children be grouped? How were the groups determined? How does the lesson fit into the unit or course of study? How will student mastery or attainment of the lesson objective be determined? Is this an introductory or culminating lesson? If not, how did the preceding lesson influence this lesson and what will the following lesson focus on?

An observational guide is a copy of the basic lesson plan the teacher will use. A suggested format for the guide is presented in Figure 1. In addition, the evaluator should have a seating chart of the class to be observed. This allows the evaluator to reference particular students by name. Preobservational data gathering is analogous to an x-ray before surgery or a flight plan before take-off. It gives the evaluator a context within which to place the observational data.

Narrowing the focus of an observation is accomplished by specifying the behaviors to be observed and the specific means for recording those behaviors. This is the purpose of the indicators defining each criterion. For example, an evaluative criterion with accompanying indicators for maximizing student time on task is presented in Figure 2.

Date: _____   Observer: _____

Time of Lesson: _____

Unit: _____   Teacher: _____

I.   Instructional Objectives:

    Long Term Goal:

    Lesson Objective(s):

    Identify level of difficulty for the lesson objectives: knowledge, comprehension, application, analysis, synthesis, evaluation.

FIGURE 1 Observation guide.

II. **Lesson Presentation:**

Basic teaching strategy to be used:

III. **Practice Activities:**

Guided practice:

Attach copy or describe the independent practice activities:

IV. **Evaluation of Results:**

Lesson:

Unit/Topic:

V. **Special Considerations:**

Group characteristics:

Special education students and/or characteristics:

VI. **Attachments**

Seating chart

VII. **Preceding Lesson Description**

Objective:

Student Activities:

Results:

VIII. **Follow-up Lesson Description**

Objectives:

Student activities:

Results:

FIGURE 1 (continued) Observation guide.

* 1. Schedules learning time in accordance with district policy.

* 2. Maintains a purposeful and orderly but not rigid classroom climate.

* 3. Establishes procedures so students know what to do upon completing a task or when needing help.

* 4. Efficiently manages time by starting class and lessons promptly and closing lessons smoothly within the allotted time.

* 5. Ensures students are engaged in task relevant activities.

* 6. Ensures students experience a high rate of task success.

* 7. Ensures a high percentage of students are on task at all times.

* 8. Minimizes time spent in collecting or disseminating materials and in making transitions between subjects, classes, or activities.

FIGURE 2 Maximizes student time on task.

The evaluator knows that data must be gathered on the eight indicators since they operationally define the criterion. An evaluator data analysis guide is useful in further narrowing the focus (see Figure 3).

The guide informs the evaluator of the number and types of judgments that must be made and the type of data required. The effectiveness of the guide, however, depends upon further narrowing the focus through training. Rather than just stipulating that the observer is expected to record time on task, it should train the evaluator how it is to be done. For example, time on task will be assessed by doing ten randomly spaced scans of each child, pausing three seconds on each student to determine whether he or she is attending to the task at hand. Again, the more preobservation data the evaluator has and the narrower the range of behaviors observed, the greater the reliability.

An issue related to the data collection is the frequency of observations. What is clear is that the frequency influences teachers' perceptions of the utility and reliability of the evaluation (Natriello, 1983). The more time spent, the greater the quantity of data, and the broader the range of teaching observed. Two observations plus a preplanning conference is a minimum, and four plus a preplanning conference is probably optimal. What is essential is that data collection is not limited solely to just classroom observations.

As mentioned above, much of what accounts for effective teaching is

LENGTH OF OBSERVATION: _____

TIME LESSON BEGAN: _____

TIME LESSON ENDED: _____

DATA ANALYSIS GUIDE
MAXIMIZING STUDENT TIME ON TASK

1. Allocated learning time for the content area observed met district guidelines? (Periods per semester or minutes per week.)

   Yes _____   No _____

2. Classroom climate could best be described as purposeful and orderly with children working constructively on the prescribed tasks without disturbing one another.

   Entire observation   _____

   3/4 of the observation   _____

   1/2 of the observation   _____

   Less than half of the observation _____

3. Were students aware of what to do upon needing help or completing a task?

   All students   _____

   Some Students   _____

   None   _____

4. During the lesson, what percentage of time did students spend on the following:

   Lesson presentation   _____

   Guided practice   _____

   Independent practice   _____

   Organizing and transitions   _____

   Dealing with misbehavior   _____

5. What percentage of students were actively engaged during:

   _____ Lesson Presentation

   _____ Guided Practice

   _____ Independent Practice

   Who were the students most frequently not actively engaged?

   _____

   _____

   _____

   _____

FIGURE 3

done outside the classroom or is nonobservable. Areas such as planning, student assessment, and parent–teacher communication are found in most evaluation criteria and are not readily observable in a classroom observation. Data can be gathered through a structured interview, which means that each teacher will be asked the same questions, not unlike the process used in job interviews. Figure 4 is a sample agenda in memorandum form for such a conference or interview. Inherent in the list of questions is an opportunity to gather data on several different criteria. Note also that at the conference the teacher will show various artifacts or work samples. It is highly recommended that these interviews be held in the teacher's classroom where the teacher's files, teaching materials, and record systems are readily available for use by the teacher. These include samples of quizzes and tests, home-

TO:

FROM:

DATE:

SUBJECT: Planning Conference

I would like to set up a time for your planning conference. This is a time for us to review your self-evaluation and previous performance as well as address any quesitons or concerns related to the evaluation process. I am also interested in having you talk about the following criteria:

1. How you assess student learning.
2. What you have done to demonstrate effective interpersonal relations with parents.
3. How you demonstrate interpersonal skills in relating to students.
4. What techniquest you use to build positive student self-esteem.
5. Areas where you have demonstrated responsibility in cooperative professional efforts.
6. Professional growth opportunities you are pursuing.

You may find it helpful to review the indicators which define the criterion listed above. They are in the evaluation packet.

If you have not already done so, you should begin to collect supportive data. Examples of the data I would like to see are:

1. Student work samples, tests and homework along with your analysis of these samples.
2. Sample substitute lesson plans.
3. Summaries of conferences with parents or students.
4. Copies of letters or memos to students or parents.
5. Student grade reports.
6. An example of a unit or group of lessons related to a unit goal.

Your conference date is listed below. Let me know if this is not convenient.

DATE SCHEDULED: _____

FIGURE 4 Memorandum.

TEACHER:

DATE OF INCIDENT	EVENT OF INCIDENT	CONFERENCE DATE

FIGURE 5 Critical incident log.

work and seat work, record keeping systems, units developed, and other materials related to one or more of the criteria being assessed. It is highly recommended that the interview be conducted in the teacher's classroom where the teacher's files, materials, and student work samples are readily available.

There is one other data source that is inherent in any evaluation system — the critical incident. This is an event, positive or negative, that is significant enough to come to the evaluator's attention and that could influence his judgment. Examples are a parent complaint, an award won, an inappropriate burst of anger, or a timely home visit to a sick child. If the event influences the evaluator's assessment of the teacher on one or more criteria, then the evaluator needs to legitimize the data by sharing it with the teacher and documenting the incident and the conference. Figure 5 is a critical incident log.

Once the evaluative criteria are determined and the indicators established, a matrix is helpful in determining the data gathering technique
to be used. Figure 6 is a sample matrix built around example criteria.

Once data gathering techniques have been developed, evaluator
training is essential. Evaluator credibility is one of the keys to effective
evaluation. Credibility is a function of the evaluator's knowledge of the
technical aspects of teaching coupled with sound familiarity with the
teacher's classroom and students (Stiggens, 1988). Evaluators must
have an understanding of what is good teaching and how it relates to the
instrument. To ensure reliability, however, they need to practice using
the instrument under the supervision of a trainer or peer coach. Ideally,
this is done in a group setting with all evaluators using the instrument
to assess the same lesson. The building of inter-rater reliability should
be an annual training activity rather than a one-time experience at the
time the instrument is developed. In addition, in the first year as an
evaluator, the group sessions should be followed up with coaching in
real classrooms. Either a trainer can accompany the evaluator or peers
can jointly evaluate the same teacher and share data and feedback.
What is critical is that evaluator skills are assessed and inter-rater
reliability is established.

ESTABLISHING VALIDITY

According to the Joint Committee on Standards for Education Evaluation, validity is the single most important issue in assessing any evaluation process (Joint Committee on Standards for Education Evaluation,
1986). Reliability deals with the accuracy with which you hit the target;
validity is the issue of whether you are hitting the correct target. Validity is a direct function of purpose (McGreal, 1982). In performance incentive systems, the purpose of evaluation is to define degrees of teaching competency and to distribute compensation based on those
determinations.

Research has identified a variety of teacher behaviors associated with
student learning gains, and theoretical models provide additional
sources of evaluative criteria. Typically, these criteria are organized
into categories or performance areas such as planning, lesson presentation, classroom management, and interpersonal relations. As McGreal

	OBSERVATION: NARRATIVE	OBSERVATION: FREQUENCY - COUNTING	OBSERVATION: RATING SCALE	ARTIFACT COLLECTION	TEACHER INTERVIEW	CRITICAL INCIDENT	SURVEY INSTRUMENTS
DEMONSTRATES EFFECTIVE LESSON PLANNING				X	X		
MAXIMIZES STUDENT TIME ON TASK	X	X					
DEMONSTRATES EFFECTIVE LESSON PRESENTATION SKILLS	X	X		X			
BUILDS POSITIVE STUDENT SELF ESTEEM	X					X	X

FIGURE 6

points out, instruments across the country tend to be very similar in the use of these categories and even in the use of the criteria within each category. Given that we all have access to the same data base and models of teaching and the willingness to exchange instruments and information, it is reasonable to expect these similarities to exist. A valid definition of teaching involves the use of research, the critical models, shared information, and consensus building by the teachers and principals responsible for using the system (Medley, 1984).

A sound research based set of criteria developed through consensus is essential but not sufficient to meet the test for validity. The instrument, methods, and procedures for gathering data must directly support the intended purposes of the evaluation and be congruent with the criteria (Joint Committee on Standards for Educational Evaluation, 1986). For instance, one common error involves including information that has no relevancy to the purpose. If your system focuses on classroom performance, then a teacher's participation on committees or punctuality in getting to meetings is irrelevant data. This use of irrelevant information to make judgments is referred to as "contamination" (Joint Committee on Standards for Educational Evaluation, 1986). Likewise, it is equally invalid to ignore or fail to include relevant information. An evaluation system that fails to include classroom observation or fails to state whether the classroom is orderly and well-disciplined suffers from "deficiency" (Joint Committee on Standards for Educational Evaluation, 1986). Another common error challenging valid assessment is failing to take into account factors over which the person being evaluated has no control. Teachers with excessive class sizes or a disproportionate number of handicapped pupils should be given consideration (Joint Committee on Standards for Educational Evaluation, 1986).

Often evaluation instruments and/or procedures are used for purposes other than what they were intended. The most glaring example is designing an entire system focused at regular classroom teachers and then using the instrument and procedures to evaluate all certified personnel, including such disparate roles as librarian and counselor. Also, many of the criteria in use today originated from research based on the teaching of basic skills, and it is questionable whether such criteria are valid for use with special area teachers such as art, music, physical education, or for special education resource teachers. Developing instruments and procedures specific to such roles enhances validity.

ENSURING UTILITY

Finally, evaluator competency is a key factor influencing validity. Specifically, Duke and Stiggens (1986) found that evaluator credibility as perceived by teachers included the following:

- knowledge of the technical aspects of teaching
- knowledge of the subject area
- years of classroom teaching experience
- years of experience in the school district
- recency of experience
- familiarity with the teacher's classroom and students

Evaluator credibility is dealt with in two ways, training and/or the use of multiple evaluators. Training must include a solid understanding of the research and models of teaching that the criteria are based upon. Not only should evaluators be able to recognize a given behavior when observed but they should be able to demonstrate it. Putting teachers and evaluators through the same training provides a common knowledge base and enhances the credibility of the evaluator.

Multiple evaluators are a good solution to both the issues of reliability and validity. However, this is not always economically feasible, nor do all districts want to commit extra administrative or teacher time to evaluation. There are two evaluation situations, however, in which multiple evaluators may be highly desirable. In termination decisions, the use of more than one evaluator ensures "fairness" and alleviates a single individual of the total responsibility. The second situation is in determining excellence beyond minimal standards. In the study of effective evaluation practices, the researchers found that the further one moves along the competency continuum from minimal to excellent, the more inferential the data becomes and the less generalizable are the specific criterion indicators, and concomitantly there is a need for greater evaluator expertise. Using two or more evaluators can offset these issues (Wise, 1984). If a district can afford the expense, multiple evaluators are desirable, but one can have a valid and reliable evaluation system using single well-trained evaluators.

Utility is the last standard to consider. Simply put, utility is the cost–benefit ratio—i.e., are the results or outcomes of the evaluation worth the effort, time, and dollars? Evaluation can require additional time and effort on the part of teachers as well as administrators. Developing portfolios, taped lessons, and conferences takes time away from instructional planning, and it is possible to reach a point of diminishing returns where the process inhibits improved instruction rather than enhances it. Likewise, administrators required to expand long hours evaluating are not able to pursue other organizational goals. Also, school districts have limited budgets and the training and/or operational costs of evaluation are not available to pursue other goals.

Finally, there is a political cost to consider (Wise, 1984). If the costs of evaluation, whether in terms of time, dollars, or effort, are viewed as excessive by either the evaluators or those evaluated, low morale and dissension will result. Wise et al. suggest three criteria to use in weighing this delicate cost–benefit ratio: decision making, communications, and personnel improvement (Wise, 1984). Does the system provide data useful for making relevant decisions? In performance compensation systems this means data that discriminates between levels of performance as well as decisions regarding termination or assignment. Does the system promote better communications among evaluators and teachers? Evaluation should build a common definition of good teaching practice and provide a vocabulary to discuss teaching and learning. It should also promote an ongoing dialogue about teaching. Whether through increased skill development or better selection, the result of evaluation should be improved performance.

To these criteria the Joint Commission adds another—a constructive orientation, or the degree to which the program increases professional competence and enthusiasm. Common errors impeding this criteria include failing to recognize both strengths and weaknesses of a teacher's performance; fostering competition to the detriment of teamwork, ignoring performance that exceeds expected standards, making unrealistic recommendations for improvement, or failing to assess whether the person evaluated is provided sufficient resources to do the job well (Joint Committee on Standards for Educational Evaluation, 1986).

The essence of utility as a standard is that the evaluation system should work for you to accomplish important organizational goals, but if you are not careful, you can end up working for the evaluation system.

The research on why performance compensation plans fail is replete with utility issues. Reliability and validity are of such immediate concern to developers that utility standards are too often not addressed until after implementation, when it is often too late. Commitment to a lengthy pilot period, coupled with the use of external evaluators to assess the pilot, can ensure a greater probability of success.

Performance based compensation is the only justifiable way to pay people. It is not sufficient to avoid performance based pay because it is a politically sensitive issue or because the evaluation system must meet high standards for validity, reliability, and utility. Our profession has a research base in both teaching and evaluating, the technical expertise is readily available, and there is a long history of experience to build upon. Any district can implement a successful performance based compensation plan — if it wants to.

REFERENCES

Aleamoni, Lawrence M. 1981. "Student Ratings of Instruction," in *Handbook of Teacher Evaluation,* Jason Millman, ed., National Council on Measurement in Education, pp. 110–141.

Carroll, Gregory J. 1981. "Faculty Self Evaluation," in *Handbook of Teacher Evaluation,* Jason Millman, ed., National Council on Measurement in Education, p. 181.

Cohen, David K. and Richard J. Murnane. 1985. "The Merits of Merit Pay," An unpublished report supported by the Stanford University Institute for Educational Finance and Governance, p. 4.

Conley, David T. 1987. "Critical Attributes of Effective Evaluation Systems," *Educational Leadership,* 44(7):62.

Duke, Daniel L. and Richard J. Stiggens. 1986. *Teacher Evaluation: Five Keys to Growth.* Washington, D.C.: American Association of School Administrators, pp. 27–28.

Epstein, Joyce L. 1985. "A Question of Merit: Principals and Parents' Evaluations of Teachers," *Educational Researcher* (Aug./Sept.):8.

Evertson, Carolyn M. and Freda M. Holley. 1981. "Classroom Observations," in *Handbook of Teacher Evaluation,* Jason Millman, ed., National Council on Measurement in Education, pp. 101–103.

French-Lazovik, Grace. 1981. "Peer Review—Documentary Evidence in the Evaluation of Teaching," in *Handbook of Teacher Evaluation,* Jason Millman, ed., National Council on Measurement in Education, pp. 101–103.

Joint Committee on Standards for Educational Evaluation. 1986. *Standards for the Evaluation of Educational Personnel.* Kalamazoo, Michigan: Evaluation Center, College of Education, Western Michigan University.

McGreal, Thomas L. 1988. "Evaluation for Enhancing Instruction: Linking Teacher Evalaution and Staff Development," in *Teacher Evaluation: Six Prescriptions for Success,* S. Stanley and W. Popham, eds., Arlington, Virginia: Association for Supervision and Curriculum.

McGreal, Thomas L. 1982. "Effective Teacher Evaluation Systems," *Educational Leadership,* 39:303–305.

Medley, Donald M., H. Cohen, and R. Soar. 1984. *Measurement-Based Evaluation of Teacher Performance: An Empirical Approach.* New York: Longman.

Natriello, Gary. 1988. *Evaluation Frequency, Teacher Influence, and the Internalization of Evaluation Process: A Review of Six Studies Using the Theory of Evaluation and Authority.* Eugene, Oregon: Center for Educational Policy Study, pp. 31–34.

Newcombe, Ellen. 1983. *Rewarding Teachers: Issues and Incentives.* Research for Better Schools, Inc., Philadelphia, p. 10.

Staff. 1989. "North Carolina's Career Ladder Nears a Crossroad," *Education Week* (February 1):14.

Stiggens, Richard J. 1988. "Revitalizing Classroom Assessment," *Phi Delta Kappan,* 69(5):365.

Wise, Arthur E., L. Darling-Hammond, M. W. McLaughlin, and H. Bernstein. 1984. *Teacher Evaluation: A Study of Effective Practice.* Santa Monica, California: Rand, pp. 44–57.

CHAPTER 10

Performance Appraisal in Education:
A Strategic Consideration

SHARON C. CONLEY – *University of Arizona*
SAMUEL B. BACHARACH – *Cornell University*

THE topic of performance appraisal seems out of vogue these days. In the early phase of this country's reform movement, Merit Pay Plans were gaining in popularity throughout the country. The central question was, how do we improve our compensation and performance appraisal systems to motivate teachers in the classroom? With the failure of many of these plans came the recognition that in concentrating on the question of teacher motivation, we had ignored other important educational issues. We had given insufficient attention specifically to questions of the work of teaching, school culture, and administrative leadership. A renewed interest emerged in how to design the compensation and performance appraisal system to capitalize on teachers' intrinsic motivations to teach. The challenge became one of providing rewards that recognized the genuine development of teachers' professional skills. In this chapter, we try to explicate a series of strategic questions that must be considered before implementing a performance appraisal system for teachers: 1) What should be evaluated in teaching? 2) How should performance appraisal be linked to organizational rewards? and 3) How can performance appraisal reflect the work of teaching?

INTRODUCTION

Researchers who have examined performance appraisal in private sector organizations have long stressed that performance appraisal is a difficult task with many obstacles.[1] All too often in education, the performance appraisal system that accompanies a change in the teacher

This article was originally published in the *Journal of Personnel Evaluation*, 3:309–319, 1990 Kluwer Academic Publishers, Norwell, MA.

compensation system is simply an afterthought. At a recent conference regarding one state's teacher Career Ladder Program, one of the authors of this article raised a question concerning the type of evaluation that would accompany the Career Ladder Program. The state commissioner of education responded by maintaining that they would "cross that bridge when they come to it."

Inevitably, the failure to deal with the strategic questions regarding what type of performance evaluation program should accompany a new compensation program creates suspicion and confusion on the part of teachers and administrators alike. Indeed, most innovative compensation programs such as career ladders do not succeed because the originators of these programs fail to strategically consider the importance of the accompanying performance appraisal system. The first issue that we examine in this regard is what should be the focus of a performance appraisal system for teachers.

CONSIDERATION ONE: WHAT TO EVALUATE—TEACHERS' SKILLS OR STUDENT ACHIEVEMENT SCORES?

Traditionally in the personnel evaluation literature, the performance of individuals may be evaluated from two perspectives: skills versus work outputs. According to a classic work by Porter, Lawler, and Hackman (1975), *skills* may be examined in terms of the activities a person performs and the inputs the person makes. Alternatively, *outputs* can be examined in terms of the results of a particular activity. Performance appraisal systems can and do focus on outputs only, skills only, or some combination of the two.[2]

Education has traditionally had a strong bias toward output measures, such as student achievement scores, as a test of teacher competency. This bias has recently been accentuated by the reform movement. We are constantly bombarded by Department of Education ratings of school quality as measured by achievement scores. In careless hands, some would have us use these measures not simply as a way of rating schools, but also as an implicit way of distinguishing among teachers. The meaning derived from such distinctions is that the lower the student achievement score, the poorer the teacher.

The assumption that students of the better teachers will achieve better test scores has been too readily accepted by many proponents of new compensation systems. However, education researchers have long argued that the use of student test scores as an indicator of teacher effectiveness is at best wishful thinking.[3] Many other factors account for the variation in student achievement other than teacher performance. The academic ability of students assigned to a class can vary markedly from year to year, a district's curriculum may change, or a teacher may be assigned additional duties or have less support staff.[4] While student achievement scores may have the attraction of being objective and clean measures, they are, at best, the most indirect measures of teacher effectiveness.

For performance appraisal to be successful, those being appraised must be motivated and challenged by the appraisal.[5] The personnel literature teaches us that it is important to evaluate workers in terms of the criteria over which they have some sense of control. Student achievement scores, when used to provide negative feedback, do not offer teachers information about what they should improve. Alternatively, test scores, when used to provide positive feedback, do not tell teachers what they are doing right. This helps explain why teachers who have been identified as "excellent" consistently maintain that they do not believe student test scores adequately reflect their performance.[6] The reality is that an excellent teacher may not guarantee excellent students. Given the ambiguous relationship between teacher effort and student achievement, the use of test scores as the primary focus of a performance appraisal fails to provide teachers with a sense of efficacy. This failure often results in teachers believing that they can do very little to control the results of their evaluation. In turn, this lack of efficacy will often result in teacher indifference and possible burnout.

While teachers may not feel that they have total control over student achievement, they can be held responsible for their own skill development, provided they are given appropriate resources.[7] A performance appraisal in a school system should help assure that all students are served by teachers whose skills have maximally developed. While we may recognize that teacher's skills may not be a sufficient condition for the assurance of quality education, we should assure that it is not an obstacle. Performance appraisal systems should thus place greater emphasis on assessing teachers in terms of their skill development.

Skill or knowledge based pay has recently received much attention in the human resource literature.[8] That literature suggests that a knowledge based approach to compensation makes pay dependent on mastery of certain skills, not on the particular job or task being performed.

Under such a system, employees' compensation increases as they show advances in skill development.

The greatest criticism of assessing employees' skills, however, is the subjectivity of the process. In education, some architects of performance appraisal systems try to duck the problem of subjectivity by simply drawing up lists of teacher's tasks, which are presented as evaluations of teachers' skills. Checklists and behaviorally anchored rating scales are examples of such task evaluations. In practice, however, these types of evaluations are often no more than sanctioning devices. Furthermore, while they may be objective, they are not valid in that they do not directly address the critical component of a successful teacher—the ability to make decisions under conditions of uncertainty and unpredictability.[9]

The personnel evaluation literature suggests that professional decision-making skills are the most difficult aspects of performance to measure. However, they are also those skills that by their very nature define what a professional is. The real problem for a performance evaluation system that attempts to evaluate teachers' skills is to incorporate teachers' skills as decision makers. A recent study of over 500 teachers found that teachers make numerous decisions on a daily—even hourly—basis. Specifically, teaching decisions are directed to teaching roles or purposes (i.e., instruction, counseling, and management), as well as teaching processes (i.e., planning, implementaton, and evaluation).[10] The interaction of these roles and processes defines teaching as a uniquely complex decision-making activity. Indeed, as Mosston observes, the notion of teaching as decision making is the "one statement that is true and universal, and can therefore serve as the basis for understanding" the necessary skills of teaching. To the degree that a peformance appraisal system ignores the decision-making skills that are most important in characterizing teaching, it will not assist teachers in improving their performance.

In sum, if a school or district is trying to create a system of performance appraisal that motivates and challenges teachers and that focuses on elements of performance that teachers can change, then assessments of skills appear to be an appropriate basis of performance appraisal. In addition, assessments of skills are potentially more valid than are work outputs in the sense that they can tap the decision-making process that is at the heart of teaching. To the degree that a performance appraisal system ignores the problem-solving skills that are most important in characterizing teaching, it will not yield an accurate "picture" of a teacher's performance, nor will it help teachers improve their performance. That is: *Performance appraisal in education should place a greater emphasis on teachers' skills rather than on student achievement.*

Implication: Skill Development

To the degree that a performance appraisal system is designed to focus on skills, "formative" appraisal (appraisal for the purpose of development) should receive primary emphasis. Such an emphasis on formative appraisal would require school districts to examine how teachers go about acquiring and building on their skills. Evidence exists that teachers increase their decision-making and problem-solving capabilities by "being teachers"—i.e., by repeatedly confronting and resolving for themselves the practical problems of managing a classroom.[11] Formative appraisal can help teachers make sense out of those experiences by helping them develop a "habit of inquiry," where they form questions about their practice.[12] That process of questioning through observation helps teachers become better decision makers.

Unfortunately, most school districts do not have mechanisms in place for that type of development to occur.[13] Currently, the pretenure period does little to help teachers acquire the skills they need; teachers are left to acquire their decision-making skills largely on their own. If districts took formative appraisal seriously, they might specify the pretenure period as an intensive period of skills development. During this developmental period, formative appraisers could help teachers expand their decision-making and problem-solving skills. Specifically, their purpose would be to provide teachers with diagnostic tools so that teachers may monitor, evaluate, and strengthen their own performance.[14] However, this is not meant to imply that skill development ends with tenure; other developmental periods can and should follow tenure.[15]

CONSIDERATION TWO: WHAT LINKAGES SHOULD BE DRAWN BETWEEN PERFORMANCE APPRAISAL AND ORGANIZATIONAL REWARDS?

The previous section stressed the need to focus on formative appraisal; the actual linkage of performance appraisal to organizational rewards require some types of *summative* appraisal. Summative appraisal is an overall, summary judgment of an employee's performance and is conducted for the purpose of making some type of personnel decision. In this context, when performance appraisal is linked to organizational rewards, it is the summative component of the appraisal that serves as the basis of reward allocation.

In the private sector, organizations attempt to link rewards to performance appraisal for the purpose of increasing the extrinsic motivation of workers. The extent to which this effect is produced consistently is a point of debate in the literature.[16]

In education, the current reforms of merit pay and career ladders have focused on two different types of rewards. Merit pay, which focuses on measuring work outputs, tends to reward performance with temporary fluctuations in pay, such as bonuses. Career ladders, to the degree that they focus on assessing skills, tend to reward employees with relatively permanent promotions.[17] In general, promotions are more appropriate when an organization wishes to reward levels of skill and proficiency that have been acquired over a period of time. Thus, the decision to grant organizational rewards, i.e., promotions, would turn on the *level of skill* that a teacher has acquired in teaching.

However, we know all too well from the private and public sector that whenever an organization tries to draw a linkage between performance appraisal and rewards such as promotion, several problems emerge. One of the problems is that most organizations try to combine formative and summative appraisal in a single session.[18] When important organizational rewards depend on the results of a performance appraisal that combines formative and summative evaluation, the organization has a dual goal: to obtain counseling and planning information about individuals for formative appraisal and to obtain information on which to base rewards for summative appraisal. In this instance, the individual being evaluated also has a dual goal: to obtain valid performance feedback and, at the same time, to obtain important extrinsic rewards, i.e., promotions. These dual goals of individuals and organizations tend to conflict with each other.[19]

Another source of potential conflict in performance appraisal is the common practice of using the *same* person(s) to conduct formative and summative appraisals. Such a system places the appraiser in the dual role of "coaching" individuals for formative improvement and making summative judgments of their performance.

Thus, potential conflicts in performance appraisal arise out of two separate issues: 1) the combination of formative and summative appraisal in a single session and 2) the use of the same person(s) to conduct formative and summative appraisal. These conflicts close off communication between teachers and those who appraise their performance, appraisers cannot make accurate assessments of performance, and teachers cannot receive important performance feedback. Thus: *If schools attempt to link the results of performance appraisal to organizational rewards, they should attempt to reduce the potential conflicts that often result from that linkage.*

Implication: Reducing Conflict in Performance Appraisal

One way to resolve potential conflicts in performance appraisal is to separate formative and summative appraisal processes. As noted previously, formative appraisal might take place during a specified period of skill development (such as the pretenure period). Following this phase of formative appraisal, the summative decision to promote a teacher would focus on whether or not particular teaching skills have been acquired.

A second way to resolve potential conflicts in performance appraisal would be to specify that the person(s) who serves as formative appraiser(s) should not be the same person(s) who makes summative judgments, i.e., promotion decisions. In such a system, while the formative appraiser(s) might play a role in advocating the teacher's promotion if he/she decides an individual teacher is ready for promotion, the person(s) who serves as summative appraiser would retain the final authority for promotion decisions.[20]

The question of who should serve as formative and summative appraisers in school districts requires that we consider another aspect of the nature of teaching, and that is the nature of work interdependence.

CONSIDERATION THREE: WHAT IS THE IMPACT OF PERFORMANCE APPRAISAL ON THE WORK OF TEACHING?

An important consideration in structuring a performance appraisal system is the nature of the work conducted in an organization. One component of the nature of the work is the degree to which workers have to rely on each other to accomplish their tasks or the degree of interdependence among the workers.

Different work groups show different degrees of interdependence. Sales people, for example, are independently responsible for their tasks of selling products to customers. Professional and craft occupations that are responsible for serving one client or customer at one point in time also have low levels of interdependence.

Teaching, however, is an occupation in which the level of interdependence is high. In teaching, the "product" of education is not something that one teacher gives to one student at one point in time. Rather, it is something that students acquire over many years, as they pass from classroom to classroom, grade to grade, and building to building. Teachers in junior high/middle school, for example, are dependent on the educational experiences that teachers in elementary schools provide students. Teachers are also dependent on each other to maintain consistent policies, such as homework and discipline practices, from classroom to classroom.[21]

This interdependency means that the "product" of schools, effective education, depends on cooperation among teachers and open sharing of information. To the degree that the school organization's performance appraisal system interferes with that cooperation, such a system is dysfunctional to the organization.

The best example of a dysfunctional system is merit pay. Merit pay forces employees to play a "zero-sum" compensation game in which one employee cannot earn significantly more without decreasing the amount of money that other employees can be paid.[22] Merit pay is based on the assumption that to motivate teachers to improve their performance, each teacher must compete with every other teacher in the school for a fixed "pot" of money. Many career ladders are also zero-sum in nature, since they specify that teachers must compete for a limited number of job positions. Of course, under such systems, teachers recognize that they are competing for a fixed and scarce number of rewards and view each other's competence as threats to their income security. This undermines the cooperation necessary to effective education. Thus: *Schools should structure performance appraisal systems that encourage cooperative efforts among teachers.*

Implication: Teacher Cooperation

To the degree that performance appraisal is a cooperative process, the interdependent work efforts of teachers are enhanced. There are two ways that districts could encourage teacher cooperation in performance appraisal. The first involves the elimination of quota systems for allocating rewards, and the second involves building peer teams for skill development purposes.

First, it is critical that if a district ties organizational rewards to performance appraisal, the district should attempt to allocate sufficient funds to reward all who qualify. Thus, if performance appraisal is linked to promotion, districts should avoid placing a quota on the number of teachers who may receive a promotion.

Some would argue that the total avoidance of quotas is unrealistic because teachers cannot generate more money for the school organization. Therefore, reward distribution must be zero-sum in nature. It should be pointed out, however, that the specification of a developmental period for formative growth preceding summative promotion decisions (described earlier) eases that situation. Specifying that the pretenure period should be a developmental period—and that teachers would not be evaluated summatively until the end of that period—would allow school organizations to appraise a smaller number of teachers for summative purposes. As such, the use of a developmental period for growth has an important practical advantage, in addition to the advantage of explicitly focusing the appraisal process on improvement, rather than on constant judgments and surveillances of performance.

With regard to the second method of increasing cooperation, the use of peer teams for purposes of formative appraisal might encourage teachers to view each other as potential allies, rather than competitors. A team, as opposed to a single "mentor," would provide a teacher with multiple inputs for pinpointing strengths and weaknesses and would reinforce collegial ties among teachers.

As noted previously, these formative appraisers might take on a quasi-summative role when it comes to a teacher's promotion decision. The peer team could act as advocates for a teacher's promotion, with the administrator retaining the final authority for the promotion decision.

Under such a system, the peer team would not have an active role to play in initiating summative appraisals or in blocking consideration of a teacher for promotion. In practice, of course, it would be difficult for a teacher to secure a promotion without the active endorsement of his/her peer team. The opposite side of the coin, however, is that it would be difficult for the summative appraiser(s) to reject a promotion if and when those who have worked closely with a teacher do give such endorsements. But having the formative appraiser(s) choose between active endorsement and passive silence would

- preserve the authority (and responsibility) of administrators for summative appraisal—and therefore not disrupt the authority structure of the school itself
- preserve the individual teacher's right to secure a summative decision from those who have final responsibility for making those decisions, if he or she feels confident that a case for a positive decision can be made
- emphasize that the specific role of the peer team would be to provide formative assistance for helping individual teachers become ready for promotion

Figure 1 summarizes these points. The figure depicts performance appraisal as a process occurring over time with two distinct time periods: pretenure and post-tenure. A specified focus of performance appraisal is skill development during the pretenure period. In this context, formative appraisal is critically important. We have argued that it is appropriate for a teacher's peers to provide this assistance, given the interdependent work context of teaching and the need to promote cooperative modes of skill assistance.

The decision to grant tenure is a summative promotion decision.[23] The focus of performance appraisal at this point is on whether or not a teacher has acquired specific teaching skills. We have proposed that the school administrator could retain the authority for such promotion decisions but that the peer team, by acting as advocates for a teacher's promotion, could influence the promotion decision.

Following the decision to grant tenure, there may be further periods

Focus of Performance Appraisal	Skill Development (Formative)	Promotion (Summative)	Skill Development/ Promotion
Person(s) Conducting Performance Appraisal	Peers	Administrator	Peers/Administrator
	Pre-tenure	Tenure	Post-tenure

TIME

FIGURE 1 Proposed structure of teacher performance appraisal system.

of development and further promotion decisions. A teacher's peers could continue to assist with formative appraisal, and administrators could make further promotion decisions.

CONCLUSION

The reform effort of the past several years has assumed that changing our system of teacher compensation to some form of merit pay or a career ladder will reinvigorate our educational system. All of these plans involve linking performance appraisals of individual teachers to a particular organizational reward (e.g., salary increases and promotions). However, many of these plans have ignored a simple but basic premise of personnel management: that the success or failure of any compensation system will depend heavily, if not totally, on the system of performance appraisal that accompanies it. We have tried to show in this chapter that only by examining the nature of the work and the structure of the performance appraisal system can we begin to overcome these obstacles.

The strategic considerations outlined reveal three areas of emphasis for performance appraisal in schools. First, performance appraisal should concentrate on teachers' levels of decision-making skill. To this end, a developmental period for formative growth becomes critically important. Second, if a school district links organizational rewards with performance appraisal, it should attempt to ease the potential conflicts that occur. To reduce these conflicts, it is suggested that school districts should: 1) address the separate processes of formative and summative appraisal and 2) specify that a different person(s) serve as formative and summative appraisers.

Finally, to promote teacher cooperation and enhance the interdependent efforts of teachers, districts should: 1) reduce the occurrence of "zero-sum" compensation games by avoiding quota systems in allocating rewards and 2) encourage teachers to facilitate each other's formative growth by providing peer assistance.

State educational leaders and policymakers who have advocated merit pay and career ladder legislation have given little consideration to how conflicts in appraising individuals can be lessened. On the whole, they have paid too little attention to lessons from the private sector concerning inter-worker cooperation, reward systems, and performance appraisals.

If we are to learn anything from the private sector, it is that monolithic solutions rarely work. Rather, each change must be strategically considered as to the ripple effects it would have throughout the educational system. In education, we have too often advocated merit pay or career ladders without seriously examining their implications for the type of performance appraisal that will have to be put in place. This failure will inevitably doom all these efforts to change the compensation and career structure of teaching.

REFERENCES

Bacharach, S. B., S. C. Conley, and J. B. Shedd. "A Developmental Framework for Evaluating Teachers as Decision Makers," Accepted for publication in *Journal of Personnel Evaluation in Education.*

Bacharach, S., D. Lipsky, and J. Shedd. 1986. *Merit Pay and Its Alternatives.* OAP Monograph.

Bernardin, H. J. and R. W. Beatty. 1984. *Performance Appraisal: Assessing Human Behavior at Work.* Boston: Kent Publishing Co.

Casey, Willian F. III. 1979. "Would Bear Bryant Teach in the Public Schools? The Need for Teacher Incentives," *Phi Delta Kappan,* 60:500–501.

Conley, S. "Career Ladders and Labor Management Cooperation," Paper presented to April 1986 AERA meeting.

Deci, E. L. 1976. "The Hidden Costs of Rewards," *Organizational Dynamics,* 4:61–72.

Feiman-Nemser, S. and M. Buchmann. 1985. "Pitfalls of Experience in Teacher Preparation," *Teacher College Record,* 87:53–65.

Lawler, E. E. III. 1977. "Reward Systems," in *Improving Life at Work: Behavioral Science Approaches to Organizational Change,* Chap. 4, J. Richard Hackman and J. Lloyd Suttle, eds., Santa Monica, California: Goodyear Publishing Co.

Lepper, M. R. and D. Greene. 1978. *The Hidden Costs of Reward: New Perspectives on the Psychology of Human Motivation.* Hillsdale, NJ: Lawrence Erlbaum Associates.

Lortie, D. 1975. *Schoolteacher: A Sociological Study.* Chicago: The University of Chicago Press.

Mahoney, T. A. 1979. *Compensation and Reward Perspectives.* Homewood, Illinois: Richard D. Irwin.

Meyer, H. H., E. Kay, and J. French. 1965. "Split Roles in Performance Appraisal," *Harvard Business Review,* 43:123–129.

Mitchell, S. "Negotiating the Design of Professional Jobs," Paper presented to April 1986 AERA meeting.

Mosston, M. 1972. *Teaching: From Command to Discovery.* Belmont, CA: Wadsworth Publishing Company, Inc.

OAP. 1985. *Criteria and Standards for Teacher Promotion.* Paper commissioned by the National Education Association.

Porter, L. W., E. E. Lawler, and J. R. Hackman. 1975. *Behavior in Organizations.* McGraw-Hill.

Shedd, J. and R. Malanowski. 1986. "From the Front of the Classroom: A Study of Teaching," Paper commissioned by the Tucson Education Association, Ithaca, NY Organizational Analysis and Practice.

Soar, R. S. and R. M. Soar. 1973. *Classroom Behavior, Pupil Characteristics and Pupil Growth for the School Year and for the Summer.* University of Florida, Gainesville, 5 ROI MH 14891 and 5 ROI MH 15626.

Weissman, R. 1969. "Merit Pay—What Merit?" *Education Digest,* 34:16–19.

Wight, D. 1985. "The Split Role in Performance Appraisal," *Personnel Administration,* (May):83–87.

Wise, Arthur E., L. Darling-Hammond, M. W. McLaughlin, and H. T. Bernstein. 1984. *Teacher Evaluation: A Study of Effective Practices,* The Rand Corporation, R-3139-NIE.

ENDNOTES

1 See Bernardin, H. J. and R. W. Beatty. 1984. *Performance Appraisal: Assessing Human Behavior at Work.* Boston: Kent Publishing Co.

2 See, for example, Porter, Lawler, and Hackman. 1975; Bernardin and Beatty, 1983; Peterson and Kauchak, 1982.

3 See, for example, Darling-Hammond, L., A. Wise, and S. Pease. 1983. *Teacher Evaluation in the Organizational Context: A Review of the Literature.* The Rand Corporation.

4 Bacharach, S., D. Lipsky, and J. Shedd. 1984.

5 See Lawler, Edward and David Nadler. 1975. "Motivation: A Diagnostic Approach," in *Behavior in Organizations.* McGraw-Hill.

6 See Jackson, P. 1968. *Life in Classroom.* New York: Holt, Rinehart and Winston.

7 Mitchell. Paper presented to AERA Convention, San Francisco, April 1986.

8 Tosi, H. and L. Tosi. 1984. "Knowledge-Based Pay: Some Propositions and Guidelines to Effective Use," Mimeographed; Jenkins, G. D. and N. Gupta. 1985. "Skill-Based Pay: A Concept That's Catching On," *Personnel,* 62(9):30–37.

9 See Bacharach, S. B. and S. C. Conley. "Uncertainty and Decision-Making in Teaching: Implications for Managing Professionals," in *Schooling for Tomorrow: Directing Reform to Issues That Count,* T. J. Sergiovanni and J. H. Moore, eds., Boston: Allyn & Bacon, pp. 311–329.

10 See Bacharach, S. B., S. C. Conley, and J. B. Shedd. "A Developmental Framework for Evaluating Teachers as Decision Makers," Accepted for publication in *Journal of Personnel Evaluation in Education.*

11 See Lortie, D. 1975. *Schoolteacher: A Sociological Study.* Chicago: The University of Chicago Press.

12 See Feiman-Nemser, S. and M. Buchmann. 1985. "Pitfalls of Experience in Teacher Preparation," *Teachers College Record,* 87:53–65.

13 See Bacharach, S. B., S. C. Conley, and J. B. Shedd. 1986. "Beyond Career Ladders: Structuring Teacher Career Development Systems," *Teachers College Record,* Summer.

14 For an illustration of a system designed to provide teachers with diagnostic information concerning their decision-making skills, see Shedd, J. and R. Malanowski. "Criteria and Standards for Career Development Systems," Organizational Analysis and Practice, Inc., Ithaca, NY.

15 See Conley, S. "Career Ladders and Labor Management Cooperation," Paper presented to 1986 AERA meetings.

16 See Deci, E. L. 1976. "The Hidden Costs of Rewards," *Organizational Dynamics,* 4:61–72. See Lawler, E. E. III. 1977. "Reward Systems," in *Improving Life at Work: Behavioral Science Approaches to Organizational Change,* Chap. 4, J. Richard Hackman and J. Lloyd Suttle, ed., Santa Monica, California: Goodyear Publishing Co. See Lepper, M. R. and D. Green. 1978. *The Hidden Costs of Reward: New Perspectives on the Psychology of Human Motivation.* Hillsdale, NJ: Lawrence Erlbaum Associates.

17 It is important to note that in such a system we would recommend that promotion be based on skills, not job tasks. The majority of "career ladders" currently being proposed in education links promotion to specific job duties, not skills. See Bacharach, S., S. Conley, and J. Shedd. 1986. "Beyond Career Ladders: Structuring Teacher Career Development Systems," *Teachers College Record,* Summer.

18 See Wight, E. 1985. "The Split Role in Performance Appraisal," *Personnel Administration,* (May):83–87.

19 See Porter, L. W., E. E. Lawler, and J. R. Jackman. 1975. *Behavior in Organizations.* McGraw-Hill.

20 See Bernardin and Beatty's (1984) description of multiple-step processes for decision making in performance appraisal. The process removes the responsibility of "final evaluation" (e.g., merit pay) from the immediate supervisor and places it with a higher level manager or supervisor. The rationale is similar to the rationale provided here: "The immediate supervisor's efforts may be directed toward a strict *description* of performance and career development." However, our proposal that formative appraisers act as advocates for individuals differs in that it casts formative evaluators in a slightly more active role.

21 This point of view may seem inconsistent with what some observers call a "professional model of schools" in which teachers are seen as independently responsible for identifying and addressing student needs. We would argue that this is an argument for teacher *discretion* in determining how they carry out their tasks and is not inconsistent with the notion that the work of teachers is interdependent in accomplishing the primary tasks of the organization.

22 See Bacharach, S., D. Lipsky, and J. Shedd. 1986. *Merit Pay and Its Alternatives.* OAP Monograph.

23 Alabama has, in the past year, passed a legislation that specifies the pretenure period as a period of development for beginning teachers. The decision to grant tenure is seen as a "summative" promotion decision.

ADMINISTERING THE ALTERNATIVE COMPENSATION SYSTEM: THE PRACTITIONERS' PERSPECTIVE

Administering an Alternative Compensation System: Reflections on the Tennessee Plan

CHARLES BURKETT – *University of Tennessee*
ROBERT McELRATH – *East Tennessee State University*

THE importance of the school principal as a change agent and his/her role in reform movements in education, including the movement to provide alternative ways of compensating educators, are highlighted in this chapter. Principals are crucial to the implementation of change; they provide the leadership in the schools, so their perceptions of anything new and their means of implementing new systems are of great consequence. Bill Clinton (1986), governor of Arkansas, stated, "Strong leaders create strong schools. Research and common sense suggest that administrators can do a great deal to advance school reform. They will lead the next wave of reform."

IMPORTANCE OF THE PRINCIPAL TO REFORM MOVEMENTS

Educational reform seems to be the current password in schools. The general public has seen the acceleration of change in technology in particular and in society in general, and has come to equate change with improvement. The attitude that new is better has invaded society and is having its impact in the schools. The general public expects the schools to change (reform) and, as a result, be improved. The public is correct in believing that we cannot have rapid reform in technology and society in general and not have rapid reform in education. Our system of education needs, at least, to be a part of the reform movement, if not in its forefront. Alternative compensation for teachers and principals is one thrust for beginning the reform.

PRINCIPALS ENGAGED IN PROGRAMS WITH ALTERNATIVE COMPENSATION AND SCHOOL REFORM

The need for a public system of education has never before been seriously challenged in modern times. Our schools have always been considered a cornerstone of our social system. Given the emphasis on reform to meet the demands of a changing society, schools as they exist now are being seriously challenged. Many of the "authorities" on change are "betting" that schools, given their history of slowness to adjust to change, will not be able to make the needed adjustments without radical reform imposed from the outside. Yet external pressure for change has become the fulcrum for the current reform movement in education. Different programs for the compensation of professional educators are one aspect of the movement. It does not seem reasonable that we can continue to compensate teachers and principals on the basis of their formal education and experience and effect needed change—we cannot continue to treat the competent and incompetent alike. If education is to attract the best, retain them, and expect high output, it will have to devise ways to effectively pay for services based on performance. If the reform is to be effective, principals will have to provide the leadership. They, too, will have to make some major adjustments and stop treating school operations as routine. They will have to exhibit much more responsiveness to initiating and implementing change.

The principal is involved, directly or indirectly, in any major reform in education; the reform effort affects him/her and those he/she is charged with leading. A principal must be well-informed about the change, its rationale, and its probable consequences. The principal must act, not react. Initial reform movements in education focused on improving teacher performance and on providing alternative compensation methods to reward effective teachers. Relatively little attention was given to providing leadership for the change; the leader's role was not well-planned in most cases and, indeed, was completely ignored in others.

Principals throughout the country have had to provide leadership for schools that have been increasingly attacked by various segments of society. During the last decade, there have been numerous reports emphasizing the poor quality of our schools. Educators at all levels, especially principals, have been frustrated by implications in numerous reports that if schools would just get tougher, educators would work harder and that if students were better motivated, the ills of the schools and society would be cured.

One of the most widely read reports on the state of education and one that got the attention of the country and that forced principals into a defensive position was *A Nation at Risk* (1983). The information presented in this document was not well-researched, and it would be difficult for the authors to defend its accuracy. Even so, the information was alarming as to the "sorry" state of education in the country. In this respect, even though inaccurate, the report may have produced the results desired by the authors by calling attention to the need for improving education.

Politicians got into the act during the early 1980s; governors devoted most of their attention to education and its possible reform, in their annual meetings. The President and Secretary of Education also became involved in the issue at about the same time. There was a great deal of rhetoric but very little action at the national level. At the state level, there was much rhetoric and some action, with several states passing legislation mandating the improvement of teachers and teaching. At the local level, educators were forced to react to the national and state concerns. The reforms, including additional compensation for those identified as better teachers, were planned at the top and edicts passed down to the locals. Some local educators perceived these edicts favorably, but many saw them as threats. The school principal, in most cases, was caught in the proverbial middle, having had little to do with the planning of the change but expected to provide leadership for its implementation.

The *A Nation at Risk* (1983) report was considered by many observers to have given the impetus to what is considered the first wave of school reform of the 1980s. The theme of the first wave centered on higher expectations and standards for schools. The movement, led by governors, state legislators, and state boards of education, dealt mostly with improved graduation requirements, and it raised questions about the qualifications of teachers and the quality of teacher preparation programs.

In the late 1980s, those promoting reform began to focus their attention on improved school leadership, empowerment of teachers, and the restructuring of schools. Compensation alternatives for teachers and principals were designed to assist in the achievement of these goals.

WHY HAVE ALTERNATIVE COMPENSATION PROGRAMS BEEN DEVELOPED?

Principals have been charged with implementing the goals, most of which were determined by others, for improving the schools. The major goal in creating alternative pay plans was to improve the quality of elementary and secondary education by varying the incentives and rewards available for classroom teachers and principals. To develop and implement such a plan, it was thought, would assist in making teaching and school administration more professional careers by paying more for a job well done. The majority of alternative compensation programs are designed to create different levels of professional status for teachers and administrators by establishing a ladder that can be climbed during one's career. This career ladder design also gives teachers a means of advancement without having to go into administration to do it.

Introduction of alternative pay plans came as a surprise to the majority of American citizens because most did not realize that teachers were paid solely on the basis of training and experience and not at all on the basis of performance. When the idea of performance based compensation was introduced to the public, they endorsed the concept. The Peter Hart Poll (1983), conducted in one state, found that 87 percent of the citizens believed that teachers should be rewarded on the basis of performance and 67 percent of those surveyed said they were willing to pay additional taxes to support such a plan. The Gallup Poll (1987) reported that 80 percent of Americans favored increased pay for teachers who proved themselves particularly capable. Comparing this poll to a similar one five years earlier, when the first incentive plan was introduced, the percentage of those favoring the plan had increased. The idea of alternative compensation based on quality of work seemed very practical and logical to the general public. Little did they realize the difficulty of developing defensible criteria for determining the differences in teacher quality or the resistance by teachers to any such plan. Therefore, principals were left with the dilemma of implementing a program for alternative compensation that was highly favored by the general public and greatly opposed by teachers.

POLITICAL INFLUENCES AFFECTING PRINCIPALS INVOLVED WITH ALTERNATIVE COMPENSATION

Politicians, especially governors, proved that change can be brought about and implemented by force, even with the persons most directly affected by it being in opposition—in this case, teachers and principals. The program for alternative compensation for teachers and principals in Tennessee was born out of a dispute between a governor and his state teachers' organization that he insisted on calling the teachers' union. The "teachers' union" had not supported the governor's educational program during his first term and chose to support his opponent when the governor ran for reelection for his second term in 1982. Therefore, educators in the public schools and state-supported universities were not included in the early planning of the program. In fact, one of the chief planners was a professor from a private university.

The news media and the public embraced the concept of the alternative compensation for teachers and principals. The "teachers' union" continued to oppose the program. The plan was introduced by the governor with much fanfare. The legislature delayed the proposal for one year, for the most part in order to appease teachers who were opposing the plan.

The principals in the state, who would be charged with providing leadership for implementing the plan, had almost no input into the political arena where the scenario was being played out. This put principals in an untenable position of being charged to implement a plan that they had no part in developing. They were also put in the position of having to decide whether to support the teachers' or the governor's position.

ATTENTION FOCUSED ON THE PRINCIPALSHIP

There is more evidence supporting the importance of the principal's impact on the effectiveness of the school than on any other subject of school leadership. We can safely say that the old adage of "as the principal goes, so goes the school" is supported by research findings. As a result, renewed focus is being placed on the principal to provide leadership in gaining greater educational opportunities for students and in rewarding the results by alternative compensation means.

The lack of valid objective means of evaluating the effectiveness of principals has always been troublesome. Appropriate alternative compensation is difficult to match to the level of performance with certainty. Reformers have been plagued with how to determine varying levels of compensation for different degrees of performance, primarily because there is a woeful lack of standards by which to judge effective principaling. Perhaps one of the most valuable results of the reform movement, as it applies to alternative compensation for principals, will be to establish such standards.

Some of the common characteristics of effective principals have been identified by research findings. While these findings are not conclusive, they do provide a starting point. Jwaideh (1984) listed desired characteristics of principals found in research reports as follows. Effective principals have vision, establish goals, balance their task performances, achieve desired human relations, are guided by school norms, are innovators, are change agents, are flexible, are effective communicators, have community support, and have central office support.

Effective principals manage schools well, but they do much more than simply manage schools. They provide leadership for evaluating and improving teacher effectiveness and the teaching/learning environment of the school. Reilly (1984) found that effective principals provided leadership in maintaining a calm school environment that was conducive to forming a positive learning atmosphere. Leithwood and Montgomery (1982) found that effective principals were attuned to the entire school, as well as its place in the school system. Top priorities for effective principals were the happiness and achievement of students. They also reported that there were specific matters to which effective principals gave attention. These matters included management tasks such as providing space, scheduling meetings, disseminating information, delivering supplies, providing finances, and caring for facilities. They also gave attention to leadership activities such as developing in-service training plans, planning in-service with consultants, assessing teacher needs and designing strategies to solve problems with new curriculum, finding means of securing resources, developing a school philosophy, and assisting teachers in implementing new programs. While this list is not exhaustive, it serves to indicate some of the responsibilities fulfilled by principals who are effective leaders. The standards for establishing alternative compensation systems for principals should be selected from these research based activities and expectations.

Lamar Alexander (1986), former governor of Tennessee, who is credited with leading the school reform movement by the governors in the 1980s, during his frequent visits to communities, said, "Washington cannot fix schools; governors, legislatures, and state boards of education cannot fix schools; but communities can fix schools." He emphasized that communities can fix schools only by selecting effective principals who will build a school climate that empowers teachers and motivates learners.

In summary, principals and those aspiring to become principals are now being perceived as the key to the success of the school reform movement of the 1980s and the alternative compensation plan. Research findings are rather explicit in indicating that the principalship position and who fills it are the most important considerations for school improvement. The quality of the principal determines the quality of the improvement program that takes place within the school.

PERCEPTIONS OF PRINCIPALS OF AN ALTERNATIVE COMPENSATION PLAN

When a dramatic change occurs in education, one can expect ambivalent feelings from those affected by it. Alternative compensation is a rather dramatic change that has been implemented in some states, causing mixed reactions. The perspectives of principals concerning the success of an alternative compensation plan for teachers in one state will be discussed here. These perceptions were taken from principals in a state where the program had been in effect for four years. Alternative compensation in this state was based on the career ladder level of teachers and principals.

A study was conducted by the Tennessee Association for School Administration and Supervision (1988) where principals were asked if they supported the program and if they perceived that instruction had improved as a result of the program. They were also asked if the "best" teachers and principals were applying for upper levels of the alternative compensation program. The major findings of the study were as follows.

Strengths of the Alternative Compensation Program as Perceived by Principals

(1) Principals rated the extended contract opportunities for teachers and administrators as one of the most significant contributions of the program. [The majority of principals and teachers in this state are employed for less than twelve months. The extended contract (more pay for additional work that is an option for levels 2 and 3) is paid by the state. The extended contract benefits provide pay for teachers and principals with compensated time to do planning, developing, and researching that they would not ordinarily be able to do.]

(2) A great majority of the principals responding to the survey (89

percent) reported that the alternative compensation was providing improved opportunities for the professional growth of teachers and principals.

(3) They reported that the program was an effective vehicle for meeting the demands of the public for improved schools.

(4) A majority (55 percent) reported that leadership at the school level had been improved as a result of the opportunities provided in the alternative compensation program. (For example, principals are required to attend a principals' academy every five years.)

(5) Classroom teaching had improved as a result of the program according to 52 percent of those surveyed.

(6) A majority (52 percent) of the principals surveyed reported that student achievement had improved as a result of the program. A study of test scores in this state from 1983–87 verified that the perception of the principals was correct.

Weaknesses of the Alternative Compensation Program as Perceived by Principals

(1) Almost one-half (48 percent) of principals surveyed reported that teacher and principal evaluations for alternative compensation should be done at the local, rather than at the state, level as it presently is done. (The evaluations were done by three state evaluators for candidates applying for level 2 and 3.)

(2) Nearly one-half (49 percent) of the principals reported that they did not feel that the most competent teachers and principals had applied for career ladder advancement.

(3) Forty-two percent reported that they did not consider the state evaluation process as an accurate indicator of the performance of teachers and principals. [Those administrators who had achieved upper level status reported less disagreement than did those who were nonparticipants. At the time of the survey, approximately 25 percent of the teachers and principals who were eligible had applied to be evaluated for alternative compensation (upper level status).]

Recommendations for Improvement as Perceived by Principals

The principals in the survey made the following recommendations for the program:

(1) The program should continue.

(2) Annual reviews should be made for improvement.

(3) The length of the evaluation cycles for both teachers and principals should be shortened from one year to one semester.

(4) Evaluations of principals for upper levels of the program should measure how well they evaluate teachers.

(5) No teacher should be recommended for upper level status without a thorough evaluation of performance. (Legislation at the time of the survey had been introduced to award upper level status for teachers and principals based on their completing staff development programs. This legislation was not approved.)

RESULTS OF STUDY OF EFFECTIVENESS OF PRINCIPALS WHEN COMPARED BETWEEN VARYING LEVELS OF COMPENSATION

Johnson (1989) conducted a study of principals who were receiving various levels of compensation. The principals involved in this study were either on level 1 or level 3 of a three-tier alternative compensation plan. Principals in both groups received some additional compensation for recognized services ($1000 for level 1 and $7000 for level 3). He compared the leadership behavior of principals on level 1 with that of principals on level 3 and the organizational climate of the school. The comparisons were made of leadership and climate as assessed by teachers in the respective schools of principals who were involved in the study.

Fifteen level 1 elementary school principals were compared to eleven level 3 elementary school principals on the basis of how teachers rated them on leadership behavior and the school on organizational climate. The Leadership Behavior Description Questionnaire X11 (LBDQ X11) was administered to teachers in the twenty-six schools to determine the teachers' impressions of the principals' leadership behavior. The Organizational Climate Description Questionnaire (OCDQ-RE) for elementary schools was administered to teachers in the twenty-six schools in order to determine their opinions of the climates of the schools. There were 305 teachers in the fifteen level 1 schools. The response rate from these teachers was 90.8 percent. There were 253 teachers in the schools administered by the level 3 principals. The response rate from these teachers was 84.1 percent. Differences were tested by using

Table 1. Comparison of organizational climate of schools administered by level 1 and 3 principals for compensation purposes.

Principal Rank	N	X	s	F	df	p
Level 1	15	46.916	22.519	63593	(1240)	.433
Level 3	11	54.214	23.780			

the ANOVA statistical test. Data for the comparisions between leadership behavior and school organization climate in schools administered by level 1 and level 3 principals are reported in Tables 1 and 2.

No significant differences were found in the perceived leadership behavior of the principal or in the organizational climate of the school between those who were on level 1 and receiving an additional $1000 in compensation and those on level 3 who were receiving an additional $7000. Therefore, it was concluded that there were very little, if any, differences between those principals who received a small amount of alternative compensation and those who received a more substantial amount, in terms of providing leadership and a positive organizational climate. However, those on level 1 were eligible to apply for level 3 yet had chosen not to do so.

Assuming that there are thousands of effective school leaders in the states that have alternative compensation programs, why do some choose to enter the upper levels of the program while others do not? Is it fear of failure, lack of confidence in the evaluation plan, lack of encouragement and support from superiors, or lack of a good self-image? These and other topics need to be researched, and the results will give direction for improving leadership training, programs, and evaluation systems. A brief summary of another recent study will illustrate the importance of continued research dealing with alternative compensation programs.

Hopson (1989) conducted a study of female principals and supervi-

Table 2. Comparison of leadership behavior scores of level 1 and 3 principals for compensation purposes.

Principal Rank	N	X	s	F	df	p
Level 1	15	368.75	21.305	.00001	(1,24)	.998
Level 3	11	368.726	29.646			

sors who were receiving various levels of alternative compensation. She compared group 1 female principals/supervisors (nonparticipants and level 1) with group 2 female principals/supervisors (levels 2 and 3) using the Self-Directed Learning Readiness Scale (SDLRS), which isolates eight factors: love of learning; self-concept as an effective, independent learner; tolerance of risk, ambiguity, and complexity in learning; creativity; view of learning as a lifelong, beneficial process; initiative in learning; self-understanding; and acceptance of responsibility for one's own learning.

Demographic and SDLRS scales were submitted to 122 female principals and supervisors of schools who were eligible to participate in the alternative compensation program. Sixty-eight percent of those chosen for the study responded to the survey. Eighteen female principals (group 1) were either level 1 or nonparticipants in the program and eighteen female principals (group 2) had achieved upper levels 2 and 3 of the alternative pay plan. These principals had successfully completed the state performance evaluation. There was a significant difference between the SDLRS scores of group 2 and group 1 (level 1 and nonparticipants). Group 2 had a mean score of 258.57 compared to the mean score of 241.60 for group 1.

The same results occurred when comparing the mean scores of the two groups of female supervisors. Group 3 (level 1 and nonparticipants) consisted of seventeen female supervisors who had a SDLRS mean score of 243.43 and group 4 (levels 2 and 3) consisting of thirty supervisors who had a SDLRS mean score of 259.97, which was significantly higher ($p = .05$). This study raises many other issues for further study such as completing an analysis of each of the eight factors of the SDLRS.

Hopson's study also considered demographic factors such as age, number of children in the family, salary, and years of experience and found no significant differences in SDLRS mean scores of the four groups. In short, self-directed learning is not related to age, experience, or salaries. The results of the study are listed in Table 3.

SUGGESTIONS FOR PRINCIPALS CONCERNING ALTERNATIVE COMPENSATION PROGRAMS

Ideally, principals in schools with existing alternative compensation plans should be responsible for the overall evaluation of teachers who

Table 3. Self-directed learning readiness scores comparing groups of principals and supervisors.

		Principals			
Variable	Mean	SD	t value	df	p
Group 1	241.667	25.042	−2.20	32	.035
Group 2	258.578	19.88			
		Supervisors			
Group 3	243.428	25.752			
Group 4	259.967	14.653	−2.24	16.92	.038

are aspiring for status or rank for higher levels of pay for better performance. The principal must supervise or carry out evaluations of teaching skills and knowledge—things that teachers know and do that contribute to good teaching. In developing the evaluation system, educational research and information from teachers must be used to clarify the skills and knowledge of effective teaching.

Principals should be responsible for seeing that teachers are evaluated in at least six major skill areas:

(1) Planning for instruction

(2) Teaching strategies

(3) Evaluation of student progress

(4) Classroom management

(5) Professional development and leadership

(6) Basic communication skills

In order for principals to insure that evaluations of teacher performance for alternative compensation purposes are somewhat objective, specific criteria under each major skill area must be examined. These criteria are often called "indicators." For instance, when measuring teaching strategies, the indicators are used in the evaluation to assess how the teacher presents subject matter and whether he/she reteaches at appropriate times. Each indicator is evaluated by using several illustrative statements called "measurement items."

Multiple Sources of Data

When principals and other evaluators are making judgments about teachers that will affect the mental health of those involved, as well as their livelihoods, safeguards must be taken to insure that evaluations are as fair, objective, and thorough as possible. Therefore, it is advisable that multiple data sources be used. This system is used in many schools and state school systems that are involved in alternative compensation for teachers. The system includes five primary sources of data in the teacher evaluation process: 1) the teacher, 2) the evaluator, 3) the teachers' respective principals, 4) peer teachers, and 5) the teachers' respective students. In addition, several means of gathering data are utilized in this system: classroom observation, dialogue sessions between the teacher and evaluators, questionnaires, and a summary of professional development and leadership activities. Some state systems administer a written test to measure pedagogical and communication skills.

THE PRINCIPAL'S ROLE IN IMPLEMENTING THE ALTERNATIVE COMPENSATION PROGRAM

Experiences in the use of an alternative compensation plan seem to indicate that teachers who participated in the program got professional satisfaction from it. The amount of satisfaction they received from it depended to a great extent on the attitudes and behaviors of their respective principals. For example, if the principal believed that effective teaching could be evaluated fairly for differentiated pay purposes, teachers would likely pursue the option of alternative compensation for different levels of behavior. If teachers perceived that their principals were capable of discriminating between effective and ineffective teaching and that they could be objective, the teachers were more likely to support the program.

A survey by McElrath (1988) of twenty selected schools in Tennessee that had a high percentage of faculty members who had achieved upper level status on the alternative compensation program revealed that all of the principals were supportive of the program. All had encouraged and assisted each teacher before, during, and after the evaluation. Teachers reported a variety of activities by principals that encouraged them to participate. Some of those activities included

- Workshops on effective teaching were conducted.
- Principals organized special sessions for those who were to be evaluated during the year and reviewed the evaluation instruments, competencies, and scoring procedures. Many mysteries of the system were eliminated.

- Principals assigned other teachers as mentors to give guidance, encouragement, and assistance. One teacher stated, "In a sense, my mentor served as a big sister during the year, giving me extra time and encouragement."
- Principals held personal conferences with teachers whom they deemed ready to be evaluated for advancement for alternative pay.
- Principals organized staff development programs for those who needed special assistance. For example, in one school three teachers requested additional assistance for improving their classroom management techniques. A twenty-hour program, spread over several weeks, enabled the teachers to review literature, observe other teachers, and put into practice the principles of good classroom management. All of these teachers were evaluated and earned additional compensation under the alternative compensation plan.

ESTABLISHING AN EVALUATION SYSTEM FOR ALTERNATIVE COMPENSATION FOR PRINCIPALS

Local and state school systems that are developing alternative compensation programs for principals are struggling with the tasks of identifying what should be evaluated, who should evaluate, and what instruments should be used to measure the skills of principals for alternative compensation programs. Other questions that are often asked are, Will the evaluation system be objective? What weights will be given to the various instruments? How will the evaluators be trained? Will staff development opportunities be offered to those principals who fall short of qualifying for alternative compensation? When may principals reapply for evaluation? These and other questions will arise when an agency has to develop an evaluation plan for alternative compensation.

Those charged with developing an evaluation plan must agree upon a set of assumptions and principles of evaluation; establish eligibility requirements (screening); choose competencies, indicators, and measurement items; develop instrumentation; and decide the data sources that will be used. The task is easier if a sound framework is established for the process.

Assumptions and Principles of an Evaluation Plan for Alternative Compensation for Principals

Knowledge of the assumptions and principles upon which the evaluation system is built will be helpful to candidates as they prepare to participate in alternative compensation programs. State evaluation systems that have been developed for principals include the following assumptions:

- The primary goal of the evaluation program is to identify outstanding principal performance.
- The main goal of the evaluation process is the improvement of instructional programs.
- The evaluation program focuses on performance rather than credentials.
- Principals want to be competent professionals.
- Organizing and implementing high quality instructional programs are the primary responsibilities of principals.
- All principals can improve their performance.
- The evaluation program must include a strong professional development program.
- Principals are best able to evaluate the performance of their peers.
- Rigorous training is essential for preparing to be an evaluator.
- Evaluation is best conducted by a team of evaluators rather than by a single individual.
- The evaluation process should not discourage diversity in school programs.
- Multiple sources of data are essential to the development of a complete picture of the principal's performance.
- The instruments must be understood by the principals who are being evaluated.
- The instruments must assess the performance of skills deemed important to effective administration of the instructional program.

Screening of Principal Candidates

Should principal candidates for alternative pay programs meet prerequisites before performance evaluation begins? Should these prerequisites include effective written and oral communication skills? Is there a certain body of knowledge that all principals should be expected to know before applying for advancement? Some state systems require that candidates pass a professional skills test before being eligible for performance evaluation. Policymakers tend to believe that the principalship cannot be considered a profession unless principals possess a basic body of knowledge needed for the effective administration of schools. Those responsible for developing the evaluation system must decide the prerequisites that must be met before the evaluation begins.

Principal Competencies, Indicators, and Measurement Items

School leaders are much in agreement that "effective schools" research suggests that some principal competencies are more important than others in facilitating improvement in student learning. The competencies found in the majority of principal evaluation plans fall into four major domains: 1) instructional leadership, 2) organizational management, 3) communication and interpersonal relations, and 4) professional growth and leadership. Those constructing the system must decide the objectives that are to be included in each domain and how each will be measured. For instance, *instructional leadership* may have multiple objectives such as

(1) Establishes and implements clear instructional goals
(2) Plans, implements, and evaluates instructional programs
(3) Provides a purposeful school environment conducive to learning
(4) Conducts an effective evaluation and utilization of teachers

These objectives are usually called *indicators* and multiple measurement items are developed to evaluate each indicator. A weight is assigned to each measurement item, usually based on the importance of the indicator to the success of the school. The mystery of the evaluation system is removed when principals know what is being evaluated and the weight that is assigned to each task.

Plans for alternative compensation for principals are currently in use in some states. Research findings in one of those states on requirements for programs for alternative compensation of principals provide guidelines for developing an adequate evaluation system of principals.

Following is an example of an indicator used in Tennessee for examining each principal candidate who is evaluated for alternative compensation.

I. Instructional Leadership (competency)
    A. Established and implements clear instructional goals and specific achievement objectives for the school (indicator)
        1. Provides in-service for teachers in developing and implementing school goals and objectives (measurement item)
        2. Ascertains that school and classroom activities are consistent with the school's instructional goals and objectives (measurement item)
        3. Evaluates progress toward instructional goals and makes needed adjustments (measurement item)

As can be seen in the above example, several indicators, with specific measurement items, are used to evaluate each competency of the principal.

Multiple Data Sources

Several data sources should be used in an effort to insure an element of objectivity and fairness when principals are being evaluated. Information about the performance of principals can be gathered from 1) superordinates, 2) observations, 3) candidate interviews, 4) questionnaires administered to teachers and students, and 5) professional skills tests when used. If a state evaluation plan for principals is used, data gathering sources should be validated and reliability established based on field test results.

Training of Evaluators

The importance of trained evaluators cannot be overemphasized. Persons charged with the responsibility of evaluating principals for alternative pay purposes must be thoroughly trained in every aspect of the evaluation process. These persons must be familiar with the identified competencies expected of effective principals and be provided time for practice in the use of instruments prior to engaging in regular scheduled evaluations. Training sessions, when well organized, provide one of the most beneficial and meaningful staff development programs offered to principals.

PRINCIPALS' PERCEPTION: THE EFFECTS OF ALTERNATIVE COMPENSATION

Several principals responsible for schools where alternative compensation plans for teachers and principals are in effect were interviewed to gauge their perceptions of the effects of varying compensation based on performance. Elementary, middle, and secondary school principals were interviewed. All the principals interviewed operate under the same system of alternative compensation. In order to receive additional compensation, teachers and principals must be evaluated by state evaluators and judged to be worthy of salary supplements for extra efforts and greater results. In these schools, some teachers had successfully completed the evaluation and were receiving salary supplements, others were evaluated and were not judged as meriting additional compensation, and others chose not to be evaluated.

The principals interviewed have from three to twenty-two years of experience in the position. All but one had achieved level 3 for principal alternative compensation. Level 3 provides $3000 incentive and $4000 for additional work called "extended contract" if the principal had not been previously employed on a twelve-month basis.

Eight questions were asked of the principals. The questions, designed to serve as indicators of their attitudes toward alternative compensation, were as follows:

(1) Has alternative compensation for teachers and principals improved the teaching/learning environment? Explain your answer.

(2) How has the change to alternative compensation for teachers under your direction affected your role regarding principal/ teacher relationships?

(3) What effect has alternative compensation had on relationships among teachers? (Include both teachers who are receiving supplements and those who are not.)

(4) What are the positive effects of added compensation?

(5) What are the negative effects of added compensation?

(6) What effect has alternative compensation had on students? What is its effect (if any) on at-risk students?

(7) How has alternative compensation affected the teachers' daily schedules? What are the effects of extended contracts?

(8) Are the best qualified teachers actually receiving the most compensation under the alternative compensation plan? Explain your answer.

We will look at each of these questions in turn.

Has Alternative Compensation for Teachers and Principals Improved the Teaching/Learning Environment?

The majority of the principals felt that extra compensation has had a definite positive impact on the teaching/learning environment. One elementary principal stated that the faculty has become more aware of the importance of setting goals and developing procedures to accomplish these goals. He further stated that the faculty stays on task with less wasted motion as a result of staff commitment to better use of instruction time.

A secondary principal perceived the expanded programs that developed as a result of the extended contract clause as making a difference in the learning environment. They have provided opportunities to directly help students that were not available before.

One middle school principal felt that alternative compensation has not improved instruction nor the learning opportunities for students. He stated that the test scores of students in his school have always been above average and that incentive pay is not as effective as people claim it is. He says, "It is not extra pay, but extra pay for extra work."

One of the principals considered two aspects of the program to be highly beneficial: the establishment of the principals' academy and the development of the instructional model. He felt that the academy gives the principals an opportunity to keep up with current happenings in public school education. In his opinion, the instructional model (a model required for those in the alternative compensation program) is useful in providing uniformity for the teaching process and is especially helpful to new teachers.

How Has the Change to Alternative Compensation for Teachers under Your Direction Affected Your Role Regarding Principal/Teacher Relationships?

The two elementary principals did not feel that the alternative compensation program had affected relationships with teachers either negatively or positively. One indicated that being selected for incentive salary based on merit made him "take a look" at a lot of different areas of leadership responsibilities and induced him to try to better meet the teachers' needs. The middle and secondary school principals did not detect a noticeable difference in their relationships with the teachers in their schools. Both reported that they felt a greater sense of responsibility for helping teachers who were preparing for evaluation to achieve higher levels of compensation.

What Effect Has Alternative Compensation Had on Relationships among Teachers? (Include Both Teachers Who Are Receiving Supplements and Those Who Are Not.)

Administrators interviewed representing middle school principals reported that they had not detected any adverse effects on the relationships of teachers. Those who were being supplemented did not "look down" on the other teachers, and they had not detected any jealousies. The teachers who were being supplemented were the same ones viewed with most respect before.

The one interviewed representing middle school principals reported that he had not witnessed any outward signs of negative effects on teacher relationships but that he had heard reports throughout the school system that teachers who were not receiving added compensation felt that they were just as effective as those who did receive the added funds. He reported that he has heard some negative comments such as, "How did *she* get approved for alternative compensation?"

Principals interviewed representing secondary school administrators contended that some teachers who were receiving the added compensation tended to overrate themselves in comparison to other teachers. One principal stated that, in some instances, those in the program may not have been as good as some teachers who were not in the program. Some of the better teachers, in his opinion, had not applied to be evaluated for alternative compensation because they had been turned off by problems in the evaluation process, by weak evaluators, and by "the horrors that some of their peers had endured in the evaluation process."

What Are the Positive Effects of Added Compensation?

The elementary principals interviewed indicated that there are several positive aspects: (a) all teachers and administrators deserve more

money, (b) it improves self-esteem, (c) it allows one to be a risk taker —
to take a chance on passing the evaluation for added compensation, (d)
it allows for teachers and administrators across the state to talk a "common language" since the evaluation criteria are standard in the state,
and (e) the program focuses on money, and that is what the program is
about.

The middle school principals also emphasized that teachers and principals deserve more money and that a real positive aspect of the program is that it provides for higher salaries for those who choose and are
chosen for the option. He felt that another positive aspect is the recognition of being "one of the best" and making one feel good about
himself/herself.

The secondary principals indicated that the positive effects of the
program were more money and status. One stated, "If there is money
out there, I am going to try to get my part."

What Are the Negative Effects of Added Compensation?

The elementary principals indicated that they know of no negative effects of the program. The middle school principals contended that the
negative factors are the risk of being turned down and the humiliation
that goes with rejection; they also mentioned some negative feelings
such as resentment, peer pressure, envy, and jealousy that surrounded
the selection process. They also said that the community sometimes
viewed those with greater compensation as the best and that it can be
an "administrative nightmare" to have parents call and request that their
children be placed with those teachers. They admitted that they knew
that the other teachers were just as good as those with added compensation.

The secondary principals contended that the confusion surrounding
some of the first evaluations had a negative effect. Because of the faulty
process and weak evaluators, some teachers were turned down who
should have been approved. Many of the other teachers were hesitant
to try the evaluation for fear of experiencing the same frustrations and
pain evidenced by other teachers.

What Effect Has Alternative Compensation Had on Students?

All of the principals interviewed indicated that the extended contract
component of the program had positive effects. The extra pay for added

services allowed them to plan programs for the students that they would not ordinarily have. They mentioned, specifically, summer school programs for at-risk students, enrichment, "prime time" programs, overnight trips, added foreign language opportunities, and extended library hours.

How Has Alternative Compensation Affected the Teachers' Daily Schedules? What Are the Effects of Extended Contracts?

Some of the principals indicated that teachers were putting in considerable amounts of additional time working with students before and after school because of this program. Other principals contended that the teachers were putting in the additional time already. One principal felt that the program left teachers "looking for things to do" in order to meet the additional time requirement for the extended contract component. Most of the principals agreed, however, that the extended contract time had positively affected the teachers' daily schedules and that they were accomplishing more for the good of students.

Are the Best Qualified Teachers Actually Receiving the Most Compensation under the Alternative Compensation Plan?

The principals indicated that some of the better teachers are, indeed, receiving the added compensation. However, they expressed concerns that many of the most effective teachers are not receiving added compensation for some of the following reasons: (a) they do not want to take time from students to prepare for the evaluation; (b) they do not need the money; (c) they are not motivated to apply; (d) they have fear of failure; (e) they feel union pressures; and (f) they have different personal reasons.

The principals' interviews indicated that principals saw many positive aspects of the alternative compensation program, especially the extended contract component. Their greatest reservations seemed to be the inequity in determining who were the better teachers and the concern over whether added compensation made for better teacher performance. The information gathered in these interviews should help the reader understand some of the perceptions of principals in schools functioning under an alternative compensation plan. Their opinions, whether positive or negative, should be considered when establishing such a program.

SUMMARY

The principals' perspective regarding alternative compensation for teachers and principals has been presented in this chapter. Principals see themselves and others see them as the "key" to educational reform. However, much of the reform has been planned by someone else and passed along for the principals to implement in the schools. They are often caught in the proverbial middle between the teachers, who will be most directly involved in the implementation, and those who are advocating reform but who do not understand the ramifications for teachers and principals. If alternative compensation is to work, principals must be involved in all levels of the planning and implementation. They must also be given the authority, funds, and support for the task of providing leadership to administer an alternative compensation program.

REFERENCES

Alexander, L. 1986. "Role of Local Community Task Forces," Speech given to the Carter County Community Task Force.

Gallup, A. M. and S. M. Elam. 1988. "The 20th Annual Gallup Poll of the Public's Attitudes toward the Public Schools," *Kappan* (Sept.):33–46.

Hart, P. D. 1983. "A Survey of Voter Attitudes in the State of Tennessee," Washington, D.C.: Peter Hart Research Associates, Inc.

Hopson, L. E. 1989. "A Study of the Self-Directed Learning Behaviors of Female Administrators in the Public Schools of the First and Second Tennessee Districts," Master's Degree Thesis.

Johnson, E. H., Jr. 1989. "A Comparison of Career Ladder III and Career Ladder I Elementary Principals' Leader Behavior and Organizational Climate," Doctoral Dissertation.

Jwaideh, A. R. 1984. "The Principal as a Facilitator of Change," *Educational Horizons,* 63:9–15.

Leithwood, K. A. and D. J. Montgomery. 1982. "The Role of the Elementary Principal in Program Improvement," *Review of Educational Research,* 52:309–339.

McElrath, R. L. 1988. "Survey of Twenty Selected Principals' Perceptions of the Career Ladder," Johnson City, Tennessee.

National Commission of Excellence in Education. 1983. *A Nation at Risk: The Imperative for Educational Reform.* Washington, D.C.: U.S. Government Printing Office.

National Governor's Association. 1986. *Time for Results: The Governors' 1991 Report on Education.* Washington, D.C.

Reilly, D. H. 1984. "The Principalship: The Need for a New Approach," *Education,* 104:242–247.

Tennessee Association for School Administration and Supervision. 1988. "Survey of Principals' Perceptions of the Career Ladder," Nashville, Tennessee.

CHAPTER 12

Performance Based Teacher Compensation: Implications for Local School Administrators

WILLIAM K. POSTON, JR.—*Iowa State University*

TEACHER salary patterns have been up for grabs in recent years. Politicians have been demanding accountability, unions have been demanding autonomy, boards have been demanding efficiency, parents have been demanding greater effectiveness, taxpayers have been demanding more results with less cost, and historical precedents have been demanding balance.

All these pressures focus on the local school administrator who is usually left to make most things work and to act compatibly with common sense. Most dramatically, today as in the past, the burden for efficacy falls upon the individual school administrator more often than not.

ORGANIZATION OF THIS CHAPTER

The challenge for local school administrators wishing to capitalize upon the manifold advantages of performance based pay and incentives demands knowledge of the problems, skill with the processes, and facility with the requirements of implementation of performance pay programs. The purpose of this chapter is to help local school administrators acquire the following skills, outcomes, or objectives:

(1) To identify sixteen reasons behind the development and popularity of performance based compensation at the local level

(2) To determine a number of distinct positive results related to teaching and learning, which distinguish successful performance based compensation programs

(3) To determine several positive effects that accrue from an organizational and management perspective with successful performance based compensation programs

301

(4) To analyze key problems relating to performance based compensation systems, which hold implications for local school administrators

(5) To evaluate the nature and significance of several dimensions of performance based compensation systems, which relate to administrative responsibilities and planning

(6) To pull together several disparate components of the performance based compensation issue for use in administrative planning

PERFORMANCE PAY RATIONALE FOR LOCAL SCHOOL ADMINISTRATORS

For decades, plans for compensating teachers for the work they do have been tied to fixed, uniform scales. This method of paying teachers has been challenged in the past few years because of its perceived ineffectiveness in delivering preferred educational results (Freiberg, 1987). Ostensibly designed to gain improvement in the quality of teaching and learning, changes from traditional salary scales for teachers to performance based compensation (PBC) plans have been proliferating nation-wide (Littleford, 1989).

Closer Focus on New Demands for Administrators in PBC Plans

Changes from traditional salary scales for teachers to PBC plans have been increasing nation-wide, ostensibly to gain improvement in the quality of teaching and learning in schools (Freiberg, 1987). As in any change, accommodation of PBC plans has created a plethora of new demands and requirements for local school administrators and teachers. These new demands create immense challenges because they frequently involve conflicting issues and could leave efficacy of accomplishment in doubt.

As is the case with most educational innovations, local school administrators have inherited the primary responsibility, if not for design of PBC systems, then for the implementation and management of performance based plans, regardless of origin. The pressure to link monies paid to teachers to "results" is a spin-off from the moves toward accountability that began in the early 1980s. Most of the push for results has come from sectors external to schools, and consequently the program may or may not be destined for success unless local school administrative efforts make it happen (Cibulka, 1989). Key to this discussion is the determination of why any school district would want to have a performance based compensation program for teachers in the first place.

TEACHING AND LEARNING RESULTS FROM INCENTIVES

Most importantly, given linkage of local district specific circumstances with what has been shown to work, performance based teacher compensation plans *can* work (Watson, Poda, and Miller, 1988). However, local school administrators worth their salt usually demonstrate pragmatic caution before attempting any innovation, and performance based compensation should be no exception. Looking carefully before leaping into something as complex as PBC makes for greater likelihood of success. Looking at some of the effects of PBC systems reveals some interesting outcomes and advantages.

In some locations where teacher performance and remuneration linkages are being attempted, several positive attributes are cited (Iowa Department of Education, 1989). For example, teaching and learning effects said to result include the following:

(1) Marked focus on learning outcomes
(2) New and expanded roles for teachers
(3) Accountability for student achievement
(4) Personalized instruction tied to individual needs
(5) Application of research and development of new knowledge

Let us look at each of these in detail.

Learning Focus

The focus on learning outcomes is congruent with recent developments in educational planning that are thought to be more productive in the teaching and learning process (Spady, 1988). Results of actions taken are far more indicative of progress and achievement than antecedents or inputs.

For example, the teacher who sets specific outcomes for students, defines in measureable terms what students should think, do, or feel, and equates instructional efficacy with reaching objectives is far more empirical about teaching than one who does not. On the other hand, the teacher who equates achievement with mere presentation of instruction, provision of materials, and normative testing and grading of student progress (i.e., grading on the curve) is without demonstrable evidence of goal completion. In other words, it's hard to tell if you've arrived if you didn't know ahead of time clearly where you wanted to go.

Teacher Role Expansion

New and expanded roles for teachers could be sufficient rationale alone for PBC programs. Teachers who get an opportunity to use expertise in different ways are afforded a larger stake in the values of the organization. In decision making, for example, participation of teachers is strongly needed. Designing curricula, planning staff development, choosing instructional materials, planning school budgeting, and even evaluating teacher performance are ways in which teachers can and should have a strong voice in any school district. As we shall see later, such role changes are important to morale as well.

Accountability for Achievement

Accountability for student achievement is high-risk behavior for teachers, but the rewards are substantial. The key reason for teaching is learning. Without responsibility for learning, the enterprise of teaching is rudderless and undirected. Without responsibility for learning, teaching is meaningless. Responsibility for learning is the foundation of effective teaching.

Individualization in Teaching

Personalizing teaching to meet specific needs of individual learners is unquestionably worthwhile. Given twenty-five to thirty students in a class, the teacher who diversifies instruction according to the needs of each student is contributing to the success of each specific, identifiable client. In effect, the teacher is making the large group into twenty-five to thirty separate groups, each with a membership of one. Undifferentiating instruction is ineffective and not worth supporting in any modern classroom.

Research Applications in Teaching

The last teaching and learning effect, that of applying research and developing new knowledge, is indicative of the new ground-breaking nature of PBC programs. Some things we now know would not have been learned without accountability reforms. For example, one study of state accountability reforms reveals that public disclosure of performance does seem to produce enhanced results (Cibulka, 1989).

Working on the cutting edge of emerging teaching know-how is exciting and commendable in a profession of service to others.

ORGANIZATION AND MANAGEMENT RESULTS FROM INCENTIVES

Teaching and learning effects are not thought to be the only noteworthy results of PBC plans. Organizational and managerial effects are also noted at the local school district level with PBC implementation, including the following:

(1) Site based decentralized control
(2) New administrative roles
(3) Accountability for success
(4) Supportive climate
(5) Expanded community relationships
(6) Financial productivity

Focus at the building level for key organizational functions provides greater flexibility in local strategies for effectiveness. In the example of staff development, local school administrators can implement programs to meet the specific training needs of their staffs at a close proximity to the source of the need.

Decentralization and Local Administrative Roles

New administrator roles, such as "management by walking around," build bridges among members of the local school team (Frase, 1990). In addition, administrative propinquity is a major contributor to supportive group relationships in change processes. The closer the administrator is to the classroom the better. Or as one wag put it, "Vince

Lombardi could never have coached from the front office during the game."

Accountability in Supervisory Behavior

As in teaching and learning above, organizational benefits include new and improved ways of accepting accountability with performance based compensation plans. Self-reported results of instruction and student outcomes tracking are benchmarks of organizational accountability, which can and should result from PBC programming. Knowledge of results is a primary part of any organizational improvement effort and may be instrumental in enhancement of learning (Cibulka, 1989).

Closer Relationships: Climate and Community

The supportive climate that characterizes PBC organizations results from application of many of the tools needed in PBC system workings such as mentoring, coaching, collaborative planning, and group processes that portray the principal as a peer in the implementation team.

Positive parent relationships are generated in PBC programs given the strong need for home–school connections. Parents, brought aboard as key crew members on the ship of learning, become increasingly supportive of the school. The positive shift in parental attitude is just one spin-off benefit from parents participating as partners in the learning process in soundly designed PBC plans.

Financial Productivity

Costs for education have increased more rapidly than financial support from legislatures, leaving greater need for improved productivity in educational programs. Curriculum-driven budgeting procedures used in performance based compensation districts have provided one avenue for improved productivity, and tools to effectively tie results to planning have become more available in recent years (Poston, 1990). Some believe that the pressure on schools to become more results-effective and cost-efficient at the same time couldn't have come at a more propitious time (Robinson, 1987). In any case, PBC systems provide fuel for the engines of productivity, in terms of satisfying taxpayers of the prudent utilization of tax monies provided for education.

LOCAL SCHOOL DISTRICT RESULTS: SUMMARY

In summarizing reasons for accepting the challenge of PBC plans, it's apparent that productive teaching–learning effects are brought into focus, and enhanced organizational–management benefits accrue as well. Local school administrators could possibly capitalize on these and other beneficial effects of performance based compensation plans for their schools.

OBSTACLES FOR LOCAL SCHOOL ADMINISTRATORS TO OVERCOME

Historically, plans to link evaluation of performance to pay have been replete with problems. The major problems have centered around the following items, which hold implications for local school administrators:

(1) Faulty teaching evaluation systems
(2) Organizational dissonance
(3) Deficient motivation and reinforcement practices
(4) Inadequate morale and staff conflicts
(5) Deficient financial support
(6) Muddled values, policies, and philosophy

School administrators need to take definitive action in each of the listed problem areas so as to minimize difficulties and to enhance success. Examining each in turn, specific implications and guidelines for the local school administrator are apparent.

Faulty Evaluation Processes and Procedures

Subjective evaluations, inadequate data in assessment, and inconclusive criteria have plagued incentive pay plans in the past (Robinson, 1984). Local school administrators need high-quality assessment tools to clinically define teacher job expectations and duties with precision. Moreover, administrators need to have superior competence and determination to evaluate with exactitude. In fact, the administrator must be the single individual most qualified by training and experience in the school to evaluate teaching.

Criteria for evaluation need to be accepted by all parties, and teachers must be stakeholders in the planning, development, implementation, and ongoing maintenance of the evaluation program. Without strong ownership, teachers will not support the process. The administrator must not only see the need for sound evaluative processes but must nurture their creation and oversee them to fruition.

Conditions, processes, and outcomes of teaching must be carefully controlled with accurate definitions and specifications. Unsound, nonempirical techniques will go a long way toward undermining PBC program success. Instrumentation is available, which accurately depicts effective characteristics of teaching (Kyrene, 1989), but classroom observation techniques should provide for acceptance of more than one model of teaching effectiveness (Freiburg, 1987).

Training programs for developing high probability of accuracy for administrators in evaluation procedures are also essential. The good news is that such training is readily available for administrators wishing to develop such high skill levels.

If local administrators are unwilling or unable to discriminate among levels of effective teaching, no performance based compensation system has a chance of succeeding. Poor discriminators could not be reasonably expected to coach poorly performing teachers to perform better.

The better the evaluation process and the better the evaluator, the better the chances for success of the locally managed performance based compensation plan. Teachers who demonstrate better performance, in order to be compensated or rewarded, must first be recognized. Unrewarded teachers who demonstrate high performance will become discouraged and ineffective.

The burden for administrators then becomes one of sorting out the good from the bad performers and being able not only to prove his/her conclusions, but also to obtain employee loyalty and support for the system.

Obviously, the administrator may be threatened by identifying the poor performer, since inadequate performance may reflect upon the employee's supervisor.

On the other hand, in the historical development of the single salary schedule, all employees generally received equal salary rewards. As a consequence, teachers who were productive and effective performers became disenchanted and discouraged with the unfair distribution of rewards. Their exit from education was unnecessary, premature, and injurious to potential quality of instructional systems. Rewards for less than satisfactory performance reinforce mediocrity and produce perceived and actual inequity among employees.

Organizational Dissonance

Organizational problems must be controlled by the local administrator. Excessive record keeping, inordinate complications, insufficient structure, deficient grievance procedures, and incomplete support systems can undermine and weaken administrative efforts to implement performance based compensation plans. Unless the administrator streamlines the process to limit the bureaucratic detail needed to operate the PBC program, dissonance will develop, which could be fatal to any hope for success.

Fundamentally, organizational goal demands have to be balanced with individual capabilities, commitment, and resources provided. Even more importantly, the local school administrator has to ensure that all available district or organizational resources are focused on the program to achieve success.

For performance compensation plans to be successful, the structure and character of educational organizations must be handled in effective ways. However, given certain operational and functional adjustments by local school administrators, and given sufficient commitment on their part to muster support and direction of the organization totally, performance based plans may have much to offer teachers and schools of the future.

Deficient Motivation and Reinforcement Practices

There are certain things local administrators may do to raise the likelihood of success in PBC systems, and those things are grounded in motivational and reinforcement research literature. For example, if the goal is to motivate teachers to higher levels of performance, the roadmap to that particular destination requires congruence with modern motivational theory.

Most administrators should already know that pay is not necessarily a motivator in and of itself (Herzberg, 1966), but insofar as pay rewards outstanding performance, it can be meaningful in nourishing and maintaining quality in performance (Atkinson, 1964; Cofer and Appley, 1964).

Moreover, pay is often important to capable employees as a feedback mechanism on performance or as a measure of work targets hit or goals met (Atkinson, 1964; McClelland, 1961). In addition, pay is often seen as a reward for achievement or success (Herzberg, 1966) but only under certain circumstances.

Effective use of pay in PBC plans must adhere to principles associated with success in reward/pay systems, like the following (Lawler, 1984):

(1) Pay policies must be public and understandable.
(2) Salaries must be viewed as important by employees.
(3) Pay increases must be seen as incentives.
(4) Incentives must be noticeably large enough to make a difference.
(5) Incentives must be clearly linked to accurately measured levels of performance.
(6) Poor or substandard performance must not be rewarded.
(7) Incentives must be scheduled with sufficient frequency to sustain a given level of performance.
(8) Coupling pay and performance together must be seen as connected with employee needs for recognition.
(9) Cost must be subordinated to organizational effectiveness.

If school organizations find it difficult to make effective use of the above principles, they may find attainment of performance based systems less than satisfactory. Given appropriate design and administration, pay for school employees can be a powerful motivator.

However, school employees are sensitive to how they stack up with others, or stated another way, level of pay for a school employee in comparison with other school employees is no less important than the actual pay itself. An employee must see his/her level of pay as achievement *in comparison with the pay of others* (Goodman and Friedman, 1971; Adams, 1963; Carrell and Ditrich, 1978).

If this is not the case, the employee will not see a relationship between his/her efforts and any dividend received for accomplishment. Inequity (such as that found in single salary schedules for teachers) in salary would arise whenever the teacher sees others in comparable jobs making comparable amounts without comparable effort or accomplishment. For example, if a teacher sees another teacher making similar pay for less performance than his/her own performance, that teacher may seek to gain equity by matching (or in this case, diminishing) work output or effort. Conversely, teachers may also seek equity by working harder if they believe they will be justly compensated.

Compensation for performance achievement is risky in terms of timing and schedule as well (Skinner, 1971). It is critical that a reward follow good performance in close proximity. If the reward doesn't follow the performance promptly, its usefulness is rapidly diminished. Further, any reward for inappropriate behavior may be disastrous and confusing. Employees must always see what it is (behavior, output) that is being rewarded, and employees must see that it is rewarded consistently.

Inadequate Morale and Staff Conflicts

In the history of merit pay, part of the reason for demise of such programs has been staff dissension arising from friction, jealousy, and charges of favoritism (Robinson, 1984). Consequently, those painful years have generated some findings useful in overcoming such problems (Freiburg, 1987).

Teacher incentive programs should incorporate teacher participation in program design and delivery, and teacher cooperation should be emphasized over competition. Teacher professional growth is a worthy goal as is goal setting (Kyrene, 1989). All members of the professional team (i.e., librarians, counselors, teachers, etc.) should have the opportunity to participate, and no surprises to participants in the program's design or implementation should occur.

Teacher consensus has long been known as a direct positive correlate of teacher morale, and the local school administrator has his/her work cut out in order to provide leadership accordingly. Effective consensus-building in PBC plans is not easy but is not unnecessary either.

Deficient Financial Support

In the motivation information presented above, a couple of things were apparent relative to financial support. First, incentives (pay) must be large enough to make a difference. Secondly, cost must be subordinated to organizational effectiveness. In addition to these precepts, local school administrators need to know that if enough monies are not provided for meaningful incentives and activities, success is strongly jeopardized.

Politically, performance incentives have obtained significant support in recent years, but some legislatures have given only a fraction of school districts access to incentives. In Arizona, only eighteen school districts were allowed by the Arizona legislature to participate in Career Ladder Plans (performance based compensation, so-called), and in some of those districts, not all teachers were allowed access to the incentives due to financial constraints. Such paltry and inadequate financial support squelches success before the program gets off the ground.

In addition, PBC should be no substitute for adequate floor levels of compensation for the teaching profession. Rather than straight single salary schedules, or incentive-rich/survival-poor compensation systems, a combination is needed. Something akin to base salary (adequate for entry) plus commission (PBC), as in commercial enterprises, may be workable. Local school administrators must be assured of sufficient monies to accommodate the plan for incentives prior to beginning any such program. If monies are not going to be available in adequate supply, the administrator would be better off not starting a performance based program in the first place.

Muddled Values, Policies, and Philosophy

The local school administrators really have their work cut out for them in building sound philosophy, goals, and policies. Central foci of any PBC program need to be anchored on improvement of teaching and learning and enhancement of productivity. Assuring that all partners in the design and delivery of the program are involved in conceptualization of values and ends is critical. Philosophy and goals must also have content and substance worth accepting and supporting.

Some philosophical rocks along the "road to goals" may include political interests desiring "to get the turkeys" out of teaching, parental pressures to place their children only in a "top performer's" classroom, economic claims that PBC can save money (or cut taxes), conformist thinking that mitigates against voluntary teacher involvement in PBC plans, arbitrary forces that mandate quota systems or limited access to incentives, and others.

Local school administrators must remember lessons learned in the past that indicate that shared decision making, in-service training, involvement of staff and others, role differentiation, and work climate are processes that imbue values underlying performance based compensation plans (English, 1985). In addition, administrators must ensure that appropriate processes are employed to assure sound value definitions and policy implementation efforts as one piece of the PBC pie for success.

KEY ADMINISTRATIVE RESPONSIBILITIES FOR PBC PROGRAM SUCCESS

As stated in the introduction, administrators carry the largest burden of responsibility for the success of performance based compensation systems. In locally managed programs with pay for results, the individual administrator generally is the qualified evaluator who must make and carry out judgments about salary allocations to employees for performance achievements.

Generally (although this is not always the case, regrettably), the building administrator should know most about the nature of the teaching job and how well it is being done. The opinions and evaluative judgments of the individual building administrator are critical ingredients in a successful and viable PBC system.

Other key ingredients include effective evaluation techniques and procedures, administrator validity and reliability in carrying out the evaluation process, process objectivity, and climate support. These "ingredients" are reflected in some of the organizational and operational effects of PBC programs and must be present for success in performance based compensation.

Another requirement for performance based compensation systems that is relevant to the local school district is equitable compensation in comparison to the marketplace. Given poor, moderate, or uncompetitive salaries overall in a school system, performance pay may be dead before it starts. Schools must offer competitive salaries to attract and retain quality employees, but schools must also offer a way for resources to be allocated in support of teaching effectiveness and performance. Each of these factors is dependent upon the other for quality enhancement over time using performance pay.

Each facet of the push to pay for performance contains new roles and responsibilities not only for teachers but for their supervisors as well. Performance based compensation for teachers is intended to provide a means for rewarding teachers who perform at high levels of effectiveness and is supposed to improve the quality of education through improving motivation of teachers. However, the prosperity of PBC systems is largely dependent upon the local school district administrative staff's skill and commitment.

FINAL COMMENTS ABOUT LOCAL SCHOOL DISTRICT ADMINISTRATIVE EFFORT

In conclusion, the main questions for local school districts are whether the end result of such systems is worth the extra effort they require and what exactly are the payoffs. If the payoffs are sufficient rationale to implement such plans, the tasks and responsibilities are achievable at the local level, given certain conditions. But as any local school administrator knows, success in anything worth doing never comes easily.

REFERENCES

Adams, J. S. 1963. "Toward an Understanding of Inequity," *J. of Abnormal and Social Psychology,* 67:422–436.

Atkinson, J. W. and D. Birch. 1978. *An Introduction to Motivation.* New York: Van Nostrand Publishing Co., Inc.

Carrell, M. R. and J. E. Ditrich. 1978. "Equity Theory: The Recent Research Literature, Methodological Considerations, and New Directions," *Academy of Management Review,* 3:202–210.

Cibulka, J. B. "State Accountability Reforms: Performance Information – Political Power," Presentation to the American Educational Research Association, San Francisco, California, March 1989.

Cofer, C. N. and M. H. Appley, 1964. *Motivation: Theory and Research.* New York: John Wiley and Company.

English, F. W. 1985. "We Need the Ghostbusters! A Response to Jerome Freiberg," *Educational Leadership,* 42(4):22–25.

Frase, L. E. and Robert Hetzel. 1990. *School Management by Wandering Around.* Lancaster, PA: Technomic Publishing Company, Inc.

Freiberg, H. J. 1987. "Career Ladders: Messages Gleaned from Experience," *J. of Teacher Education,* 38(4):49–56.

Goodman, J. S. and A. Friedman. 1971. "An Examination of Adams' Theory of Inequity," *Administrative Science Quarterly,* 16:271–288.

Herzberg, F. 1966. *Work and the Nature of Man.* Cleveland, Ohio: World Publishing Company, pp. 71–91.

Iowa Department of Education. 1989. Report to the Iowa City Superintendents Association Conference: Excellence in Education – Phase III, September 24, 1989, Newton, Iowa.

Lawler, E. E. 1984. "Whatever Happened to Incentive Pay?" *New Management,* 1(4):37–41.

Littleford, J. C. 1989. *Independent School Salary Systems: The Shift to Career Ladders.* National Independent Schools Association, Booklet.

McClelland, D. C. 1976. *The Achieving Society.* New York: Irvington Publishers, Distributed by Halstead Press.

Poston, W. K., Jr. *Curriculum Driven Budgeting.* Lancaster, PA: Technomic Publishing Company, Inc. Forthcoming.

Robinson, G. E. 1984. "Incentive Pay for Teachers: An Analysis of Approaches," *Educational Research Service Concerns in Education,* Booklet.

Skinner, B. F. 1971. *Beyond Freedom and Dignity.* New York: Knopf, Inc.

Spady, W., N. Filby, and R. Burns. 1986. "Outcome Based Education: A Summary of Essential Features and Major Implications," San Carlos, California: Spady Consulting Group, Paper, pp. 1–6.

Watson, R. S., J. H. Poda, and C. T. Miller. 1988. "State Mandated Teacher Incentives and School Improvement Plans," *Educational Research Service Spectrum,* 6(1):21–24.

CHAPTER 13

Independent School Salary Systems: The Shift to Career Ladder Options

JOHN C. LITTLEFORD – *Headmaster, University School of Milwaukee*

INTRODUCTION

INDEPENDENT schools in the United States, particularly those that are members of the National Association of Independent Schools, have traditionally guarded and valued their independence. They do not like the title "private" schools and prefer the label "independent," by which is normally meant as independent as possible from regulatory agencies and federal and state restrictions. Independent schools also traditionally have had a great deal of flexibility in their internal management structure. One of the traditional broad areas of discretion has been the head of school's management prerogative to negotiate individual salaries with each member of the teaching staff.

Over the years the individually negotiated salary structure within independent schools has shifted towards unpublished scales, guidelines, or in rare cases, lane and track salary systems similar to those in operation in most public schools. The movement has been gradual, reluctant, and often resulted from pressure from teachers.

In a study done for NAIS in 1983, this author and Valerie Lee, currently an Assistant Professor at the University of Michigan, did research for the National Association of Independent Schools (NAIS) on the subject of faculty salary systems in independent schools. Nine case studies were developed. All of the schools studied offered competitive salaries in comparison with other NAIS schools. Yet the salary systems by which these salaries were paid differed dramatically one from the other. The nine schools were organized in groups of three, ranging from least structured to most structured in terms of salary delivery systems.

The three in the least structured format were those in the traditional independent school mode where the head of the school normally negotiated individual salary increases with each teacher, based on the

317

head's perception of the merit of that teacher and his or her performance. The third group of the three schools looked very similar in salary structure to public school systems. There was often a B.A. track, an M.A. track, and an M.A. plus 30 track with individually guaranteed steps for each year of service. The fact that there is no research supporting a relationship between advanced degrees and effective teaching or longevity of service and effective teaching did not seem to dissuade these independent schools from moving into a highly predictable guaranteed salary structure. Some of the teachers in these schools appreciated the predictability of the structure and the scales, while others bridled at the restrictions and looked for some opportunity for differentiation based upon performance.

The most interesting schools were those three in the middle cluster where teachers were offered a degree of predictability of future earning power while the school retained a substantial amount of discretion for the head of the school to make performance based salary decisions. Within these three schools was one that used a corporate salary structure and another that used a rapidly rising salary ladder that tapered off very quickly and flattened out after a teacher reached twenty years of service. The third salary structure involved a school that had a program very similar to that of a college with separate designations for beginning teachers, senior teachers, and master teachers or faculty leaders. These labels were not used in this particular school, but there were three distinct salary ladders and movement from one to the other was based on a specific evaluation process and published criteria.

Patterns and Directions

Historically, independent schools have operated with highly discretionary salary systems, where salaries negotiated individually between the head and teachers have been the rule rather than the exception. Many schools still operate without reference to any salary scale, guideline, or structure, published or unpublished. The past fifteen years, however, have seen rapid, almost precipitous, movement from highly unstructured, traditional salary systems toward more highly structured, explicit salary systems that rely on one or more scales. These newer salary systems are characterized by highly explicit scales, little or no performance pay, highly explicit scales for extracurricular pay, and considerably greater involvement of faculty members in decisions about salary matters through faculty compensation committees.

This trend seems to have been prompted by the knowledge that teachers want to be able to plan their financial future more reliably and therefore want a greater degree of predictability in their earnings. It also seems to have been prompted by increased reluctance on the part of school heads to make value judgments about teachers' performance that affect compensation. Public school practices, a stronger faculty voice in decision making, a greater demand for information about how salary systems work, and better informed faculty members have all influenced the move in this direction.

Perhaps the greatest single element of the move toward more explicit salary systems and scales has been the relatively low salaries offered by independent schools. Low pay has prompted teachers and schools to attempt to raise salary levels significantly, in turn creating greater faculty interest not only in actual amounts paid but in how these amounts are distributed.

Offsetting this fifteen-year trend is a countervailing phenomenon that has come to the fore in the last five years. Schools that have highly traditional, unstructured salary systems are moving very slowly, if at all, in the direction of more explicit pay structures. In addition, some schools that have highly structured salary systems are studying the possibility of injecting into those systems a greater degree of discretion, flexibility, and opportunity for recognizing individual differences in performance among teachers. These schools are, however, encountering faculty resistance to their attempts to move toward greater flexibility. Where discretion has been eliminated, boards of trustees are pressing for its reinstatement. The most recent and popular salary structure compromise for independent schools is the career ladder.

The Structure of School Salary Systems

Following are some of the patterns that have been developing in the salary structures of independent schools over the past several years. The diagram shows five of the six themes of *Faculty Salary Systems in Independent Schools.*[1]

Structure

Low--High

Performance Pay

Low--High

Extracurricular Pay

Low--High

Faculty Involvement in Decision Making

Low--High

Faculty Satisfaction

Low--High

It appears that schools that are highly unstructured and traditional in their approach to salaries tend to have high levels of discretionary pay. These same schools tend to have little or no formal process of evaluating teachers or criteria for performance pay. They also tend to pay little or nothing for extracurricular activities, regarding them as a basic part of the teaching assignment. Teachers at these schools are involved in decisions about salaries only a little or not at all.

Many schools that have unstructured systems seem to experience high faculty morale and regard for the school's salary system. But the schools that achieve this level of faculty support are also those that are paying high salaries, that enjoy high faculty trust in the leadership, and whose leadership is strongly committed to increasing faculty salaries. These schools are likely to be small enough for communication among all levels of administration and faculty to be open and unencumbered. Even the absence of a formal evaluation system and explicit performance pay criteria does not prevent faculty support for the overall salary system. These schools would find it easier to move gradually toward a moderately explicit salary system.

Some of the schools that have moved rapidly toward highly structured and explicit pay scales have moved almost totally away from performance pay. They appear to have no formal system of faculty evaluation. Schools in this group have begun to pay substantial amounts for participation in extracurricular activities and have made faculty salaries higer and more explicit for a wide range of other activities. Many of them have launched faculty salary committees that have proved to be quite active and that have had a noticeable effect on salary structures and modifications from year to year. Whether a faculty salary committee is formed at the behest of the head or the faculty often depends on the level of trust in the school and on how cooperatively administrators and teachers work on the issue of salaries. Schools having an explicit salary system encounter more difficulty in injecting a discretionary element into the salary system because teachers, regardless of their philosophical position on performance pay, like predictability and explicitness. And, once an explicit salary system is in place, teachers are reluctant to give it up.

One of the best examples of an interesting accommodation between faculty and administration on the subject of performance pay is Wetherly Academy, one of the nine pseudonymous schools in *Faculty Salary Systems in Independent Schools*. Wetherly, a well-known boarding school, had one of the most highly explicit pay structures of any independent school in the country, with multiple scales that provide predictable future earnings for teachers. This same school, however, has a highly unexplicit, undefined, and unpublished performance pay system. Even so, the faculty did not object to this system or lobby to eliminate it, perhaps because so much of the rest of the system was explicit and standardized.

Substantial regional differences exist in the structure of independent school salary systems. Schools in the New York area tend to have highly explicit salary scales that do not differ markedly from those of their public school counterparts. Experience and advanced degrees are the basis of increased earning power. Schools in the West and in New England seem to have a much wider range of approaches, evenly distributed. Schools in the Southeast and Midwest tend to have a sizable number of schools with highly explicit salary systems balanced by a similar number that have retained traditional systems having little or moderate structure. Although several regions of the country seem to have a bipolar approach to salary structure, many schools are looking at more moderate, middle of the road approaches that combine an explicit salary system with some sort of performance pay. Again the career ladder approach is seen as a healthy compromise.

NAIS member schools seem to fall into one of four categories of salary structure: (1) those that still have traditional negotiated systems — and those that have moved only a slight distance from this approach; (2) those that have moved dramatically toward one or more explicit scales; (3) those that employ highly explicit salary scales with a performance pay option that may be either explicit or ambiguous; and (4) those that have employed the "discretionary band" concept, where a scale operates in tandem with a certain amount of discretionary latitude. This last idea, gaining momentum and popularity in several regions of the country, is best represented in *Faculty Salary Systems in*

Independent Schools by the Neville School, a coeducational school in the Northwest. At Neville, opportunities for performance pay are numerous, operating within a general framework of minimum and maximum salary levels that a teacher achieves after a certain number of years of experience. Figure 1 is a chart of Neville's faculty salary system.

Performance Pay

Before the original salary study was begun, the authors thought that performance pay in independent schools would usually turn out to consist of sizable amounts of money paid to a small number of "master" teachers generally recognized by their colleagues as being outstanding performers. Instead, in the schools studied, we found that much smaller amounts—usually ranging from $100 to $1000—were paid to as much as 80 or 90 percent of the teaching faculty of a given school. The goal of this method of performance pay seemed to be to make most or all of the teachers feel like winners and to send negative signals to a small percentage of teachers, who were asked to improve their performance. A few schools had an approach that combined both models, allocating enough money so that a small number of teachers received a much larger amount of performance pay than the rest.

From salary seminars, several polls, and many individual conversations, the following patterns and characteristics seem to hold true for many independent schools:

(1) Most of the schools using "performance pay" do not define it as such; they regard it simply as a discretionary form of additional money.

(2) Most schools that offer performance or discretionary pay, with or without a scale, do not have any published criteria for awarding performance pay.

(3) Most schools, even those that have or are working toward creating a faculty evaluation system, do not actually tie the results of such an evaluation explicitly to the amount of salary a teacher is paid.

(4) Many school heads seem reluctant to ask marginally competent teachers to leave or to give negative comments to instructors. Reluctance is even greater about making salary decisions based on an open evaluation of a teacher's performance—decisions that must then be defended.

The most important issue on the minds of teachers is faculty evalua-

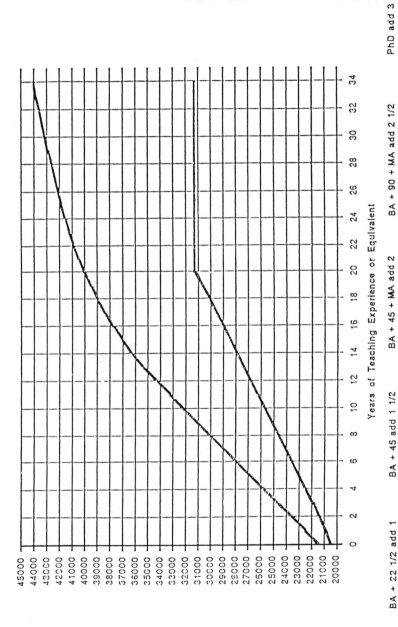

FIGURE 1 Neville school salary chart—1989–1990.

Years of Teaching Experience or Equivalent

BA + 22 1/2 add 1   BA + 45 add 1 1/2   BA + 45 + MA add 2   BA + 90 + MA add 2 1/2   PhD add 3

tion. They feel that performance pay should be addressed only after establishing a system of faculty evaluation based on due process and having clear-cut guidelines and expectations for teachers. Many schools have some type of system of evaluation or are developing one. No more than 5 to 10 percent of the schools, however, have any kind of formal faculty evaluation system with a published procedure for regular and written reviews of a teacher's performance.

A frequent response of the teachers is that a performance pay system could succeed best in a school that was already offering competitive salaries and investigating performance pay as a way to increase the overall level of salaries. They feel that any school paying poor, moderate, or uncompetitive salaries should concentrate on raising basic salary levels before diverting money to performance pay. Heads and trustees, on the other hand, tend to agree that it is those schools having modest or scarce resources that must be the most courageous in allocating those resources according to some measure of teaching effectiveness and performance.

Two of the schools in *Faculty Salary Systems in Independent Schools* were frequently referred to as models worthy of consideration in the area of performance pay. The first was the Neville School, with its "discretionary band" in addition to an explicit salary scale. The longer a teacher has been at Neville, the greater is the discretionary band within which the head may make specific salary decisions. This approach tends to be particularly interesting to trustees and heads who see in it both predictability of future earnings for teachers and discretion for the head in recognizing performance and extracurricular commitment.

The second most frequently mentioned system is that of the Hawthorne Country Day School, which has a very explicit salary system for those holding bachelor's and master's degrees and an equally explicit performance pay schedule with annual performance increases of up to $1000, which are accrued from year to year. Hawthorne publishes its performance pay criteria, which consist of points for extracurricular commitments and evaluation of performance as teacher, adviser, and coach. Like Neville, Hawthorne offers a structural compromise between a system that relies exclusively on discretionary pay and one that relies solely on rigid pay scales.

No more than 5 percent of any of the schools interviewed indicated that their schools were paying over $1000 in differential performance pay to teachers of similar backgrounds and experience. No more than 10 percent were philosophically in favor of providing more substantial sums of money to a much smaller group of highly valued teachers. Most heads are convinced that their schools have a certain small number of master teachers, but they indicate that these teachers are not necessarily paid a great deal more than others having similar experience and education.

Regional differences in approaches to performance pay are quite noticeable. Performance pay is almost nonexistent in the New York area and is rarely evident in the Midwest. It is somewhat more popular among southeastern schools, but there is a bipolar split among schools in the Southeast, with approximately half supporting the idea and the other half opposing it. Peformance pay seems to be an option exercised more frequently in the West, New England, and the Southwest, and to a lesser extent in the Middle Atlantic states.

Some schools confronted a very difficult problem in that most of them have not yet developed explicit faculty evaluation systems and do not feel that salary levels are high enough to warrant moving into an explicit performance pay system. But this is changing as salary increases over inflation. However, a clear danger is felt by some schools: schools with moderate or poor salary levels, and without a careful system of faculty evaluation in place, should be very cautious about moving in the direction of explicit performance pay systems. Those schools that have highly ambiguous performance pay systems may be living on borrowed time and may confront serious difficulties when the heads now in office—the ones who have earned the trust that now exists—leave their posts.

Very few schools had explored the concept of performance pay exemplified by Westmore in *Faculty Salary Systems in Independent Schools*—multiple scales, with the low one reflecting probationary status and the high one reflecting a nonprobationary performance pay track (see Figure 2). This model, also found in institutions of higher education, is being used by more and more schools. It is a system well worth examining for schools that seek some flexibility in salary decisions but do not wish to place much pressure on the head to make value judgments about performance that affect specific salaries paid to teachers. It is, in effect, the model for the increasingly popular career ladder concept.

Extracurricular Pay

Faculty Salary Systems in Independent Schools indicated that extracurricular pay was becoming one of the more important issues in inde-

Step	Level I	Level II	Level III
15		37,000	43,500
14		36,053	
13		35,003	
12		33,983	
11		32,994	
10	30,506	31,725	
9	29,333	30,646	
8	28,205	29,610	
7	27,121	28,608	
6	26,078	27,641	
5	25,075	26,706	
4	24,111	25,803	
3	23,409		
2	22,950		
1	22,500		

FIGURE 2 Westmore salary guidelines—1989–90.

pendent schools as teachers questioned the equity of extracurricular assignments when extracurricular pay was not provided for specific activities. The problem centered around inequitable assignments, concern about vacation time used for extracurricular duties, and a feeling that extracurricular activities should be more explicitly defined and compensated for, depending on the number of hours spent in a given activity. Some schools had the traditional view of extracurricular assignments as a basic expectation of an independent school teacher. Others reduced teaching loads to accommodate extracurricular assignments as part of the basic duty day.

Recent school visits have confirmed that the issue of extracurricular pay is causing growing unhappiness among teachers. But schools that have adopted highly explicit "pay for everything" systems are also encountering difficulties from burdening the budget with a new and sizable annual salary expense and having to devise an equitable way of allocating these extracurricular dollars. At schools using the traditional negotiated salary approach or having an unpublished salary schedule, extracurricular pay either does not exist or is incorporated in base pay. Several heads indicate that the systems of highly explicit extracurricular pay they have developed have led to the inclusion of a wide range of activities that once would have been considered a part of the regular teaching day. The career ladder alternative is appealing to these schools because it offers a definition of a full-time position that is broad-based.

Teachers are looking at extracurricular pay as one way to earn more money, often by doing something that they enjoy anyway. Because they can choose or not choose a specific extracurricular activity, this gives them some control over how to earn their pay. More and more teachers are asking to be paid for extracurricular activities, particularly those that occur after school, according to an explicit schedule based on some rational measurement of the time and skills needed to conduct the activity. Schools and heads are confronted with how to address these concerns while trying to keep costs under control and avoid creating a system that will eventually be expected to give teachers extra pay for all kinds of supervisory duties.

Teacher Involvement in Decision Making

Faculty Salary Systems in Independent Schools indicated that significant faculty involvement in creating and monitoring salary systems occurs either when the head of the school invites the faculty to form a committee to deal with these questions or when a faculty committee forms right after a change of head without the formal approval of the new head or the board and begins to ask for specific involvement in decisions on salary matters. Where highly influential faculty salary committees exist, schools tend to develop and use highly explicit salary scales, often including explicit compensation for extracurricular activities. In cases where the head has created the committee, the move toward highly explicit salary scales is somewhat more gradual.

Feedback from a series of salary seminars indicated that faculty salary committees are becoming more common in independent schools. Where they are formed with the support and involvement of the head, they participate constructively in the salary process. Where they come into existence without the express involvement and support of the school head, the results are more mixed, and the opportunities for conflict between head, board, and faculty are more likely.

As indicated earlier, schools that have moved toward highly explicit salary scales over the last several years are now trying to introduce a discretionary component into their faculty salary systems. Where strong faculty committees already exist, and particularly those elected by the faculty, the effort to reduce rigid salary scales meets strong resistance. In other schools, conflict between trustees and faculty members has resulted from boards feeling that too little discretion is included in the compensation package. Both types of schools are now examining the career ladder approach.

This area of salary administration is perhaps one of the most delicate at this time. Where trust is high between faculty and head and where relatively high salaries are already being paid, faculty salary committees have proved to be constructive and useful forums for developing and carrying out salary practices. Where they lack administrative support and approval and in schools where trust and salary levels are lower, such committees often move in directions the administration and board may deem harmful to the long-term interest of the school.

The consensus of many heads is that this area needs to be explored carefully and slowly and that schools that move toward forming faculty salary committees should give serious consideration to specific guidelines for their functioning and expected outcomes.

Faculty Satisfaction with Salary Systems

The schools described in *Faculty Salary Systems in Independent Schools* were, as has been indicated, already paying relatively high salaries, at least according to NAIS norms. Teachers were highly satisfied with the systems these schools used to distribute money and with the levels of salary paid. In later discussions, however, where a much wider range of schools was represented, evidence of faculty satisfaction was much less consistent. Trustees, heads, and business managers, as well as teachers, said that faculty members in many schools were not satisfied with either the level of salaries being paid or with the way salaries were distributed.

Summary

A strong salary pattern existed in independent schools in the past: individually negotiated salaries, informal salary systems, high discretionary pay, low extracurricular pay, and little involvement of faculty members in decisions about matters of salary. This pattern has been counterbalanced by the trend, over the last five to ten years, toward more highly structured salary systems that include little or no performance pay, highly codified extracurricular pay, and high faculty involvement in developing and monitoring salary systems.

Contrasted with this pendulum swing is a newer trend, about five years old. Salary structures are being developed that have a fairly high degree of flexibility for rewarding excellence through some form of performance pay increasingly using a career ladder approach. In these situations, faculty involvement tends to be at the invitation of the head, and some form of faculty evaluation based on due process is now beginning to influence salary increases and performance pay.

The move from unstructured to highly structured systems seems to correlate closely with low pay, high turnover of heads, and a faculty need to have more predictability of earning power. Schools able to make the transition from an unstructured to a moderate approach or schools that back off successfully from a highly structured approach appear to be those that have a commitment to paying higher salaries, high trust in the head, faculty evaluation based on due process, and/or explicit criteria for determining performance pay.

Schools are increasingly concerned about their diminished ability to reward excellence in the face of the move toward iron-clad salary scales during the last decade. In spite of these difficulties, some schools have achieved or are working toward a compromise between these contrasting patterns.

THE CAREER LADDER

Since the publication of the NAIS study on salary systems in 1983, the strongest movement in independent schools' salary administration has been toward one form or another of the Career Ladder Format. One of the interesting aspects of this movement has been that schools with published salary scales have also been moving towards a Career Ladder Format. That has been an extremely sensitive issue, one fraught with political and social issues, as it is much easier for teachers to accept movement in the direction of predictability of earning power than it is for them to accept the opposite, as in moving from a highly structured salary system to one that is less structured and provides more room for discretion.

The Career Ladder Concept is quite simple. It assumes that teachers new to the school will stay at some lower level of compensation until they have proven themselves to be effective, potential long-term members of the core faculty, at which time by some evaluation system, they are appointed, nominated, or elected to move to the second career ladder (often referred to as the senior teacher ladder). There is often a

major increase in salary at the time of such a move and a major increase in status, as the teacher moves from what is a probationary stage
to an informal tenure stage. There is a third career ladder position,
often called master teacher or faculty leader, to which someone may be
appointed or nominated based on some specific additional criteria. Appointment to this third category is usually limited to a set percentage of
faculty, perhaps 20 percent at the most. Quite often, certain additional
standards are set for eligibility for the faculty leader category, which
may include such things as a minimum of a master's degree, at least ten
years of teaching overall, or at least five years of teaching at a particular school.

The instructor step is very similar to the assistant professorship position at a university or college. It is an untenured role in which one must
prove oneself before moving onto the more secure position of senior
teacher (or at the college level, associate professor). The faculty leader
or master teacher category is quite similar in nature to the appointment
at the college level to a full professor.

In some schools the faculty leader or master teacher category relates
only to taking on additional assignments or responsibilities, curriculum
leadership, or a twelve-month contract. Most of the independent
schools that are considering a career ladder concept look upon the
third category as one where income increases directly in relation to
evaluated performance, not additional workload. The criteria that
might be associated with movement to such a third category would certainly include willingness to take on extracurricular responsibilities,
willingness to mentor fellow faculty, and willingness to serve the public
relations interests of the school and community.

One of the intriguing questions about the new approach to independent school career ladders is whether or not administrators are eligible.
Some schools include all administrators, as well as teaching faculty, in
the career ladder structure, and administrators do not necessarily
receive more salary than do teachers of comparable experience. In
some schools department heads who might receive a formal stipend of
anywhere from $1000 to $4000, are not included in the career ladder
until such time as they might resign their department head position.
The purpose here is not to encourage excellent teachers to move into
administration simply because of salary incentives, but rather to have
people seek administrative positions because of the desire to influence
policy and direction of the institution. Ultimately, those who have
served in the department head roles effectively and who choose no

longer to do so may apply for the faculty leader category and thereby maintain or increase the level of salary they might have been receiving as a department head.

In some schools the movement from the instructor to the senior teacher category is accompanied by a base pay increment that is added permanently to annual salary. In other settings, the salary increment in moving from category one to two is a merit based commitment that is reviewed on a periodic basis. If one assumes that approximately 20 percent of the teachers would be in the instructor category and no more than 20 percent in the faculty leader category, the bulk of career teachers (approximately 60 percent) are in the senior teacher category.

At one school studied the additional salary paid in the faculty leader category came in the form of an annual bonus paid at the end of June in the amount of $4000. It was a two-year appointment that was biannually reviewed and evaluated to determine whether or not that teacher would continue in the faculty leader status. In future years a teacher might choose not to commit the kind of time and energy that would be required to remain in the faculty leader position. In that case, the teacher might voluntarily choose to step down from that category.

An additional intriguing question about the Career Ladder Concept is whether information on the placement of each teacher should be made public. Several schools that have explored this concept have decided not to make anything public and to notify only the teacher of his or her status.

Many independent schools have discretionary pay, but few have criteria based performance pay systems where the criteria are publicly known and accepted by the faculty. In a few schools where such publicly based performance pay systems exist, it is critical for the department head and/or division head to be able to concretely demonstrate to the teacher why he or she did or did not receive appointment to the senior teacher category or the faculty leader category. In some schools that have adopted the Career Ladder Concept, there is also a performance pay based salary increase that would occur from year to year, *within* each career ladder. Thus, a teacher might receive a percent of salary across the board as an inflation-related increase. The same teacher may be eligible for movement from career ladder step one to two or two to three, which would provide an additional stipend, in some cases added to the base salary. Finally, teachers would also be evaluated based on regularly understood, accepted, and published evaluation criteria as to how their performance measured during that year. Specific performance pay increases are then offered for this aspect of performance. These may or may not be added to base, but in most schools studied, such increments are added to the base salary.

The Career Ladder Concept offers some fascinating incentives to the administration and boards of independent schools. First, it allows the school to spend its scarce dollars in ways that specifically reward particular groups of faculty that are designated as having more importance to the institution. It is clear that those appointed to the master teacher or faculty leader category are viewed as having the most important long-term leadership impact on the school, and therefore a greater amount of scarce dollars are put into that category. It is also clear that the instructor or beginning category is a training or probationary period where the school provides fewer dollars. On the other hand, the Career Ladder Concept can attract intelligent and capable young teachers to the school and signal them that growth in salary in this particular school *can* be rapid. The career ladder can provide for rapid advancement. A teacher, new to the profession and coming to a school with a career ladder, would be brought in as an instructor. After one year of proving his or her skills as a classroom teacher, that teacher might then have an opportunity to be placed into the second or senior teacher category, or such an evaluation based shift might take as long as five years. If it took that long, the assumption is that the teacher would no longer be a member of the faculty.

After the first year, a new teacher would receive a substantial increase in moving from the first career ladder to the second. After meeting the criteria of the faculty leader or master teacher category, such a teacher might then conceivably be named to the top category within a period of as little as three to five years from the time of arrival. This is clearly an educational "fast track" that is not currently available in schools with published salary scales, nor is it often available in schools where there are individually negotiated increases. A Career Ladder Concept, such as that described above, provides a rationale for clearly differentiating among different faculty groups and rewarding them differently.

Schools that have developed lane and track type salary scales would certainly find resistance to moving to the more open-ended Career Ladder Concept. On the other hand, it is possible to do this, particularly if the school examines the relationship between its benefit levels and its career ladder levels. One school found that it had a locked step salary system from which it wanted to extricate itself. In order to do this, it used the defined benefit retirement plan in its school to place a freeze on the salary ladder by arguing successfully with its faculty that a defined benefit plan results in substantially higher increments of dollars from the school as the teacher comes closer to retirement. Thus, a freeze on salary at the higher levels, particularly when those increases are based simply on experience, was accepted by the faculty. This particular school divided its faculty into three groups even though they were already placed on a salary scale. As it moved them off the salary scale and into the three tiers of a career ladder, teachers were notified whether they were in the instructor, senior teacher, or faculty leader status.

Teacher involvement in decision making while creating such plans can be a critical issue. Where there is substantial teacher involvement in decision making, the movement from a lane and track salary scale to a career ladder is not likely to occur. Where there is substantial faculty involvement in decision making, it is very difficult to move a lane and track salary scale to a faculty career concept without simply imposing one. Where a school has individually negotiated faculty contracts, it is far more productive to have faculty involvement as a new career ladder is developed. This move is from flexibility to predictability. Anyplace along this continuum where faculty involvement is encouraged, greater predictability of salary earnings will occur and less flexibility or discretion for the administration will also result.

The Career Ladder Concept is a midpoint between a complete performance pay base salary system and a complete lane and track salary system. The Career Ladder Concept can be developed with a high degree of predictability by providing specific steps for years of experience within each category. Alternately, the Career Ladder System may provide substantially more flexibility for the administration by not publishing formal step increases within each career ladder. Again, the development of a career ladder depends very much on the school's current salary structure.

Independent schools seem to be moving not only in theory, but in practice, to adopting some basic outline of a Career Ladder Approach primarily because of the recognized needed balance between predictability of earning power for teachers and flexibility and discretion in hiring and rewarding performance for administrators. The options that can be developed in such a system are numerous. The concept is clearly attractive today to independent schools.

NON-SALARY BENEFIT APPROACHES

Many independent schools are also developing non-salary programs to help attract and hold faculty. Some of these do indeed cost the institution substantial sums of money. Others are basically morale boosters that are relatively cost free.

Independent schools are increasingly considering the concept of offering faculty day care. Such day care may be paid for by the faculty participants, but by virtue of the school offering the facility without charging overhead, the program is subsidized and the fees are less than the teachers might pay in local day care facilities. This is a very attractive program in the corporate setting and is increasingly attractive to teachers.

Teacher recognition opportunities abound in independent schools, including faculty appreciation weeks (or days) and faculty photo galleries of honor where teacher photographs are displayed and service is proudly recognized. Teacher recognition and appreciation can occur in school publications that have regular sections on celebrating teachers and their accomplishments. Holidays, major social events, or parties can recognize the length of service and quality of performance in individual teachers or in groups of teachers. Schools may also use staff development dollars to reward, enhance, and enrich the professional growth of faculty through leaves of absences, summer grants, workshop development, or graduate school tuition assistance.

Some independent day schools are also offering free meals. A free lunch, if one considers sitting with students and providing supervision as "free," is common practice in many independent schools, both boarding and day. A new concept gaining momentum and often urged by John Shank, Professor of the Amos Tuck School of Management, is additional meals, such as a free breakfast for faculty and faculty families. Dr. Shank has publicly recommended this approach at a series of salary seminars held in the fall of 1983, 1984, and 1985 and sponsored by Carney, Sandoe, and Associates. Such a program can bring together groups of faculty including those who may already be on campus during the early hours of a day. The professional dialogue and collegial relations can be enhanced by coming together around a meal provided by the school, even in day school settings. Such meals can often be inexpensive.

Written commendation notices, birthday cards, regularly publicized accomplishments on school bulletin boards, or other forms of personal attention to faculty are also used in independent schools.

Other independent schools have taken the concept of sick leave, particularly where it can be accumulated to a certain level, and turned it into an incentive for faculty not to use it. Such sick days, when not used, may be permitted for additional workshop days, conference-attending opportunities, and time off for visiting other schools. In other words, there is a direct connection between good health and having more flexibility and opportunity to develop professional growth opportunities. A few independent schools do allow faculty to take unused sick leave days as vacation time, while others allow such accumulated days to be used as part of coverage in the case of a long-term disability.

SUMMARY

Independent schools in the past have been extremely reluctant to share information about teacher salary systems and levels. The reason for this reluctance is understandable. Independent schools have traditionally not published salary information and have relied heavily on discretionary pay decisions to reward and retain faculty. For teachers to talk extensively about the salary issue or for schools to publish their salary scales or salary decision-making approaches might undermine the flexibility and discretion of school administrations.

As the National Association of Independent Schools has increasingly called attention to the need for independent schools to compensate faculty more competitively, the whole subject of faculty salary distribution systems, as well as salary levels, has been a more frequent topic of discussion at conventions and meetings and among teachers themselves.

It is clear that in the future, the once prevalent "gentlemen's agreement" not to discuss salaries in the faculty lounge may break down as more and more nontraditional teachers enter independent schools and ask for more information about their current and future compensation opportunities. This pressure will certainly grow. Yet in responding to it, independent schools have more options than simply to mimic the once traditional public school lane and track salary structure, which even today public schools are increasingly rejecting in favor of more flexible performance based systems. Independent schools will need to permit a dialogue about salary and salary structures to occur among the faculties of our schools, and the career ladder may be the middle ground on which faculties and administrations might agree.

It is quite possible that independent schools, with their tradition of discretionary nonpublished salary systems and public schools with their tightly locked published lane and track salary scales might move toward one another onto some sort of central turf where evaluation based performance pay accompanies salaries that are related as well to degrees and experience using the career ladder as a model.

The National Association of Independent Schools has just produced a video for use in front of independent school faculties, trustees, parents, and donor prospects. It is entitled *A Profession at Risk.* If this film is shown to the faculties of independent schools, it will result in an even greater demand on the part of independent school teachers that they know more about salary decisions and the basis of these decisions to the extent that performance is a part of such decisions. Faculty will insist that there be published and mutually agreed-upon criteria as part of a faculty evaluation system that would be connected to performance pay decisions.

Thus, the future for independent school salary administration is both challenging and potentially rewarding. It will require a delicate balancing act of tact, forthright communication, negotiation, and participation by faculty as well as administration for flexible but predictable salary systems for the future.

ENDNOTE

1 The enumeration of some materials included are reprinted by permission from *Faculty Salary Systems in Independent Schools* by John C. Littleford and Valerie Lee, copyright © 1983 by the National Association for Independent Schools.

PART VI

ALTERNATIVE COMPENSATION PROGRAMS IN ACTION

CHAPTER 14

Trends and Issues: Incentive Programs for Teachers and Administrators

LYNN M. CORNETT – *Career Ladder Clearinghouse, Atlanta, Georgia*

MORE than eight of ten Americans favor "increased pay for teachers who prove themselves particularly capable." According to the Gallup Poll, this is a higher percentage than seven years ago, when the nation's first incentive plans for teachers were being debated and established. Career Ladder and other incentive pay programs are the largest educational experiment in the United States today. Thousands of teachers and administrators are receiving hundreds of millions of dollars through these programs. Such a situation naturally raises some questions.

- Are attitudes of teachers and administrators toward incentive pay changing?
- Is education improving because of these programs?
- Will states and school districts continue the commitments to incentive pay programs for the long term so that their effectiveness can be evaluated?

States and districts are now in the difficult stages of implementing Career Ladder Programs for teachers and administrators. Much of the glamor is gone. Headlines do not tell of dramatic developments or heated controversy about new programs as they did in 1984 and 1985 when some twenty-five states legislated or mandated that programs be developed.

SREB's Career Ladder Clearinghouse continues to compile information about questions that are frequently asked:

- Have states increased or decreased funding for incentive programs?
- What changes are occurring in the evaluation of teachers or administrators for Career Ladder or other incentive programs?
- Is student achievement being used in evaluating teachers or administrators for Career Ladder or other incentive programs?

339

- What has changed in schools because of these incentive programs?
- Will Career Ladder and the incentive programs get a fair test?

Legislatures that have financed pilot programs now have to make decisions about additional funding. Teachers' organizations in some districts are influencing the development of career ladders or incentive plans; other teachers' groups continue to resist any plan that calls for evaluation of teachers for rewards or that limits additional duties to only career ladder teachers.

Each year is a test of the long-term resolve that these programs will improve education. Because the headlines are gone, some assume that career ladders are another passing "educational fad"—another idea that sounds good but goes awry. But an analysis of reports from across the nation shows continuing support for Career Ladder Programs from many leaders in education and government. Educators who are designing and implementing incentive programs see them as a way to change "business as usual" attitudes in the schools by paying more to teachers who do a better job, providing rewards for those who will take on extra duties, and by seeing that exemplary teachers are more involved in decisions about teaching and learning.

Not all incentive pay programs have enjoyed continuing support. In 1988, programs without strong support or that were not funded in 1987 remained that way. In Alabama and Florida no funding was provided for the programs, and as a result the legislation was repealed. In Nebraska, a date for implementing a project was set aside. Career Ladder and incentive programs are very vulnerable to funding decisions. Legislators continue to get letters stating that a Career Ladder Program evaluation system has problems—that it doesn't choose the best teachers or that teachers can't succeed in the classroom because of the evaluation system.

These may be legitimate concerns—ones that need to be weighed as decisions are made. On the other hand, teachers also make strong positive comments such as, "My reaction to the career development plan is that it provides a new sense of accountability and a great many new opportunities for the teaching profession," and "Career ladder makes me want to set high, attainable goals." The third-party evaluation of the four-year-old Utah Career Ladder Program by the Far West Laboratory interpreted the strong feelings of teachers as showing that the Career Ladder Program is *changing the instructional climate in schools* (Amsler, Mitchell, Nelson, and Timar, 1988). If the Career Ladder

Program did not bring about strong feelings, this would signal that the changes were probably only at the surface and that they represented no real difference in the schools. School districts in Utah are at different stages in implementing programs, even though they began at the same time. Some districts focused only on paperwork and were hung up on procedures—afraid of being sued. Other districts were using the program to manage instruction and align teacher and district goals. These latter were the districts where most change was occurring.

From the vantage point of the SREB Career Ladder Clearing-house (Cornett, December 1988), the status of career ladders and other incentive programs across the United States appears to be as follows:

- Twenty-five states have career ladders or incentive programs with state funding or assistance; nine state programs are planned or under development.
- South Carolina has expanded the Teacher Incentive Program state-wide after a three-year pilot project; North Carolina has more than tripled funding for its program; Arizona continues to expand its project; in 1988-89 California's mentor teacher program was fully funded for the first time; Indiana's pilot mentor program is now state-wide.
- Funding for incentive programs has generally fared well, but the programs are new; in most cases there is still debate about them, and the costs of fully operational programs are substantial. All of these factors can make funding vulnerable to cuts. To determine if the programs can achieve intended results, they will need to be funded for several more years.
- Florida and Alabama repealed legislation for programs; in Nebraska legislation mandating a date for starting a program was struck. (These Career Ladder Programs never received funding and never got under way.) In Wisconsin, pilot programs (funded since 1985) were not funded for 1988–89.
- School incentive programs (awards are school based) continue in Florida and South Carolina; legislation in Louisiana and Colorado has established programs, and programs are being proposed in Kentucky and Texas.
- The public supports the incentive pay concept, but many teachers continue to question the fairness of evaluation systems and whether, in fact, teachers should be rewarded for exemplary teaching.

- Administrators (principals and other supervisors) are included in only a few programs (Tennessee, North Carolina, Georgia, and South Carolina).
- A comprehensive third-party evaluation of the Utah program shows that changes are occurring in managing instruction in schools and "that the program is supporting school effectiveness."
- Teachers' organizations appear to support programs in which teachers assume additional duties and responsibilities more readily than they do pay-for-performance programs.
- Programs continue to be refined (especially evaluation procedures within programs); more time is needed for a fair test of the career ladders and incentive programs.

FUNDING

Have States Increased or Decreased Funding for Incentive Programs?

In most states that have put substantial funding into incentive programs, funding increased or held steady in 1989; if states had provided no funding for plans, that remains the case (see Table 1).

North Carolina and South Carolina have tripled the money that was initially provided for pilot projects. Tennessee's funding was up slightly for 1988–89 to a total of $99 million. Texas continues to provide several hundred million state dollars, with districts providing additional funds. In South Carolina, the Teacher Incentive Program went state-wide in 1988–89, with an increase in funding from $12 million to $22 million. Funding for the School Incentive Program was $3.9 million, and funding for the Principal Incentive Program increased from $600,000 to $1.1 million. The North Carolina pilot project, in its fourth year, was funded at $46.5 million, an increase of $15.5 million above 1987–88 and $30 million more than the second year of the project when teachers received money for moving to career level I.

The Arizona pilot project was funded at $4.6 million in 1985–86; $9.1 million was spent in 1987–88, and over $10 million was projected for each of the final two years of the pilot project. Utah continued to fund its career ladder at $41 million. In California, the Mentor Teacher Program was fully funded for the first time. Funding for 1988–89 was $63.5 million, up from $30.8 million in 1984–85. Over 10,000 teachers can now be mentor teachers. (Legislation allows up to 5 percent of a

Table 1. Incentive programs—1989.

	Local Initiative	Pilots with State Funding and/or Assistance	Full Implementation of State Program	State Program under Development	Discussion No Legislative Action Pending	Type of Program
Alabama						
Alaska	X					Teacher Incentive
Arizona		X				Career Ladder
Arkansas		(Not funded)				Career Development
California			X			Mentor Teacher
Colorado		X(1)		X(2) (Not funded)		(1) Teacher Incentive (2) Teacher/School Incentive
Connecticut				X		Teacher Incentive Mentor Teacher
Delaware						
Florida			X			School Incentive (2 Programs)
Georgia				X (Not funded)		Career Ladder
Hawaii				X		Mentor Teacher

(continued)

Table 1 (continued).

	Local Initiative	Pilots with State Funding and/or Assistance	Full Implementation of State Program	State Program under Development	Discussion No Legislative Action Pending	Type of Program
Idaho				X		Career Compensation Mentor Teacher
Illinois	X					Teacher Incentive
Indiana		X(1)	X(2) X(3)			(1) Career Ladder/ Development (2) Mentor Teacher (3) School Incentive
Iowa			X			Teacher Incentive
Kansas	X					Teacher Incentive
Kentucky		(Completed in 1987)				Career Ladder
Louisiana		X(1)		X(2)		(1) Career Options (2) School Incentive
Maine			X			Tiered Certification
Maryland	X					Career Development Incentive

Table 1 (continued).

	Local Initiative	Pilots with State Funding and/or Assistance	Full Implementation of State Program	State Program under Development	Discussion No Legislative Action Pending	Type of Program
Massachusetts			X(1)	X(2)		(1) Teacher Incentive (2) Mentor Teacher
Michigan	X					Teacher Incentive
Minnesota	X(1)	X(2)				(1) Teacher Incentive (2) Mentor Teacher
Mississippi				(Proposed)		School Incentive
Missouri			X			Career Ladder
Montana	X				X	Teacher Incentive
Nebraska						Teacher Incentive
Nevada	X					Teacher Incentive
New Hampshire	X					Teacher Incentive
New Jersey			X			Teacher Incentive
New Mexico					X	Teacher Incentive

(continued)

345

Table 1 *(continued)*.

	Local Initiative	Pilots with State Funding and/or Assistance	Full Implementation of State Program	State Program under Development	Discussion No Legislative Action Pending	Type of Program
New York	X(1)	X(2)	X(3)			(1) District/School Incentive (2) Mentor Teacher (3) Teacher Incentive
North Carolina		X(1)		X(2)		(1) Career Ladder (2) Differentiated Pay
North Dakota	X					Career Development
Ohio	X	X		X		Career Ladder
Oklahoma	X			(Proposed)		Teacher Incentive
Oregon		X				Career Development Mentor Teacher
Pennsylvania		X(1)	X(2) X(3)			(1) Career Development (2) Career Development/Mentor Teacher (3) School Incentive
Rhode Island					X	Mentor Teacher

Table 1 (continued).

	Local Initiative	Pilots with State Funding and/or Assistance	Full Implementation of State Program	State Program under Development	Discussion No Legislative Action Pending	Type of Program
South Carolina			X(1) X(2) X(3)			(1) Teacher Incentive (2) Principal Incentive (3) School Incentive
South Dakota	X					Mentor Teacher
Tennessee			X			Career Ladder
Texas			X(1)	X(2)		(1) Career Ladder (2) School Incentive
Utah			X			Career Ladder
Vermont				X		Mentor Teacher
Virginia	X	(Completed in 1986)				Career Ladder/ Teacher Incentive
Washington		X(1)	X(2)			(1) School Incentive (2) Mentor Teacher
West Virginia					X	Teacher Incentive
Wisconsin	X					Mentor Teacher
Wyoming	X					Career Ladder/ Teacher Incentive

district's teachers to be designated mentors.) The Iowa Educational Excellence Program was funded at $92 million for 1988–89 – the same as the previous year – when $41 million of that amount went to district-designed programs of supplemental pay, pay for performance, or a combination. Eighty-seven percent of the districts, through negotiated plans, developed additional pay for additional duties; 12 percent developed a combination plan. Only three of the over 400 districts developed pay-for-performance plans. In Missouri in 1987–88, the state's share of funding for the Career Ladder Programs was $7.3 million for 120 districts. In 1988–89, it was anticipated that thirty-one additional districts (of the state's 545 districts) would participate. The funding for 1988–89 was $10 million, but a supplemental budget request for $1.4 million went to the legislature. About 6000 teachers were eligible for career ladder pay, compared to 2300 who participated in 1986–87.

If states provided no funding previously, that situation remained the same for 1988–89. Funding for the Alabama and Florida programs was not forthcoming during the 1988 legislative sessions and in both states the programs were repealed. In Wisconsin, a two-year pilot project was funded at $1 million for 1985–87, with an additional $214,000 for 1987–88. The legislature provided no funding for 1988–89. In states that in the past have provided no funding for programs (Arkansas, Idaho, Nebraska, and New Mexico), funding is still not available.

EVALUATION

What Changes Are Occurring in the Evaluation of Teachers as a Result of Career Ladders and Incentive Programs?

From the beginning, the primary questions about career ladders and other incentive programs have focused on how the evaluation decisions will be made. Early issues were state versus local evaluation; whether to include observation of classroom teaching; who would observe and evaluate teachers – principals or other teachers; and whether criteria for advancement would be decided at the state or local level. Some states, for example Tennessee and North Carolina, developed classroom instruments for use state-wide. Texas used local evaluation while a state process was being developed. Utah permitted states to use local instruments initially but tightened guidelines later; districts in Utah now use similar instruments. Teacher evaluation has changed and is changing.

According to the third-party evaluation completed by the Far West Laboratory on the Utah program, the "Career Ladder System focuses teacher and principal attention on teacher evaluation. More frequent and effective teacher evaluations is the single greatest effect of the Career Ladder System" (Amsler et al., 1988). According to the evaluation, two of the parts of the Utah program—performance bonus and career ladder levels—have focused attention on the quality of teaching. Principals and teachers did not agree, however, on whether more evaluation is actually more effective. About 57 percent of the principals agreed that the performance bonus plan helps principals carry out better evaluations; 47 percent of the teachers agreed.

A review of the North Carolina Teacher Performance Appraisal Instrument, by a committee from outside the state, concluded that it was a "quality instrument, one that is highly suited to its purpose" (Brandt, Duke, French, and Iwanicki, 1988). The group did recommend some changes, such as reviewing teaching practices included in instruction to be sure that the practices reflect current literature on effective teaching—especially effective models of teaching based on coaching and modeling rather than direct instruction only. The committee recommended that the instrument be used for certification and career levels I and II but not as the primary measure for career level III decisions, the highest level. Another recommendation was that all evaluators be certified and be required to demonstrate competency on a regular basis.

A report by the North Carolina Department of Public Instruction recommended procedures to determine the reliability across districts of the ratings of teachers (North Carolina Department of Public Instruction, 1987). The wide variations in distributions of ratings may be explained by the level of training or the fact that the procedures have been in place only a short time. Evidence to date is that performance ratings tend to be inflated, rather than otherwise. Ratings of criteria that are not observable in the classroom (lesson planning, interaction with colleagues and parents, and noninstructional duties) tend to receive higher ratings than ones that are drawn from research and can be observed in the classroom. The appeal process for career development procedures was reviewed by the North Carolina State Department of Public Instruction and by an outside consultant in 1988. The need for training local school board members (who review local decisions) was highlighted (Brandt, 1988).

The North Carolina Teacher Performance Appraisal Instrument is used not only for placing persons on the career development levels but for all teachers across the state. A study was conducted by the Department of Public Instruction on the use of the system from 1985 to 1987 to evaluate the process and to determine if there were differences when the process was used in the Career Development Program (Stacey, Holdzkom, and Kuligowski, 1988). A survey of evaluators and teachers who were evaluated was conducted in twenty-two districts and fifteen career development pilot projects. Results showed that a majority of teachers and evaluators agreed that the procedures include standards against which teachers are willing to be judged, and they did not see major revisions as necessary. Both teachers and evaluators were more positive about teacher observation than about the conference that followed the classroom observations. Eighty-four percent of the evaluators said the final evaluation decision was "an accurate indicator of overall performance to a large extent," compared to 70 percent of the teachers. There was more agreement with this statement by evaluators in career development pilots than in those districts without pilot projects. The outcome and benefit of the appraisal process rated highest by both evaluators and teachers was "better teaching." More evaluators in the career development units than evaluators in districts without the career development component said better teaching and job satisfaction were positive outcomes. Teachers took the opposite view—those in the career development districts saw job satisfaction as an outcome of the appraisal process to a lesser degree than those in districts without programs.

In Fort Bragg, North Carolina, a career development project (not one of the state's pilot projects) has developed a new evaluation instrument for teachers who want to advance to career status II. While teaching is the only major area assessed for the career status I teachers, additional functions have been added for the next level that are school based and show a teacher's development in working with colleagues and school principals. The new process has been developed to recognize different points of development for teachers. Teachers will be assessed as to how well they identify and meet school goals, and teacher skills will be viewed in the context of moving toward an effective school. In addition, teachers will choose from a variety of other activities to be assessed, such as being a mentor teacher, sharing knowledge with colleagues (demonstrating techniques or presenting workshops), and providing leadership through such activities as curriculum review and design or being a team leader. The instrument was designed using the literature on organizational theory and school-site management.

The Charlotte-Mecklenburg Career Development Program began its developmental planning stage in 1981 (Cornett, 1988). Prior to the beginning of the plan, in each of the schools an administrative position was created – assistant principal for instruction. A Career Development Program for beginning teachers formed the heart of the program. A second part, the "cross-over" program, was designed for experienced and tenured teachers who wanted to become career teachers. Originally, it was designed with a heavy emphasis on the use of multiple outside observers visiting the classroom on several different occasions. Over the years the evaluation process for veteran teachers has been changed to include principals. (Six years ago teachers said they wanted independent fellow teachers to observe and to report on their performance in the classroom – they didn't want their principals and other teachers in their schools doing that.) The number of observations was reduced at all levels; however, there are still multiple observations by different observers. The original evaluations focused on numerical scores only; word descriptions now provide additional information about a teacher's performance. The school committee – headed by the principal, with the assistant principal for instruction and teacher members – uses evaluation data as a part of the career ladder decision process.

A study of district incentive programs in Virginia noted that the programs have resulted in a complete overhaul of traditional teacher evaluation (Brandt and Gansneder, 1987). Rating scales of general teacher behaviors have been replaced with research based, instructional behaviors to be observed in the classroom. In half the districts teachers serve as evaluators or collectors of classroom data. In districts where a comparatively low proportion of eligible teachers was selected for incentives, more attention was given to teacher assessment and the number of formal and informal observations was increased dramatically.

USING STUDENT OUTCOMES

Is Student Achievement Being Used in Evaluating Teachers or Administrators for Career Ladders or Other Incentive Programs?

Several states – Utah, South Carolina, Arizona, and Georgia – mandate that student achievement be included in making decisions about teachers advancing on the career ladder. The Kentucky Career Ladder Pilot Project included a study to identify promising ways to examine student achievement. The 1987 Texas legislature called on the State

Department of Education to study the use of student achievement in assessing teacher performance.

School based incentive programs that award money to schools to use for instruction or for school personnel on the basis of student outcomes, such as achievement and attendance, continue in both South Carolina and Florida; a similar new program was established in Louisiana by 1988 legislation; Georgia's program is in the pilot stages. School incentive plans have been proposed in Kentucky and Texas.

The Teacher Incentive Program in South Carolina uses student achievement as a major factor in determining awards. Teachers document student achievement that exceeds "expected growth." The State Department of Education and the University of South Carolina have provided technical assistance to districts in developing ways to document student achievement.

In Utah, student achievement is required as one piece of evidence in evaluating teachers. Plans are now placing greater emphasis on the use of teacher- and district-designed tests using a comprehensive test item bank that has been developed by the State Department of Education. Most districts use a conference process for teachers to set goals— measurable goals that can be part of a written plan.

The Arizona Career Ladder Pilot Project is designed to focus on teacher performance and student achievement. All pilot sites have student achievement goals as top priorities and have developed different uses of achievement measures. Teachers move to higher levels based on teaching performance, student academic progress, higher level responsibilities, and professional growth. Student progress is measured through pre- and post-testing using standardized tests and other district measures. A center at Northern Arizona University is examining teacher performance and the relationship to student achievement as part of a continuing evaluation of the pilot projects.

Georgia's Career Ladder Program includes student achievement as a criterion for advancement. A district review team will make recommendations for advancement on the ladder, based on evidence presented by the teacher. Teachers who demonstrate sustained excellence in performance on the job (as measured by the state-wide assessment procedures); productivity (as shown in academic achievement of students); service (through professional activities in working with other educators); and self-growth (professional development, such as coursework, staff development, and conferences) will move up the ladder.

Kentucky's Career Ladder Pilot Project for teachers used a goal setting approach in measuring student outcomes to determine if a common core of goals might emerge and whether the approach might be useful (Redfield, 1988). Each teacher met with the principal, reduced the plan to one page, and negotiated the plan with the principal. Teachers had to include from four to eight goals, at least one from categories that included academic outcomes across the curriculum, academic content specific to a subject, and nonacademic areas such as skill or affective outcomes. Goals were categorized according to their significance for education and the level of difficulty in reaching them. Teachers wanted to be sure that if very high standards were set for student achievement, the difficulty level for these standards would be considered. Teachers and principals met in a final conference at the end of the year to examine progress in reaching goals. Among the project's findings were 1) principals, parents, teachers, and students wanted student outcomes defined more broadly than only academic achievement and 2) teachers and principals, as with other techniques, need training to successfully implement a goal setting process.

At the end of 1987, a review of incentive pay programs in Virginia showed that thirteen districts had or were developing incentive programs; student performance was a criterion for awards in half of the plans and the sole criterion in two (Brandt and Gansneder, 1987). For instance, in one district, teachers receive a $600 bonus if 75 percent of their students "maintain or exceed expected achievement levels"; if three-fourths of the teachers in a school achieve this, then all teachers in the school receive the bonus.

School based programs continue. The Florida District Quality Instruction Incentives Program was funded at $10 million for 1988–89 and continues today. This program, created by 1984 legislation, is negotiated at the district level and provides incentive money for schools that exceed expected student achievement. At least half of the available money (determined on the basis of student enrollment in the district) must go to school employees at meritorious schools. Schools qualify by exceeding expected student achievement results. Other standards can include vocational placement, students who are winners of science fairs, student attendance, and parent participation. The State Department of Education provides technical assistance to schools, including several models for determining student achievement progress.

The South Carolina School Incentive Reward Program began in 1984. Rewards are based on schools meeting criteria that include student achievement gains and improved student and teacher attendance.

The achievement gain criterion must be met for a school to receive a reward; attendance rates qualify reward winners for additional funds. Money is distributed to the school for instructional purposes and may be used for materials or equipment. Students' scores are also tracked from one year to the next to determine students' progress over time. The student results are grouped at the school level, and the top quarter of schools are rewarded in each of the five school comparison groups. The comparison groups are based on student backgrounds (socioeconomic factors) and school resources.

The Group Productivity Bonus, a part of the Georgia Career Ladder Plan piloted in 1988–89, rewards entire school and central office instructional staff for student achievement that exceeds what might be expected when student socioeconomic characteristics are taken into account. The bonus plan is designed to reward cooperation among staff for improving instruction and student achievement. Awards range from $125 to $600 and include certified staff and instructional aides in schools and each central district office.

Louisiana's "Children First" education reform package, approved in 1988, called for two incentive programs—the School Profile and Incentive Program and the Model Career Options Package. The School Profile and Incentive Program includes the creation of profiles of schools, including test results, drop-out rates, graduation rates, students in Advanced Placement classes, expenditures, and other information approved by the board of education. Profiles on every school and school system will be prepared annually. The School Incentive Program is designed to reward schools making significant progress and to increase local accountability. Initially, at least 100 schools will be rewarded (schools will be grouped into categories based on factors such as similar socioeconomic status of students, size of school, and urban or suburban location). The cash awards will be used for instruction, not to increase salaries. A school council of teachers, community members, and students will assist the principal in determining use of the award.

OUTCOMES AND EVALUATION OF THE PROGRAMS

What Has Changed in Schools Because of These Incentive Programs?

Rewarding excellence, promoting better teaching, improving education for children—these are the intentions of "the career ladder movement." Teachers will take on different responsibilities; they will become master teachers and will not have to leave the classroom to receive higher pay; teaching will become more attractive; and teachers whose students learn more will be rewarded—these are desired outcomes of the programs. Questions do remain:

- Are students learning more?
- Have these programs changed schools?
- Have these programs made teaching more attractive?

While many factors contribute to improved schools, several evaluations of programs are beginning to provide information about the early effects of these incentive programs. The most comprehensive to date has been completed in Utah. A third-party evaluation of the North Carolina Career Development Plan is being completed, and a multiyear effort in Arizona is evaluating that state's pilot project. Early indications are that short-term effects have occurred (the change in evaluation procedures has already been mentioned).

In North Carolina, a 1988 study by the State Department of Public Instruction asked the question: "What effects has the Career Development Pilot Program had on student achievement in sixteen participating districts" (North Carolina Department of Public Instruction, 1988)? The study made a comparison from 1985 to 1988 of student achievement in the sixteen career development districts (the duration of the pilot project) and to comparable districts that did not participate. Average daily membership, per pupil expenditure, percentage of students planning to attend college, and geographic location were taken into account in matching districts. Results showed that at grades 3, 6, and 8, the number of career development districts having student achievement levels below the national median *declined*. In the matched districts, the number declined only for grade 3; in grade 6 the number of districts below the median *increased*. While the study is careful to point out the difficulties in attributing the change to one program, the report states, ". . . If we fail to discover similar patterns of achievement in a matched sample of students, then clearly some effect of Career Development is present and is influencing students' achievement." During the pilot project, the State Department of Education reported that superintendents, principals, and teachers in the career development districts said that teaching and student performance have improved. In 1986, 57 percent of responding teachers said, "Participating in the program has helped me perform my role more effectively." In 1988, 64 percent thought,

"Observation and evaluation have helped me to improve specific aspects of my teaching" (North Carolina Department of Public Instruction, 1988).

The objective of the Utah study (Amsler et al., 1988), conducted by the Far West Laboratory, was to provide policy leaders with an assessment of the overall impact of the Career Ladder System on schools in Utah. The study reported, "Together, the four components of the Career Ladder System create a powerful mechanism for school improvement. The system is changing both individual teacher behavior and the ways schools are organized to define goals, delegate authority, and complete tasks."

Utah's policies for its incentive programs are comprehensive. The policies have several parts: extended contract year, "job enlargement," performance bonus, and career ladder levels (additional duties and responsibilities). The four parts of the Utah Career Ladder System have had powerful, but slightly different, effects on schools and teachers. The extended contract year focuses on individual teachers and is affecting their work. For example, it has been very important in expanding the definition of basic teacher work to include planning activities, which are always associated with good instruction but which traditionally have remained unpaid. The researchers found that the extended contract had an organizational level effect. It was changing the day-by-day operations of the schools by acknowledging that the school, as an organization, has transition periods for which planning is needed.

"Job enlargement" was designed to allow districts to pay teachers for short-term activities that expand their work responsibilities in the schools. The researchers likened this to venture capital, or the R&D unit in a corporation. Job enlargement involves allowing schools to provide innovations that simply were not happening before. Short-term job enlargement activities in the districts included mentoring programs, curriculum development activities, homework hotlines, and after-school enrichment programs. The Utah review found that job enlargement allows schools, which can be notoriously slow, bureaucratic structures, to make innovations and try new ideas.

The third part of the Utah program, according to the study, is the most controversial and the one that teachers and principals liked the least—performance bonus. The legislative intent was to improve the quality of teaching by awarding bonuses to the teachers rated the best in a district-developed evaluation instrument. The study found that the major benefit of performance bonus has been to focus teacher and principal attention on evaluation. Principals said it helped them to understand effective and noneffective instruction. In nine of the twelve districts that were studied, bonuses were awarded to approximately 70 percent of those teachers who applied. "That there is a reward simply for effective classroom performance is really powerful, even if many of your colleagues are also receiving one." Because of performance bonus, a shared language has developed about what good teaching is and how it can be evaluated and improved.

The career ladder is designed to create different levels of professional status for teachers by creating a "ladder" that one can climb to receive increased pay through increased work responsibilities and status. The Utah researchers (Cornett, 1988) noted that the career ladder has the potential for making real changes in the structure of the teaching profession. Differences among teachers in terms of skills and abilities can be recognized in a way that does not destroy collegiality. The performance bonus and the extended contract year focus on changes at the individual teacher level. The two other parts—career ladder and job enlargement—focus on organizational levels of change, and the researchers reported changes in the schools, such as teachers taking on new duties.

Evidence showed a reorganization of the principal's work role without an increase in compensation. In terms of the survey data, despite the workload increases, principals—more than teachers, actually—were very supportive of the program. They felt that even though they were working much harder, their schools were being better run.

The Utah researchers concluded that the total program is supporting changes in school effectiveness, especially in the extended contract and in the career ladder levels. The research found that the performance bonus was the most controversial and most difficult to implement. The total Career Ladder System is providing a substantial reallocation of teacher salaries across the state, according to the study.

Trends have recently been identified by the Utah State Office of Education in examining the program after several years. The career ladder levels appear to be taken more seriously in a growing number of plans. Job enlargement and career ladder levels are often overlapping and need further study to sort them out. Several districts use the career levels to promote continuing and meaningful career development. Performance bonus is considered the most difficult to implement—evaluation to identify high performing teachers and appropriate pay is considered difficult. Evaluation procedures have improved and will continue to do so, according to the Utah Office of Education. While districts are using more of the funding (a 50 percent cap exists) to support additional contract days, many legislators who want a reward system for excellence are questioning this move. The successful parts of the program, according to the department, are that

- Plans focus on improving student achievement with educator advancement.
- Plans are locally owned and driven by local boards of education.
- Legislation allows innovation practices within guidelines and new directions for the system.

The Utah State Office of Education and districts are now exploring refinements that may be proposed for the next legislative session.

A third-party evaluation made several recommendations for improving the South Carolina Teacher Incentive Program (MGT, 1988). First, the evaluators recommended more equitable funding for the incentive program operations. Each district gets 20 percent of its total district allotment (on a per pupil basis) for administrative purposes. For many of the smaller districts, 20 percent is not adequate; a few districts are so large that 20 percent is actually more than they need, according to the report. The districts need more technical assistance, according to the study. (Beginning in 1989–90, evaluation instruments for teacher performance had to be approved by the State Department of Education.) Documenting student achievement continues to be a problem. The study recommends that districts provide information to all teachers (participating and nonparticipating) about expected student achievement levels and whether students have exceeded those levels.

One-third of the participants reported that the Teacher Incentive Program had helped them show more initiative in their job. Many believed it was too early to expect changes in schools, such as in curriculum or productivity, due to the program. Nearly 80 percent of the participants agreed that the program requirements were consistent with the goals of their school. The additional paperwork continues to be a problem although one-fourth of the teachers in Bonus Model to one-half in Campus/Individual Model districts who had participated more than one year have seen a decline in the paperwork load. A majority of the participating teachers thought it was possible to implement an unbiased way to identify and reward superior teachers. However, less than one-half of the participating teachers said their concept of a superior teacher was consistent with the award requirements. The study noted that this is not surprising, since one-half of the participants and non-participants believed they were in the top 10 percent of teachers in terms of on-the-job performance and productivity. The program has contributed to improvements in teacher and student performance assessments, according to the South Carolina study.

Program revisions, based on the pilot project, include changes in the attendance requirement (more flexibility) and in activities that teachers can include in their self-improvement plan (more focus on direct work with student teachers and additional study).

In Missouri during 1987–88, teachers, librarians, and counselors could move to the first and second levels of a career ladder in participating districts. During the year, the State Department of Education studied levels of teacher morale and job satisfaction for teachers participating and not participating in the program. When compared with years of experience, teacher morale for Missouri career ladder teachers remained the same and then rose sharply for those with over twenty-four years of experience. For noncareer ladder teachers there was a comparable high level of morale for the inexperienced but a steady decline as experience increased. Job satisfaction between the two groups was fairly consistent for inexperienced teachers. For those not participating, no increase in job satisfaction was evident for those teachers with more experience. The study found high levels of morale across all age groups for career ladder teachers; it was opposite for noncareer ladder teachers—decreasing morale between the ages of twenty-five and forty-nine, increasing only after age fifty.

The Arizona Career Ladder Project reports that the most impressive results of the project are the increased awareness of and focus on examining student achievement. Districts have stepped up training of teachers in student assessment and evaluation.

An evaluation of the first year of Rochester City School District's Peer Assistance and Review Program (1986–87), a pilot project to provide assistance to beginning teachers, showed that interns were positive about their experiences with mentors (Gillett and Halkett, 1988). (This program is now a part of the district's Career in Teaching Program.) Most relied on their mentor for improving instructional skills and classroom management. Interns said that their greatest need was the moral support and encouragement that was provided by the mentor; 90 percent of interns felt they needed help in developing teaching skills. Findings from the evaluation support the notion that beginning teachers are often placed in difficult assignments, such as classes with many students who have behavior problems, split grades for elementary teachers, and, for high school teachers, large classes or several different teaching subjects (Halkett, 1988). The evaluation of the program noted that a good evaluation process with objective criteria that are clearly understood by new teachers is needed for a successful mentor/internship program. The Career in Teaching Program in the school district (negotiated through a 1988 contract) includes the intern as the first level of four rungs on a career ladder; the mentor teacher position is one category of lead teacher (the top rung on the ladder). To address the problem of placing inexperienced teachers in difficult positions, lead teachers will have to have proven their teaching ability in difficult situations and be willing to assume those kinds of assignments.

COMMITMENT TO CHANGE

Will Career Ladders and the Incentive Programs Get a Fair Test?

Support for career ladders, pay for performance, or other incentive programs are getting a fair test in some states. A "fair" test means that the funding situation is fairly stable, policymakers show a continuing commitment, programs are being fine-tuned, and results or changes in schools are being reported.

The fate of other programs may be in a tenuous position—original promoters of programs are no longer on the scene, state budgets have been cut, and resistance to change is heard from school personnel. In these situations it is not clear whether programs will continue long enough to determine their effects. Some programs may simply be the wrong approach. A serious problem is that few comprehensive evaluations of programs are being conducted or are planned. Decisions are made on the basis of surveys of "attitudes" toward programs only. States such as Arizona, North Carolina, and Utah are to be commended for incorporating a comprehensive look at what is working and what is changing in the schools. Evidence from almost every program shows that teacher evaluation is improving and that persons outside the classroom—for example, school principals—are focusing more on instruction. Teachers and school administrators in many districts are aggressively working to develop new ways to teach and deliver instruction.

Most programs have not been in existence long enough for a fair test.

Educators will need to urge necessary refinements in programs, and state and school leaders will need to be diligent to see that the changes do not alter the original intent of the programs. Additional time and effort by all will be needed to determine if real change and improvement in schools is occurring.

REFERENCES

Amsler, M., D. Mitchell, L. Nelson, and T. Timar. 1988. "An Evaluation of the Utah Career Ladder System: Summary and Analysis of Policy Implications," Far West Laboratory for Educational Research and Development.

Brandt, R. M. 1988. "An Evaluation of the Career Development Pilot Program Appeals Process," Report submitted to the Education Subcommittee of the Joint Legislative Commission on Government Operations, North Carolina General Assembly.

Brandt, R. M., D. L. Duke, R. L. French, and E. F. Iwanicki. 1988. "A Review with Recommendations of the North Carolina Teacher Performance Appraisal Instrument," Report submitted to the Education Subcommittee of the Joint Legislative Commission on Government Operations, North Carolina General Assembly.

Brandt, R. M. and B. M. Gansneder. 1987. "Teacher Incentive Pay Programs in Virginia," Curry School of Education, University of Virginia.

Cornett, L. M. 1988. "Teacher Incentives: The Outsiders' View," Southern Regional Education Board.

Cornett, L. M. 1988. "Is 'Paying for Performance' Changing Schools?" Southern Regional Education Board.

Gillett, T. and K. A. Halkett. "RCSD Mentor Program Evaluation: The Policy Implications," Paper presented at the annual meeting of the American Association of Colleges for Teacher Education, February 1988.

Halkett, K. A. 1988. "Peer Assistance and Review Program 1986/87 Local Evaluation Report," Report submitted to Rochester City School District.

MGT Consultants. 1988. "An Evaluation of the Teacher Incentive Program 1987–88 Pilot Test Implementation," Report submitted to the South Carolina State Department of Education.

North Carolina Department of Public Instruction. 1987. "Performance Appraisal—Cornerstone of Career Development Plan," Report submitted to the North Carolina State Board of Education.

North Carolina Department of Public Instruction. 1988. "Student Achievement in Career Development Program Pilot Units 1985–88," Report submitted to the North Carolina State Board of Education.

Redsfield, D. L. "Expected Student Achievement and the Evaluation of Teaching," Presentation at the Annual Meeting of the American Educational Research Association, 1988.

Stacey, D. C., D. L. Holdzkom, and B. Kuligowski. 1988. "Effectiveness of the North Carolina Teacher Performance Appraisal System," Raleigh, NC: Department of Public Instruction.

CHAPTER 15

A Work Redesign View of Career Ladders in Utah

ANN WEAVER HART —*The University of Utah*

In an attempt to improve teaching and learning and, subsequently, student performance, changes in the work structures in schools and the rewards offered teachers are being undertaken across the country. Ways to make teachers more proficient, to reward and retain the best teachers, and to attract an increased share of academically able students to teaching careers are being widely explored. Proponents of these reform efforts reason that current ways of organizing schools are not necessarily best suited to the demands placed on modern education systems and that teaching lacks appeal for a sufficient number of talented and motivated people. Increasing this appeal and exploring new designs of work could create a better work force and improve schooling (Carnegie Commission, 1986; Holmes Group, 1986; Rosenholtz, 1987; Rosenholtz and Smylie, 1984). Policymakers and school leaders say they are "making radical changes in the belief these changes will produce better students" (Pierpont, 1989).

A variety of education reforms have arisen. In 1984 and 1985, twenty-five states either legislated such programs or mandated that they be developed. At one time, as many as forty states were looking at teacher incentive, career ladder, or restructuring alternatives. This legislative interest in education reform reflects the attitudes of the American public. Eight out of ten Americans favor some form of increased pay for particularly capable teachers, a higher percentage than five years ago when the changes began. Currently, twenty-five states have funded incentive or Career Ladder Programs, and nine additional programs are under development (Cornett, 1988). The increases in pay associated with these reforms can be substantial, potentially providing annual salaries as high as $70,000, and the public investment is high. In Florida, taxpayers have invested a 1/2 percent increase in the state corporate income tax, a state lottery, and a billion dollar bond issue into education reform (Pierpont, 1989).

363

Many theories of compensation and work incentives have been applied to these reforms. Merit pay (Murnane, 1986), mentor/novice (California, 1985), professionalization (Metzger, 1987), and school based management (Fiske, 1988; Sizer, 1985) models are used by scholars and practitioners to develop and assess reforms. A perspective on work organization in the management sciences known as work redesign provides another model helpful in understanding the dynamics and potential impacts of work restructuring in schools. In this chapter, I apply a work redesign conceptualization of education reform to an analysis of Career Ladder Plans for teachers in Utah. This approach is useful for three reasons. (1) Stereotypical and ambiguous constructs of career ladders, merit pay, and other teacher incentives isolated from their specific work and reward features obfuscate the potential impacts of restructuring on recruitment and retention goals and on teaching and learning in schools. (2) Work redesign is a broad conceptual approach that makes teaching reform comparable to research and practice in other work settings. (3) Work redesign provides a structural and social framework with the complexity necessary to examine the human work context in which all education reform must prosper or perish.

UTAH CAREER LADDERS: PHILOSOPHIES AND THEORIES OF TEACHER INCENTIVES

In 1984 the legislature of the state of Utah joined this diverse movement of teacher incentive reforms. It enacted legislation that allowed each district to plan a career ladder for teachers and provided funds to support the systems. Forty different Career Ladder Plans were designed and implemented. Each year for the next three years the legislature appropriated additional funds. By 1986–87, the yearly appropriation was about $35 million, or about $1900 for each of the state's teachers. The 1988 funding was about $41 million. Because the most comprehensive evaluations of Career Ladder Plans to date have been completed in Utah and the forty plans vary substantially, the state provides a wealth of information about the early results of different features of these efforts to improve the effectiveness of schools (Amsler, Mitchell, Nelson, and Timar, 1988; Cornett, 1988; Malen, Murphy, and Hart, 1987).

The original impetus for the career ladder in Utah came from a group of political and educational leaders (Governor Scott Matheson, influential legislators on the Utah Education Reform Steering Committee, a few superintendents, and others on concurrent task forces) who worked together through 1983 to design an education intervention in response to *A Nation at Risk* (1983). Proponents lacked the power to push their original initiative, which relied primarily on a promotion ladder, through the legislature. So, while a variety of beliefs and assumptions drove the reform, the final legislation was an eclectic collection of teacher incentives. Added to this original plan to restructure and redesign teacher work, career paths, and compensation were two new features—salary increases to all teachers through additional contract days and merit pay. The plan consequently had three parts, sometimes described as "a camel with three humps": 1) an extended contract year based on existing salary schedules, 2) a performance bonus or merit stipend based on classroom teaching performance, and 3) a component permitting staff differentiation and work redesign. The extended contract provision was necessary to "buy the support of the UEA," and the merit pay component was the "price to pay" to maintain the support of dominant political groups (Malen and Campbell, 1985). By 1985–86, the state board of education reported that 34.1 percent of funds were spent by districts for various forms of differentiated staffing, 38.7 percent for the extended contract year, and 27 percent for performance bonuses (see Figure 1). While these features are conceptually and operationally very different, each is a part of the Utah Career Ladder Plans.

Extended Year

The extended contract provision of the career ladder provided the chance for teachers to focus on their work without students present, while being compensated at their professional rate. Based on the assumption that teaching involves more than lectures and presentations to student audiences, it proved to be by far the most popular of the three parts with teachers and principals. Most districts allocated the maximum amount of money permitted to the extended year. Typically, districts used the days for activities teachers previously reserved for weekends, evenings, and after school—grading and report cards, workshops, class preparation (Amsler, Mitchell, Nelson, and Timar, 1988; Hart, 1987; Hart and Murphy, 1987, 1990b; Malen, Murphy, and Hart, 1987).

While critics point out that this provision bears little or no relationship to a career development or promotion plan, diluting the integrity of the

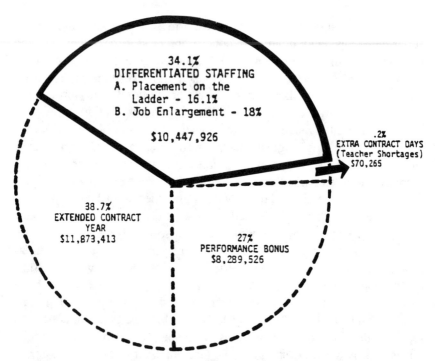

FIGURE 1 Total dollars and percent budgeted for the career ladder levels/differentiated staffing component. Source: *Career Ladders in Utah: A Content Analysis of Utah's Career Ladder Plans for 1985-86.* A Report from the Utah State Board of Education, November 1985.

reform (Malen and Hart, 1987), its defenders counter that it addresses other problems in the profession. For example, it begins to move teaching closer to a "full-time profession." The part-time nature of teaching is frequently mentioned as a disadvantage in the recruitment and retention of high quality teachers, ample reason to consider restructuring the work (Carnegie, 1986; Holmes, 1986). In addition, it provides some relief for the crushing teaching loads carried by most teachers in Utah, where student/teacher ratios are the highest in the country.

Merit Pay/Performance Bonus

In 1985, the legislature chose to expand the classroom teaching merit requirements in the initial legislation. In 1986, this portion of the plan was again extended by the state board of education, which until 1991 required that 10 percent of career ladder money be spent on the performance bonus (25 percent in the area vocational centers, which had no need for an extended year). While it was highly criticized and external evaluation reports repeatedly labeled it the least productive aspect of the career ladder, merit pay has been described by legislative analysts as nonnegotiable, a fundamental feature of the initial legislative intent to "identify the few outstanding salesmen and reward them for outstanding performance." It is necessary to maintain support for continued funding. Although many people recognize that merit pay is "still a problem area," they argue that it "deserves time for improvement. To categorically eliminate it is unjustified and would jeopardize the funding." District and school educators, however, describe the performance bonus as the "biggest frustration" associated with the career ladder (Jensen and Denler, 1989).

The evaluation of individual teachers' merits for the distribution of benefits posed a major challenge for this provision. The most common techniques used—1) the observation of teaching and completion of an evaluation instrument by principals or peers and 2) "multiple lines of evidence" collected and submitted by teachers—are often accused of being a "staged set-up." Some teachers argued that "anybody can put on a dog and pony show for fifty minutes" or put together "a great looking box full of tests, lesson plans, and credentials" that doesn't reflect what "students experience with a teacher every day." Other problems with the merit bonus also arose. Eligibility requirements were often written closely parallel to the current salary system based on experience, degrees, and college credit hours, limiting the pool of applicants. Awards tended to include all or almost all applicants. Teachers on award committees felt they had to provide evidence to "defend any decision to withhold the bonus" (Hart and Murphy, 1987; Hart and Murphy, 1990b), and informal agreements among teachers often crippled attempts to differentiate. Teachers sometimes decided in advance who would apply for positions, divided bonuses among colleagues after the cash award was distributed, or employed strategies that guaranteed all "deserving" applicants identical scores (four fours and all other scores five—on a scale of one to five—randomly distributed) on evaluation instruments (Amsler et al., 1988; Hart, 1985, 1987, 1990a; Malen and Hart, 1987; Malen, Murphy, and Hart, 1987; teacher interviews, 1989). Supervisors have countered by sanctioning principals and peer evaluators whose ratings are too high or have too narrow a range. Some teachers characterize these strategies as "groveling for dollars."

Problems with merit pay are not unique to Utah, however, nor are they unique to teaching. While the "past decade has seen a boom in 'pay for performance' plans—in schools, the federal government and private companies—. . . many organizations have run into snags putting performance pay into practice." Problems encountered include worker jealousy, indecisive or poorly trained administrators, and an "ubiquitous perception that everyone is excellent or superior. Surveys show that roughly 80% of American workers believe that they are better than the norm. 'We have this American myth, like Lake Wobegon, that everyone's above average' " (Waldman and Roberts, 1988, p. 45). The Utah State Office of Education has taken steps to address problems arising from the merit component of the career ladder. Districts with overly narrow eligibility requirements such as prohibiting teachers without tenure from applying for the bonus currently are being told to revise their plans, a form of probation. Limits are set on the percentage of teachers who apply who can receive the bonus. Additionally, state-sponsored conferences are organized where districts of similar size and makeup can share evaluation instruments and techniques and talk about their plans. While ways can be found to circumvent the most careful regulations through informal agreements and while pro forma and procedural compliance are still a problem, people recognize and are attending to criticisms of this component.

Renewed interest in student outcomes sparked by difficulty with teacher evaluation has spread from the bonus component to other aspects of the career ladder. A focus on outcome accountability for the career ladder in general is receiving increased attention. Evidence of impacts on student achievement, conceived broadly, is now required of all Career Ladder Plans. Student achievement evidence has included such things as standardized and criterion referenced test scores and student products and performances. While educators acknowledge that student achievement "implies norm referenced tests," they are seeking ways to gain some comparability of outcomes without retreating into a too narrow definition of achievement. Teachers participate in the goal setting process in most districts, tying their classroom goals to career ladder activities with increasing frequency. The State Office of Education is also developing a test item bank criterion referenced to the state's core curriculum requirements that eventually will be able to be used as a resource by any district or school. The test item bank, planned as part of a core curriculum initiative, illustrates an increased integration of career ladders with other curriculum and student outcome activities at the state level. Although the achievement of "some equality and comparability" of outcome of measures is one of the greatest challenges facing the career ladders, it is being confronted with increasing openness and energy (Cornett, 1988; Jensen and Denler, 1989).

Job Enlargement / Work Redesign

A work redesign conceptualization of a career ladder includes a series of stable promotional positions characterized by increased salary, expanded influence over the work of others, increasing authority over system-wide decisions, growth-promoting responsibilities, and noticeable differentiation among teachers in status, pay, and tasks. Opportunities for career growth, both horizontal and vertical, are deliberately structured into the organization of work, and teachers can plan career paths to make maximum use of the opportunities they most value for professional growth and renewal (Bacharach, Conley, and Shedd, 1986; Hart, 1987, 1990a). Simultaneously, the organization of tasks, roles, and working relationships is designed to maximize the use of available human resources to accomplish desired outcomes.

This conceptualization of a career ladder was uncommon during the early stages of enactment and implementation in Utah. Legislators and teachers tended to view the reform as "merit pay by another name" or as a way to "get a little money to teachers" by playing "the only game in town" (Hart, 1990a; Hart, Kauchak, and Stevens, 1986; Malen and Hart, 1987). Even the term *work redesign* elicited puzzled expressions from educators, legislators, and parents. Over time, however, the "job enlargement" and "career ladder levels" encompassed within this view of a career ladder have received increasing attention. Governor Scott Matheson was an ardent advocate of promotional steps, and by May 1986 Governor Norman Bangerter had labeled the career ladder the "backbone" of education reform in Utah, a "first step toward restructuring the teaching profession" (*Salt Lake Tribune,* 1986, p. B7). External evaluators and researchers often concurred that the work redesign/job enlargement/restructuring features of the Career Ladder Plans focused on school-wide improvement, and student outcomes stood the greatest chance of having a long-term impact on the quality of teaching and learning in schools (Amsler et al., 1988; Hart, 1987, 1990b; Malen and Hart, 1987; Malen, Murphy, and Hart, 1987). Leaders at the State Office of Education are increasing the emphasis on long-range planning and staff differentiation in their interactions with superintendents and career ladder representatives across the state, including a move toward three-year approval of plans that must now be reviewed and approved annually (Jensen and Denler, 1989).

The idea of career levels and differentiated work assignments for teachers also worried those who remembered the long fight for uniform salary schedules or who feared that the camaraderie of their working environment would be eroded. The uniform salary schedules were developed to protect teachers from ubiquitous salary caprice. In some districts in Utah, male teachers and principals and those with large families were paid more than those who were unmarried or had small families well into the 1960s. People openly worried about competition and jealousy among teachers and their possible effects on cooperation and good feelings in schools. The experiences of teachers in vocational education and sports with differentiated pay opportunities based on expanded roles did not dispel these fears. Equality and civility norms were manifested in numerous interviews and open-ended survey responses (Amsler et al., 1988; Hart, 1986, 1987; Malen and Hart, 1987). The growth of a critical mass of teachers who could establish a norm for change in the schools was an early need and is an ongoing need (Berman and McLaughlin, 1978).

In the general management literature, work redesign refers to "the deliberate, purposeful planning of the job, including any or all of its structural or social aspects" (Umstot, Bell, and Mitchell, 1976, p. 379). Although discussions of the Utah career ladders sometimes distinguish between "job enlargement"—designed to pay teachers for short-term projects and activities in schools that expand work responsibilities, innovate, and accomplish specific, small-scale tasks—and the "ladders"—promotion systems including increased pay through increased work responsibilities and status—these aspects both are consistent with a broader conceptualization of work redesign (Hart, 1990b). A more unified understanding of the Utah career ladders can be achieved by including all components of the ladders under the more extensive definition of work redesign commonly used in other work settings. Using this more inclusive framework, all components of the plans can be examined in unison and their individual and collective impacts better assessed.

A WORK REDESIGN VIEW OF UTAH CAREER LADDERS

A work redesign framework facilitates understanding of Utah career ladders as attempts to affect the effectiveness of work and outcomes of work in schools. This framework, including task structures, moderating variables, and work perceptions serving as the basis for action, provides a useful means for examining the current and potential impacts of Utah's experiment with teacher work and compensation reform on educational outcomes.

The formal structure is only part of this view of work. Although formal structures of work (like the curriculum development systems, teacher leader jobs, or mentors' tasks common in career ladders) have been found to be the most influential factors affecting performance and attitudes in research on work redesign, many outcomes are independent of objective job characteristics. A number of variables moderate relationships between work structure, perceptions, and outcomes. Scholars often investigate factors intervening between the structures of work and people's perceptions of its nature and significance that guide their actions. Work structures are judged and interpreted through information cues in the social system (school, district, and environment), teachers' and principals' individual differences, and various group differences. The resulting perceived career ladder work characteristics may differ significantly from objective features of the new work and among teachers and schools. The framework illustrated in Figure 2 combines three elements of work design and their interactions to help explain a work redesign view of school reform: work structures, moderating variables, and perceived work characteristics.

The effects of these three elements of work redesign are multidirectional. Information and judgments about the desirability and appropriateness of career ladder structures affect all stages of work design and redesign. Multidirectional and interaction effects are important components of the eventual outcomes and are illustrated in the figure with arrows.

Teacher Work Structures

Utah's career ladders alter the structure of the work year, the kind of tasks performed by different people in schools, responsibility and interaction patterns, supervision, and pay. All this structural change aims to improve teaching and learning. Theories of work redesign and empirical studies of work redesign provide insight into emerging outcomes of this structural reform. One important model applied to the design of work is the job-characteristics model.

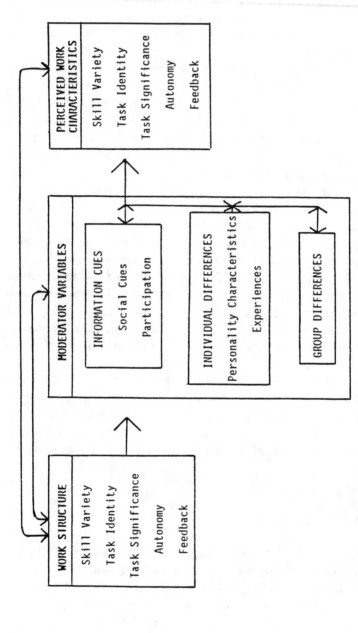

FIGURE 2 Work redesign framework. Source: Hart, A. W. 1990b. "Work Redesign: A Review of Literature for Education Reform," in *Advances in Research in the Management of Schools*, S. Bacharach, ed., Greenwich, CT: JAI Press.

Job-Characteristics Model

Much of the research on work structures tests, replicates, and expands the job-characteristics model developed by Hackman and his
colleagues (Hackman and Lawler, 1971; Hackman and Oldham, 1980).
It also explores effects of task interdependence and organizational constraints on job structures and their outcomes. In this model, job dimensions are hypothesized to affect critical psychological states associated
with high levels of internal motivation, satisfaction, and quality of performance. The five core dimensions of work affecting psychological
states in the job-characteristics model are skill variety, task identity,
task significance, autonomy, and feedback. The critical psychological
states are meaningfulness (resulting from skill variety, task identity,
and task significance), knowledge of results (resulting from feedback),
and experienced responsibility (resulting from autonomy). Individual
differences—in skill, knowledge, and, particularly, need for professional growth or achievement—moderate the potential of job characteristics for influencing work behavior and attitudes.[1] A linear relationship resulting in a motivating potential score (MPS) for a job is the
central feature of the model (see Figure 3). *Skill variety* describes the
need for many different skills to accomplish tasks. *Task identity* involves the completion of a whole task or piece of work. *Task significance* is the degree to which a job affects other people or their jobs
in the school, district, or community. *Autonomy* is freedom, independence, and discretion in scheduling and carrying out work assignments, and *feedback* is information on performance provided by the job
itself.

While the job-characteristics model undergoes continual refinement
and investigation, the relationship of career ladders' features to the mo-

```
skill      task        task
variety + identity + significance  X   autonomy   X   feedback  =>
              3


                          EXPERIENCED   KNOWLEDGE  = tested
   MEANINGFULNESS          AUTONOMY     OF RESULTS     MPS


(Job Characteristics => Psychological States = MPS)
```

FIGURE 3 Job-characteristics model.

tivating potential of these reforms can be important evidence of their incentive power for various groups (Hart, 1990b). Evidence of the potency of reforms whose aim is consistent with the concept of work embodied in the model is mounting. For example, an extensive external evaluation of Utah career ladders (including a random sample of teachers and principals across the state and case studies of twelve districts), a policy report compiled from multiple case studies, surveys, and institutional reports, and individual research projects over the last five years identify issues congruent with the model (Amsler et al., 1988; Hart, 1987; Hart and Murphy 1987, 1988, 1990a; Malen and Hart, 1987; Malen, Murphy, and Hart, 1988). These findings point to conceptual consistency between the new structures and skill variety, task identity, task significance, autonomy, and feedback, regardless of the specific mathematical relationship among the elements, in several ways.

First, the opportunity to acquire new knowledge and experience is repeatedly identified by participants as a major advantage of roles that expand or enlarge work. This feature provides a lateral growth opportunity and the skill variety identified as critical in work and career development literature as well as ladder promotions (Bacharach, Conley, and Shedd, 1986; Hackman and Oldham, 1980). Participants value the personal growth they experience, the contributions they make to their schools, and the chance to self-select in and out of extra responsibilities depending on their individual circumstances. Other work settings also have been found to benefit from short-term entrepreneurial projects and additional compensation for quality work. Because opportunities for hierarchical mobility always will be limited by the number of top positions available in any organization, stimulating, short-term assignments will be worthwhile (Kanter, 1983).

This element is not without its problems. Poor articulation of the relationship of projects and tasks to the core work of the school—teaching and learning—and retreat into conventional activities redefined and renamed as career ladders to avoid the censure of peers has resulted in accusations that many tasks and activities undertaken under career ladder sponsorship are "Mickey Mouse," "busy work," or "redundant." Adherence to career ladder regulations from the State Office of Education then sinks to the level of "pro forma" or "procedural" compliance or completely breaks down (Amsler et al., 1988). However, careful attention to task identity and task significance *at each school site* could go far in alleviating these problems, particularly if the importance of the tasks to the work and performance of others is high and clearly understood. Where these connections are made and widely recognized, career ladder participants and their colleagues have praised the contributions of the new roles to the overall quality of teaching and learning in their schools (Hart, 1986, 1987, 1990a; Hart, Kauchak, and Stevens, 1986; Hart and Murphy, 1990a; Murphy and Hart, 1988). While personal development for career ladder teachers is critical to tap recruitment or retention advantages, the contribution of the new roles to the good of the whole appears to be a vital component of their social acceptance in schools (Hart, 1987; Hart and Murphy, 1990a).

Second, when teachers accrue more decision-making authority over professional issues in schools, their autonomy and the significance of their work for others increase. Professional autonomy and task significance are enhanced for those in the new authority roles. They have more freedom, independence, and discretion in scheduling and carrying out work assignments and more effect on other people or their jobs in the school, district, or community. Mentors and supervisors have an impact on new members of the profession; teacher leaders affect curriculum, materials, methods, task structures, schedules, student assignments, and class organization (Amsler et al., 1988; Hart, 1987; Hart and Murphy, 1987).

The career ladder levels are more likely to include these multifaceted career opportunities, and they have been slow to develop in the Utah plans. Early data from survey and case studies suggested that the ladder levels were less popular with teachers than were the short-term job enlargement tasks. They violated equality norms more openly and directly than did job enlargement. However, teachers complained that the ladders were "step ladders. You step up and you step down." They had difficulty giving up their part-time supplemental employment, fearing that long-range family income could not be dependent on career ladders when "you fall off every two years" (Hart, 1987; Hart and Murphy, 1987). "For all I know, it will disappear anyway next year, but I'll still be working here with these people" (Amsler et al., 1988, p. 32). Over time, teacher opinions of these roles seem to be evolving. In 1987, a comprehensive state-wide survey found that the job enlargement component was judged less useful than the career ladder levels component by teachers (Amsler et al., 1988, p. 108). Principals, however, may have difficulty accepting permanent and powerful leadership positions for teachers. In the same survey and by a much wider margin, they labeled the ladder levels less useful than the job enlargement tasks.

Case studies may offer some insight into teachers' growing support for career ladder levels. Hart and Murphy (1990a) and Murphy and Hart (1988) found that teachers condemned tasks and roles that had little or distant relevance for their core responsibilities associated with teaching and learning. The job assignments of teachers appointed for several years were more permanent and more likely to be well-integrated into the routine work and clearly understood goals of the school. Amsler et al. (1988) found that only two of the twelve districts they studied in depth had achieved "substantial benefits" from the ladder levels. "In these, teachers and administrators are carefully scrutinizing requirements for each level to ensure that the distinctions do reflect increasing work responsibilities and proof of sustained excellence" (p. 131). Where "subversion" was the case, the "Career Ladder Component is the one that can be made to look very much like step and lane awards" (p. 130). Thus, teachers may be making sense of their experiences with career ladders through their commitment to their work over time, even when differentiation, unfamiliar and difficult to accept, makes them uncomfortable and requires a serious rethinking of their expectations and careers. When connections between the new work and the core goals of the school are made, reformers avoid many pitfalls of top-down structural redesign. As Fenstermacher (1978) points out, one must transform behavior rather than simply persuade or command.

> To have a "transformation" effect rather than a "conversion" effect on teachers . . . all evidence offered to teachers as an inducement to change their beliefs and practices . . . must be related to the "subjectively reasonable" beliefs teachers already have, in order to make them more "objectively reasonable." . . . The conversion schema . . . merely ignores teacher beliefs or tramples upon them on its way to writing mandates and interdicts. (pp. 174–175)

An additional explanation for teacher support for tasks and roles that contribute visibly to school-wide teaching and learning can be found in studies designed to test the job-characteristics model. The model relies on the creation of critical psychological states through task design — meaningfulness, knowledge of results, and responsibility. Walsh, Taber, and Beehr (1980) point out that task identity (measured by the Job Diagnostic Survey) may be a summary of each individual's evaluation of the meaningfulness of the job rather than an assessment of the ability to complete a whole piece of work. Meaningfulness, tying new roles to valued outcomes, may relate task identity to task significance and substantially affect judgments about the worth of the new roles.

A third link between the job-characteristics model and Utah career ladders is also related to critical psychological states and can be found in the increasing importance of teacher evaluation, task completion, and student outcomes associated with the career ladders in Utah. While improvements in teacher evaluation are possible without work redesign, the demands of promotion and reward structures associated with the career ladders have increased attention on the processes of teaching and on student outcomes and have provided resources for improvements in feedback and evaluation (Amsler et al., 1988; Jensen and Denler, 1989). Knowledge of results is enhanced, and teachers are more responsible for their work (and often for peer evaluations). Certainly, evidence that evaluations sometimes are subverted is prevalent (Malen, Murphy, and Hart, 1987), but teachers, principals, and district and state leaders continue to emphasize the role of the new structures in providing feedback to teachers about their work and in linking that feedback to student outcomes. As teachers work more closely together in new structural arrangements, the feedback they receive from each other will be on a routine basis and will be tied more closely to the work itself.

A final tie between the career ladders in Utah and the job-characteristics model of work redesign is related to growth need strength, the most powerful moderating variable identified in the research. While this factor has a significant influence over the motivating potential of a job structure in the model, it describes an individual difference among the people doing the work and will be discussed in that context in the following section on moderating variables.

The job-characteristics model can be used to more comprehensively analyze progress toward the integration of career ladder structures into the fundamental work of schools and to decrease the retreat to pro forma and procedural implementation that occurred early in the program in Utah (Amsler et al., 1988). This integration is vital, otherwise "isolated, in segmentalist fashion, and not allowed to touch other parts of the organization's structure and culture," the "innovation will never take hold, fade into disuse, or produce a lower level of benefits than it potentially could" (Kanter, 1983, p. 299). For example, for some time teachers and principals have described "regular" evaluation processes and "career ladder" evaluation as separate and distinct. One teacher recently remarked that she was just observed and evaluated twice in one week—once by the principal for her "regular" evaluation and once by a peer observer for her "career ladder performance bonus." Observers and committees were asked to distribute career ladder positions and bonuses tabula rasa, without contamination by other sources of information. Additionally, the conceptual distinction between isolation and autonomy is not clear in education.

Integration will require a new equilibrium or consensus about the meaning of autonomy. Some researchers warn that the autonomy/equality/civility norms in schools are violated by work redesign (Lortie, 1975; Malen, Murphy, and Hart, 1987). Yet studies in all kinds of work populations, including professionals and managers, differentiate autonomy from the isolation common to teachers. Autonomy in other professional settings includes control over the time, decisions, important resources, and information necessary to accomplish the work. Isolation, increasingly described as dysfunctional (Little, 1982), is not equivalent. For decades, organizational analysts have argued that integration, interdependence, and collaboration increasingly will characterize work as expertise and the complexity of work problems increase (Bennis, 1967). Schools are not immune to these trends. New knowledge about learning disabilities, individual learning styles, and diverse instructional techniques join conceptualizations of "student as worker" (Sizer, 1985) and the teaching of "critical thinking skills" (Cohen, 1988) as expectations for education in the 21st century. The "egg carton school" will not suffice in meeting these needs for integration.

Interdependence, Collaboration, and Integration

The increasing need to accommodate interdependence also is addressed by structural analyses of job characteristics. One of the five core features of work in the job-characteristics model, task significance (see Figure 3), acknowledges the effects of one job on other jobs in a school. The statement that third grade reading teachers depend on the quality of reading instruction in the first grade is painfully obvious. But teaching work proceeds in relative isolation as though no such interdependence existed. Not only are teachers dependent on the successful completion of the work of other teachers and of "students as workers," they are dependent on the social and economic environments of the schools in which they work. Task interdependence often is defined as a connection between jobs in which the performance of one person depends on the successful performance of others (Kiggundu, 1983). Teaching fits this definition.

Experienced responsibility, a critical psychological state in the job-characteristics model, provides the conceptual link between interdependence, work restructuring, and autonomy. People experience responsibility for their work as a function of both interdependence and autonomy. These features may seem contradictory, but actually they function in concert. Two main characteristics of task interdependence in work design explain the harmony in this apparent contradiction. First, task interdependence does not erode autonomy. When people feel responsible for the performance of others, it can contribute to efficacy, the belief that one's efforts will have an impact on one's own and others' work outcomes. And autonomy makes people feel more responsible for their own work (Brass, 1981; Kiggundu, 1983). Second, interdependence causes chain reactions when work is redesigned in schools. It creates new roles, responsibilities, tasks, and authority structures. People feel responsible for their own and others' success. Those who supervise teachers also are affected. The work of immediate supervisors is profoundly altered when the work of those they supervise is redesigned. Tinkering with teachers' work will affect principals' work. Even in the very early stages of career ladders in Utah when work redesign was a nascent concept, principals experienced changes in their work and predicted far-reaching impacts in the future. Principals who interpreted new roles as a human resource for the improvement of schools applauded the reform. Those who interpreted the changes as a threat to their legitimate authority found formal and informal ways to limit its impact (Hart, Kauchak, and Stevens, 1986).

The interaction of autonomy, interdependence, responsibility, and meaningfulness influences the incentive power of new structures of teaching work for the purpose of recruitment, retention, and performance enhancement. Teachers are accustomed to working alone, isolated from each other. They ignore their interdependence although they readily acknowledge the accumulation of student knowledge and the impact of the social and intellectual environment in which children live and learn. However, Utah teachers working in career ladder assignments describe deep satisfaction from helping other teachers, contributing to teaching and learning in their schools, and personal growth (Hart, 1987, 1990a; Malen and Hart, 1987).

This newfound enthusiasm is purchased at a price. Increased interdependence and collaboration have their problems as well as their benefits. The transition period, when opportunities presented by career ladders are available only to limited numbers of a work force accustomed to no differentiation among teachers, strains the egos and professional commitment of those not appointed to the new roles. The new corps, young people entering the profession, takes its chances for promotion. The existing corps sometimes experiences promotion as favoritism. After five years with career ladders in Utah, some school faculties were still "seriously divided" with the "40% not on the career ladder" seeking ways to eliminate it and the "60% of teachers on the career ladder strongly in favor of keeping it. This means a lot of money and influence for some teachers." Those who are dependent on others in their work or who do not initiate interdependence (teachers supervised by teacher leaders or mentor teachers) are less satisfied with their work than those they depend on. Teachers not in career ladder roles often oppose the differentiation, peer supervision, and vulnerability of their new work arrangements (Lipsky, 1976). Principals describe some resolute opponents as "vehement," "fundamentally opposed to any differentiation among teachers as a matter of principle" (principal interviews, 1989).

The Organizational Environment for Redesign

Internal and external environmental characteristics form a final major feature of work structure critical to this discussion of work redesign in schools. Although most studies provide more evidence for a "within-person, cognitive consistency model than for a person-situation theory of task design" (Roberts and Glick, 1981, p. 204), the relationship of teachers' tasks to the school environment is important to understanding school reform.

One environmental factor in teacher work restructuring is resource availability (Mitchell, 1986; Peters and O'Connor, 1980). Resources both constrain and shape reform. The resources identified in research on work include 1) information; 2) materials, supplies, or clients; 3) budget; 4) human support service; 5) training or knowledge; 6) time; 7) physical work environment and space; 8) tools and equipment; and 9) authority. All these resources exist in schools and affect the work of teachers. In many cases their scarcity disrupts teaching and limits learning (Lipsky, 1976).

Resource constraints pose a particular challenge to Utah's career ladders. Without the necessary resources to sustain the basic effort, redesigned work is unlikely to improve education substantially. Utah faces a challenging future with the highest investment in education per taxpayer in the nation and the highest teacher/pupil ratios in the nation. Lipsky (1976) argues that teachers will have little or no energy or commitment to devote to rethinking and reorganizing their work if they lack the basic resources to do well what they are already expected to do. While current resources could be redistributed to create a more attractive work structure and increase teacher career growth opportunities (Mitchell, 1986), continued attention to the resource environment in education is necessary to protect reforms.

A second feature of the organizational environment, widespread comfort with the status quo, also affects the success of work redesign. The almost universal experience people have with schools as they are now structured poses a major limitation. Universal public education translates into universal inertia. Many people ask, "Why should schools differ substantially from the schools we graduated from? We've done all right. Our education prepared us for responsible and productive citizenship." Parents recognize and are comfortable with schools as now structured.

Familiarity is a seductive trap. Scholars find that society by and large is willing to trade dramatic, though uncertain, performance for predictable, though mediocre, performance from its institutions (Hannan and Freeman, 1984). Schools seeking the capacity to respond quickly to changing needs and demands must compete with those that emphasize reliability and accountability (Freeman, 1982; Hannan and Freeman, 1980). Alterations in the design of work may improve performance dramatically but make the outcomes less reliable and less controllable. This tension between immediate and long-range purposes, between reform and preservation goals of schooling, is characteristic of America's relationship with its schools throughout its history (Hofstadter and Metzger, 1955). The alternative perspective chronicles mounting pressures to prepare for continuous change (Bennis, 1967).

The inertia facing career ladders in Utah is evident in the selection criteria often used for new teacher roles and bonuses. Initially, schools typically promoted from within and offered seniority based rewards. In the career ladders studied by Hart (1986b; 1987) and Hart and Murphy (in press) all attempts to open jobs to teachers outside a school, even *within the district,* were blocked, limiting access to promotional opportunities. While promotions continue to be from within, bonuses are more broadly distributed. Some observers pointed out that continued insistence on narrow eligibility for rewards and an emphasis on seniority jeopardized the reform in Utah. But the opposite situation also is a problem. As probationary teachers are added to the pool of eligible applicants and more and more established teachers see that the bonuses are widely awarded, more teachers receive bonuses, and they become smaller and smaller.

Leadership is a third organizational factor influencing the success of educational work redesign. Superintendents, principals, and policymakers are capable of crippling a redesign initiative by promoting "vanishing effects" rather than "sustaining effects" (Malen and Hart, 1987). Many approaches to teacher work redesign neglect supervision, although supervisors play several important roles (Cordery and Wall, 1985). They provide salient information, shaping the views of others (Smircich, 1983). This function is discussed at length in the moderating variables section that follows. Their influence also is apparent in other areas. They may 1) fail to follow through on efforts that heighten teachers' expectations; 2) be unwilling to reduce supervision and materially increase teachers' influence in critical decisions; 3) fail to reduce turnover, making it difficult for the redesigned and enlarged work to be effectively executed and promoting the return to convention and familiar practice; 4) fail to contend with the expansion of teachers' work and their increased power in schools; and 5) yield to pressures for greater predictability and closer supervision (Hart, 1990b). Failing to recognize that leadership can be an organizational characteristic and resource, principals and other administrators may view increased power and opportunity for teachers as a threat to their own authority (Ogawa and Bossert, 1989).

These problems with leadership appeared in Utah. For example, some principals were unable to manage or even to adjust to new power and work relationships with lead teachers. Their responses to work redesign influenced the effect of new structures on the goal accomplishment, quality, and adaptibility of schools (Hart, Kauchak, and Stevens, 1986; Hart and Murphy, 1990a; Murphy and Hart, 1988). District and state leaders often focused on tight regulation, control, and process evaluation rather than on growth opportunities and student outcomes, resulting in a retreat to pro forma and procedural compliance with the law (Amsler et al., 1988; Bacharach, Conley, and Shedd, 1986; Cornett, 1986; Malen, Murphy, and Hart, 1987).

These three aspects of organizational structure—job characteristics, interdependence, and the organizational environment—demonstrate both the complexity and the potential benefits of work redesign. In spite of limitations, redesigning may be well worth the effort.

Bacharach and Conley (1986, pp. 12-13) make the argument for education:

> . . . [I]n education, we never appropriately design the jobs of teachers, and rarely specify what it is they do in their jobs. Therefore, we spend disproportionate amounts of time . . . appraising the *individual* rather than evaluating the *task.* . . . Contemporary management recognizes that workers *must* have opportunities to develop themselves and must have a sense of career movement. . . . A genuine career development system, concerned with the development of professionals . . . would have as its primary concern the expansion of teacher skills, and with promotion would come further opportunities for teachers to expand their skills.

Moderator Variables

While the thrust of most reform commission reports is structural, social and psychological factors at each work site (social information, individual differences, and group differences — see Figure 2) moderate the outcomes of work redesign. Comparative case studies of schools implementing identical career ladder structures are congruent with findings of work design research in many work settings identifying critical moderating variables (Shaw, 1980). The structure provides only the foundation of reform.

Scholars of organizational behavior have accumulated evidence over many years that the social environment and the work group influence outcomes of work redesign, regardless of the objective features of the work itself. Barnard (1938), Merton (1957), Argyris (1957), Bennis (1967), French (1969), and others argue in classic exposes on human behavior in organizations that personality and the human organization shape the performance of the structural organization. The importance of human interpretations and of belief and culture in schools has received increasing attention from scholars and practitioners in recent years (Bolman and Deal, 1984; Deal and Kennedy, 1982; Meyer and Rowan, 1977).

Many human resource factors intervene between structure and outcomes. It cannot be shown that "task attributes are mutually exclusive, collectively exhaustive, and universally salient" (Griffin, 1983, p. 186). Differences among teachers and principals and between schools molded responses to the career ladders in Utah schools in isolation of the objective structural features of the plans (Adler, Skov, and Salvemini, 1985; Hart and Murphy, 1990a). Moderating variables identified included 1) the information cues sent and received at each school site, 2) individual differences, and 3) group differences (see Figure 2).

Information Cues

One critical moderating variable shaping the success of a new work structure, information cues, operated in the implementation of Utah's career ladders. Cues to which teachers and principals responded came from the public media, the legislature, principals, superintendents, teachers' associations, and individual teachers. These cues often conflicted, and the relative importance of each referent group to the individual teacher shaped their impact.

Social Cues

While task structure affects job attitudes, motivation, and performance more than do social cues, the influence of cues from the social environment is important enough to shape the ultimate success or failure of a work reform program (Griffin, 1982; Vance and Biddle, 1985). Cues are strong determiners of people's attitudes about work, including teaching. ". . . [P]eople deciding on their careers pay attention to what the society tells them" (Pierpont, 1989). This human factor—called social cues, social meaning, or social information processing (SIP) in the general work literature—deserves more attention than it currently is receiving from education reformers. Social cues function at many levels, from national policy arenas to the school. Although social information is a critical school site factor amenable to direct human resource intervention, legislation in Utah expressly forbids any expenditure of career ladder funds for implementation, training, or human resource intervention (Jensen and Denler, 1989; Malen, Murphy, and Hart, 1987). All funds must be distributed directly to teachers. "There is a feeling here that organizational development money is wasted money." While it maximizes the salary impacts of the career ladders, this policy ignores the high likelihood of failure of work redesign in the absence of carefully planned implementation and socialization strategies (Hackman and Oldham, 1980).

Social information processing has long been of interest to organizational behavior scholars. Research predicts and career ladder data affirm that teachers, principals, and students evaluate information relevant to school reform according to personal relevance, using people similar to themselves for comparison (Hart, 1987, 1990a; Salancik and Pfeffer, 1978). In schools, this information came from 1) individual perceptions and judgments of the desirability of the new roles and tasks in schools; 2) information from the social context about appropriate attitudes; and 3) self-perception, mediated by attributions explaining their past behavior as educators (Salancik and Pfeffer, 1978).

Examples from case studies illustrate the impacts of information in schools processed from these three sources. A new role common to many career ladders is that of peer supervisor or mentor. Clinical supervision and other observation techniques are being used in many districts in Utah. In one district, where clinical supervision was touted as a way to improve feedback to new teachers for their professional development, two extreme attitudes existed in different schools. These judgments—1) that peer supervision was a wonderful means to get help, a "resource pool within [the school's] own faculty focused on improvement of the entire school" or 2) that "a mentor can also be a tormentor" and peer supervision caused "dissension, pain, and anguish"—prevailed once they developed, in spite of identical training for lead teachers throughout the district and very similar job descriptions at the different schools. By the end of the first year of the career ladder, teachers clamored for more observation visits in one school and paralyzed the teacher supervisors in another (Hart, 1990a).

In these and other districts and schools, some lead teachers learned that they should keep quiet about their work, that it was inappropriate to openly support the career ladder, that advocacy of the structure by promoted teachers was seen as self-serving. Although proud of the quality of their work and their contributions to instruction, curriculum, and special programs in the schools, they described how they "downplayed their jobs" in lunchroom conversation, denigrated the importance of what they had done, and, like good students ashamed of their grades, concealed their hard work and accomplishments. These teachers said they often felt compelled to "explain" why they had applied for career ladder roles, often using short-term financial need as an excuse (Hart and Murphy, 1987, 1990a). Peers who accused teachers in new roles of "exalting themselves above other teachers" or "kissing up to the administration" (Hart, 1986, 1990a; Malen and Hart, 1987) provided clear social cues to those who ventured to change. Where these statements were repeated often, teacher attitudes about the redesigned work deteriorated.

Yet another source of information that influenced teachers' interpretations of career ladder roles was their self-perception and a need to affirm their past behavior. A prevalent belief that the reform was temporary, yet another fad "imposed on teachers by the legislature," and a loyalty to the belief that "all teachers are equal" made many teachers and principals reluctant to commit much emotional or intellectual energy to the career ladders (Hart, Kauchak, and Stevens, 1986). One adamant opponent to the whole concept said that career ladders violated "everything that attracted me to teaching in the first place" and that differentiation would "destroy the camaraderie and sharing" that characterized the profession. Others pointed out that they had left employment in business expressly to get away from the competition and backstabbing they experienced there (Hart, 1990a). While many teachers said they were making plans to prepare for career ladder positions in the future and applications for career ladder roles and bonuses has increased (Hart and Murphy, 1990a; interviews, 1989), discomfort with the implicit criticism of their past career choices implied by their participation continues.

The impact of social information processing is common during work redesign and is not unique to education. Hackman and Oldham (1980) point out that early discomfort with new job configurations, even for those who approve the changes and help design them, can contribute to the "vanishing effect" — small incremental changes designed to make people more comfortable but capable of returning the work gradually to its earlier forms. Pfeffer and Lawler (1980) suggest that work attitudes may be as much a result of past behavior, serving to justify or explain choices, as they are a cause of behavior. Once committed to a job people describe the rewards they value in terms congruent with available rewards and their past decision to accept them. Once committed to remaining in a job, they argue, people unconsciously rationalize their decision by developing attitudes consonant with their behavior.

Vivid, timely, and compelling information can profoundly alter, even overwhelm, work restructuring. Because belief change accompanying work redesign is inversely proportional to the amount of prior information accumulated (Blau and Katerberg, 1982), teachers with long experience in the current form of work, good memories of their own student days, and familiarity with the long-lived institution called school face a major challenge. When teachers, principals, and others involved in work restructuring activities accumulate experience based information that overwhelms a "logical" analysis of potential benefits from new structures, the implementation of reform can be crippled. As scholars point out (Blau and Katerberg, 1982; Fenstermacher, 1978), changes in attitudes or beliefs about work are a direct function of the discrepancy between currently held beliefs and new information and inversely proportional to the amount of information at the time of change. This aspect of school restructuring reform deserves careful attention from educational leaders. Strong social cues are needed to support constructive perceptions of the new roles and authority relationships in education.

As was pointed out in the preceding discussion of work structures, the active participation of educational leaders in the information processing and sense making attendant to work reform played a major role in its usefulness as a resource for teaching and learning in Utah schools. Articulation of goals and purposes of the new structures — from principals, superintendents, teacher association leaders, and policymakers — appears to be a critical component of their use (Malen and Hart, 1987; Murphy and Hart, 1988). Information cues come from many sources of varying salience to the recipient, and the interpretation of social cues can be a major function of school leaders in work redesign:

> [O]rganizing involves not only the structuring of behaviors, a process that must be continually reaccomplished, . . . but also the structuring of information and meaning, a process that must also be continually reaccomplished. Indeed, what the social psychological experimenter does in the laboratory may be one of the more important tasks of management — making certain information salient and pointing out connections between behaviors and subsequent attitudes . . . creating meaning systems and consensually shared interpretations of events for participants. (Pfeffer and Lawler, 1980, p. 54)

Principals and respected veteran teachers can provide information cues to other educators that actually change their perceptions of the tasks and roles associated with career ladders or other new work structures. Experimental research demonstrates the power of salient information cues. Manipulated information about work from supervisors can explain significant differences in descriptions of jobs and in performance (Green and Novak, 1982; Griffin, 1983; O'Connor and Barrett, 1980).

In Utah, the role of leaders in helping people make sense of the usefulness or uselessness of new structures of work and rewards was quickly apparent (Hart, 1990a; Hart and Murphy, 1987; Malen and Hart, 1987; Murphy and Hart, 1988). Principals were found who interpreted, judged, praised, promoted, and subverted redesigned teacher work. Murphy and Hart (1988) identified significant impacts of principals on the functioning of new structures in schools and responses to changes in authority structures and leadership. Principals responded to shifting demands and role transitions in several ways. Only when they functioned as instructional leader—managing and developing capacity among teachers and focusing discussions on the core technology of the school—or as "chairman of the board"—managing meaning, interpreting new roles, securing resources, and organizing and formalizing tasks and roles—was the fundamental work of schools affected in the perceptions of teachers in those schools.

Coworkers are a vital source of social cues, and teachers provided a major source of information about the potential and legitimacy of the career ladders to other teachers. In research in other settings, people receiving positive rather than negative social cues from coworkers are found to be more satisfied and more productive. In one laboratory study "the comments of coworkers were a more powerful motivating force than the actual properties of the task" (White and Mitchell, 1979, p. 8). Teachers' cues to each other about the desirability of a new role or reward can substantially affect the satisfaction and productivity of promoted teachers. The more frequent, intense, and extended these cues, the more powerful their effect. "[O]n the job, individuals may develop positive or negative feelings about their work due to factors wholly unrelated to any set of work characteristics . . ." (Adler et al., 1985, p. 274; see also Caldwell and O'Reilly, 1982). When career ladder roles are "Mickey Mouse" and bonuses are "groveling for dollars," the meanings are clear.

Conflicting information cues from many levels also muddy teachers' responses to career ladders. While numerous public policy reports describe teaching in less than glowing terms and news reports chronicle a list of ills in the organization of schools, teachers often support the fundamental organization and norms dominating their work, and scholars describe "teaching work" in normative terms (Lortie, 1975). The effects of these conflicting cues cannot be accurately predicted, but their presence and potential influence deserve attention (Blau and Katerberg, 1982; Hogan and Martell, 1987).

Teacher incentive reforms like the Utah career ladders depend for their effectiveness on the assumption that rewards and work structures valued by teachers and potential teachers can be identified, created, and distributed. But the Utah experience and research in other settings suggest that attitudes and behavior are shaped by social information as well as structural design. Current teachers may identify the rewards they have chosen to accept in the past as the rewards they value (Salancik and Pfeffer, 1978; Skinner, 1971). Their reliance on intrinsic, relational rewards could be as much a result of the lack of sufficient extrinsic rewards (or the interaction between insufficient extrinsic rewards and the prevalence of intrinsic rewards) as it is a natural preference.

One final aspect of information processing that played and continues to play an important part in response to the Utah career ladders is broad participation in the design and revision of Career Ladder Plans. The local ownership that resulted from participation is credited with much of the success of the career ladders in the districts (Cornett, 1988). Indeed, it has been described as "the absolute difference between success and failure." Much of the literature exploring the impact of information cues in work redesign focuses on participation in the process by those who perform the work (Strauss, 1977), and participative management is highly praised aspect of many education reform structures (Pierpoint, 1989). Jans (1985, p. 394) states:

> People will tend to become involved in their jobs if they can participate in decision making in the work group and if they are doing work which matches their self-images. This requires managers who are willing and able to share authority with their subordinates. . . .

And teacher union leaders praise the reforms implementing school based management for involving "teachers directly in the improvement of schools," emulating practice in the "best businesses," and treating teachers as "decision makers" (Shanker, 1989).

But experimental manipulations of participation during work redesign fail to validate participation's long-term impacts (Griffeth, 1985). Participation does affect overall satisfaction and early perceptions of the quality of new job features, but effects are short-term and limited to immediate participants (Seeborg, 1978). These findings mirror comments of teachers about the increased authority of some of their peers promoted under Career Ladder Plans. While some teachers approved that "at least a few teachers [were] more involved in decision making," others criticized the "new oligarchy of teacher leaders and principals" created by the new system and perceived no benefit to teachers as a group when some teachers accrued more power (Hart and Murphy, 1990a).

A variety of explanations have been offered for findings about participation effects that appear to conflict. Short-term jobs with little importance to those doing them (the object of most experimental research) may lack salience for participants (Jans, 1985). The level of political maneuvering associated with the decisions may also contribute to the effects. Teacher work redesign that affects core values and norms may require participation, at least in the formative stages. On the other hand, if the changes are trivial or the features of the work that are changed are a matter of indifference to teachers (Hoy and Rees, 1974), participation will have little effect. Because of its inconsistent outcomes, participation is sometimes labeled an ideological, rather than a practical, issue (Locke and Schweiger, 1979). In a strongly worded defense of participatory decision making, Sashkin (1986) calls it "an ethical imperative." It functions very much in this role in Utah. However, if lack of participation stimulates resistance, disruption, and intransigence in the early stages of education reform, its political and practical importance should not be overlooked. Others may expect too much from participation. In Dade County, Florida, enthusiasts predicted that school based management in which they "really involve everybody" in decisions and "develop a sense of ownership" would result in "radical" changes (Shanker, 1989).

The ownership that develops when widespread participation is used as a device to promote early acceptance of school reform also carries with it liabilities. In Utah, participation led to early acceptance and institutionalization within a few years. Those who sought ongoing improvement aimed at student outcomes within the new system see dangers in this rapid institutionalization. "My greatest fear is that they've owned bad practice, and the mood to make change is [now] missing, . . . locking people in." Ongoing innovation and adaptation are features of healthy and effective school organizations, and a too vigorous defense of plans once designed limits the ability of school districts to continue to adapt their work and reward structures when they are found to be inappropriate. So much effort has gone into the design and implementation of the plans that relatively little energy has been devoted to modifying or changing them as flaws are uncovered. Many teachers are unaware of significant adaptations to career ladders (Hart and Murphy, 1990a). Instead, people have begun to defend "their" plans. Consequently, concerted effort from the State Office of Education is now directed toward encouraging assessment and adaptation (Jensen and Denler, 1989).

Individual Differences among Teachers, Potential Teachers, and Principals

Individual differences among people confound the basic assumptions of teacher work redesign (O'Connor and Barrett, 1980; Schneider,

1985), but they also stimulate the original interest in reforms as teacher incentives. To attract a larger percentage of the target population of young people to teaching careers, policymakers and educators depend on the appeal of work and reward features they can manipulate (Murphy, Hart, and Walters, 1989). The effects of a variety of these differences among people on work preferences are examined in research. Individual differences studied in association with work redesign tend to fall into two interactive categories: 1) personality/disposition and 2) work experiences.

Personality

Personal differences affecting response to the design of work are diverse. They include growth need strength, field independence, self-esteem, age, income, job and organizational tenure, education, urban or rural origin, current urban or rural setting, Protestant work ethic, anomie, expectancy and valence, general mental ability, need for achievement, self-actualization, need for autonomy, need for affiliation, locus of control, and authoritarianism (Blood and Hulin, 1967; Hulin and Blood, 1968; Gangster, 1980; O'Connor and Barrett, 1980; Thomas and Griffin, 1983; Vecchio, 1980; White, 1978).

The most powerful and consistent of these characteristics is growth need strength. This characteristic includes measures of higher order need for achievement and for personal and professional growth. Other characteristics moderate responses to work design, but their impacts are interactive. For example, general ability level is a desired trait in the target population of teachers, but organizational constraints have a more detrimental effect on high-ability individuals, thereby obscuring ability–performance relationships (Peters and O'Connor, 1980). Work features that lessen dysfunctional turnover (or attract desirable employees) must affect both satisfaction (present-oriented attitudes about the current work) and attraction/expected utility (future-oriented judgments of work) for present and alternative roles (Mobley, Griffeth, Hand, and Meglino, 1979). Longitudinal studies of work redesign suggest that a job designed to mesh well with current personality and individual situations may be very different from the kind of job desirable in the future (Brousseau, 1978). However, researchers have found significant relationships between adolescent traits and job attitudes and career and job satisfaction at varying stages of adult life (Quinn and Staines, 1979; Staw, Bell, and Clausen, 1986; Staw and Ross, 1985).

The continued strength of individual differences in shaping attitudes toward work structures in research on work redesign ratifies the belief that teaching work can be designed to attract and retain a larger proportion of those who possess desired individual traits. The design of teaching and school structures to promote improved performance must be followed by the testing of the attraction of features of these plans for target populations of current and prospective teachers. This task lies ahead in Utah as well as in other states, however. The challenge can be met in a variety of ways.

First, although individual differences traditionally have been measured for research purposes using psychological instruments, this process may be unnecessarily elaborate in everyday practice. Performance and satisfaction have been linked to job enrichment, and desire for enriched work significantly moderates this outcome relationship. Administrators and supervisors may simply ask how much responsibility, autonomy, or participation someone would like in his/her work rather than being concerned with growth need strength, need for self-actualization, or other abstract personality measures (Cherrington and England, 1980). Researchers might identify the kind of student educators they wish to attract to teaching and ask them the same questions to augment psychometric research.

Second, because preference and choice are central features of the individual differences/work design link, the exploitation of individual differences applied to the recruitment and retention of teachers requires more variance in task structures and work opportunities (Bacharach and Conley, 1986). Wide variety currently is not the reality in most Utah career ladders or in other school restructuring reforms. Major differentiation of tasks and roles and public knowledge of these differences is just developing. Satisficing (accomplishing the minimum necessary to satisfy), pro forma and procedural compliance, and conventional behavior could cripple any potential recruitment benefit from work restructuring.

Finally, task changes must be visible and significant. Another dynamic observed in Utah emanated from a lack of substantial task changes. These reforms (including those in other parts of the country) often alter governance structures but not work structures. While work redesign includes all human and structural aspects of the work, participation in decision-making processes is a very small portion of the total option of choices for reform. For example, in Utah, much talk of "paying teachers more for what they are now doing" circulates. The prevalence of this practice and tacit approval of this goal are apparent in interviews, case studies, and survey evaluations. Teachers (73.0 percent) and principals (87.3 percent) agree or strongly agree that the job enlargement component of the career ladders is "an effective incentive for teachers to . . . be paid for work they once did for no pay" (Amsler et al., 1988, p. 37). Teachers see the tasks provided by short-term jobs as ancillary to their careers, interesting but not central to their concept of work. They also see the financial rewards that accompany the ladders as temporary. Providing a telling illustration of the add-on nature of career ladder financial benefits and the still nascent recruitment and retention incentives they offer, one teacher pointed out, "I can't assure my bank that this money will continue, so I'm not able to use it for credit purposes" (Amsler et al., 1988, p. 16).

All these issues are pertinent to the evaluation of education reform as a teacher incentive. Recruitment and retention goals make individual differences important to teacher work redesign. If changes in teachers' roles, authority, and work patterns are meant to appeal to people with specific characteristics, then the impact of restructuring on those possessing the desired traits requires assessment.

Experiences

Work history and life experience also influence work preferences. In the current debate over changes in teaching work and school structure, the established norms and customs of teachers and teaching receive much attention. Acknowledging the importance of experience, some scholars argue that personalities are partly a result of qualitative differences in the work people experience as they move along their career paths (Brousseau, 1978). Research reveals "strong early experience effects on attitudes" (Vance and Biddle, 1985, p. 262). Like personality differences, experiences affect the work features people value and the relative power of changes in work structure to influence their attitudes and performance. As the information processing research suggests, even rewards and work structures that people say motivate them may reflect congruence with available rewards and structures more than inherent differences (Pfeffer and Lawler, 1980). This sense-making process may lead some experienced teachers, after years committed to their profession with few avenues for attainment, to denigrate the importance of new opportunities in order to reduce the dissonance between their decision to remain and the rewards available in the past.

But experience does not completely obscure the role of inherent differences, and many teachers currently abandon the career because their options are limited to administration, exit, or bitterness (Schrag, 1983).

The effects of experience on work attitudes and performance are complex and illustrate the possible need to conceptually and operationally separate recruitment features from retention features when thinking about and assessing teacher reforms. While many experiences shape work attitudes, a few examples from the literature can illustrate the relationships that develop. Longevity in a particular job, longevity in a career field, chronological age, group or isolated work, supervisory experiences, and many other experience factors have been found to influence judgments about work.

Longevity, in a job or in a career, can have a variety of impacts, for instance. Katz (1978) found that the strength of the relationships between the five core job dimensions of the job-characteristics model and satisfaction depends on longevity in the job. For new employees, only task significance was related positively to job satisfaction while autonomy had a strong negative correlation. Other researchers who focus on young people entering a career also emphasize the importance to young workers of feedback from respected and experienced colleagues, knowledge of results, and opportunities to grow and develop in the job (Hall, 1976). Under these circumstances autonomy can be alienating and frustrating. Katz additionally found that

> . . . [G]roups of employees with progressively greater job longevity
> . . . have progressively weaker correlations between job satisfaction and
> the various task dimensions. . . . [A]ll of the task dimension–job satis-
> faction correlations are insignificant and close to zero for employees
> assigned the same job for at least 15 years. (Katz, 1978, p. 213)

Chronological age, too, is related to job satisfaction (Kalleberg and Loscocco, 1983). Older workers tend to be more satisfied.

Research and practice affirm the power of experience and personality to shape work preferences. This knowledge supports the expectation that new structures should affect the recruitment and retention of teachers. The target population, highly qualified and able people, will be more likely to seek opportunities not valued by some teachers and by some prospective teachers, and people considering a teaching career do so in part because of their own experiences as students. Student teachers' responses to work redesign plans support the contention that previous experience influences the decision to teach. They sometimes object to collegial work arrangements:

> I chose teaching because I like being my own boss. I liked [student teaching] because [my cooperating teacher] would leave me alone. I could do what I wanted and this behavior showed that he trusted me. (Hart and Adams, 1986, p. 61)

They also "pay attention to what the society is telling them" about the rewards and importance of their chosen field (Pierpont, 1989).

Because experience is an influential factor in work attitudes and in adjustment to various work configurations, work redesign requires important transitions of people. No matter how productive or farsighted new structures potentially may be, no matter how effectively they promote and improve student learning, the career transitions undergone by those who implement a work restructuring reform will affect attitudes and performance at every school (Van Maanen, 1977; Nicholson, 1984). Role and career transitions, when professional identities are often reframed, occur during any work redesign such as the Utah career ladders. Role transition research, including any changes in employment and job content, and the ongoing experiences of Utah educators with their career ladders provide evidence of the importance of attending to the human resource issues of work role transition (Bacharach, Bamberger, and Conley, 1988; Nicholson, 1984). Teachers and principals undergo major work role transitions during the restructuring of teaching and schools.

Those undergoing transition need accurate information, assistance interpreting role and setting changes, relationships with others who can serve as sounding boards, opportunities to test reality with others in similar roles, and freedom to take action to fill their own needs (Louis, 1980a). Transitions also affect people differently. They can be overstretched, fulfilled, or growing (Oldham and Hackman, 1980). Depending on their career transition state, teachers' and principals' responses to reforms such as the career ladders should differ. When they have weak needs for growth or knowledge or they lack skills needed to meet the demands of new roles, the changes designed to enrich their work could be threatening, and they could feel "pushed or stretched too far by the work. . . ." (Oldham and Hackman, 1980, pp. 263–264). Fulfilled teachers could be satisfied with the responsibilities and challenges of their jobs and have "no particular desire to move upward" (Oldham and Hackman, 1980, p. 264). As one teacher in Florida explained, they might "tend to resent anything that takes [them] away from" classroom preparation and presentation tasks (Pierpont, 1989). These people may require lateral career paths for variety and opportunity (Schein, 1978). Finally, the growing teacher or principal will be one who responds to work by moving into a "growth cycle so stimulated by the enriched nature of their work that they seek even higher levels of responsibility and additional opportunities for on the job learning" (Oldham and Hackman, 1980, p. 265). Without a variety of options and multiple paths, only a few of the career needs of teachers will be met.

Transitions alter organizations as well. As teachers in Utah worked in career ladders, they helped create features of the plans. This evolution took place through the innovative behaviors of those holding the new roles. As they felt their way, they shaped the structure of their work (Hart, 1987, 1990a; Hart and Murphy, 1990a; Nicholson, 1984). New roles and unfamiliar boundaries between roles also were created by career ladders (Latack, 1984), and role ambiguity and role overload common in all substantial career transitions stimulate increased need for assistance. Teachers complained about "administrative work" and "unrealistic expectations and demands." They had no role models and no experience in the new configurations of work and authority to guide their actions.

Feedback played an important part in the success of teachers' transitions and in the personal and role development that occurred as a result. Because veteran employees in transition require high quality and frequent feedback on their potential and performance, feedback for the promoted teachers was a critical need. But feedback for promoted teachers often was shortchanged in Career Ladder Plans. These plans tended to focus on providing supervision and mentors for new teachers. They evaluated veterans only to distribute bonuses or select for positions. Lead and mentor teachers were anxious about their performance (Hart, 1990a; Hart and Murphy, 1987). However, when "teachers and administrators are carefully scrutinizing requirements for . . . *proof* [emphasis added] of sustained excellence" and their expectations "are clear," "districts are realizing substantial benefits from the Ladders" (Amsler et al., 1988, p. 131).

Ambiguity and overload are two side effects of transition during work redesign with which teachers in Utah are coping. Hart (1990a) and Hart and Murphy (1987) found that promoted teachers wondered what to do, even when given elaborate job descriptions, and felt the ambiguity keenly. Overload arose from unrealistic expectations for the new roles from district administrators, principals, and other teachers. Elaborate and unreasonable job descriptions sometimes were written. The perception that reforms were temporary caused additional overload because teachers were reluctant to relinquish their outside jobs (Hart, 1990a; Near, Rice, and Hunt, 1980).

Case studies of schools in Utah revealed some of the dangers of role overload during transitions to career ladders. Somewhat ironically, teachers backed away from career ladder participation in two schools where a work redesign career ladder seemed to enjoy great support. Teachers expended so much effort that they experienced "burnout" in these schools. At the end of the first year, many teachers did not reapply for their positions. Again, an absence of human resource support for the transitions experienced or for the role development necessary for the success of the new structure may have contributed to this outcome (Hart and Murphy, 1990a).

Group Differences

Although the fine distinction between group and individual differences remains cloudy, group membership is a widely studied factor in attitudes toward work. In education reform, teachers' preferences often are offered as evidence that new structures will or will not work. Their effect on responses to work structures is of interest to educators. The norms, expectations, and characteristics of "teachers" form the basis of much of the debate on education reform (Lortie, 1975; Murnane, 1986; Malen, Murphy, and Hart, 1987). Evidence suggests, however, that while members of a profession share a significant number of similar experiences, diverse work attitudes exist within careers (McKelvey and Sekaran, 1977). Greater variance within, rather than between, groups appears to be the rule (Schwab and Cummings, 1976; Ilgen, Campbell, Peters, and Dugoni, 1978; King, 1974), providing additional support for a continued emphasis on work redesign as part of education incentive reform for individuals.

Researchers returned to the work site for insight into the reasons for the strength of within-group differences in attitudes toward work features and found that work attitudes and preferences may primarily be related not to careers or the differences between groups attracted to various careers but to three features of work settings: 1) job properties — the characteristics of everyday tasks, 2) interaction context — characteristics of the day-to-day interpersonal environment of work, and 3) organization policies—characteristics of general rules and standards enforced in each school (Van Maanen and Katz, 1976, p. 602; Katz and Van Maanen, 1976). Work site variables affect desires for responsibility and scope in work more than do career, job category, or membership in the larger organization (Dunham, 1977). Overall work satisfaction and attitudes about work features are linked, then, to role design factors at the school level. Hart and Murphy (1990a) and Hart (1990a) found that differences between schools significantly affected the successful use of career ladders to accomplish instructional goals and promote healthy and effective school organizations. Each school was critical to teacher work reform success. Teachers working under almost identical Career Ladder Plans sometimes voiced contradictory attitudes and very different work behaviors resulted (Hart, 1986, 1990a; Hart and Murphy, 1987).

When they are firmly entrenched, group differences constrain as well as facilitate work redesign. Brief and Downey (1983) found perceptions or "implicit theories" of what the organization is or ought to be as one such contraint on work redesign. Implicit theories may limit the consideration of potentially powerful work structure options and may exist at the societal, career, organizational, or work site levels. One often hears teachers articulate implicit theories: individualized instruction is good; teachers should not evaluate other teachers; uniform salary schedules protect teachers from capricious evaluations; all teachers are equal. These theories do not need to be rational or correct in an objective sense to be powerful.

> The fact that "incorrect" implicit theories may continue to serve a social glue function does not mean that other dysfunctional consequences may not also flow simultaneously to the organization or its members because of the "correctness." . . . In some cases, the more embattled the organization, the greater the organization members' perceived need to preserve the traditional arts. (Brief and Downey, 1983, p. 1079)

Investigations into individual and group differences shed light on some questions unanswered in Utah. Data on the attitudes of teachers tend to be aggregated and summarized without regard to sub-group or individual characteristics of interest to reformers. Simple averages fail to reveal the power of characteristics, values, and norms, in parsimoniously defined sub-groups. Teachers are likely to differ when they enter the profession and at varying career stages. Studies in work redesign do not support the prediction that all teachers will respond to incentives aimed at "average" attitudes, and the deliberate disaffection of teachers in some sub-groups was and continues to be a goal of the reform. Utah data also fail to address the attitudes ot young people in target populations choosing other professions or leaving teaching. Additionally, group and individual differences are interactive, and the effect of working as a teacher (e.g., leadership, secondary or elementary, urban or rural, collegial and experimental settings) on values, desires, and norms should be taken into account. Lack of options over time reduces the likelihood that diverse people with many experiences and varying needs for growth and achievement will choose teaching as a career or, if they do choose teaching, will long remain.

What data have been collected confirm the importance of many of these issues. Teacher attitudes toward work redesign career ladders differ significantly with longevity in teaching, level of teaching (elementary or secondary), and experience in the new roles (Hart, 1987; Hart and Walters, 1988). Within-group differences among teachers have been identified by other researchers. DeLong (1982, 1983) found differences in teacher career orientations on two career factors. Factor 1 — managerial competence, autonomy, variety, and creativity — described preferences of teachers interested in supervision, organization, and creation. He argued that many bored teachers are in this group. Autonomy is a central theme of the group, and members say they are comfortable with the thought of leaving education. Factor 2 — technical competence and security — describes teachers who take their greatest career satisfaction in knowing that others see them as excellent teachers.

Although new teachers choose the career because of established conceptions of the nature of "teaching" work, the socialization period is an opportune time for interventions promoting the success of teacher work redesigns (Louis, 1980a, 1980b; Van Maanen, 1978; Van Maanen and Schein, 1979). Student teachers can be amenable to changes in their attitudes toward work patterns requiring more interdependence and collegiality (Hart and Adams, 1986). Vivid and early experience with work characterized by experimentation, freedom from isolation, and high performance expectations — features identified as characteristics of effective schools (Little, 1982) — can create preferences for these work patterns leading to an expectation for increased scope of influence, collegial work, and accountability.

Problems with the current work force do arise when work redesign is based on the individual and group characteristics of those in target populations. While McKelvey and Sekaran (1977, p. 301) argue that "managers should . . . design jobs with the expectation that different types of employees look for different things," to admit that a structure is designed to encourage some people to leave teaching and discourage other from choosing a teaching career may be difficult. Not only will outcomes be long in coming and the design of appropriate measures challenging, teaching and learning in schools must continue while the changes take place. Even if teaching is poorly organized to recruit and retain those who do not choose or who self-select out of the profession, the needs of current teachers cannot be ignored, yet another reason to increase the variety of opportunities in teacher incentive plans.

PERCEIVED WORK CHARACTERISTICS

Objectives and perceived job characteristics may differ significantly, and this difference forms the final feature of a work redesign view of Utah's career ladders discussed in this chapter. People's descriptions of the same work often are dissimilar. While some characterize a job as satisfying, productive, and significant, others express boredom and complain that it is unsatisfying. Assessments of tasks, autonomy, and feedback differ. These perceptions of work characteristics intervene between work structure and outcomes (Caldwell and O'Reilly, 1982) because it is on the basis of perceptions about work that people act. However, some see a reliance on perceptions to assess work as dangerously decoupled from work outcomes. By using attitude data to assess the progress of work redesign and restructuring reforms in education, policymakers and researchers follow in the footsteps of other restructuring reforms (Roberts and Glick, 1981). They also become subject to some of the same pitfalls, providing evidence of perceptual changes within teachers rather than evidence of objective changes in teaching work structures and outcomes. Attention should continually refocus on the structures actually altered as well as on attitude and perceptual changes.

However, work redesign for education requires that teachers' and potential teachers' perceptions of the career change as a result of re-structuring and is premised on the assumption that these perceptions are proportionally related to attitude and behavior change (Terborg and Davis, 1982). Perceptual data cannot be rejected or it would be impossible to measure the incentive power of the new structures.

[W]hen the intent is to predict or understand employee attitudes or behavior at work . . . , employee ratings of the job dimensions are *prefer-
able* to use, since it is an employee's own perception of the objective job
that is causal of his [sic] reactions to it. . . . (Hackman and Oldham,
1976, p. 261)

In education, researchers and practitioners have yet to use the most
common perceptual measure of job characteristics, the Job Diagnostic
Survey developed by Hackman et al. or other instruments (Arnold and
House, 1980), to assess the new work structures. To date in Utah,
assessments have relied on incumbent reports, and pre-post measures
of teachers' perceptions of changes in the motivating potential of their
work structures have not been collected. Were psychometric instruments to receive wider use, a large data base comparable to other work
settings would become available. Validated instruments, in concert
with interviews, observational data, and researcher descriptions of
work characteristics, could provide a fuller view of the actual and perceived changes taking place.

Because Utah's career ladders already are in place and new structures
are being implemented in school systems across the country, the opportunity to study impacts on a variety of outcomes in schools using
pre-/post-/redesign evaluation designs has passed. The frames of reference people apply to their assessment of work structures change
substantially in the process of redesign as well. Expectations are raised
and work is reconceptualized [Terborg and Davis (1982)]. Because
many restructuring reforms are well underway, and publicity for the
reforms already implemented is widespread, teachers' expectations and
attitudes have already been altered. Some ways to overcome these
assessment problems are suggested by redesign research. In addition to
pre- and post-tests, where possible, evaluations can tap attitudes or
construct careful examinations of retrospective attitudes in the absence
of pre-tests. Satisfaction and performance retrospectively rated can
provide one view of the job prior to an intervention (Terborg and
Davis, 1982; Oldham and Brass, 1979; Golembiewski, Billingsley, and
Yeager, 1976).

In addition to job-characteristic perceptions, a variety of other outcome measures are used to assess work redesign: 1) measures of job
satisfaction and motivation, 2) absenteeism, 3) turnover, 4) productive
quantity, and 5) work quality. While the debate over appropriate outcome measures for education rages, many have high value for a majority of Americans. Drop-out rates, student products, student attitudes

about school, and standardized achievement data could be collected. Changes in teacher and principal attitudes, behaviors, and job satisfaction—factors falling under the immediate influence of work perceptions—will surface most quickly during restructuring and should be used to assess the progress of reforms while more long-range outcome data are collected and analyzed over time. Utah, where attitude survey and case study data were collected from the beginning of the initiative, is in the forefront of evaluations of career ladders (Cornett, 1988). But the impacts of the well-documented perceptual changes on more long-range measures of effects—teacher retention, teacher recruitment, and student outcomes—require more time and a variety of measures for meaningful assessment. Additionally, job satisfaction (psychometrically evaluated), absenteeism, and turnover can provide reliable monitors of the effects of Utah's career ladder initiative on a continuing basis.

In summary, the full spectrum of work redesign factors applied to an analysis of Utah Career Ladder Plans provides a complex yet useful view of the structural, psychological, and social factors affecting work restructuring in human organizations. A careful examination of these factors points out issues deserving vigilant attention if education reform is to prosper and survive over the long term. First, education reform, to tap the full spectrum of options for school improvement, cannot be limited to a narrow range of options—to compensation systems, decision-making systems, or promotion ladders. Other alternatives can be considered: 1) new ways of organizing instruction; 2) the task, autonomy, and feedback structures of the work itself; 3) the lateral and vertical growth opportunities available over the full spectrum of an education career; and 4) the current and future utility of incentives for people moving through adult professional development. The wider the variety of opportunity structures, the more diverse the appeal.

Second, to function as an incentive, to retain and recruit teachers from a target population of people possessing desired attributes and skills, the plans must include features of work valued by these people. These work features may differ substantially from the norms and established practice of current school organizations. Surveys of currently working teachers that rely on their average perception of the reforms ignore the significant moderating effects of individual and group differences on work attitudes and perceptions. While research on the individual and group characteristics that moderate work attitudes and behavior has yet to identify all critical factors, much is known about the impact of growth needs or need for achievement on the valued work characteristics. Ongoing, long-term assessments of the impacts of new structures on sub-groups of teachers and young people in target populations are needed (Hart and Murphy, 1990b; Murphy and Hart, 1989).

Finally, the time-consuming and difficult task of designing new structures of authority and work for teachers based on features of work valued by those in target populations will be wasted if the effects of the immediate work context on sense making, resultant perceptions and attitudes about work, and subsequent task structures are ignored by policymakers and educational leaders. The successful management of work restructuring in schools requires on-site intervention into the social information processing that shapes perceptions and, ultimately, work behavior. Teachers and principals undergoing major role transitions require and deserve assistance.

FUTURE OF CAREER LADDERS IN UTAH

While Utah pours millions of dollars into its Career Ladder Plans, the complexity of the undertaking is not widely acknowledged. To a large number of people, the ladders are still a set of salary distribution systems stimulating better teacher evaluation. Rather than adapting the existing initiative to develop more opportunities for teachers, public figures in the state sometimes call for reform as if no effort had been expended. T. H. Bell (1989, pp. 18–19), former U.S. Secretary of Education, has joined the continuing rhetoric of reform and regulation in the state:

> Utah is missing out on the school reform drive. The governor, legislature, state school officers, and the board of education should write a major school reform act for the state of Utah. Utah never even set high school graduation standards at the level of the *Nation at Risk.* We are coming up short on rebuilding our system.

Other critics call the Utah career ladders a "disaster" or complain that "it's never been fully funded so it's not at all what was intended" (Jacobsen, then Campbell, quoted in Swinton, 1989). This reform rhetoric could result in an over-reliance on the appearance of continual revolution as proof that Utah educators care about schools. Currently, two new programs are being pursued in Utah. A move to join the Coalition of Essential Schools—a view of school restructuring sparked by the work of Ted Sizer that relies on site-based management—and a block grant experiment are being undertaken. The Coalition for Essential Schools group could integrate their restructured high schools with the career ladders. The block grants could have two very opposite effects— leading to more creative restructuring or returning to previous practice and uniform salary increases for all teachers. These reform movements, diverse and potentially powerful, require conceptual integration so that the effect on teaching and learning, teachers' work, and students' schooling can become the focus of each new endeavor.

The "vanishing effects" that threaten any work redesign are well documented in Utah (Malen and Hart, 1987). They emanate partially from a lack of strong articulation of social and structural changes at the work site and from a vulnerability to calls for quick fixes—increased regulation and the elimination of poor teachers, "those that ought not be teaching" (Jacobsen, quoted in Swinton, 1989, p. 24). To permanently affect the way young people view teaching careers, major workplace changes visible to every student, parent, and teacher and influencing perceptions of the variety, status, and opportunities available in teaching careers will need to become firmly entrenched. As the Utah Career Ladder System now stands—an add-on program that must be funded each year by the legislature—it is temporary, still viewed "as a safety valve [the legislators] can use if they have to scramble for money at the last minute." As a temporary program, its recruitment and retention potential is seriously crippled. New pressures to dilute the emphasis on work differentiation in career ladders continually develop and further dilute the incentive effect of restructuring. For example, House Bill 206, a measure that would permit school districts to use career ladder money to pay teachers for taking college courses in their specialty areas, advanced out of the Education Committee of the Utah House of Representatives in February 1989. Kolene Granger, associate state superintendent, "warned that if every teacher took a three credit-hour course, it would take more than $3 million out of the . . . career-ladder program" (Scarlet, 1989). This measure would have simply taken money from restructuring and added it to the conventional practice of paying teachers for college credit by advancing them on the uniform salary schedule.

But "sustaining effects" also function in Utah and can lead toward the larger goal of permanent change in the structure of work in schools. Financial problems in the state required a major tax increase in 1988 but did not kill career ladder funding. A remarkable openness and commitment to the assessment of programs, demonstrated by the prevalance of policy and research reports and outside evaluations in the state, has led to expanded views of the potential uses of career ladders. Increasingly, attention is directed toward the substantive contribution to teaching and learning in schools provided by career ladder resources. Educational leaders currently are seeking to replace the current system of annual review and approval by the State Office of Education with a three-year approval system. These trends need to continue.

"In the long run, of course, it is the end product that counts, whether higher pay or new management responsibilities of the teachers will result in better educated students" (Pierpont, 1989). In the furor and disruption of reform in a long-lived public institution like schools, this goal is easy to lose sight of. Inertia and discouragement over the pace of change are major challenges. A renewed focus on the school level will help. Multiple structural, social, and psychological factors—leadership, career opportunities, role transitions, sense making, instructional processes and task structures, goal accomplishment, and valued outcomes—attendant to school reform deserve attention in addition to the procedural and regulatory functions more easily emphasized. A broader scope of intervention and assessment will help Utah achieve a substantive change in teaching and learning with its career ladders.

Several changes in focus will help move Utah career ladders closer to the benefits available through restructuring/redesign: 1) discrete assessment of the many and varied work and pay features available under Career Ladder Plans, 2) avoidance of blanket statements about "The Career Ladder," 3) increased focus on outcomes moving away from procedural and pro forma compliance with regulation, 4) stable long-term plan approval and funding, and 5) a constant emphasis on the school level impacts of the reforms on instruction and the complex social–psychological environment in schools that shape these impacts. These changes in emphasis could make substantive work reform possible with little or no change in the legislation that began the Utah career ladder experience.

REFERENCES

Adler, S., R. B. Skov, and N. J. Salvemini. 1985. "Job Characteristics and Job Satisfaction: When Cause Becomes Consequence," *Organization Behavior and Human Decision Processes*, 35:266–278.

Amsler, M., D. Mitchell, L. Nelson, and T. Timar. 1988. *An Evaluation of the Utah Career Ladder System.* San Francisco, CA: Far West Laboratory for Educational Research.

Argyris, C. 1957. "The Individual and Organization: Some Problems of Mutual Adjustment," *Administration Science Quarterly,* 2:1–24.

Arnold, H. J. and R. J. House. 1980. "Methodological and Substantive Extensions of the Job Characteristics Model of Motivation," *Organization Behavior and Human Performance,* 25:161–183.

Bacharach, A. B. and S. C. Conley. "Educational Reform: A Managerial Agenda," paper presented at the annual meeting of the American Educational Research Association, San Francisco, 1986.

Bacharach, S. B., P. Bamberger, and S. C. Conley. 1988. "Work Processes, Role Conflict and Role Overload: The Case of Nurses and Engineers in the Public Sector," Unpublished paper.

Bacharach, S. B., S. Conley, and J. Shedd. 1986. "Beyond Career Ladders: Structuring Teacher Career Development Systems," *Teachers College Record,* 87(4):563–574.

Barnard, C. I. 1938. *The Functions of the Executive.* Cambridge, MA: Harvard University Press.

Bell, T. H. Cited in Swinton, H. 1989. "Utah Public Education Still Riding a Horse and Buggy," *Utah Holiday* (January):18–26.

Bennis, W. 1967. "Organizations of the Future," in *Classics of Organizational Behavior,* W. E. Natemeyer, ed., Oak Park, IL: Moore Publishing Company, Inc., pp. 281–293.

Berman, P. and M. W. McLaughlin. 1978. *Federal Programs Supporting Educational Change, Vol. VIII: Implementing and Sustaining Innovations.* Santa Monica, CA: Rand.

Blau, Gary J. and R. Katerberg. 1982. "Toward Enhancing Research with the Social Information Processing Approach to Job Design," *Academy of Management Review,* 7(4):543–550.

Blood, M. R. and C. L. Hulin. 1967. "Alienation, Environmental Characteristics, and Worker Responses," *Journal of Applied Psychology,* 51:284–290.

Bolman, L. G. and T. E. Deal. *Modern Approaches to Understanding and Managing Organizations.* San Francisco, CA: Jossey-Bass.

Brass, D. J. 1981. "Structural Relationships, Job Characteristics, and Worker Satisfaction and Performance," *Administrative Science Quarterly,* 26:331–348.

Brief, A. P. and H. K. Downey. 1983. "Cognitive and Organizational Structures: A Conceptual Analysis of Implicit Organizing Theories," *Human Relations,* 36: 1065–1090.

Brittain, J. and J. Freeman. 1980. "Organizational Proliferation and Density Dependent Selection," in *Organizational Life Cycles,* J. Kimberly and R. Miles, eds., San Francisco: Jossey-Bass, pp. 291–338.

Brousseau, K. R. 1978. "Personality and Job Experience," *Organizational Behavior and Human Performance,* 22:235–252.

Caldwell, D. F. and C. A. O'Reilly III. 1982. "Task Perceptions and Job Satisfaction: A Question of Causality," *Journal of Applied Psychology,* 67:361–369.

California Commission on the Teaching Profession. 1985. *Who Will Teach Our Children? A Strategy for Improving California's Schools.* Sacramento, CA: California Commission on the Teaching Profession.

Carnegie Forum on Education and the Economy. 1986. *A Nation Prepared: Teachers for the 21st Century.* Hyattsville, MD: Carnegie Forum on Education and the Economy.

Cherrington, D. J. and J. L. England. 1980. "The Desire for an Enriched Job as a Moderator of the Enrichment-Satisfaction Relationship," *Organizational Behavior and Human Performance,* 25:139–159.

Cohen, D. 1988. *Teaching Practice.* Issue Paper 88-3. East Lansing, MI: Teacher Education Research Center.

Cordery, J. L. and T. D. Wall. 1985. "Work Design and Supervisory Practice: A Model," *Human Relations,* 38:425–440.

Cornett, L. 1986. *Implementing Plans: Success and Change.* Atlanta, GA: Career Ladder Clearinghouse.

Cornett, L. 1988. "Is 'Paying for Performance' Changing Schools?" The SREB career ladder clearinghouse report 1988. Atlanta, GA: Southern Regional Educational Board.

Deal, T. E. and A. Kennedy. *Corporate Cultures.* Reading, MA: Addison-Wesley.

DeLong, T. J. 1983. "Career Orientations of Rural Educators: An Investigation," *The Rural Educator* (Winter):12–16.

DeLong, T. J. 1982. "Reexamining the Career Anchor Model," *Personnel* (May/June):50–61.

Dunham, R. 1977. "Reactions to Job Characteristics: Moderating Effects of the Organization," *Academy of Management Journal,* 20(1):42–65.

Fenstermacher, G. D. 1978. "A Philosophical Reconsideration of Recent Research on Teacher Effectiveness," *Review of Research in Education,* 6:157–185.

Fiske, E. B. 1988. "Lessons: Schools Are Beginning to Adopt an Innovator's Idea about Where Learning Should Begin," *The New York Times,* August 17.

Freeman, J. 1982. "Organizational Life Cycles and Natural Selection Processes," in *Research in Organizational Behavior,* B. M. Staw and L. L. Cummings, eds., Greenwich, CT: JAI Press, pp. 1–32.

French, W. 1969. "Organization Development: Objectives, Assumptions and Strategies," *California Management Review,* 12:23–34.

Fullan, M. 1982. *The Meaning of Educational Change.* New York: Teachers College Press.

Gangster, D. C. 1980. "Individual Differences and Task Design: A Laboratory Experiment," *Organizational Behavior and Human Performance,* 26:131–148.

Golembiewski, R. T., K. Billingsley, and S. Yeager. 1976. "Measuring Change and Persistence in Human Affairs: Types of Change Generated by OD Designs," *Journal of Applied Behavioral Science,* 12:133–157.

Green, G. and M. A. Novak. 1982. "The Effects of Leader-Member Exchange and Job Design on Productivity and Satisfaction: Testing a Dual Attachment Model," *Organizational Behavior and Human Performance,* 30:109–131.

Griffeth, R. W. 1985. "Moderation of the Effects of Job Enrichment by Participation: A Longitudinal Field Experiment," *Organization Behavior and Human Decision Processes,* 35:73–93.

Griffin, R. W. 1982. *Task Design.* Glenview, IL: Scott-Foresman.

Griffin, R. W. 1983. "Objective and Social Sources of Information in Task Redesign: A Field Experiment," *Administrative Science Quarterly,* 28:184–200.

Hackman, J. R. and E. E. Lawler III. 1971. "Employee Reactions to Job Characteristics," *Journal of Applied Psychology Monograph,* 55(3):259–286.

Hackman, J. R. and G. R. Oldham. 1976. "Motivation through the Design of Work: Tests of a Theory," *Organizational Behavior and Human Performance,* 16:250–279.

Hackman, J. R. and G. R. Oldham. 1980. *Work Redesign.* Reading, MA: Addison-Wesley Publishing Company.

Hall, D. T. 1976. *Careers in Organizations.* Pacific Palisades, CA: Goodyear Publishing Company, Inc.

Hannan, M. T. and J. Freeman. 1984. "Structural Inertia and Organizational Change," *American Sociological Review,* 49:149–164.

Hart, A. W. "Career Ladder Investment in School Level Improvement," paper presented at the annual meeting of the Northern Rocky Mountain Educational Research Association, Jackson Hole, Wyoming, 1985.

Hart, A. W. "Career Ladders in Utah: The School Site Perspective," paper presented at the annual meeting of the American Educational Research Association, San Francisco, 1986.

Hart, A. W. 1987. "A Career Ladder's Effect on Teacher Career and Work Attitudes," *American Educational Research Journal,* 24(4):479–504.

Hart, A. W. 1990a. "Impacts of the School Social Unit on Teacher Authority during Work Redesign," *American Educational Research Journal,* 27:503–532.

Hart, A. W. 1990b. "Work Redesign: A Review of Literature for Education Reform," in *Advances in Research in the Management of Schools,* S. Bacharach, ed., Englewood Cliffs, NJ: JAI Press, pp. 31–69.

Hart, A. W. and G. Adams, Jr. 1986. "Preservice Socialization for Teacher Career Ladders," *The Journal of Teacher Education,* 37:59–64.

Hart, A. W., D. Kauchak, and D. Stevens. "Teacher Career Ladder Effects on the Work of the Principal," paper presented at the annual meeting of the American Educational Research Association, San Francisco, 1986.

Hart, A. W. and M. J. Murphy. "Career Ladders in the Salt Lake City School District: A Study of Implementation," Report prepared for the U. S. Department of Education and the Salt Lake City School District, 1987.

Hart, A. W. and M. J. Murphy. 1990a. "Career Ladders and Work in Schools," in *Educational Reform in the 1980s.* Joseph Murphy, ed., Berkeley, CA: McCutchan, pp. 215–242.

Hart, A. W. and M. J. Murphy. 1990b. "New Teachers React to Redesigned Teacher Work," *American Journal of Education,* 98:224–250.

Hart, A. W. and L. C. Walters. "Teacher Responses to Work Redesign: Attitude Indexes from Data Envelopment Analysis," paper presented at the annual meeting of the American Educational Research Association, New Orleans, Louisiana, 1988.

Hofstadter, R. and W. P. Metzger. 1955. *The Development of Academic Freedom in the United States.* New York: Columbia University Press.

Hogan, E. A. and D. A. Martell. 1987. "A Confirmatory Structural Equations Analysis of the Job Characteristics Model," *Organizational Behavior and Human Decision Processes,* 39:242–263.

Holmes Group. 1986. *Tomorrow's Teachers.* East Lansing, MI: Holmes Group Inc.

Hoy, W. K. and R. Rees. 1974. "Subordinate Loyalty to Immediate Superior: A

Neglected Concept in the Study of Educational Administration," *Sociology of Education,* 47:268–286.

Hulin, C. L. and M. R. Blood. 1968. "Job Enlargement, Individual Differences, and Worker Responses," *Psychological Bulletin,* 69:41–55.

Ilgen, D. R., D. J. Campbell, L. H. Peters, and B. L. Dugoni. "Individual and Situational Contributions to Work-Related Role Perceptions," Working paper, Purdue University, West Lafayette, Ind., Department of Psychological Sciences, 1978.

Jacobsen, G. and J. Campbell. 1989. Quoted in Swinton, H. 1989. "Utah Public Education Still Riding a Horse and Buggy," *Utah Holiday* (January):18–26. Timpagne, "Sunday Morning," January 22, 1989.

Jans, N. A. 1985. "Organizational Factors and Work Involvement," *Organizational Behavior and Human Decision Making,* 35:382–396.

Jensen, Carl E. and C. B. Denler. 1989. Interview.

Kalleberg, A. L. and K. A. Loscocco. 1983. "Aging, Values, and Rewards: Explaining Age Differences in Job Satisfaction," *American Sociological Review,* 48:78–90.

Kanter, R. M. 1983. *Changemasters.* New York: Simon and Schuster.

Katz, R. 1978. "Job Longevity as a Situational Factor in Job Satisfaction," *Administrative Science Quarterly,* 23:204–223.

Katz, R. and J. Van Maanen. 1976. "The Loci of Work Satisfaction," in *Personal Goals and Work Design.* P. Warr, ed., New York: Wiley.

Kiggundu, M. N. 1983. "Task Interdependence and Job Design: Test of a Theory," *Organizational Behavior and Human Performance,* 31:145–172.

King, A. S. 1974. "Expectation Effects in Organizational Change," *Administrative Science Quarterly,* 29:221–230.

Latack, J. C. 1984. "Career Transitions within Organizations: An Exploratory Study of Work, Nonwork, and Coping Strategies," *Organizational Behavior and Human Performance,* 34:296–322.

Lipsky, M. 1976. "Toward a Theory of Street-Level Bureaucracy," in *Theoretical Perspectives on Urban Politics,* W. Hawley et al., eds., Englewood Cliffs, NJ: Prentice-Hall, pp. 196–213.

Little, J. W. 1982. "Norms of Collegiality and Experimentation: Workplace Conditions of School Success," *American Educational Research Journal,* 19(3):325–340.

Locke, E. A. and D. M. Schweiger. 1979. "Participation in Decision Making: One More Look," *Research in Organizational Behavior, Vol. 1.* Greenwich, CT: JAI Press, Inc., pp. 265–339.

Lortie, D. C. 1975. *School Teacher: A Sociological Study.* Chicago: University of Chicago Press.

Louis, M. R. 1980a. "Career Transitions: Varieties and Commonalities," *Academy of Management Review,* 5:329–340.

Louis, M. R. 1980b. "Surprise and Sense Making: What Newcomers Experience in Entering Unfamiliar Organizational Settings," *Administrative Science Quarterly,* 25:226–251.

Malen, B. and R. C. Campbell. 1985. "Public School Reform in Utah," in *The Fiscal, Legal and Political Aspects of State Reform of Elementary and Secondary Education,* V. D. Mueller and M. P. McKeown, eds., Cambridge, MA: Ballinger, pp. 245–275.

Malen, B. and A. W. Hart. 1987. "Career Ladder Reform: A Multi-Level Analysis of Initial Effects," *Educational Evaluation and Policy Analysis.*

Malen, B., M. J. Murphy, and A. W. Hart. 1987. "Restructuring Teacher Compensation Systems: An Analysis of Three Incentive Strategies," in *Education Finance Association Yearbook*. K. Alexander, ed. Cambridge, MA: Ballinger, pp. 91–142.

McKelvey, B. and U. Sekaran. 1977. "Toward a Career-Based Theory of Job Involvement: A Study of Scientists and Engineers," *Administrative Science Quarterly*, 22:281–305.

Merton, R. K. 1957. *Social Theory and Social Structured*. New York: The Free Press.

Metzger, H. 1987. "The Spectre of 'Professionism.' " *Educational Researcher* (August–September).

Meyer, J. W. and B. Rowan. 1977. "Institutionalized Organizations: Formal Structure as Myth and Ceremony," *American Journal of Sociology*, 83:340–363.

Mitchell, S. M. "Negotiating the Design of Professional Jobs," paper presented at the annual meeting of the American Educational Research Association, San Francisco, 1986.

Mobley, W. H., R. W. Griffeth, H. H. Hand, and B. M. Meglino. 1979. "Review and Conceptual Analysis of the Employee Turnover Process," *Psychological Bulletin*, 86(3):493–522.

Murnane, R. J. 1986. "Surviving Merit Pay," *IFG Policy Notes*, 6:5–6.

Murphy, M. J. and A. W. Hart. "Preparing Principals to Lead in Restructured Schools," paper presented at the annual meeting of the University Council for Educational Administration, Cincinnati, Ohio, 1988.

Murphy, M. J., A. W. Hart, and L. C. Walters. "Satisfaction and Intent to Leave of New Teachers in Target Populations under Redesigned Teacher Work," paper presented at the annual meeting of the American Educational Research Association, San Francisco, 1989.

National Commission on Excellence in Education. 1983. *A Nation at Risk*. Washington, D.C.: National Commission on Excellence in Education.

Near, J. P., R. W. Rice, and R. Hunt. 1980. *Academy of Management Review*, 5(3):415–429.

Nicholson, N. 1984. "A Theory of Work Role Transitions," *Administrative Science Quarterly*, 29:172–191.

O'Connor, E. J. and G. V. Barrett. 1980. "Informational Cues and Individual Differences as Determinants of Subjective Perceptions of Task Enrichment," *Academy of Management Journal*, 22:697–716.

Ogawa, R. T. and S. T. Bossert. "Leadership as an Organizational Characteristic," paper presented at the annual meeting of the American Educational Research Association, San Francisco, CA, 1989.

Oldham, G. R. and D. J. Brass. 1979. "Employee Reactions to an Open Plan: A Naturally Occurring Quasi-Experiment," *Administrative Science Quarterly*, 24:267–284.

Oldham, G. R. and J. R. Hackman. 1980. "Work Design in the Organizational Context," *Research in Organizational Behavior, Vol. 2*, Greenwich, CT: JAI Press Inc., pp. 247–278.

Peters, L. H. and E. J. O'Connor. 1980. "Situational Constraints and Work Outcomes: The Influences of Frequently Overlooked Construct," *Academy of Management Review*, 5:391–398.

Pfeffer, J. and J. Lawler. 1980. "Effects of Job Alternatives, Extrinsic Rewards, and Behavioral Commitment on Attitude toward the Organization: A Field Test of the Insufficient Justification Paradigm," *Administrative Science Quarterly*, 25:38–56.

Pierpont, B. 1989. "The Price of Excellence," *CBS Sunday Morning*, January 22.

Principal interview, 1989.

Quinn, R. P. and G. L. Staines. 1979. *The 1977 Quality of Employment Survey*. Ann Arbor, MI: Institute for Social Research.

Roberts, J. and W. Glick. 1981. "The Job Characteristics Approach to Task Design: A Critical Review," *Journal of Applied Psychology*, 66:193–217.

Rosenholtz, S. J. 1987. "Education Reform Strategies: Will They Increase Teacher Commitment?" *American Journal of Education*, 95:534–562.

Rosenholtz, S. J. and M. A. Smylie. 1984. "Teacher Compensation and Career Ladders," *Elementary School Journal*, 85(2):149–166.

Salancik, G. R. and J. Pfeffer. 1978. "A Social Information Processing Approach to Job Attitudes and Task Design," *Administrative Science Quarterly*, 23:224–253.

Salt Lake Tribune. 1986. May 26, p. B7.

Sashkin, M. 1986. "Participative Management Remains an Ethical Imperative," *Organizational Dynamics*, 14:62–75.

Scarlet, P. 1989. "Panel OKs Using Career-Ladder Cash to Pay Teachers for Extra Education," *Salt Lake Tribune*, February 14, p. 4A.

Schein, E. H. 1978. *Career Dynamics: Matching Individual and Organizational Needs*. Reading, MA: Addison-Wesley.

Schneider, B. 1985. "Organizational Behavior," *Annual Review of Psychology*, 36:573–611.

Schrag, F. 1983. "It's Time for Merit Pay," *Learning*, 11(8):28.

Schwab, D. P. and L. L. Cummings. 1976. "A Theoretical Analysis of the Impact of Task Scope on Employee Performance," *Academy of Management Review*, 1:23–35.

Seeborg, I. S., 1978. "The Influence of Employee Participation in Job Redesign," *Journal of Applied Behavioral Science*, 14(1):87–98.

Shanker, A. 1989. "The Price of Excellence," in *Sunday Morning*, B. Pierpont, January 22.

Shaw, J. 1980. "An Information-Processing Approach to the Study of Job Design," *Academy of Management Review*, 5:41–48.

Sizer, T. R. 1985. *Horace's Compromise: The Dilemma of the American High School*. Boston: Houghton Mifflin Company.

Skinner, B. F. 1971. *Beyond Freedom and Dignity*. New York: Knopf.

Smircich, L. 1983. "Concepts of Culture and Organizational Analysis," *Administrative Science Quarterly*, 28:339–358.

Staw, B. M., N. E. Bell, and J. A. Clausen. 1986. "The Dispositional Approach to Job Attitudes: A Lifetime Longitudinal Test," *Administrative Science Quarterly*, 31:56–77.

Staw, B. M. and J. Ross. 1985. "Stability in the Midst of Change: A Dispositional Approach to Job Attitudes," *Journal of Applied Psychology*, 70:469–480.

Strauss, G. 1977. "Managerial Practices," in *Improving Life at Work: Behavioral Science Approaches to Organizational Change*, J. R. Hackman and J. L. Suttle, eds., Santa Monica, CA: Goodyear.

Swinton, H. 1989. "Utah Public Educaton Still Riding a Horse and Buggy," *Utah Holiday* (January):18–26.

Terborg, J. R. and G. A. Davis. 1982. "Evaluation of a New Method for Assessing Change to Planned Job Redesign as Applied to Hackman and Oldham's Job Characteristic Model," *Organizational Behavior and Human Performance*, 29:112–128.

Thomas, J. and J. Griffin. 1983. "The Social Information Processing Models of Task Design: A Review of the Literature," *Academy of Management Review*, 8(4): 672–682.

Umstot, D. D., C. H. Bell, Jr., and T. R. Mitchell. 1976. "Effects of Job Enrichment and Task Goals on Satisfaction and Productivity: Implications for Job Design," *Journal of Applied Psychology*, 61:379–394.

Van Maanen, J. 1977. "Experiencing Organizations: Notes on the Meaning of Careers and Socialization," in *Organizational Careers: Some New Perspectives*, John Van Maanen, ed., New York: Wiley International, pp. 15–48.

Van Maanen, J. 1978. "People Processing: Strategies of Organizational Socialization," *Organizational Dynamics* (Summer):19–36.

Van Maanen, J. and R. Katz. 1976. "Individuals and Their Careers: Some Temporal Considerations for Work Satisfaction," *Personnel Psychology*, 29(4):601–616.

Van Maanen, J. and E. H. Schein. 1979. "Toward a Theory of Organizational Socialization," in *Research in Organizational Behavior, Vol. 1*, B. M. Staw, ed., Greenwich, CT: JAI Press, pp. 209–264.

Vance, R. J. and T. F. Biddle. 1985. "Task Experience and Social Cues: Interactive Effects on Attitudinal Reactions," *Organization Behavior and Human Decision Processes*, 35:252–265.

Vecchio, R. P. 1980. "Individual Differences as a Moderator of the Job Quality–Job Satisfaction Relationship: Evidence from a National Sample," *Organizational Behavior and Human Performance*, 26:305–325.

Waldman, S. and B. Roberts. 1988. "Grading 'Merit Pay.' " *Newsweek*, November 13.

Walsh, J. T., T. D. Taber, and T. Beehr. 1980. "An Integrated Model of Perceived Job Characteristics," *Organizational Behavior and Human Performance*, 25:252–267.

Weaver, C. N. 1978. "Job Satisfaction as a Component of Happiness among Males and Females," *Personnel Psychology*, 31:831–840.

White, J. K. 1978. "Individual Differences and the Job Quality–Worker Response Relationship: Review, Integration, and Comments," *Academy of Management Journal*, 21:36–43.

White, S. E. and T. E. Mitchell. 1979. "Job Enrichment Versus Social Cues: A Comparison and Competitive Test," *Journal of Applied Psychology*, 64:1–9.

ENDNOTE

1 Hackman and his colleagues use a psychometric measure of growth need strength (GNS) to capture the general need to grow and achieve. Other researchers measure need for achievement or some other general higher order need strength to represent this individual psychological characteristic.

CHAPTER 16

Pay for Performance in Fairfax County, Virginia

ROBERT R. SPILLANE—*Superintendent, Fairfax County Public Schools, Virginia*

PLANS to change the way a group of workers is compensated should begin with a new conception of that group of workers. Much has been written, especially over the past five years, about teachers as a group of workers. Most of this writing (and a lot of the talking that has accompanied this writing) has focused on the term *profession.* Is teaching a profession or not, and how much of a profession is it, and what needs to be done to make it one or more of one? This is an important issue, since no educational reform will succeed unless teachers have the will, the wherewithal, and the opportunity to make it succeed, and only truly professional teachers—who are self-motivated, self-confident, highly skilled, and knowledgeable—will be able to provide the kind of education that the Carnegie Foundation's report, *A Nation Prepared,* describes as necessary for the twenty-first century, an education in which "our schools . . . graduate the vast majority of their students with achievement levels long thought possible for only the privileged few." Increasing teacher professionalism is the *raison d'etre* for teacher pay for performance, and any program to restructure teacher compensation must be based on a concept of teacher professionalism. The concept and development of teacher pay for performance in Fairfax County, Virginia, illustrates this imperative.

Because Fairfax County's pay-for-performance program is founded on a belief in teacher professionalism, it does not depend on outside funding. While state funding is an important ingredient in the school system's budget, paying teachers is a local function; the structure of teacher compensation should not depend on targeted outside funding, which may or may not respond to local beliefs about compensation. Teachers, through their associations and individually, must be involved in planning and implementing a program to improve the profession. Pay to increase professionalism must be carefully used to bring about the kind of professionalism that will truly improve instruction; other-

413

wise, the extra money is wasted. If all teachers are to be considered professionals, *all* must be well compensated and the opportunity to be identified for "merit pay" must be voluntary. Those with the ambition to apply and the high quality professional performance to qualify should receive substantial additional pay and be expected to provide professional leadership while not being expected to do specific additional work in return. Fairfax County's pay-for-performance program begins and ends in a concept of professionalism that, as I said in 1985, means "making teachers responsible to each other and to the highest standards of the teaching profession for the quality of their teaching."

Fairfax County had conducted a small pilot test of teacher performance evaluation in five schools in 1984–85, and had researched many other attempts at teacher performance evaluation linked to pay by the time I became Fairfax County's superintendent in 1985. Through its experience and research, the school system had learned a lot about what *to* do and about what *not* to do.

When I arrived as superintendent in 1985, I began to lay out my views regarding the factors that had to be in place if a pay-for-performance program were to be successful. In particular, I believed that such a program had to

- involve teachers and their representatives throughout planning and implementation
- raise salaries for all teachers while implementing performance evaluation, never sacrificing base salaries to fund merit pay
- ensure that the extra pay is substantial enough to make a real difference in a teacher's pay
- train evaluators sufficiently to ensure inter-rater reliability
- establish and allow no arbitrary limits on the percentages and numbers of teachers who could receive merit pay

Using the 1984–85 pilot test as a learning experience rather than as a failure and using my concept of how pay for performance could be made to work as a basis, in 1985 the school board and I began working with the two teachers' associations on a Teacher Performance Evaluation Plan that all parties could live with and that could serve as a foundation for the kind of teacher professionalism that all parties wanted to see.

In January 1986, I appointed a "Blue Ribbon Commission on Strengthening the Teaching Profession in Fairfax County Public Schools," comprising representatives of teachers; state, local, and federal governments; the academic community; local business; and the PTA, along with experts on the teaching profession. The commission met biweekly for several months and used various sources of data and various studies and reports to deal with the following issues:

- identifying weaknesses in the then current system of teacher compensation
- specifically defining appropriate changes in the compensation structure and examining the issue of merit pay
- suggesting methods of differentiating staffing and examining such concepts as "master teachers" and "career ladders"
- suggesting methods for building respect for teaching and teachers
- recommending a process for licensing teachers
- defining the essentials in professional development

In July 1986, a FCPS Blue Ribbon Commission submitted a report that endorsed features such as

- internships for new teachers
- peer review and assistance for teachers
- self-appraisal and staff development opportunities
- clearly defined teacher performance standards
- delineation of levels of performance
- involvement of teachers, specialists, and principals in evaluation
- prescriptive supervision for marginal teachers
- involvement of master teachers in activities that will improve instruction

Their report also called for a three-level salary schedule that would reward excellent teachers, terminate employment of poor teachers, and raise salaries overall to be competitive. The commission noted that "the people of Fairfax County are willing to pay more for good teachers if there is assurance of quality control and accountability."

Meanwhile, I had been meeting regularly with leaders of the dominant local teachers' organization—The Fairfax Education Association (FEA)—to discuss a salary agreement that would go into effect in September 1987. The result of these discussions was a "pay-for-performance" proposal to which the FEA leadership agreed in July 1986. This proposal called for a restructured pay scale that substantially raised teacher salaries across the board while using a performance evaluation system to reward excellent teachers (those who apply for and meet the rigorous evaluation standards for the higher "Career Level II" salary schedule) and to provide special help to and/or withhold pay increases from and/or terminate employment of teachers who do not meet the high standards of "FCPS teachers"; a seven-member "Career Advancement Review Board" (including at least four teachers) would hear appeals of "Career Level II" (CL II) decisions. This proposal was accepted by a 76 percent vote of the FEA membership in September 1986 and publicly supported by members of the school board and county board of supervisors (on whom the school board is fiscally dependent) in the spring of 1987.

With this agreement in place, Fairfax County instituted a second pilot test of its performance evaluation program in eight schools during 1986–87. The pilot test included all major aspects of the Teacher Performance Evaluation Program (TPEP), which were eventually part of the system-wide TPEP implementation. The program was based on the belief that evaluation is a positive process for encouraging professional growth and an essential element in the improvement of instruction. The performance evaluation program involves teachers in a meaningful appraisal program and the county's teachers' organizations have been involved from the beginning.

The program's goals are to

- Offer professional growth opportunities for all teachers.
- Recognize outstanding teaching performance.
- Give special assistance to beginning teachers.
- Provide intensive assistance to teachers rated "marginal."
- Identify teachers not meeting school board adopted standards.
- Provide training for evaluators, teachers, and observers.

Both the pilot test and the plan as fully implemented used a set of "Standards of Teaching Performance," which were developed with teachers to include all aspects of a teacher's professional performance. (There were seven standards for the pilot, and an eighth — on monitoring and evaluating student outcomes — was added for implementation.) The eight standards are

(1) Demonstrate a knowledge of content and curriculum.

(2) Provide appropriate learning experiences.

(3) Demonstrate appropriate planning.

(4) Manage instruction and behavior of learners.

(5) Demonstrate human relations and communication skills.

(6) Monitor and evaluate learner/program outcomes.

(7) Use available resources.

(8) Fulfill professional responsibilities.

The standards state what is expected of teachers in Fairfax County Public Schools, and all standards are considered essential to effective performance. Each standard has "guidelines" and "performance indicators" that specify a variety of ways that each standard can be achieved, but they are not intended to provide observers with an exhaustive checklist and they are not to be used quantitatively.

During the pilot and the first two implementation years, TPEP has used a five-level rating system to identify how well a teacher had implemented the "Standards of Performance." The principal determines evaluation ratings after all required data are collected. When determining evaluation ratings, the principal considers the quality, intensity, and frequency with which the observed behaviors occur. The five ratings and their definitions are

(1) Exemplary—Performance far exceeds all standards. The teacher has demonstrated complete job mastery and serves as an example or a leader for other teachers.

(2) Skillful—Performance exceeds all standards. The teacher is fully qualified for all aspects of the position and has made contributions significantly above those expected of effective teachers.

(3) Effective—Performance meets all standards.

(4) Marginal—Performance does not meet one or more standards. Objectives are only partially achieved. Improvement is needed, and there is a reasonable expectation that improvement can be achieved.

(5) Ineffective—Performance does not meet one or more standards. Objectives are not being achieved. Termination of employment will be recommended.

After much discussion and suggestions by the FEA and other groups, I recommended, and the school board approved, reduction from five to four ratings. Since all evaluations through the phase-in were based on the five-rating system, I refer to this system in the following.

In order to provide planned and sustained assistance to teachers whose performance is rated "marginal," those teachers are referred to an intervention program and are evaluated again during the next school year. If a teacher rated "marginal" does not achieve a rating of "effective," "skillful," or "exemplary" on the next evaluation, he or she is recommended for termination of employment. Teachers referred to the intervention program receive assistance from an intervention team composed of the evaluator, a curriculum specialist or other staff member, and a consulting teacher. The team develops an improvement plan with the teacher and suggests ways for the teacher to implement the plan. Team members may make classroom observations and discuss problems and strategies with the teacher. The evaluation process continues while a teacher is in the intervention program. With the exception of the evaluator, members of the intervention team do not participate in the evaluation.

Teachers may progress through a career ladder consisting of three levels: Entry Level, Career Level I, and Career Level II. Entry Level comprises the first three years of teaching experience, during which time teachers have prescriptive guidance and professional assistance available to provide them with whatever special assistance and support they may need. They are formally evaluated during each of the three years—the first year by the principal after at least three observations and the second and third years by the principal after at least three observations or (at either the principal's or the teacher's request) by a two-member team of the principal and a curriculum observer (curriculum specialist, peer observer, or other staff member with expertise in the teacher's field, content area, or grade level). If the team approach is chosen, each member of the team observes the teacher at least twice for a total of not less than four observations. The observation process includes conferencing, feedback, and suggestions. Evaluation of Entry Level teachers provides recommendations concerning the teacher's continued employment. Decisions for continuing a contract can thus be the result of a rigorous and extended evaluation process.

Entry Level teachers who have been rated "effective," "skillful," or "exemplary" move to "Career Level I" (CL I) at the beginning of the fourth year and are evaluated during year five. Career Level I includes a three-year cycle of prescription, evaluation, and self-assessment. The CL I evaluation is similar to that for the Entry Level, including the option of principal alone or team evaluation. During the two nonevaluative years, teachers work on goals identified during prior evaluations and self-assessment, which include student input gathered through appropriate surveys and/or other methods; student input is not used as evaluative data for the principal.

Career Level II eligibility begins when a teacher meets the following requirements: is currently in the seventh or any higher year of credited experience; has been a full-time teacher in Fairfax County Public Schools during the year preceding the CL II evaluation or has been on a leave of absence for not longer than one year; is a full-time teacher during the CL II evaluation; and has received a rating of "effective," "skillful," or "exemplary" on the most recent CL I evaluation.

Teachers who meet all eligibility requirements for CL II may apply for CL II the first year they are eligible. Teachers who meet all eligibility requirements for CL II but who do not wish to apply for CL II remain at CL I and continue to follow the three-year CL I evaluation cycle. The principal may elect to evaluate any teacher on CL II during any year using the CL II observation process.

Teachers seeking CL II status are evaluated by their principals after a three-member team completes its observations. The team consists of the principal, a curriculum observer, and a generalist observer (i.e., a curriculum specialist, peer observer, or other staff member). Each member of the team observes the teacher at least twice, for a total of not less than six observations. The observation process includes conferencing, feedback, and suggestions. Once the CL II evaluation process is completed, the principal awards CL II status if the teacher achieves a rating of "skillful" or "exemplary."

There are no arbitrary limits on the number of teachers who may attain CL II. Teachers who attain CL II are evaluated on a four-year cycle and work on identified goals and self-assessment in nonevaluation years similarly to CL I teachers.

Teachers who meet all eligibility requirements and have been rated "effective" on the most recent evaluation may reapply for CL II after one prescriptive/self-assessment year. After two unsuccessful attempts for CL II from an "effective" rating, teachers will be placed on the normal three-year CL I cycle. They may then reapply for CL II from an "effective" rating during their next scheduled evaluation year.

Teachers who have achieved CL II and elect to remain at that level must receive "skillful" or "exemplary" evaluation ratings every 4 years to retain CL II status. If they are rated "effective" or "marginal," they return to CL I at the end of the year. If the teacher is rated "ineffective," the principal recommends termination of employment.

Teachers who perform duties other than standard classroom teaching (e.g., librarians, counselors, resource teachers) are evaluated using similar processes, which in some cases means that the evaluating supervisor is an administrator other than a principal.

Teachers who participated in the 1986–87 pilot were aware that evaluation decisions made during the pilot year would be official if TPEP was implemented the following year. All teachers in the pilot schools with fewer than three years of service were evaluated as Entry Level and all those with five years of service were evaluated as Career Level I teachers. Evaluations were based on reports of observations and on other information available to the principal. At least three observations were required for Entry Level teachers and two for Career Level I teachers, and the teacher could choose to be observed by the principal alone or by a two-member team including a curriculum observer. Teachers with more than six years of service who had been rated at least "satisfactory" under the old evaluation system could choose either a Career Level I evaluation or a Career Level II evaluation. If they were identified as Career Level II by the latter type of evaluation, they would be eligible for extra monetary compensation in Fiscal Year 1990 if TPEP was eventually implemented system-wide and if the extra compensation for CL II was eventually approved by the school board.

Preparation for the pilot test included training of all observers and evaluators in "The Skillful Teacher"—a system for observing classroom performance, which was developed by Jon Saphier in Cambridge, Massachusetts. This training provided a framework and a vocabulary that teachers and administrators could use to observe and talk about teaching. The Skillful Teacher is distinctly *not* a method of teaching. Rather, it is a complex but understandable and coherent framework for observing and discussing the different aspects of teaching (*any* teaching—highly controlled or open-ended, or any other style). Among the aspects of teaching for which The Skillful Teacher supplied a vocabulary are attention, momentum, discipline, clarity, learning styles, and evaluation. This training is a critical element of the inter-rater reliability (and inter-observer reliability) on which TPEP depends.

The 1986–87 pilot test in eight schools successfully showed that TPEP could be effective. Of the 412 teachers in the pilot schools, 317, or 77 percent, were eligible to apply for Career Level II evaluation (i.e., had seven years of service and satisfactory ratings on their last previous evaluations); 209 of that 317, or 66 percent, selected the more rigorous Career Level II evaluation. Of these 209 who submitted themselves to the rigorous evaluation, 138, or 66 percent, were evaluated as meeting Career Level II standards. Besides showing that TPEP was viable, the evaluation of the pilot program provided valuable information about how the process could be improved. In particular, it led to strengthening of training for observers and evaluators (principals) to better ensure the validity and reliability of observation reports and evaluation ratings.

Based on the pilot experience, the school system geared up for a two-year phase-in of TPEP in all 184 schools and centers in Fairfax County. I created a "Career Advancement Review Board" (CARB), made up of four teachers elected by the teachers and three superintendent appointees. One of the early elected CARB members was the president of the FEA. Training became a major system-wide priority, since all observers and evaluators needed training before they could perform their tasks. Observers were trained in The Skillful Teacher and conferencing, and principals were trained in The Skillful Teacher, conferencing, rater reliability, and other areas. Based on popular demand, a school-based Skillful Teacher course was developed and made available to all teachers who were interested.

During the two-year phase-in, all teachers eligible for CL II evaluation were evaluated. Considering both the phase-in and the 1986–87 pilot, 6107 were eligible, and 3263, or 53 percent, chose CL II evaluation. Of these, 2198 (or approximately 26 percent of the total number of teachers in the school system) were identified as "Career Level II teachers." At the other end of the scale, twenty-three, or 0.3 percent of the total number of teachers, were identified as "ineffective" and were recommended for dismissal, and 175, or 2 percent of the teachers, were identified as "marginal" and provided with assistance from three-member intervention teams. The phase-in was an immense undertaking in a school system of this size, involving teachers, principals and other school-based managers, and area- and central-office administrators. Perhaps the most important reason for the success of this undertaking was the support of the FEA, which helped gain teacher support for the program and which held a number of membership votes on the program and on possible changes in the program's operation. Both the FEA and the other teachers' association—the Fairfax County Federation of Teachers (FCFT), which opposed TPEP from the beginning—were represented on the superintendent's advisory council on TPEP, and both recommended changes in procedures during yearly discussions with the FCPS personnel services department. The school system made some changes based on these suggestions, and the system did, in fact, work.

In the spring of 1989, after two pilots and two phase-in years, FCPS was in a position to recommend additional pay for the 2198 teachers who had been identified as Career Level II. My proposed FY 1990 budget included a provision for a separate CL II pay scale that was an average of 10 percent above the pay scale for Career Level I teachers. In February 1989, the school board considered this proposal and substituted for it a 9 percent bonus that would not be part of base pay. While the difference in take-home pay between the two proposals was minuscule, the bonus would not trigger additional pension credit. However, the FEA interpreted this change as a betrayal of the agreement they thought they had secured with me, an agreement for a separate pay scale for CL II, which would be 10 percent over the CL I scale. Shortly before the February school board vote, Mary Futrell, President of the NEA (of which FEA is an affiliate), had spoken forcefully to the Fairfax County Chamber of Commerce about the importance of that vote; this was somewhat surprising, considering the traditional NEA opposition to any kind of "merit pay." After the February school board vote, the FEA held a vote of its membership on merit pay "as amended by the School Board," which predictably drew overwhelming opposition, and both FEA and NEA went into opposition to Career Level II, while continuing to support the rest of TPEP.

Ironically, of course, this places the teacher unions in the untenable position of opposing the additional pay that 2198 teachers—members of their unions—are receiving. That explains, to a great extent, why the rhetoric of their opposition has been more sporadic and perfunctory than substantive, especially since the bonus survived a second school board budget unscathed. The school board approved the FY 1991 budget without any attempt to eliminate or reduce the bonus. The hurdle of the second budget vote softened the voice of the cynics who said financial support would be withdrawn once the evaluation component was in place. The vote effectively institutionalized merit pay.

At this point (spring 1990) FCPS has in place a performance evaluation program that has resulted in highly trained observers and evaluators, much more attention to and discussion of instruction among teachers and administrators, almost 400 teachers having left the system because of TPEP, hundreds of teachers provided with special help to improve performance, a clear understanding of professional standards among all teachers, and identification of 2198 teachers as outstanding among their peers. These 2198 began receiving the 9 percent bonus in their paychecks this school year. Whatever the future of TPEP, it has already created a more professional atmosphere among teachers and administrators, and systems for selection, training, and evaluation of all educational administrators have been developed and are now being phased in.

Change is always difficult. Around the turn of the 19th century, English factories based on new technologies brought masses of farmers into cities and towns and drastically changed their lifestyles. Today, many say that an "Information Revolution"—based on current technologies—will cause social and lifestyle changes as drastic as those caused by the Industrial Revolution. We tend to perceive these changes caused by technology as inevitable, and they probably are. To some extent, we will all be forced to adapt to new lifestyles and new types of social organization. But what about changes in the way we provide education, which people like Ernest Boyer, Marc Tucker, William Bennett, and John Goodlad are calling for? All human change may be difficult, but planned change to improve and adapt is better than unplanned change at the mercy of forces we cannot control. If we cannot change aspects of our educational systems to conserve and improve the quality of education we provide our young people, either they will not be prepared for the challenges of adult life or our educational systems will be changed drastically by forces beyond our control. But, because change is difficult, many educators and many in the communities they serve become skittish when needed changes are about to be implemented. Fairfax County's pay-for-performance plan is a case in point.

A major reason that needed changes, which initially receive substantial public support, fail in implementation is that either the implementers or the public—or both—underestimate the price of human change.

The purpose of Fairfax County's pay-for-performance plan is to strengthen the teaching profession and answer public demands for excellent schools. It provides teachers with a package: 1) substantially higher salaries across the pay scale (well above cost-of-living increases), 2) the possibility for outstanding teachers to receive salaries that are even higher than those on this already substantially increased scale, and 3) performance evaluation for all teachers to identify the outstanding and to help or terminate the employment of those who should not be teaching. The elements of this package are inextricably linked and offer much to teachers, which is why Fairfax County's teachers largely bought into the plan early in its development.

It is interesting that, even in politically stable, non-union, and affluent Fairfax County the traditional problems of "merit pay" have played major parts. Changes in the personnel of the school board and board of supervisors have altered the calculus of political support over the past four years. Agreements with the dominant teachers' organization have been loosely structured, which is good for a developing program but not so good when things get tough. Financial arrangements are necessarily annual, which means that pay-offs must be projected into a not completely certain future. Any school system that develops and implements pay for performance will have to deal with political, teacher organizational, and financial problems. But the message from Fairfax County is that these can be overcome and a working pay-for-performance system *can* be developed and implemented.

Talk about professionalism is cheap and action difficult and risky, but Fairfax County has taken action and achieved a great deal. While Fairfax County's Teacher Performance Evaluation Program has lost some of the support it had in the beginning and the mechanism for "merit pay" has been changed, the program is in place and is being implemented—over 2100 teachers began receiving their bonuses in September 1989. The real test will be to see where performance evaluation and teacher professionalism are five years from now in Fairfax County.

PART VII

RESTRUCTURING AND COMPENSATION PROGRAMS IN ACTION

The Reform of Public Education in Rochester, New York, and the Professionalization of Teaching

MANUEL J. RIVERA — *Deputy Superintendent, Rochester Public Schools, New York*

PART 1: THE ROCHESTER STORY

THE City School District of Rochester, New York, is typical of many urban districts that have experienced drastic changes in enrollment and demographics over the past twenty years. In 1970, the Rochester schools enrolled 46,000 students; approximately two-thirds were white and one-third was minority (black, Hispanic, Asian, and native American). During the next five years, the proportion of minority students rose dramatically (from 37 percent to 50 percent), due largely to the loss of white families to the suburbs and increased enrollment of white students in private and parochial schools. This trend continued in the late 1970s and early 1980s. Today, Rochester is a school system of approximately 32,000 students; the majority, 72 percent, are black, Hispanic, native American, Asian, and other minorities (Rochester City School District, *District Data Base,* 1987–88).

A significant portion of these students lives in poverty, and an increasing percentage lives in single-parent homes. According to the most recent census, 14.5 percent of families in the city have incomes below poverty level, compared to a much smaller percentage (2.8 percent) of families below the poverty level in Rochester's suburbs. Forty-one percent of city families are single-parent households. Twenty-one percent of Rochester's families with children between the ages of six and seventeen years and 40 percent of families with school-aged children headed by women exist on incomes at or below the poverty level (Rochester City School District, *Data Analysis,* 1985).

Commitment to Education

In general, the Rochester community has regarded the City School District favorably throughout its history. From inception, the industrial community's interest in promoting excellent schools complemented local boards' desire to improve the quality of education. By the early twentieth century, the Rochester district had evolved into a system that offered a well-rounded program of academic studies, civics, fine arts, foreign languages, practical arts, vocational training, home economics, and health. A superficial analysis of student performance in the district suggested that the Rochester schools were doing a fine job. The schools had their share of high achievers—students enrolled in honors and advanced placement courses. Recipients of local, state, and national scholarships attended some of the finest universities in the country. Despite these signs of excellence, other less publicized indicators attested to performance problems in the system: the increased numbers of children in compensatory services, high retention rates at the early grades, high drop-out rates, a rise in special education referrals, and the steady loss of middle- and high-income families to parochial and suburban schools.

In the early 1970s, Rochester, like many other school districts, selectively released student performance data that emphasized the system's successes. At the end of the decade, the election of a school board composed primarily of parents whose children were students in the Rochester schools proved to be a turning point in the history of the district. Informed about educational issues and involved in many of the system's federally funded and local programs, the new board members sought broad-based political support for education initiatives designed to improve student performance and achievement.

The movement to initiate major educational reform began with the selection of a new superintendent, Laval S. Wilson, in 1980. Early in his tenure, Wilson developed a long-range plan to improve district services and promoted an open, participatory budget process that substantially increased board and community involvement in determining resource allocations.

Central Assessment and District-wide Planning

The cornerstone of Wilson's plan was the development of the district's data base, a comprehensive assemblage of information on achievement, attainment, attendance, mobility, student loss, suspension, enrollment, and placement. Developed to assess the system's strengths and shortcomings, the data base contained information not previously available, including analyses of student achievement by race and ethnicity. Release of the data in 1982 revealed a district profile that confirmed what many school system personnel already knew.

Student failure rates were unacceptably high, and differential achievement rates for the various racial and ethnic groups characterized the schools. These findings belied the public's image of the district and substituted the following facts:

- District demography had changed radically during the previous fifteen years. For the first time in 1976, minority students became the majority (53 percent).
- During the same fifteen years, overall enrollment dropped by 12,000 students.
- Two of three students enrolled in non-Regents courses rather than in the New York State Regent-level courses.
- Only one of five students graduated with an academic diploma from the New York State Board of Regents.
- Three of four students enrolled in non-Regents courses were minority.
- Failure rates in core subjects (English, mathematics, science, and social studies) were approximately twice as high among students enrolled in non-Regents courses.
- Consistently, the twelfth-grade class was 50 percent smaller than its ninth-grade cohort.
- The most severe problems of achievement, attendance, and behavior appeared at grades 7, 8, and 9.
- Achievement, advanced placement, attainment, and behavior problems (evidenced in suspension) were characterized differentially by race and socioeconomic status (Rochester City School District, *Data Base,* 1981–82).

Using the data base to assess the school system's productivity, Wilson prepared a policy analysis and long-range plan intended to strengthen district services. His three-year plan, a centrally designed improvement program, contained approximately thirty initiatives directed towards various aspects of district operation. Areas targeted for improvement included curriculum and instruction, attendance, school environment, special services (special education, career education, sex education, and family life), and management. The district successfully implemented a number of these initiatives, including the introduction of a new social studies and science curriculum at the elementary grades and the creation of separate clusters for junior high students housed in comprehensive high schools (grades 7–12). Most importantly, Wilson's appraisal of the district's status and his commitment to improvement generated community interest in the needs of the city schools and forged new political alliances. Thus, conditions were set under which the district could gain greater financial support at a time when constraints on the national economy severely limited resources for education.

The district's program in the early 1980s resulted in incremental improvements in student performance measured by conventional indices. For example, the junior high school cluster program was responsible for the following changes that occurred during 1983 and 1984:

- Attendance rose by 3.1 percentage points, from 85.5 percent in 1981–82 to 88.6 percent in 1983–84.
- Seventh-grade reading achievement improved by 6 percentage points, bringing junior high school students' performance above the national norm.
- Seventh-grade math achievement rose by 8 percentage points.
- The percentage of junior high students involved in short-term suspensions was cut by two-thirds.
- A higher proportion of students enrolled in Regent-level courses at grade 9 (increasing from 32.7 percent in fall of 1982 to 39.2 percent in fall of 1985) (Rochester City School District, *Data Base,* 1983–84).

The improvements, however, were not uniform. Results varied from one school to another, even though the same requirements and support systems were applied throughout the district. Some clusters realized increases in student achievement and attendance and decreases in discipline problems at rates that far exceeded district-wide averages.

These initiatives, however, were not sufficient to meet growing community dissatisfaction with a public school system that was failing the majority of its black and Hispanic students and suspending them from school in record numbers. Public discontent reached an all-time high in 1983. Increased student assaults and suspensions in schools and strained racial tensions prompted a city-wide focus on improving the quality of education in Rochester's schools. The Urban League of Rochester organized a series of task forces involving all segments of the community (clergy, school staff, school board, union members, parents, community, and business). This collective concern culminated in the March 1986 release of the highly publicized report, *A Call to Ac-*

tion (1986). The report challenged all individuals, groups, and organizations in Rochester to accept responsibility for the "crisis in education" and to contribute to finding solutions.

The report addressed such issues as teacher professionalism, academic standards, multicultural education, parent involvement, and school–community relations. During this period, the school board appointed a new superintendent, Peter McWalters. Keenly aware of the pervasive and persistent problems, McWalters worked closely with staff, community, and school board members to develop a new mission for the district. The mission recognized that the most important interactions in a school system take place between teachers and students; further, it emphasized the need to create a school system distinguished by high achievement, one that does not predict success or failure of its students by their socioeconomic circumstances or racial or ethnic background.

Over the next three years, McWalters called on his staff to affirm the inherent ability and worth of each child. He stressed the school's need to support each student's success, emphasized the involvement of parents and the community in successful schools, and recognized the individual school as the essential unit of district productivity (McWalters, 1989).

The Reform Initiatives: An Overview

In 1986 and 1987, the superintendent and school board introduced a number of new initiatives to address the system's inequities. The Rochester School Board approved recommendations to

- establish a Peer Assistance and Review Program
- target resources to early childhood education
- reduce class sizes for kindergartens and first grades throughout the school system
- assign teacher aides to every kindergarten and first-grade class
- provide staff development in order to better meet the needs of a diverse student body
- reorganize secondary schools (grades 7–12) into middle schools and senior high schools
- support school-based planning efforts, consistent with "effective schools" research

These and other initiatives developed during 1986–87 altered our basic assumptions and changed the underlying philosophy that guided our policies and programs. As a result, we began to redefine our roles and professional relationships. Our new mission statement, goals, and strategies for attainment clearly represented the district's efforts to respond to the concerns of the community.

The school board ratified a new contractual agreement with the Rochester Teachers' Association (RTA) in August 1987. This contract set new expectations for teachers' roles in school governance, decentralized district operations, and created school communities accountable for student progress. The contract attracted much attention from educators, civic and community leaders, and the general public. Rochester had taken a bold step towards redefining the role of the teacher in urban schools.

The much acclaimed publication in 1986 of two significant educational reform reports greatly influenced Rochester's plan for local school reform. *A Nation Prepared: Teachers for the 21st Century* (Carnegie Forum on Education and the Economy, 1986) cites the need for fundamental change in the structure and working conditions within schools in response to trends in the national economy. Rapid changes in technology and methods of production dictate that future workers will require dramatically different skills. Minimum competency will not be sufficient to meet the demands of the next century. A broad knowledge base will best prepare our graduates for labor market competition and success in college. Clearly, as shifting economic trends demand a more sophisticated labor pool, schools must better serve those students for whom the current structures and practices have been the least effective (McWalters, 1989).

The Carnegie proposals, several of which are being implemented in Rochester, will, it is hoped, lead to fundamental change in the structure and working conditions of our schools. The proposals, as outlined in *A Nation Prepared: Teachers for the 21st Century,* call for

sweeping changes in educational policy to:

- Restructure schools to provide a professional environment for teachers, freeing them to decide how best to meet state and local goals for children while holding them accountable for student progress.
- Restructure the teaching force, and introduce a new category of *Lead Teachers* with the proven ability to provide active leadership in the redesign of the schools and in helping their colleagues to uphold standards of learning and teaching.

- Relate incentives for teachers to school-wide performance, and provide schools with the technology, services and staff essential to teacher productivity.
- Make teachers' salaries and career opportunities competitive with those in other professions. (p. 3)

The report of the Holmes Group, *Tomorrow's Teachers* (1986), offers similar recommendations regarding the restructuring of schools and the teaching profession. The Holmes Group recommends a differentiated structure for professional opportunity. Three levels are proposed:

- the *Career Professional Teacher,* capable of assuming responsibility not only within the classroom but also at the school level
- the *Professional Teacher,* prepared as a fully autonomous professional in the classroom
- the *Instructor,* novices who would practice only under the supervision of a Career Professional

Finally, the Holmes report asserts that the existing structure of schools and the working conditions of teachers will have to change if we are truly earnest about our attempts to professionalize teaching.

Superintendent Peter McWalters and Adam Urbanski, president of the Rochester Teachers' Association, believed that a fundamental restructuring of schools and redefinition of the teaching profession must occur in order to better prepare students for the challenges of the future. The district also must recognize schools as the essential unit of productivity. To achieve this end, the district would "provide school staff with wide latitude in decisions that affect performance—assignment of staff, allocation of funding, curriculum emphasis, placement and grouping of students, design of instruction, use of instructional time—and afford them a resource base that allows substantive improvement to proceed" (McWalters, 1989, p. 7).

The school board concurred that the "transfer of wider latitude and authority to individual schools [was] only possible when the district [had] assurances that school efforts [would be] directed to improved student performance, and accompanied by parents' and community's satisfaction with the quality of [academic and support] service provided" (McWalters, p. 7).

McWalters called for the reorganization of the district in a manner very different from the traditional conception of the way public schools operate. His model would have more in common with American corporations, which have been most successful in restructuring and decentralizing their organizations into smaller units more responsive to change.

With this in mind, the teachers' contract, ratified in 1987, set the parameters for the restructuring of the Rochester City School District—a system that would be specifically tailored to meet the needs of the communities served. The contract included the following major elements.

School Based Management

The district's movement toward school based management built upon the experience gained during the mid-1980s. Primary responsibility for the design of school improvement programs rested with school based planning teams composed of elected representatives of the entire school community (teachers, parents, administrators, support staff, school neighbors). In accordance with school based planning guidelines, each school team, chaired by the principal, would assess student performance and school productivity, set goals for improvement, and design instruction and other services consistent with the school's goals. Decisions would be reached by consensus. The process provided for participation of faculty, parents, and others who share a genuine interest in education. While the planning team holds primary responsibility for the design of the school's program, innovation is not restricted to members of the team. Individual staff members, faculty groups, departments, houses, and clusters may also contribute ideas for school improvement. The board of education is responsible for establishing new policies in support of school based management issues, such as staffing, budget, program design, performance standards, and assessment of student progress.

Redefining the Teaching Profession

The success of the redesign of Rochester's schools depends critically upon the commitment and competence of building staff and upon their willingness to accept increased responsibility for the design of school programs (McWalters, 1989, p. 8). The teachers' contract provided the impetus for educators to accept responsibility for the delivery of quality instruction, to participate in the governance of schools, and to set standards for their profession.

The contract called for the establishment of a Joint Governing Panel (five members appointed by the union and five appointed by the superintendent) to develop the *Career in Teaching Program* (CIT). The CIT plan delineates four career levels: Intern, Resident, Professional Teacher, and Lead Teacher. The intent of the plan is twofold: "to develop and maintain the highest caliber teaching staff; and to provide [Rochester] teachers with career options that do not require them to leave the classroom in order to assume additional responsibility and leadership roles" (Gillett and Halkett, *Career in Teaching Program: An Overview of CIT,* 1989, p. 5). The attainment of these goals requires a greater level of highest quality staff interaction than in the past, expanded professional expectations, and district-wide accountability, defined to some extent by improved student performance.

One of the major ongoing concerns of the Joint Governing Panel is those policies that affect the recruitment, selection, and hiring of teachers. The panel is expected to recommend new policies and procedures based on an analysis of the best hiring practices in both the private sector and other urban school districts. An annual staff recruitment campaign, including aggressive affirmative action strategies, would incorporate recommendations made by the Joint Governing Panel.

PART 2: THE PROFESSIONALIZATION OF TEACHING—FROM THEORY TO PRACTICE

The *Peer Assistance and Review Program* (PAR) and the *Career in Teaching Program* (CIT) constitute the heart of the initiatives to restructure the teaching profession in Rochester. An analysis of these reform initiatives reveals the extent to which Rochester's plan reflects lessons learned from the past, as well as concerns raised by contemporary educators and researchers.

In a recent research report entitled "Steady Work: Policy, Practice, and the Reform of American Education" (1988), Elmore and McLaughlin conclude that some of the federal reform initiatives in the 1950s and 1960s were not very successful. They believe federal policies "exercised limited leverage on the course of innovations because they did not critically influence those factors most responsible for effective implementation—the *motivation* [emphasis added] of actors within the institutional setting and the locally designed implementation strategies" (p. 22).

A local reform initiated in some school districts, merit pay, also proved to be highly controversial and ineffective in motivating teachers. One study concludes that merit pay "is unlikely to *motivate* teachers to work harder" (Murnane and Cohen, 1986, p. 15).

To say that all reform initiatives or federal policies have been ineffective is misleading. For the most part, however, many of the earlier reforms did not knit the roles and incentives among policymakers, teachers, and administrators, nor did they necessarily focus on the fundamental aspects of schooling—conceptions of knowledge and learning. In essence, the more successful policies and programs of the past and today are those where the individuals responsible for their implementation have been involved in their formulation and development.

If we consider the lessons of past reforms, then the proposals outlined in the Holmes and Carnegie reports hold promise for the future—promise for substantive educational reform that can lead to a more *motivated* teaching work force, improved knowledge of the learning process and teaching skills, and more innovative and effective programs. *Improved student performance* is the anticipated outcome of such reforms.

In referring to the Holmes and Carnegie reform proposals, Harvard University researcher Susan Moore Johnson notes that "even where the recommendations resemble earlier initiatives, as with career ladders or elevated standards for certification, the intent behind the new formulations seems different. Teachers are to be the agents rather than the objects of reform" (Johnson, 1989, p. 95). Johnson's observation is insightful, and, to some extent, one can apply "lessons learned" from earlier reforms when assessing the potential impact of the Holmes and Carnegie proposals.

The Holmes proposals, and particularly the Carnegie proposals, recognize the school as the essential unit of improvement. "The quality of education improves, the argument goes, as the quality of classroom instruction improves; the quality of classroom instruction improves as the schools function more effectively; and schools function more effectively as all features of the larger system concentrate on the prerequisites of effective school performance" (Elmore and McLaughlin, p. 55). These proposals to substantially involve teachers in setting school policy and practice, curriculum development, and establishing standards in many other aspects of schooling represent a fundamental change from the nature of past reforms. Teachers, in essence, would become the *change agents* of the future in public education. The involvement of educational practitioners and the focus on teaching and learning in these proposals are the major differences from reform efforts of the past.

The successful outcome of such far-reaching proposals depends in large measure on how skillfully and with what understandings local districts develop and implement the suggested reforms. Restructuring the teaching force and restructuring schools (as proposed in the Carnegie and Holmes reports) differently than in the past can lead to a more motivated and skilled work force. In a recent study involving twenty-five high school teachers whose work is highly valued by their principal, Susan Moore Johnson found that many of the teachers believed that their work was unappreciated and ". . . their best efforts as teachers went unrecognized by administrators and parents . . ." (Johnson, p. 97). She further noted that ". . . most also resented non-teaching duties, lamented relentless demands on their time, [and] regretted the isolation of their work . . ." (p. 100). Johnson also indicated that many teachers thought peer observations in classrooms would be useful, although such supportive peer interaction occurred rarely.

An analysis of their responses indicated that ". . . staged careers could document professional progress and provide well-deserved financial compensation" (p. 109). If career ladders could be designed to overcome problems (such as creating new hierarchies akin to existing administrative structures and addressing shortcomings of the current performance appraisal system), this group of teachers would likely support them.

> By instituting different roles and career patterns and by redistributing authority, other changes might occur in schools that would improve them as workplaces. Isolation might diminish. Expertise might be shared. Instructional values might gain a new currency. Groups of teachers might redirect school policies. Gradually, teachers might gain public recognition and respect. (pp. 109–110)

Thus, while I do not recommend that the specific proposals of the Carnegie Forum ought to be universally implemented, there is much that is applicable to particular districts. The suggestions of both the Carnegie Forum and the Holmes Group deserve the attention of teachers and school officials throughout the nation. I am convinced that these reforms can lead to positive outcomes for teachers and students. The ultimate success of any reform measure, however, is dependent upon how local school systems interpret, formulate, and implement the call to restructure schools and the teaching force.

A number of questions arise on which I base this analysis of Rochester's efforts to implement one reform proposal: the restructuring of the teaching profession.

What was the role of the Rochester teachers' union with regard to the formulation and implementation of this reform? Maeroff (1988) paraphrases Johnson and Nelson (1987) when he states that "the ultimate success or failure of the reform movement will depend on the reaction of local contract bargaining units" (p. 101).

- To what extent have teachers been involved in formulating the plan and implementing efforts to restructure the teaching profession?
- Do Rochester's efforts to restructure the teaching profession address some of the problems and concerns expressed by earlier researchers?
- What is so unique about Rochester's Career in Teaching Program?
- Is it just another cover-up for merit pay?
- What isn't working? What have been some of the problems with implementation?
- What does the future hold for the restructuring of the teaching profession in Rochester?

The Development of the Peer Assistance and Review Program (PAR)

In 1985, the Rochester superintendent and teachers' union president worked collaboratively on a program that was the precursor to the unprecedented agreements in the 1987 teachers' contract. They spearheaded the development of the Peer Assistance and Review Program as a pilot project to provide internships for new teachers and to create attractive alternatives for tenured teachers to remain in the profession.

The union president and the superintendent of schools did not work in isolation on this important initiative. During the 1985–86 school year, the proposed PAR Program went through a series of changes based on input from teacher union representatives from every school in the city and central office administrators. Both the superintendent and union president remained actively involved in negotiations throughout the process. The administrator's union (ASAR), however, which represents principals, vice principals, and other administrators, did not support the project and declined invitations to participate in program development.

The Peer Assistance and Review Program was patterned after a mentor program in Ohio known as the Toledo Plan. "Like the Toledo Plan, the PAR Program agreement provided for mentors to: (1) assist and assess the progress of beginning teachers [interns], and (2) help improve the performance of experienced teachers in need of remediation. Under both the Toledo Plan and the PAR Program agreement, the mentors are charged with the responsibility of recommending which teachers are competent to teach beyond their first year" (Gillett and Halkett, *An Overview of CIT,* p. 1).

The goals of the PAR Program were to (a) retain good teachers, (b) develop effective new teachers, (c) provide opportunity for professional growth of mentors, (d) help remediate peers in need of assistance, and (e) help teachers feel a greater ownership and engagement with teaching through increased accountability in professional matters.

Once agreement was reached, a panel, composed of three administrators appointed by the superintendent and four teachers appointed by the president of the RTA, shared responsibility for the development of guidelines and procedures and for program administration and implementation. At the end of each school year, the PAR panel also reviewed evaluations conducted by each intern's mentor and supervisor and recommended their continued employment or termination.

The development of criteria to select the mentors was an important first step. The panel agreed that the selection of mentors should be based on "competence." All mentor applicants were required to have demonstrated outstanding teaching ability (as determined by their record of service in the district for at least ten years). In addition, successful applicants had to agree to decline appointment to any administrative or supervisory position during their service as mentors and for a two-year period thereafter. The RTA and City School District viewed mentorship as a step on the teacher career ladder, not as a stepping stone to an administrative position.

The district's first mentor teachers were available to assist interns in September 1987. During the program's first year, 22 mentors assisted 176 interns to develop and refine their skills. The role of the mentor as designed was not intended to be a new hierarchy or another administrative structure in our schools. The mentors, released full-time from their regular assignments, observed the interns at work and offered expert advice on how to improve classroom teaching and student learning. The mentors served as a sounding board for ideas, provided emotional support and encouragement, and helped the interns to gain confidence in their teaching abilities. Mentors helped reduce the sense of "isolation" expressed by teachers in Johnson's study and provided demonstration lessons or arranged for interns to observe other teachers.

PAR: A Successful Beginning

At the end of the first year, Halkett (1988), in her evaluation report, declared the PAR Program a success for both interns and mentors. "Most interns were satisfied with the PAR Program, felt positive about their experiences, and were satisfied with their mentor. For assistance in areas of critical import—using motivation techniques, improving instructional skills, classroom management and providing for individual student differences—most interns relied on their mentor. For moral support and encouragement—the interns' greatest expressed need— most interns relied on their mentor. Mentors felt that they made a positive difference in their intern's first year with the district. Mentors felt positive about mentorship as an option on the career ladder" (p. 1). This summary finding was based on surveys developed by the PAR panel and administered to all the interns and mentors.

Mentors also had the responsibility to assess and document the progress, skills, and needs of interns in a number of areas, including teaching procedures, classroom management, and knowledge of subject/academic preparation. They were required to submit a final report and meet with the panel to discuss each intern's progress. Given this role, it is also interesting to note some of the interns' responses regarding the assessment and evaluation process.

- [Only] 66.2% of the interns felt their supervisor was knowledgeable enough about their strengths and weaknesses to evaluate their performance, [whereas] 80.4% of the interns felt their mentor was knowledgeable enough about their strengths and weaknesses to assess their performance
- 58% of the interns felt their supervisor provided adequate follow-up assistance in areas identified as in need of improvement; while 81.8% believe that their mentor provided adequate follow-up assistance. (Halkett, 1988, p. 8)

The City School District's evaluation of the Peer Assistance and Review Program provides some evidence to suggest that this reform initiative was a successful start towards restructuring the teaching profession in Rochester. I have cited only a few of the findings from the evaluation report. They do, however, demonstrate that the involvement of the union and teachers collaboratively with the superintendent and other administrators produced an effective educational reform. The PAR Program addressed several of the issues and concerns raised by teachers in Johnson's study.

The "master teacher" proposal, described by Elmore and McLaughlin in *Steady Work* (1988), is similar in nature to Rochester's mentor teacher initiative. In their work, the authors state that "the success of the reform will depend, to a large degree, on the competence of the people we select . . ." (p. 57). I believe that the involvement of teachers in the formulation of this initiative and special attention in identifying the most "competent" mentors are, in large measure, important reasons for the success of Rochester's initial effort.

PAR: Weaknesses and Problems with Implementation

While the program's first year could be viewed as a success, there were weaknesses, problems with implementation, and other areas of concern that emerged. The PAR Program's evaluation report identified some of the concerns and problems, but not others.

As mentioned earlier, the administrator's union (ASAR) chose not to participate in the development of PAR. Thus, while the superintendent was creating new alliances with the RTA president, his relationship with the leadership of ASAR became more strained. ASAR considered mentor teachers participating in the performance evaluation of interns to be in direct conflict with the role of administrators, particularly principals, vice principals, and other building-level supervisors. Also, the PAR Program appeared to conflict with certain statutory requirements and regulations of the Commissioner of the New York State Department of Education. These issues triggered a lawsuit initiated by ASAR against the district. Although the charges were dismissed, the suit was evidence of new problems associated with the reform proposals. A year later, the new teachers' contract, which awarded to some teachers salaries in excess of those earned by administrators and formalized the expanded role for classroom teachers, exacerbated the rift between the superintendent, teachers, and administrators.

The evaluation of the Peer Assistance and Review Program also provided evidence that administrators in the field and mentor teachers were not necessarily working collaboratively. The report cites the following: "27.3% of the mentors said that they worked consistently and constructively with all of the supervisors of their interns, and 59.1% said they worked with most of the supervisors" (Halkett, 1988, p. 9).

The resistance of the administrator's union presented another problem for implementation. Administrators referred very few tenured teachers in need of assistance to the PAR Governing Panel for intervention. In one case, where a tenured teacher was referred, the PAR panel chose not to assign a mentor (following their assessment of the teacher's performance), despite the documented record of poor performance provided by the principal. Clearly, providing assistance to tenured teachers was an issue that would have to be resolved.

Other weaknesses and problems of the PAR Program's first year existed:

- Communication between the PAR Governing Panel and the mentors was poor—roles and responsibilities of both were unclear for some mentors.
- Because of budget constraints, only a limited number of mentors (twenty-two) could be hired, and for the many qualified teacher applicants, this new career option never materialized as a real career opportunity.
- The twenty-two mentors were assigned first-year teachers (interns) at an 8:1 ratio, and "while 91.2% of the interns felt that their mentor was accessible enough, only 58.1% of the interns said that it was easy to reach their mentor during the day" (Halkett, 1988, p. 3).
- Mentor teachers expressed dissatisfaction with being away from the classroom on a full-time basis.
- Lastly, the evaluation report indicated that there was not a clear, common understanding of the intent of the Peer Assistance and Review Program among staff.

Although the district offered internships to develop the pedagogical skills of new teachers, many believed that they served ". . . merely a mechanical function, that is, assisting interns to learn how to do paperwork, how to discipline their class, what to teach, etc." (Halkett, 1988, p. 2). The program needed a clearer definition of purpose and a stronger focus on the development of teaching skills for new practitioners.

The 1986–87 evaluation of the PAR Program was based on survey results. It provided good firsthand information about what interns and teachers "believed" and "felt" about certain professional issues. Future evaluations ought to assess the extent to which stated goals have, in fact, been met. For example, portfolios of teacher performance may be more appropriate inclusion in the evaluation of a program that establishes improving teacher skills as one of its goals. Future evaluations will also need to address the extent to which student performance has improved as a result of this or any other similar initiative.

Recognizing the soundness of many of the Carnegie Forum's and Holmes Group's proposals and based on its initial success with the Peer Assistance and Review Program, the Rochester City School District now was ready to face an even greater challenge: the restructuring of the teaching profession. The opportunity for taking such a daring step presented itself in 1987 when the teachers' contract came up for negotiation. This landmark event irrevocably changed the course of teaching in Rochester and spawned a program destined to restructure the profession: the Career in Teaching (CIT) Program.

Compensation Provisions and the Contractual Agreement

Prior to the development of the new contract, there were thirty-nine separate steps and seven salary brackets by which a teacher's salary could be determined. This salary schedule was typical of the traditional bureaucratic system of seniority advancement, with additional incremental salary increases available to individuals upon successful completion of course work, in-service training, or advanced degrees. The schedule reflected and reinforced a system that depended upon a stable and plentiful work force. As in many districts, teachers advanced their careers by promotion into administrative positions, not through new or additional teaching assignments. Although teachers could acquire greater salary benefits by completing additional course work or degrees, few mechanisms existed to financially reward excellence for classroom performance. Furthermore, few formal incentives existed to encourage the type of collegial support that is typical of other highly skilled professions.

The teachers' contract, ratified in 1987, received national attention for its 40 percent pay hikes over a three-year period (see Tables 1, 2, 3 and 4). However, altering the compensation structure alone was only one step in a process to transform the effectiveness of the district as an educational institution.

Equally important to the sizable compensation package was a commitment to the proposition that every child within the district could

Table 1. Bracket T-I salary schedule—July 1, 1987–June 30, 1988.

Step	C Bach. Deg. Amount	D Bach. Deg. +15 Hrs. Amount	E Bach. Deg. +30 Hrs. Amount	F Mast. Deg. Bach. Deg. +45 Hrs. Amount	G Mast. Deg. +15 Hrs. Bach. Deg. +60 Hrs. Amount	H Mast. Deg. +30 Hrs. Bach. Deg. +75 Hrs. Amount	I Doctorate Amount
1	23,483	24,243	25,002	25,761	26,521	27,280	28,799
1.5	23,958	24,717	25,477	26,236	26,995	27,755	29,273
2	24,433	25,192	25,951	26,711	27,470	28,229	29,748
2.5	24,907	25,667	26,426	27,185	27,944	28,704	30,222
3	25,382	26,141	26,900	27,660	28,419	29,178	30,697
3.5	25,951	26,711	27,470	28,229	28,989	29,748	31,267
4	26,521	27,280	28,039	28,799	29,558	30,317	31,836
4.5	27,280	28,039	28,799	29,558	30,317	31,077	32,595
5	28,039	28,799	29,558	30,317	31,077	31,836	33,355
5.5	28,609	29,368	30,128	30,887	31,646	32,406	33,924
6	29,178	29,938	30,697	31,456	32,216	32,975	34,494
6.5	29,748	30,507	31,267	32,026	32,785	33,544	35,063
7	30,317	31,077	31,836	32,595	33,355	34,114	35,633
7.5	30,887	31,646	32,406	33,165	33,924	34,683	36,202
8	31,456	32,216	32,975	33,734	34,494	35,253	36,772
8.5	32,026	32,785	33,544	34,304	35,063	35,822	37,341
9	32,595	33,355	34,114	34,873	35,633	36,392	37,911
9.5	33,165	33,924	34,683	35,443	36,202	36,961	38,480
10	33,734	34,494	35,253	36,012	36,772	37,531	39,050
10.5	34,304	35,063	35,822	36,582	37,341	38,100	39,619
11	34,873	35,633	36,392	37,151	37,911	38,670	40,189

Table 1 (continued).

Step	C Bach. Deg. Amount	D Bach. Deg. +15 Hrs. Amount	E Bach. Deg. +30 Hrs. Amount	F Mast. Deg. Bach. Deg. +45 Hrs. Amount	G Mast. Deg. +15 Hrs. Bach. Deg. +60 Hrs. Amount	H Mast. Deg. +30 Hrs. Bach. Deg. +75 Hrs. Amount	I Doctorate Amount
11.5	35,348	36,107	36,867	37,721	38,480	39,239	40,753
12	35,822	36,582	37,341	38,290	39,050	39,809	41,323
12.5	36,297	37,056	37,816	38,765	39,524	40,378	41,897
13	36,722	37,531	38,290	39,239	39,999	40,948	42,466
13.5	36,922	37,681	38,670	39,714	40,473	41,422	43,035
14	37,072	37,831	39,050	40,189	40,948	41,897	43,605
14.5	37,072	37,831	39,200	40,568	41,328	42,277	44,080
15	37,072	37,831	39,350	40,948	41,707	42,656	44,555
15.5	37,072	37,831	39,350	41,098	41,857	42,806	44,705
16–19	37,072	37,831	39,350	41,248	42,007	42,956	44,855
19.5	37,396	38,155	39,674	41,572	42,332	43,281	45,179
20	37,721	38,480	39,999	41,897	42,656	43,605	45,504
20.5	37,871	38,630	40,149	42,047	42,806	43,755	45,654
21–24	38,021	38,780	40,299	42,197	42,956	43,905	45,804
24.5	38,345	39,105	40,623	42,522	43,281	44,230	46,128
25	38,670	39,429	40,948	42,846	43,605	44,555	46,453
25.5	38,820	39,579	41,098	42,996	43,755	44,705	46,603
26	38,970	39,729	41,248	43,146	43,905	44,855	46,753

Note: From The Contractual Agreement between The City School District of Rochester, New York and The Rochester Teachers Association (NYSUT/AFT—AFL-CIO), p. 97.

445

Table 2. Salary schedule—July 1, 1987.

Intern		Resident		Professional		Lead*	
Index	Amount	Index	Amount	Index	Amount	Index	Amount
1.00	$23,483	1.11	$26,067	1.11	$26,067		
		1.22	28,650	1.22	28,650		
		1.33	31,233	1.33	31,233		
		1.44	33,816	1.44	33,816		
				1.55	36,399		
				1.66	38,982		
				1.77	41,565		
				1.88	44,149		
				1.99	46,732		
				2.10	49,315		
				2.21	51,898		

*Lead teacher designation to be negotiated for implementation July 1, 1988.

Table 2 is for conversion purposes only. Unit members whose 1987–88 salary (Table 1) falls within 2% plus or minus any salary amount shown in Table 2 will be placed on that index number. Unit members placed on this Salary Bracket (Table 2) will retain the same index number for determining 1988–89 and 1989–90 salaries (Tables 3 and 4).

Note: From *The Contractual Agreement between The City School District of Rochester, New York and The Rochester Teachers Association (NYSUT/AFT—AFL/CIO)*, p. 98.

Table 3. Salary schedule—July 1, 1988.

Intern		Resident		Professional		Lead*	
Index	Amount	Index	Amount	Index	Amount	Index	Amount
1.00	$26,067	1.11	$28,935	1.11	$28,935		
		1.22	31,802	1.22	31,802		
		1.33	34,670	1.33	34,670		
		1.44	37,537	1.44	37,537		
				1.55	40,404		
				1.66	43,272		
				1.77	46,139		
				1.88	49,006		
				1.99	51,874		
				2.10	54,741		
				2.21	57,609		

*Lead teacher designation to be negotiated for implementation July 1, 1988.

Note: From *The Contractual Agreement between The City School District of Rochester, New York and The Rochester Teachers Association (NYSUT/AFT—AFL/CIO)*, p. 99.

Table 4. Salary schedule—July 1, 1989.

Intern		Resident		Professional		Lead*	
Index	Amount	Index	Amount	Index	Amount	Index	Amount
1.00	$28,935	1.11	$32,118	1.11	$32,118		
		1.22	35,301	1.22	35,301		
		1.33	38,484	1.33	38,484		
		1.44	41,667	1.44	41,667		
				1.55	44,850		
				1.66	48,033		
				1.77	51,215		
				1.88	54,398		
				1.99	57,581		
				2.10	60,764		
				2.21	63,947		

*Lead teacher designation to be negotiated for implementation July 1, 1988.

Note: From *The Contractual Agreement between The City School District of Rochester, New York and The Rochester Teachers Association (NYSUT/AFT—AFL/CIO)*, p. 100.

learn—regardless of background or social circumstances. In addition, recognition of teaching as a valuable function in its own right—not as a stepping stone to an administrative position—was also necessary. Experience, extra training, and demonstrated success would be acknowledged by incentives to remain in the classroom.

Largely influenced by the Carnegie proposals, Superintendent McWalters and the president of the RTA, Adam Urbanski, agreed to a contract that would increase the status of the district's teaching profession by significant changes in the salary schedule and work responsibilities of teachers. One of the most important agreements was the decision to establish the Career in Teaching Program (CIT). The intent of the Career in Teaching Program was to redefine the teacher's role in school organization and development as a means of improving student performance (Gillett and Halkett, *An Overview of CIT,* 1989). The contractual agreement called for the establishment of a Joint Governing Panel to develop the basic principles and agreements. The Career in Teaching Program would have two primary goals: "(a) to develop and maintain the highest caliber teaching staff, and (b) to provide [Rochester's] teachers with career options that do not require them to leave the classroom in order to assume additional responsibility and leadership roles. Both goals assume greater collegial interaction and expanded professional expectations; both assume accountability defined, in part, by improved student attainment" (p. 5).

The plan would include four levels: *Intern*—first-year teachers, *Resident*—successful interns working for certification and tenure (second through fifth years), *Professional Teacher*—fully certified and tenured staff, and *Lead Teacher*—successful teachers with ten years' experience who apply and are selected for roles requiring additional responsibilities and time requirements. Lead Teacher designation carried a stipend that for some would boost their salaries to more than $60,000.

Although the compensation package attracted widespread attention, the Career in Teaching Program provided Rochester's professional staff with unprecedented opportunities for promotion within the profession. For example, Lead Teachers continue to teach—at least part-time. In recognition of their expertise, they receive the "most challenging" teaching assignments. Lead Teachers also participate in peer review, curriculum design, the mentor teacher program, staff development, and as adjunct faculty at local colleges.

Under the CIT Program, opportunities for advancement within the field are more available than before. By rejecting the traditional practice of assigning the least experienced staff to the most difficult classrooms or schools—a practice based on a more narrow vision of seniority—teachers assume a level of responsibility commensurate with their experience and ability.

The Development of the Career in Teaching Program

Similar to the Peer Assistance and Review Program, the development of the essential facets for the Career in Teaching Program required several months and the involvement of many teachers and district administrators. A ten-member governing panel (five teachers appointed by the Rochester Teacher's Association and five administrators appointed by the superintendent) worked throughout the first half of 1988 to establish a set of initial objectives. They agreed that they would (a) define the roles, responsibilities, expectations, and success measures for the four new career levels—Intern, Resident, Professional, and Lead Teacher; (b) develop policy recommendations and a plan to ensure the recruitment, selection, and hiring of the "best" candidates for teaching positions; (c) ensure that only teachers with potential to become top educators are employed after their first year or granted tenure; (d) develop a plan for monitoring the tenure process, one that would be developed in condjunction with establishing the responsibilities and success measures of the Resident Teacher; (e) redesign the performance appraisal system for teachers; (f) work to incorporate staff development as an integral part of a teacher's advancement through the levels of the career ladder; and (g) provide an opportunity for exemplary teachers to inspire excellence in the profession, to share their knowledge and expertise with others, and to participate actively in instructional decision making (Gillett and Halkett, *An Overview of CIT,* 1989).

Implementation and refinement of the CIT Program will take many years. It is clear, however, that achieving these objectives can result in a cadre of better skilled and highly motivated teachers—a profession better prepared to meet the needs of our changing urban population.

Although no formal evaluation of the CIT Program as yet exists, there is general agreement in the district that it represents another important step towards restructuring the teaching force. Progress in refining the CIT Program continues at a steady pace. For example, in 1989 the classification of Lead Teacher was expanded to include those who serve as *mentors* for new teachers, *demonstration specialists* (teachers who provide instructional demonstrations district-wide), and *intervention specialists* (teachers who provide assistance and support to tenured teachers experiencing severe difficulties in the classroom). To strengthen its commitment to providing additional career options for its professional staff, the district more than doubled the number of Lead Teachers in 1988–89.

The complete redesign of the performance appraisal system for teachers is still another bold step that the district has undertaken. The new system will "(a) be based on an assumption of teacher competence, (b) focus on and promote developmental and professional growth of teachers, (c) include peer review and provisions for student and parent input, (d) reflect student achievement, and (e) provide for cyclical, but not necessarily annual, reviews" (Gillett and Halkett, *Career in Teaching: Performance Appraisal Redesign for Teachers,* 1989, p. 1).

Currently, the district is implementing pilot projects at selected sites to test various models of performance appraisal. Two Lead Teachers coordinate the performance appraisal redesign project. They meet regularly with teachers, administrators, parents, students, and others to provide information, to do research and gather data regarding teacher evaluation, to design innovative performance appraisal methods, and to identify sites for "field testing." Ultimately, they will oversee evaluation of the project.

CONCLUSION

Still in its infancy, certain elements of Rochester's Career in Teaching Program address many of the problems identified by researchers in the field. The additional compensation afforded local teachers does not resemble some of the failed efforts of *merit pay* that have often resulted in further isolating teachers (Murnane and Cohen, 1986). Rather, it is compensation in recognition of professional competence based on criteria established by teachers. The importance of the union and its willingness to depart from the traditional industrial model of unionism cannot be underscored enough. There is no written evidence to date to support findings that teachers are, in fact, more motivated or more skilled, or that student performance has improved as a result of the early implementation stages of this reform. But structures have been put in place and are still being developed that have greater promise for meeting these goals than any previous reform. Unlike earlier reform efforts, such as those described in *Steady Work* (Elmore and McLaughlin, 1988), the development of professional expectations for teachers includes a focus on teaching and learning. Restructuring the teaching profession in Rochester, thus far, has taken time and much effort, involving many individuals. I firmly believe that a "skillfully" managed process involving as many teachers as possible in shaping the teaching profession can result in a greater sense of ownership and willingness to accept the proposed changes. In many respects, teachers in Rochester are the agents rather than the objects of reform.

Changing the culture of an organization and the behavior of its work force is a slow and oftentimes painful process. Clearly, different perspectives will exist and conflicts inevitably will arise over many aspects of the process. Regardless, I believe that the strides the Rochester City School District is taking towards restructuring the teaching profession will result in improved student performance and teacher motivation. In the long term, improved student performance is the standard by which success of Rochester's plan will be measured. There is much work to be done!

REFERENCES

Carnegie Forum on Education and the Economy. 1986. *A Nation Prepared: Teachers for the 21st Century: The Report of the Task Force on Teaching as a Profession.* New York: Carnegie Forum on Education and the Economy.

Elmore, R. F. and M. W. McLaughlin. 1988. *Steady Work: Policy, Practice, and the Reform of American Education.* National Institute of Education Report No. 400-79-0023, Santa Monica, CA: The Rand Corporation.

Gillett, T. D. and K. A. Halkett. 1989. *Career in Teaching Program: An Overview of CIT.* Rochester, NY: City School District/Rochester Teachers' Association.

Gillett, T. D. and K. A. Halkett. 1989. *Career in Teaching: Performance Appraisal Redesign for Teachers: A Report on Initial Efforts.* Rochester, NY: City School District.

Halkett, K. A. 1988. *Peer Assistance and Review Program: 1986/87 Local Evaluation Report: Executive Summary.* Rochester, NY: City School District.

Holmes Group, The. 1986. *Tomorrow's Teachers: A Report of the Holmes Group.* East Lansing, MI: The Holmes Group.

Johnson, S. M. 1989. "Schoolwork and Its Reform," in *The Politics of Reforming School Administration,* J. Hannaway and R. Crowson, eds., *Politics of Education Association Yearbook 1988.* New York: Falmer Press, pp. 95–112.

Johnson, S. M. and N. C. Nelson. 1987. "Teaching Reform in an Active Voice," *Phi Delta Kappan,* pp. 591–598.

Maeroff, G. I. 1988. *The Empowerment of Teachers: Overcoming the Crisis of Confidence.* New York: Teachers College Press.

McWalters, P. 1989. *Superintendent's Proposal to the Board of Education: Position Paper on the Redesign of Public Education in Rochester.* Rochester, NY: City School District.

Murnane, R. J. and D. K. Cohen. 1986. "Merit Pay and the Evaluation Problem: Why Most Merit Pay Plans Fail and a Few Survive," *Harvard Educational Review,* 56(1): 1–17.

Rochester City School District. 1981–82. *Data Base.* Rochester, NY: Rochester City School District.

Rochester City School District. 1983–84. *Data Base.* Rochester, NY: Rochester City School District.

Rochester City School District. 1985. *Data Analysis.* Rochester, NY: Rochester City School District.

Rochester City School District. 1987. *The Contractural Agreement between the City School District of Rochester, New York and the Rochester Teachers Association (NYSUTAFT–AFL/CIO), July 1, 1987–June 30, 1990,* Rochester, NY: Rochester City School District.

Rochester City School District. 1987–88. *District Data Base.* Rochester, NY: Rochester City School District.

The Urban League Community Task Force on Education. 1986. *A Call to Action.* Rochester, NY: The Center for Educational Development/Urban League Community Task Force on Education.

CHAPTER 18

Empowering Teachers and Enhancing Student Achievement through School Restructuring

THOMAS W. PAYZANT – *Superintendent, San Diego City Schools, California*

SPREADING rapidly through American public education is a new wave of reform. It is called "restructuring," and it represents a significant departure from reforms of the past.

We will trace the origins and development over the past three years of a dynamic and promising new reform movement in a major urban school district. The work has led to many exciting changes, and many others are being planned. However, challenges and obstacles remain, and it will be years before we will be able to evaluate our efforts fully. But at this point, we are extremely encouraged by what we see.

The current school restructuring movement is fundamentally different from the school reform ideas that have been considered in the past. Today's movement challenges traditional assumptions about the best way to organize our schools for teaching and learning. It raises questions about roles and responsibilities of those involved with schools and admits that schools as they are do not work for many students. Most importantly, it forces us to acknowledge that we must do a better job of providing meaningful educational programs for all students and that more of the same will not be good enough.

Most schools in America are structured today much as they were at the turn of the century, i.e., they function like factories, selecting, sorting, grading, and processing students. The curriculum has scope and sequence. The lessons are explicit and timed. There is an assembly line process that propels students through a maze that, if successfully negotiated, leads to annual promotion and ultimately a high school diploma. Too many, however, fall off the assembly line—we call them dropouts. And in the name of quality control, we test to emphasize failure rather than success.

While this approach may have served us in the past, it no longer meets all of the students' needs. As our society has become more diverse, the needs of our schools vary greatly, considerably more than they did only a decade ago. For example, in San Diego children come to our schools speaking over sixty different native languages. They represent many races and come from an even greater number of ethnic and social backgrounds. Our challenge is to provide equal and excellent educational programs for all of them.

Many people, both in and out of education, are coming to the realization that further tightening of the present system is not the answer. They point, for example, to a growing mismatch between the skills of high school graduates and the needs and expectations of employers. They see an unacceptably high drop-out rate, and far too many students who do remain in school are at risk of failing.

It is not possible for us to know the exact nature of the society in which today's children will live as adults. While the traditional purposes of the schools are still relevant, the context in which they are pursued is changing dramatically. To prepare young people for an unknowable future calls for a shift of emphasis in our approaches to learning and teaching. For example, it will be necessary to strengthen the teaching of problem-solving and thinking skills. We must stress the importance of maintaining our political and governmental institutions and train students to be able to make intelligent public policy. We must pay attention to ethical dilemmas and character development and find ways to link the world of school, the world of work, and the world of social responsibility.

The new restructuring movement proposes that much more of the decision-making authority, responsibility, and accountability for student achievement be placed with teachers at each school. The idea is that teachers, working with the advice and involvement of parents and other staff members, know best how to meet the particular needs of the school's students. However, giving teachers a greater say in how the school is organized and how and what students are taught is not a simple matter. Traditions die slowly. Educators pride themselves on stability and accept change cautiously. But despite the many obstacles, school restructuring seems to offer the promise that schools can be much better and can graduate students ready to meet the complex demands of the world in the twenty-first century. It is already clear that once some of these fundamental shifts in authority and responsibility are made, the changes that take place can be significant and lasting.

DEFINING RESTRUCTURING

Restructuring must be seen as a process for renewal, not as an outcome. The restructuring process involves questioning fundamental assumptions and practices that shape education and schooling. It includes assessing the successes and failures of children in schools as a prerequisite for enhancing learning and teaching. The process also calls for formulating new roles and relationships that lead to collaboration between and among staff members, students, parents, and the community as decision making and shared responsibility for student outcomes move from the central office to the schools. Finally, the restructuring process requires the development of action plans to make schools places where *all* students learn and teachers want to teach.

As we begin to give schools the authority to make decisions about how they are organized, what the curriculum should be, and how it should be taught rather than mandating those things from the top of the bureaucracy down, questions and concerns are raised from many quarters. People ask

- Can waivers of union contracts, board policies, administrative procedures, state mandates, and federal regulations be secured to support restructuring?
- Will there still be school district goals, standards, and expectations?
- What will change mean for the least successful and most successful students in the school?
- What role will the school principal play in a restructured school?
- How will working conditions in schools change to enable teachers to function as professionals?
- What will happen to the administrators and other staff members at the central office?
- Who will be held accountable for the students' learning, and how will the results be assessed?
- How will the reward and incentive system be changed?
- How will decisions about budgets and the allocation of resources be made?
- How will teachers and parents work together?
- How do we know these kinds of changes won't make things worse rather than better?
- Isn't there a danger that teachers and students in every school will be tempted simply to do their own thing?

At this point in the brief history of the restructuring movement, no one has complete and final answers. We have general ideas and assumptions and realize that there may not be one best answer to each question. We have much more to do.

THE ORIGINS OF THE RESTRUCTURING MOVEMENT

One major impetus to the school restructuring movement in America was the release in 1986 of the report of the Carnegie Forum on Education and the Economy, *A Nation Prepared: Teachers for the 21st Century.*[1] The report called for drastic improvements in the standards of schools and teachers. Among other things, it recommended the establishment of a national board for professional teaching standards and dissolution of undergraduate degrees in education. A central component of the Carnegie report was a call for restructuring schools to significantly improve the quality of student learning and achievement by professionalizing teaching and giving teachers a greater say in how the school is organized and how the students are taught.

The earlier efforts, including the "excellence" movement which stemmed primarily from the 1983 report, *A Nation at Risk,* of the National Commission on Excellence in Education,[2] basically emphasized quantitative changes imposed from the top down. They called for more instructional days in the school year, more hours in the school day, more homework, and more and tougher course requirements for graduation. Many of the reforms initiated by the states, such as California, during the 1980s followed this same pattern. Each of these changes was implemented in San Diego City Schools with strong policy direction by the board of education and administrative direction of the superintendent.

The new school restructuring movement calls for changes that are much more fundamental. It recognizes that schools would be organized and function in very different ways if educators acted on what we know about how people learn how best to teach them. Change, proponents argue, must begin at the bottom of the educational bureaucracy where the real business of public education takes place, i.e., in the classroom between teachers and students. The movement acknowledges that there is not one best way for all students to learn and all teachers to teach, and on this basis it concludes that different schools can and should be organized differently. It recognizes that people in every school must establish a vision of what the school can be, set high expectations for students, and collaborate on strategies for making sure students learn.

That implies making basic changes in the way our school district bureaucracies are organized. Support personnel in central offices must become enablers, facilitators, and coaches rather than enforcers, controllers, and directors. Superintendents and board members must learn how to share power with principals, teachers, and parents while still providing leadership through a vision for education and goals and expectations for the entire school district.

BEGINNING RESTRUCTURING IN SAN DIEGO

The origin of the restructuring movement in the San Diego City Schools can be found in the report and recommendations of the Schools of the Future Commission. The commission, which was appointed by the superintendent in the summer of 1986, had as its membership seventeen prominent San Diegans representing a board cross section of the community including business and industry, the military, higher education, the media, and the arts. They were given the charge of addressing the question, "What should the San Diego public schools be like in the year 2000?" A $25,000 grant from the Stuart Foundations matched by local corporate and foundation funds enabled the commission to function independently. The superintendent insisted that school district officials provide access to all information requested by the commission, but the analysis of the information was left to the commission and the person it hired to work on the preparation and writing of the report.

After a year of extensive examination, interviews, and discussion, the commission members arrived at consensus on a vision for San Diego's future schools. In June of 1987 it released its report, *Which Way to the Future? San Diego and Its Schools at a Crossroads.*[3] The commission made five general recommendations:

(1) *Build a new schools–community coalition to support the long-term excellence of the educational system, based on mutual responsibility and measurable goals.* To increase the education and employability levels of great numbers of students, an unprecendented effort will be needed to coordinate San Diego's resources with the public school system. Rather than operating independently of one another, with minimal interaction, the city's future educational system must be a planned, cooperative endeavor between the community and the schools.

As the first step in building this new coalition, parents, businesses, government, universities, civic and cultural organizations, and the military should join together with the city's public schools in a San Diego Compact for Educational Excellence.

(2) *Begin a fundamental restructuring of schools with pilot "Schools of the Future" to experiment with new approaches and organization that help all students attain productive futures.* The last thirteen years of the twentieth century can and should be an exciting period of innovation for San Diego City Schools. Today's schools are not reaching all students. While the schools are integrated, achievement levels are not equal across racial/ethnic groups. Adequately preparing far greater numbers of graduates for the increased demands of the workplace and world of the twenty-first century will challenge educators to experiment with new methods of teaching students and organizing schools.

Five key principles can guide the design of pilot "Schools of the Future":

- Empower individual schools to determine how best to teach students, within clear expectations set by the superintendent and board of education.
- Encourage principals and teachers to work together in managing schools and the learning process.
- Allocate resources, incentives, and recognition to enhance school based authority and the retention of good teachers in the classroom.
- Use diverse teaching approaches and curricula to respond to the diverse learning needs of students.
- Provide more rigorous school based accountability—with fair, equitable, and objective methods to evaluate school performance—in return for more school based authority.

(3) *Integrate technology into every classroom and school administrative office to enhance teaching, learning, and managing.* Technology has the potential to provide enhanced group and individualized instruction for students, improved incentive systems and status for educators, and greater visibility of school results for the community. Pilot projects should be undertaken, which demonstrate a working vision of technology's benefits, which adequately train staff, which build broad support for expanding successful programs, and which are cost-effective.

(4) *Take advantage of San Diego's unique location as an international gateway to Latin America and the Pacific Rim by encouraging all students—beginning in the primary grades—to learn a second language in addition to English and to better understand world cultures.* San Diego is a border community and a gateway to Pacific Rim nations. Trade with the city's Latin American neighbors and Asian countries is on the rise. The ability of San Diego companies to successfully compete for international markets will depend in part on the language training and cultural awareness students receive from the schools. A native San Diegan who learns the Spanish language and Mexican history can more effectively conduct business with Mexico or work to resolve long-standing problems between the two countries.

(5) *Aggressively pursue a stable, independent, and increased funding base for public education.* San Diego City Schools cannot plan today for tomorrow's schools. Every year school district officials must wait for the state legislature and governor to work out an education budget before funds can be allocated to school programs. The future of the city and the state are too important for the schools to be an annual political bargaining chip.

A "California Educational Trust Fund" is needed to provide a long-term independent, and increasing source of funds for the state's public schools. The funding mechanism should remove public education from annual political competition with other essential services.

It was the second recommendation calling for a fundamental restructuring of schools that became the catalyst the superintendent and board of education wanted in order to begin moving the district directly toward the restructuring activities taking place in schools today. In its full report, the commission not only outlined in some detail the general direction it thought restructuring should take, it also set forth the steps the district should take to get the process started.

APPOINTMENT AND INITIAL ACTIVITIES OF THE INNOVATION AND CHANGE LEADERSHIP GROUP

These recommendations included establishing a leadership group representing the major school district and community constituencies to begin designing a restructuring process. The superintendent responded in the fall of 1987 by creating the district's Innovation and Change Leadership Group (ICLG). Its general charge was to plan, encourage, and guide the district's restructuring initiatives.

Membership in the ICLG represents a broad cross section of the school district's community. Originally, twenty-seven staff and community members were selected to serve, and that number grew to thirty-one representatives in 1988. Membership includes

- equal representation of teachers and administrators (eleven members each), including the current and past presidents of the San Diego Teachers' Association and Administrators' Association of San Diego
- representation of classified employees by the current presidents of the Classified Employees' Association and the California School Employees' Association
- the current board of education president
- community representation by the San Diego Unified PTA Council president and a school site PTA representative, two members from the original Schools of the Future Commission, one member from the San Diego Dropout Prevention and Recovery Round Table, and the dean of the University of San Diego's School of Education

The ICLG first sought to broaden the district's knowledge and the public's awareness of reform issues. The ICLG with the joint sponsorship of the San Diego County Office of Education, University of San Diego, San Diego State University, and the Association of California School Administrators conducted a four-part seminar series entitled, "Preparing Schools for the Future: Restructuring Schools." This took place between November 1987 and March 1988. The seminar featured the principal author of the Carnegie report and teachers, principals, and district officials from three school systems across the country who are at the forefront of the restructuring movement.

Marc Tucker, executive director of the Carnegie Forum, gave an overview of the principles of restructuring. Administrators and teachers from Schenley High School in Pittsburgh described the creation of the Schenley High School Teachers Center by teachers in 1983 and reviewed its current activities. Operated by teachers, the school based center offers each Pittsburgh secondary teacher an intensive professional development experience when they are released full time from their regularly assigned teaching responsibilities.

Representatives from Jefferson County, Kentucky, described the teacher development and support activities the Gheens Professional Academy offers to restructuring schools. At the academy, teachers from twenty-four schools are developing the skills they need to become facilitators/trainers for school based management; in turn, their schools will become models (similar to teaching hospitals) for other schools in the district.

Representatives from Dade County, Florida, described the "School Based Management/Shared Decision Making" program that resulted from a contract between the local teachers' union and board of education. Under the auspices of the Task Force on Professionalization in Schools, thirty-two schools are now in the pilot program stage. They are given maximum flexibility in budgeting, operations, and programming and are granted latitude in waivers from district policy.

The ICLG's next step addressed the complex process of defining the purpose and goals of the schools of the future initiative by generating a purpose and belief statement[4] and by designing the criteria and process for enlisting in the restructuring effort. The core beliefs set out by the ICLG defined the purpose and parameters of restructuring. Restructuring

- is a commitment to a long-term strategic planning process
- is rooted in the findings and recommendations of the Schools of the Future Commission
- can be accomplished with existing district resources and within district policies and contracts
- requires an environment of trust, flexibility, and risk taking
- requires a balance between greater autonomy and more responsibility for schools
- can be successful in San Diego and result in a valuable model for other school districts

To launch the restructuring process and heighten awareness of and interest in the initiative, ICLG sponsored "Super Saturday: School Restructuring Work Session" in April of 1988. Teams of five (a principal, two teachers, a classified staff member, and a parent) from thirty-eight schools convened voluntarily for a day-long in-service planning session to learn about the restructuring process. "Super Saturday" was cosponsored by the Matsushita Foundation, which has formed a partnership with San Diego City Schools for long-term support of the district's restructuring efforts.

"Super Saturday" began with comments from the president of the board of education expressing the board's commitment to restructuring, followed by an overview by the deputy superintendent of the district's goals and progress in restructuring. In the keynote address, Ken Tewel, a Matsushita Foundation consultant, provided an overview of the foundation's goals and activities in supporting restructuring programs, drawing upon his own experiences as a principal in three public high schools in New York City.

With this as an introduction, smaller workshops convened to review the draft "Purpose and Belief Statement" and to discuss the process for enlisting schools. This enlistment process required meetings with faculty, staff, parents, and students to discuss the information received at "Super Saturday." According to the guidelines, if two-thirds of faculty and staff voted to support the belief statements and if parents and students generally indicated their support, a school could then express its written intent to participate. Following their enlistment, each school would then elect a steering committee responsible for coordinating the planning process at its site. Twenty-five schools had committed to participate in restructuring by late spring 1988.

At the end of June 1988, teams from fifteen elementary schools, six middle or junior high schools, and four senior high schools met for "Super Planning Week," a four-day strategic planning workshop to develop the skills needed to lead school staffs through the planning process. The superintendent started the week with a presentation outlining his hopes for restructuring. Using case study and role-playing in groups, each school team participated in a model-planning and team-building exercise that included how to develop a vision and goal statement, how to generate options for achieving that vision, how to develop an implementation plan, and how to design ongoing evaluation and assessment procedures. Several teams of central office administrators also worked on similar tasks. The Matsushita Foundation again provided support to bring consultants from Harvard University, the Dade County school district, and school systems in Seattle, Santa Fe, and Rochester to the session. The Stuart Foundations provided stipends for the participating teachers.

In the weeks following "Super Planning Week," the district initiated several activities to support restructuring efforts in the schools. Support groups formed at all school levels to facilitate communication and collaboration among restructuring schools. These groups meet regularly to share ideas and build momentum for restructuring.

At the same time, managers at the divisional level began to meet with their staffs to discuss how central offices can best support restructuring schools. Their discussions focused on the effects of greater school autonomy on the relationship between the central office and restructuring schools and what new systems, procedures, and policies might need to be developed in order to promote successful restructuring.

The superintendent delivered a progress report to the larger school community in his annual address to district leaders in August 1988. The message conveyed support, enthusiasm, and hope that school restructuring would be a key theme for the 1988–89 school year.

Carrying this theme forward, beginning in October 1988, the district sponsored a series of workshops geared to the professional development of teachers. Topics included how to increase the number of minority students graduating from high school and entering four-year colleges and how to utilize Socratic teaching methods most effectively. In December 1988, the district hosted a two-day city-wide dropout prevention conference that brought together experts on the issue of dropout prevention to examine, in part, how restructuring could help more students succeed in school.

THE ADOPTION OF A BOARD POLICY ON RESTRUCTURING

The school restructuring initiative was formally recognized by the board of education in its policy statement[5] on school restructuring, approved on November 8, 1988. This particular school board meeting was held at a restructuring school, Linda Vista Elementary, and featured comments from staff members and parents representing various restructuring schools and from members of the ICLG. The district received a great deal of media and public attention from this meeting.

Along with its policy statement on school restructuring, the board adopted a series of belief statements to help shape and encourage restructuring efforts. The policy and belief statements follow:

Policy

The policy of the Board of Education is to support school restructuring as a process to achieve a fundamental change in school organization and instruction that will prepare all students for the future. The purposes of school restructuring are to improve the quality of instruction and student achievement. School restructuring will require greater site autonomy and control over budgets; shared decision making among staff members, parents and students; and appropriate accountability standards for student outcomes.

Belief Statements

The Board of Education established the following set of belief statements that are the rationale for promoting school restructuring:

About Change—We believe:

- that school restructuring is not a passing fad but is a long-term strategic planning effort to improve the quality of student instruction by changing the organization of schools.
- that the environment for change must allow for flexibility and risk taking.

About Students—We believe:

- all students can learn and that public education should enable all students to fulfill their unique potential.
- all students deserve to be at school, that each child should feel welcomed by the school staff, and that each student should achieve success at school.
- that students learn in different ways, and that current instructional methods must change to meet each student's learning needs.
- that with the rapid increase in knowledge, students must learn to effectively process information and become lifelong learners.
- that parental involvement is an essential element of effective student learning.

About Schools—We believe:

- that the school is the locus of change.
- that schools should have greater autonomy and foster shared decision making among administrators, teachers, classified staff, and parents.
- that greater school autonomy and shared decision making must be accompanied by the acceptance of responsibility and accountability for student learning.
- that changes in school organization, instructional practices, and staff roles will occur in phases and that they will need time to evolve. It will take several years before major change is evident.
- that schools can restructure within their resource allocations.

About District Organization—We believe:

- that the district organization exists to set district goals and objectives, provide support and help for schools, establish district standards, and assist schools in assessing results.

About Changing Roles — We believe:

- that desired change in school must have significant involvement from teachers and place primary emphasis on teaching and the instructional process.
- that principals should lead all employees in schools to create an environment for change by encouraging collaboration; shared decision making; and teamwork involving parents, students, and the community.
- that granting schools greater autonomy and encouraging shared decision making, collaboration, and teamwork will change the roles not only of school staffs, parents, and students but also of board members, employee organizations leaders, cabinet members, and district certificated and classified support staff. Relationships must become more enabling, supportive, and empowering.

About San Diego City Schools — We believe:

- San Diego City Schools is in a unique position to be a model for school restructuring nationally given the composition of students, quality of staff, and district reputation for innovation.

Requirements

The Board of Education encourages schools to explore new and more effective ways to educate students and to request changes or waivers of present requirements that unnecessarily restrict schools. Until such changes are made or waivers granted, schools will need to adhere to the following requirements:

- Work to achieve district goals.
- Adhere to board policy.
- Conduct activities that are legal and ethical.
- Adhere to collective bargaining agreements.
- Operate within resource allocations.
- Avoid activities that negatively impact other schools.

Change or Waiver Process

The Innovation and Change Leadership Group will assist schools with requests to waive local, state, and federal policy, laws, regulations, and collective bargaining agreements to facilitate school restructuring efforts. The Innovation and Change Leadership Group will recommend for approval waivers or adjustments to policies or agreements to the Board of Education or the appropriate employee organization.

Process and Planning

The Board of Education establishes the following as important for each restructuring school to observe:

- Commit to the purpose and belief statements of the Board of Education's restructuring policy.
- Engage in broad-based decision making involving the school administration, faculty, staff, parents, and students as appropriate.
- Engage in a planning process to create a vision statement, define school needs, establish goals and priorities, design implementation plans, and develop measures of success and an ongoing assessment process.
- Establish goals and implementation plans for improved student learning which are as good or better than what currently exists.
- Apply for a change or waiver as necessary.
- Seek additional outside funds and in-kind contributions to support restructuring if needed.

This commitment and support from the board greatly strengthened the restructuring movement in the district.

THE PARTICIPATION OF THE TEACHERS' UNION

Restructuring was also given an enormous boost late in 1988 when the board and the teachers' association reached a landmark agreement on a new four-year contract. The contract is based on collaboration, shared decision making, and trust building, leaving behind ten years of adversarial, conflict-ridden bargaining. The agreement also led to similar multiyear contracts with the district's other employee bargaining units.

The teachers' contract[6] recognizes that restructuring may call for a variety of changing roles and responsibilities, including more teacher involvement in decision making at the school level, new systems of accountability, and changes in how the school is organized and how learning activities take place. Article XXV of the contract reads as follows:

Section 1: Statement of Intent

The District and the Association agree that it is in the best interest of the San Diego City Schools to cooperatively engage in exploration of an experimentation in the current wave of educational reform proposals being discussed by educators nationally, and further to explore the various reform proposals which the creativity of City Schools staff may generate.

Such a venture may call for a variety of changing roles and responsibilities within the schools, including but not necessarily limited to:

A. Involving school staff members in decision making at sites.
B. Devising new systems of school site accountability.
C. Organizing and staffing schools in new ways.
D. Altering schedules and learning activities to accommodate different levels of student learning.
E. School staff member involvement in budget development.

Section 2: Restructuring/Educational Reform Plans

As a part of the educational reform process, the parties encourage local staffs considering restructuring efforts to consider the development and submission of proposals which involve:

A. Peer group coaching.
B. Team performance reviews.
C. Observation schedules.
D. Greater interaction between staff members.
E. Sharing of teaching techniques and strategies.
F. Such proposals should remain separate and distinct from performance evaluation which is set forth in Article XIV, unless a contract waiver is obtained.

Section 3: Board and Association Agreement

A. In restructuring/educational reform areas, the District and the Association recognize the need for flexibility in any restructuring effort and will, where appropriate, consider waiving or modifying contract provisions.
B. Restructuring/education reform proposals shall be referred to the Contract Administration Committee to review to determine whether contract waivers are necessary.
C. All agreements to modify, amend or otherwise change contract provisions will be by mutual written agreement of the parties. Each party will determine its own procedures for ratifying any written agreements which modify existing contract provisions.

FURTHER ACTIVITIES OF THE INNOVATION AND CHANGE LEADERSHIP GROUP AND DEVELOPMENT OF THE WAIVER PROCESS

Meanwhile, the ICLG continued to assertively encourage and assist restructuring. The group expanded its role during the 1988–89 school year. In addition to promoting district-wide seminars and workshops on various restructuring topics, the leadership group established a sub-committee on educational technology and assumed policy, staffing, and budgeting responsibilities. These activities included

- appointment of a high profile technology subcommittee co-chaired by the local area vice president of Pacific Bell and the assistant superintendent of the district's Educational Services Division to develop plans for implementing the Schools of the Future Commission's educational technology recommendation
- selection of a resource teacher to assist schools in restructuring planning
- oversight of $60,000 in foundation and district funds that are available to schools and central offices for small planning and staff development grants

The board policy on restructuring cited the need for a waiver process. Without a process allowing schools to waive state and federal regulations, administrative procedures, board-adopted policy, or negotiated contracts, schools could not attempt major organizational changes. The ICLG developed such a process, which was approved by the board in early January 1989.

The following is a description and a flow chart depiction (see page 469) of the proposed waiver process.[7]

Stage I. School Site Requests Waiver

- Idea emerges from school planning discussions.
- Idea is found to be inconsistent with policy, contract provisions, or state and federal regulations after discussion with School Operations Division and appropriate central office support departments
- Idea is discussed with broader school community, including teachers, administrators, classified staff, parents, and, as appropriate, students and/or community representatives. Idea is justified among the school community in terms of improved student learning achievement.
- Consensus is reached among school community, with support of School Operations Division, to pursue a waiver to implement idea.

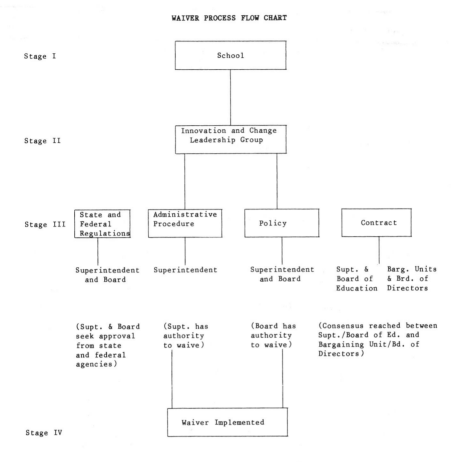

WAIVER PROCESS FLOW CHART

Stage II: School Presents Waiver Request to Innovation and Change Leadership Group

- Idea is presented to ICLG by school representatives with support of School Operations Division representatives.
- Consensus is reached among ICLG members that school proposal for waiver should move forward in the process.

Stage III: Regulation, Policy, Procedure or Contract Waived

- ICLG identifies whether waiver relates to state and federal regulation, administrative procedure, board-adopted policy, or negotiated contract. Waiver proceeds in process depicted in flow chart. If consensus is reached among various individuals and groups, waiver is approved by either superintendent, board of education, or superintendent and board of education simultaneously with bargaining units and their boards of directors.

In February 1989 the first waiver was granted to a school, enabling teachers, other school staff members, and parents to participate in the selection of a principal.

A NEW VISION STATEMENT AND NEW EXPECTATIONS

As the restructuring movement has gained momentum in the district, the top administrative staff, superintendent, and board of education began to reexamine the organization of the district and its instructional programs and consider the direction the district should be going. One thing these discussions led to was the writing of a new vision statement for the San Diego City Schools. It is in three parts and addresses change, excellence, and empowerment:

Change: We have a vision of an environment where innovation and change are encouraged and all ideas are heard and respected; where everyone believes that all children can learn and deserve to be taught.

Excellence: We have a vision where excellence in teaching and learning is our principle theme. Striving for that excellence will be reflected in everything we do . . . in our relationships, our attitudes toward work, and in every decision we make.

Empowerment: We have a vision where the school district promotes trust, believes in fair practices, recognizes the whole person, provides opportunities for growth and development, and rewards achievement . . . a district where the board, administrators, teachers, classified employees, parents, community, and students work together through shared decision making for a common goal; where multicultural differences are cherished, and all are accountable for results and share responsibility for student learning.

Growing out of the same staff discussions that resulted in the new vision statement was a set of what are called "expectations for action." They are concise statements to guide us as we work toward our goal of serving all children well:

Expectations for Teaching:

- We will act on what we know about how children learn.
- We will stop the search for the one best way to teach all children.
- We will accommodate the different learning styles that children have.
- We will use a variety of approaches to motivate children to learn.
- We will teach children in different ways by using a variety of teaching strategies.
- We will together accept responsibility for the outcomes of children's learning.
- We will judge everything that we do based on its impact on children—what they learn and how we teach them.
- We will have the courage as leaders to hold ourselves accountable for all children making progress from year to year.
- We will have the fortitude and integrity—the character to make tough decisions which must be made to protect the interests of children and ensure their progress in meeting the high expectations we set for them.

Expectations for Schools:

- We will structure and organize our schools based on what we know about teaching and learning.
- We will create schools where parents, teachers, classified employees, administrators, and students collaborate and share in making decisions about how to meet the purposes of education.
- We will work creatively with neighborhoods to develop schools as important community resources.

Expectations for Educators:

- We will become motivators, enablers, facilitators, and helpers and make our district offices into resource centers which are less impersonal and bureaucratic and more approachable and responsive.
- We will deal forthrightly with the tensions that exist between stability and change, patience and impatience, central direction and school site decision making, and school level accountability and district accountability.
- We will reflect in our actions a strong commitment to a shared belief that all children can learn and an understanding that more of the same will not be good enough.

EFFORTS TO INVOLVE ALL EMPLOYEES

Communicating the district's commitment to restructuring to all of the district's more than 10,000 employees is a major challenge. For restructuring to be successful, it is necessary that everyone understands how it can help us reach our goal of providing the best possible educational program for every student and in what ways it changes his or her role and responsibilities. It has become clear that informing people about the restructuring movement is an ongoing process that requires planning and resources.

Existing district publications are useful, and the ICLG has begun publication of a restructuring newsletter designed to help keep employees informed about restructuring activities. Principals and department heads are encouraged to keep themselves informed and help their employees understand restructuring.

In November of 1989 what was called a Restructuring Revue Kick-Off Conference was held. It was a half-day session that the principal of each school was required to attend and to which each principal was asked to bring his or her school's teachers' union representative and a member of the classified employee association. The leadership of the teachers' union and the administrators' association worked with the district Staff Development and Training Department to plan the conference and develop the materials for it. The presidents of four employee organizations and the superintendent all spoke in the opening session.

This conference was historic. For the first time teams including union officials, administrators, teachers, and classified staff came together in district-wide meetings to work together collaboratively. It underlined the high priority the district was placing on school restructuring activities, and it helped staff members better understand what restructuring is. It was especially significant that the conference was jointly sponsored by the district and the employee organizations. It reinforced the new spirit of cooperation and joint commitment in the district.

This spirit of cooperation was reflected in an article written for the ICLG's restructuring newsletter by Hugh Boyle, president of the San Diego Teachers' Association.[8] Mr. Boyle wrote

What are my greatest hopes and fears in restructuring as a union president? If I am allowed to have three greatest fears, these are the three: first, the fear that nothing substantive will happen. Writing for an article in the September *Kappan,* Mary Hatwood Futrell, immediate past president of the National Education Association, said, "History will view the 1980's not as the decade of education reform, but as the decade of education debate." I agree. The time for debating is over. It's not enough to simply raise consciousness, to hold summits, or to point accusing fingers. It's time to act.

My second greatest fear is that our reform will result in something like the spate of math and science grants which followed our national crisis created by the Soviet launching of Sputnik. As Ernest Boyer has said: "The harsh truth is that school reform is failing the inner city because the diagnosis is wrong. Formulas for renewal—more homework, more testing, more requirements of graduation—work best for schools that are already succeeding and for students who are college bound." Unless our reform reaches all our students, we will have failed.

My third greatest fear has already been realized. The headline of the *San Diego Union* story reported on the salary increase for this year read: "Board Grants Teachers 6.4% Raise." The message the headline sent may have been totally missed by most people, but to those of us who negotiated the four-year agreement, the point couldn't have been clearer: when a salary increase comes about through anything but protracted, acrimonious negotiations including the threat of strike, the union has not won. The pay increase has been given to the teachers by the generosity of their employer. The union leader knows that some union members will see this and ask, "Why belong to a union when the Board of Education is so generous? Who needs a union? Are not the district and its teachers working together toward a common goal?"

I may be naive in believing that the present cooperative spirit between the district and SDTA is genuine and that it will lead to meaningful changes in both the way in which we educate children and the conditions in which teachers do their teaching. However, I am not so naive as to believe that there are not and there will never be administrators who believe that their job is to administer—manage the school—and the teacher's job is to teach—labor in the school. Under those conditions and others, there will be a clash of priorities. Indeed, at the point when we are beginning the restructuring movement in San Diego, barely over 50% of the district's budget goes into teachers' salaries, benefits and other direct costs. If reform is to center in the classroom, how will individual teachers or groups of teachers at sites change that priority? I believe it will occur only through the collective voice of teachers through their professional union because if the money is not allocated to the school sites, it is not there for the staff to spend. However, my fear is that teachers will be lulled into a state of euphoric cooperation which sees teachers working harder and longer with the same resources and for the same remuneration.

Now to my hopes. Hmmmmmmmmmm. It seems on reading over what I have written about my greatest fears really covers my hopes. I hope that my fears are not realized. I hope I am wrong in my perception that teachers view our new contract and new relationship with the district as a sign to them that they no longer need SDTA. I hope that our planning will result in positive changes that will improve the education for all our children, but especially for those we have failed in the past. I hope that the careful and patient beginning we have been involved in for the past two years results in an educational system in San Diego that everyone — parents, students, teachers and other employees, and the community at large — can sincerely claim to be America's Finest School District.

For the Restructuring Revue Kick-Off Conference in November, the superintendent built his presentation around responses to a series of questions about restructuring and the district's restructuring efforts. Here is a selected list of those questions and a summary of his responses to them.

Is Restructuring Voluntary or Mandatory?

For schools it is voluntary to become an official restructuring school, but no school can ignore the vision of the district and expectations for action. Schools will find different ways to work toward the vision and meet the expectations, one of which is through the restructuring process.

For the central office it will be mandatory because unless we change our roles we will be unable to serve restructuring schools.

Is Shared Decision Making Voluntary or Mandatory?

It is neither at present. There is no single shared decision-making model that all schools must implement by a specified time. It is a goal that we should all work toward.

Some years ago many believed parent involvement was optional at schools. Today, we all know it is a necessity, and we actively work in many different ways to get it. Before long, I think our beliefs and action with shared decision making will follow a similar pattern, and we will wonder how we ever worked without it.

Is There One Shared Decision-making Model or One Best Way to Restructure?

No. However, there are some common characteristics of restructuring and shared decision making that are usually considered in various models. For example, a school wouldn't really have shared decision making if it systematically locked a stakeholder group or an individual out of the process.

Is There a Final Decision Maker in Shared Decision Making?

Yes. Sometimes it is a group which reaches a decision by consensus or majority vote. Sometimes it is a committee chair, a principal, an assistant superintendent, superintendent, or the board of education.

The goal is to have more decisions made by those most affected by and responsible for them, but there will still be lots of opportunity for individuals in leadership positions to make decisions. Leaders will be willing to relinquish more decisions to groups when groups are willing to take responsibility for the consequences of them. Shared decision making still requires strong leadership.

What Are the Expectations for Those Schools That Are Not Restructuring Now?

All schools must look carefully at what they are now doing and test their current practices against the district's vision and expectations. Unless *all* students are making progress consistent with these expectations, the status quo is not acceptable. If any school staff can honestly say that they are meeting the needs of the least successful student in the school, they might convince their colleagues that more of the same is all that is needed. Here are a few examples of what I mean:

- *Is Juan successful in school?* Juan is a recent immigrant with little formal education, limited skill in English, who lives in a crowded apartment, and rarely gets three meals a day. Yet his parents love him and want him to be success in his new country.
- *Is Dolores successful in school?* Dolores is a shy, quiet child whose parents are divorced and whose mother works all day and is exhausted at night. She drifts through and perhaps out of school with mostly Ds and a few Cs, and hardly anyone takes notice.
- *Is Rebecca successful in school?* Rebecca's mother and father are both working in high powered professions. Rebecca has a high I.Q. and is in the seminar for gifted students, but she is

bored with life and is beginning to miss school and to experiment with drugs.

- *Is Tyrone successful in school?* Tyrone has an African American father and a Vietnamese mother. He is constantly being referred to the principal for behavior problems. He has been evaluated for special education, and his father reluctantly has signed an Individual Education Program (IEP) for him to be assigned to a special class for learning handicapped students.

After the very successful Restructuring Revue Kick-Off Conference in November, which was attended by teams of administrators, teachers, and classified employees from schools, it was decided that a similar conference should be held for central office and other district support personnel. The conference was held in mid-December and was attended by teams of administrators and classified employees from every division and department in the district. As was the earlier session, the conference was sponsored by the teachers' union, the administrators' association, and the classified employees' associations. The conference opened with presentations from the presidents of each of the three groups and the superintendent. The superintendent's remarks were again built around responses to the series of questions about restructuring used at the earlier conference but also included additional questions directed to the roles of support service employees such as follows.

Will Restructuring Lead to Reorganization of the Central Office?

There will not be a major administrative reorganization of the district, but without question, there will be some reorganization within divisions.

How Will Restructuring Affect My Job?

Some assignments will change, as will the expectations for how we do our jobs. However, it is not likely that any positions will be eliminated simply because of restructuring. Everybody's role will be affected to some degree. We will have to become service-oriented. Our behavior must be more enabling, helping, and facilitating. We must find ways to encourage and support reorganization and change in the schools, and we must change ourselves. If people in the schools are not calling us for help and support, then we have to question our reason for existing.

What Is the Role of Central Office Staff When a Restructuring School Implements a Program That, According to Latest Research, Is Not in the Best Interests of Students?

Restructuring is not a license to make bad decisions for children. Anyone who sees actions and practices that are contrary to the children's interest must speak out.

If Central Office Personnel Share Power with People at the Schools, Will Responsibility for Outcomes Be Shared as Well?

Yes, and that is one of our major challenges. We must be alert to changes in schools that affect our roles as service providers and design assessment programs as action plans are developed.

How Will We Know Whether What We Do in the Future Is Better for Students?

Assessment design must be included in our action plans. Traditional norm-referenced tests will not be sufficient to measure student progress. The standards all students must meet call for more than fundamental basic skills that the standardized multiple choice tests measure. New performance based instruments that show what students know and can do are needed. Portfolios, writing samples, exhibitions, and teacher judgment are some types of authentic assessment that must be created, used, and explained to the public. Individual school, as well as school district, accountability report cards can be used to inform the public about how well we are doing. The data in these report cards can be valuable as we engage parents and staff members in the strategic planning process to improve teaching and learning.

The superintendent concluded his presentation with a charge to the central office:

> I envision that together we serve as a customer-focused resource center; that we are accountable for our services; and that we work collaboratively with each other and school sites in our continuing goal to ensure excellence in teaching and learning.

The conference did a lot to help many support employees who are not assigned to school sites to better understand restructuring and how it affects their work.

Another communication technique we have employed is the use of videotape. A ten-minute video was produced in which the superintendent presented the district's recently developed vision statements and explained our restructuring efforts. Copies of the video were sent to all principals and heads of departments with the request that they preview it with the team that attended the Restructuring Revue Kick-Off Conference, show it in a staff meeting, and have the team lead a discussion of it.

There is no question that attitudes and relationships are changing because of restructuring activities. More and more people in the district are beginning to understand that it is permissible to talk and work together in different ways, to question past practices, to think about creative methods to improve teaching and learning, and to experiment with new forms of decision making.

However, much work lies ahead. It takes time for attitudes to change and trust to increase. For example, keeping people excited and enthusiastic about the restructuring movement and eager to continue to work to enhance the educational programs will be a major challenge. There certainly will be occasional disappointments, setbacks, and differences of opinion. Staff morale, while high now, could slide. We must be prepared to provide the necessary support and appropriate staff development opportunities for employees who need help.

RESTRUCTURING AND TEACHER PROFESSIONALISM

At the same time, most observers believe that restructuring activities can lead to greatly improved teacher professionalism. If a teacher makes a commitment to be part of an effort to develop a new organization for the school and a new instructional program in the school that will teach all children well, he or she immediately begins to apply more of his or her professional knowledge. The teacher is more challenged, has greater interaction with his or her colleagues, and is less dependent on a centralized curriculum and mandated instructional methods. The teacher is free to be more creative and experiment with new approaches, and as a respected professional, the teacher is more willing to take responsibility and be accountable for student achievement.

All of this leads to a need for greater access to new ideas and additional staff development programs. Restructuring has the potential to create an exciting and stimulating intellectual atmosphere in a school where the professionalism of a teacher can thrive.

RESTRUCTURING AND PARENT INVOLVEMENT

We already see that restructuring activities improve the participation of parents in their children's education and in the school. In fact, our board's restructuring guidelines specify that not only must a restructuring proposal have the support of two-thirds of the faculty and staff of a school, but parents must generally indicate their support as well. This means parents must be involved from the start. If a school that is beginning to develop a restructuring proposal does not have sufficient active parent involvement, it must recruit it.

Because the primary reason for restructuring at a school is to better fill the needs of the students in that particular school, it follows that the school must work with parents in order to fully access those needs. Also, most restructuring proposals aim for greater parent involvement because teachers know their chances for success are greatly enhanced when parents become part of the educational process.

Efforts are also being made in most restructuring schools to involve more parents in the ongoing decision-making process at the school. Parents are helping with such things as developing the school's budget or in the selection of a new principal. When parents know they will be involved in meaningful ways, the level and quality of their participation increases.

FINAL THOUGHTS AND OBSERVATIONS

Many of the questions that are most often asked about the restructuring movement have to do with assessment. How do we know if the changes being made are actually improving the educational program? How will we know if things really are better for all students? What skills should we be trying to test? How do we align our tests with the curriculum?

These questions and concerns come at a time when there is a growing national debate over how students should be tested, and in many ways the restructuring movement and the search for new assessment systems are closely related. They both stem from the same sets of concerns.

At the beginning of a new decade it is clear that more of the same will not be good enough if we are to be successful in helping all students acquire knowledge and demonstrate skills that in years past we only requested of a select few. The reforms of the 1980s urged us to recapture the halcyon days of the 1950s. Reflecting on what really happened in those years suggests that they were not all that we think they were. Our memories play tricks on us.

In the 1980s our measure of accountability was compliance. In the decades of the 1990s we will be judged by outcomes—what do students really know? What can they do? There never can be true accountability unless there are consequences—rewards when things go well and goals are reached, and withholding of rewards for poor results. In education we do not like this reality. We have no real tradition that causes us to deal with the consequences of our actions. Whether things go well or poorly, very little changes.

A formidable challenge for restructuring is for us to use the process of collaboration to devise new reward and incentive systems that reward team work and team responsibility. In the 1980s we learned that we could rely on monitoring and compliance activities performed by emissaries of central bureaucracies to expel the blatantly poor and unacceptable practices from schools and school districts. We also humbly learned that you can legislate or regulate exemplary practice and performance through compliance activities.

It will take new forms of collaboration building on a revitalized teaching profession, renewed parent interest and active involvement, caring leadership of administrators, and innovative policy-making to enhance learning for all students.

San Diego City Schools are off to a good start, but there is a long way to go to make the vision for the 1990s reality for an increasingly diverse, growing, multicultural community. In the last decade we viewed our diversity as a problem. In this decade it must be an opportunity. How exciting it will be to accept the challenge of the Schools of the Future Commission and make substantial progress toward having all students become bilingual by the year 2000.

It is time to embrace the vision of change, excellence, and empowerment that leads educators to change their behavior as well as their rhetoric. This process will not be easy, since it involves altering traditional views about change and power. We will have to strive to provide access for all students to a curriculum that is intellectually challenging, engaging, and personally fulfilling, as well as one that prepares young people for a transformed world of work and ever-increasing political and social responsibilities. It will be necessary to empower people to participate in the process of change and to devise ways to hold them accountable for what students learn, while at the same time moving away from special interest politics as we make decisions about the allocation of scarce resources. One important step will be for educators to reach out to providers of services for children and youth—social service, juvenile justice, health, churches, employment agencies, and others—to pool their limited resources and share creative ways of improving through collaboration the quality of what we all want to do for children. We will have to develop new kinds of assessment instruments that are credible, valid, and reliable. Most important will be to withstand the pressure to demonstrate quick results when five to ten years are needed to make the fundamental systemic changes necessary to reach the goals of the 1990s.

All of these steps will be difficult, and the alternative to success in this endeavor is not pleasant to contemplate. If we fail, we may be facing the demise of public education and public schools as we know them. However, if we take what we know about learning and teaching and shape our practices accordingly, we will successfully enhance teaching and learning for all children. The reward at the end of the decade as a new century begins will be an abundance of evidence that confirms that the decade of the 1990s was one where enhanced teaching and learning truly made a difference in the lives of all children.

ENDNOTES

1 1986. *A Nation Prepared: Teachers for the 21st Century.* The Report of the Task Force on Teaching as a Profession of the Carnegie Forum on Education and the Economy.

2 1983. *A Nation at Risk: The Imperative for Educational Reform.* A Report to the Nation and the Secretary of Education, United States Department of Education by The National Commission on Excellence in Education.

3 1987. *Which Way to the Future? San Diego and Its Schools at a Crossroads.* The Report of San Diego City Schools' Schools of the Future Commission.

4 1989. "Purpose and Belief Statement," *Restructuring San Diego City Schools, A Brief History.* Planning, Research, and Evaluation Division, San Diego City Schools.

5 *Policy Statement on School Restructuring.* Office of the Superintendent, San Diego City Schools, Adopted by the Board of Education, November 8, 1988.

6 *Collective Negotiations Contract between the Board of Education of the San Diego Unified School District and the San Diego Teachers Association.* San Diego, California, July 1, 1988 to June 30, 1989.

7 *Waiver Process for School Restructuring.* San Diego City Schools, Adopted by the Board of Education, January 3, 1989.

8 1990. *Restructuring in Our Times.* Innovation and Change Leadership Group, San Diego City Schools, Vol. 2, No. 1.

CHAPTER 19

Kyrene Career Development Ladder:
A Case Study

CAROLYN J. DOWNEY — *Superintendent, Kyrene Public Schools, Tempe, Arizona*
CAROL PARISH — *Assistant Superintendent, Kyrene Public Schools, Tempe, Arizona*

THIS chapter is a case study of the Career Development Ladder Plan developed for the Kyrene School District in Tempe, Arizona. The chapter will describe the background of the district and the underlying framework used in planning the model for the career development ladder. The description of the plan itself will reveal the complexity necessary to incorporate a differentiated compensation plan that would meet the varying motivational needs of staff. Finally, the authors will describe the difficulties encountered in implementing the plan and those aspects that have been most successful. Recommendations for revisions will be included, particularly in those areas that resulted in difficulties for the Kyrene District: 1) the salary schedule and 2) the form of compensation.

BACKGROUND AND FRAMEWORK OF THE PLAN

A District Background

The Kyrene School District is located near Phoenix, Arizona, in the fastest growing part of the state. The district's boundaries cover approximately 140 square miles, serving segments of the cities of Phoenix, Tempe, Chandler, and Guadalupe, as well as the Gila Springs Indian Reservation. In the fall of 1984, the student population was 4209 and increasing rapidly. By the fall of 1989, the student population exceeded 9200, a gain of approximately 17 percent per year.

In the fall of 1984, the Kyrene District was a risk-taking district of young administrators and staff. It was becoming known as the premier small district in Arizona and was building a national reputation for excellence. Working relationships between the teachers' organization, superintendent, and board were good. Employees were proud to be

483

part of the district and most adjusted to the ongoing changes being implemented in "state-of-the-art" curriculum and instruction programs. A strong staff development program on effective teaching practices and clinical supervision had been in place for two years. A teacher evaluation committee had been established in spring 1983 to begin work on a comprehensive and challenging teacher assessment procedure that would include higher level teaching skills, with a focus on professional growth and formative evaluation, including a variety of assessment/diagnostic approaches.

The decade of the 1980s was an exciting time in the Kyrene District. When the Arizona state legislature passed a career ladder bill, administrators and leaders of the teachers' organization agreed to submit a proposal to develop a Career Ladder Model. The legislation allowed schools to submit proposals for a career ladder, and, if approved, the school district board was permitted to increase taxes to their constituents on a graduating scale over a five-year period, up to .05 percent of the maintenance and operation budget. For the 500 Kyrene teachers employed during the 1989–90 budget year, this meant a plan with over one million dollars available for its implementation.

A very short time line was available to develop the Career Ladder Plan. Kyrene's proposal was approved in August 1984, and the district was given three months to design a plan acceptable to the majority of staff. A shared decision-making approach was used, providing for structured input and resulting in a large committee. A technician was hired to work with the committee, conducting literature searches and drafting and revising the policy document.

After three intense months of weekly meetings and high teacher input, a complex Career Development Ladder Plan was designed. Teachers were asked to endorse the plan, and 82.5 percent of the staff voted. Of that group, 85.1 percent endorsed the majority of the plan. In the fall of 1985, the first year of implementation, only two teachers chose not to enter the plan. Now, six years later, the Career Development Plan is still in existence and 100 percent of the teachers have elected to participate.

Since its original design, only two major modifications in the plan have been implemented. The first, required by the state legislative education committee, has had a major negative impact on the plan, and the second, while enhancing the plan, also poses problems. These modifications and their impacts will be discussed later in this chapter.

For the most part, however, the plan is intact as originally designed and has proved successful.

Basic Framework

Four major areas of consideration influenced the design and current implementation of the Kyrene Career Development Ladder Plan. These are presented below:

- strategies, based on an examination of the literature on failed plans, designed to avoid identified pitfalls
- statutory constraints
- motivational theory influences
- purposes of the plan

Strategies Built into the Plan

Very early in the design stages, a literature search was undertaken to determine why merit and incentive plans failed in the past. A list of factors contributing to plan failure was identified, and strategies for increasing the likelihood of success for the Kyrene model were identified. The following list identifies areas considered and corrective strategies used in the Kyrene model:

Factors Contributing to Plan Failure	Kyrene's Strategy
Poor evaluation procedures that lack specificity and measurable criteria	A comprehensive plan including specific, observable competencies
Use of peers in the evaluation process	Evaluation as part of the normal principal–teacher evaluation process
Poorly prepared evaluators	Extensive training for principals in teacher competencies to obtain inter-rater reliability
Teacher opposition to the plan	Extensive teacher involvement in the design and implementation of the plan with various forms of communication feedback loops and opportunities for input

Factors Contributing to Plan Failure	Kyrene's Strategy
New compensation plan was a substitute for raising salaries of all teachers, and funding was inadequate	Design model not as a salary plan but as an incentive plan for professional growth
Permanent merit	Fund the base salary component of the ladder with regular district monies; use external funding for add-ons and options
Difficult to administer	Incorporate into the on-going evaluation plan for teachers
A quota system that limited or froze opportunities for all teachers	No participation limit in most options, sharing a pool of money, a flow system from one option to the next, renewal required for options
Minimum-year requirements that eliminated young teachers and teachers new to the system	A fast-track system, using no requirements for some of the first year to determine skill placement and placing no requirements on some incentive options
Once qualified, a person never had to meet standards again	Continual demonstration of skills required, renewal required for options
Teachers were in competition and were rated against the performance of others	Performance rated against a standard; most options do not have quotas
Created staff dissension	Group options designed to promote cooperation
Penalized unsatisfactory teachers	Counsel out or terminate such teachers. Freeze the salary schedule during intervention if not terminated after one year. If contract is renewed because of satisfactory performance, reinstate on the first level of the career ladder only. Other skill

Factors Contributing to Plan Failure	Kyrene's Strategy
	levels would not be used for dismissal purposes.
Publicity caused morale problems	Low media coverage, no publicity on individual teacher awards
Parents required "superior" teachers	Limited publicity
No yearly evaluations of the plan	Evaluation designed as part of the plan
Program was underfunded	Set up options to fund plan and identify priorities, defer low-cost reward options, flow-through option plan, provide different forms of recognition

Statutory Constraints of the Plan

Several requirements for implementing the district's Career Development Ladder Plan were mandated by the state legislature. One interesting aspect is that no state funds were appropriated for implementation. Instead, by exercising state control over local dollars, the legislative education committee allowed the district, upon approval of their proposal, to increase the taxes to its constituents up to .05 percent of the maintenance and operation budget. In addition, the statute influenced the design of the plan in three significant areas by 1) placing limitations on restructuring the salary schedule, 2) requiring employee approval, and 3) mandating increased student achievement.

Restructured Salary Schedule

The statutory constraint on restructuring the salary schedule proved to be the most difficult from a design perspective. It may also be the reason for the governing board deciding to no longer ask for the plan to be funded. As designed, the plan allows teachers to have a higher earning power over time. However, because teachers do not receive a raise each year, many have found this to be a dissatisfier. This may result in failure of the plan.

The statute requires that the restructured salary schedule *not* be a linear, step-by-step increase in salary based on years of experience and education. Teachers' organizations have historically fought for such schedules, and rightfully so, when there were many pay inequities. Despite the fact that most inequities have now been rectified, teacher organizations are still uneasy about relinquishing this type of schedule. In the Kyrene plan, a new approach was required.

How does one surrender such a plan, maintain the integrity of the schedule, and yet emphasize performance and growth? The initial effort by the task force resulted in a ladder based on an idea adapted from Robinson's (March 1984) Educational Research Service paper. This approach placed the career ladder or incentive dollars on top of the linear step-by-step salary schedule, as shown in Figure 1.

The lowest step of the salary schedule is at the bottom of the figure. The first level of the ladder incorporates the entire linear salary schedule, and levels above that first level are additive dollars and requirements to the first level.

PERFORMANCE EVALUATION COMPONENT	PROFESSIONAL COMPETENCE COMPONENT	EDUCATIONAL PRODUCTIVITY COMPONENT
INPUT AND PROCESS MEASURES OF TEACHER PERFORMANCE	— INDICATORS — OF • STATUS • GROWTH • PERFORMANCE • CONTRIBUTIONS • CRITICAL NEED	RESULTS AND OUTPUT MEASURES OF STUDENT LEARNING
BASIC SALARY SCHEDULE		

FIGURE 1 Components of incentive pay plans (taken from page 20 of the Educational Research Service Report entitled, "Merit Pay for Teachers," March 1984).

Table 1. Traditional certified salary schedule (1989–1990)

	1 BA	2 BA + 15	3 MA BA + 30	4 MA + 15 BA + 45	5 MA + 30 BA + 60	6 MA + 45 Doct*	Teacher Comp
A	19,881	20,615	21,540	22,465	23,634	24,803	544
B	20,554	21,288	22,312	23,237	24,576	25,745	544
C	21,227	21,961	23,084	24,009	25,518	26,687	544
D	21,900	22,634	23,856	24,781	26,460	27,629	544
E	22,573	23,307	24,628	25,553	27,402	28,571	544
F	23,246	23,980	25,400	26,325	28,344	29,513	544
G	23,919	24,653	26,172	27,097	29,286	30,455	544
H	24,592	25,326	26,944	27,869	30,228	31,397	544
I	25,265	25,999	27,716	28,641	31,170	32,339	544
J	26,031	26,765	28,566	29,491	32,170	33,339	544
K	26,797	27,531	29,416	30,341	33,170	34,339	544
L	27,563	28,297	30,266	31,191	34,170	35,339	544
M	28,329	29,063	31,116	32,041	35,174	36,343	544
N	29,095	29,829	31,966	32,891	36,178	37,347	544
O	29,861	30,595	32,816	33,741	37,182	38,351	544

*Stipend provided dependent upon qualification.

This design is still one the authors would recommend. Such an approach has been successfully used in other states. It provides a transition from one type of salary plan to another that is more easily understood by the employee. However, the legislative aide overseeing the design of the Kyrene model would not accept this approach, placing the success of the plan in jeopardy. At the time of this writing, an attempt is being made to deal with this situation in a positive way.

As a result of the rejection of this salary plan, another approach had to be designed. The Kyrene model eventually took the form of an upward collapsing schedule that was to the advantage of the teachers, taking fewer educational credits and less teaching experience to obtain more pay. It was also considered important, as the district moved to the Career Development Plan, that no person be hurt financially in the move. As a result, the following steps were taken to create the new salary schedule.

Step One turned the current step-by-step linear salary schedule upside down. Instead of the lowest salary being at the top of the salary schedule, it is now at the bottom. Table 1 shows a typical linear step-by-step salary schedule. Table 2 shows the same schedule turned around so that the lowest salary is at the bottom left-hand side of the salary schedule.

Step Two — Next the schedule was collapsed upward and to the left into fifteen cells with corresponding ladder titles (Table 3): Residency Level, Career Development Level I, Career Development Level II, Career Development Level III, and Career Development Level IV. The skills placed in each of these levels will be explained.

To create these cells, every three years of experience and at least two educational levels (e.g., Bachelor's and Bachelor's plus eighteen credits) were collapsed into the cell with the highest salary. Figure 2 illustrates how this would be accomplished. This resulted in a 1989–90 salary schedule that looked like that in Table 4.

The traditional salary schedule is also provided, giving teachers the option of whether to choose the career development ladder salary schedule. For comparison purposes, Table 5 shows the 1989–90 traditional salary schedule.

It was determined by the governing board that this upward collapsing

Table 2. Traditional certified salary schedule (1989–1990).

	1 BA	2 BA + 15	3 MA BA + 30	4 MA + 15 BA + 45	5 MA + 30 BA + 60	6 MA + 45 Doct*
O	29,861	30,595	32,816	33,741	37,182	38,351
N	29,095	29,829	31,966	32,891	36,178	37,347
M	28,329	29,063	31,116	32,041	35,174	36,343
L	27,563	28,297	30,266	31,191	34,170	35,339
K	26,797	27,531	29,416	30,341	33,170	34,339
J	26,031	26,765	28,566	29,491	32,170	33,339
I	25,265	25,999	27,716	28,641	31,170	32,339
H	24,592	25,326	26,944	27,869	30,228	31,397
G	23,919	24,653	26,172	27,097	29,286	30,455
F	23,246	23,980	25,400	26,325	28,344	29,513
E	22,573	23,307	24,628	25,553	27,402	28,571
D	21,900	22,634	23,856	24,781	26,460	27,629
C	21,227	21,961	23,084	24,009	25,518	26,687
B	20,554	21,288	22,312	23,237	24,576	25,745
A	19,881	20,615	21,540	22,465	23,634	24,803

*Stipend provided dependent upon qualification.

Table 3. Traditional certified salary schedule (1989–1990).

	1 BA	2 BA + 15	3 MA BA + 30	4 MA + 15 BA + 45	5 MA + 30 BA + 60	6 MA + 45 Doct*
O	29,861	30,595	32,816	33,741	37,182	38,351
N	29,095 5	29,629	31,966 10	32,891	36,178 15	37,347
M	28,329	29,063	31,116	32,041	35,174	36,343
L	27,563	28,297	30,266	31,191	34,170	35,339
K	26,797 4	27,531	29,416 9	30,341	33,170 14	34,339
J	26,031	26,765	28,566	29,491	32,170	33,339
I	25,265	25,999	27,716	28,641	31,170	32,339
H	24,592 3	25,326	26,944 8	27,869	30,228 13	31,397
G	23,919	24,653	26,172	27,097	29,286	30,455
F	23,246	23,980	25,400	26,325	28,344	29,513
E	22,573 2	23,307	24,628 7	25,553	27,402 12	28,571
D	21,900	22,634	23,856	24,781	26,460	27,629
C	21,227	21,961	23,084	24,009	25,518	26,687
B	20,554 1	21,288	22,312 6	23,237	24,576 11	25,745
A	19,881	20,615	21,540	22,465	23,634	24,803

*Stipend provided dependent upon qualification.

Table 4. Certified salary schedule (1989–1990).

		BA to BA + 15 Column 1	BA + 30–45 MA-MA + 15 Column 2	BA + 60 MA + 30–45 Doct. Column 3
Pro. Level 4	O N M	30,599	33,747	38,356
Pro. Level 3	L K J	28,299	31,197	35,345
Pro. Level 2	I H G	25,999	28,647	31,345
Pro. Level 1	F E D	23,980	26,329	29,517
Resid. Level	C B A	21,961	24,011	26,689

	1 BA	2 BA+15
C	21,227	21,961
B	20,554	21,615
A	19,881	20,615

NEW CELL

$\longleftrightarrow$ 21,961

FIGURE 2

salary schedule would be incorporated into the regular budget over a three-year period. Recognizing that the additional tax base for the career ladders might not exist, the board members also decided they would not use career ladder dollars to accomplish this collapsing. It was their commitment to institutionalize as much of the plan as fiscally possible.

This resulted in teachers obtaining higher increases than other employee groups over the next three years, which did create some morale problems within the other employee groups. Also, it set up an expectation by the teachers' organization leaders for higher than usual salary increases. This led to two years of salary impasse between the teachers' organization and the board. Apparently, the teachers' organization leaders forgot the "extra" effort in the salary schedule and came to expect such increases each year.

During the 1988–89 Meet and Confer efforts between the teachers' organization and the board, a salary impasse existed. Ultimately, the board passed a salary schedule that represented one of the better salary increases in the state, yet teachers were upset. The overall average increase was 5.45 percent, while the Arizona cost of living rose only 3 percent. In the 1989–90 discussion, there was salary agreement using a concept collaboration approach. However, the teachers' organization collaboration team recommended that teachers not ratify the agreement. The board went on to pass an average salary increase of 7.1 percent, which, again, was one of the better ones in the state. Staff were still disheartened because most believed the raise was a poor increase, although the total dollars exceeded the 3.9 percent cost-of-living increase. In essence, it was a second year of impasse. This has created great mistrust between the board, administration, and the teachers' organization leaders.

Because of the plan's design of three years on a salary step, two-thirds of the teachers received less than the cost-of-living increase, although their overall earning power for the three years is greater. For example, even with no increase each year, this can be illustrated as shown in Table 6.

In the spring of 1990, as of the writing of this chapter, an extensive compensation study is being undertaken. It is hoped that a positive outcome will be forthcoming. Recommendations regarding this problem will be made in the last section of this chapter.

Employee Approval

The legislative statute also required employee endorsement of the plan. As mentioned earlier, the vote was most positive, with 83.4 percent endorsing the majority of the components. Several factors that may have contributed to this high rate of endorsement follow (p. 494):

Table 5. Traditional certified salary schedule (1989–1990).

	1 BA	2 BA + 15	3 MA BA + 30	4 MA + 15 BA + 45	5 MA + 30 BA + 60	6 MA + 45 Doct*
O	29,861	30,595	32,816	33,741	37,182	38,351
N	29,095	29,829	31,966	32,891	36,178	37,347
M	28,329	29,063	31,116	32,041	35,174	36,343
L	27,563	28,297	30,266	31,191	34,170	35,339
K	26,797	27,531	29,416	30,341	33,170	34,339
J	26,031	26,765	28,566	29,491	32,170	33,339
I	25,265	25,999	27,716	28,641	31,170	32,339
H	24,592	25,326	26,944	27,869	30,228	31,397
G	23,919	24,653	26,172	27,097	29,286	30,455
F	23,246	23,980	25,400	26,325	28,344	29,513
E	22,573	23,307	24,628	25,553	27,402	28,571
D	21,900	22,634	23,856	24,781	26,460	27,629
C	21,227	21,961	23,084	24,009	25,518	26,687
B	20,554	21,288	22,312	23,237	24,576	25,745
A	19,881	20,615	21,540	22,465	23,634	24,803

*Stipend provided dependent upon qualification.

Table 6. Example of earning power over three years.

Certified Career Ladder Schedule	BA	BA + 15
Teacher A	21,961	21,961
(Salary Steps A, B, C)	21,961	21,961
	21,961	21,961
Total 3 Year Earnings	65,883	65,883
	MA	**MA + 15**
	BA + 30	**BA + 45**
Teacher B	28,647	28,647
(Salary Steps G, H, I)	28,647	28,647
	28,647	28,647
Total 3 Year Earnings	85,971	85,971
Traditional Schedule	**BA**	**BA + 15**
Teacher A	19,881	20,615
(Salary Steps A, B, C)	20,554	21,288
	21,227	21,961
	61,662	63,864
	MA	**MA + 15**
	BA + 30	**BA + 45**
Teacher B	26,172	27,907
(Salary Steps G, H, I)	26,994	27,869
	27,716	28,641
	80,832	83,607
Three- (3) year difference for Teacher A	4221	2019
Three- (3) year difference for Teacher B	5139	2364

- Good relationships existed among teachers, administrators, and board members.
- A highly structured, two-way input and feedback approach was used by the career development ladder task force. All teachers had ample opportunity to be informed about the proposed plan prior to the vote. The advisory council met almost weekly during the three months available for the design stage. Each week the task force representative from each of the schools submitted the work completed to date to faculty to obtain their input, and each task force meeting began by considering that input. A "Career Ladder Communique" was also distributed to all staff between meetings and continues to be used as needed.

These techniques resulted in excellent communication and shared decision making.

- There was trust in the principals' knowledge of effective teaching practices (the skills at the various career development levels) and their ability to evaluate and supervise based on these skills for employee growth.
- A separate committee, constituted in the spring of 1983, was working on a comprehensive teacher evaluation system to fit perfectly into the career development ladder. Several committee members served on both committees. The evaluation system at the summative stage divided teaching skills into "basic" and "advanced" skills. Termination of employment could only be based on deficiency of basic skills. These skills, later named "Residency Skills," became the first rung of the career development ladder and were the skills required for "tenure."

It is interesting to note that the basic skills included in most Career Ladder Plans across the nation are the only skills required for even the top rungs of the ladders. Kyrene's model truly became a ladder of higher level effective teaching skills. It has proven to be a professional *development* ladder.

Increased Student Achievement

The third legislative requirement was that the plan be structured with a focus on increased student achievement. The Kyrene plan has a strong student achievement focus as illustrated in the following ways:

- Teachers show evidence of appropriate student progress criteria for advancement in all base salary levels.
- Teachers demonstrate appropriate level skills that are correlated with increased student achievement.
- Three in-class incentive pay options exist, which focus on increasing student achievement.
- Workshop participant options are provideed, which are directly related to skills that increase student achievement.
- There is a school-wide incentive for increasing student achievement (not yet implemented).

Motivational Theory Influences

In addition to studying why plans failed in the past and constraints in the law, employee motivational theory as it related to the teaching profession was studied. Several motivational theories influenced the plan. Strategies from both "content" and "process" theories were used. Content theory suggests that one is motivated by rewards both intrinsic and extrinsic, such as those identified by Herzberg (1966) and Maslow (1920). Herzberg's (1966) findings regarding work itself, job achievement, recognition for achievement, responsibility, growth, and advancement, as well as Maslow's (1920) belongingness theory are content theories incorporated into the plan. Process theories, according to Sample (1984), "suggest motivation is a combined function of an individual's perception that effort will lead to performance and of the desirability of the outcomes that could result from such performance." Casio's (1982) definition indicates that "it is the anticipation of reward that energizes behavior and the perceived value of various outcomes that gives behavior its direction." The process theories that influenced the plan included the expectancy theory of Vroom (1964), Casio's (1982) theory, and equity theory. Using these theories, the following ideas were formulated.

Have a Professional Growth Focus with Higher Level Teaching Skills on Each Step of the Ladder

The Kyrene plan was designed to be a challenging and growth-producing model. The task force wanted skill levels that would be difficult to obtain, except over an extensive period of time, through experience and professional growth situations. Where possible, there was to be a hierarchy of skills. For example,

- *Professional Level IV 2.24:* supplements basic materials with media materials (films, video, audiotapes, etc.) that correspond to objectives.
- *Professional Level III 2.20:* establishes written short- and long-term goals for individual students based on learning rate and learning needs.
- *Professional Level II 2.16:* when needed, specifies additional entry level, enroute, and terminal sub-objectives based on a task analysis of an objective.

- *Professional Level I 2.15:* when needed, modifies objectives to reflect correct level of difficulty for individual students.
- *Professional Level 2.04:* instructional plans are based on diagnostic data gathered frequently prior to new learning as needed throughout the year.

Most career ladders have a single set of skills, and the degree to which a teacher achieves these skills determines the level of the ladder on which the teacher is placed. The Kyrene career development ladder is different. For each level of the ladder, the skills are different and more complex. After the Kyrene plan was designed, it was found that the skills placed in the first level (Residency) were typically the skills for the complete ladder in other Career Ladder Plans across the nation. This can be illustrated as shown in Figure 3.

Also, the Kyrene plan was different from most plans in the nation in that the level on which the teacher was placed was the one containing the skills on which the person was working as opposed to skills currently demonstrated. The term "development" was purposely included in the name of Kyrene's plan to state symbolically that this was not a merit plan but a professional growth plan. The 1989–90 list of skills is as shown in Figure 4 (see Appendix A for skill descriptions). This approach links to Herzberg's (1966) growth and achievement and recognition for achievement work satisfiers, as well as Vroom's (1964) expectancy theory.

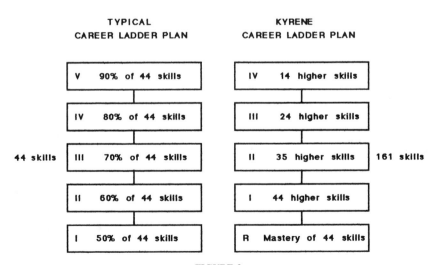

FIGURE 3

PROF IV		
2.41	5.17	7.09
3.38	6.15	7.10
3.39	6.16	7.11
4.21	6.17	7.16
5.16	6.18	

PROF III		
2.06	3.32	5.15
2.16	3.33	5.30
2.17	3.34	6.12
2.27	3.35	6.13
2.23	3.36	6.14
2.38	3.37	7.08
3.06	4.20	7.14
3.31	5.14	7.15

PROF II		
2.05	3.27	5.12
2.14	3.28	5.13
2.15	3.29	5.28
2.23	4.04	5.29
2.24	4.05	6.10
2.25	4.06	6.11
2.26	4.07	7.02
2.36	4.13	7.04
2.37	4.14	7.05
3.24	4.18	7.07
3.25	4.19	7.13
3.26	5.11	

PROF I		
2.02	3.16	5.08
2.03	3.17	5.09
2.04	3.18	5.10
2.11	3.19	5.24
2.13	3.20	5.25
2.22	3.21	5.26
2.32	3.22	5.27
2.33	3.23	6.05
2.34	4.10	6.06
2.35	4.11	6.07
3.04	4.12	6.08
3.05	4.16	6.09
3.13	4.17	7.02
3.14	5.06	7.12
3.15	5.07	

RESIDENCY (Basic Skills)		
1.01	3.07	5.04
1.02	3.08	5.05
1.03	3.09	5.18
1.04	3.10	5.19
2.01	3.11	5.20
2.07	3.12	5.21
2.08	4.01	5.22
2.09	4.02	5.23
2.10	4.03	6.01
2.21	4.08	6.02
2.30	4.09	6.03
2.31	4.15	6.04
3.01	5.01	7.01
3.02	5.02	7.06
3.03	5.03	

FIGURE 4

Provide a Plan for All Staff—Help All Teachers
to Be Exceptional Rather Than Awarding the Exceptional Few

This was the major difference between the Kyrene plan and most other incentive or Career Ladder Plans. Most plans attempt to identify a few very exceptional teachers and recognize them. The Kyrene plan has a professional growth focus that provides incentives for growth to assist all teachers in becoming exceptional. This became a particular issue with the legislators, who wanted the plan to reward the "master teachers" and "get rid of the poor teachers." It took and still takes a lot of convincing each year for the Kyrene plan to be approved.

This belief, which links to Herzberg's (1960) work satisfier of growth and advancement as well as Vroom's (1964) expectancy theory, is incorporated into the plan in several ways:

- All staff who choose to participate after their first year in the district, which is the year in which placement level on the career development ladder is determined, are eligible.
- Pay for growth is the focus rather than pay for performance. Instead of being rewarded for the demonstration of certain skills, teachers are given an incentive for working on the next ladder level of skills, once mastering the previous level skills. This is a subtle change from most career ladders but an important symbolic message.
- Most of the incentive and supplemental pay options are of a professional growth nature, for instance, peer coaching.
- The inclusion of the word "development" (career development ladder rather than career ladder).

Provide for Collegial Efforts

Recognizing the isolationism of the teacher's workplace, the plan supports collaborative and collegial efforts of the teaching staff. This translates into incentives such as

- professional growth mini-grant options requiring a joint proposal prepared by at least two staff members
- incentive pay options for learning about and participating in peer coaching experiences
- supplemental pay options for serving as a "buddy" to a new teacher or a mentor to a more experienced teacher

Focus on Cooperation Rather Than Competition

An informal agreement with the teachers' organization and administrators restricted the district to recognizing groups of schools and district staff, not individual schools or individual teachers. It had been decided that to single out one school over another or one teacher over another could create a negative climate in the system and affect cooperative efforts. Therefore, the district had not for several years employed such recognitions as "Teacher of the Year."

This proved to be a major area of discussion during the development of the Career Development Ladder Plan. The task force strongly felt this informal agreement should be maintained. This belief was translated into the plan in several ways:

- Instead of awards to individual teachers for increased student achievement, awards for school-wide achievement gains against the school's own past performance are utilized.
- Pools of money are shared by those who achieve or participate in a particular part of the plan, thus eliminating competition for the top few incentives.
- Recognition is confidential in most situations, and notice of awarded options is placed in the person's official personnel file.
- There is no media "hype" on the program or awarded incentives.

Reward the Teacher for a Commitment to Teaching in the Classroom

Rather than providing pay incentives that take the teacher out of the classroom, the Kyrene model mainly focuses on rewarding classroom effort. Most career ladders in the nation "award" the teacher with supplemental pay. The contract is extended by one, two, or three months — months in which the person is not teaching, but instead works on curriculum development or training efforts. Alternatively, the teacher is given extra pay for being a mentor — an additional job during the school year.

The task force rejected early the idea that teachers at the "top" of a career ladder would become involved in and responsible for activities that took them out of their classrooms. A plan that encouraged and valued excellence in teaching and a commitment to the profession of teaching would be foremost in the design. Extra pay for higher level responsibilities that exceeded teaching would only be an option for those interested in such duties.

Recognize That Some Teachers Are Interested in
a Job Ladder and Supplemental Pay

Although the majority of the plan focuses on rewarding the classroom teacher for staying in the classroom, it was felt that there should be some opportunities built into the plan for those who wished other career paths. The task force was influenced in the definition by Bacharach (1984). A distinction was made between three terms:

- *Career Ladder*—a hierarchical ordering of levels within a single position, where promotion from level to level represents acknowledgement of increasing competence in the position—in this case, classroom teaching.
- *Career Development Ladder*—a hierarchical ordering of levels within a single position, where promotion from level to level represents mastery of the previous level's competencies and a professional growth focus on the skills of the current position level.
- *Job Ladder*—a hierarchical ordering of jobs with distinctly different sets of responsibilities—aide, assistant teacher, teacher, curriculum developer, teacher trainer. Often, this is translated into differentiated staffing.

The difference between the first two terms is subtle and has been described elsewhere in this chapter. The Kyrene plan is a career development ladder for the most part but does include opportunities for career paths outside of teaching. These job ladder opportunities are translated into supplemental pay incentives (extra pay for extra work) by providing some funds for

- mentor teachers
- buddy teachers for new staff
- curriculum writers (although as of fall 1989, funds had not been expended on this option)
- teacher trainers

In addition, the following supplemental pay options are provided:

- career ladder advisory council
- workship participants

Provide a Variety of Incentive Options

The Kyrene model recognizes that teachers' reasons for entering and remaining in the field of teaching are varied. Consequently, a variety of incentive options are needed to meet the differential needs of staff. The reasons teachers are initially attracted to the field are not necessarily the reasons why they stay in teaching. Attraction or lack of attraction into the field of teaching is linked to such things as entry pay (Brederson, Fruth, and Katen, 1983; Page and Page, 1982), prestige (Lortie, 1975), number of career options, and working conditions (Cresap, McCormick, and Paget, 1984). Teachers more frequently cite the importance of working with students and facilitating student learning as reasons for being attracted to the profession (Frase, Hetzel, and Inman, 1987; Rosenholtz and Smylie, 1983).

Some of the factors for retaining teachers leaving the field include low public esteem and limited opportunities for recognition (Rosenholtz and Smylie, 1983; Goodlad, 1984; Boyer, 1983). Other conditions that influence retention include lack of opportunity for professional growth and conflict with or lack of support from administrators. Rosenholtz (1984) cites teachers' overriding doubt about their ability to succeed with students as a major reason for leaving the teaching profession. He also states that recognition or approval from colleagues increases the teacher's likelihood of remaining in the profession. As a result, multiple ways of receiving compensation were designed in the Kyrene plan.

Design a Plan to Be Institutionalized

It was recognized that the tenuousness of the funding term, as well as the amount of money available, would not allow the plan to create financial comparability with similar professions. The Kyrene model, unfortunately, would not be a plan to "pay teachers what they are worth." The career ladder task force examined the teaching profession in relation to similar professions in terms of education and found that in order to compare teachers' salaries with those of other professions, the number of teacher work days, which is less than the average number of work days of other professions, needed to be considered. Although it was recognized that teachers often obtain summer employment, this is seldom comparable to their daily pay rate for teaching.

The use of figures that extrapolate teachers' salaries over a twelve-month period may, therefore, be misleading. Such figures were used for hypothetical comparison purposes only. The teacher salary in Kyrene was estimated for a twelve-month period. Teachers worked an average of 180 days; most other professionals in comparison jobs had 230 work days. (The comparison includes all nationally recognized holidays plus twenty vacation days.) In 1984–85, the Kyrene teacher with a Bachelor's or Master's degree and no teaching experience would have received a comparable annual salary computed as follows:

BA Calculation: $16,125 ÷ 180 = 89.58 daily rate × 230 = $20,604
MA Calculation: $17,501 ÷ 180 = 98.23 daily rate × 230 = $22,363

Using data from the *College Placement Council* (July 1984), the following professional salary comparisons were made for college graduates entering the job market. The salaries did not include fringe benefits.

Profession	Bachelor's Degree	Master's Degree
Accounting	$19,524	$23,196
Marketing	$18,660	$27,348
Humanities	$17,724	$18,732
Civil Engineering	$22,764	$26,724
Mechanical Engineering	$26,280	$30,288
Agriculture	$17,016	–
Computer Science	$24,552	$30,060
Mathematics	$23,400	$28,764
Health Profession	$18,912	–
Business Management	$18,660	$27,348
Chemical Engineering	$27,420	$30,684
KYRENE TEACHER 1984	$20,604*	$22,363*

Examining these data, it was found that the Kyrene teacher's salary was about in the middle of the scale using the Bachelor's level, but at the Master's level the Kyrene teacher's salary was among the lowest. It should be noted, as mentioned earlier, that teachers usually cannot ob-

*Hypothetical pay based on 230 work days rather than 180 work days.

tain summer employment at equivalent hourly rates. As the task force examined the dollars available, it became apparent quite quickly that to achieve comparability with other professionals for the beginning teacher with a Master's degree was not feasible considering the statutory limits on available funds.

Therefore, the Kyrene plan was not designed to be a salary plan. It was felt that if a plan were devised under such tenuous circumstances, the task force would be designing a plan for the hygiene-dissatisfier side of Herzberg's (1966) motivational theory. However, the plan was revised one year later to meet legislative approval in one year, which increased the likelihood that the plan would become a salary plan. A skill incentive bonus was added to each career level.

Purposes of the Plan

The purposes and rationale of the plan were developed during the design phase using ideas from the previous three areas of influence. The objectives and rationale of the Kyrene plan are as follows:

(1) Objective No. 1: to improve the status of the teaching profession

Rationale: In order to motivate public willingness to pay teachers a professional-level salary schedule, teacher instructional competencies and job responsibilities must be raised in direct proportion to teacher salary increments.

(2) Objective No. 2: to reward teachers for full-time commitment to teaching as a career

Rationale: Teachers must have incentives to remain in the teaching profession.

(3) Objective No. 3: to attract and retain quality teachers

Rationale: Teachers must be provided with opportunities offering intrinsic and extrinsic rewards such as personal instructional skill development, educational career advancement, and financial rewards and incentives for professional work.

(4) Objective No. 4: to reward and recognize excellence in teacher performance.

Rationale: Exceptional teacher performance positively impacts student learning. To maintain high performance levels, quality teachers must be recognized and rewarded.

(5) Objective No. 5: to provide interested individuals with career paths that might lead to other professional roles in the district.

Rationale: Some teachers need opportunities for continuing advancement in their educational career paths.

(6) Objective No. 6: to improve student learning.

Rationale: Student learning is the inherent function of schools and will be improved in direct proportion to betterment of teacher instructional effectiveness skills.

THE PLAN

The Kyrene plan has two major components:

- Base salary professional growth component with a focus on 168 teaching behaviors grouped into seven competency areas and placed into five levels on the ladder. The component is primarily concerned with the development of teaching skills and the salary schedule. Movement from one level to the next involves evaluation in four major areas: skill demonstration, student progress, professional growth, and professional development.
- Incentive and supplement pay option component with numerous in-class, school-specific, district-wide, and job ladder options. These options are available to teachers at all levels. Teachers may apply for one or more of these options.

Participation in the base salary component is concurrent with participation in any of the options. In other words, teachers who participate in one of the options will not leave the base salary component. Participation in optional areas is renewable annually. A teacher may choose to join or leave the career development ladder at any time but may only rejoin once in their career in the district.

A visual framework of the Career Development Ladder Plan is presented in Figure 5.

Base Salary Component

The Kyrene career development ladder incorporates into its plan a restructured version of the "single salary schedule." It includes criteria for movement to four career levels:

- Professional Level IV

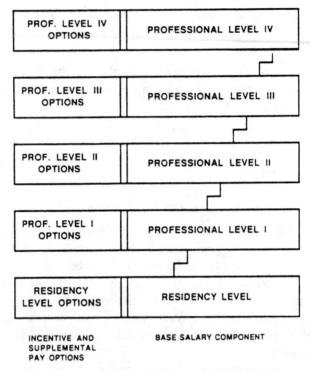

FIGURE 5 Career development ladder levels.

- Professional Level III
- Professional Level II
- Professional Level I
- Residency Level

Four Criteria of the Base Salary Component

Advancement on the career development ladder is determined by a teacher's demonstration of competency in four areas. These areas are described below.

Criteria One – Skills Demonstration

The major feature of the base salary schedule is a list of teaching skills at each level of the ladder. The skills (161 total) are quite comprehensive and encompass the latest research and expert thinking about effective teaching practices. There are forty-four skills in the Residency Level, which are called "basic skills." These skills must be demonstrated for a teacher to continue to receive a contract for teaching and are linked to "tenure" in the district. There are 117 advanced skills with a range of fourteen to forty-four skills in the other levels of the ladder.

Advanced
Professional Level IV	14 skills
Professional Level III	24 skills
Professional Level II	35 skills
Professional Level I	44 skills

Basic
Residency Level	44 skills

Teachers are assessed on all basic skills (Residency Level Skills) regardless of current level. They are also assessed on the Advanced Level Skills for the present career development ladder, as well as all preceding level skills. The formal year-long evaluation cycle, using the Kyrene District Competency Summary Evaluation form, constitutes the process for assessing skills demonstration.

Appendix A is a list of the 1989–90 skills for each level. There has been some evolution of the skills over the past six years as part of the pilot testing of the ladder. The skills are logically or dependently sequenced with the more difficult skills at the higher levels of the plan. For instance, here are some sample skills in the area of reinforcement:

- *Professional Level IV 5.22:* demonstrates consideration for the health and safety of students by maintaining a safe physical environment.
- *Professional Level III 5.21:* establishes a positive classroom climate.
- *Professional Level II 5.17:* fosters student self-responsibility and critical thinking skills by providing opportunities for students to resolve problems.
- *Professional Level I 5.12:* develops effective individualized behavior management plans for students demonstrating chronic behavior problems.
- *Residency Level 5.07:* manages unacceptable behavior and minor

discipline problems by teaching and reinforcing the desired behavior.

When teachers demonstrate the skills of one level, they move to the next level. The level a person is currently on is his/her professional growth level, and that person will focus on his/her own development with respect to these skills. All teachers participating in the career development ladder who are not in their first year in the district receive a compensation amount tied directly to the professional growth level at which they are placed.

The amount is separate from the district operational budget. The career ladder bonus is established through a weighted index beginning with the first professional level. This level is assigned an index of 1.0, with the higher levels indexed on this figure. The bonus amount is tied to a cost-of-living index each year. The bonus amounts and index for 1989–90 are as follows:

Level	Amount	Index
Professional Level IV	$1150	1.9
Professional Level III	$960	1.6
Professional Level II	$776	1.3
Professional Level I	$589	1.0
Residency Level	$217	no index

This bonus was added during the second year of the plan as a requirment of the legislative committee, which approves the plan each year. This was a mistake in that it becomes a disincentive when the career ladder money is no longer available. This will be discussed later in the chapter.

A minimum of three years is required in each level unless a person is "fast tracked." The Residency Level requires only two years unless "fast tracked." The reason for this difference is that during the first year in the district, teachers are assessed and then placed on the appropriate level by performance the second year.

"Fast track" means the teacher has requested an opportunity to receive recognition for demonstrating skills at a level higher earlier than the three-year period. It allows a teacher to share a higher level on the career ladder bonus described above. Application to fast track is made to the principal in the fall or during the previous spring's summary evaluation conference. The annual full evaluation cycle is the process used by the supervisor to determine if fast tracking has been achieved.

Hypothetically, teachers may fast track one level per year, but it usually takes at least two or three years in a level to achieve competency in the required skills.

Criteria Two—Demonstration of Student Progress

The second area for movement on the career development ladder is tied to student acheivement. Each teacher is appraised on his/her demonstration of appropriate student progress. Data sources such as norm-referenced and criterion-referenced tests, student products, and other sources of information are established by each teacher and supervisor early in the evaluation cycle. This is part of the ongoing teacher evaluation system each year.

Criteria Three—Professional Growth Plan

In conjunction with the supervisor, a third area for movement on the ladder is tied to each teacher's annual professional growth plan. One to three professional growth objectives are identified, and progress on these is monitored through a year-long evaluation cycle. Accomplishment of objectives is assessed at the completion of each cycle. Appendix B provides a sample of the professional growth plan.

Criteria Four—Professional Development

The fourth area for movement on the ladder focuses on continuing development of effective teaching behaviors. Ongoing development of teaching skills, knowledges, and competencies is an essential part of the system. Teachers are given credit for moving up the ladder for participation in

- district staff development offerings
- external-to-district workshops and seminars
- university courses/hours in appropriate areas
- internships and field work

Professional development activities must be approved in advance. Acceptable activities shall be of such a nature that the work done acquiring the credit will directly improve the teacher's services to the district's students. Professional development activities must correlate with the individual's professional growth plan or with school and/or district priority goals.

Point System

The point requirements in these four areas for each of the five career development ladder levels are delineated below. A minimum of three years is required at each level, unless a teacher has qualified for fast tracking.

Residency

Skills Demonstration	70–92 points
Demonstration of Student Progress	1–5 points
Professional Growth Plan	1–5 points
Professional Development	1–10 points

	Column 1:	74 points minimum
	Column 2:	80 points minimum
	Column 3:	88 points minimum

Professional Level I

Skills Demonstration	93–109 points
Demonstration of Student Progress	1–5 points
Professional Growth Plan	1–5 points
Professional Development	1–10 points

	Column 1:	97 points minimum
	Column 2:	103 points minimum
	Column 3:	111 points minimum

Professional Level II

Skills Demonstration	110–128 points
Demonstration of Student Progress	1–5 points
Professional Grwoth Plan	1–5 points
Professional Development	1–10 points

	Column 1:	118 points minimum
	Column 2:	125 points minimum
	Column 3:	134 points minimum

Professional Level III

Skills Demonstration	129–143 points
Demonstration of Student Progress	1–5 points

Professional Growth Plan		1–5 points
Professional Development		1–10 points
Column 1:	140 points minimum	
Column 2:	146 points minimum	
Column 3:	155 points minimum	

Professional Level IV

Skills Demonstration		144 points
Demonstration of Student Progress		1–5 points
Professional Growth Plan		1–5 points
Professional Development		1–10 points
Column 1:	158 points minimum	
Column 2:	164 points minimum	
Column 3:	174 points minimum	

These points are then translated into the salary schedule in Table 7 (example provided for 1989–90).

Failure to Demonstrate Basic Skills

According to state statute, a teacher who does not meet district standards on the evaluation of basic skills (Residency Level Skills) may be rehired for one additional year. That teacher will be on formal notice for possible nonrenewal or dismissal. If a contract is offered for another year, the teacher will remain on the same experience step regardless of experience and in the same educational range regardless of additional educational work until notice is removed.

Strategies for improvement are made available to the teacher. If notice is removed because the teacher has begun functioning at a satisfactory level, the teacher will immediately move to the appropriate level and salary.

Downward Movement

A person in the advanced levels of the career ladder may actually move up and down the ladder. In those instances when a teacher has not demonstrated the skills sufficient to maintain current level placement, he/she may be moved to a lower career ladder level, one consistent with demonstrated skill proficiencies. The teacher maintains the current salary level at the time of this lower placement but does not receive the career ladder based salary component bonus. The teacher is also eligi-

Table 7. Certified salary schedule (1989–1990).

		BA to BA + 15 Column 1	BA + 30–45 MA-MA + 15 Column 2	BA + 60 MA + 30–45 Doct. Column 3
Pro. Level 4	O N M	30,599	33,747	38,356
Pro. Level 3	L K J	28,299	31,197	35,345
Pro. Level 2	I H G	25,999	28,647	31,345
Pro. Level 1	F E D	23,980	26,329	29,517
Resid. Level	C B A	21,961	24,011	26,689

ble for only the career ladder options provided within the lower level he/she is placed. Residency level skills must still be demonstrated; otherwise, the process that was described above under "Failure to Demonstrate Basic Skills" is initiated.

Evaluation System

The Kyrene School District's Certified Employee Evaluation System (CEAS) is a critical support system for the career development ladder's based salary component. The evaluation system is a very comprehensive system with a major emphasis on formative evaluation. In all cases, the immediate supervisor is the assessor and is responsible for the teacher's evaluation and recommendation for movement on the ladder. There is a formal appeal process (see Appendix C) as well.

The evaluation system includes the following major ingredients (see Figure 6):

- supervisory observations and conferences

- optional input activities
- evaluation of student progress
- self-evaluation of competencies
- supervisor's evaluation of competencies
- professional growth plan

A minimum of one twenty-minute formal observation followed by a post-observation conference is conducted each year for every continuing teacher. Probationary teachers receive a minimum of two twenty-minute observations and conferences each year. Most teachers participate in several observations and conferences each year as part of the district's focus on instructional coaching by administrators. Obviously, teachers in their "career development ladder" movement year receive

COMPONENT	FORM TO BE USED BY SUPERVISOR	MINIMUM REQUIREMENT PER YEAR	
		CONTINUING	PROBATIONARY
Supervisory Observations and Conferences	Observation/ Conference Record	One (1) 20-minute formal observation followed with a conference	Two (2) 20-minute formal observations each followed with a conference
Optional Input	Competency Evaluation Summary form (if input is gathered)	Optional throughout year	Optional throughout year
Demonstration of Student Progress	Competency Evaluation Summary form	Once	Once
Self-evaluation of Competencies	(Uses Competency Evaluation Summary form, but this is not collected)	Once prior to summary conference	Once prior to summary conference
Supervisor's Evaluation of Competencies	Competency Evaluation Summary form Sections I and II	Once with conference	Once with conference
Professional Growth Plan (PGP)	Professional Growth Plan (PGP)	Completed once; monitored at least once	Completed once; monitored at least twice

FIGURE 6 Evaluation components and frequency requirements.

numerous formal and informal observations in order for the supervisor to place the individual properly on the ladder. Observations may be teacher-initiated.

Incentive and Supplemental Pay Option Component

There are four major categories of incentive and supplemental pay options in the Kyrene plan. The two terms are defined as

- *Incentive Pay:* extra pay for exemplary work in *regular* work setting; compensation for effort beyond the expected but occurring during existing work hours
- *Supplemental Pay:* extra pay for extra work *beyond* existing work hours

There are four incentive pay options and ten supplemental pay options. These options are integrated into the different career levels of the plan as shown below. Eligibility for an option is based on specific career levels. The specific level for determining eligibility for each option is shown in Figure 7.

Incentive Pay Options

These incentive pay options, which occur during the normal work hours, are designed to provide incentives for professional advancement, to foster cooperation among teachers, or to meet district needs in critical areas. The four options are

- mini-grants
- peer coaching
- critical needs educator
- school-wide outstanding student achievement program

Of the four options, three have been operational for four years. A pool of money is allocated each year to each option. Most options have a ceiling amount of $500 or $564 plus three substitute days ($150 value) if used in a professional growth experience. It was determined that most options should be of equal value so as not to compensate individuals differently based on different motivational needs.

The following is a brief outline of purpose, eligibility, and description for each incentive pay option, as well as financial incentive information.

			Teacher Mentor	Teacher Mentor
	*Instruction Specialist I	Instruction Specialist II	Instruction Specialist III	Instruction Specialist IV
	Administrative Assistant	Administrative Assistant	Administrative Assistant	Administrative Assistant
	Administrative Intern	Administrative Interm	Administrative Intern	Administrative Intern
	*Curriculum/ Staff Develop. Specialist I	Curriculum/ Staff Develop. Specialist II	Curriculum/ Staff Develop. Specialist III	Curriculum/ Staff Develop. Specialist IV
	Teacher Consultant	Teacher Consultant	Teacher Consultant	Teacher Consultant
	Dept. Area Chairperson	Dept. Area Chairperson	Dept. Area Chairperson	Dept. Area Chairperson
*Staff Develop Instructor R	Staff Develop Instructor I	Staff Develop Instructor II	Staff Develop Instructor III	Staff Develop Instructor IV
Design/Develop Spec. Tasks	Design/Develop Spec. Tasks	Design/Develop Spec. Tasks	Design/Develop Spec. Tasks	Design/Develop Spec. Tasks
Buddy Teacher	Buddy Teacher	Buddy Teacher	Buddy Teacher	Buddy Teacher
Dist. Workshop Participant	Dist. Workshop Participant	Dist. Workshop Participant	Dist. Workshop Participant	Dist. Workshop Participant
Summer School Instructor/ Director	Summer School Instructor/ Director	Summer School Instructor/ Director	Summer School Instructor/ Director	Summer School Instructor/ Director
School Workshop Participant	School Workshop Participant	School Workshop Participant	School Workshop Participant	School Workshop Participant
After School Student Activity Instructor/ Coordinator	After School Student Activity Instructor/ Coordinator	After School Student Activity Instructor/ Coordinator	After School Student Activity Instructor/ Coordinator	After School Student Activity Instructor/ Coordinator
Peer Coaching	Peer Coaching	Peer Coaching	Peer Coaching	Peer Coaching
School-Wide Outstanding Student Achieve.	School-Wide Outstanding Student Achieve.	School-Wide Outstanding Student Achieve.	School-Wide Outstanding Student Achieve.	School-Wide Outstanding Student Achieve.
Instructional Innovation Mini-grant	Instructional Innovation Mini-grant	Instructional Innovation Mini-grant	Instructional Innovation Mini-grant	Instructional Innovation Mini-grant
Critical Need Area Educator	Critical Need Area Educator	Critical Need Area Educator	Critical Need Area Educator	Critical Need Area Educator
RESIDENCY LEVEL	**PROF LEVEL I**	**PROF LEVEL II**	**PROF LEVEL III**	**PROF LEVEL IV**

* Assignments based on skills/competency at appropriate Career Development Ladder level.

FIGURE 7 Incentive and supplemental pay options.

Incentive Pay Option One: Instructional Innovator Mini-Grants

Purpose: The purpose of this option is to provide teachers with opportunities for career enhancement, collegiality, and group cooperation toward a goal. It encourages teaching projects designed to improve one's own professional growth, as well as improve student learning.

Eligibility: All teachers in the plan are eligible to participate. This option is designed to be completed in teams of two or more teachers.

Description: A mini-grant is designed by teachers to address the needs of students and their own professional growth innovatively. To apply for a mini-grant, teachers complete a proposal form that includes strategies for improved student learning, rationale, and a plan for monitoring and evaluating student growth. The principal must approve the proposal, and then a screening committee appointed by the Career Ladder Advisory Council will recommend approved proposals to the administration. Teachers apply in the spring of each year for the next academic year funding. A catalog of previously completed mini-grants is available, as well as a training session on how to write winning mini-grant proposals.

Incentive: is up to $500 per teacher (or $564 and three substitute teacher days).

Incentive Pay Option Two: Peer Coaching

Purpose: The purpose of this option is to support individual growth toward specific instructional goals through collegial interaction.

Eligibility: All teachers on the plan are eligible. At least two teachers from the same school must apply as a team.

Description: Peer coaching is an option that encourages collegiality. Participants attend six hours of training, participate in reciprocal observations and feedback sessions, participate in reflective interviews, videotape and self-analyze one lesson, choose two additional activities, and complete a log of their peer coaching activities. Selection is made in the spring for implementation in the next academic year.

Incentive: is up to $500 per teacher (or $564 and three substitute teacher days).

Incentive Pay Option Three: Critical Need Area Educator

Purpose: The purpose of this option is to attract qualified teachers to teach subjects where critical staff shortages exist or where there are students with special needs. Currently, the areas where incentive pay is offered are in limited English proficient certificate, speech, and language specialist. Areas of critical shortage are analyzed annually and redefined as needed. An area identified as critical one year may not be so identified the next year.

Eligibility: Any certified staff member currently employed in the identified critical need area is eligible to apply. Qualifications include appropriate state certification, appropriate coursework as identified by the district, and appropriate skills for the specific students served.

Description: Teachers are assigned to areas of critical need.

Incentive:
- $2080 per year for Language English Proficiency program teachers
- $1000 per year for Language English Proficiency endorsed classroom teachers who qualify
- $2500 per year for teachers of visually handicapped students
- $2500 per year for teachers of hearing handicapped students

Incentive Pay Option Four: School-wide Outstanding Student Achievement (as yet to be implemented)

Purpose: The purpose of this incentive option is to recognize excellence in teaching that results in increased student achievement.

Eligibility: The entire faculty of a school, given a majority vote of all certified staff at that school.

Description: The faculty apply for this incentive through a written form. The approach for determining student achievement gains is through the district's criterion-referenced and norm-referenced assessment tools or through school-generated assessment approaches approved by the district. The increase in achievement is based on a repeated measure approach from one year to the next so that a school is, in essence, competing against itself based on the previous year's scores.

Incentive: is $1000 per school enrolling under 600 students with a $100 increase for every additional 100 students. The award is given to the entire faculty in the next fiscal year.

Supplemental Pay Options

These options are, in essence, extra pay for additional work beyond the normal work day, although some of the activities may occur during the regular work situation. The purposes vary based on need. Some of the options are typical extra pay options like department chair, while others are for more recent career ladder type positions such as mentor. There are ten supplemental pay options:

- mentor
- buddy teacher
- staff development instructor
- department chair/team leader/coach
- summer school instructor
- after-school student activity instructor
- workshop participant
- designer/developer (not funded to date)
- teacher on special assignment (job ladder)
- administrative internship (job ladder)

The following is a brief outline of purpose, eligibility, and description for the first two incentive pay options, as well as financial incentive information.

Supplemental Pay Option One: Mentor

Purpose: The purpose of this option is to provide mentors for new and veteran teachers in the areas of curriculum and instruction and to coordinate district programs at the building level.

Eligibility: Teachers must have taught at least three years in the district and be on Professional Level III or IV. Applications for these positions are accepted in the spring for the following year. Selections are made by the principal or supervisor.

Description: There is one mentor per school in addition to special area mentors (music, gifted, speech/language, library, physical education, Language English Proficiency, special education, kindergarten, art). They are responsible for demonstrating successful instruction and/or classroom management for teachers to observe, assisting teachers in developing and implementing the instructional and classroom management plans, assisting new teacher workshops, and coordinating district testing programs and special area program inventories.

Incentive: is $1250 per year.

Supplemental Pay Option Two: Buddy Teacher

Purpose: This option is designed specifically to assist teachers new to the Kyrene district in entering the system and developing residency level skills.

Eligibility: Participants must apply for these positions in the spring for the following school year. Selections are made by the principal. The teacher must be a participant in the Career Ladder Program with at least three years' teaching experience, one of which must have been in the Kyrene School District.

Description: Buddy teachers assist new teachers during orientation week and throughout the school year by providing assistance with classroom management, instructional planning, and access to local district information and by demonstrating teaching skills.

Incentive: is $750 per year.

The remaining supplemental pay options are typical options that schools have within their systems. They involve pay for extra duties, for participating in workshops, or for developing and designing specific tasks. Two areas that are part of a job ladder are the teacher on special assignment and the administrative internship. These options are paid through the regular maintenance and operation budget for people to work part-time or full-time in quasi-administrative roles. In 1989–90, there were eleven teachers on special assignments and two administrative interns.

Forms of Compensation

One important feature in the Kyrene Career Development Ladder is the form of compensation available to the individuals opting for the Incentive/Supplemental Pay Option. Many Career Ladder Plans have failed based on the assumption that money serves as an effective motivator in all cases. With respect to most of the incentive pay options in this plan, the amount of money tied to the compensation is miniscule. The options have been based on the motivational theory of Herzberg (1966). Herzberg's theory asserts two separate and distinct sets of factors accounting for satisfaction (motivation) and dissatisfaction (hygiene). According to Herzberg's theory, the factors that serve as motivators of satisfiers are tied to work content. They include achievement, recognition for achievement, expanded responsibilities, intrinsic interest work for itself, professional growth, and advancement. These factors serve people's motivational needs.

Using this theory as suggested by Frase, Hetzel, and Grant (1982b), compensation must serve not only as a reward but also as a motivator. The major purpose of the compensation plan was to motivate staff to continue excellent practices and to make additional improvements. The task force studied this problem carefully to identify compensation options that would serve as motivators.

The form of compensation for the Residency, Professional I, II, III, and career levels is the base salary compensation package, which includes an annual bonus stipend. The forms of compensation for the various incentive and supplemental pay options are determined annually. The forms of compensation include, but are not limited to, the following:

- direct financial compensation in the form of salary (e.g., $1000 stipend, $500 bonus, or percentage of salary increase)
- additional fringe benefits package (e.g., additional medical, psychological, or counseling, legal aid, etc., could be "cafeteria plan")
- professional growth experience
- extended leave
- extended contract (e.g., ten, eleven, or twelve months)
- reimbursement for tuition
- reimbursement for conference participation (registration and expenses)
- reimbursement for professional association dues (other than the teachers' association)
- reimbursement for professional magazine subscriptions and/or books
- additional instructional materials and supplies including computer software

Career Development Ladder Advisory Council

The following section describes the composition, role, purpose, and functions of the Career Development Ladder Advisory Council.

Composition

The Career Development Ladder Advisory Council is composed of a career ladder specialist (chairperson of the council), in addition to members appointed by the superintendent.

The specific composition of the advisory council is as follows.

- career ladder specialist, chairperson
- teacher representative from each school with an attempt to balance across curriculum areas
- staff development coordinator
- elementary principal
- middle school principal
- member of the governing board (observer, resource)
- education association representative
- technicians (ex-officio members): director of personnel, assistant superintendent of educational services, career ladder specialist

Selection is made no later than three weeks following the completion of the teacher transfer process. Members serve on the council at least one year and no longer than three consecutive years. Members may be given one-year, two-year, or three-year appointments in order to maintain a balance between new and continuing members on the council.

Meetings are held on an on-call basis. The council meets at least twice a year. Minutes of each meeting are submitted to the chairperson.

As the district increases in population, the composition and size of the advisory council will be reviewed periodically; regional representation could be an option should the size of the district council become unwieldly. Parent representation on the advisory council will be maintained on an ad-hoc basis.

Role

The advisory council's primary focus is to advise and assist district personnel regarding the ongoing assessment and evaluation of the Kyrene Elementary Career Development Ladder Plan. The council has no governing authority but is a recommending body to the administration.

Purposes and Goals

The purposes and goals of the council are

- to obtain information that will update, modify, expand, and improve the quality of the Career Development Ladder Plan
- to make recommendations that will expand and strengthen the effectiveness of the Career Development Ladder Plan
- to assist in implementing the recommendations

- to assist in identifying ongoing needs
- to assist in reviewing and evaluating the Career Development Ladder Plan

Function

The primary function of the council is to facilitate the planning and conducting of the ongoing assessment and evaluation of the Kyrene Career Development Ladder Plan and to facilitate the appeal process.

The council will implement the following general procedures to facilitate the ongoing assessment and evaluation of the Career Development Ladder Plan:

- Formulate key assessment and evaluative questions to be addressed.
- Select appropriate assessment and evaluation activities.
- Identify specific data to be collected with each assessment and evaluation activity.
- Select and assign personnel to be involved in facilitating the evaluation.
- Develop a time line for collecting data.
- Develop data collection instruments.
- Compile, review, and analyze data collected.
- Develop a format for reporting the assessment and evaluation information.
- Communicate the assessment and evaluation findings to the appropriate personnel.
- Assist the appropriate personnel in implementing change based on the assessment and evaluation findings.

RECOMMENDATIONS

The majority of the Kyrene Career Development Plan is very functional. Some of its greatest strengths lie in its professional growth nature and the fact that it is a "development" ladder. This author would recommend to any group designing a career ladder to use a comprehensive list of skills rather than a percentage of the skills for each ladder and that as people advance on the ladder, the skills they are working on are those on the ladder.

Another excellent part of the plan, which is recommended for use elsewhere, is the variety of incentive and supplemental pay options that provide diverse activities to meet the various motivational and professional needs of staff.

A third functional area is the use of a compensation plan that is, for the most part, not based on quotas. A pool of money is placed into a particular option and depending on the number of people participating, there is a sharing of the pool. An important factor in this area, however, is the placing of a ceiling for the top amount of money or incentive any person can receive.

The following changes are recommended by the author to alleviate difficulties encountered in implementing a Career Development Ladder Plan:

- Use incentive money for non-salaried compensation choices. The funds are best used for professional growth opportunities, especially professional trips to conferences and workshops. The benefits reaped are much greater than those of any salary option (Frase, Hetzel, and Grant, 1982a). Also, if the plan must be discontinued, it should not be replaced with a decrease in salary, which would serve as a disincentive.
- Keep the district's current salary schedule and overlay the career ladder onto that salary schedule. Attempting to completely restructure salary schedules is too great a change for the majority of staff, both in terms of financial perspective, as well as logistics. Some of the strategies suggested earlier in the chapter, which were attempted initially in the Kyrene plan, are still those that would fit most systems. Other districts in the nation have used these with great success.

There are several questions in designing a Career Ladder Plan. Some of the factors that need to be considered are as follows:

- number and types of rungs
- basis for determination
- rewards at each rung (type and amount)
- numbers of roles
- increased roles and responsibilities
- quotas
- linkage to performance evaluation
- linkage to personal and professional goals
- difference between remediation and skill enhancement

- amount of reward
- use of quotas
- frequency of rewards

Prior to initiating any compensation program, it is important first to determine the purpose of the plan. Among those that should be considered are the following:

- Provide performance pay.
- Provide professional growth opportunities.
- Recognize the exceptional few.
- Assist all staff.

Many questions need to be addressed in the design of a career ladder. It is hoped that the case study of the Kyrene plan will provide insight into those particular aspects that have worked and those that have not worked.

APPENDIX A

1.0 Fulfills Professional Responsibilities and Assignments

R   1.01   Accepts and fulfills assigned responsibilities and duties in a prompt and efficient manner.

R   1.02   Follows or implements governing board policies, school procedures, and any other rules, regulations, or procedures that may be established by central office or school administration.

R   1.03   Maintains accurate, complete records as required by law, district policy and administrative regulations.

R   1.04   Participates in school/district activities as specified in meet and confer agreement.

P-I   None
P-II   None
P-III None
P-IV   None

2.0 Plans and Organizes Instruction

A. *Diagnostic Evaluation*

R   2.01   Instructional plans are based on diagnostic data gathered primarily at the beginning of the year or semester.

P-I 2.02 Instructional plans are based on diagnostic data gathered primarily from formal assessment measures (such as district tests, published pre-tests, or placement tests).

P-I 2.03 Instructional plans are based on diagnostic data gathered from informal assessment techniques such as teacher observation of oral responses and written classwork.

P-I 2.04 Instructional plans are based on diagnostic data gathered frequently prior to new learning as needed throughout the year.

P-II 2.05 Instructional plans are based on diagnostic data gathered from assessment measures including some designed by the teacher which are based on district course of study learning objectives.

P-III 2.06 Instructional plans are based on diagnostic data gathered from many sources including school records and data gathered by other school personnel.

P-IV None

B. Learning Objectives

R   2.07 Specifies objectives for groups of students.

R   2.08 Specifies objectives based on district course of study.

R   2.09 Specifies objectives for each lesson.

R   2.10 Specifies objectives for weekly plans.

P-I 2.11 Specifies objectives for individual students as needed.

P-I 2.12 Specifies objectives based on diagnostic data gathered.

P-I 2.13 Specifies objectives for quarterly plans or longer.

P-II 2.14 Incorporates special education students' IEP objectives into plans.

P-II 2.15 When needed, modifies objectives to reflect correct level of difficulty for individual students.

P-III 2.16 When needed, specifies additional entry level, enroute, and terminal sub-objectives based on a task analysis of an objective.

P-III 2.17 Is knowledgeable of the sequence of skills along the continuum of objectives listed in the district course of study.

P-IV 2.18 Prioritizes objectives within a curriculum area to identify the most critical learning outcomes.

P-IV 2.19 When possible, organizes curriculum objectives into interdisciplinary instructional units.

P-IV 2.20   Establishes written short- and long-term goals for individual students based on learning rate and learning needs.

C. Materials

R   2.21   Selects materials from district-adopted materials.
P-I   2.22   Demonstrates planning for use of media by previewing materials.
P-II   2.23   Selects materials that facilitate instructional objective(s).
P-II   2.24   Supplements basic materials with media materials (films, video, audiotapes, etc.) that correspond to objectives.
P-II   2.25   Selects materials that facilitate learner needs for remediation or enrichment.
P-II   2.26   When appropriate, selects supplemental materials that enhance learning by drawing up student interests.
P-II   2.27   When needed, adapts materials to match objective and/or learner needs.
P-III 2.28   When needed, supplements available materials by creating materials that enhance learning.
P-IV   2.29   Selects materials that enhance interdisciplinary transfer.

D. Instructional Design and Planning

R   2.30   Develops a daily or weekly schedule that corresponds to allocated time guidelines for subject areas.
R   2.31   Develops plans for lesson content based on learning objectives.
P-I   2.32   Develops coordinated plans for special needs students with appropriate support personnel.
P-I   2.33   Plans to group students for learning using survey-level diagnostic data.
P-I   2.34   Plans for instruction reflecting knowledge of developmental characteristics of children.
P-I   2.35   Designs instruction to provide for regular review of key concepts and skills related to new learning.
P-II   2.36   Plans to group students for learning using diagnostic data on specific instructional objectives.
P-II   2.37   Plans to group students for learning by forming flexible groups on an "as needed" basis.
P-III 2.38   Plans instruction to provide for the transfer of learning.

P-IV 2.39 Designs instruction systematically incorporating strategies that promote higher-level thought process, responses, and critical thinking.

P-IV 2.40 Develops plans for instruction that reflect consideration of individual differences among learners by including re-teaching of deficiencies in student's prior learning.

P-IV 2.41 Develops plans for instruction that reflect consideration of individual differences among learners by including remedial and/or enrichment activities based on diagnosis or differentiated assignments.

3.0 Provides Effective Lesson Delivery

A. Content/Subject Matter Presentation

R   3.01 Demonstrates understanding of content/subject by providing accurate, current, and relevant information.

R   3.02 Demonstrates understanding of content/subject by clearly communicating the critical attributes.

R   3.03 Demonstrates understanding of content/subject by presenting the content in an organized manner.

P-I   3.04 Demonstrates understanding of content/subject by cueing students to critical pieces of content.

P-I   3.05 Demonstrates understanding of content/subject by showing what is accurate and precise modeling.

P-II None

P-III 3.06 Demonstrates understanding of content/subject by modeling, when appropriate, correct thought processes and strategies.

P-IV None

B. Principles of Learning

R   3.07 Establishes a mental set for a lesson when appropriate.

R   3.08 Augments student motivation by expressing an appropriate level of enthusiasm during the lesson.

R   3.09 Facilitates retention of learning by guiding group practice for initial practice sessions.

R   3.10 Gives precise directions for tasks and clearly communicates standards for finished products.

R   3.11   Teaches students study skills and strategies necessary for successful completion of tasks.

R   3.12   Prescribes assignments that provide additional practice of critical content.

P-I   3.13   Provides for active participation of students by eliciting both covert and overt responses from students.

P-I   3.14   Augments student motivation by using both formal and informal means of recognition.

P-I   3.15   Facilitates transfer of learnings by previewing content.

P-I   3.16   Establishes closure for a lesson when appropriate by summarizing relevant learning.

P-I   3.17   Provides for active participation of students by creating a variety of response opportunities.

P-I   3.18   Augments student motivation by giving praise/rewards privately or publicly as appropriate.

P-I   3.19   Facilitates retention of learning by monitoring responses during practice and giving group and individual feedback.

P-I   3.20   Prescribes assignments that are manageable proportions and coordinated with respect to total student load.

P-I   3.21   Gives students prompt and relevant feedback on assignments.

P-I   3.22   Establishes closure for a relevant lesson when appropriate by helping students summarize relevant learning.

P-I   3.23   Uses a variety of ways to establish a mental set for a lesson when appropriate.

P-II   3.24   Augments student motivation by consciously maintaining an appropriate level of concern.

P-II   3.25   Facilitates retention of learning by reviewing prerequisite concepts and skills prior to new learning and reteaching if needed.

P-II   3.26   Provides for active participation of students by using techniques to encourage participation of passive learners.

P-II   3.27   Augments student motivation by consciously using appropriate feeling tone.

P-II   3.28   Augments student motivation by providing success opportunities for each student into lessons.

P-II   3.29   Facilitates retention of learning by providing regular, focused reviews of priority concepts and skills.

P-II 3.30 Facilitates transfer of learnings by bridging unfamiliar content with the familiar.

P-III 3.31 Provides for active participation of students by involving most of the students most of the time.

P-III 3.32 Augments student motivation through using creative instructional techniques.

P-III 3.33 Augments student motivation by providing appropriate feedback for learning that is immediate and specific (as related to objective, concise, and clear).

P-III 3.34 Facilitates retention of learning by making the learning meaningful by relating to students' interests, prior knowledge, and past experiences.

P-III 3.35 Facilitates retention by providing a high degree of initial learning.

P-III 3.36 Facilitates retention of learning by scheduling massed practice for new learning and distributed practice for old learning.

P-III 3.37 Facilitates retention of learning by differentiating individual practice assignments as needed.

P-IV 3.38 Provides challenging and creative assignments.

P-IV 3.39 Facilitates transfer of learnings by modeling and teaching strategies and frameworks for organizing new learnings.

4.0 Evaluates and Communicates Student Progress

A. Evaluation Tools and Methods

R   4.01 Selects assessment measures that match all components of learning objectives.

R   4.02 Assess student performance daily or weekly as appropriate.

R   4.03 Administers standardized tests (ITBS, district tests) in a reliable manner by adhering to test directions.

P-I   None

P-II 4.04 Selects assessment measures that are suitable for specified purpose(s); diagnosis, measuring progress, normative comparison, and program evaluation.

P-II 4.05 Constructs assessment measures that match components of learning objectives.

P-II 4.06 Constructs assessment measures that include observations of products, processes and oral responses.
P-II 4.07 Demonstrates understanding of standardized test results.
P-III None
P-IV None

B. Record Keeping

R   4.08 Places test results, as required, in appropriate files.
R   4.09 Maintains a record keeping system that has records for performance of individual students.
P-I   4.10 Maintains a record keeping system that records performance on academic objectives and on social/behavioral objectives.
P-I   4.11 Demonstrates understanding of formative and summative evaluation.
P-I   4.12 Establishes high yet reasonable standards for evaluating student achievement.
P-II 4.13 Maintains a record keeping system that has records for performance of groups of students.
P-II 4.14 Maintains a record keeping system that includes objectives from IEPs developed by child study teams.
P-III None
P-IV None

C. Uses

R   4.15 Maintains confidentiality of individual student records and uses group data in ethical manner.
P-I   4.16 Uses results of evaluation to guide instructional planning.
P-I   4.17 Uses results of evaluation to identify special needs students for referral.
P-II 4.18 Uses results of evaluation to differentiate instruction to meet individual learning needs.
P-II 4.19 Uses results of evaluation to assess and modify instruction to increase effectiveness.
P-III 4.20 Effectively communicates test data and student progress.
P-IV 4.21 Uses results of assessment data to evaluate instructional research and application techniques.

5.0 Organizes and Manages the Classroom/School Environment

A. *Student Behavior*

R   5.01   Establishes classroom rules, procedures, and consequences that are based on high behavioral expectations and consistent with the school code of conduct.

R   5.02   Establishes classroom rules, procedures, and consequences that are directly taught, practiced, and reviewed and which are clearly communicated to parents as well as students.

R   5.03   Deals effectively with discipline problems by focusing on inappropriate behavior allowing students to maintain dignity.

R   5.04   Deals effectively with severe discipline problems by seeking the appropriate assistance.

R   5.05   Provides consistent support to school-wide discipline programs and procedures.

P-I   5.06   Classroom rules, procedures, and consequences are routinely applied.

P-I   5.07   Manages unacceptable behavior and minor discipline problems by using techniques such as eye contact and proximity.

P-I   5.08   Manages unacceptable behavior and minor discipline problems by teaching and reinforcing the desired behavior.

P-I   5.09   Deals effectively with dangerous discipline problems.

P-I   5.10   Involves specialists and parents in establishing a system for individual behavior management.

P-II   5.11   Uses praise and rewards that are age and developmentally appropriate.

P-II   5.12   Develops effective individualized behavior management plans for students demonstrating chronic behavior problems.

P-II   5.13   Assesses management strategies of student behavior and adjusts if needed.

P-III 5.14   Prompts students toward behavioral self-management.

P-III 5.15   Fosters student self-responsibility and problem solving.

P-IV 5.16   Promotes the transition of student reinforcers from extrinsic to intrinsic.

P-IV 5.17 Fosters student self-responsibility and critical thinking skills by providing opportunities for students to resolve problems.

B. Learning Environment and Climate

R 5.18 Maintains order in the classroom by establishing and teaching procedures for handling routine tasks.

R 5.19 Maintains order in the classroom by having materials and equipment ready to use.

R 5.20 Organizes the classroom space to facilitate teacher/student proximity.

R 5.21 Establishes a positive classroom climate.

R 5.22 Demonstrates consideration for the health and safety of students by maintaining a safe physical environment.

R 5.23 Demonstrates consideration for the health and safety of students by teaching and reviewing safety rules and procedures.

P-I 5.24 Maintains order in the classroom by keeping all students involved in the desired learning.

P-I 5.25 Encourages student participation and leadership by providing opportunities and reinforcing students' participation in class activities.

P-I 5.26 Organizes the classroom space to facilitate an effective learning environment.

P-I 5.27 Establishes a positive classroom climate by facilitating comfortable interpersonal relationships among students.

P-II 5.28 Encourages student participation and leadership by providing opportunities for students to be involved in decision making.

P-II 5.29 Fosters creative thought valuing student contributions through recognition and use of student ideas.

P-III 5.30 Provides opportunities for cooperative learning.
P-IV None

6.0 Demonstrates Interpersonal Skills

R 6.01 Promotes healthy teacher/student relationships by reinforcing and encouraging all students in a fair and empathic manner.

R   6.02   Maintains and communicates expectations for courteous and caring student to student interaction.

R   6.03   Maintains high standards of confidentiality and professionalism concerning student records.

R   6.04   Views colleagues as a valuable resource.

P-I   6.05   Recognizes and values student interests, concerns, and contributions.

P-I   6.06   Initiates and maintains parent/teacher communication both formally and informally.

P-I   6.07   Plans for appropriate use of volunteers and instructional aides when available.

P-I   6.08   Participates in and demonstrates enthusiasm for curricular and extracurricular functions.

P-I   6.09   Applies problem-solving skills to conflict situations.

P-II 6.10   Directs operative parent/teacher conferences.

P-II 6.11   Communicates clear information to parents of student progress on academic and behavioral goals.

P-III 6.12   Encourages students to develop a sense of responsibility and self-reliance.

P-III 6.13   Provides ongoing opportunities for success for all students.

P-III 6.14   Uses a variety of appropriate forms of parent/teacher communication.

P-IV 6.15   Encourages parental support of and involvement in school learning activities.

P-IV 6.16   Works collaboratively and cooperatively with colleagues to foster school/district goals.

P-IV 6.17   Shares instructional resources and seeks input from colleagues.

P-IV 6.18   Demonstrates an awareness of the broad educational perspective in decision making.

7.0 Demonstrates Professional Growth and Collegiality

A. *Self-Growth*

R   7.01   Engages in professional self-development by writing professional growth plans that include goals and plans for achievement.

P-I   7.02   Engages in professional self-development by acquiring new knowledge about content areas or teaching strategies through means such as reading professional literature, taking coursework, or attending conferences, workshops, or other staff development activities.

P-II 7.03 Engages in professional self-development by applying newly acquired knowledge.

P-II 7.04 Engages in professional self-development by using student achievement data to evaluate and modify instructional effectiveness.

P-II 7.05 Engages in professional self-development by gathering data from formal and informal techniques to evaluate teaching behavior.

P-III None

P-IV None

B. Colleagues

R 7.06 Fosters collegiality by giving feedback on successes and supporting colleagues' efforts.

P-I None

P-II 7.07 Assists colleagues in handling discipline problems by providing suggestions and support.

P-III 7.08 Contributes to professional growth of colleagues by formally or informally sharing new knowledge and ideas.

P-IV 7.09 Assists colleagues in constructing, administering, or interpreting formal and informal measures of student performance.

P-IV 7.10 Assists colleagues in developing plans, strategies, or materials to improve instructional delivery.

P-IV 7.11 Contributes to professional growth of colleagues by engaging in coaching/mentoring activities, including instructional analysis and conferencing.

C. School/District

R None

P-I 7.12 Contributes to the improvement of the school/district program by recognizing and offering assistance in resolving problems within the school environment.

P-II 7.13 Contributes to the improvement of the school/district program by periodically participating on school-level/district committees.

P-III 7.14   Contributes to the improvement of the school/district program by periodically providing leadership on school-level/district committees.

P-III 7.15   Contributes to the improvement of the school/district program by assisting with a special program, project, or event that addresses school or district goals.

P-IV 7.16   Contributes to the improvement of the school/district program by providing leadership and assuming responsibility for a special program, project, or event that addresses school or district goals.

APPENDIX B

The following form is an example of a professional growth plan.

PROFESSIONAL GROWTH PLAN

FOR:

NAME:_____ SUPERVISOR:_____

SCHOOL/DEPT._____ CYCLE:____/____/____ TO____/____/____

PROFESSIONAL GROWTH OBJECTIVE   1:
(Verb, content area, level of thought process)

PLAN OF ACTION:
These are the learning strategies I will use enroute to Objective 1:

These are the resources (material, staff development, etc.) I will need to complete Objective 1:

I estimate the completion date to be: _____ /_____ /_____

CRITERIA:
The following criteria will be used to determine accomplishment of Objective 1:

(continued) . . .

PROFESSIONAL GROWTH PLAN

FOR:

NAME:_____ SUPERVISOR:_____

SCHOOL/DEPT._____ CYCLE:____/____/____ TO____/____/____

PROFESSIONAL GROWTH OBJECTIVE 2:
(Verb, content area, level of thought process)

PLAN OF ACTION:
These are the learning strategies I will use enroute to Objective 2:

These are the resources (material, staff development, etc.) I will need to complete Objective 2:

I estimate the completion date to be: _____/_____/_____

CRITERIA:
The following criteria will be used to determine accomplishment of Objective 2:

This plan was approved on: _____/_____/_____

Signature of EMPLOYEE   _____

Signature of SUPERVISOR   _____

WHITE:	Initiated by EMPLOYEE/Held by SUPERVISOR/To PERSONNEL when completed
CANARY:	To SUPERVISOR when completed
PINK:	To EMPLOYEE when completed
GOLDENROD:	To EMPLOYEE when initiated

APPENDIX C

Process for Reconsideration of Placement on the Career Ladder

A process for reconsideration of placement on the career ladder has been designed to assist teachers and supervisors regarding placement decisions. An informal and/or formal process may be used to help determine this decision. The informal process will be between the

teacher and his/her immediate supervisor; the formal process will in
volve an appeals panel. The process may be used for

- initial placement reconsideration of the determination of the
  growth focus onto the career ladder
- placement for movement from one level to the next one on the
  Career Ladder Plan

There will be no placement decision reconsideration for

- a person who has asked to be "fast tracked" to a higher level
  (The final decision for fast tracking will be made by the
  immediate supervisor.)
- a person who is in either intervention or documentation/
  dismissal phases of the Certified Employee Evaluation System.

Informal Review of Placement

After a year-long series of contacts and conferences with the
employee, the supervisor makes the placement decision based on the
evidence observed. This decision is recorded on the Competency
Assessment Summary Form. In some cases, an employee may feel
that additional evidence brought to the attention of the supervisor
might change the placement decision.

If an employee wishes an informal reconsideration, he/she initiates
a conference with the immediate supervisor to take place as soon as
possible, preferably within a week of the placement decision. Additional conferences may be scheduled, if deemed necessary. The
teacher and supervisor may agree on an approach for reviewing additional evidence. This could include

- reviewing the situation from the teacher's perspective
- reviewing definitions of skill indicators
- providing additional artifact evidence to support teacher
  demonstration of the skill indicator
- scheduling mutually agreed upon additional observations
  (announced and/or unannounced) to observe for demonstration
  of skill indicators

The first level of placement reconsideration, therefore, is the
teacher's immediate supervisor, who will meet with the teacher to
analyze sources of agreement and disagreement about the teacher's

placement and to problem solve in regard to appropriate subsequent action to be taken. This portion of the process may include examination of additional evidence submitted by the teacher.

Upon completion of the informal process, Section I of Form A will be completed by the supervisor and signed by both the teacher and the supervisor, providing documentation of the process. If the teacher does not agree with the decision, he/she may formally appeal.

Formal Appeal

If a teacher wishes to initiate a formal appeal, a pre-appeal orientation session will be held with the appellant and the director of personnel to

- review the purposes of the placement process
- clarify the Career Ladder Plan approach
- reveiw the process for determining placement on the Career Development Ladder Plan
- discuss reasons for the appeal
- review the informal appeal process
- describe the purpose of formal appeals
- specify procedures for formal appeal, including how the decision will be communicated to the teacher

Should the teacher then wish to initiate the formal appeal process, the following steps are required:

- Complete Section II (which states the reason for the appeal) of Form A within fifteen working days of receipt of Form A, Section I. An exception to the above may be made by mutual agreement between the parties involved.
- Obtain the signature of the supervisor on Section II.
- Send the form to the director of personnel who will coordinate the process.

The appeals panel shall consist of three qualified evaluators other than the immediate supervisor of the teacher. The panel shall be appointed from the district's list of qualified evaluators. Should there be more than one appeal from the same school within the year, the composition of the panels will be different. The panel shall be selected by the director of personnel in consultation with the teacher making the appeal. Following the selection of the panel, the director of personnel shall appoint one member as chairperson.

The appeals panel shall request from the teacher a schedule for a two-week period showing when the teacher will be teaching and which subject areas will be taught. During this period, the panel will be conducting observations. Each member of the panel shall make a minimum of one unannounced and one announced observation independently on different days and at different times. There will be a total of at least six independent observations. Panel members will notify the teacher of the times they will be making the announced observations. Each observation shall be at least thirty minutes in length.

An interview of the teacher shall be conducted to collect additional data. Prior to the interview, a list of the skills that are not readily observable in the classroom shall be given to the teacher. It is the teacher's responsibility to be prepared to show evidence that supports the demonstration of those skills.

Each panel member shall complete a Kyrene Teacher Competency Assessment Summary form for each of the two observations. Each panel member shall then summarize the two observations and interview information to complete one evaluation report. In the case of disagreement, additional observations may be scheduled at the request of the panel with mutual agreement of the teacher.

The appeals panel shall meet within twenty working days from the date of its selection as the appeals panel and compare evaluations. The panel shall make a decision either to (1) recommend that the original decision be maintained or (2) recommend a new level, higher than the level recommended by the immediate supervisor.

The decision of the appeals panel is final and will be communicated to the teacher in writing using Form B within six working days after the panel meets. If the panel is unable to reach consensus in support of the supervisor's decision, the appeal of the teacher will be upheld.

The original of the written appeal, together with the decision of the appeals panel, is given to the teacher. Copies are given to the immediate supervisor and placed on record in the official personnel file.

REFERENCES

Bacharach, S. B., D. B. Lipsky, and J. B. Shedd. 1984. *Paying for Better Teaching: Merit Pay and Its Alternatives.* Ithaca, New York: Organizational Analysis and Practice Monograph.

Boyer, E. 1983. *High School: A Report on Secondary Education in America.* New York: Harper and Row.

Brederson, P. V., M. J. Fruth, and K. L. Kasten. 1983. "Organizational Incentives and Secondary School Teaching," *Journal of Research and Development in Education,* 16.

Casio, W. F. 1982. *Applied Psychology in Personnel Management.* Reston, VA: Reston Publishing.

Cresap, McCormick, and Paget. 1984. *Teacher Incentives: A Tool for Effective Management.* Reston, VA: National Association of Elementary Principals.

Frase, L., R. Hetzel, and R. Grant. 1982a. "Merit Pay: A Research-Based Alternative in Tucson," *Phi Delta Kappan,* 64(4):266–269.

Frase, L., R. Hetzel, and R. Grant. 1982b. "Promoting Instructional Excellence through a Teacher Reward System: Herzbergs' Theory Applied," *Planning & Changing,* 13(2):67–76.

Frase, L., R. Hetzel, and D. Inman. 1987. "Is There a Sound Rationale behind the Merit Pay Craze?" *Teacher Education Quarterly,* 14(2):90–101.

Goodlad, John I. 1984. *A Place Called School: Prospect for the Future.* New York: McGraw Hill.

Herzberg, F. 1966. *Work and the Nature of Man.* Cleveland: World.

Lortie, D. C. 1975. *School Teacher: A Sociologist Study.* Chicago: University of Chicago Press.

Maslow, A. H. 1970. *Motivation and Personality, 2nd Ed.* New York: Harper and Row.

Page, F. M., Jr. and J. A. Page. 1982. "Perceptions of Teaching That May Be Influencing Current Shortage of Teachers," *College Student Journal,* 16.

Robinson, Glen E. 1984. "Merit Pay for Teachers," Educational Research Service Report. Arlington, VA: Educational Research Service, Inc.

Rosenholtz, Susan J. and Mark A. Smylie. 1983. "Teacher Compensation and Career Ladders: Policy Implications from Research," paper commissioned by the Tennessee General Assembly's Select Committee on Education, December.

Rosenholtz, Susan J. 1984. "Political Myths about Reforming the Teaching Profession," Denver, Colorado: Education Commission of the States.

Sample, J. A. 1984. "The Expectancy Theory of Motivation: Implications for Training and Development," *The 1984 Annual: Developing Human Resources.* San Diego, California: University Associates, Inc.

Vroom, V. H. 1964. *Motivation and Work.* New York: John Wiley and Sons.

CHAPTER 20

Paying for Performance in Lake Forest, Illinois

ALLEN J. KLINGENBERG – *Superintendent, Lake Forest Public Schools, Illinois*

OVERVIEW

IN District 67 the idea of "merit pay" is much more complex and encompassing than simply "more pay for more work." Merit pay, or Performance Evaluation Pay System, as it is called, means an all-inclusive program involving the commitment, cooperation, and caring for each of the members of the District 67 family. Performance compensation means not only salary and benefits, but more importantly self-satisfaction.

For one to understand the system, let's begin by telling you a little about the characteristics and flavor of the district and the community it serves. Lake Forest Elementary School District 67 and Lake Forest, Illinois, were chartered by the state in 1861. The district consists of six schools: four grade schools housing grades K–3, a middle school for grades 4 and 5, and a junior high school for grades 6–8. In 1990–1991, the schools are attended by 1870 students and staffed by 162 certificated and 60 noncertificated employees. A nine-member board of education is appointed by the mayor and governs the district. The district's 1990–1991 budget is $11.2 million, 93 percent of which is funded by local property taxes, fees, and returns on investments. The remaining revenue comes from state and federal sources.

The parent community is actively involved in the education process. Over 95 percent of our 1146 families belong to the Association of Parents and Teachers and many serve as volunteers in every area of the district's program, from classroom aides to guest speakers, helping to produce poetry anthologies and sponsoring coffees and open houses. Parents sit on the superintendent's Curriculum Advisory Committee and frequently are asked to critique new program ideas and are periodically surveyed to determine their perception of the district's programs, goals, and support for new initiatives.

541

Lake Forest has had a "merit" performance compensation program since 1861. During the past eighteen years, however, the district has moved to formalize the concept of performance pay and during the past eight years has been using a computer projection model to determine parameters of equitable compensation recommendations for staff members.

To understand the Lake Forest model, one must understand the management concept under which the school system operates. The system of operation used in management is akin to that of the private corporation (see Table 1). The board of education is like the corporate board of directors; corporate management is similar to the superintendent and his management team. The corporate product is analogous to the educational programs and services of the district. The consumers of the corporate product are the students, parents, taxpayers, and community groups. The stockholders in the school corporation are taxpayers.

To put this in perspective, the school system operates as an integrated system providing services to its consumers. In terms of the school system, the board of education is in control and determines the overall vision, mission statement, and goals of the district, with management implementing a program to achieve the purposes and goals of the organization. Teachers are responsible for implementing specific programs necessary to provide these services for the consumers, our students. The community members are our ultimate consumers. The consumers are made up of students, parents, and nonparents. Parents who have children in our schools (less then 20 percent of taxpayers) are the most direct consumer/observers of our programs in terms of their children's learning and are therefore asked to give us periodic feedback on the quality of our product. We have conducted five surveys in eighteen years.

The basic concept of management in the district is really no different

Table 1. Corporate model versus school district.

Stockholders	Taxpayers
Corporate Board	Board of Education
Corporate Management	District Management Team
Corporate Employees	District Teachers and Support Staff
Corporate Product	School Program and Services
Consumers	Students/Parents/Residents

from that existing in most school districts. However, the major difference may be in the extent to which the Lake Forest Model uses standards and yardsticks for measuring the acceptability of its programs
and the performance of its personnel.

In this system of management the community expresses goals and
values for the school organization through a variety of means. These
include the various paper and pencil surveys that are conducted periodically and comments to the board of education and to the management
and teaching staff via formal superintendent/principal coffees and
various informal avenues. The board of education takes these expressions from the community and staff and transmits them into values and
goals through its policies and goal statements. One of the yardsticks
used by the board of education is a yearly evaluation of its policies asking, *"Are they adequate to meet our needs? Are they current in terms of
Federal and State laws and recent court decisions?"*

The board and management team working together select specific
programs to implement the board policies and objectives. These programs usually result from teacher and management suggestions. Information is solicited through an annual site-based process, through an
annual needs assessment by the superintendent with each employee
having an opportunity to give ideas, and via an extensive committee
structure for teacher empowerment, which the schol district provides
and where over 95 percent of the staff participate. However, the board
has the final responsibility in selecting the recommended programs
based on the recommendations of the superintendent of schools. The
standards and yardstick which the board applies to these programs: *Are
the programs adequate? Are results suggested observable and measurable?*

Once the program is decided upon, the superintendent, his management team, and the teaching staff together establish the procedures to
implement the programs and keep them in motion to achieve the objectives. The check and yardstick that is used is this: *Does the administration and staff have adequate resources to implement the programs and
achieve the results?* The information looked at is the results of the programs measured by test results, parental feedback, and other measures.

EVALUATION SYSTEM DRIVES COMPENSATION MODEL

With this background, let's examine how the performance evaluation
system works. It begins with the board's commitment to "set the highest

standards of excellence for the school program, staff, facilities, and materials."

The board believes that the district staff—both certificated and non-certificated—is its most precious asset and that the success of the entire educational program rests upon the skills, efficiency, creativity, thoroughness, and dedication of each staff member, whether he/she be the cafeteria aide, classroom teacher, the administrator for buildings and grounds, or the superintendent. Therefore, only the best are hired, and to each individual goes the following message: "The board believes you are the best possible person to perform the task you have been assigned. We have great confidence in your abilities, your good judgment, and your desire to give full measure to the work that you do. We promise you generous material rewards in the form of salary and benefits, but more importantly, we promise you deep satisfaction that comes from being a successful part of an outstanding team."

The district is committed to providing the highest caliber of leadership. Each of the building principals has served the district in a teaching capacity, each has obtained his administrative credentials with the encouragement and financial assistance of the board, and each has participated in the district's own Management Training Program.

Whether the employee is management or whether the employee is a classroom teacher, the evaluation system for professionals in District 67 recognizes that evaluation and supervision are integral to the continued professional development and improvement of the instructional program that is the district's product.

The evaluation system is set up to achieve a sensible balance of flexibility and consistency that takes into account the need to do the best possible job of supervision, adapted to the unique needs of the teacher and the school program. The process of evaluation and how it operates is described in detail since it drives the compensation model. The parts of the evaluation system are crucial. Table 2 describes the Teacher Evaluation System.

Table 2. Parts of the teacher evaluation system.

1. Classroom Observation Checklist (Rating Scale)
2. Overall Professional Performance Checklist and Rating Scale
3. Development and Attainment of Mutually Determined Personal Professional Goals
4. Student Feedback, Parent Feedback, Student Learning Results

LAKE FOREST EVALUATION PLAN

Going back into the district's historical records, it's clear the system did not have a salary schedule where compensation was based on years of service or numbers of graduate hours completed. The district has moved during the past eighteen years toward formalizing the evaluation system underlying its performance pay program so as to make it more objective and easily communicated to staff. The emphasis in the remainder of this chapter is how the Lake Forest evaluation system functions and drives the compensation system.

The district uses a very comprehensive evaluation system to determine whether the management and teaching staff are achieving the results desired for the total district program. The information for monitoring district performance includes the results of educational programs measured by standarized test results and/or parent, student, and teacher feedback. Test results are one of the ultimate effectiveness yardsticks used to measure the extent that the education programs are successful. The goal each year is for the district to be two years above national norms on all subtests of its adopted standardized test (Stanford Achievement Test). This test was selected because of its comprehensiveness, difficulty level, and the fact that it best mirrors the district's basic skills curriculum. The information for determining individual staff effectiveness is based upon the results of the personnel evaluation system.

Whether the employee be a manager or a classroom teacher, the evaluation system for the professionals of the district recognizes that evaluation and supervision are important to the continual professional development and improvement of the instructional program that is its product. The evaluation system is set up to achieve a sensible balance between staff teaching practices and consistent evaluations of all staff members by the responsible supervisor. The evaluation process for teachers includes a classroom performance checklist, an overall performance checklist, and an annual review of mutually determined personal staff member objectives developed by the teacher and his/her supervisor.

Teacher evaluation in Lake Forest is based upon the averaged scores of the three evaluation instruments: the Teachers' Classroom Performance Checklist, the Teachers' Overall Performance Checklist, and the Management by Objectives (annual goals and objectives) Control Form.

Classroom Teaching Evaluation Instrument

The Teachers' Classroom Teaching Performance Checklist is the most important and contributes 60 percent of the total weighted factor for the final evaluation rating. The classroom teacher is the mediator of learning. In Lake Forest we contend that 90–95 percent of all academic learning goes on under the direction of teachers and therapists in the classroom or therapeutic setting. We believe that if one is to improve the quality of education and learning most efficiently and effectively, one must concentrate efforts where the majority of that education is taking place – between the teacher and the student.

Once the teacher understands, assimilates, and consistently implements the most commonly accepted learning theories, the primary role of the teacher then becomes the development of a classroom environment where those conditions that will provide the best chance for student motivation, learning, and growth to take place actually occur. This becomes the first functional step for the teacher in Lake Forest.

Adult learning processes, achievement, motivation, and growth operate under the same identical learning principles for teachers as they do for students. The role of the principal or administrator is therefore to develop conditions that are most conducive to *teacher* learning, achievement, and growth.

While the job of the teacher is developing and clarifying attitudes, behaviors, and skills in students, the principal or supervisor is accountable for providing the same for teachers. Since the majority of learning is taking place in the classroom and the priority is to increase the effectiveness of the mediator of learning, then planning, teacher observation, conferencing, and evaluation should become the primary role of the administrator responsible. Creating an atmosphere and conditions to achieve these ends in order that the administrator function most effectively is the job of the superintendent implementing the vision mission statement and goals of the board of education.

While students learn best by doing or being actively engaged in the learning process and activities, teachers likewise improve their teaching skills in this manner. The ongoing evaluation process, then, actually becomes "on the job training" by reinforcing and placing into final practice those things learned in instructional feedback conferences, evaluation goal conferences, staff development activities, and formal coursework. All of these activities are based upon the realization that the most effective learning experiences for our student consumers result from the classroom practices of teachers.

Research shows that effective teachers actively involve students in planning, learning, and evaluating. In Lake Forest, teachers were actively involved in deciding what criteria *they* felt would best describe the various levels of acceptable and unacceptable teacher performance for purposes of their evaluation. Their total involvement at each step of the entire process was the major objective of the committee developing the instruments now used. Those instruments are reviewed at least every five years to make sure current research findings are being applied.

What is good performance? What factors should be evaluated in classroom teaching? The Staff Committee in 1972 decided to start with "The California Definition of Teacher Competence." This was a study involving the ideas of thousands of teachers, describing traits and observable activities or behaviors that they thought were synonymous with good teaching. The findings of that study and other research into successful teaching has formed the basis for the items in both the Classroom Teacher and Overall Performance Instruments now used.

The most recent *major* merit evaluation modification project was undertaken in 1982. That process involved committees of teachers and administrators who accepted the responsibility for designing a more objective system and process of evaluation and for writing specific items within these instruments that would describe and numerically rank differing levels of observable teaching behaviors, activities, and performance.

This committee adopted a forty-point rating scale from 1.0 to 5.0 for each item on the checklists (1 . . . . . 2 . . . . . 3 . . . . . 4 . . . . . 5). This forty-point scale was then carried through to report an average for all items on the individual instruments and to report the final teacher rating, which is the average rating score on the three instruments used in the system. The classifications given these scores were and are: 1.0 to 2.9, Unsatisfactory; 3.0 to 3.8, Satisfactory; 3.9 to 4.1, Excellent; and 4.2 and above, Superior Performance. The current staff is rated from 3.1 low to 4.8 high (see Figure 1).

The teachers and administrators developing the instruments also agreed that the final product should result in teachers competing against the items in each instrument rather than teachers competing against other teachers for ratings. The ideal goal of the evaluation process in Lake Forest is that each professional reach a superior level of performance. Those decimal points found between these numbers are vital. These points show growth, lack of growth, or declining performance, no matter how minimal, so as to provide positive reinforcement

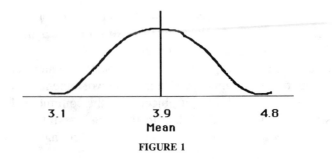

3.1   3.9   4.8
                   Mean

FIGURE 1

in order to furnish intrinsic motivational fuel for that person being evaluated. The goal of evaluation is to help each employee become increasingly more effective, so that he or she can feel and perceive movement toward higher levels of performance.

Through the documentation generated by this process of observation, conferencing, and evaluating, those teachers and administrators who cannot effect positive changes in their performance or level of functioning can be either placed immediately on a formal remediation plan (with the data in place) or dismissed, providing the deficiencies are deemed uncorrectable. This strategy has proven to be extremely effective, especially if it is undertaken during the first two years of employment.

This evaluation process has proven useful in that the final average of the three instruments in force translates directly into a final rating, which, in turn, relates to the amount of each teacher's merit or performance compensation in the district. Though continuously modified, 90 percent of the original items for the classroom checklist are still in effect and have been there since 1972. Merit salary compensation *is* still in effect in Lake Forest.

Classroom teachers, therapists, and specialists utilize a self-evaluation instrument applied to their teaching that is identical to the one used by their administrators. This self-evaluation document is used for comparison between the evaluator and evaluatee and serves as a basis for dialogue during the summative evaluation conference.

It was the choice of the administration that the staff help develop and approve of the items on all instruments so that a sense of ownership would be developed. The staff insisted that the administration conduct the observations, immediate instructional improvement conferences, and final evaluation conference and provide the final decision on the

score or level of performance attained on each item, on each instru
ment, and on the final rating.

The administrator for personnel shares the responsibility for observing, conferencing, and evaluating, along with the principal or other administrator, during the first two years (probationary phase) of a teacher's service. This is carried out regardless of the number of years of
experience of a teacher when employed. This practice also serves as a
benchmark or second party comparison between departments such as
special education, regular classroom, related arts, physical education,
etc., and between evaluations of teachers at different grade levels and
in different buildings.

The justification for the items in this fifteen-year-old instrument and
the descriptors that indicate different levels of performance are based
on construct validity. Each item was approved by total staff *consensus*,
and most items are validated by the current super research on teacher
effectiveness. The criteria have to be as objective as possible. One must
remember that learning activities and teaching behaviors and the student reaction can all be seen and, therefore, can be objectively described and determined to be at a given level of performance.

Since the primary job of the classroom teacher is to direct the learning environment of his/her students, it follows logically that the greatest weight of the evaluation should be placed upon that teacher's functioning at the time and the place that the learning situation is taking
place. That place is in the classroom teaching.

Succinctly, the teachers' ongoing involvement in the planning, selection, execution, evaluation, and modification of the entire evaluation
process and system are deemed crucial to its success in Lake Forest.
The items and instruments designed by the teachers became *their* criteria and not simply that of the administration. In 1990–91 the superintendent's advisory council will conduct a study of the evaluation
system.

The Overall Teacher Evaluation Instrument

Teachers are also rated on their overall performance—first, as a
classroom teacher, then as a member of the building and district team,
and as a professional educator. This instrument, in addition to the
classroom one, effectively constitutes a job description for certificated
staff members in the district. This instrument was developed using the

same research strategy as was the classroom instrument described in the previous section.

While the classroom instrument carries 60 percent of the total weight, the overall teacher evaluation instrument and the Goals and Objectives Control Form, which is described later in this chapter, carry a weighting of 20 percent each.

High evaluation scores on the overall instrument, such as item 9, professional growth; item 3, assistance and support; item 7, accepting constructive criticism; and item 13, English usage, are usually reflected in higher level classroom teaching performance as well. One strand of the district's current staff development program, for example, uses an outside contracted professional who has been conducting Madeline Hunter Teacher Effectiveness Workshops monthly for interested staff and administrators. This staff development experience is aimed directly at the professional growth item of the current instrument, but its main impact will be on the classroom performance of the teacher.

The measurement of the teacher as a professional, as well as a caring and sharing coworker, is directly rated by items 4, assistance and support; item 8, volunteering suggestions; item 12, relationships with staff; item 14, honestly and tactfulness; and item 15, building morale.

These items call for documentation on the part of both the principal and the teacher as opposed to the more objective data-observed characteristic of the classroom evaluation items. The teachers and administrators who made up the writing committee and the total staff who approved this instrument asserted their belief and trust in the district's management staff when they approved this instrument. Again, involving teachers in choosing the criteria for evaluation was an essential component and a top priority in the selection of items for this part of the evaluation plan.

The need for joint teacher and administrator involvement in the evaluation processes is demonstrated by item 2, district activities; item 3, building activities; item 8, volunteering suggestions; item 10, attendance and punctuality; item 18, routine tasks; and item 20, building objectives. All of these require some form of record keeping by the supervisor and teacher.

In many districts, one hears the complaint, "I see the same people on all the committees." This is not the case in Lake Forest, where teachers and administrators have bonded together to ensure broad involvement. At committee meetings administrators want participating teachers, and so they coach their teachers to be active participants. Teachers have responded positively, and the involvement this has engondered has brought nothing but benefits to Lake Forest.

Teacher Goals and Objectives

Teacher goals and objectives are initially developed between the teacher new to the district and his/her principal or supervisor following several observations in the fall of each year. With experienced teachers, these goals are developed or modified during the final evaluation conference in the spring. Items may be added or modified at any schedule conference during the year. Each teacher has between five and ten goals he/she is working on each school year.

Specific items either from the classroom or from overall instruments that are found to be in need of improvement may be translated into or added directly to the management by objectives control form. Table 3 serves as the means for tracking progress on yearly goal accomplishment. The administrator must prioritize those goal statements in order to pinpoint objectives that can most quickly yield increased overall teacher efficiency and effectiveness. The administrator must be able to give suggestions and assistance to improve performance levels that are tailored to and lend themselves most readily to the teachers' respective strengths and styles. The highly motivated teacher can make great strides in improving teaching effectiveness by concentrating efforts on these priority goals. Additional weight is really given to specific goals if they are listed both as a goal *and* included on an instrument.

Other goal items may be furnished by the administrator or the teacher and are usually related to items common to all teachers in the district or a particular building, department, or grade level. These other goal items may come from the results of the student feedback instrument, standardized test scores, the Committee Participation Evaluation Form, parent surveys, etc.

As noted on the control form (Table 3), each goal item is given a priority and a date it is to be accomplished. A minimum of three reviews of these objectives is formally scheduled during the course of the year to check and discuss progress or lack of it and to provide administrative coaching.

The same forty-point (1.0 to 5.0) scale is used to rate the level of accomplishment for each goal as well as to determine an average for the instrument itself. This instrument, like the overall instrument, carries 20 percent of the weight of the total evaluation.

Table 3. The city of Lake Forest, School District Number 67.

Management by Objectives Control Form
Personal Objectives for 1990–91 School Year

Teacher ___xxxxxxxxx___   Building ___xxxxxxxxx___   Position ___xxxxxxxxx___

Scales
Review Ratings: (5—Excellent) to (1—Low)
Priority: (5—High) to (1 = Low)
Objectives: (A—Accomplished) (Continued) (M—Modified)

Personal Objectives	Priority	Date to Be Accomplished	1st Review by November 1	2nd Review by February 1	3rd Review End of March	Objective
						A C M
						A C M
						A C M
						A C M
						A C M
						A C M

1st Review Date _____ , 19--   2nd Review Date _____ , 19--   3rd Review Date _____ , 19--

Role of Student Feedback Information

The student is the most important consumer of every school program, and therefore in Lake Forest students are given regular opportunities to "feed back" impressions of teacher performance and school performance. The questions and techniques involved in surveying students are simple and straightforward, although the interpretation of the information is more complicated.

In Lake Forest the district uses forms specifically designed for kindergarten and first grade students, second and third grade students, and fourth through eighth grade students. These forms were developed jointly by Dr. William Coats and Dr. Allen Klingenberg while professors at Western Michigan University, and the instruments have been field-tested and validated with thousands of students in Michigan and Illinois. Lake Forest has made necessary adaptations to the instruments over the years for its specific needs.

To collect information on teacher performance from young children (K–1), the principal or a person known to the student administers the questionnaire to the class, explaining that the information will be helpful to the teacher in improving his or her teaching. If the children are not capable of reading the questionnaire, the principal reads it to the class. He also assures the children that the teacher will not see their individual responses.

Once the questionnaires are filled out, they are machine-scored and the teacher is presented with a summary of pupil responses, which is compared with the teacher's own self-assessment on the same instrument.

The two right-hand columns of Table 4 show the class average and teacher's self-evaluation summary to illustrate the process. Items where the students indicate need for improvement may be considered by the principal and teacher for inclusion in next year's goals.

Obviously, no hard and fast conclusions can be drawn from such comparisons, but the information is of great value to the teacher in understanding how the class views the teacher, and for the principal in helping teachers identify areas to improve upon and provide appropriate strategies to use.

Once such information is assembled, the teacher and principal review the data together. Favorable implications of the data are discussed, but the principal's major task is to help the teacher develop alternative ways to improve performance where the feedback indicates

Table 4.

	Class A	Class B	Composite
My teacher explains things so that I understand them.	4.07	3.36	3.71
My teacher treats everyone fairly.	3.79	2.93	3.36
The kids in my class behave.	3.03	2.82	2.91
My teacher is friendly toward all students.	4.00	3.11	3.55
My teacher makes school seem fun and interesting.	3.21	2.75	2.98
My teacher laughs and enjoys jokes in the classroom.	1.50	2.33	1.91
My teacher enjoys teaching school.	3.86	3.57	3.71
My teacher lets students tell about their ideas in class.	2.68	3.11	2.69
I do interesting things in my teacher's class	2.02	2.61	2.71
My teacher looks neat and dresses nicely.	4.87	3.82	3.95
My teacher controls his/her anger.	3.00	3.18	3.89
My teacher is able to answer questions about school work.	3.96	3.87	3.52
My teacher thinks what I say is important.	2.08	2.64	2.33
My teacher likes me.	3.36	3.11	3.23
My teacher wants me to ask questions and give my ideas in class.	2.09	2.64	2.76
I feel free to give my ideas in class.	3.4	3.18	3.28
I feel like I learn a lot in class.	3.58	2.93	3.24
I think my teacher is a good teacher.	3.64	3.46	3.55
Average of the above 18 items	**3.27**	**3.84**	**3.15**

it is necessary. Figure 2 is a graph of the responses by a class, which is the most effective way of communicating the perceived strengths of various facets of the teacher's performance.

With older students (7–12 grades) more complicated questions are used. It is at the middle school level (4–5), that student judgment becomes a more mature evaluation of teacher performance. The student feedback instruments used in this district reflect this. The rationale for using student feedback is that teacher communication with students is essential to learning. Classroom feedback input from students provides a measure of the teacher's success in achieving objectives in class and is the first step in helping that teacher do a better job. However, having the information is not enough. The teacher's immediate supervisor should help interpret and apply the information to improve performance. The teacher then must make specific plans for improvement. Most people have difficulty being objective about their own performance; however, performance information from multiple sources encourages objectivity and a more realistic look at the situation. Counseling with the teacher on the implications of the results, even where performance is extremely good, is essential. In fact, such information is usually of greatest value to the better teachers, who are often their own best critics.

Objectivity collected, student feedback is constructive and has a positive effect on staff morale. Teachers find the information valuable in self-development, and principals find that it supplements and often confirms their judgment in determining the strengths and weaknesses of teachers. The use of such information requires maturity and common sense on the part of the teaching staff and the supervisor, so that it is constructive and healthy and not a disruptive factor in teacher/ management relations.

The district's experience is that feedback from students should be recorded longitudinally and shared with teachers. Responses of each student must be disguised and not discussed on an individual basis. Summaries or overall impressions should be used instead. Student opinions are a part of a comprehensive program of staff appraisal and are not used alone. Often such input substantiates observations that supervisors make. This substantiation helps make the evidence con-

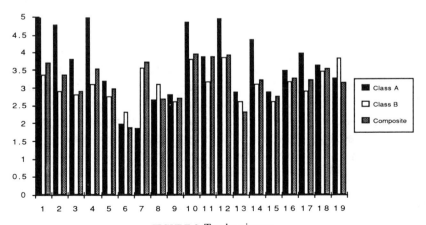

FIGURE 2 Teacher image.

vincing to the teacher, whose understanding and acceptance is essential for change in behavior to occur.

PAYING FOR PERFORMANCE

Performance appraisal and the resulting monetary compensation serve the public interest by ensuring that increases in salary are not awarded unless they are deserved.

The largest operational item in the school budget is employee salaries—usually 70 to 80 percent of total operating expenditures. That's an impressive figure, but even more significant is how the salary budget is used. Compensation can have a positive effect on employee morale, satisfaction, and, most important, productivity. Conversely, it can be a source of considerable dissatisfaction and decreased morale. In either case, compensation is an important management tool. In education, no less than in any other field, people ought to be paid according to the difficulty of their work and their contributions to the overall results achieved by the organization.

Many educators and laymen who read articles about merit pay become infatuated with its apparent advantages. It seems important to review the subject with two purposes in mind: first, to provide an understanding of the weaknesses as well as the strengths of current teacher compensation plans and, second, to present the challenges and advantages of changing teacher compensation methods.

Teacher compensation today follows a single, almost universal pattern. This is a lock-step salary schedule of from eight to twenty levels of predetermined increments. Salaries are differentiated on the basis of two factors—experience (expressed in years of service within a district) and additional college credits or degrees earned beyond the bachelor's degree. Under this system all teachers with the same credits and years of service earn the same salary regardless of the results they attain.

A variation of the lock-step salary schedule is the index system. It incorporates the same two factors—experience and credits or degrees—but expresses salary increases as a percentage of a starting salary rather than in terms of absolute dollars. In such a plan, the beginning salary is all-important. For example, the system might provide for a starting teacher with a bachelor's degree to earn $20,000 and for a teacher with twenty years of experience and a master's degree to earn 2.5 times as much, or $50,000. In addition to the problems associated with the standard salary schedule, the index system has this drawback: a $100 increase at the base is worth $100 times 2.5, or $250, at the top of the schedule. A district may be unable to raise its beginning salary because of the impact on its top salaries.

It can be reasonably argued that these traditional approaches to teacher compensation have some advantages. They recognize, for example, that the basic satisfactions and motivations of teachers may not be financial, and they remove salaries as a competitive or divisive factor among the teaching staff. However, there are serious disadvantages, too. Many teachers find the traditional plans quite frustrating. Unlike almost any other profession, teaching affords no opportunity for advancement, promotion, or reward based on performance, competence, dedication, effort, and, most important, achievement of results. Although a teacher certainly develops rapidly during the first few years of practical experience, most educators agree that, beyond a period of three to five years, performance is not determined mainly by years of service, but rather by skill and dedication. Therefore, to pay teachers with fifteen and twenty years' experience considerably higher salaries than are paid to those with three to five years' experience—and to disregard their performance—seems illogical and unfair to the teachers themselves as well as to students, parents, and community.

Even in districts with traditional teacher salary schedules, boards can take the initiative in seeing that teacher performance appraisal is operating and that action is taken where performance is unsatisfactory. An individual might ask, for example, "How many teachers have been frozen at a step on the salary schedule because their performance was not satisfactory, and what measures does the district use to determine this?"

In the face of these criticisms of teacher compensation, one might ask, "Why aren't board members taking action?" However, one also should recognize the difficulties of doing so. Some boards have adopted incentive compensation approaches that simply are not appropriate in education. Others have made mechanical and technical mistakes in their plans. Probably the biggest obstacle to merit pay is the resistance of teacher unions and mandated laws in many states that require boards to bargain collectively. For many districts, unfortunately, this may preclude the desirability of the whole idea.

There are two requirements for performance based compensation. First, the district must develop a plan that is satisfactory to teachers, workable in practice, and advantageous to the district. This is a challenging but by no means impossible task. Without such a plan, the district will have no basis from which to move toward a better system than it now has. Second, negotiations will be required to achieve such a system, at least in bargaining districts. In some districts it may be possible to move quickly; in others it may take a period of years, and indeed full implementation may never be achieved. However, if the district has a plan, it is possible to move gradually and intentionally toward it.

Lake Forest, like other districts that use merit pay, has found that it works extremely well in practice, although true performance pay is an endangered species with only Ladue, Missouri, having a similar program in place. Its primary benefits are greater teaching effectiveness, student learning consistently achieved, and better consumer (student/parent) acceptance of the school program. Paying more to better performers retains the best people and encourages others to seek careers elsewhere. In most professional organizations, higher compensation for better performers results in improved morale; school districts are no exception.

Lake Forest, with 1870 students, does not use a salary schedule. But because it is larger and more complex (six attendance centers) than most pure performance districts, its program for evaluating and paying teachers is considerably more elaborate as is its process for determining teacher compensation. Beginning salaries for new teachers are set by the marketplace (comparisons with twenty-two nearby districts) and by negotiations with individual teachers with experience when hired. After that, pay increases are based on the overall composite of the extensive performance evaluation ratings developed by principals and teachers described earlier.

"It is direct performance with school children that counts," says Ron Dristle, personnel director. "We aren't impressed with college degrees, except that the teacher must meet the statutory minimum standards. Obviously, we don't discriminate against staff members with advance degrees. But some of our best teachers have only a bachelor's degree, high grade point averages, and have done additional formal and informal study to continually improve."

The teacher's salary is directly tied to the evaluation system for the staff of District 67, recognizing that supervision and evaluation are integral to the continued professional development and the improvement of instruction. The system has been developed to achieve a sensible balance of flexibility and consistency that takes into account the need to do the best possible job of supervision and adapt it to the unique needs of the individual teacher and building. The process of evaluation is an ongoing one that includes formal and informal observations and evaluation conferences and interviews.

The parts of the teacher evaluation system for salary determination are Classroom Observation Checklist—Rating Scale, the Overall Professional Performance Checklist—Rating Scale, and attainment of mutually determined (by principal and teacher) personal professional goals.

The general procedures for implementing this system include

(1) An evaluation procedure that results in an overall assessment developed by considering each of the components of the program according to these percentages: 60 percent for classroom teaching, 20 percent for the overall professional performance, and 20 percent for the attainment of the goals mutually determined with the principal

(2) A requirement that all components of the evaluation system be brought together, analyzed, and shared with the teacher in a conference

(3) A requirement that the teacher be provided an opportunity to have entered into his/her file remarks and information clarifying statements in the evaluation done by the principal

(4) Retainment of a copy of the teacher's evaluation forms in the teacher's personnel file in the principal's office

(5) Use of discussion at this evaluation conference to develop new or revised personal objectives for the teacher for the next school year

(6) Requirement that a numerical value be derived from the data recorded on the two instruments and the administrator's assessment of the attainment of the teacher's personal objectives

(7) An evaluation process consisting of classroom observations and conferences to secure information supporting or clarifying the observation data according to the *Time Line* (five times for probationary staff and two times minimum for tenured staff).

The development of a numerical value describing the teacher's overall performance serves as a "check point" against which the principal or administrator can evaluate his/her own impressions and judgment of the teacher's performance relative to other teachers he/she evaluates. The numerical value is computed as follows:

(1) An average numerical value is determined for the classroom observations (60 percent).
(2) An average is determined for the overall teaching performance (20 percent).
(3) An average is determined for teachers' professional goals (20 percent). The personal professional goals are mutually established and written according to these requirements: (a) these goals are established as the need arises but at least once annually; (b) the goals are assessed by the teacher and principal at least three times each year; (c) the principal makes a determination of the relative degree of attainment of these goals on a five-point scale to be included in the numerical rating; (d) the teacher is provided a copy of these goals and is allowed the opportunity for input to the extent that it is given prior to the principal's evaluation of attainment.
(4) Each instrument is independently weighted according to the percentages for teachers (60 percent, 20 percent, 20 percent).
(5) The three weighted values are totaled to produce the composite numerical value.

The exact procedure for hypothetical teachers, Mrs. Jones and Mrs. Smith, is detailed in Table 5. The system provides for using a variety of sources for gathering evaluation data. It also is noteworthy that a major source of evaluation input comes from the teacher being assessed through a process of "management by objectives." That is, the teacher and the administrator agree on a set of objectives for each school year.

Table 5. Performance rating Mrs. Jones and Mrs. Smith.

Mrs. Jones			
Classroom Observation Scale	3.0 × .6 (60%)	=	1.8
Total Testing Performance	4.0 × .2 (20%)	=	0.8
Personal Objectives	5.0 × .2 (20%)	=	1.0
Average rating is 3.6 on the five-point scale.			3.6
Mrs. Smith			
Classroom Observation Scale	4.0 × .6	=	2.4
Total Teaching Performance	4.0 × .2	=	0.8
Personal Objectives	5.0 × .2	=	1.0
Average rating is 4.2 on the five-point scale.			4.2

Then they confer periodically to assess progress toward those objectives, and direct principal/teacher coaching occurs to move the teacher toward goal accomplishment. Sources for these personal objectives include

(1) Student feedback using standardized forms

(2) Parental feedback in letters and conferences

(3) Student learning results from standardized tests

(4) Performance on specific items of classroom and overall rating instruments

Specific Salary Determination Process

Each year the administration studies the salary ranges of its twenty-two comparison districts and the consumer price index for the past twelve-month period. This information yields information that describes the relative standing and deviation of each teacher in comparison to the ranges of actual salaries being paid in the comparison group (the marketplace). Figure 3 outlines the range concept for the salary plan. The salary range concept has the following advantages:

(1) It is competitive with surrounding districts.

(2) The salary range concept includes years of Lake Forest experience.

(3) Entry level exists to top of the range placement.

(4) Performance progress is possible within the range.

(5) Salary administration is not tied to degree held.

For these ranges the staff projects what inflation will be in the next twelve months and what we believe the competition will be paying. These ranges are adjusted using this information. Each year the board of education comes up with a total dollar amount for salary increases that it believes will keep the average salaries competitive within the ranges. The administrative staff allocates the salary amount provided to those teachers who are most deserving based on the performance indicators described in Table 5 previously.

In order to determine how much each building principal has to give out, the superintendent takes the total full-time equivalent staff contingent in each building and allocates to that building principal an amount of money based upon the district average salary for the previous year multiplied by the increase factor. Usually 1 percent is held back so that

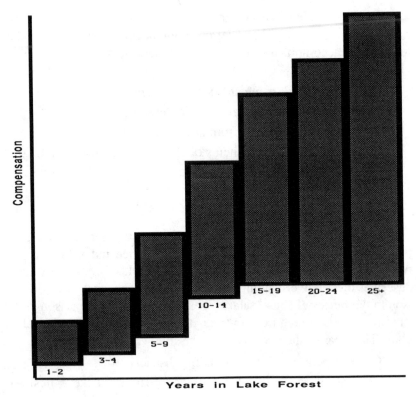

FIGURE 3 Salary range sample.

individual situations between buildings can be addressed where individuals with the same rating, same years, etc., are treated inequitably because one principal may have more money available than another because of retirement, etc. The process is not totally scientific; however, by using computers we are able to project, given the rating of a teacher in a specific building, what he or she should be receiving given the amount of monies we have available and what the competition will be paying. The district's philosophy of salary compensation is analogous to the sign hanging over the University of Michigan football locker room that reads, "Those who stay will be champions." Those who stay in District 67 and perform at a superior level (above 4.1) will be compensated very appropriately in comparison to the twenty-two neighboring districts up and down the north shore of Chicago. Figure 4 indicates how District 67's salaries compared to its twenty-two comparison districts.

New BA teachers with no experience will start with at least $22,000 in 1990–91, new MA teachers at least $24,000. Approximately one-half of the teachers new to the district have prior experience and are individually placed in the ranges. The top salary increase figure in 1990–91 was $5500.

Each teacher's salary is developed individually by his/her principal using data from the teacher's classroom performance, overall performance, and objectives accomplished during the year. If the teacher is dissatisfied with the evaluation or increment he can appeal through his principal to the superintendent and the board. Individual teacher salary conferences are also used to explain evaluation results, to hear the teacher's side, and to set performance goals for the coming year. The principal and teachers use test results, student–parent feedback, principal observation, and teacher observations to develop goals for the next year. School and building objectives are also incorporated to formulate some of the teacher's professional goals for the next year.

Why Performance Compensation Works

The district's director of personnel, Ron Dristle, points out that the district would, in all probability, get by with lower salary increases by

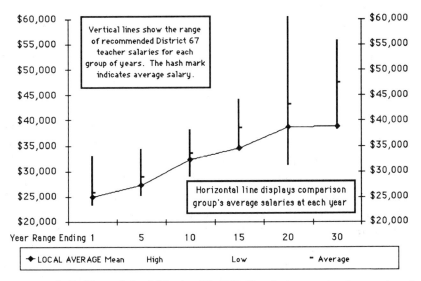

FIGURE 4 Lake Forest School District 67: 1990–91 salaries compared to projected groups.

going into collective bargaining, but he believes the benefits of performance compensation far outweigh the costs for staff and students. The evaluation program provides a basis for freezing the salary of a teacher who doesn't perform adequately and for eventually terminating employment if improvement doesn't occur. The evaluation process is part of the system for recommending continued employment, as well as for identifying strengths and weaknesses in classroom performance and allocating salary increases. In District 67, the teacher's expertise and knowledge as an educator are highly valued. Teacher empowerment is evident and their input is visible through participation on the various district committees. In 1989–90, over 95 percent of the teachers participated in two or more of the twenty district committees and building committees. The Superintendent's Advisory Council (SAC) consists of elected and appointed teachers from each building. This committee reviews district policies and procedures and assists in long-term district planning. CAC, or Curriculum Advisory Council, reviews the district's curriculum decisions. Other committees, such as the Summer School, Gifted, Study Skills, or Teacher Center Committees exist so teachers can provide input and give assistance in these important areas. Reading, Language Arts, Science, Social Studies, or Math committees focus on particular issues within these subject areas. These committees are not simply opportunities for teachers to rubber stamp administrative or board decisions. Rather, they are working committees, which in many cases have helped establish district procedures and build the district's program from the ground up. For example, during the last two years, the Reading Committee conducted an extensive review of the reading program. After many surveys, evaluations, and considerable teacher input, the decision was made to pilot three different series before consensus was achieved on one.

The board of education recognizes and respects the varied professional talents of its teachers. In order to facilitate teachers' research and development of unique projects and programs, a special fund exists for teachers who wish to work on original research projects. Over the past years, teachers have developed new computer projects, kindergarten consonant and vowel books study skills programs, and written expression projects, to name just a few. The board encourages all teachers to pursue these endeavors and stands behind their commitment by providing the necessary funds.

Another way teachers are empowered is to provide additional leadership opportunities. Individuals who have demonstrated the interest and potential are selected for lead teacher roles. Lead teachers coordinate the activities of their grade level. Their role is especially important for articulation between the various buildings.

Selective recruiting is another reason why performance compensation works in Lake Forest. Teachers hired are selected because the district's interview process indicates that they are risk takers. They thrive in a merit system because they know their efforts will be recognized and rewarded. In addition to participating in extensive in-service and institute day activities, teachers utilize the evaluation system results to continually analyze their own performance and attempt to perfect it. Self-analysis and goal setting provide an individualized form of staff development.

The board backs its commitment to the teachers by providing them with the means and opportunity to further develop their professional talents. Each year, an extensive staff development program is set up by teacher committees based upon faculty input. By understanding the various levels of professional development needed and then providing a variety of options, the district is able to offer relevant staff development opportunities to all its teachers. The board further stands behind its commitment by providing generous financial advances and reimbursement for workshops, and in 1990 the board adopted a policy to pay nearly 100 percent of graduate coursework leading to an approved advanced degree.

All district principals have also received extensive training in the evaluation process and are upgraded yearly on evaluating teacher performance. The administrators attend evaluation seminars both on an individual level and as a group. Because all supervisors have also been District 67 teachers, they bring firsthand knowledge and understanding to the merit pay plan implementation. These experiences as classroom teachers within a performance evaluation system are most valuable to principals. They better understand the questions a new teacher might have and are able and willing to clarify the process whenever needed. District evaluators must also maintain their own training as educators. An administrator who demonstrates competence in the classroom is more credible in the eyes of teachers and is better equipped to provide educational leadership and instructional coaching for his or her staff.

Another factor necessary for acceptance is the communication via the district needs assessment. The superintendent meets with every district employee to conduct a needs assessment yearly. These private meetings to discuss needs, questions, or concerns give each employee the "Boss's ear." Every comment is listened to; every request is noted. All suggestions, from necessary P.E. equipment, lights in the parking lot, extra computers and software, to new coffee pots, are written down. A needs assessment list is then compiled and advisory council members review the requests and assign a priority recommendation to each item.

Cooperation, communication, and commitment on the part of all staff members are crucial in a performance compensation system. The programs and activities that are described in this chapter reflect these values and help to establish the special climate in the district. It is because of this climate that the performance pay system is a success. The district's performance pay plan has gone through an evolutionary process over the years, and the current program has been reviewed, revised, and reshaped several times. What currently exists reflects the shared efforts of teachers and administrators.

What is important to note is the word *shared*. Not only were the evaluation instruments created as a result of pooled ideas, but the performance pay system itself encourages teachers to contribute ideas, share with each other, participate in the decision-making process, and assume leadership roles.

An important element in the performance pay process is the strong sense of trust that exists. Teachers believe that they will be evaluated fairly and they are confident that their performance pay increase will reflect their efforts. Because they have had a part in writing the evaluation instruments, teachers are not suspicious of the items on the instruments, and they know that the evaluation items reflect agreed-upon characteristics and descriptors of good teaching. Further, they can appeal concerns without fearing retribution.

To quote one of our principals reflecting on her experience as a teacher, "I knew that my principal was aware of my long hours and dedication, and I saw the benefits of this at evaluation time. I felt I was treated fairly. My teaching was observed on a regular basis 2 to 4 times a year. This initially made me somewhat anxious—what if the map flipped up on me? What if the students were having a bad day? What if I were having a bad day? But I soon learned that supervisors were understanding. They wanted me to succeed. Observation conferences were positive, suggestions were helpful and on-target. I know my teaching ability was enhanced greatly by these observations and conferences." She continues, "Now as a principal, I make sure that I am aware of each evaluation item as they relate to every teacher. I pull no punches at evaluation time. If someone does have difficulty with a particular area, I make sure that this is clearly communicated and coaching provided for improvement long before evaluation time."

SURVEY RESULTS ENDORSE PROCESS

Overall Attitudes toward District 67

Overall, residents, parents, and teachers seemed very pleased with the school district as a whole in the 1990 spring survey of all groups (see Figure 5). Both parents and residents gave the district an average grade of B+, with residents giving a grade point average of 3.3 and parents giving a grade of 3.4 on a four-point scale. The average grade given by teachers for all schools was 3.5 or an A−.

Parents expressed very high satisfaction with the quality of their children's education in reporting an overall mean score of 4.12 (on a five-point scale) on the school evaluation forms. Of those parents and residents who indicated they had sent children from District 67 schools on to high school, most seemed well satisfied with the preparation their children received for high school. Residents reported a mean satisfaction score of 3.8 (on a five-point scale) and current parents reported a satisfaction score of 4.0. Whereas residents indicated their attitudes toward District 67 have remained relatively constant over the past five years, respondents to the parent survey indicated a significant positive shift in attitudes toward District 67 schools in the past five years.

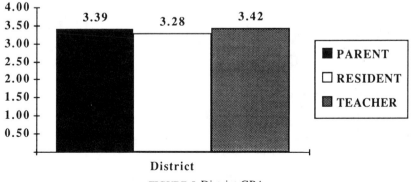

FIGURE 5 District GPA.

(Forty-seven percent expressed a favorable change in attitude compared to 27 percent expressing an unfavorable shift in attitude over that time.)

Finally, very positive support for the school district was expressed by residents, parents, and teachers who have moved into the district from other school districts. Fully 63 percent of residents, 69 percent of parents, and 70 percent of teachers who indicated they had transferred from another school district felt that the quality of children's education in the district was better than that which they experienced elsewhere (see Figure 6).

Specific District 67 Attributes

The overall satisfaction parents and residents expressed with regard to their children's preparation for high school (4.0 and 3.8, respectively) was broken down into specific subject areas of preparation. Parents whose children had completed algebra or geometry in District 67 schools (a new program) were most satisfied with their children's transition to high school math (4.34 on a five-point scale). Residents and parents whose children had completed only pre-algebra in District 67 schools were less satisfied, but still reasonably so (3.61 and 3.71, respectively). Satisfaction with the transition to high school English was high, with parents reporting a mean satisfaction score of 4.01, and residents reporting a mean score of 3.76. Finally, while still achieving a positive satisfaction score, Foreign Language preparation received the lowest score from both residents and parents in terms of transition to high school; residents gave a mean satisfaction score of 3.5, and parents

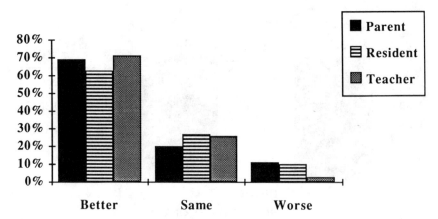

FIGURE 6 Transferees' attitude toward District 67 versus previous districts.

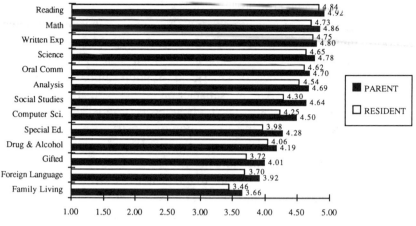

FIGURE 7 Importance of educational program.

expressed a 3.6 level of satisfaction. Figure 7 shows responses ranking the importance of individual subjects.

Parents were queried on their satisfaction with their children's progress in a variety of specific subject areas (Figure 8). Although all subjects received a satisfaction score above the midpoint, there were significant differences between those subjects that received the highest satisfaction ratings for student progress (Social Science—4.1, Math—4.1, Reading—4.1, Art—4.0, Music—4.0, Spelling—4.0, and Science—4.0) and those that received the lowest satisfaction ratings for student progress (Computer Skills—3.2, Critical Thinking—3.7, Study Skills—3.7, Foreign Language—3.7, and Penmanship—3.7).

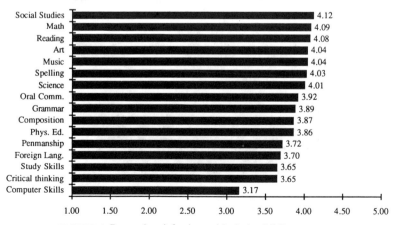

FIGURE 8 Parents' satisfaction with their child's progress.

The school evaluation form requested satisfaction ratings from parents on a variety of educational and physical attributes of individual schools (Figure 9). As previously reported, the aggregated grade average for all schools was 3.4 (B+) on a four-point scale. The satisfaction ratings for specific aspects of District 67 schools support this rating, since all items received average satisfaction ratings well above the midpoint 3 on a five-point scale. The highest levels of satisfaction were reported for comfort expressing an opinion or constructive criticism to a child's teacher—4.4; the physical location of schools—4.3; the concern teachers demonstrate for the students' progress—4.3; the comfort level parents feel in expressing opinions to the principals—4.3; the degree to which parents perceive their children enjoy school—4.3; and the level of effectiveness of teachers—4.3. Those items that received substantially lower, although still positive, ratings for satisfaction level are student bus service—3.8; the amount of instructional time allotted to basic skill areas—3.9; and the security procedures for controlling access to school buildings during school hours—3.9.

When asked how Lake Forest teacher and administrator salaries should compare to those paid in other North Shore school districts, most parents and residents felt that Lake Forest salaries should be at

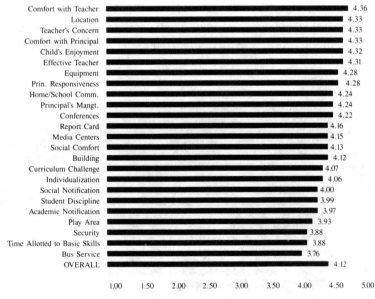

FIGURE 9 Parent's satisfaction with their child's school.

least comparable to other districts. Fifty-one percent of responding parents and 64 percent of residents felt that teachers should be compensated at the same rate as other districts; 58 percent of parents and 66 percent of residents felt that Lake Forest administrative salaries should be the same as other North Shore districts. Parents, particularly in evaluating teacher salaries, were inclined to be more generous than residents, with 35 percent of the parents suggesting that Lake Forest teachers be paid slightly more than teachers in other districts and 13 percent of the parents expressing the view that Lake Forest teachers should be paid significantly more. This parental view was cross-validated in a separate item that asked parents to indicate which educational priorities should receive increased, similar, or reduced levels of support in the future. The single item receiving by far the highest number of responses was faculty salaries, with 56 percent of the respondents suggesting an increase in the future level of support. The next highest priority items for parents were staff development, with 40 percent of the responding parents recommending an increase in support; the English program for seventh and eighth grade students, with 38 percent of the parents recommending increased levels of future support; and the library/resource center, with 38 percent of responding parents suggesting increased support.

CONCLUSION: SUPERIOR SALARY FOR SUPERIOR PERFORMANCE

The district demonstrates its commitment to quality education in the various programs and opportunities, materials, resources, and benefits it provides for the teachers. District 67's commitment to its staff is reflected in its provision of a superior salary for superior performance. When teachers believe that they have been dealt with fairly, the channels of communication are strong, different parties work together cooperatively to achieve what is best for students, and the district is committed to backing its promises, then a climate is established wherein performance pay can thrive. This climate and strong performance evaluation works in Lake Forest. The superior salaries of many district teachers attest to this fact.

CHAPTER 21

The Career Ladder Plan of the Cave Creek Unified School District: A Case Study

DAVID ALEXANDER – *Superintendent, Cave Creek Unified School District, Arizona*
RICHARD P. MANATT – *Director, School Improvement Model, Iowa State Univ.*

THE Career Ladder Project in Arizona was initially designed by the legislature as a five-year pilot project. In 1990, the initial legislation was extended and modified. The program is a fundamental restructuring of education designed to test various ways to attract and retain good teachers and to reward good teaching.

Since the spring of 1984, fourteen school districts have been approved to pilot a Career Ladder Program. Each district designed and implemented its own pilot program within the general guidelines established in enabling legislation. These pilot projects provide for teachers to advance professionally, receive high compensation, and accept higher levels of responsibility for school improvement/restructuring. Additionally, each project serves to promote increased accountability in areas of teacher performance, evaluation, and student academic progress within Arizona's public school system (Joint Legislative Committee, 1990).

PILOT DISTRICT REQUIREMENTS

School districts participating in the program must design and implement a totally new teacher performance based pay system, Career ladder salary schedules cannot incorporate traditional salary schedules, which pay teachers for seniority (experience) or education credits beyond basic certification.

All of the initial pilot projects had to create some form of governance in which teachers constituted the majority in membership, to assure teacher input in program development and implementation. Criteria for teacher placement on a district's Career Ladder Plan had to incorporate increased student achievement as part of the teacher's evaluation for advancement. Participation was voluntary by districts, and each plan had to be voluntary for veteran teacher participation.

Participating school districts were legislatively funded by an increased weighted percent (0.5 percent for planning, up to 5.0 percent after the fourth year and thereafter) above the budget limit established in the state's schooling funding formula.

THE CAVE CREEK STORY

Visualize being a superintendent at the end of the first three months of your first superintendency. Seated before you are three well-known, experienced members of the Arizona legislature and one very prominent corporate executive who are members of the Joint Legislative Committee on Career Ladders. This is their second monitoring visit in as many years. Their conclusions stun you. They are of the opinion that the Career Ladder Program in Cave Creek is "unhealthy" and it will be their recommendation to the legislature that Cave Creek's participation in the program should be discontinued.

After considerable negotiation the district was granted sixty days to prepare a proposal for revising the district's plan. In addition, the district's plan had to address five specific issues felt by the Joint Legislative Committee on Career Ladders to be troublesome:

- the preparation of a report to the legislature delineating the lessons learned from previous mistakes
- a plan to revise the teacher evaluation system
- a shift in the "burden of proof" for evaluation and salary placement from the principal to a state of shared responsibility on the part of teachers and administrators
- the initiation of a staff development program to support career ladder teachers
- freeze, cap, or other slowdown in the salary escalation of previous plans

Sixty days later the superintendent, governing board president, and four teachers presented a plan for total revision of the district's career ladder effort. This plan was approved by the legislature and the district received a one-year "conditional" approval.

The state's Career Ladder Program, during its first five years, was designed to be experimental. The pilot districts were to test various designs and implementation strategies and report to the legislature results. Obviously, the experimental nature of the pilot programs allowed for "doing it right" and "doing it wrong." In Cave Creek, as characterized by the corporate executive who was a member of the Joint Legislative Committee on Career Ladders monitoring team, the experiment was best described as "how *not* to implement a Career Ladder Program." What happened? A recapitulation of the first three years of career ladder may clarify what went wrong.

In the spring of 1984, the district responded to a state mandate to develop a comprehensive teacher and administrator evaluation system. The district hired a local consultant to devise a system. It was adopted for use in the fall of 1984 without being field-tested prior to implementation.

Also in the spring of 1984, the district made application to be a career ladder pilot district. The dialogue surrounding the governing board's decision to permit application centered on the lack of competitiveness in teacher salaries. The receipt of career ladder supplemental funding was seen as a means of increasing teacher salaries without intrusion into the regular budget.

Again using a local consultant, a Career Ladder Plan was developed and submitted in an attempt to garner the supplemental funds for teacher salaries. After months of negotiations the district was approved for inclusion in the fall of 1985.

This initial plan was characterized by the following components:

- Use was made of the nonfield-tested teacher evaluation system, with added emphasis on certain criteria judged to be commendable performance areas, if present at the time of observation by the principal.
- An elaborate portfolio system was set up, in which teachers accumulated and documented points earned for various activities, both instructional and extracurricular. Points were awarded for a very broad range of criteria, including such disparate activities as writing letters of support for seniors seeking college admission or coaching football. A Portfolio Council reviewed and rated the portfolio contents submitted by the teachers. Their ratings were used as a weighting factor (multiplier) for salary increases.
- Part of the placement criteria included length of prior experience and coursework beyond certification requirements.
- Teachers were placed on one of the first three of five career ladder levels based on years of experience in the district and academic (degree and coursework) standing.

The first year of implementation resulted in large salary increases requiring a salary cap. Initial salary increases ranged from $5000 to over $14,000. Salary raises had to be capped at $8000 and the remainder was scheduled for distribution the next fiscal year. The first year of implementation was also characterized by strident concern for the inequities of the portfolio system. Not all teachers had equal opportunity to garner points. All teachers did not have an equal chance to be a coach, club sponsor, letter writer, or many of the other activities for which points were awarded.

Revisions were made for implementation in the fall of 1986. These changes represented attempts to improve the portfolio system, but in the eyes of teachers these attempts failed and a new group of teachers and administrators took on the task of rewriting and revising the plan for the district.

A new plan was approved for the fall of 1987. However, due to previous salary escalations, a combination of salary freezes and caps were necessary. New career ladder teacher placements were required to maintain that placement for two years in an attempt to slow salary escalation.

The governing board had been continually frustrated with the failure to achieve labor peace throughout the three years of career ladder attempts. Since the program was voluntary for teachers, career ladder participation hovered around 50 to 55 percent of the total staff. The district was facing continual student growth and therefore was adding staff. In an attempt to eventually stabilize labor negotiations, the board required that all new teachers be placed on the Career Ladder Program regardless of prior experience so that attrition would eventually leave all teachers on the career ladder.

It was soon apparent that the newly revised plan was suffering implementation problems. A further revision was begun in the fall of 1987 and a draft was available for review in the spring of 1988. This latter version was characterized by a supplementary teacher evaluation document designed to "bridge" the gap between classroom observation of teacher performance and the previously adopted teacher evaluation system. This revision was slated for implementation in the fall of 1988. The bridge was an attempt to clarify the performance criteria via descriptors.

It was in the early months of the 1988–89 school year that the Joint Legislative Committee on Career Ladders monitored the district and found the conditions "unhealthy" for continuation in the experimental program.

REMEDIAL PLAN

The president of the governing board, the superintendent, and four teachers formed a committee to prepare a remedial plan for presentation to the Joint Legislative Committee on Career Ladders. Part of that remedial plan included submitting to a vote of the full faculty the issue of whether or not teachers wanted to continue pursuing a Career Ladder Program. A vote was taken and 67 percent of the 78 teachers voted for continuation.

Following the positive vote, extensive discussions were held with teachers to develop the remedial plan. The remedial plan approved by the Joint Legislative Committee on Career Ladders provided the following recommendations:

(1) Replace the teacher evaluation system with a system that focuses on teacher classroom performance.

(2) Establish a permanent career ladder governance committee in which the majority of members are teachers.

(3) Develop a system whereby the assessment of student achievement is fair to all teachers as a component of advancement on the ladder.

(4) Devise a method whereby a second appraiser is involved in teacher observation and evaluation.

(5) Provide for staff development.

(6) Provide for professional development based in predetermined areas for need for improvement.

(7) Establish a training program for principals that achieves inter-rater reliability of observation, conferencing, and teacher evaluation.

Also included in the plan were two areas of concern noted by the Joint Legislative Committee on Career Ladders:

(8) Shift the burden of proof for teacher evaluation and salary placement from the principal to the teachers and administrators.

(9) Restructure the compensation plan to end the salary escalations of the past.

The remedial plan was approved by the Joint Committee on Career Ladders in the spring of 1989. Parameters of the plan's implementation will be discussed later in this chapter.

After four years of struggling to design and implement a Career Ladder Program, ten issues emerged as critical to success. These ten issues, discussed below, have been reported to the legislature. Many of these critical issues were addressed in new legislation, which made the Career Ladder Program permanent in 1990.

Avoid "Job Ladders"

Avoid developing a program that is geared to duties performed by teachers. Cave Creek's initial Career Ladder Plan allowed teachers to gain points for doing job-related tasks such as writing letters of reference for college-bound students, coaching, play directing, and completing committee assignments, regardless of importance. The list of duties was exhaustive and lacked equity. Not every teacher was eligible to perform all duties, and some duties were assumed to be more valuable than others regardless of whether or not a teacher had an equal chance at performance.

Career Ladder Plans should be based on teaching skills that have been determined prior to initiation of placements. These predetermined performance areas should be valid, reliable, and legally discriminating between levels of performance.

Administrator and Board Stability

This area is extremely important to small school districts. Cave Creek is more similar (in all areas of demographics) to other small- and medium-sized school districts throughout the state than are most of the other career ladder experimental districts.

During the first two years of the Career Ladder Plan in Cave Creek, there was a 100 percent turnover in the principalship (four people). By the fourth year of the project, 100 percent of the entire administrative staff had turned over, including the superintendency. Small districts, due to salary restrictions, often cannot compete with larger districts for administrators. Thus, a revolving door approach is not uncommon. The negative impact of this trend is tremendous on Career Ladder Programs in the following ways:

- All Career Ladder Plans depend on teacher evaluations for placement and advancement. Principals are the most important people in these evaluation reviews. Constant changes in evaluators (principals) frustrates teachers and makes the system inequitable.

- Few small districts have comprehensive training for principals in how to evaluate using the system adopted in a given district. It only takes one principal evaluating his/her building teachers differently from others to spark the charge that a Career Ladder Program is unfair and inequitable.
- Few districts set aside time and funds to train principals in all facets of Career Ladder Program documentation, program history, placement criteria, precedents, and decisions. This again results in charges of unfair treatment by teachers.

Administrator stability has been reached (for now) in Cave Creek and administrator training is underway. Plans have also been approved for training principals and peer evaluators in all facets of the program.

Governing board stability also is crucial to effective Career Ladder Programs. The governing board,which originally approved the program, saw the Career Ladder Plan as a means of raising salaries. In fact, the original plan has been characterized as a salary escalation plan. Since the original approval, only one governing board member remains on the board. Maintaining a continuing commitment by succeeding governing boards is imperative to assuring continuity within the Career Ladder Program.

We realize that administrative and governing board stability is not always possible. However, after careful analysis by teachers who have been part of the Career Ladder Plan (CLP) since its inception, most of the mistakes and problems of the Cave Creek Career Ladder Program can be attributed to administrator/governing board instability and the lack of leadership in training for specific district criteria.

Teacher Performance Evaluation vs. Non-Career Ladder Teacher Evaluation

Teachers in Cave Creek perceived this to be the most critical CLP implementation issue. Two major mistakes had been made in the original planning:

- The originally approved evaluation system was not designed to be used to discriminate between levels of teacher performance.
- A revised Career Ladder Plan for 1987–88 had a document specifically designed for career ladder participants, but this

additional document was used as an evaluation "bridge" to the original, untested evaluation system.

Although these mistakes were made, they point out the importance of why this venture was an experiment.

With any evaluation system, human evaluators must be used. Principals bear the brunt of evaluating. The reliability of ratings between principals must be consistent, and there must be continuity. If a principal rates a teacher on the same performance criteria *differently* from another principal and the result is that one teacher achieves career ladder advancement while another teacher does not, serious inequities will exist in the system. Inter-rater reliability is required of all principals. To assure this reliability, all principals *must* be trained to view evaluation/performance criteria in the same way. The lack of inter-rater reliability among Cave Creek principals caused an emotionally laden reaction from teachers. Training of all principals as reliable raters is paramount.

Teachers must also be trained in the evaluation criteria. A district cannot adopt an evaluation system that affects an individual's salary without training each teacher on what the expected performance will be. Clearly each teacher, prior to placement/advancement, must fully understand the expected performance behavior on which their evaluation and salary will depend. Once these performance behaviors are agreed to, subsequent reinterpretations of the performance cannot be made during the same evaluation period. Cave Creek also made mistakes in this area. Presently, a list of thirteen performance criteria, each accompanied by a series of behavioral descriptors, is being reviewed and field-tested for teacher acceptance. Acceptance is necessary prior to implementation.

Define Terms

Each CLP must have a comprehensive set of definitions to accompany any career ladder handbook, procedures, guidelines, etc. Interpretation of guidelines needs to be spelled out, and one person or a small committee must be appointed to be the keeper/historian of decisions and precedents. Career Ladder Programs, by their nature, are subject to continuing interpretation as new challenges to the program arise. Cave Creek made the mistake of not designating an individual or committee to be the repository of decisions and interpretation, thus, teachers were again angered over inconsistent interpretations and "new" precedents. These constant changes caused considerable morale problems.

Avoid Career Ladder Programs Designed Solely to Escalate Teacher Salaries!

In retrospect, it appears that many of the initial discussions surrounding the district's participation in career ladders were based on the fact that career ladder funding would assist the district in raising teacher salaries. It is clear from this experiment that the first decision that must be made by the governing board, teachers, and administrators is whether or not the employees genuinely want a pay-for-performance plan. To create a plan to justify the money is inappropriate. To design a pay-for-performance plan that rewards performance with state funds is appropriate. The legislature must be convinced of the true motivation of a district choosing to participate.

Avoid Voluntary Exits from the Program

Presently, Career Ladder Programs are structured so that participants may volunteer to participate and voluntarily choose to terminate participation. In Cave Creek, some teachers went on career ladder, received large salary increases, then after one year they went off career ladder. This was very demoralizing to those who were committed to the program and were struggling toward advanced levels.

Suggestions from Cave Creek teachers include

- The volunteer commitment to career ladder must be for a minimum of five years.
- After five years, a teacher who exits must be frozen in salary for the length of time it takes for regular, non-career ladder salary increments/raises to equal that individual's prior career ladder salary.

Governance

Any Career Ladder Program should include a governance structure. The governance participants should serve staggered four-year terms. This brings consistency and continuity to decision making. In Cave

Creek in the early years of the experiment, as conflicts, problems, and confrontation arose, new "power" groups emerged and manipulated the end results in their favor, thus alienating previous participants. Granted, the likelihood of this happening always exists, but a structured, representative group with terms of office that exceed the year-to-year "issues" serves to stabilize the program.

Vision

A district's board, community, and all of its employees need to develop jointly a vision of where the district is headed and how a Career Ladder Plan fits into that vision. The following fundamental questions were not asked in Cave Creek and must be answered in Cave Creek now:

- What is professionally competent teacher behavior?
- What is the district's philosophy of education?
- What is the district's philosophy of instruction?
- Does a Career Ladder Program contribute to this vision?
- How will career ladders benefit teachers, individually and collectively?
- On what criteria will performance is based? Clearly describe performance that exceeds expectations.

Hire Professional Help

Small districts are frequently staffed with three or four principals and a superintendent, all of whom may wear numerous administrative hats in addition to their primary responsibility. Being expert in teacher performance behavior for pay is not something common to either administrative or teacher training. It was not until the 1988–89 school year that it was recognized that the expertise did not exist within the Cave Creek district to answer all of the questions that arose regarding teacher performance behaviors and evaluation. For a Career Ladder Plan to work in small districts (like CCUSD), teachers must trust that decisions made about career ladder performance criteria are well grounded in teacher performance research, that such criteria can actually legally discriminate between various teachers' levels of performance, and that the accepted criteria are reliable across all classroom teaching situations. Larger districts with sufficient funds to have release-time teachers or administrators to research, train, and implement a Career Ladder Plan may garner the necessary expertise. But in small districts, limited funds *seriously* restrict their ability to develop implementation expertise.

Once this condition was realized in Cave Creek, a comprehensive bid was released to twenty potential bidders who, according to educational research literature, had prior experience in designing and developing teacher performance-for-pay programs. The district was able to obtain the services of an internationally known team of experts who had developed pay-for-performance plans in over 100 school districts. The School Improvement Model Program of Iowa State University, headed by professor Richard Manatt, agreed to assist Cave Creek. Work is in progress and the report from teachers, patrons, and administrators is clear: the district should have had this type of assistance from day one. Only by freezing career ladder salaries was the district able to afford this level of expertise.

The district has recommended to the legislature that a list of qualified persons/groups (who have published records of their expertise) be created to assist small districts seeking assistance in the design, development, and implementation of pay-for-performance programs.

Establish Eligibility Criteria

Small districts usually can be characterized as intimate, familiar places where teachers, students, patrons, administrators, and board members are close friends and neighbors. Larger districts are often characterized by big, impersonal bureaucracies where teachers are familiar only with their local school colleagues and administrators. In small districts (especially in small towns), district teachers know each other regardless of school or school level. Therefore, in this familiar setting, small districts more often try to please all teachers who volunteer to participate in the Career Ladder Plan by designing criteria that make any volunteers eligible for placement and advancement. This was wrong in Cave Creek, and we feel it will be wrong in other small districts. Prequalifying criteria, which take into account the following, should be considered minimal to establishing career ladder placement eligibility for teachers.

- There should be an induction period for all personnel new to the district. During this induction period, the new employee should receive the district's basic staff development. Employees should be trained in teaching skills, district institutions, rituals, and culture, and, most importantly, they should be given a thorough review of expected teacher behaviors on which pay for performance is based.

- New employees and potential career ladder veteran employees should be able to demonstrate, to some degree, the prescribed pay-for-performance criteria before being allowed to petition for career ladder placement.
- Documentation of student achievement must exist, be reviewed, and judged acceptable prior to a teacher petitioning for eligibility or placement.

Although there are other specific examples of implementation problems in Cave Creek, most if not all of them can be categorized into the previous ten issues. Some of these problems are directly attributable to the problems generally found in small districts.

THE CONSULTING TEAM

The monitoring visit from the Joint Legislative Committee on Career Ladders, which labeled the Cave Creek career ladder "unhealthy," began a process that resulted in the School Improvement Model (SIM) research team joining forces with the district's faculty and administration. SIM is centered in the College of Education at Iowa State University. The SIM team helps public and independent schools improve student achievement by an organizational renewal process. Sometimes the effort is limited to creating teacher and administrator performance evaluation systems; at other times a school restructuring is undertaken. Recently, some client districts have been developing a mastery learning system with outcome based education, criterion-referenced testing, and pay for performance. Approximately one dozen team members (professors of education and research associates) form a "stakeholders' committee" appointed by the local board of education to measure, analyze, and improve the performance of all students, teachers, and administrators. The joint team strives for the "information organization" so essential to success in the decades ahead.

The SIM approach to performance evaluation systems development is research based and has repeatedly shown that teacher morale, school climate, and student achievement improve (Manatt et al., 1976; Stow and Sweeney, 1981; Manatt and Stow, 1986; Manatt and Daniels, 1990).

Ever since our first modest effort to study teacher performance criteria twenty years ago, we have maintained a consistent set of principles (a credo) that guides our work with a client district. First and foremost is the belief that SIM is a process, not a product. Each project is unique because it is planned, operated, and controlled by the teachers and administrators of that school organization. Therefore, the components vary but the philosophy does not. These guiding principles worked particularly well in the Cave Creek Unified School District where the repeated failure of previous career ladder attempts had built an aura of mistrust and had caused principals to become extremely wary of any future career ladder efforts.

The stakeholders' committee is appointed by the superintendent. The initial charge to the group makes clear that the task is important and that each member has been appointed for special knowledge or skills. Stakeholders represent teachers, administrators, parents, students, and board members. No more than half of the stakeholders are teachers, who are typically selected by the leaders of their assocation or union. Stakeholders are informed at the outset that they are an ad hoc group serving at the pleasure of the board of education and that their assignment is to "decide to recommend"; the board must make the final policy decision. Stakeholders' committees vary from fifteen to twenty-five members, depending on the size of the school organization.

At first glance it would appear that the preponderance of teacher members would result in a watered down performance appraisal system. This never happens for several reasons. Most important, teachers have higher standards than other stakeholders — a fact that may surprise some who have not listened to teachers as individuals express their desires for professional respect and accomplishment. Second, teachers and administrators quickly become caught up in the challenge of creating an administrator performance evaluation system and a teacher performance evaluation system simultaneously. The opportunity to work toward a mutual benefit appraisal system boosts expectations on all sides. Furthermore, teachers and administrators generally behave in a very professional manner when their clients (parents and students) are present.

Stakeholders are expected to serve for at least three years. In Year One, committee members plan a performance evaluation system for all professional positions. During the second year, and after approval by the board of education (and the collective bargaining process where required by law), each principal and a couple of teachers in each building test the proposed system. After careful analysis of the test, the system is refined and resubmitted to the collective bargaining process if required. Once approved, this new system is operated in its entirety during Year Three, with final adjustments made by the stakeholders' group at the end of the project.

From the viewpoint of the district's professionals, the ten issues previously described (job ladders, board instability, definition of terms, etc.) were paramount. The SIM team, perhaps because of the detachment provided by distance, believed from the outset that a viable career ladder was possible once a valid, reliable, and discriminating performance evaluation system could be installed and operated long enough to produce solid information. By the time the SIM researchers had become involved (1989), the Joint Legislative Committee on Career Ladders had decided that all Career Ladder Plans (CLPs) must include the concept of job enlargement at the higher rungs and that student achievement must be a factor in the pay-for-performance equation. Both of these decisions helped to overcome the reluctance of both teachers and administrators to broaden the performance data gathered beyond classroom observations. While performance evaluation of administrators, classified personnel, and governing board members was included in the project, only systems performance evaluations of teachers will be described. For a full discussion of all SIM developmental procedures, see the ASCD publication, *Teacher Evaluation: Six Prescriptions for Success* (1988).

OVERVIEW OF THE SYSTEM

The stakeholders' committee recommended that all teachers, those on the career ladder and on the traditional two-cell salary schedule (based on years of experience and education), would be evaluated using the same criteria insofar as was possible. Career ladder participants would be awarded points for advancement on the ladder which would be components of a formula or algorithm. The CLP composite score is explained in Figure 1.

The major component of the system is the summative evaluation report (SER). The peer evaluation is used only for the career ladder par-

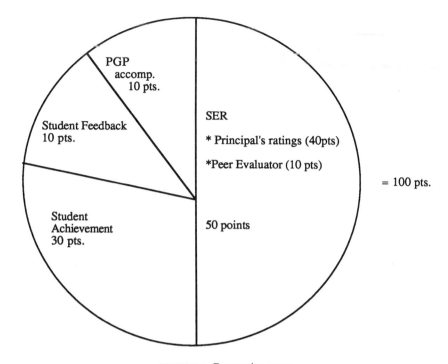

FIGURE 1 Composite score.

ticipant. All teachers are required to work on a professional growth plan (PGP) and to solicit student feedback. While all teachers will submit measures of student achievement, only the career ladder participant will use student data for a report to the validating committee.

The Career Ladder Program requires an oversight body to be called the "Career Ladder Validating Committee." Rules for the validating committee include

(1) Initial committee membership will include six teachers (one from each building plus two career ladder teachers from the stakeholders who will be elected by the faculty and will serve at-large) and one administator.

(2) Memberships will be established on a rotating basis. In starting up the committee, four teachers will have two-year terms; two teachers will have three-year terms. Thereafter, teachers will have two-year terms. Teachers may not be reelected until one year has passed.

(3) Responsibilities of the committee will be

- to tabulate summative evaluations from principals and peer evaluators, teacher's PGP, student feedback, and student achievement
- to schedule and supervise the application process
- to provide portfolio advisement
- to certify and monitor placement and maintenance of level on the career ladder
- to serve as a clearinghouse for questions
- to provide the superintendent with a written recommendation about career ladder placement of teachers

The Career Ladder Plan offers an alternative form of teacher recognition and compensation that is based on the following components: teaching competencies, student achievement, student feedback, and professional growth. The CLP's primary purpose is to increase student achievement through a system of teacher incentives and job enlargement. Additional compensation at all levels of the career ladder is made possible through special funding from the state legislature.

The career ladder also is intended to attract, retain, motivate, and reward effective teachers for the Cave Creek Unified School District. The CLP does this through a higher level of compensation for the beginning teacher, the teacher in midcareer, and the senior teacher who assumes a higher level of leadership. The Cave Creek Unified School District Career Ladder Plan details different standards and requirements for each level of the ladder. Some sample levels are shown in Table 1.

Four sets of unique, district-specific instruments were developed by the stakeholders' committee with technical assistance from the consul-

Table 1.

Level	Title
0	Newly Employed Teacher
I	Entry Teacher
II	Resident Teacher
III	Associate Teacher
IV	Senior Teacher
V	Advanced Teacher
VI	Master Teacher

Table 2. Teacher evaluation: performance areas and criteria.

A. Productive Teaching Techniques
  1. Uses effective planning skills
  2. Implements the lesson plan
  3. Communicates effectively with students
  4. Motivates students
  5. Ensures student time-on-task
  6. Provides opportunities for individual differences
  7. Uses appropriate evaluation activities
B. Organized, Structured Class Management
  8. Provides evidence of classroom organization for effective instruction
  9. Demonstrates accountability for student achievement
  10. Sets high standards for student behavior
C. Positive Interpersonal Relations
  11. Demonstrates effective interpersonal relationships
D. Employee Responsibilities
  12. Demonstrates responsible conduct
  13. Demonstrates a willingness to keep curriculum and instructional practices current

tants. The most important is the summative evaluation report (SER) which contains thirteen criteria in four performance areas. This is illustrated in Table 2. All teachers, career ladder, and framework will be evaluated yearly on these criteria by both the supervising principal and the peer evaluator. The peer evaluator does not rate the performance of "employee responsibilities," criteria 12 and 13.

The SER is published in the district's *Teacher Performance Evaluation Handbook.*[1] A separate publication, *Performance Criteria with Examples,* was written to provide clarity for each of the teacher performance criteria. The term *examples* was chosen rather than *descriptors* or *indicators* to avoid any misunderstanding on the part of teachers and their evaluators. The behaviors used as examples are just that. They do not totally define "good teaching" or suggest robot-like performance (or for that matter, robot-like teacher evaluation).

Table 3 expands the performance area "Productive Teaching Techniques" and criterion 1 "Uses effective planning skills" from Table 2 to illustrate.

The *Career Ladder Plan* constituted the third publication and was a detailed explanation of how a teacher who was a candidate for ladder placement or advancement was to proceed. Each applicant was to as-

Table 3. Performance criteria with more examples.

A. Productive Teaching Techniques
  1. Uses effective planning skills
    a. Prepares course objectives from the prescribed curriculum
      • Formulates instructional objectives, based on the curriculum guide, which identify the learning, level of thinking, and student behavior
      • Uses an organizational system for planning short- and long-term instructional objectives
      • Matches individual lesson objectives and unit objectives to the prescribed curriculum
      • Can analyze and articulate use of planning skills, which assures consistency of these skills
    b. Selects lesson objectives at the correct level of difficulty
      • Uses data that were collected for diagnostic and prescriptive purposes
      • Develops short- and long-term instructional objectives that are individualized
      • Uses a variety of sources to identify correct level of difficulty
      • Uses a task analysis to identify prerequisite and essential skills
      • Can analyze and articulate how the correct level of difficulty was identified, which assures consistency of this skill
    c. Develops lesson plans that are designed to accomplish the objectives
      • Develops an introduction and/or an anticipatory set for the lesson
      • Determines how the objective will be communicated to the students
      • Determines how the importance of the learning will be communicated to the students
      • Organizes information in an appropriate sequence
      • Organizes information so learners see the relationship of the parts to each other and to the whole
      • Plans necessary time frames for each lesson segment
      • Plans information, questions, and activities that are relevant to each sub-objective
      • Identifies effective models and examples
      • Plans activities that check students' understanding and/or application of the essential sub-objectives
      • Structures massed and distributed practice activities to reinforce the objective(s) being taught
      • Plans a closure for the learning
      • Can analyze and articulate how the lesson is designed to accomplish the objective, which assumes consistency of these skills

semble a portfolio containing his/her summative evaluation report from both appraisers, student feedback data, student achievement data, and the results of the professional growth plan.

To start the process the teacher must apply and agree to participate in and complete the following requirements:

(1) Submit a letter of intent requesting consideration for placement. The letter is sent to the Career Ladder Validating Committee.

(2) Meet the requirements and standards of the level of placement.
   • *Teaching Competencies* — Allow the specified observations of classroom instruction. These are to be conducted by a team of qualified evaluators (principal and peer evaluator) who, after formative data gathering, will complete a summative evaluation report (SER) at the end of the year.
   • *Student Achievement* — Document evidence of pupil progress to determine success in improving student achievement.
   • *Student Feedback* — Survey students in each semester and year-long course to determine their perceptions of teaching effectiveness and classroom environment.
   • *Professional Growth* — Specify and attain professional growth plan(s) based upon needs indicated by the performance evaluation profile.
   • *Job Enlargement* — evidence documenting the job enlargement activities of the candidate's present CL level.

Job Enlargement

The district stakeholders' committee was aided by changes in the state's career ladder specifications in the most recent attempt to create a career ladder. By 1989, guidelines provided by the Joint Legislative Committee made it clear that job enlargement and student achievement must be the foundation of any new ladder plan. The new guidelines simply specify that career ladder teachers must have job enlargement responsibilities at upper levels of the ladder. Specific assignments will be made as indicated by district-wide needs assessment. Possible Cave Creek examples are shown in Table 4.

The fourth publication necessary to operate the plan was the *Student Feedback Report*. This intrument was provided for four levels of students: K–2, 3–5, 6–8, and 9–12. The survey instruments each have twenty questions, which, using a Likert-type scale, result in a compos-

Table 4.

I. Entry Teacher

   1. School level committee—short-term
   2. Special assignment

II. Resident Teacher*

   1. School level committee—short-term
   2. Grade representative

III. Associate Teacher

   1. Subject specialist
   2. Grade representative
   3. Year-long committee

IV. Senior Teacher

   1. Department chair
   2. Building coordinator for curriculum
   3. Grade level leader
      a. Team leader
      b. Special projects leader

V. Advanced Teacher

   1. Curriculum alignment tasks
   2. Validating committee
   3. Peer evaluator
   4. District-wide committee

VI. Master Teacher

   1. Research specialist
   2. Staff developer
   3. Peer evaluator/coach
   4. Chair district-wide committees
   5. Curriculum and testing specialist
   6. Validating committee

*Each CLP participant may also fulfill job enlargement tasks listed for levels above and below their current placement.

ite score which may total 100 points. A portion of the K–2 instrument will serve as an example:

(1) My school day is interesting. {No O} {? O} {Yes O}

(2) My teacher gives us enough time to do our work. {No O} {? O} {Yes O}

(3) I pay attention in class. {No O} {? O} {Yes O}

(4) Our discussions are about the lesson being studied. {No O} {? O} {Yes O}

Professional Growth and Student Achievement

While not requiring a separate publication, both professional growth of the teacher and *improvement* of student achievement are important values for the CLP algorithm. The professional growth plan is contained in the *Teacher Performance Evaluation Handbook* and includes the following data:

- performance area and criterion to be improved
- goal of improvement
- specific, measurable behavior
- procedures
- progress check
- documentation/appraisal method for final accomplishment
- comments from evaluator and evaluatee
- career ladder professional growth plan score (for ladder teachers only)

The career ladder applicant is given very specific instructions for preparing a portfolio for consideration by the validating committee. First, the CLP handbook describes all of the requisites for each teacher rank (Levels I–VII) including the salary to be recieved. The requisite for Senior Teacher is shown in Table 5.

Student achievement, and its improvement, is the underlying purpose of the career ladder. Eventually, all student achievement gains used for the purposes of the career ladder will be measured by curriculum-referenced testing. Achievement gains will be aggregated across three years when using curriculum-referenced measures, to compensate for single-year highs or lows. For the next three years or until curriculum-referenced measures are available, the following procedures will be used to provide time to create the array of needed curriculum-referenced measures.

Teachers will select a testing instrument from an approved list. The test(s) chosen or developed must have grade-level, cross grade-level, departmental, and/or principal input. The validating committee must approve the choice of tests and subjects each year by October 1.

Elementary school teachers (K–6) will test two subjects, either mathematics and language arts or mathematics and reading. Secondary teachers (grades 7–12) will submit test results from two preparations (two sections). Students tested and included in the tabulation must have

Table 5.

Level IV	Senior Teacher
Salary	$
Educator Requirements	• Must submit portfolio • Completed curriculum alignment training • Attends CL in-service • Has teacher's certificate
Experience Prerequisite	• One-year minimum
Job Enlargement	• Department chair • Grade level curriculum leader • Team leader • Specials projects leader • Building curriculum coordinator
EOY Composite Score	• 80–85 points
Requirements for Next Vertical Movement	• Peer evaluator/coaching training • Staff developer training • One year minimum

been in a year-long class for at least seven months or fourteen weeks in a semester course. Test choices include

- Iowa Test of Basic Skills (ITBS)—"preferred" for grades K–6
- Test of Academic Proficiency (TAP)—"preferred" test for grades 9–12
- Arizona Student Assessment Plan (ASAP) (when available)
- Teacher prepared test (pre-/post- or post-test only)
- Publisher prepared test (textbook)
- Independent testing materials

A total of thirty points in the composite score of 100 are derived from the student achievement gains. Scoring is to be as shown in Table 6.

Scoring

Computation of a teacher's composite score and recommendation to the superintendent for placement or advancement on the ladder is the responsibility of the career ladder validating committee. This committee, comprised of six teachers elected by their peers and one administrator, receives the portfolio prepared by the teacher applicant. Using the documents assembled by the applicant, the validating committee

Table 6.

Non Normed Test Points Awarded	10	15	20	25	30
Percentage of students receiving 75% or better on testing	75–77	78–82	83–87	88–92	93–95
Norm-Referenced Test Points Awarded	10	15	20	25	30
Percentage of students meeting or exceeding one grade equivalent increase	75–77	78–82	83–87	88–92	93–95

checks the accuracy of each subtotal value, i.e., the SER scores from the principal and peer appraiser, the student feedback score, etc., and places the values in the algorithm and adds to obtain the composite score (Table 7). The point range of the composite automatically determines the ladder placement (Table 8).

The use of the validating committee takes the burden from the principals (who, in the past iterations of the district's ladder, had recommended placement) and moves the decision point to the compiled evidence. The evidence speaks for itself—the teacher's professional performance and accomplishments actually determine the placement. The committee merely serves as a "validating" mechanism.

EPILOGUE

The career ladder legislation passed by the Arizona Legislature in 1984 has been a success. A joint university study of the career ladder

Table 7.

Components	Possible Points
1. Summative Evaluation Report—Principal	(40)
2. Summative Evaluation Report—Peer	(10)
3. Student Feedback Summative Report	(10)
4. Student Achievement	(30)
5. Professional Growth Plan Accomplishment	(10)
EOY Composite Score	(100)

Table 8. Placement legend.

Point Range	Level	Title
55–60	0	Newly Employed
61–65	I	Entry Teacher
66–70	II	Resident Teacher
71–79	III	Associate Teacher
80–85	IV	Senior Teacher
86–92	V	Advanced Teacher
93–100	VI	Master Teacher

in the fourteen pilot districts indicated that significant student achievement gains were obtained. As a result, in 1990 the legislature expanded the project to include seven new districts by 1993 and placed the entire program in a permanent status. Oversight for the program has moved from the legislature to the state board of education. A state advisory committee oversees and monitors implementation.

Arizona is spending a great deal of money to assure the success of the Career Ladder Plan and, as a result, the state has very high expectations for participating districts. Funding is provided through a formula based on student count and planned annual increases up to 5 percent to cover higher participation rates and the cost of teachers moving up the ladder. Funding for 1988–89 was $13.5 million. Funding for 1990–91 was estimated to be $20 million.

Based on the success of the pilot districts, new districts will be required to meet additional guidelines:

- New teachers to a district will be required to participate.
- Differentiated evaluation criteria will be developed for each of the various levels of the ladder.
- Multiple evaluations must be used to judge teacher performance.
- Teachers at the top of the levels of the ladder will be required to take on additional instructional responsibilities.

Cave Creek Unified School District struggled to revise and redraft its Career Ladder Plan to conform to the anticipated changes in the standards. The district's Teacher Performance Evaluation System, Principal Performance Evaluation System, and the Superintendent and Board Evaluation Systems were completely redeveloped. At this writing, Cave Creek Unified has been approved for continued funding, having met all of the criteria as an initial pilot district and having met the new criteria.

REFERENCES

1990. Joint Legislative Committee on Career Ladders 1989 Annual Report to the Thirty-Ninth (Arizona) Legislature, Second Regular Session.

Manatt, R. P. and B. Daniels. 1991. "Relationship between Principals' Ratings of Teachers' Performance and Student Achievement," *Journal of Personnel Evaluation in Education*, 4:189–201.

Manatt, R. P. 1988. "Teacher Performance Evaluation: A Total Systems Approach," in *Teacher Evaluation: Six Prescriptions for Success,* S. J. Stanley and W. G. Popham, eds., ASCD. 79–108.

Manatt, R. P., K. Palmer and E. Hidlebaugh. 1976. "Evaluating Teacher Performance with Improved Rating Scales," *NASSP Bulletin*, 60:21–24.

Manatt, R. P. and S. Stow. 1986. "Developing and Testing a Model for Measuring and Improving Educational Outcomes of K–12 School," Technical Report. Ames: Iowa State University.

Stow, S. B. and J. E. Sweeney. 1981. "Developing a Teacher Performance Evaluation System," *Educational Leadership*, 38:538–541

ENDNOTE

1 Each of the district's career ladder publications is copyrighted. They may be obtained by calling the district office: 602/488-2703.